Homegrown Hate

Homegrown Hate

Why White Nationalists and Militant
Islamists Are Waging War against
the United States

Sara Kamali

UNIVERSITY OF CALIFORNIA PRESS

University of California Press
Oakland, California

© 2021 by Sara Kamali

Library of Congress Cataloging-in-Publication Data

Names: Kamali, Sara, author.
Title: Homegrown hate : why white nationalists and
    militant Islamists are waging war against the United
    States / Sara Kamali.
Description: Oakland, California : University of
    California Press, [2021] | Includes bibliographical
    references and index.
Identifiers: LCCN 2020029262 (print) | LCCN 2020029263
    (ebook) | ISBN 9780520360020 (cloth) |
    ISBN 9780520976115 (ebook)
Subjects: LCSH: Domestic terrorism—United States—
    Prevention. | White nationalism—United States. |
    Islamic fundamentalism—United States. | Religious
    militants—United States.
Classification: LCC HV6432 .K344 2021 (print) |
    LCC HV6432 (ebook) | DDC 363.3250973—dc23
LC record available at https://lccn.loc.gov/2020029262
LC ebook record available at https://lccn.loc
    .gov/2020029263

Manufactured in the United States of America

30 29 28 27 26 25 24 23 22 21
10 9 8 7 6 5 4 3 2

For my mother
and
for the warriors of peace, of all creeds and colors,
who strive against inequity, oppression, and
impunity

America is a unique sociological fabric, and it bespeaks poverty of imagination not to be thrilled at the incalculable potentialities of so novel a union of men. To seek no other goal than the weary old nationalism,—belligerent, exclusive, inbreeding, the poison of which we are witnessing now in Europe,—is to make patriotism a hollow sham, and to declare that, in spite of our boastings, America must ever be a follower and not a leader of nations.

—Randolph S. Bourne, *Atlantic Monthly,* July 1916

Contents

Acknowledgments   *ix*

Introduction. Empathizing with the Enemy: The Threat Within   *1*

PART ONE. WHO THEY ARE

1. The Fourteen Words: The Racist Beliefs of White
   Nationalists   *39*
2. Loyalty and Disavowal: The Exclusionary Ideology of
   Militant Islamists   *83*

PART TWO. WHY THEY FIGHT

3. #WhiteGenocide: Grievances of White Nationalists   *113*
4. The Crusades Redux: Grievances of Militant Islamists   *137*

PART THREE. WHAT THEY WANT

5. (RA)HOWA: (Re)Claiming the United States through
   (Racial) Holy War   *161*

6. America the Beautiful: Establishing a White Ethnostate
   or Constructing a Caliphate   181
7. Encouraging the End of Days: The Apocalyptic Rhetoric
   of Political Violence   204
8. The Myth of the Lone Wolf: Joining Virtual Packs Online 219

PART FOUR. WHAT CAN BE DONE

Conclusion. Securing the Homeland: Counterterrorism and
the Need for Holistic Justice   249

Notes   273
Selected Bibliography   359
Index   395

Acknowledgments

I begin this note to you, the reader. *Wherever* you are, *whenever* you are, and *however* you are, thank you for spending time with these pages. Our paths may never cross physically, nor indeed during the same time period, and there may be a whole host of dissimilitudes separating us. I believe, however, that differences, including of colors and languages, are to be celebrated, as they evidence the artistry of The Sublime; moreover, while identity politics focuses on that which sets us apart from each other, we must also embrace that which brings us together: our common humanness. As the poet Saʿdi wrote movingly centuries ago:

> The children of Adam are limbs of each other
> Having been created of one essence.
>
> When a calamity affects one limb
> The other limbs cannot remain at rest
>
> If you have no sympathy for the troubles of others
> You are unworthy to be called by the name "human."

My official study of the many academic disciplines this book brings together did not begin until I was an undergraduate at the University of St Andrews, where I also worked at what was then the RAND Centre for the Study of Terrorism and Political Violence. I had the sincere good fortune to be there during the time of the late Paul Wilkinson, CBE, a pioneer in the field of terrorism studies, whose scholarly guidance and humanity shaped my views as a student then and continue to influence my approach as an educator in and out of the classroom now.

Warmest thanks also to Michael Jerryson, Distinguished Professor of Religious Studies and director of the James Dale Ethics Center at Youngstown State University, whose support of my scholarship means a great deal, because he is not only an excellent scholar on religion and violence but also, and even more importantly in my estimation, he is a thoroughly good human being.

Furthermore, my time as an undergraduate student at the American University in Cairo was invaluable in affording me an understanding of the world through the perspective of Egyptians in what was then a nation on the precipice of political destabilization. This period greatly impacted my views on global security and violence, as well as human rights, in myriad ways. I will not be able to do justice to the Egyptians whose many instances of kindness and hospitality were, at times, literally lifesaving and can only send a sincere note of gratitude.

My warmest thanks to Professor Eugene Rogan, FBA, director of the Middle East Centre at St Antony's College; Professor Faisal Devji, director of the Asian Studies Centre at St Antony's College; and Dr. Halbert Jones, who was then the director of the North American Studies Programme at St Antony's College and is now the director of the Rothermere American Institute, for their collegiality and support, and the opportunity to lecture and engage with a wide variety of audiences while I was conducting postdoctoral research at St Antony's College and at the Faculty of Oriental Studies at the University of Oxford.

Additionally, the staff at the Codrington Library at the University of Oxford (one of my favorite places to write and think and write some more), all deserve a very hearty thank you, as do the staff at the Bodleian Library and at the Middle East Centre Library. So, too, do the staff and student workers at the UC Santa Barbara Library, from the tireless individuals behind the scenes at the Interlibrary Loan Department to the people with whom I had the pleasure to directly interact at the Services Desk and the Department of Special Research Collections. I truly commend librarians everywhere for so diligently helping to garner the countless materials I have requested over the years. Libraries, and books in particular, have always been safe havens in which I could explore and discover and, ultimately, be immersed in worlds of wonderment.

Thank you, too, to all of the custodians in these spaces, especially at the UC Santa Barbara Library, whose friendliness in the wee small hours of the morning was—and is—so appreciated. Their immaculate maintenance of the library, which often goes unseen because of the hours they work—as is the case for most custodians who work the night shift—will always be valued.

I would be highly remiss if I did not express my sincerest appreciation for the team at UC Press (in alphabetical order): Jessica Moll, production editor; Eric Schmidt, acquisitions editor; and Lia Tjandra, art director.

Jessica steered the book through the minutiae of the last stages of publication with aplomb. Thank you for your attentiveness and patience.

Eric championed my vision for this book when White nationalism was out of sight for many. He also cheered me on throughout the process, heartening me immensely, particularly when this project seemed, at times, Sisyphean due to the ever-evolving nature of current events and related source material, as well as the tumult of global geopolitics, climate change–related disasters, and the COVID-19 pandemic. The "thank you" is officially in print now—finally!

For the cover of my book, Lia marvelously brought to fruition the concepts I had detailed during the initial design stages. Though it's unfair to judge a book by its cover, Lia's artistry fully captures the complexity of *Homegrown Hate* in elegant simplicity. Thank you for realizing (in all meanings of the word) what has hitherto been a series of doodles in my mind and on paper.

Significantly, I have had many teachers in life, some more stringent than others. Though exacting instructors, their lessons are the ones that have left the most indelible imprints on my continuing education. For them all, I am grateful:

To poverty, for teaching me nonjudgment.

To illness, for teaching me humility.

To wealth, for teaching me the substance of true richness.

To health, for teaching me about privilege.

To worry, for teaching me faith.

To hunger, for teaching me patience.

To loneliness, for teaching me fortitude and perseverance.

To disregard, for teaching me thoughtfulness.

To empty words, for teaching me the importance of integrity.

To superficiality, for teaching me the value of sincerity.

To bigotry, for teaching me respect.

To oppression, for teaching me the might of justice.

Lastly, I end these acknowledgments with gratitude to my family—to my brother, who always believed I could (and would), to my sister, and, most especially, to my mother, Dr. Shakera Azimi, who instilled in me a profound love of literature and of the musicality of language, ever encouraging me to witness the poetry in the seemingly mundane. She is an inimitable exemplar of grit and grace—one I can only hope to begin to emulate—and whose wit, elegance, and beauty is surpassed only by her intelligence, patience, and compassion.

Empathizing with the Enemy

The Threat Within

The sleepy college town of Charlottesville, Virginia became the violent epicenter of racism, religion, and politics in 2017. Now a byword for White nationalist agitation, Charlottesville was the site of what would become the largest gathering of American White nationalist groups thus far this century.[1] One counterprotester, Heather Heyer, was killed after James Alex Fields Jr. purposefully struck her with a car, a murder that then U.S. attorney general Jeff Sessions described as an act of "domestic terrorism."[2]

Organized by Jason Kessler, founder of the White nationalist advocacy group Unity and Security for America and a self-styled "white civil rights leader," the Unite the Right rally was held to protest the removal of a statue of Robert E. Lee.[3] Lee was a commander of the Confederate forces during the U.S. Civil War—a hero not only to the Confederacy but also to many of the rally's attendees. Though the monument was a symbol of the nation's racist history, its proposed removal became symbolic of other issues aggrieving the participants, such as the perceived displacement of White people, evidenced by the demographic rise of people of color in the United States; threats to White cisheteronormative masculinity; as well as cancel culture and political correctness, which serve only to stifle expressions of White identity—all of which heightened their shared sense of victimhood.[4] These themes, which are omnipresent in White nationalism today, were also present in the cries chanted by the protesters, many of whom marched wearing militia uniforms and openly carried firearms, already prepared for the race war in which they collectively envisioned themselves taking part: "Blood and soil"; "You will not replace us"; "Jews will not replace us"; "White lives matter."[5]

A range of White nationalist organizations were present at the rally, from those with a documented history of violence to those engaging mainly in vitriolic rhetoric, including the Patriot movement, paramilitary members, neo-Confederates, neo-Nazis and skinheads, and identitarians, in addition to the National Socialist Movement, the Traditionalist Worker Party, the League of the South, Identity Evropa (the American Identity Movement), Vanguard America, and the Proud Boys, among others. Prominent individuals, such as David Duke and Richard Spencer, were also in attendance, attesting to the rally's appeal to generations of White nationalists. David Duke once held the highest office within the Knights of the Ku Klux Klan; Richard Spencer is credited with coining the term *alt-right* and is the president of the National Policy Institute, whose goal is the creation of a White ethnostate.[6]

Further reflecting the complexity of White nationalism within the United States and around the world, the attendees also represented a plethora of religious views. They comprised agnostics and atheists, as well as adherents of racist religions such as Christian Identity, which originated in nineteenth-century England; Creativity, founded in 1973, its Golden Rule stating, "What is good for the White race is the highest virtue; what is bad for the White race is the ultimate sin"; and Wotanism, a reinterpretation of the ancient pagan Norse religion Odinism.[7]

Irrespective of their organizational affiliation and religious self-identification, what the Unite the Right demonstrators had in common was adherence to White nationalism, which is the desire for the United States to be exclusively White, or a White ethnostate. This goal may be achieved in various ways, including eliminating everyone deemed to be a person of color by exclusion, deportation, killing, or a combination thereof. Militant White nationalism may seem like a one-dimensional racist phenomenon made up of angry White men anxious about the demographic changes in the United States. However, as subsequent chapters will make evident, White nationalism is a complex assemblage of organizations, personalities, theologies, credos, and motivations. In the aggregate, White nationalists, militant and nonmilitant, seek to protect what they conceive of as the White race from what they perceive as cultural and racial genocide in an imminent race war.[8] As this book will discuss, from the perspective of many White nationalists, the war has already begun.

White nationalists, such as those who displayed such a strong show of force in Charlottesville, are not the only internal threat to the United States. American militant Islamists, many of them influenced by organizations like al-Qaʿida and Islamic State (Dāʿish), as well as by individual figureheads like the late Anwar al-Aulaqi, also pose a powerful menace to the nation. American militant Islamists share a perceived lack of belonging and a fractured sense of identity, yet there is no single determining factor or profile for these individuals; individuals do not become militant simply because they are immigrants, the children of immigrants, or people who identify as practicing Muslims. What is knowable from their own reports, however, is that they frequently identify with the suffering of the Muslim civilians who are the overlooked casualties of the many U.S.-led wars in Muslim-majority nations, including Iraq and Afghanistan, or who are victims of a U.S. foreign policy that turns away from their anguish, as in the case of the Rohingya in Myanmar. Their sense of victimhood, emblematized by their self-described association with Muslim civilian casualties overseas, is similar to that of their White nationalist counterparts in that it is constructed and exploited to justify their violence. The online media of al-Qaʿida and Islamic State (Dāʿish) reinforces this narrative by reciting the injustices perpetuated during the Crusades and European colonialism on Muslim-majority countries. The divisive and Orientalist narrative of Islam versus the West that is flagrantly exploited by White nationalists to perpetuate Islamophobia is also used by organizations such as al-Qaʿida and Islamic State (Dāʿish) and by ideologues like Anwar al-Aulaqi who advocate militant Islamism even posthumously.[9] In this framework, militancy becomes the only recourse for such historical and global injustices.

Seeking retribution for members of the *umma,* the global community of Muslims, seemingly out of a desire for connection with believers outside their own nation, militant Islamists ironically reject fellow Muslim Americans. Compelled to act as would-be heroes in the grander narrative of avenging Muslims in Muslim-majority countries targeted by the United States, they hypocritically target Americans, including fellow Muslim Americans, on shared soil. Many American militant Islamists go further than discounting the lives and beliefs of other Muslim American citizens, actively labeling them as apostates for their patriotism and pride in the United States, a nation held in contempt for exacting violence on beleaguered Muslims in Muslim-majority countries.

Perhaps the greatest menace posed by these militant Islamists is, in fact, a mutual war of attrition. Throughout its brief history, the United

States has long been lauded by the international community as the leader of the free world, a bastion of civil rights and liberties, and a righteous bulwark against dictatorship and oppression, though it has undoubtedly struggled to uphold these ideals in practice. The threat of terrorism is leveraged to issue counterterrorism policies that erode freedom, encourage fear, and pit Americans against one another in the name of national security. This takes the shape of not only the surveillance of millions of innocent Muslim Americans by law enforcement agencies but also the monitoring of any who are deemed a political threat. The true danger of American militant Islamists is that they target America's very social fabric.

As the subsequent chapters will detail, there are striking parallels and marked differences between White nationalists and militant Islamists, so it is important to note the contextual divergences and convergences of these groups. Primarily, the historical embeddedness of White nationalism in the United States from the country's founding has resulted in overlapping groups and affiliations demanding a White ethnostate. By contrast, despite the deep roots of Islam in America, American militant Islamism is a diffuse post-9/11 phenomenon.

Another substantial difference is the relationship between state action and political violence carried out in the name of these ideologies. Whereas many White nationalists regard the political landscape as currently in their favor, because they have been both tacitly and explicitly endorsed by President Donald Trump, American militant Islamists view themselves as directly opposed not only to the U.S. government and all of the institutions constituting its bureaucracy but also, by extension, to their fellow Americans. Whereas militant White nationalists seek to restore and purify the United States by reinforcing existing sociopolitical and historical inequities, militant Islamists seek a cessation of the oppressive policies of the United States by overthrowing the country's existing political structures and those of the ruthless international dictatorships it supports hypocritically through the use of violence.

Militant Islamists share with their White nationalist counterparts a strong element of misogyny, or the enforcement of hostility toward women who violate patriarchal norms and expectations.[10] This is not to claim that all misogynists are terrorists or that all terrorists are misogynists. But as traditional gender roles are threatened by shifting norms, research increasingly shows that violence toward women is often linked with other types of violence, including mass shootings and politically motivated violence. Certainly, a number of White nationalists and

Islamists identify as women; nevertheless, the overwhelming majority of the subjects of this study are men. Moreover, just as it is important to acknowledge misogyny as an important predictor of a predisposition to violence for both ideologies, it is just as important to acknowledge the tension between misogyny and the role women themselves play in reinforcing misogyny, or at the very least sexism, within this context. Specifically, women normalize and mobilize the particularly violent strands of these ideologies through social networking and recruitment. While a full discussion is outside of the sphere of this book, there have been many scholarly works dedicated to these topics.[11]

As the chapters that follow will explore at length, adherents of both groups identify intensely with a sense of their own victimhood, both collective and individual. The mantle of victimhood they don in the pursuit of political aims frequently cloaks isolation, frustration, and a fractured sense of belonging, all of which are ultimately expressed as violence. Whatever their self-identified religiosity, including none, their longing for a White ethnostate or a caliphate is frequently, at least in part, a desire for a sense of purpose and community. They commit their acts of terrorism, while declaring them to be in the name of the Fourteen Words or religious tenets, in an attempt to redress their perceived marginalization by defending themselves or avenging the deaths of those they regard as innocent victims.

Though the specific motivations and aims of militant White nationalists and militant Islamist activists differ, the politically charged religious and sacred rationales they rely on, the grievances they seek to assuage, the goals they wage war to fulfill, and the dangers they pose are strikingly similar. Neither group must be underestimated.

THE ORIGINS OF *HOMEGROWN HATE*

This is the first book to directly compare American militant White nationalists and American militant Islamists, who both mutually—and exclusively—target America for the purposes of claiming the nation as theirs and theirs alone, either as a White ethnostate or as part of a global caliphate.[12] Weaving together the strands of many scholarly disciplines, the book aims to outline the organizations, articulate the worldviews, and examine the motivations of these Americans, whether citizens by birth or by naturalization, who are waging war on the United States by calling for violence or by committing acts of terror. The book's title, *Homegrown Hate,* is a direct reference to how their resentment and rage manifest into animosity and enmity toward their own country.

The bedlam and output of violence created around the world by militant Islamist groups such as al-Qaʿida and Islamic State (Dāʿish) have long been a focus of U.S. media attention and popular concern. Even so, for decades, U.S. government agencies and personnel involved in national security, in addition to academic and research institutions, nonprofit agencies, and civil rights organizations, have uniformly recognized militant White nationalism as a more perilous threat to American national security than militant Islamism.[13] These sources conclude that American militant White nationalists, specifically, and militant groups on the political far right, broadly, are responsible for more attacks and more fatalities than their American militant Islamist counterparts.[14]

This has been true for at least the past decade. In 2009, the U.S. Department of Homeland Security's Office of Intelligence and Assessment, in coordination with the FBI, concluded that "lone wolves and small terrorist cells embracing violent right wing extremist ideology are the most dangerous domestic threat in the United States."[15] The report caused a furor due to its use of the label "right wing extremist," as well as the fact that it examined the recruitment of military veterans by those it labeled extremists.[16] Its author, Daryl Johnson, then a senior analyst with the Extremism and Radicalization Branch of the Homeland Environment Threat Analysis Division, experienced the dismantling of his unit as a result.[17] The secretary of Homeland Security at the time, Janet Napolitano, rescinded the report. Resources formally allocated to keep track of the political far right, which is now concomitant with White nationalism, was scaled back, if not fully stopped. In the interim, militant White nationalism has become so widespread that the FBI has categorized it a "persistent" threat.[18]

A database of nine years of domestic terrorism incidents (2008–16) compiled by the Investigative Fund at the Nation Institute and published by the Center for Investigative Reporting likewise concluded that "terror plots and actions by far-right right groups and attacks outnumbered Islamist domestic cases by more than 2 to 1."[19] Similarly, in a 2017 report, the U.S. Government Accountability Office, a nonpartisan congressional research agency, released statistics on the fatalities caused by "domestic violent extremists" from September 12, 2001, to December 31, 2016. As utilized in the report, "domestic violent extremist" encompasses the categories of "far right wing violent extremist groups" and "radical Islamist violent extremists." The following statistics are included in the report:

In ten of the fifteen years, fatalities resulting from attacks by far right wing violent extremists exceeded those caused by radical Islamist violent extremists.

In three of the fifteen years, fatalities resulting from attacks by far right wing violent extremists were the same as those caused by violent radical Islamist extremists.

Of the eighty-five violent extremist incidents that resulted in death, far right wing violent extremist groups were responsible for sixty-two (73 percent).

Of the eighty-five violent extremist incidents that resulted in death, violent radical Islamist extremists were responsible for twenty-three (27 percent).[20]

In 2020, the Triangle Center on Terrorism and Homeland Security issued its annual report on Muslim American involvement in terrorism. In 2019, twenty-four Muslim Americans were arrested for alleged terrorism involvement. By the center's count, the number of fatalities attributed to American militant Islamists in the United States from September 11, 2001, to December 31, 2019, was 141. Over this same period, it cited approximately 290,000 murders in the United States. The report also cited that in 2019 alone, 254 Americans were killed in mass shootings, including 22 people killed by White nationalist Patrick Crusius at a Walmart in El Paso, Texas.[21] Crusius's twenty-third victim died of his injuries in 2020.

Despite the alarming statistics, violent expressions of White nationalism are often ignored by federal counterterrorism agencies, which have remained slow to robustly fund and organize units examining the phenomenon; jettisoned by the criminal justice system, which does not have a federal criminal statute for domestic terrorism (if enacted, such a statute could itself be problematic for the civil liberties and civil rights of minoritized groups); and neglected by the media, which often personalizes the stories of the perpetrators when they are White.

Militant White nationalists, by virtue of White privilege, are portrayed and perceived as individuals, so they are not collectively criminalized.[22] White privilege is defined as the inherent and unearned advantages, opportunities, and benefits White people are afforded simply because of their skin color. It also insulates White people while simultaneously disadvantaging people of color. By contrast, instances of militant Islamism are prosecuted as terrorism, criminalized in the court of public opinion, and covered by the media in a way that reifies

Islamophobia.[23] Furthermore, innocent Muslims in the United States and around the world are similarly prosecuted by guilt through association.

White privilege is also made evident in successful attempts to suppress legislation that would address the increasing numbers of White nationalists, most vividly shown in the myopic focus of funding and legislating for counterterrorism programs addressing militant Islamism.[24] During Donald Trump's presidency, the U.S. Department of Homeland Security's Office of Community Partnerships, which oversaw White nationalist terrorism and had a budget of $21 million under President Obama, was relabeled the Office of Terrorism Prevention Partnerships and had its budget cut to less than $3 million.[25]

Signaling a potential shift to the minimizing of White nationalist violence at the federal level, FBI director Christopher Wray acknowledged to the House Judiciary Committee in 2020 that militant White nationalists "collectively pose a steady threat of violence and economic harm to the United States."[26] Recognizing that militant White nationalists, which he defined as "racially/ethnically motivated violent extremists," are "the primary source of ideologically-motivated lethal incidents and violence in 2018 and 2019 [in the United States], and have been considered the most lethal of all domestic extremism movements since 2001," Wray further stated that violence in the name of this ideology would be "on the same footing in terms of our national threat banding as ISIS and [American militant Islamism]."[27]

Though Wray's language indicates a new tone, as does the U.S. State Department's designation of the White nationalist group the Russian Imperial Movement as a global terrorist organization, whether or not terrorism perpetrated by American militant White nationalists and American militant Islamists will ever truly be regarded on the same plane from a national security perspective will be made evident by funding priorities and the language framing the urgency of the threat.[28] Despite the recognition within the Trump White House that "racially motivated extremism" concomitant with militant White nationalism exists as a terrorist threat, former FBI supervisor Dave Gomez, who oversaw terrorism cases, stated, "There's some reluctance among agents to bring forth an investigation that targets what the president perceives as his base."[29] Moreover, the affinity President Trump has for many of the racist and exclusionary worldviews of the militant and nonmilitant White nationalist groups within the broader political far right also factors into why scant federal resources have been allocated to keeping track of and dealing with this ideology during his administration.

PRESIDENT DONALD TRUMP AND
HOMEGROWN HATRED

It is impossible to talk about the need for this book without reference to the presidency of Donald Trump. White supremacy and White national-ism have long had outsized influence on American politics—including economic, criminal justice, immigration, military, and foreign policies—resulting in systemic inequities that are rooted in racism and manifested according to class, gender identity, sexual orientation, and ability, for example. But the election of President Donald Trump has normalized White nationalist rhetoric and policies, including conspiracy theories, all of which are now explicitly part of the American political establishment.[30] Many Americans who support him self-identify in seemingly innocuous terms, including *race realist, White identitarian,*or *White racialist,* that are in fact derived from White nationalist discourse.[31] Within these circles of the political far right, Christianity is often upheld as a cultural entity that encompasses Whiteness, and racialized Christendom reifies the Ori-entalist notion of Western civilization as demarcating Whiteness from the Other. The White nationalist belief that the United States is a land solely for White people gives cause for violence, rhetorical and physical, in the pursuit of establishing America as a White ethnostate.

Indeed, Trump's 2016 election was met with fanfare by an array of White nationalists, militant and nonmilitant, who are united in viewing themselves as victims of a world that is on the brink of collapse on sev-eral levels: they feel that their economic livelihoods are threatened by immigrants of color, their cultural identity is being displaced by people of color, and their social values are being upended by women and nonbi-nary gender identities. White nationalist Richard Spencer, an ardent sup-porter of President Trump, gave a speech celebrating Trump's election at the National Policy Institute's 2016 annual conference: "America was, until this past generation, a white country designed for ourselves and our posterity. It is our creation, it is our inheritance, and it belongs to us. . . . Hail Trump! Hail our people! Hail victory!"[32] Spencer was met with a standing ovation, the crowd raising their arms in Nazi salutes.

Trump's election was also greeted as a triumph by the very popular White nationalist websites the *Daily Stormer* and *Counter-Currents,* and in a front-page article in *The Crusader*, the KKK's official newspaper, which calls itself "the political voice of White Christian America."[33] The openness of these demonstrations of support, harking back to a dark time in global history, indicates how standardized White nationalism and its platform of racism, nativism, and misogyny have become since President Trump's election.

Even while refraining from explicitly utilizing words like *White* or *Black*, and, in fact, denying that he is a racist, Trump employs dog whistles—highly inflammatory but coded language—in addition to covert displays of racism and other forms of discrimination to incite his base of supporters.[34] Oscillating between displays of covert and overt racism, President Trump labeled himself a nationalist in 2018, though not explicitly deeming himself a White nationalist, at a political rally in Houston, Texas: "You know what I am? I'm a nationalist, okay? I'm a nationalist. Nationalist. Nothing wrong. Use that word. Use that word."[35] In 2019, he hosted the Presidential Social Media Summit and invited politicians and online provocateurs within the political far right.[36] That same year, he also tweeted that four Democratic congresswomen of color—Alexandria Ocasio-Cortez, Rashida Tlaib, Ayanna Pressley, and Ilhan Omar—should "go back and help fix the totally broken and crime infested places from which they came," implicitly equating American citizenship with White identity.[37] (Three of the four of them were born in the United States, and all are American citizens.)

The inference is that the United States is a nation not for people of color but for White people only. Coating his racist remarks with conspiracies, Donald Trump engaged in falsehoods before his presidency as well. In an interview with Fox News talk show host Bill O'Reilly in 2011, Trump, at the time a reality TV host, declared that the then presidential candidate Barack Hussein Obama, who would go on to become the nation's forty-fourth president, had not been born in the United States, claiming, "He doesn't have a birth certificate. He may have one, but there is something on that birth certificate—maybe religion, maybe it says he's a Muslim; I don't know"—as if being Muslim and American are juxtaposed and contradictory identities.[38] As president of the United States, Trump has levied similar birther attacks on his political rival Senator Kamala Harris, claiming her status as a natural-born citizen of the United States is questionable due to her parents' citizenship status at the time of her birth.[39] These conspiratorial attacks signal the conspicuous Islamophobia that has become the hallmark of White nationalism, along with antisemitism and the demarcation of who qualifies as an

American and who does not. Donald Trump is aligning with those who make up his base, upholding the view that to be American is to belong to the institution of Whiteness, portraying himself as their protector from the Other.

Brazenly, he has also consistently used Twitter as a bully pulpit to overtly promote racism. He has called the Black Lives Matter movement a "symbol of hate" and stated the Black Lives Matter mural painted in front of Trump Tower in New York City denigrates Fifth Avenue.[40] Repackaging the Fourteen Words, the slogan of White nationalists, which will be discussed in chapter 1, President Trump tweeted in the run-up to the 2020 presidential election, "This is a battle to save the Heritage, History, and Greatness of our Country! #MAGA2020."[41] MAGA, or "Make America Great Again," was Donald Trump's 2016 presidential campaign slogan. When placed in the context of his speeches, his actions, and the policies of his administration, MAGA became a byword for racism, with the red hats emblazoned with the logo synonymous in the eyes of many Americans with the Ku Klux Klan hood or the Confederate flag.[42] Signaling victimhood of the present besieged state of White America, the "again" is meant to hark back to an America of undisputed White privilege in which White people were not only the demographic majority but also the sole voices of power. Even though many people of color may posit that this America has never ceased to exist—if not demographically then certainly within the scope of White people possessing unearned privilege due to their skin color and unchallenged cultural hegemony—it is this nostalgic America that White nationalists seek to reclaim, the concept of which will be discussed in detail in chapter 5.

During his impeachment hearings in the U.S. House of Representatives, President Trump seemingly warned about an impending civil war should the impeachment ultimately be successful, tweeting a quote from pastor and Fox News contributor Robert Jeffress, "If the Democrats are successful in removing the President from office (which they will never be), it will cause a Civil War like fracture in this Nation from which our Country will never heal."[43] The nod to civil war is coded language for the racial holy war, or RAHOWA, which many members of Trump's White nationalist base view themselves as taking part in. The Oath Keepers, an antigovernment White nationalist organization, affirmed the president's tweet by responding, "This is the truth. This is where we are. We ARE on the verge of a HOT civil war. Like in 1859."[44] The discourse on a civil war is leveraged as a call to arms for White nationalists, signaling that violence is the only recourse to protect the United States from immigrants and people of color and keep the country as the Founding Fathers always intended it to be: for White people and by White people.

In 2020, in the run-up to his bid for a second term in the White House, President Trump also posted and then deleted a video of a senior citizen and Black Lives Matter supporters in a heated exchange. In the video, an elderly man driving a golf cart with America First and Trump 2020 signs repeatedly shouts "White power" at Black Lives Matter supporters. Trump also published a tweet thanking the "great people of the Villages," the community in Florida where the video was reportedly taken.[45] Such tweets function as shout-outs to long-standing elements of the political far right, including White nationalists, who uphold Whiteness as an exclusive identity marker of rightful Americans.[46]

On July 4, 2020, in the midst of global Black Lives Matter demonstrations protesting systemic racism and subsequent calls for the removal of Confederate symbols—like the Confederate flag, which Trump defended as a "freedom of speech" issue; statues commemorating heroes of the Confederacy, erected primarily in the Jim Crow era; and the names of military bases named after Confederate leaders—President Trump gave a speech at Mount Rushmore lambasting the Americans who took part for seeking "the end of America."[47] Addressing his supporters who see themselves as victims in a race war, his speech at Mount Rushmore in 2020 recalled his response to the Unite the Right rally. Though his comments may seem like innocuous equivocation, they are notable for their lack of outright condemnation of the violence and racism of the White nationalist protesters: "You had some very bad people in that group, but you also had people that were very fine people, on both sides. . . . You had people in that group that were there to protest the taking down of, to them, a very, very important statue and the renaming of a park from Robert E. Lee to another name."[48] Donald Trump's language normalizes racism by embedding it into national rhetoric. Much as the appearance of racists is no longer demarcated by white hoods, racism is no longer solely in the purview of blatant diction but can also be found surreptitiously inserted in speeches and seemingly offhand remarks, all of which insidiously thwart our national bearings of equity and justice.

White nationalists, including propagators of racist vitriol and those who perpetrate violence, have also responded to messages that appear to be targeted to their fears and resentments. Specifically, White nationalists and many members of the overarching political far right view Trump as preventing White genocide—the erasure of people deemed to be White and of White cultural values—through his executive orders, laws, and agency directives, many of which appear to be directly aimed at their perceived enemies, including people of color, immigrants, Queer Americans, and especially Muslims in the United States and around the world.[49]

The energization of White nationalists has had predictable and deadly consequences. Trump's political rhetoric and policies at the federal level have corresponded to an increase in membership in White nationalist organizations, as well as a wave of hate crimes, harassment, and intimidation targeting people of color, Queer people, Muslim Americans, and Jewish people that swept the country in the immediate aftermath of Election Day in 2016.[50] Trump's presidency, which has been marked by racism, misogyny, antisemitism, Islamophobia, and ableism, as well as opposition to immigration and Queer rights, has normalized the systemic oppression of minoritized communities, validating the political and social aims of White nationalists and normalizing their worldviews, including conspiracism, particularly fears of the "Deep State."[51]

Donald Trump's presidency has also galvanized militant Islamists, who propagandize his Islamophobic rhetoric and racist policies by warning online that they are stoking tensions when the United States is on the precipice of civil war, eerily mirroring the language of White nationalists.[52] Militant Islamists have been energized by the presidency and administration of President Trump, going so far as to declare him "the perfect enemy" and feature him in propaganda videos online. While many Muslims around the world, including Muslim Americans, often view the Trump administration's policies as expressions of a deep-seated antipathy toward Islam and Muslims, American militant Islamists regard these same policies as opportunities to gain followers—in essence, they use the same covert and overt tactics that President Trump deploys to appeal to his constituency. However, instead of signaling Trump's messages of White nationalism, encompassing White supremacy, antisemitism, Islamophobia, and victimhood perpetuated by people of color, militant Islamists leverage the Trump administration's own oratory and agenda to portray the U.S. government and the American way of life as antithetical to Islamic ethics and morals.[53]

On the Dark Web, the day after Trump's 2016 election, various Islamist outlets predicted his leadership would be the downfall of America, theorizing that his presidency would lead sincere Muslims around the world to seek the refuge of a caliphate due to the atrocities that would be committed in what they envisaged to be a blatant war against Muslims everywhere. One user on al-Minbar Jihadi Media, a popular militant Islamist website on the Dark Web affiliated with Islamic State (Dāʿish) and named after the pulpit used by an imam in a masjid, called Trump a "donkey" (an animal culturally representing idiocy) who would cause the destruction of the United States. The individual wrote, "The world is going to experience a change, and this change will put Islam in the leadership position as the end result. In fact, the election of Trump is but an indication of the end of the American empire, so that it draws its last breath at the hands of this fool."[54]

For many militant Islamists, President Trump provides the perfect foil in that his administration's overt hostility toward Muslims around the world and the religion of Islam justifies their anti-American stance. On President Trump's election, Abu Muhammad al-Maqdisi, a prominent ideologue of militant Islamism, tweeted in Arabic to his tens of thousands of followers: "#Trump reveals the true mentality of the Americans, and their racism toward Muslims and Arabs and everything. He reveals what his predecessors used to conceal. So his victory further exposes #America and its appendages."[55]

Many militant Islamists dismissed what they regarded as wan attempts by President George W. Bush and President Barack Obama to position the U.S.-led wars in Iraq and Afghanistan and drone strikes in many Muslim-majority countries as part of the global War on Terror rather than solely as attacks against Muslims and Islam. President Obama, for instance, declared in a widely praised speech in 2009, "America is not—and never will be—at war with Islam."[56] Militant Islamists, who, like their White nationalist counterparts, harness rhetoric and imagery to justify their violence, no longer have to interpret hidden messages or rely only on vilifying American foreign policy to draw members to their cause. They can now simply cite the conspicuous rhetoric and policies of the Trump White House to fuel the clash of civilizations narrative sustaining their political cause. The Muslim travel ban upheld by the U.S. Supreme Court, the move of the U.S. embassy in Israel to Jerusalem (interpreted by many White nationalists as the fulfillment of a biblical prophecy indicating the imminent return of Jesus Christ and the subsequent End Times), and Islamophobic commentary and tweets vilifying Muslim Americans all energize militant Islamist groups.

Notably, both American White nationalists, especially those who carry out violence, and American militant Islamists view Donald Trump's presidency as ammunition to spark the epic conflict they have envisioned to fulfill their respective political aims of a White ethnostate or a fully realized caliphate. Militant White nationalists and militant Islamists have a spiraling effect on one another: each group gives cause to the other's fears. In true parallel fashion, each is, for the other, the primary enemy and positioned as the true infidel.

METHODOLOGY OF *HOMEGROWN HATE*
Distinguishing Violence in the Name of Religion from Religious Violence

This book describes in detail the religions and religious concepts within the configuration of White nationalism and militant Islamism. To be clear, these discussions do not presuppose that religion is an instigator of violence. Religion in and of itself does not cause terrorism, nor does exposure to violent ideas. There are a multitude of social and political factors, as well as psychological factors in some instances, that must converge in order for an individual to commit an act of violence. In fact, many studies have shown that most mass shootings in the United States, which are often carried out to achieve political aims, thus fulfilling the legal definition of terrorism, cannot be attributed to psychopathology.[57] Further complicating the understanding of the drivers of terrorism is the fact that two individuals may have the same experiences but not react in the same way.

In reality, an individual's decision to exact revenge against the United States by targeting fellow Americans is a confluence of psychological, social, and political factors, including self-perception as a victim, a fragmented sense of identity, and, for those who identify as religious, sparse religious knowledge. Additionally, the vast majority of individuals who experience these elements will never commit acts of violence. Indeed, empirical evidence has shown repeatedly that the conveyor belt theory undergirding the current U.S. counterterrorism approach has no basis in reality.[58] Conveniently, and incorrectly, linking exposure to ideas promoting violence with the carrying out of violence creates the myth that there are stages to becoming a terrorist, which can be used to justify the criminalization of many marginalized groups, including Muslim Americans and people of color more broadly.

Certainly, the topic of religion's role in the planning and perpetration of violence is widely debated in policy and academic circles. For these reasons, this book examines how religious concepts are leveraged to legitimize political violence. For the subjects of this book, irrespective of actual belief, religion is merely a tool to justify violence in order to achieve social and political ends.

Furthermore, I maintain, much like religious studies scholars William Cavanaugh and Karen Armstrong, that religion does not incite terrorism; rather, religion is exploited to sanctify terrorism.[59] Cavanaugh's thesis is that there is nothing particular to violence that is deemed "religious" that cannot be applied to other forms of violence, such as those carried out under the banner of nationalism, Marxism, or free-market ideology.[60]

Additionally, as Karen Armstrong argues, secularism, or the now taken-for-granted division between religion and the state, would itself be incomprehensible to eighteenth-century Europeans.[61] What constitutes religion in the modern Western European framework—delineating between the religious and the secular, between the private and the public—is not how religions are understood in many non–Western European cultures, and this renders any definition of religion a politicized construct.[62] Illustrating this point is the Arabic word *dīn*. Translated into English as *religion*, it actually encompasses one's entire mode of being, fusing, in Western terms, the religious and the secular. The projection of the Westernized construct of religion onto non-Western systems of belief and practice mean that labeling violence as "religious" is problematic, if not erroneous.

It is therefore crucial to understand that it is not the *sources* of knowledge that make one a terrorist but rather *how* these sources are wielded as weapons of war. In other words, I demarcate a stark difference between violence in the name of religion, which is violence cloaked in religious frames of reference, but only for legitimacy, to achieve sociopolitical aims, and religious violence, or violence motivated directly by religion. This book wholeheartedly supports the former definition.

Conducting Comparative Analysis

When systematically conducted, comparisons serve to illuminate rather than obfuscate. As defined by religious studies scholar Sam Gill, comparison is "not conformity with a pre-existing pattern."[63] I employ a comparative approach to parse the many parallels and differences between White nationalism, militant and nonmilitant, and militant Islamism. On the contrary, the comparative framework was the natural outcome of examining the historical, social, and political contexts of both militant White nationalism and militant Islamism in the United States. My comparative approach is grounded by the work of religious historians Bruce Lincoln and Cristiano Grottanelli, who identify the elements that determine valid comparison, which include studying a relatively small number of factors closely, granting equal attention to similarities and differences, and attributing equal dignity and intelligence to all parties considered.[64]

This book also extends its comparative analysis by applying the principle of defamiliarization. Taken from twentieth-century Russian formalism by noted scholar of religious studies Jonathan Z. Smith, this concept means to make "the familiar strange in order to enhance our perception of the familiar."[65] Defamiliarization is particularly important in the context of the two ideologies compared in this book because it calls for the juxtaposition of something we think we know with the seemingly incongruous. Defamiliarization reminds the reader to critically question assumptions. Building off of comparativism, defamiliarization allows for a faceted understanding of the social and political context driving these ideologies by defamiliarizing White nationalism in relation to militant Islamism.

Achieving Empathy through Epistemic Worldview Analysis

Over the course of two years, I conducted in-depth personal interviews with a number of key figures, both American White nationalists and American militant Islamists. However, due to the maelstrom that ensued when the FBI contacted me in relation to these interviews, I will not be identifying the subjects or quoting them directly. Rather, I have integrated the substance of our interviews into the subsequent chapters. In these interviews, we discussed their views of the United States, their grievances, their justifications of violence, motivations, and aspirations. Though these interviews were laden with difficulties, they were necessary to understanding the internal motivations of adherents to the ideologies comprising what law enforcement agencies agree are the greatest threats to America's national security.

In the research that forms the heart of this book, I employ the methodology of epistemic worldview analysis to enter into my subjects' worldviews completely and fully comprehend their rationales for violence according to their logic, not what I thought they were or may have been. In other words, empathy. Though in writing this book I utilized a comparative approach, out of which stems defamiliarization, or making the familiar unfamiliar, the research I undertook beforehand relied on the inverse. In fact, by employing empathy, or making the strange familiar, I was able to cognitively connect with the subjects of this book, whose views are so different than my own, and understand why they see the world in the way they do. The process of doing so included identifying my own assumptions and worldviews in order to set aside any assumptions and bias about the truth of their points of view, removing myself morally from the case studies within this book, and refraining from projecting my own value system. Actively listening without prejudice, I was then able to conduct productive interactions on what it meant to my subjects to act appropriately within their perceived understanding of the world.[66] While the interviews aided in this process of coming to a greater understanding of the Other and of the reasons why America has become a target for its own citizens, there are limitations to what can be known about all of the factors that culminate in beliefs, goals, and the carrying out or planning of violence. Some of these factors may not even be conscious but are shaped implicitly by individual upbringings and sociopolitical contexts.

Even though there is a dire need for this type of approach to interviewing, and indeed for the hermeneutics of suspicion, or contextualizing the interviews themselves rather than condemning the interviewees, this approach might seem like unpatriotic appeasement. It might also seem more appealing to forego objective inquiry into their motivations and thus dismiss them.[67] I maintain that on the contrary, objectively analyzing the world from the vantage point of those whose values I do not share has a solid foundation in the American aspirations of pluralism and freedom from tyranny.

My own worldview, based on the multiplicity of my identities as a first-generation Muslim American (i.e., my American identity, my Muslim identity, and my Central Asian cultural heritage), renders the predominant narrative dividing East from West nonsensical, diminishing, and simply incorrect. As a result, my professional areas of interests have largely dealt with conflict and its equitable resolution. And, though my religious identity, most especially, may raise a reflexive cri de coeur from those who believe it renders any analysis I undertake to be inherently biased, this particular identity, in fact, makes me all the more mindful of exercising nonjudgment, especially because of the Islamophobia I myself have experienced, providing an unfiltered platform for all of the subjects of this book.

Just as readers may question if I harbor any inherent bias, so, too, did some interviewees. Certainly, both White nationalists and militant Islamists reacted to my last name, Kamali, throughout the course of this research. Tipped off to my Central Asian background by my surname, some were jubilant, others wary. Many militant Islamist interviewees erroneously assumed I would be sympathetic to their cause, while some White nationalists I contacted believed I would denigrate their beliefs and fail to portray them in a fair manner. In such instances, the reasons individuals gave for denying an interview request could be as telling as the interview itself might have been.

To give an example, for one prominent White nationalist, my last name acted as an explicit deterrent. This figure, a bestselling author, shares the conspiratorial mindset of many White nationalists, notably a deep mistrust of the U.S. government. Because he is an outspoken survivalist and sovereign citizen who calls for the establishment of a fortified home for fellow Christians in the Northwest, I contacted him through his popular website to request an interview. Shortly thereafter, he replied. He informed me that my surname led him to believe I would have an implacably negative bias against him and instructed me not to contact him again.

For every interview I conducted, many more people declined or did not respond. Interviewees were apprehensive not only about my positionality but also about attracting the attention of law enforcement officials; this caution at times made it difficult or impossible for me to make personal contact with key militant figures, whose communications are carefully monitored by federal agencies. Amid the increasingly vociferous debates about civil liberties, government transparency, and the rights of academics and journalists, the perils of interviewing alleged militants would make for a worthy book on its own.

A trove of primary source documents was used to corroborate the interviews, including personal correspondence such as letters and journals, as well as ideological literature, constituting mainly of handbooks, booklets, magazines, leaflets, speeches, posters, and artwork. Other source material for this book consists of government reports, trial transcripts, academic books and academic journals, news sources and content from social media sites. Because domestic terrorism and homegrown violent extremism are constantly evolving, as are the terms and definitions themselves, selectively using news outlets on the Internet has been useful in providing the most up-to-date contextual information with regard to certain individuals and groups.

DEFINITIONS AND TERMINOLOGY

Because terminology is often contested territory, it is important to discuss definitions, including why this book uses the term *terrorism* instead of labels such as *extremism, fundamentalism, radicalism,* or *activism;* how to delineate between the political far right and White nationalism, militant and nonmilitant; why *White nationalism* is a more precise term than *White supremacy, White separatism,* or *White power;* the contours of Islamism; identifying Salafiyya; reorienting *jihad;* and the significance and rationales for employing and capitalizing *Black, White, Brown, Queer, Indigenous,* and *Latinx.*

Terrorism

The word *terrorism,* which long-standing scholar of terrorism studies Bruce Hoffman defines as "violence—or equally important, the threat of violence—used and directed in pursuit of, or in service of, a political aim,"[68] is, in his estimation, overused, pejorative, and intended to portray anyone accused of it as someone appropriate to hate and demonize.[69] It is for precisely these reasons that I am using the term *terrorism* in this book.

Because the application of the term *terrorism* is not uniform, it is used herein to redress this imbalance. In many instances, media labeling and public discourse, as well as criminal charges and sentences, differ depending on whether an individual or group self-identifies or is perceived as being a White nationalist or a Muslim. American news outlets focus on militant Islamist threats in the United States and abroad to the detriment of other types of terrorism, so that for most Americans the term *terrorism* is solely associated with militant Islamism.

As Bruce Hoffman also points out, the usage of the designation *terrorism* is divided along partisan lines and is politically loaded; this book therefore refers to violence or threats of violence by White nationalists in pursuit of their political aims as *terrorism* in order to apply the term evenly. Due to the systemic racism underpinning the criminal justice system, including the reification of White supremacy, acts of violence perpetrated by American militant Islamists are likely to be classified—and charged—as *terrorism,* whereas acts of violence committed by militant White nationalists may be labeled as domestic terrorism but are not able to be prosecuted as such. The label only establishes the federal government's jurisdiction and the scope of the inquiry.[70] In fact, though the 2001 USA PATRIOT Act expanded the legal definition of *terrorism* to include domestic terrorism—alongside international terrorism—there is currently not a federal criminal statute for domestic terrorism.[71]

Because domestic terrorism is not an actual legal charge in and of itself, a person committing such a crime can only be "arrested and convicted under existing criminal statutes."[72] This means that violent acts perpetrated by militant White nationalists—which could be prosecuted as domestic terrorism if there was a criminal federal statute for that charge—are often categorized in the criminal justice system as mass shootings or hate crimes and explained away as the result of individual pathology or mental illness.[73] Nonsensically, at the present time, in order for a White nationalist to be prosecuted as a terrorist, that individual must have ties to a militant Islamist organization.[74]

The issues that arise due to the lack of a federal criminal statute to prosecute White nationalist violence are also apparent in the separation between *domestic terrorism* and *homegrown violent extremism*. According to the U.S. Department of Homeland Security, a domestic terrorist is "based and operating entirely within the United States or its territories without direction or inspiration from a foreign terrorist group," whereas a homegrown violent extremist is acting "in furtherance of political or social objectives promoted by a foreign terrorist organization, but is acting independently of direction by a foreign terrorist organization."[75] So while a domestic terrorist is perpetrating acts of violence with no foreign influence, a homegrown violent extremist is influenced by (but not directly commanded by) a foreign authority.[76] Though this may change over time, what this means in practice currently is that domestic terrorism, which relates to White nationalism, is not as prioritized in terms of counterterrorism funding or language depicting it as a similar threat as homegrown violent extremism, which relates to militant Islamism.

Other disqualified terms for terrorism in the global lexicon include *extremism*, which suggests an aberration rather than a serious phenomenon, and *fundamentalism*, which is rooted in Christianity and thus not appropriately applied to other contexts.[77] *Radicalism* misguidedly connotes something inherent in a religion that can be modified to incite violence, a concept that reveals an integral flaw within current federal counterterrorism initiatives which employ the term.[78]

Other alternative terms to *terrorism*, such as *activism*, buttress the systemic racism of U.S. policies that target minoritized communities. Utilizing the term *activism*, which has been supported as a replacement for the term *terrorism* by religious studies scholars, most prominently by American sociologist Mark Juergensmeyer, would actually postulate that activists, who are often mistaken by governments as security threats, are, in fact, worthy of criminalization.[79] Political activism has consistently been suppressed by American federal authorities through surveillance and policing. The kind of activism that is targeted, however, is that which is undertaken by communities of color. Under the COINTEL-PRO program, run by the FBI from 1956 to 1971, the purported purpose of which was to investigate "various Klans and hate organizations," (what I now term White nationalist groups), mass surveillance of "black nationalist, hate-type organizations" was also conducted.[80] Leaders of the civil rights movement in the 1960s, including the Reverend Dr. Martin Luther King Jr., were also investigated by federal agencies. Today, this legacy lives on for people of color. Black Lives Matter and Standing Rock activists are similarly surveilled and criminalized, as are immigration activists and other human rights activists.[81] Applying the term *activists* to those who commit acts of violence based on hate risks conflating them with activists who are striving for positive change in their communities.

Similarly, the primary reason I have not included an appendix with a list of actors, their planned and/or carried out acts of violence, and the resulting devastation, is that practices of entrapment and coercion of individuals by law enforcement agencies, including the FBI, raise questions about whether all those accused in such cases were truly planning acts of what would legally be considered terrorism.[82] Such operations include undercover surveillance, which was employed by the FBI in the PATCON program against members of the political far right in the 1990s but has since 9/11 been largely redirected to target Muslim Americans and political activists such as Black Lives Matter and Standing Rock protesters.

The Political Far Right

The challenges faced in defining and applying the term *terrorism* are also present when attempting to define what is commonly referred to as the *right wing,* or what I name the *political far right,* which includes White nationalism, in the United States. Namely, a uniform definition does not exist. Historically, the political far right itself is amorphous, fluctuating with the social and political norms of the day. Since the mid-1990s, labels for it have included: extreme right, far right, radical right, right, right-wing populism, national populism, new populism, neopopulism, exclusionary populism, xenophobic populism, populist nationalism, ethnonationalism, anti-immigrant, nativism, racism, racist extremism, fascism, neofascism, postfascism, reactionary tribalism, integralism, and antipartyism.[83] Multiple proposed typologies categorizing the political far right put forth by scholars and analysts have proved ineffective due to the cross-pollination of ideas, values, and motivations among various groups.[84] By way of illustration, a self-styled neo-Nazi may find he has much in common with an antigovernment Patriot, and either one could also be a Christian Identity adherent, a Wotanist, or an atheist. Furthermore, figureheads of one group often move on to form other groups, leaving behind a legacy of ideas that may branch out and take shape under the stewardship of a successor, or fizzle out due to a lack of leadership. The ideological consolidation and division of the elements within the political far right has only been heightened by social media and the ability to communicate uninhibitedly in real time with anyone around the world across multiple platforms.

As chapter 1 will discuss in detail, the contours of the political far right broadly encompass groups and individuals challenging the political status quo through the following four elements, in varying degrees and combinations: an agenda of establishing America as a White ethnostate, a belief in White supremacy, religious adherence, and an antigovernment stance. Though White nationalism, in both its militant and nonmilitant expressions, is intertwined with the objectives of the political far right, there do exist elements within the political far right that are not explicitly affiliated with White nationalism, such as some individuals who identify as tax protesters, survivalists and preppers, and sovereign citizens.

White Nationalism

White nationalism is not a euphemism for White supremacy but rather an ideology that reaches past the constraints of White supremacy, White separatism, and White power, in fact encompassing them. I thus define *White nationalism* as an ideology concerned with White racial consciousness, White identity, and White cultural hegemony, in addition to the political and economic dominance of the sociopolitical and historical construct of the White race. Its militant expression is endorsed, supported, condoned, and/or undertaken with the aim of safeguarding Whiteness and establishing a White ethnostate. The term *White nationalism* itself does not concretize an individual as a violent actor, and no one belief system is a predictor of violence. Therefore, the descriptor *militant* is carefully applied to differentiate between those who do and those who do not undertake violence.

Notably, within the constellation of White nationalist groups and individuals, the term *White nationalist* is not wholly accepted or applied.

Nick Fuentes, an attendee of the Unite the Right demonstration in Charlottesville and host of the podcast *America First*, is also one of the leaders of the Groypers, or the Groyper Army, a White nationalist group named after the meme of Pepe the Frog, which was co-opted in 2016 as an antisemitic symbol.[85] Groypers advocate for political conservatives to adopt explicit White nationalist positions upholding what they believe to be the values of America First, an America that is exclusively for White people. President Trump has also retweeted a video clip from the America First Clips Twitter account, which the Groypers embraced as an endorsement of their racist views.[86] Though Fuentes's views align with White nationalism as I define it above, he eschews the designation because it is "used almost exclusively by the left to defame." Moreover, as Fuentes stated in an interview alongside American Richard Spencer with the French Canadian White nationalist Jean-François Gariépy, he prefers the term *nationalist,* explaining, "I think in a way it's almost redundant that you're a 'White' nationalist. We know that the word 'nation' almost implicitly talks about ethnicity and biology. So I think if I call myself a nationalist, it's almost implicit in that word that it's, 'Well, America does have a heritage of being a European country.'"[87] By depicting himself as a nationalist, instead of a White nationalist, Fuentes seeks to normalize the many racist tropes of White nationalism through a verbal sleight of hand.

Much like how *extremism, fundamentalism, radicalism,* and *activism* are inadequate replacements for *terrorism,* there are terms that are similarly deficient when discussing White nationalism. Specifically, though White supremacy, White separatism, and White power are often conflated with White nationalism—indeed, just as nationalism itself may be confused with patriotism—these designations are not adequately descriptive and fail to demarcate ideological principles.[88] Specifically, the term *White supremacy* is too narrow in that it refers solely to the notion that Whiteness is inherently superior both biologically and culturally to all other identities; by extension, White people have the natural right to control people of color, who are considered as less than human.

White separatism is likewise an inadequate label for many of the groups and individuals in this book because it calls only for the White race to live apart from people of color. While I maintain that White nationalists are White supremacists because they believe that White people are innately better than people of color, I also contend that White nationalists go beyond this conviction in their desire to live in a White ethnostate entirely for White people and governed by White people. Because of this goal,

White nationalists advocate not just for White separatism but also, in many instances, for the eradication of people of color.

There are also definitional distinctions between White nationalism and White power. As defined by historian Kathleen Belew, the term *White power* includes "radical tax resisters, white separatists, . . . and proponents of white theologies such as Christian Identity, Odinism, and Dualism."[89] I categorize many of these same groups as being not under the umbrella of White power but part of the cosmos of the political far right, within which some exist as White nationalists, some militant and others not. Though both terms underscore the claim for victimhood, *White nationalism* is more precise in that it emphasizes the primary aim of a White ethnostate to protect what is upheld as the White race, while *White power*—an appropriation of a slogan from the American Black Power movement—emphasizes a more general demand for self-determination for White people.

One further note: generally, when I use the term *race* in this book, unless it is qualified, I am doing so to reflect the point of view of White nationalists, militant and nonmilitant, who understand race to be a biological phenomenon. Though I believe that there is only one race, the human race, and genomicists as well as social scientists concur that the current application of race to categorize people is a sociopolitical and historical construct, White nationalists maintain that race is not the outcome of external circumstances but a scientific reality.[90] According to this logic, there are distinguishing biological factors that make the White people innately superior to people of color, warranting not only a physical hierarchy, with White people entitled to institutional power, but also, in many instances, a spiritual taxonomy that divinely ordains White domination, as will be discussed in chapter 1.

Islamism

Many of the definitional challenges and confusion already discussed with regard to terrorism and White nationalism are also present in defining Islamism. The term is often misapplied to describe violence against state or civilian targets not adhering to a particularly narrow rendering of Islam.[91] In actuality, the parameters of what constitute Islamism and, by extension, an Islamist, are by no means universally agreed on.[92] Islamism's underlying, universal proposition is that the failures of Muslim-majority nations can be attributed to neglecting Islam. Islamism thus broadly refers to political movements that take their inspiration from various interpretations of Islam. This is why many Islamist political parties, whatever their particular platforms and methodologies, use the slogan "Islam is the solution."[93]

In this book, I define *Islamism* as an ideology that seeks to comprehensively order politics and society in accordance with Islamic law; the definition, interpretation, and application of Islamic law is dependent on the actor or actors interpreting and applying it. It is precisely because the word *Islamism* does not presuppose violence of any kind, or lend any insight into a definitive value system or clearly indicate a clear set of political or religious ideals, that I use the qualifier *militant*.[94] This same qualifier is also utilized to carefully delineate between White nationalists who undertake violent action and those who do not. Moreover, the usage of the term *Islamism* is not intended to obscure important distinctions between militant and nonmilitant groups regarding their religious beliefs, nationalities, and political aspirations. Indeed, Hamas, Hezbollah, Islamic State (Dāʿish), and al-Qaʿida, as well as countless other Islamist organizations that leverage violence as a tool in disparate political conflicts, all have different beliefs, goals, and interests. This term is meant to acknowledge the maneuvering of religious concepts to sanctify violence in furtherance of distinct sociopolitical aims.

Of course, the religion of Islam itself, though based on a core set of beliefs and texts, has had a panoply of expressions across historical and cultural contexts. Indeed, outlets within academia, criminal justice, and journalism have put forward a range of definitions of Islamism.[95] Noah Feldman, an American professor of constitutional and international law, defines Islamism as "a comprehensive political, spiritual and personal world-view defined in opposition to all that is non-Islamic." Olivier Roy, a French political scientist specializing in Islamism, prefers to focus on motivation, defining Islamism as "the attempt to create an Islamic state."[96] CIA official Graham Fuller references potential political views, defining an Islamist as someone "who believes that Islam as a body of faith has something important to say about how politics and society should be ordered in the contemporary Muslim world and who seeks to implement this idea in some fashion."[97] The term itself has been featured so often in the media that the Associated Press has its own definition: "An advocate or supporter of a political movement that favors reordering government and society in accordance with laws prescribed by Islam."[98]

To briefly discuss related basic terminology, Islam is the name of the religion, while a Muslim is a person who adheres to the religion of Islam. Muslim is used to describe people but rarely as a descriptor, save for in the phrases "Muslim-majority government" or "Muslim-majority nation." To describe places and objects related to Islam as a religious civilization, the adjective Islamic (rather than the noun Muslim) should be used, as in "Islamic history" or "Islamic art and architecture."

Salafiyya

Another key related term in the field is *Salafiyya,* or *Salafism,* which is often confused with militant Islamism, much as White supremacy is with White nationalism. In actuality, *Salafiyya* is a neologism referring to as-Salaf as-Salihin (meaning "the Pious Predecessors"), the companions (men and women) of the Prophet Muhammad who lived during the Prophet's lifetime, as well as those closest generationally to the him.[99] In order to claim the legitimacy of piety and of God's favor, present-day militant Islamists declare themselves to be Salafiyya, co-opting the term Salaf and exploiting the connotations Muslims around the world have of the people who truly bear this title. Many Muslims who practice Sunni Islam consider as-Salaf as-Salihin to be the most righteous people in Islamic, if not world, history, as well as those who understood and practiced Islam best. I employ the term only when directly quoting militant Islamists who use it to define themselves.

Jihad

Another word that demands clarification is *jihad.* Much like Salafiyya or Salafism, jihad has mistakenly become synonymous with militant Islamism. To use *jihad* in a violent context, as in the phrases "jihadist terror" or "jihadist warfare," is a misnomer. The word itself comes from the Arabic root *j-h-d* and means to struggle or to persevere; in its appropriate usage, the term lacks any immediate connotation of violence. The correct Arabic term for war is *ḥarb* (root *ḥ-r-b*), and the word for fighting, but not necessarily killing, is *qitāl* (root *q-t-l*).[100] Using *qitāl* in lieu of *jihad* when referring to the use of force would go far in rectifying the misapplication and misappropriation of the concept of *jihad.* In this book, I avoid mischaracterizing messages and actions as jihad, unless I am directly quoting a source.

Finally, a note on what to call the militant Islamist organization ad-Dawla al-Islamiyya fi-l-ʿIraq wa-sh-Sham, or the Islamic State of Iraq and Syria / the Levant, for which there is no universally agreed-upon name. The organization calls itself ad-Dawla al-Islamiyya, or the Islamic State, even though many Muslims around the world do not accept the organization's claim to be a definitive state or caliphate, which, according to Islamic teachings, requires a leader legitimated by the support of the majority of the *umma*. Meanwhile, some global leaders and media outlets refer to the movement as Dāʿish, a pronounced version of the acronym of the group's full Arabic name that mimics the Arabic words *dāʿis* (*d-ʿa-s*), meaning "one who crushes something underfoot," and *dāḥis*, "one who sows discord." The acronyms ISIL and ISIS are also often used interchangeably. In this book, the term Islamic State (Dāʿish) reflects both the name that the group uses for itself and the acronym that has gained currency in the media and international public discourse. I refrain from using the article "the" because this would connote that Islamic State is a definitive caliphate and widely recognized by the global *umma*, when it is not.

Black, White, and Brown

The Black Lives Matter movement started out in 2013 as a Facebook post by Alicia Garza, a Black woman and American civil rights activist, in response to the acquittal of George Zimmerman, who shot and killed Trayvon Martin, a Black teenager, in Florida in 2012. Garza then cofounded what would eventually become a global network of chapters with fellow activists and community organizers Patrisse Cullors and Opal Tometi. Black Lives Matter protests around the world gained traction in 2020 after the murder of George Floyd, a Black man, by police officers in Minneapolis, Minnesota, in May of that year. With the purpose of creating "a world free of anti-Blackness where every Black person has the social, economic, and political power to thrive,"[101] these protests sparked editorial debates throughout news outlets and scholarly publications over capitalizing words such as *Black* and *White*. Because this book is concerned with racism and justice, it is important to explain the terminology and capitalization exercised herein.

Capitalizing *Black* is out of recognition and respect for people within the African diaspora and within the African continent. Different from the label *African American,* which was popularized by the Reverend Jesse Jackson in the 1980s, *Black* recognizes and is an umbrella term for African Americans, Afro-Caribbeans, Afro-Latinxs, African immigrants in the United States, and people who choose to solely identify as Black. Because the institution of slavery stole the traceable identities from enslaved people, *Black* is also sometimes applied as the preferred sole designation of one's cultural background.[102]

Capitalizing *White* may seem like the obvious response to capitalizing *Black*. That is, on the surface, *White* initially seems to be the opposite of *Black,* so the logic would appear to follow that they should be concurrently capitalized. However, recognizing how White people and Black people move in the world will quickly render this line of thinking moot. White people, by virtue of White privilege, are not forced to confront Whiteness because of their skin color. It may seem like this is not the case anymore with discussions on race, racism, and privilege becoming part of the vernacular across communities of all skin colors. Yet it remains true that to be White is to not be held hostage to the same concerns that Blackness confers on an individual due to the sociopolitical construct of race. It is because White is the dominant category of power, indeed the default in many ways, that it must be capitalized. This is intended not to reinforce the White nationalist worldview of biological and cultural supremacy but to recognize the specificity of Whiteness and the histories of privilege embedded therein.[103]

As American professor of philosophy Sally Haslanger has written, capitalizing *Black* and *White* serves "to highlight the artificiality of race in contrast to the apparent naturalness of color."[104] Race is a sociopolitical construct, designed with the intent to subjugate. This oppression must be brought to attention via capitalization in juxtaposition to the homonyms of colors.

Brown is a term that has not been as deliberated in media discourse. Sometimes used alongside *Black,* as in Black and Brown people, or Black and Brown lives, *Brown* should be used sparingly because it does not reflect the heterogeneity of all the people to whom this designation is often applied. By way of illustration, a Brown person may be someone who is Latinx, Indigenous American, Middle Eastern, South Asian, Central Asian, Pacific Islander, or a member of one or more of these backgrounds. There are, of course, a panoply of outlooks and views across these geographic areas, none of which are automatically recognized by the word *Brown*. While Brown is seemingly a collective identity, similar to Black and White, it cannot reflect the myriad histories and cultures within, which is why a more specific description should be used when possible.

Queer

Though *Queer* carries the weight of its usage as a pejorative, it is also being reappropriated as an umbrella label to acknowledge people who do not identify as cisgender, cissexual, or heteronormative. *Queer* counters the notion that biological sex, gender, and gender expression should align and that one's sexual orientation should be heterosexual. *Queer* is also a remedy to the long history of the increasingly factional nature of acronyms such as LGBT, LGBTQ, LGBTQ+, LGBTQIAA+, and LGBTTIQQ2SA. The Q and the + are meant to be inclusive of the myriad combinations of gender identity, gender expression, and sexual orientation, given their fluidity. Moreover, intersex and asexual organizations have argued against those terms being included in the acronyms. Given the list of acronyms, and the Q at the end of LGBTQ, which may mean Queer or Questioning, the plus sign was attached. However, this may seem like a throwaway symbol that neither uplifts nor speaks to the many people who are meant to be recognized by it.

While *Queer* may be rejected by some for flattening the identities the acronyms attempt to address individually, it is because *Queer* is a fluid term, encompassing the heterogeneity of the gender identities, gender expression, sexual orientations, and levels of monogamy of people within it, and rejecting any fixed categories, that it is preferred over acronyms.[105]

Indigenous

Alongside enslaving people for free labor, the United States was also able to fulfill its so-called manifest destiny because it carried out the genocide of the many nations of people who were already living here. *Indigenous* is used to indicate the prior relationship to the land that these nations had, which the misnomer Indian American and the term Native American fail to adequately convey. Much like the specificity required when discussing people who would otherwise be labeled *Brown,* utilizing the tribal affiliation(s) of a person or people is respectful and the preferred form.[106]

Latinx

There are many names that have been used to describe people living in Latin America or descendants of people from Latin America, including, but not limited to, *Hispanic, Latino,* and *Latinx*. *Latinx* is meant to encompass all gender identities, and yet its popularity among and usage by those whom it is meant to signify is debated. Moreover, there is a debate over the elitism of the term. Often, older generations prefer to identify with their country of origin, while younger people signal their political leanings with the use of *Hispanic, Latino, Latinx,* or even *Chicano* or *Chicanx* (though these last two terms do not apply to the entirety of Latin America). People who are more politically conservative identify as Hispanic, or as Latina or Latino, and people who are more politically liberal apply the term *Latinx,* with young women most likely to use the term to self-identify. In the spirit of diversity, I use the term *Latinx,* or the plural *Latinxs,* cognizant that it is not necessarily a common appellation.[107]

Transliteration and Translation

For transliterating Arabic into romanized script, this book uses the widely respected transliteration standards created by the *International Journal of Middle East Studies (IJMES).* Despite the guidance of this system, however, there is still no one universally accepted norm for transliterating Arabic words and names into English, which leads to certain difficulties. In some cases, the spellings and diacritics that I use within the text may differ from what appears in quotes from other sources.[108]

Also, while I do apply diacritical marks to particular plurals that in the singular have none (e.g., *madāris,* the plural for *madrasa;* and *masājid,* the plural for *masjid*), there are certain words to which I would have liked to have applied diacritical marks, if only to reiterate proper pronunciation, but have refrained from doing so because of the ubiquity of their simplified forms in everyday expression and in this book— as well as the consideration that too many diacritical marks would perhaps be off-putting for many readers. One case that illustrates these points is *jihad.* It is often pronounced *jee-had* by English speakers when it is, in fact, pronounced *ji-haad* in Arabic, with an almost guttural *h* and an elongated second vowel. Its correct transliteration is *jihād,* but because the word is commonly recognized, albeit misunderstood, as *jihad,* I present it here without diacritics. Other words that appear in their conventional English spellings for the same reasons, despite their common mispronunciation, are Islam and Qur'an, both of which have elongated second vowels as evidenced by the diacritics in the following: *Islām* and *Qur'ān.*

Where approaches to understanding religious texts are concerned, I have used the New Living Translation of the Bible, a widely accepted contemporary version, and *The Qur'an: A New Translation,* by Muhammad Abdel Haleem, OBE, professor of Islamic Studies. Both provide accessible verses for a general readership. Rather than calling these "translations," I prefer the phrase "approaches to understanding," which acknowledges the myriad issues arising from using a language different than the direct source material—namely, differences in context, nuance, and depth of meaning.

THE CHAPTERS AHEAD

This book consists of four parts. The first asks who White nationalists and militant Islamists are, providing an overview of their histories and organizational structures, defining the key groups and figures, and analyzing their worldviews. The second interrogates why they fight, deconstructing their grievances against the United States and related enemy groups, and also examining how religion is made use of in order to license these grievances. The third investigates what they want, comparing their respective visions for government, which are often shaped by their respective exegeses, scripturalism, and conceptions of holy war, in addition to examining the myth of the lone wolf in both contexts. Each of these chapters begins with a case study of the actions or writings of an American terrorist. The fourth details what can be done, calling for a more just, and thus more effective, counterterrorism strategy.

Chapters 1 and 2 focus on the seeds of hate, providing the foundation of understanding for the complex environment in which homegrown hate is cultivated. Chapter 1 discusses the centrality of the Fourteen Words to White nationalism and the tenets of the most influential racist theologies on this transnational phenomenon. The chapter includes an examination of points of convergence and divergence between Christian Identity, Creativity, and Wotanism, as well as other White racist religious traditions, and outlines the religious principles behind their collective desire to establish the United States as a White ethnostate. The diverse strands of White nationalism in the United States are also presented, providing a nuanced landscape of White nationalist organizations and figureheads, religious and secular, and taking care to also delineate between those that engage in violence and those that do not.

Chapter 2 examines the religious concepts that are ultimately exploited by militant Islamists to legitimize their war against the United States. This chapter details the evolution and structure of two militant Islamist groups, al-Qaʿida and Islamic State (Dāʿish), and pinpoints key differences and similarities in their aims and tactics, both for acts of violence and for outreach to American militant Islamists, would-be and actual. It then analyzes militant Islamism through the Islamic and Islamist terminology corrupted by these terrorist organizations. Because each of these terms could easily warrant an entire book or series of books, the focus is on how such religious rhetoric is utilized by American terrorists to justify their violence in pursuance of political aims.

Building on these organizational histories and ideological principles, chapters 3 and 4 consider the focal grievances of American White nationalists and American militant Islamists in the twenty-first century—in essence, the roots of their hate. Chapter 3 delves into how a belief in imminent White genocide, as asserted in the Fourteen Words, detailed in chapter 1, shapes the defensiveness of White nationalists, impacting their attitude toward and treatment of immigrants, people of color, and minoritized communities, including Jewish Americans, Muslim Americans, Queer people, and women. This chapter concludes with a discussion on how the deaths and devastation that occurred at the hands of law enforcement in Ruby Ridge, Idaho, and Waco, Texas, are emblematic of the long-standing grievances of White nationalists against the power of the federal government, including the enduring issue of gun rights, and how these events reinforce their narrative of victimhood.

Chapter 4 evaluates how the concepts detailed in chapter 2 forge the current grievances of American militant Islamists, whose acts of violence are then propagandized by al-Qaʿida and Islamic State (Dāʿish). Sharing a similar sense of victimhood that galvanizes many White nationalists, militant Islamists are preoccupied with defending what they interpret to be true Islam against what they interpret to be the Crusader-Zionist alliance of the United States, Israel, and their political allies, or the Muslims and Muslim-majority governments deemed by these militants to have apostatized. From the vantage of the political figures discussed in chapter 2, as well as that of present-day militant Islamists, the narrative of oppressive Crusaders is validated by American foreign policy and America's support of dictatorships in Muslim-majority nations. The chapter concludes with a discussion of how Palestine and Guantánamo encapsulate their grievances against what they believe to be the Crusader-Zionist alliance.

Within the next section of the book, each chapter explores a different facet of violence, substantially investigating the flowering of hate. Chapter 5 overviews the development of the concepts of racial holy war, or RAHOWA, and of jihad, examining how these terms came to encompass holy war against the United States, how they are understood between and within groups, and how warfare gives purpose and identity to (racist) holy warriors. This chapter then analyzes how the Fourteen Words and religious texts are leveraged to support modern-day calls for warfare.

Chapter 6 discusses how religious scripture and the Fourteen Words are interpreted to justify either establishing the United States as a White ethnostate or constructing a caliphate. It analyzes how Christian Identity adherents use the Old and New Testaments to sanctify their belief that the Founding Fathers were true Christians and that the Declaration of Independence and the Constitution were divinely inspired, and explores the more caustic view of the Founding Fathers held by Creativity and Wotanism. It also delves into the Islamist conception of government, exploring how present-day militant Islamists are able to distort the notion of *ḥākimiyyat Allah,* that nothing is outside the sovereignty of God, to argue for their vision of a caliphate. Finally, the chapter scrutinizes how Islamic State (Dāʿish) was able to declare a caliphate and considers the significance of the caliphate not only to militant Islamist thought but also to the psyche of many nonmilitant Muslims around the world.

Chapter 7 directly compares the apocalyptic visions of both White nationalist–related theologies and militant Islamism, detailing the depictions of the final battle of Armageddon within them and the role of Jesus in both militant Christian–related theologies and militant Islamism. Discussing how violence carried out to further political aims is sanctified by employing eschatological rhetoric, this chapter also investigates how both ideologies use the concept of the End Times as a motif, calling for the regeneration of the world that only they can fulfill by achieving their respective political goals of a White ethnostate or caliphate.

Chapter 8 deconstructs the myth of the so-called lone wolf within the frameworks of both militant White nationalism and militant Islamism. It highlights how the concept of leaderless resistance was first promoted by Ku Klux Klan leaders, then debates the role of technology in perpetuating militancy, giving particular focus to the function of the manifesto in actualizing transnational White nationalism and to the role of the Internet in encouraging martyrdom. This chapter ultimately questions how alone lone wolves really are.

Finally, building on a premise of this book, which is that American militant White nationalism must be regarded as just as much, if not more, of a threat to national security than American militant Islamism, the conclusion advances a counterterrorism approach based on holistic justice, submitting that American counterterrorism strategies will be effective in securing the homeland when they focus on achieving equity for all rather than maintaining White hegemony and perpetuating the criminalization of people of color. I assert that in today's world, in which national security is militarized, the armaments of education, engagement, and equity are needed more than ever before because they provide the foundations for justice that weapons cannot achieve.

PART ONE

Who They Are

CHAPTER I

The Fourteen Words

The Racist Beliefs of White Nationalists

On August 5, 2012, in the Milwaukee, Wisconsin, suburb of Oak Creek, a forty-year-old bearded man dressed in military fatigues walked into a house of worship filled with congregants. The solitary figure unleashed a Springfield 9 mm semiautomatic handgun, killing six people and wounding four others. Though he acted by himself, as a so-called lone wolf, targeting those who did not look like him or share his beliefs, he had previously posted hundreds of messages on Internet hate sites glorifying violence, sharing his ideas about an impending holy war with friends, like-minded individuals, and sympathetic groups.[1] Local police and the FBI would later call these horrific murders an act of domestic terrorism.

This terrorist was Wade Michael Page, a U.S. Army veteran who envisioned himself as taking part in what he and fellow White nationalists conceive of as a racial holy war, also known as RAHOWA. The targets of his violence were innocent Sikhs, whom he murdered and wounded if not because of Islamophobia, mistaking them for Muslims, then out of antipathy for their Brownness and their adherence to a non-Christian religion. Even though his name is not typical of those who have become inextricably linked with violence in the name of religion, Wade Michael Page is actually illustrative of the face of domestic terrorism in the United States: a White warrior striving to protect and defend White identity, perceiving himself as a victim of racial and religious pluralism, and disgruntled with political correctness and cancel culture.

Photos of Page show a stern, slightly overweight man with a dark-brown goatee, thick eyebrows, and a shaved head. His most significant features, however, were not found on his face but emblazoned on his skin. Several tattoos served as visible symbols of his allegiance to militant White nationalism. Page embodied, quite literally on his person, the confluence of present-day militant White nationalist groups.[2]

The letters *W* and *P,* standing for "White power," were tattooed on the backs of his hands. His right bicep was marked with the number 838, indicating that he had pledged allegiance to the Hammerskins, which developed into the Hammerskin Nations, one of the most violent White power skinhead groups in the United States.[3] (Page had also sought to join the Ku Klux Klan; however, he forgot his application on his desk after he was fired from a Harley-Davidson shop in Fayetteville, North Carolina, because he had a problem with authority and working with women.)

While many White nationalist organizations incorporate some elements of antigovernment or religious motifs into their platforms, there are others, like the Hammerskin Nation, that include neither, instead proselytizing solely White supremacy and the creation of a White ethnostate.[4] The Hammerskin Nation is part of the skinhead subculture that emerged from 1960s working-class England, and it is also affiliated with White power music. Page, who like his skinhead counterparts sported a shaved head, Doc Martens boots, and tattoos, spread his message of hate through music, playing in a White power band called End Apathy.[5] A description of the band on its MySpace page reads, "The music is a sad commentary on our sick society and the problems that prevent true progress."[6]

On Page's upper left arm was a Celtic cross, a circle with an oversized plus sign extending from its borders, a symbol often used by skinheads. The symbol itself does not connote militancy, but the number 14, tattooed inside the cross, corresponds to the number of words in a battle cry widely adhered to by White nationalists, some of whom justify political violence through religious rhetoric and imagery: "We must secure the existence of our people and a future for white children."[7] As this chapter will discuss, this slogan, known as the Fourteen Words, was penned by David Lane, a member of the terrorist organization The Order (Brüder Schweigen), and the founder of Wotanism. Page's tattooed affiliation therefore linked him with a virulent portion of White nationalists who imagine themselves to be upholding the values of The Order.

According to the logic of his worldview, Page's violence was justified because the United States was made ill by racial and ethnic diversity and religious pluralism.[8] Wade Michael Page is not the first terrorist to construct the narrative that the United States is weakened by immigrants and citizens of color, threatened by women's rights, and diminished by changing social values. As detailed in the introduction, White nationalism includes a belief in the cultural and genetic superiority of Whiteness and concomitant support for a White ethnostate.

Setting the foundation for in-depth exploration in later chapters of the grievances and aims of the American White nationalists, militant and nonmilitant, this chapter will detail the contours of the American political far right and delineate its various constituencies that support White nationalism within the United States, as well as highlight those that are not primarily concerned with establishing America as a white ethnostate but are still part of the American political far right, such as antiabortionists. As the introduction discussed, White nationalist aims are promulgated by President Donald Trump's administration, the rhetoric and policies of which are covert dog whistles to his primarily White constituents, as well as overtly discriminatory in terms of religion and the sociohistorical construct of race. This chapter first analyzes the Fourteen Words as a moral imperative for White nationalists and then considers the role played by White evangelicalism in the growth of White nationalism. It then details the development and central beliefs of the most prominent theologies prevalent within White nationalism: Christian Identity, Creativity, and Wotanism.

Finally, the chapter considers the complex network of groups that compose the White nationalist cosmos according to their primary motivations, which rotate around the axis of establishing a White ethnostate, including religiosity, antigovernment conspiratorial views, and racism. Even though all of these groups are within the scope of White nationalism, it is important to note that not all of their members are militant and to point out the fluidity of religious adherence. The purpose of this chapter is to understand their beliefs and their overlapping networks with the explicit understanding that not all who hold these beliefs will carry out of acts of violence.

SECURING WHITENESS AND THE FOURTEEN WORDS

The Fourteen Words is a collective mission statement for all White nationalists, penned in 1988 by revered ideologue David Lane, who himself fluctuated between Christian Identity and his own version of Odinism, which he called Wotanism. This statement—"We must secure the existence of our people and a future for white children"—is a non-negotiable truth central to the identity, belief system, and political aims of White nationalists. It propounds the concept of White people as a genetically and culturally superior race to all others. It demands militancy to assert this status while maintaining an ethos of victimhood. Not open to internal or external questioning, the Fourteen Words shapes the lens through which White nationalists view themselves.

The Fourteen Words is a battle cry to the vast array of individuals within the ecology of White nationalism, and each of its elements has important resonance. "Our people" is a declaration of inclusivity for all White people, setting aside religion while upholding racial identity. It is also a statement of exclusivity, building a distinct barrier against people of color. The phrase "must secure" projects a sense of urgency, asserting that White identity is in need of protection, endorsing the sense of victimhood pervasive across White nationalism as well as reinforcing the need for militancy. The components of "existence" and "White children" underscore this exigency. White women, willingly or not, are thus integral to this project, which is dependent on their servitude as vessels of reproduction. Not only is the very survival of those who are deemed to be part of the White race at stake, but the all-encompassing threat of the Other will detrimentally affect White children, who are the essence of vulnerability and purity. The Fourteen Words invokes fear of White genocide, emphasizing a portrayal of racial, cultural, and economic victimhood that legitimizes violence.

By articulating the raison d'être of White nationalism without evoking religious tenets, the Fourteen Words appeals to a broad swathe of individuals affiliated with the racist religions and myriad organizations this chapter will discuss, including those who identify as atheists, agnostics, or spiritual but not religious. The next part of the chapter will discuss the many theologies aligned with the Fourteen Words and supportive of White supremacy—that is, the belief that White people are genetically and culturally superior.

EVANGELICAL AMERICA AND WHITE NATIONALIST CHRISTIANITY

Before turning to the racist religions most explicitly associated with White nationalism and their violent articulations—Christian Identity,

Creativity, and Wotanism—it is vital to acknowledge the prominent role that White nationalist evangelicalism and other American religious traditions play in offering theological support to the idea of the uniqueness of White identity as set apart from and above that of people not deemed to be White. Though not a precursor to militancy by any means, twenty-first-century White evangelicalism in the United States has come to intersect with White nationalist beliefs, specifically the idea that the United States must become a Christian theocratic state.

As this chapter will examine, the wielding of expressions of Christianity to justify violence is built on centuries-old sociopolitical racism cloaked in religious and sacred expression.[9] Certainly, the imaginings of Jesus as a White, fair-skinned man and the notion of the United States as a nation abiding by Christian laws made for White people by White people have long underpinned the theologies of many American religions endorsing versions of theocracy. To understand the significant connections between American White evangelicalism and White nationalism some definitions are in order.[10]

Evangelicalism itself has many definitions, depending on who is asked, particularly because, since the 1970s, the term has come to signal a political group rather than a religious demographic and has now seemingly become synonymous with Donald Trump's base of support.[11] While the boundaries of the term *evangelical* and to whom it should be applied are points of contention across a spectrum of Christian affiliations, the National Association of Evangelicals uses the following four criteria for doing so: "The Bible is the highest authority for what I believe. It is very important for me personally to encourage non-Christians to trust Jesus Christ as their Savior. Jesus Christ's death on the cross is the only sacrifice that could remove the penalty of my sin. Only those who trust in Jesus Christ alone as their Savior receive God's free gift of eternal salvation."[12] Other historians have added slightly different elements to this list, including born-again experiences and activism.[13] Essentially, White, Latinx, Black, and Asian evangelicals share the same evangelical theology of belief in the literal truth of the Bible, a personal relationship with Jesus Christ, and the significance of the born-again experience, though they differ over social issues, such as racism, abortion, and immigration.

Within the American White evangelical Protestant community, a prominent brand of evangelicalism is based on the notion that the United States is meant by God to be a White Christian nation and must be reclaimed as such.[14] Certainly, the constituencies of White evangelical

Christians and White nationalists overlap. I term these adherents "White nationalist evangelicals," and throughout this book I distinguish them from "White evangelicals," by which I mean simply evangelicals who are White.

Within the White nationalist evangelical movement, any person who threatens the cultural values of a bygone White America that perhaps never was—but that they seek to safeguard and maintain—is not welcome. This includes people of color; all non-Christians, especially Muslims; and Queer people. They also seek to constrict the rights of groups with which they disagree, particularly around the issues of abortion, immigration, and religious freedom. In brief, intensely apocalyptic and increasingly political, White nationalist evangelicalism espouses not only White supremacy and the creation of a White ethnostate as a refuge for the soon-to-be minority of White Christian Americans but also what is perceived as the God-given right and responsibility to ensure the national preservation of their particular understanding of White Christian identity.[15]

Prominent figures in this tradition include Pastor Paula White, also known as Paula White-Cain, who preaches the prosperity gospel, is President Trump's personal pastor, and was appointed to a position within the administration's Faith and Opportunity Initiative; Pastor Robert Jeffress, who is on President Trump's Evangelical Advisory Board and the White House Faith Initiative and is host of Pathway to Victory, a national radio and television ministry; James Dobson, founder of the prominent organization Focus on the Family, which promotes its evangelical views in public policy; Charlie Kirk, founder and president of Turning Point USA, an organization committed to countering what it perceives as political progressivism on college campuses; Jerry Falwell Jr., namesake and son of Moral Majority founder Jerry Falwell and president of Liberty University, a private evangelical institution of higher education; Tony Perkins, president of the Family Research Council, an influential anti-Queer organization; and Franklin Graham, eldest son of Billy Graham, who was a prominent evangelist who oversaw the alignment of this faction of White Christians with the Republican Party late in the second half of the twentieth century.

Since the election of Donald Trump in 2016, White evangelicalism, which has long been a potent political force in the United States, has become intertwined with the political far right, and particularly with White nationalism.[16] Notably mirroring this trend is the striking rate at which Black evangelicals in particular have left majority-White evangelical churches since the election of President Trump.[17] Individuals who self-identify as White evangelical Christians made up 26 percent of the U.S. voting electorate, and 81 percent of this group voted for Trump in 2016, helping propel him to the White House.[18] Many of his White evangelical supporters would not call themselves White nationalists, but numerous studies suggest that a large number of them were motivated by racism and sexism rather than economic worries exclusively.[19] Specifically, many were prompted by anxiety over perceived threats to White identity in a country that is witnessing a demographic shift away from a White Christian majority, prompting fears of losing the power that comes with White racial privilege and of a dwindling Christian-centric nation, as well as concerns over immigration and shifting gender roles.[20] White evangelicals are supportive of Trump in spite of the ways in which his behavior has at times affronted traditional stances.[21] In fact, more of this demographic supported him than it did previous presidents Jimmy Carter, an evangelical; Ronald Reagan, a Presbyterian; and George W. Bush, a Methodist, all of whom were heavily supported by and reached out to evangelicals during their campaigns.

However, reflecting the heterogeneity of each demographic in the United States, including religious constituencies, not all White evangelicals support Donald Trump's presidency—indeed, a small but eager contingent now seeks to reject the label completely because of this connotation.[22] There have been many prominent evangelical detractors, including Russell Moore, head of the Southern Baptist Convention's public policy arm, and Tim Keller, pastor of Redeemer Presbyterian Church in New York City. In 2019, Mark Galli, the general editor of *Christianity Today,* a magazine founded by the Reverend Billy Graham, wrote an editorial titled "Trump Should Be Removed from Office." Galli writes that Trump's effort to coerce the president of Ukraine to discredit a political opponent "is not only a violation of the Constitution; more importantly, it is profoundly immoral."[23] Galli makes mention of the president's immorality several times throughout his editorial. Both backlash against and support for Galli's words were swift. Franklin Graham claimed his father had voted for President Trump and would not have supported Galli's editorial.[24] Nearly two hundred evangelical leaders also condemned Galli's position and dismissed his support of impeachment.[25] But while the magazine lost hundreds of subscribers, the total number of subscribers to the magazine tripled.

These varied responses demonstrate the contentious history of the multitude of expressions of evangelicalism, and most especially White evangelicalism, in the United States. The evangelical tradition has been used to legitimate centuries of the institution of slavery, Jim Crow segregation, eugenics, White nationalism, structural racism, prejudice, discrimination, and groups like the Ku Klux Klan, but it has also been called on to validate abolition, integration, equality, justice, and diversity.[26]

Other American religions, while not explicitly espousing White supremacy, focus on the merging of church and state, a political aim central to certain segments of White nationalism today calling for establishing the United States as a theopolity. Within the teachings of both Christian Reconstructionism and Christian Dominionism, God ordained the United States to be a Christian nation in which Mosaic law is implemented in all institutions of American culture.[27] According to this interpretation of Genesis 9:2 as a direct mandate for mankind to dominate all other species, people are starkly divided into believers (who follow Mosaic law) and unbelievers (who follow secular law). Dominionism seeks to create a completely Christian culture via total dominion over the United States, and eventually the world, while Christian Reconstructionism calls for the sociopolitical and religious reconstruction of America back to the Christian nation it purportedly was under the Founding Fathers.[28]

MILITANT LATTER-DAY SAINTS

Militants who identify as Mormons, also known by the Church's preferred term of Latter-day Saints (LDS), like Cliven Bundy, the orchestrator of a 2014 armed confrontation with the federal government, and his sons, Ammon and Ryan, cite as inspiration the stories of antigovernment resistance found within the Book of Mormon.[29] The elder Bundy sought to avoid paying fees for grazing cattle on millions of acres of public land near his ranch in Nevada, which was part of a decades-long dispute over recognition of the federal government's ownership of this area. In 2016, Ammon Bundy led an armed occupation of the Malheur National Wildlife Refuge in Oregon, resulting in the death of Robert LaVoy Finicum, a friend to the Bundys, who is now regarded as a martyr by many within the movement. As with the 2014 standoff headed by Cliven Bundy, this, too, was essentially an antigovernment protest. While 2014 was specifically about land use, this time umbrage was taken because of the imprisonment of a pair of father and son ranchers, Dwight Hammond Jr. and Steven Hammond, who were convicted of arson after setting fires in

2001 and 2006 that damaged tracts of land adjacent to their ranch in Oregon that were managed by the U.S. Bureau of Land Management. (In a show of support to his base, President Trump issued pardons for both Hammonds in 2018.) The day before the 2016 standoff began, Ammon Bundy posted a YouTube video in which he cited Alma 60:28 in the Book of Mormon to explain why he believed God wanted him to defend the Hammonds: "Yea, behold I do not fear your power nor your authority, but it is my God whom I fear; and it is according to his commandments that I do take my sword to defend the cause of my country." So central is the U.S. Constitution to the cause of the Bundys and like-minded Latter-day Saints that Bundy called his group of armed militants Citizens for Constitutional Freedom.[30]

Though the Church of Latter-day Saints issued a statement rebuking Ammon Bundy's response to the Hammonds' sentencing, the belief that the U.S. Constitution is a divine document was also central to the teachings of the founder of the Church of Jesus Christ of Latter-day Saints, Joseph Smith, and his successor, Brigham Young.[31] Like Smith and Young, current Latter-day Saints believe that only theocracy can redeem the corruption of the United States.[32] In a well-known speech recorded in the church's *Journal of Discourses,* Young publicized his dismay that the hallowed document was being perverted by secular politicians in Washington: "If the Constitution of the United States were saved at all it must be done by this people"—meaning Latter-day Saints. Bundy and his many associates exploit religious rhetoric about the divinity of the U.S. Constitution to further their political aims, which are shaped by their specific understanding of their faith. The belief that the U.S. Constitution is a divinely inspired document is not one that is exclusive to the Bundys and their acolytes but one that is deeply ingrained in the teachings of the Church of Jesus Christ of Latter-day Saints.[33] The interpretation of the U.S. Constitution that has been openly dismissed by the LDS Church—despite being adopted by prominent Latter-day Saints, including media personality Glenn Beck and supporters of the politician Mitt Romney—is the White Horse Prophecy, which is a secondhand report by Englishman Edwin Rushton of Joseph Smith foretelling that the U.S. Constitution will one day "hang like a thread as fine as the finest silk fiber," only to be "preserved and saved by the efforts of the White Horse and the Red Horse."[34] The prophecy is a lengthy one that describes the White Horse as the "great and mighty people" established in the Rocky Mountains, which is interpreted to mean the Latter-day

Saints.[35] The White Horse Prophecy, along with the orthodox belief in the divinity of the U.S. Constitution, sustains the Bundys' quest against the federal government in what they see as the holy fight for constitutional and thus religious freedoms. Framing violence as a religious duty against the immorality of the federal government, they conclude that bloodshed is not only justified but necessitated.[36]

Certainly, the religious and political convictions of the Bundys and like-minded militants are intertwined. Cliven Bundy's neighbor and fellow rancher Keith Allen Nay compiled an anthology of religious writings that included snippets of scripture and speeches from prominent members of the Church of Latter-day Saints, affirming their mutual views in what would be called *The Nay Book*. On the cover, under the words "Freedom, Liberty, for God We Stand" is an illustration of Betsy Ross stitching the American flag, telling of the mélange of religious and political writings to be found within. After Nay's death, Bundy, with Nay's widow's support, shared this book widely.

The introductory letter, written by Cliven Bundy, poses its central themes as questions: "What is the Constitutional duty of a member of the Lord's church? How am I to understand the 12th Article of Faith to obey and sustain the laws?"[37] (The 12th Article of Faith states, "We believe in being subject to kings, presidents, rulers, and magistrates, in obeying, honoring, and sustaining the law."[38]) Directly responding to these inquiries are the subsequent photocopied documents included after this letter, which reference the color-coded index, with yellow used "for mentions of the Constitution as a sacred document," and pink "for references to calls to 'save and maintain the Constitution.'"[39] *The Nay Book* heavily relies on Ezra Taft Benson, the president of the Church of Latter-day Saints from 1984 to 1995 and the U.S. secretary of agriculture during the Eisenhower administration, who personifies this twinning of religion and politics.[40]

Bundy, Nay, and fellow adherents of their distinct interpretation of the tenets of the Church of Jesus Christ of Latter-day Saints believed that the American Founding Fathers and scribes of the U.S. Constitution would have sided with Bundy and his armed associates as they defended what they regarded as their land against federal overreach. Given this worldview, the Bundys' confrontations with the federal government attracted a wide range of antigovernment supporters, among them groups such as the Praetorian Guard (referencing the elite soldiers who protected the Roman Emperor), the Oath Keepers, and the White Mountain Militia, and individuals like Matt Shea, a six-term Washington state legislator.[41]

In 2019, the Washington State of House of Representatives found that Shea "planned, engaged in and promoted a total of three armed conflicts of political violence against the United States Government in three states outside the state of Washington over a three-year period," which include his promotion of the 2014 armed standoff in Nevada and his direct support to Ammon Bundy before and during the 2016 takeover in Oregon.[42] The same report determined that because of this involvement, Shea "participated in an act of domestic terrorism against the United States" and that in 2016 he "engaged in and supported the training of youth and young adults to fight a Holy war."[43] Shea, who hosts *Patriot Radio*, a weekly show on the American Christian Network, also authored "The Biblical Basis of War," a four-page document encouraging adults and children to train to take part in a holy war to establish the United States as a Christian nation, a theopolity that would "obey Biblical law."[44] Of the rules of engagement in this upcoming racial holy war, Shea wrote, "If they do not yield, kill all males."[45]

Deeply involved with Latter-day Saints like Ammon Bundy, though Christian himself, entrenched in the Patriot movement (detailed later in this chapter), and affiliated with several antigovernment groups within it, including the Lightfoot Militia and the closely linked Three Percenters and the Oath Keepers, Shea demonstrates the degree to which White nationalist views are acceptable to and even advocated by portions of the electorate, as well as the complexity of the affiliations within.[46] As will be made evident throughout this chapter, Shea is certainly not singular in either regard.

According to the theologies of certain segments of White evangelicalism, particularly its White nationalist expression, as well as militants who claim adherence to the Church of Jesus Christ of Latter-day Saints, it is both a prime religious imperative and a mechanism of survival to restore the United States to what they regard as its divinely willed status as a nation for White Americans and governed by White Americans in accordance with their respective interpretations of God's law.

Irrespective of their religious affiliations, these militants uphold violence as the sole remedy to current political ills and the most direct means to achieve the ultimate aim of establishing the United States as a White nation in keeping with its true heritage and rightful destiny. The next section will examine the development of three of the most impactful religions that endorse the Fourteen Words, influencing the rhetoric of White nationalists in their political pursuit of a White ethnostate.

CHRISTIAN IDENTITY

One of the most influential religions within contemporary American White nationalism—in terms of adherents, longevity, and thematic resonance—is Christian Identity. It is not possible to understand contemporary White nationalism without understanding Christian Identity, both its historical origins and its theological precepts. Preaching a message of White racial and cultural superiority while adjuring violence in support of ultimate, divine victory for the White race, Christian Identity's teachings of White genetic superiority, White cultural victimhood, and intolerance of people regarded as non-White, Queer people, and those who follow other religions have been exploited by many within White nationalism to sanction violence.

The primary principle in the logic of White nationalism is that science proves the concept of intrinsic differences between races and, more specifically, the biological preeminence of the White race. One of the most prominent vehicles for these interwoven concepts is the racist religion of Christian Identity. (Belief in the inherited, genetic inequality of humans is also present in the racist theologies of Creativity and Odinism, as will be discussed below.[47])

Beginning in the mid-nineteenth century, Christian Identity developed alongside eugenics, a newly established science that attempted to prove that social inequalities had their basis in biology and genetics and was promoted by post-Darwinian writers such as Sir Francis Galton, Arthur de Gobineau, Houston Stewart Chamberlain, and Madison Grant.[48] Some proponents of eugenics proposed a hierarchy within the White race, favoring Aryans due to their putative "pure" blood; White people from Eastern Europe, for example, were considered secondary, and Black and Brown people were deemed the lowest in the racial pyramid.[49]

The doctrine of Christian Identity subverts the Creationist creed found within Christianity and posits instead that different races have different origins, a theory known as polygenism. According to Christian Identity, Adam and Eve are not the primordial parents of all mankind. Rather, during the first four days of Creation, God created the earth as well as people who are not White, or "mud people," a term that signifies not only the color of their skin but also their subhuman status. On the fifth day of Creation, God realized the imperfections of the mud people, so He decided to create His perfect version of humanity, Adam and Eve, who were White, Protestant, and cisheteronormative. White people are thus God's chosen and preferred race.

In addition to this polygenist understanding of human origins, Christian Identity also preaches the "two-seed theory," which is the belief that Jewish people are descendants not of Adam and Eve's other children but of Cain, who they believe is the offspring of Satan and Eve. Christian Identity's antisemitic view of Jewish people affirms the non-Whiteness of Jewish people and the religious and racial superiority of Christian Identity adherents.

Judaism is considered incompatible with Christianity by Christian Identity adherents for several reasons.[50] Firstly, Jewish people are regarded as having denigrated the first five books of the Bible, or Pentateuch, by distorting them with notes, commentaries, and additions from oral law stemming from the teachings of the Pharisees. Because Christ explicitly spoke out against the Pharisees (Matthew 23:1–39), Christian Identity adherents consider the concept of Judeo-Christianity, or indeed any reconciliation between Judaism and Christianity, to be impossible.[51] Christian Identity thus excises Jewish people from the Abrahamic tradition, which usually encompasses Judaism, Christianity, and Islam, because, they argue, the current iteration of Judaism is not even remotely linked to the religion in the Bible and is fundamentally opposed to Christianity.[52] Secondly, Christian Identity condemns Jewish people as an evil race whose hands have been bloodied by killing Christ (Matthew 27:25) and slaying all of the righteous people on earth (Matthew 23:35).[53] Thirdly, Christian Identity asserts that Jewish people's ancestry is—if not Satanic— actually a combination of Mongol, Finnish, and Turkish, believing, as do most White nationalists, that Jewish people are considered non-White.[54]

From its origins in England in the 1840s to its growth in the United States in the twenty-first century, many figures have shaped Christian Identity's theology. However, this section will focus on seven key thinkers in order to trace the development of Christian Identity within present-day American White nationalism: John Wilson, Edward Hine, Howard Rand, William Cameron, Wesley Swift, William Potter Gale, and Bertrand Comparet.

The nucleus of Christian Identity theology is the theory of Anglo-Israelism, also called British-Israelism, which was first formulated by the Reverend John Wilson in his book *Lectures on Our Israelitish Origins,* published in England in 1840. Considered to be one of the first publications on Christian Identity, Wilson's book advanced the central principle of Anglo-Israelism: White Anglo-Saxons of Northern Europe are the direct offspring of the Prophet Abraham and the literal descendants of the lost tribes of Israel. They, instead of Jewish people, who are actually part

Satanic, are the true claimants to the prophetic destiny promised by God to Abraham and his offspring through the generations—Isaac, Jacob, and then Joseph in Genesis 12:1–3. White people, and only White people, are thus entitled to special status from God.

Though multitudes of people have claimed to be the lost tribes of Israel throughout the centuries, Christian Identity, under Wilson's tutelage, became a theology preaching that the rightful inheritance of the White race was to be blessed with the successful nations of Great Britain and the United States, referred to in the Bible as Ephraim and Manasseh.[55] Believing otherwise is tantamount to rejecting Jesus as Savior.[56]

Given the sociopolitical contexts of the United Kingdom and the United States in the nineteenth century, Wilson's theory of Anglo-Israelism soon found firm footing among the White British public, who were attracted to claims of their own racial superiority. The British Empire was at its height of industrialization and colonialism, and the expanding United States was fulfilling its "manifest destiny."

After hearing Wilson's lectures on the subject, American banker Edward Hine began publishing pamphlets promoting Anglo-Israelism in the United States. He went on to write a book on the subject for the American public, *Identification of the British Nation with Lost Israel,* published in the 1870s. Howard Rand, a lawyer from Massachusetts, also promoted Anglo-Israelism decades after it was first developed. In the early 1900s, Rand oversaw several branches of the London-based British Israel World Federation across the United States, including the Anglo-Saxon Federation of America in Detroit.[57]

It was in Detroit that Howard Rand would meet William Cameron, the public relations representative of American industrialist Henry Ford and editor of the *Dearborn Independent.*[58] In the 1920s, under Cameron's supervision, the *Dearborn Independent* became infamous for publishing a set of antisemitic articles titled *The International Jew,* including "The Protocols of the Elders of Zion," one of the most significant antisemitic documents of the twentieth century.[59] William Cameron not only managed the publication of such materials but also proved to be a promoter of American Anglo-Israelism. During the rise of xenophobia in United States in the 1920s, which also saw the growth of the Ku Klux Klan, Cameron's access to and utilization of the media only further solidified support for Anglo-Israelism, which brandished religion to sanction racism and promote White supremacy.

In the 1930s, under the triumvirate of Wesley Swift, William Potter Gale, and Bertrand Comparet, Christian Identity was more overt in its antisemitism and in its denigration of "mud people," which at that point included all non-White, nonheterosexual, non-Christian "seed."[60] While Swift proselytized antisemitism via polygenism and Gale promoted Anglo-Israelism though science, Bertrand Comparet provided the exegesis to support Christian Identity's antisemitism.

Wesley Swift was a Ku Klux Klan member who founded the Church of Jesus Christ Christian in 1946, an instance of cross-pollination that was emblematic of how the disparate elements of the political far right were already coalescing around White nationalism. In his book *God, Man, Nations, and the Races,* Swift positions himself as a true Christian and argues that the White race is the chosen race; it is thus the God-given purpose of White people everywhere to establish and rule God's kingdom on earth in the name of Christianity. Swift equates fighting for White nationalism with a divinely sanctioned destiny. White people are the only true children of God, which is manifested in their biological and cultural superiority.[61] To protect and maintain this status, the United States must be a White ethnostate. The book contains both a message of triumph and a call to self-defense: "Our destiny is to keep our race intact, to repudiate all policies of integration and mongrelization, to retain the supremacy and leadership in this our country, and to carry out our destiny for the building of God's Kingdom."[62] Swift's combination portends the Fourteen Words, which the founder of Wotanism, David Lane, writes decades later.

An early convert to Wesley Swift's church was William Potter Gale, who became a minister within the Church of Jesus Christ Christian in 1956, even though he was part Jewish.[63] Gale published a regular newsletter, *Identity,* and in the 1970s he helped build Posse Comitatus, a racist antigovernment group (discussed below).[64] Advancing John Wilson's theory of Anglo-Israelism, Gale writes of the divinely ordained genetic superiority of White people in his own book, *Racial and National Identity.* As evidence, he maintains that archaeologists have scientifically proven that there is a distinct echelon of elevated humans comprising the White race who directly descend from the family of Abraham and appeared on earth after non-Whites.[65]

Bertrand Comparet was a Christian Identity pastor, as well as a writer and speaker who published copious speeches and booklets sermonizing Christian Identity teachings. Ironically, Comparet often warns his followers not to misinterpret scripture, even though many Christians would accuse him of unusual readings of conventional biblical passages.[66]

In the booklet *The Cain-Satanic Seed Line,* Bertrand Comparet cites specific verses he interprets as Christ's confirmation of polygenism, the belief that Jewish people are the children of Satan, not the descendants of Abraham.[67] According to Comparet, the verses of John 8:31–44 are evidence of the seduction of Eve by Satan, which results in Cain, the father of the Jewish people. Merging eugenics with Christian Identity theology, Comparet declares Jewish people will be forever marked as the spawn of Satan by "that big Jew nose," in contrast to God's favored White race, whose noses are straight. Comparet further states that these claims are supported by valid scientific facts.[68] In another booklet, *Your Heritage: An Identification of the True Israel through Biblical and Historical Sources,* Comparet seemingly seeks to reassure his readers about their place at the pinnacle of divine favor by arguing that Jesus Christ was not Jewish but, in fact, "a true Israelite in battle against the Jewish people."[69] He states that the White race is God's favored people, evidenced by the etymology of the word "Adam," which Comparet asserts means "rosy" or "fair."[70] All true children of God must have the same complexion as Adam did, and therefore only those who are fair-skinned, or White, can claim this lineage.

CREATIVITY

Christian Identity is not the only belief system focused on the superiority of White identity and the inferiority of people of color, those who follow other religions, and Queer people. The racist theology now known as Creativity also concentrates on the issues that are crystallized in the Fourteen Words.

Since its founding by Ben Klassen in 1973, Creativity has also been called the Church of the Creator, the New Church of the Creator, the World Church of the Creator, the Church of the RAHOWA, the White Crusaders of RAHOWA!, and the Creativity Movement (related to, but distinct from, the Creativity Alliance).[71] After the death of Klassen by suicide in 2003 and the arrest of his successor, Matt Hale, some followers of Creativity decided to merge their beliefs with Cosmotheism, a religion founded by White nationalist vanguard William Pierce.[72] Adherents of Creativity refer to themselves as Creators. As chapter 5 will detail, the concept of RAHOWA, or racial holy war, which is widely used in White nationalist rhetoric, can be attributed to Creativity, but like followers of the other White nationalist groups described here, Creators do not necessarily engage in acts of violence, though some do endorse them.

Born to a Mennonite family in what is now Ukraine, Ben Klassen emigrated first to Canada and then to the United States. Treading the path of many other prominent White nationalists, Klassen became a member of the John Birch Society, but he left when he felt it was too sympathetic to Jewish people and thus impotent to accomplish his agenda of creating a White ethnostate. Klassen then attempted to start his own political party, the Nationalist White Party, in 1970, which became the precursor to Creativity. The party's logo—which would later be reused for Creativity—was a *W* (for the White race) with a crown on top and a halo above the crown. In later writings, Klassen stated that the crown refers to White superiority, while the halo represents the need to safeguard the White race.[73] Like Anglo-Israelism and David Lane's Fourteen Words, Klassen's logo is indicative of the entrenched White superiority, White nativism, and racist militancy that continue to motivate the present-day White nationalists who seek to transform the United States into a White ethnostate.

While Klassen takes what many non-Creators would deem to be liberties with the traditional understanding of religion in order to garner support for his message of violent racism, it is important to note that many definitions of religion do not rely on a theistic framework. That is to say, despite Creativity's distinct lack of any deity, of any belief in an afterlife, and arguably even of any moral or spiritual ethics, it is not any less of a religion, and Klassen himself utilizes terminology like *religion, church,* and *worship.* Klassen's depiction of heaven is a mortal world in which the "brilliant future potential" of the White race is realized.[74] He also referred to the concept of a deity as "spooks in the sky" and derided religion as such as "hocus-pocus."[75] Because Creativity did not fit what was then viewed as a traditional religious mold, it struggled to draw followers away from Christian Identity, which particularly during Klassen's development of Creativity had large congregations attending churches and a strong social network of adherents. Certainly, like Klassen's denial of a deity, his rejection of mainstream Christian texts may have hindered the growth of Creativity as a belief system because it failed to appeal to the panoply of Christians, who were the majority of the proponents of White nationalism during the mid-twentieth century.

All of the texts Klassen wrote as the scriptural canon for Creativity—including the compilations of the newsletter *Racial Loyalty,* in addition to *Nature's Eternal Religion, The White Man's Bible, Salubrious Living,* and *RAHOWA*—center on the need to invalidate other religions, including Cosmotheism, Christian Identity, and what he calls Odinism, as well as Islam.[76] Despite his condescension toward these religions specifically, Klassen borrows from them, desiring Creativity to emulate the influence and impact of the Abrahamic faiths, such as Judaism and Islam.[77] For instance, he takes antisemitism, the concept of "mud races," and the use of eugenics from Christian Identity and Pierce's Cosmotheism to propagate White superiority and to preach what he terms "a Whiter and Brighter world."[78]

With regard to tenets of faith, within the racial theology of Creativity, the sole dogma is that race is one's religion, a stance that is not only influential within the ecology of White nationalism but also symbiotic to its growth because it eschews the strictures of conventional religion. For Klassen, the purpose of life is not to prepare for life after death, as it is with most systems of faith, but "THE SURVIVAL, EXPANSION AND ADVANCEMENT OF THE WHITE RACE," as he stated in a letter to militant White nationalist vanguard figure William Pierce, signing off "For a Whiter and Brighter World, Creatively yours, B. Klassen, P.M."[79] Good deeds and sins are to be seen through the lens of power dynamics, not morality: "What is good for the white race is the highest virtue, what is bad for the white race is the ultimate sin. Period."[80] On a public-access television program called *Race and Reason,* hosted by White Aryan Resistance leader Tom Metzger, who would later convert to Creativity, Ben Klassen defined Creativity's goals: "What is the Church of the Creator? It is a dynamic, new religious movement constructed basically for the survival, expansion, and advancement of the white race, and the white race exclusively. . . . It *is* our program that the white race expand by natural means and inhabit all the good lands of the planet Earth— exclusively and finally. . . . We want to formulate a program for the white race and unite them into *one big racial* army."[81] Demonstrating the mutuality of worldviews among the seemingly disparate White nationalist constituencies, Klassen's endorsement of violence in the cause of defending the White race presages David Lane's Fourteen Words.[82] Moreover, though Klassen popularized the term RAHOWA, he borrowed the idea from Pierce, who similarly regarded violence as vital to the preservation of the White race.[83]

Much like Christian Identity, Creativity maintains that the world is in upheaval and that it is the purpose of Creators to rectify the defensive position the White race is in today, supporting the credo of the Fourteen Words. However, the discord between the two racist religions is laid bare in their respective treatments of the role of Christianity.[84] Whereas Christian Identity sees itself as the only real Christianity, practiced by "true" (non-Jewish) Israelites descended from Abraham, Creativity asserts that Christianity is not a valid religion because it was built on Judaism, as Jesus himself was actually Jewish. These divergent perceptions of Christianity are apparent in Klassen's writings. In *Building a Whiter and Brighter World,* he describes Christianity as a Jewish conspiracy to mongrelize and destroy the White race. For the White race to survive, Christianity must be replaced with the "healthy racial religion" of Creativity.[85]

Alongside his vehement opposition to Christianity, Klassen was also nonplussed by Christian Identity, despite borrowing concepts from it. He did not believe that the notion that the lost tribes of Israel "wandered into and populated Europe" is suggested by either the Old Testament or the New Testament—in fact, he did not accept the divinity or historical accuracy of the scriptures themselves. Historical evidence, he argued, does not provide evidence for the existence of the lost tribes or that they were in Europe; rather, he posited, "the Celts and Teutons lived in Europe long before 721 B.C.E." and could therefore not possibly be related to the lost tribes of Israel, should the latter have indeed actually existed.[86]

The next section examines Wotanism, which shares with Creativity a virulent racism, a rejection of Christianity, and ardent support for antisemitism.[87] To give an understanding of Wotanism's racist theology and its impact on American White nationalism, this section will first discuss the religion's resurgence, then consider its core beliefs, and finally highlight how it relates to Christianity, Christian Identity, and Creativity.

WOTANISM

Wotanism is a reconstructed Norse pagan polytheistic religion whose name references both the German word for Odinism and the acronym WOTAN, which stands for "Will of the Aryan Nations." Adherents sometimes refer to it as Ásatrú, from Æsir, Old Norse for "many gods."[88] Though the terms Wotanism, Odinism, and Ásatrú are sometimes used interchangeably, many differentiate between them, with Wotanism often regarded as a racist and *völkisch,* or folkish, version of Ásatrú that emphasizes the importance of blood and soil, or genetic lineage and tribal affiliations.[89] Furthermore, some Ásatrúers maintain that neither Odinisim nor Wotanism is a legitimate interpretation of their faith, because the former places too much emphasis on Odin and the latter espouses militancy. For the sake of coherence, I will use the term Wotanists to differentiate adherents who support, endorse, and/or carry out violence to support their political objectives from Ásatrúers, who do not condone violence.

Odinism, which is the root of both Wotanism and Ásatrú, is a polytheistic religion that is also seen as a complete way of life, dictating one's private life and public self in attitudes, ideas, and behavior.[90] Odinists believe that the Æsir, or gods, are everywhere and in everything and that humans have a spiritual kinship with nature, making them godlike. Odinism also teaches that each individual possesses all the physical parts of the world within himself or herself, as well as a soul that is attuned to vegetative and animal life. In addition to Odin as the Allfather (the first and eldest of the gods, the all-pervading spirit of the sun, the moon, the stars, the hills, the plains, and humans), other gods and goddesses include Odin's son, Thor, as well as Frey, Frejya, Frigga, Baldur, and Braggi. Rather than "worshipping" these gods per se, Odinists regard themselves as in communion with the gods within themselves.

Odinism is attractive to many in part because its texts are often regarded as myths and not to be literally believed. The scripture of Odinism is the Poetic Edda, also called the Elder Edda, a collection of anonymous songs and poems about Norse gods, heroes, and the beginning and end of the world that were passed on through oral tradition before being written down in the thirteenth century CE.[91] Some Odinists understand these texts to be the literal truth, while others see them as symbolic.[92] Odinist lore lays out the evolution of the world in five acts linked to the four seasons of the year, the last of which is Ragnarok, or the end of the world, which will be followed by rebirth; out of the ruins of the world, a new epoch will be ushered in with a new pantheon of gods led by the sole survivor, Baldur.[93]

According to Wotanist literature, the White race is the "true image of the gods."[94] Wotanists believe that their religion is solely for White Anglo-Saxons, basing this belief on heritage (blood) and tribalism (soil), which is why many White nationalists today will include the cry "Blood and Soil" at gatherings, rallies, and events.[95] This concept was utilized in German nationalism in the nineteenth century and in Nazi Germany, and was also employed by David Lane, who was the main force behind the reconstruction of present-day Wotanism into its current militant form.

Lane created present-day militant Wotanism by employing the concepts of blood and soil to make the religion's primary purpose the holy war to defend the White race and secure its existence for future generations. It was Lane who encapsulated this belief in the Fourteen Word credo, which is today accepted as a sacred truth throughout both religious and nonreligious White nationalism: "We must secure the existence of our people and a future for white children."

Like other prominent White nationalist figures Pierce and Klassen, Lane moved through the John Birch Society, the Ku Klux Klan, and Christian Identity before he created contemporary militant Odinism while in prison serving a 190-year sentence for taking part in the killing of Jewish radio host Alan Berg as a member of The Order (see below).[96] As the trajectories of the aforementioned figures have shown, such pathways are not uncommon and are evidence of the thematic confluence of the many organizations within the political far right that focus on White nationalism in America.

Much as Christian Identity thinkers rely on elaborate false etymologies in their rereadings of biblical passages, Wotanists co-opt the work of secular Western thinkers to support their call for a restoration of their potent collective Aryan nature.[97] Among the most prominently referenced work is that of German philosopher Friedrich Nietzsche, particularly his theories about eternal recurrence, the will to power, and the Übermensch; and that of Swiss psychoanalyst Carl Jung, particularly his theory of the existence of archetypes, or universal, mythical principles that reside in the global unconscious.[98] Both men are often cited in arguments justifying the superiority of the White race and the exclusivity of Wotanism.

Wotanists also claim to be inspired by Jung in their theory of metagenetics, which asserts that "tradition and culture are a matter of genetic inheritance."[99] In *An Odinist Anthology,* published by the Asatru Free Assembly, founded by White nationalist Stephen McNallen in the 1970s, McNallen claims, "The gods inhered in hearts and souls of generations of folk but lay dormant until the gods deemed it propitious for the resurrection of the Norse religion."[100] McNallen bolsters this assertions by claiming Jung "stated explicitly that the archetypes were not culturally transmitted but were in fact inherited—that is to say, genetic. . . . He went on to say that because of this biological factor there were differences in the collective unconscious of the races of mankind. . . . Thus the link between religion, which expresses itself in terms of archetypes in the collective unconscious, and biology—and hence race—is complete."[101] While McNallen reads Jung as supporting his own racist beliefs, this is far from a conventional interpretation of Jung's thinking on archetypes.[102]

Given Wotanism's focus on Aryan genetic superiority, it is not surprising that the same matrix of Norse and Aryan themes that independently gave rise to Lane's religion were also utilized in Nazi Germany. Though perhaps not a direct influence, Odinist themes and imagery were "an integral part of the initiation rites and cosmology of the elite Schutzstaffel (SS), which supervised Adolf Hitler's network of death camps, as well as of George Rockwell's American Nazi Party."[103] Many Wotanists revere Hitler as a strong patriarchal figure and regard the "success" of Nazi Germany as a direct consequence of what they take to be his Odinist practice. While many Wotanists would like to make a direct link between their understanding of Odinism and Nazism by claiming that Hitler and his followers believed and practiced as they do, this view is rejected as presentism by some.[104]

Both Odinism and Wotanism have been growing steadily, in marked difference to Christian Identity and Creativity. Christian Identity has been on the decline since the 1980s due to the federal government's focus on quieting the religion's antigovernment elements and to increased internal factionalism.[105] Creativity, for its part, has always attracted fewer followers than either Christian Identity or Odinism. By contrast, in 2013, signaling the growth of Odinism in the United States, the U.S. Department of Veterans Affairs authorized the use of the "hammer of Thor," Mjölnir, on the grave markers of U.S. service personnel. And in one case, the U.S. Army allowed an Odinist to grow a beard in observance of his faith.[106] This acknowledgment at the federal level is in addition to several legal rulings recognizing Odinism's legitimacy as a religion.

The increasing interest in both Odinism and Wotanism is attributable to several factors. One dominant element is the waning of traditional religiosity as a whole in the United States. With a growing number of Americans attending more than one site of worship and identifying as atheist, agnostic, religiously unaffiliated, or spiritual but not religious, institutionalized religion, from belief to devotional practices, is on the decline in the United States.[107] Rather than be confined inside a church, Odinism and Wotanism emphasize social forms of worship like *blots,* which are meetings held in natural settings, where adherents drink mead from a communal horn, read ancient poetry, and occasionally slaughter animals in sacrifice to the gods.[108]

Odinism and Wotanism thus appeal to many who feel left out of religions like Christianity and who seek a way of belief they regard as nondogmatic. Moreover, Wotanists maintain that Christianity hypocritically insists on the inherent equality of all people. Considering themselves to be adherents of a reconstructed pre-Christian religion, Wotanists understand it as their duty to return their religion, free of Christian influence, to its ancient independence.[109] Many Odinists also disdain Christianity because they regard it as responsible for Odinism's lack of status for centuries. Wotanists in particular view their cause of White supremacy as having been hindered by the conversion, sometimes forced, of Scandinavian peoples to Christianity between the eighth and twelfth centuries CE, resulting in the loss of their ancient traditions and beliefs.[110] For many, Thor's hammer is directly opposed to the Christian cross.[111] Christianity's status as a legitimate religion is discredited by its hypocritical stance on violence (unlike Wotanists' open admiration for dying in battle), its doctrine of submission to God, and its view of nature. What are understood to be the cowardly Christian doctrines of humility, self-denial, and deference are held in contempt, because Wotanists believe that the White race will always be superior to people whom they regard as non-White.[112] They similarly refuse the emphasis on the performance of good deeds and avoidance of sin preached by the Abrahamic faiths, describing their faith as the "the true religion of Western Civilization" and claiming to reunify science and religion, which in their view were bifurcated by Christianity.[113] Finally, Christianity is looked down on by many Wotanists for hypocritically insisting on a message of peace while historically being associated with wars undertaken in the name of religion.[114]

Another factor in the growth of Wotanism as a dominant racist theology affiliated with American White nationalism is its proselytization in prison. It remains particularly widespread within America's prison population. The Asatru Alliance's publication, *Vor Trú*, lists seven prison ministries in five states: Arizona, California, Colorado, Florida, and Indiana.[115] In 2005, the Supreme Court ruled in *Cutter v. Wilkinson* that "nontraditional faiths" such as Ásatrú must be recognized and accommodated in prisons.

Else Christensen, a Danish émigré to the United States, is also credited with spreading Wotanism in prisons; she started an outreach program to spread the religion in the 1980s. Influenced by Alexander Rud Mills (aka Tasman Forth), a prominent Australian Odinist, Christensen also founded what would be called the Odinist Fellowship in the United States in 1969, the first organized Wotanist group in America.[116]

Ben Klassen, the founder of Creativity, corresponded with Else Christensen, and their letters touch on tensions within the White nationalist movement that persist today. Klassen, who disparaged all religions except his own, considered those he labeled as Odinists not militant enough yet saw them as second-best to his own belief system, writing to Christensen in 1986, "I have the least disagreement with, and the most respect for, the

Odinists."[117] Klassen qualifies his support, however, because, even though Odinism shared Creativity's primary purpose to preserve and defend the White race, any religion that would deign to include a deity was one that he would hold in contempt.[118] Comparing the two movements, he declared Creativity "more militantly pro-White, and more militantly anti-Jew, anti-nigger and anti-mud [than Wotanism]."[119] He also deprecated Norse mythology due to his admiration of Greek and Roman mythology, which he viewed as more ancient and thus far superior.[120]

Those debates aside, Klassen and David Lane both valued religion insofar as it justified violence through the veneration of the White race. Moreover, while many Christian Identity proponents of eugenics created hierarchies among the White race based on their national origin, both Klassen and Lane veered from stringent delineations of the White race, determining who was White based on skin color alone. For Klassen and Lane, Whiteness was not limited to the Aryan stereotype of blond hair and blue eyes and Northern Europe heritage, such as historically found within Aryan, Indo-European, Germanic, Norse, Scandinavian, and Icelandic populations.[121] Ultimately, the systems of belief they respectively founded and reformulated were similarly exclusionary in order to achieve their political purpose of a White ethnostate to ensure the survival of the White race.[122]

In addition to shared antisemitism and contempt for those they mutually regard as non-White, there have been moments of alliance between Christian Identity, Creativity, and Wotanism. In accordance with the Fourteen Words, all three racist religions emphasize establishing a White ethnostate through violence. Militancy thus becomes the means by which to attain their mutual political goal of restoring White people to their rightful positions as the rulers, if not the only inhabitants, of the United States. Preaching that solely through bloodshed can the White race reclaim the United States for themselves, they veneer violence with holiness.

FAITH, FLAG, AND FURY: THE CONFIGURATION OF AMERICAN WHITE NATIONALISM

The landscape of White nationalism in the United States—an ideology defined by belief in the supremacy of Whiteness as an identity and culture, and by the demand for the creation of a White ethnostate, to be achieved primarily by excising people of color from the American landscape—is complex for many reasons. Firstly, various White nationalist groups are entangled with one other in terms of coalescing membership, with individuals belonging to multiple groups at the same time or in succession. The leadership of these organizations also often fluctuates among affiliations. Some individuals abstain from formally joining any organization but remain inspired by the concepts of White nationalism, including the Fourteen Words.

Furthermore, many White nationalist organizations and individuals are strongly marked by their antigovernment views, often infused with conspiracism, which collectively regard the federal government as the enemy of the people. These groups include people who refer to themselves as Patriots, sovereign citizens, militias and paramilitary groups, and Ghost Skins, as well as conspiracy theorists.[123] Antigovernment elements have been long been extant in the United States, often infused with a survivalist, or prepper, mindset—though not all survivalists or preppers are antigovernment, and not all antigovernment groups are White nationalist.[124] The sovereign citizen movement, for example, is the only significant facet of the political far right that counts a high number of people of color within its ranks; sovereign citizen groups of color include both Moorish sovereign citizens and people who refer to themselves as the Washitaw Nation, who claim their sovereignty within the United States. Notably, the most impactful theology adhered to by a majority of people of color within the political far right is Black Hebrew Israelism, which mirrors Christian Identity and is antigovernment and religious, though it is not a homogenous movement, and not all of its members are violent.[125]

Still other White nationalist organizations and individuals are more strongly characterized by taking advantage of religious rhetoric to advance their political goals, such as the Ku Klux Klan (which is largely affiliated with Christianity and Christian Identity) and neo-Nazis (whose beliefs are often aligned with Wotanism). More groups endorse concepts loosely sourced from the several of the aforementioned racist religions to legitimize their support and endorsement of violence for political aims.

Lastly, some groups and individuals also intersect on all three fronts: they are at once White nationalist, religious, and antigovernment. Such groups include neo-Confederates, who support the creation of White, Christian separatist states; and Constitutional Sheriffs, who refuse to acknowledge federal or state authority and employ the Bible to justify their calls for White rule. Finally, some White nationalist organizations, like the Hammerskin Nation, the skinhead group that inspired Wade Michael Page, are explicitly neither religious nor antigovernment.

While outliers exist and groups may overlap or remain distinct depending on context, it is still possible and useful to divide White nationalist organizations and individuals into these four main subsets that acknowledge their primary rhetorical emphasis: (1) conspiratorial, antigovernment sentiment; (2) religious adherence; (3) a combination of antigovernment and religious views; (4) neither antigovernment nor religious.

Antigovernment Organizations: Conspiracism, the Patriot Movement, and Opposing Tyranny

Conspiracy theories are not exclusive to the political far right.[126] However, the conspiracies that do feature within this group serve to exacerbate and exploit antigovernment sentiments that are often intertwined with antisemitic and Islamophobic rhetoric. The narrative of victimhood that is integrated within White nationalism in particular and in the political far right in general is also central to conspiracy theories, the formal definition of which is, "an explanation of past, ongoing, or future events or circumstances that cites as a main causal factor a small group of powerful persons, the conspirators, acting in secret for their own benefit and against the common good."[127] According to the FBI, conspiracy theories are potent weapons that "very likely motivate some domestic extremists, wholly or in part, to engage in criminal or violent activity."[128] A conspiracy theory is thus not a mere flight of fancy to be derided from an outsider's perspective but a belief that is to be considered vital as legitimating the worldview of its adherent.

Reflecting the complexity of White nationalism as an ideology, the conspiratorial mindset is to be found in fluctuating degrees across its many facets. One long-standing conspiratorial belief of many antigovernment adherents within the political far right is that the federal government is comprised of a secret group of globalists seeking to institute a New World Order, a transnationalist socialist government that would impinge on the constitutional rights of Americans. The institutions of the federal government must be dismantled and discarded because this cabal of globalists are seeking to implement restrictive measures on freedoms and values, like gun control measures and civil rights. "Globalist" is the latest version of vituperation in centuries of antisemitism in the United States and Europe conflating Jews with the supposed *éminence grise* believed to be behind the disarray of world events and encroaching lack of freedoms for White America.[129] In its current manifestation, globalism is leveraged as an existential threat. White nationalists like Thomas Rousseau, founder of the Patriot Front, an influential organization that grew from Vanguard America, one of the groups present at the 2017 Unite the Right protest, warn followers that their lives and freedoms are at stake. In 2017, he alerted his listeners in a speech at the University of Texas, Austin, ominously stating, "A corrupt, rootless, global and tyrannical elite has usurped your democracy and turned it into a weapon, first to enslave and then to replace you."[130] He claimed that the nation is at stake from this nebulous yet imminent threat and so, too, are the "The lives of your children, and your children's children, and your prosperity beyond that, [all of which] dangle above a den of vipers."[131] During what would ultimately be an unsuccessful reelection bid in 2020, President Trump issued the same warning, drawing a stark disparity between patriotic Americans and the globalist exploiters, stating, "We're fighting for Main Street, not Wall Street. We have rejected globalism and embraced patriotism."[132] While this may seem like innocuous wording on the surface, this is actually coded language drawing a definitive line between those who are considered real Americans and those who are not.

The issue of who is a true American, and thus a White American, is also essential to Donald Trump's birtherism claims against his political opponents in both of his presidential campaigns, sending doubt about his political opponents of color in 2016 and 2020. As president, Donald Trump has spread conspiracies about the origin of the COVID-19 pandemic, indeed even questioning its veracity, highlighting his racist views and seeking to appeal to his primarily White political far right base during an election year. During his 2020 reelection campaign, which also coincided with the first months of the COVID-19 pandemic in the United States, he tweeted that the Food and Drug Administration (FDA) was tantamount to the Deep State, claiming the agency was delaying releasing lifesaving treatment in the global effort to create an effective vaccine: "The deep state, or whoever, over at the FDA is making it very difficult for drug companies to get people in order to test the vaccines and therapeutics. Obviously, they are hoping to delay the answer until after November 3rd. Must focus on speed, and saving lives! @Steve-FDA."[133] By equating the agency to the Deep State, President Trump was also setting the groundwork to scapegoat the agency if the election results that November were unfavorable to him. Like racist themes and language, the conspiratorial mindset is now normalized.

The belief in a cabal of nefarious elites is a long-standing notion within the political far right that has become euphemized, much like displays of racism. While the New World Order is twentieth-century language, antigovernment conspiracies have been repackaged in the twenty-first century as QAnon. Preying on those looking for answers in a period of worldwide social instability and economic turmoil, QAnon was founded on a conspiracy theory pointing to a cabal of political, media, and business elites who make up the Deep State and are in fact Satanists and pedophiles on a collective quest for global domination.[134]

Gaining followers and a foothold within the political far right in tandem with Donald Trump's presidency and with candidates running for Congress in the 2020 election who have signaled their support, QAnon is not only a new iteration of the conspiratorial mindset within the political far right but also signifies its synthesis with conspiracism.[135]

Now with millions of followers across social media platforms, QAnon began with a series of messages by a person (or people) who goes by Q on 4chan, a popular and anonymous imageboard website frequented by members of the political far right and its subset of White nationalists. With the claim of top security clearance within the government, as referenced by the name, Q's messages often reverberate with White evangelical messages about the End Times, portraying the showdown between the cabal comprising the Deep State and QAnon adherents as the ultimate battle between good and evil. The messages, known as Q Drops, are read as cryptic prophecies in the quest to take down the Deep State and dismantle the cabal.

Moreover, Donald Trump is often believed to be Q by QAnon adherents. Weeks before Q's first post, in 2017, Trump stood for a photo with military leaders at the White House and asked reporters, "You guys know what this represents?" He proceeded to trace an incomplete circle in the air with his index finger—the letter Q, supposedly—and said, "Maybe it's the calm before the storm." Trump has since retweeted dozens of QAnon hashtags and released a campaign video for his 2020 reelection bid that showed two supporters holding signs marked with Qs.

President Trump praised Marjorie Taylor Greene, a supporter of QAnon who won the Republican primary nomination for Georgia's Fourteenth Congressional District in 2020, describing her as a "future Republican Star" who is "strong on everything and never gives up—a real WINNER!"[136]

In 2020, President Donald Trump stated of QAnon adherents, "They like me," describing them as "people that love our country." When asked about the perception that he is in fact Q, Trump repeated the conspiratorial notion of the Deep State threat that needs to be combated, essentially reifying the QAnon mindset: "We are saving the world from a radical left philosophy that will destroy *this* country."[137]

The conspiracy theories propagated by QAnon, including the narrative that the United States is on the precipice of imminent demise by the liberal forces of the Deep State, which are seeking to control events and institutions for iniquitous purposes, naturally attract those who are deeply mistrustful of the institutions of government. Ironically, they are drawn to conspiracy theories precisely because they are seeking to make sense of a world in disarray and deluged by disinformation in which authority figures no longer hold the public trust.

Adding further intricacy to the antigovernment contingent is the Patriot movement, which is an umbrella term for antigovernment militants on the political far right who consider themselves to be acting as the nation's true patriots, sincere citizens upholding the U.S. Constitution as it should be interpreted. Because they believe that the U.S. Constitution has become corrupted, they also regard themselves as exempt from the laws of the U.S. federal government, viewing it as an institution infringing on the rights of the people, often in disobedience to God's will. Highlighting the complexity of the affiliations among White nationalist groups, while all Patriot movement groups are antigovernment, some also invoke religious justifications for their White nationalist and antigovernment views. (As chapter 6 details, the religious contingent within the Patriot movement believes that the Bill of Rights, the first ten amendments of the U.S. Constitution, was divinely inspired.)

One example of a Patriot separatist movement is the American Redoubt, whose moniker was coined by survivalist writer James Wesley, Rawles (the comma is part of his name). The American Redoubt seeks to strategically group people across Montana, Idaho, Wyoming, and eastern parts of Oregon and Washington as a reaction to perceived threats to liberty and the White Christian way of life by the government and people of color. Exemplifying the complexity of the Patriot movement is Chuck Baldwin, who is both a well-known antigovernment proponent and a neo-Confederate pastor. Baldwin, who once harbored presidential aspirations as a member of the Constitution Party, relocated himself and his followers to Montana under the American Redoubt, which under Baldwin's leadership can be seen to fulfill neo-Confederate separatist goals, marked with the racism on which the Confederacy was initially founded.[138]

Sovereign Citizens

A central group within the Patriot movement are sovereign citizens, who refuse to recognize federal, state, or local laws that they deem to be illegitimate and in violation of the U.S. Constitution. One notable example of a sovereign citizen is Terry Nichols, Timothy McVeigh's accomplice in the 1995 Oklahoma City bombing, the deadliest domestic terrorism attack perpetrated by an American on U.S. soil to date, which killed 168 people, including nineteen children, and injured hundreds.

The beliefs of sovereign citizens usually also include White nationalism and sometimes include religion—though, again, these layers within the expansive category are not universally present. For example, while all sovereign citizens are antigovernment, not all of them focus on defending White identity, like tax protesters and the Moorish sovereign citizens, mentioned above. The website of the Three Percenters, for instance, declares that its members are not racists or antigovernment, despite the fact that members of the group participated in the 2017 Unite the Right rally.[139]

Tax protesters, in particular, have been a part of American history for centuries. There was the Boston Tea Party in 1773, the Whiskey Rebellion in 1794, and the Sagebrush Rebellion in the 1970s and 1980s.[140] While part of the tax protest movement is made up of left-wing protesters who refuse to pay taxes on the grounds that their tax money will be spent on foreign wars, most tax protesters refuse to pay on antigovernment grounds. Not paying one's taxes as way of protesting against the federal government also overlaps with tactics used by militant white nationalist groups, including the ones also motivated by religion, such as the Aryan Nations, which adheres to Christian Identity, and individuals who support militancy to overthrow the federal government.[141]

In 2010, one such individual, Joseph Stack, whom President Obama mentioned in a 2013 speech about "violent jihad,"[142] flew his private plane into a two-hundred-person Internal Revenue Service office in Austin, Texas, killing himself and one other person. After his murder-suicide, Stack's daughter told news outlets that while she did not condone his actions, she agreed with the antigovernment views that motivated him: "I do not agree with his last action with what he did. But I do agree about the government." She called him "a hero" because "now maybe people will listen."[143] Stack proclaimed his disgust and disenchantment with the federal government's taxation policies, detailing his history of woe with the IRS: "In a government full of hypocrites from top to bottom, life is as cheap as their lies and their self-serving laws." He also compared himself to those who serve in the armed forces and die in service of the nation: "It has always been a myth that people have stopped dying for their freedom in this country. . . . I also know that by not adding my body to the count, I insure nothing will change." His conclusion: "I saw it written once that the definition of insanity is repeating the same process over and over and expecting the outcome to suddenly be different. I am finally ready to stop this insanity. Well, Mr. Big Brother IRS man, let's try something different; take my pound of flesh and sleep well."[144] In the wake of his act of terrorism, several pro-Stack groups were created on social media, garnering hundreds of members and posts on Internet message boards echoing Stack's daughter's appraisal of her father as a hero and patriot.

Militias and Paramilitary Groups

Militias and paramilitary groups are self-styled Patriot groups that train in preparation for a showdown with government forces and are often characterized by elements of White nationalism, as well as sometimes by elements of racist religions or Christianity, though their membership can be representative of many religions and skin colors.[145] Both militias and paramilitary organizations train martially and see themselves as upholding the mission of defending the United States against all enemies, foreign and domestic. Many cite inspiration from the American Revolution and the minutemen of the 1770s, as well as from the South's secession in the Civil War.[146]

Many more describe the allure of joining a paramilitary or militia group. The primary motivation centers on a foreseen future reality in which the government would encroach on the constitutionally protected rights and liberties of American citizens. To prepare for what they regard as the inevitable battle between the U.S. government and its citizens, such groups conduct field training exercises, just as active military units would. While some outsiders may dismiss this line of thinking as paranoia, within the conspiracy-tinged worldview of many militia members the reality is that the current world is on the brink of economic, moral, and social collapse—and armed resistance is the only logical response.

Ghost Skins

Ghost Skins are military veterans, active military members, and veteran and active-duty law enforcement personnel who seek to apply the technical know-how learned in the armed forces and law enforcement agencies to fight for White nationalism and the Fourteen Words.[147]

Not to be confused with skinheads, the term Ghost Skins refers to "those who avoid overt displays of their beliefs to blend into society and covertly advance white supremacist causes," as documented in the FBI report *Ghost Skins: The Fascist Path to Stealth*.[148] To be clear, Ghost Skins make up only a tiny fraction of the Americans who serve within or are veterans of the armed services and law enforcement agencies, many of whom would be appalled by any association between the U.S. military and White nationalism.

Ghost Skins constitute a foreboding menace to the United States.[149] Feeling alienated from America's "true" ideals, as interpreted by them, and threatened by racial integration, religious diversity, and potential economic collapse, they seek to save America from what they perceive as the degradation of becoming a majority-minority nation.

As reported in a 2008 intelligence assessment prepared by the FBI's Counterterrorism Division, *White Supremacist Recruitment of Military Personnel since 9/11*, recruits are rewarded for their "discipline, knowledge of firearms, explosives, and tactical skills and access to weapons and intelligence" with positions of authority within the groups to which they belong.[150] There is a long history of White nationalist organizations in the United States recruiting from active-duty and veteran populations.[151] Particularly, the military training that veterans bring to the Ghost Skins—and the potential to pass this training on to others—can be akin to a terrorist finishing school for the group, giving it tools to advance what is portrayed as a racial holy war. Members' time in the military or law enforcement is a training camp for war—not against a foreign enemy but against their fellow American citizens. Though officially, the U.S. Armed Forces have a zero-tolerance policy toward hatemongering, in practice, the military and law enforcement have been struggling with the issue of how to deal with Ghost Skins in their ranks.[152]

Within law enforcement, police departments across the nation have been accused of aiding White nationalists in rallies and targeting counterprotesters.[153] Indeed, online message boards demonstrate the affinity many White nationalists feel toward law enforcement, which they believe is a source of protection rather than of fear.[154] Some police departments have particularly strong associations with White nationalism. For example, the Los Angeles County Sheriff's Department has had a long history of a racist subculture, including clandestine affiliations with what one federal judge called "neo-Nazi, white supremacist" gangs, such as the Vikings, Regulators, Grim Reapers, and Jump Out Boys, who are often tattooed to symbolize their membership in these cliques.[155]

In a 2017 *Military Times* poll of more than 1,131 active-duty American troops, nearly one in four respondents stated they had witnessed examples of White nationalism in the military. Forty-two percent of non-White respondents said they had personally experienced White nationalism in the military, as opposed to only 18 percent of White respondents. The pervasiveness of White nationalism in the military is also supported by the fact that nearly 5 percent of the people who were polled left comments on the survey complaining that human rights movements like Black Lives Matter and similarly focused organizations were excluded among the options given for threats to national security, which signaled an attempt by these respondents to claim reverse racism.[156]

Some Ghost Skins have taken prominent actions. Wade Michael Page, discussed above, was a disgruntled Iraq and Afghanistan veteran. Dillon Ulysses Hopper, the leader of Vanguard America, which played a major role in the 2017 Charlottesville White nationalist protest, is a former Marine Corps recruiter.[157] In 2012, with the goal of "giving the government back to the people," a small Ghost Skins unit of four members of the U.S. Army stationed at the Fort Stewart-Hunter Army Airfield in Georgia founded a group they called FEAR, an acronym for "Forever Enduring, Always Ready." They plotted to overthrow the U.S. government and potentially assassinate President Obama; forcibly take over Fort Stewart; bomb the vehicles of local and state judicial and political figureheads and federal representatives; bomb a Georgia monument and a Washington State dam; and poison Washington State's apple crop.[158]

In 2019, Christopher Hasson, a Ghost Skin and a former lieutenant in the U.S. Coast Guard and a self-described "longtime White Nationalist," was arrested for having planned attacks on prominent leaders and media personalities on the political left, including House Speaker Nancy Pelosi, members of progressive political organizations, and MSNBC and CNN journalists. He also stockpiled a cache of weapons in his home in preparation for a civil war. Authorities found thousands of searches for White nationalist literature in his Internet history and a copy he had kept of his correspondence with a prominent ideologue, Harold Covington.[159] Hasson's language provides a telling example of his belief that violence was the sole method by which a White ethnostate could be established: "I fully support the idea of a white homeland. . . . I was and am a man of action you cannot change minds protesting like that [at the Unite the Right rally]. However you can make change with a little focused violence. . . . We need a white homeland as Europe seems lost. How long we can hold out there and prevent nig-gerization of the Northwest until whites wake up on their own or are forcibly made to make a decision whether to roll over and die or to stand up remains to be seen."[160] After pleading guilty to federal gun and drug charges, Hasson was sentenced to thirteen years in prison in 2020.[161]

The prominence of the Ghost Skins phenomenon has sometimes resulted in members of the military being asked to leave their units. In 2019, Tech. Sgt. Cory Reeves was demoted after being identified as a leader of a local chapter of Identity Evropa, one of the White nationalist groups with national reach present at the 2017 Unite the Right protest in Charlottesville, Virginia, which has since rebranded itself as the American Identity Movement.[162] That same year, the independent media collective Unicorn Riot released communication between members of Identity Evropa, including two Marines, two Army ROTC cadets, an Army physician, a member of the Texas National Guard, and one mem-ber of the Air Force.[163] Also that year, two members of the Alabama National Guard were sent separation notices after reports surfaced identifying them as leaders of Ravensblood Kindred, part of the Asatru Folk Assembly, an Odinist group.[164]

Despite growing alarm about White nationalist worldviews within the military, an amendment to the National Defense Authorization Act proposed in 2019, specifically aimed to screen military enlistees for White nationalist views, was not approved by the Republican-control-led Senate. The final version of the NDAA now calls for the Pentagon to screen military enlistees for general "extremist and gang-related activ-ity" rather than for White nationalism specifically.[165]

Religious Organizations: Deific Imagery and Worshipping Whiteness

Moving away from the primarily antigovernment section of the White nationalist spectrum toward the segment that primarily emphasizes reli-gion, the two most prominent religiously oriented White nationalist groups are the Ku Klux Klan, or the KKK, and neo-Nazis. Reflecting the complexity of the White nationalist landscape, the former is affiliated with a broad spectrum of Protestant, evangelical, and Christian Identity churches, while the latter is increasingly associated with Wotanism, though historically it was more likely to claim association with Christianity, and many White nationalists who identify as neo-Nazi may also identify as agnostic or atheist.

The Ku Klux Klan

As a symbol and integral part of America's racist and religious history, the KKK has seen several waves of development. First mobilized as a vigilante group aggressively pursuing a pure White society in December 1865, at the start of Reconstruction, the Klan's first resurgence began in the 1920s, during a particularly xenophobic period in American politics.[166] The year 1915 witnessed the KKK portrayed as the hooded heroic saviors of White women who were victims of sexually aggressive Black men in D. W. Griffith's silent film, *Birth of a Nation*.[167] During the 1950s and the 1960s, the Klan grew again in response to the civil rights movement and school desegregation, which was mandated by the 1954 Supreme Court decision *Brown v. Board of Education*. In the 1980s, the KKK began to align itself with seemingly disparate White nationalist organizations, including the Posse Comitatus, Christian Identity ministries, and neo-Nazi groups such as the Nationalist Socialist Movement, which was similar to William Pierce's National Alliance.[168]

Protestantism and Christian Identity theology undergird the KKK's rites, rituals, and membership, which exploit religion to justify racism.[169] This amalgamation fuses together White nationalist motifs of politics, religion, and militancy. One of the first White nationalist websites, established by KKK Grand Wizard and neo-Nazi Don Black in 1996, is Stormfront.org, which remains popular today. During the early 2000s, there were 221 Klan groups in existence, the highest number in recent history, which is consistent with the overall rise in White nationalist groups during that period, attributable to a number of factors, including the Black identity of President Barack Obama. Demonstrating the ongoing fusion of politics, religion, and White nationalism, the Klan's official newspaper endorsed Donald Trump in the 2016 presidential election.

Neo-Nazis

Though neo-Nazis may seem to be synonymous with White nationalists due to the history of state-sponsored racism and terrorism of Nazi Germany and the parallels with the fascism and White nationalism elements of the current political far right, conflating neo-Nazism with White nationalism paints the former with too wide of brush while also diminishing the depth and breadth of the latter.[170] As a subset of White nationalism, neo-Nazism mainly promotes the antisemitic attitudes and fascist policies of the regime from which it borrowed its name, promoting conspiracy theories about Jewish people, such as their desire to take over the world.[171] Some neo-Nazis are Holocaust deniers, while others celebrate that the Holocaust systematically exterminated millions of Jewish people.

Reflecting the changing religious dynamic threading through White nationalism at various points, one neo-Nazi affiliated group, the National Socialist Movement, changed its logo from the Nazi swastika (which it understands as a tetramorph of Matthew, Mark, Luke, and John, to whom the Gospels are attributed) to an Odal rune, which, though also utilized by Nazis in Germany in the twentieth century, is not always a symbol of racism, in order to promote its views in more subdued methods and also to appeal to Odinists and Wotanists as well as to agnostics and atheists.[172]

Antigovernment and Religious Organizations: Faith and Defending against Federal Forces

Though affiliation with a White nationalist group does not directly translate into carrying out violent acts, some of the most active groups historically have been those that combine antigovernment views with stances sanctioned by the racist religions. Before discussing current groups within this category, it is useful to examine the genesis and reverberations of a mostly defunct group, The Order, which utilized both religious and antigovernment stances to powerful effect and continues to inspire contemporary White nationalists today.

Demonstrating the interchanging and overlapping alliances within American White nationalism, William Pierce, a vanguard figure of White nationalism, was also the founder of the National Alliance. As a prominent and prolific White nationalist organization, the National Alliance spread its racist message through multiple media platforms, including weekly radio addresses, racist video games and websites, and its own White power music label, Resistance Records.

In 1978, Pierce, under the alias Andrew Macdonald, published *The Turner Diaries*, a dystopian novel that has become something akin to the Bible for many White nationalists.[173] Pierce's book inspired not only numerous individual plots and acts of violence but also the real-life organization The Order (aka Brüder Schweigen), which was named after the fictional organization dramatized in *The Turner Diaries*. National Alliance member Robert Jay Mathews founded The Order in September 1983 in response to the death of Gordon Kahl, a Korean War veteran, Christian Identity adherent, and leader of Posse Comitatus (discussed below), who was killed during a shootout with the FBI and others that also left a county sheriff dead.[174] Mathews gathered a group of experienced and inexperienced White nationalist terrorists, including Christian Identity adherents and Wotanists, together calling themselves The Holy Order of Aryan Warriors, or The Order. In the group's initiation, members entrusted themselves with the "sacred duty to do whatever is necessary to deliver our people from the Jew and bring total victory to the Aryan race."[175] Acts of violence committed by The Order include the 1984 murder of Jewish radio host Alan Berg and numerous bank robberies. Both Pierce's fictional organization and the real-world group were also important influences on David Lane, an original member of The Order.

Another Army veteran inspired by The Order and revered as a White nationalist martyr was Timothy McVeigh, who had ties to a Christian Identity compound of Elohim City in eastern Oklahoma.[176] McVeigh himself linked his bombing of the Alfred P. Murrah Federal Building in Oklahoma City to *The Turner Diaries*. The fertilizer and fuel-oil bomb used by McVeigh in the bombing was almost identical in size and components to that described in Pierce's book. Eerily, the very passage depicting the explosion from *The Turner Diaries* was found glued to an envelope in the car Timothy McVeigh was driving at the time of his arrest.[177] *The Turner Diaries* continues to be a significant source of inspiration for White nationalism because of its antigovernment themes.[178]

As the trajectories of the aforementioned figures have shown, such pathways are not uncommon and are evidence of the thematic confluence of the many organizations within the political far right that uphold White nationalism in America. This fluctuation between memberships and affiliations suggests it is not the ideas themselves that incite violence but that people predisposed to violence will seek out a narrative to justify their own political ends. Though The Order is no longer active, other groups have taken up its mantle of White nationalism, religiosity, and violent opposition to the federal government.

Neo-Confederates

A segment of White nationalism that combines antigovernment views with religion is the neo-Confederate movement, which draws on symbols of White nationalism, such as the Confederate flag, as well as those of Christianity. Members of this movement claim that the current United States is not upholding its true White, Christian values as detailed in the U.S. Constitution, which is why many neo-Confederates want to break away from the federal government and establish their own government and borders. Neo-Confederates express conviction that they are or will be persecuted by the federal government and thus must defend themselves by creating their own White ethnostate.

Neo-Confederates express racism more overtly by calling for the secession of the eleven Southern states that separated from the Union during the American Civil War, from 1861 to 1865, and using the same appellation: the Confederate States of America.[179] Present-day organizations espousing these views include the League of the South, which wants to reestablish "a free and independent Southern republic" and advocates secession from the United States.[180] The League of the South states that its neo-Confederate platform exists because the United States has lost its ideals and the government is no longer ruled by White Christianity, as it believes the Founding Fathers intended. Its founder, Michael Hill, adjures followers to fight for the survival of their race, further impressing on them that the racial holy war has already begun.[181] Framing the battle in religious terms, he guarantees the crowds that God is on their side, assuring victory. He claims that God is waiting not for His followers to establish peace but to take violent action. For many Christian-related militant White nationalists, God is not the God of love and reconciliation but of war.

Constitutional Sheriffs

Founded in 2011 by two former Arizona sheriffs, Richard Mack and Joe Arpaio, the Constitutional Sheriffs and Peace Officers Association seeks to establish sheriffs as the highest law enforcement authority in the country, making even federal agents and agencies subservient.[182] Many members of this association are racist as well as antigovernment and anti-immigrant. Their worldview is often shaped by a particular interpretation of Christianity that views the U.S. Constitution as a divinely inspired document, thus imbuing it with the same reverence as the Bible (for more on this belief throughout White nationalism, see chapter 6).[183] Broadly referred to as Constitutional Sheriffs, they are a recent iteration of the antigovernment organization Posse Comitatus, a formerly prominent organization named after a Latin phrase from English common law referring to the practice of heeding no authority higher than that of the county sheriff, a concept believed by its founders to also be upheld by the Ninth and Tenth Amendments.[184] Founded in 1970 by Christian Identity minister William Potter Gale and Henry "Mike" Beach, Posse Comitatus became one of the most violent political far right groups in American history in the 1970s and 1980s, establishing chapters nationwide and killing several law enforcement officials.[185]

Today, Constitutional Sheriffs may not explicitly refer to these roots in Christian Identity, but their rhetoric is in many cases infused with religious language, and their stances on Queer rights, for example, align with those of religious conservatives. Though not all Constitutional Sheriffs wield religious imagery or refer to religious concepts in their speech, they all share a focus on survivalism and separatism that continues to appeal broadly to the disparate groups within the American political far right and that has now come to characterize antigovernment sentiment within White nationalism.

Antiabortionists

Many American antiabortion activists are motivated by their understanding of Christianity and often compare abortions to the Holocaust. Certainly, while antiabortion activism is regarded as special-issue terrorism, targeting doctors who perform the procedure and the clinics themselves, the motivations behind the attacks are often motivated by Christianity in particular. (There are also nonmilitant Christian-influenced groups, such as Survivors of the Abortion Holocaust, that oppose the organization Planned Parenthood, which provides sexual healthcare across the United States.)[186] One notable antiabortion terrorist incident was the murder of a doctor and his bodyguard in 1994 by Paul Jennings Hill. Hill was affiliated with the Army of God, an organization inspired by Presbyterian theologian Francis August Schaeffer, who is also credited with stoking the rise of the militant religious segment of the political right by publishing A Christian Manifesto in 1981, which called for a violent overthrow of the government should the landmark 1973 U.S. Supreme Court case Roe v. Wade, affirming a woman's right to have an abortion, not be reversed.[187]

The Army of God is blatantly vocal about its militant antiabortion stance, naming the Reverend Michael Bray, Paul Hill, Eric Rudolph, and Scott Roeder as American heroes for their acts of terrorism. The Reverend Bray, who wrote a book explaining why he thinks the Bible justifies the killing of abortion doctors, was charged in 1985 with conspiracy related to the bombings of several clinics in the Washington, DC, area. Hill murdered a doctor who performed abortions and his bodyguard in 1994. Eric Rudolph, who was connected with Christian Identity, an interpretation of Christianity that teaches that White people are God's chosen people, killed and wounded many throughout his reign of terror. He was charged with bombings of abortion clinics and a lesbian nightclub in the 1990s and was also the perpetrator of the Centennial Olympic Park bombing in Atlanta during the 1996 Summer Olympics.[188] Roeder murdered a doctor who performed late-term abortions in 2009. The Army of God website profiles these individuals as "warriors" alongside passages of scriptures to justify the acts of violence, such as, "Yea, they sacrificed their sons and their daughters unto devils and shed innocent blood, even the blood of their sons and of their daughters" (Psalm 106:37–38).[189] After being captured in 2003, Rudolph explained his actions, which were based on his antiabortion views that incited what he viewed as his necessary war against the government: "It is solely for the reason that this govt has legalized the murder of children that I have no allegiance to nor do I recognize the legitimacy of this particular government in Washington. . . . And whether these agents of the government are armed or otherwise they are legitimate targets in the war to end this holocaust, especially those agents who carry arms in defense of this regime and the enforcement of its laws."[190]

Antiabortion terrorism is one more example of how religion and politics often overlap to create a culture of violence that often targets the federal government.

Neither Religious nor Antigovernment: Racism and Fighting for White Privilege

While most of the more prominent White nationalist organizations incorporate some elements of antigovernment or religiously justified beliefs into their stances, there are White nationalist groups that include neither, relying solely on their support for White supremacy and the creation of a White ethnostate.

Historically, the primary such group was skinheads, members of a subculture that emerged from 1960s working-class England. Racist skinheads are often associated with easily identifiable traits: shaved heads, Doc Martens boots, tattoos, and White power music. Wade Michael Page, discussed above, was a member of the Hammerskin Nation, a prominent White nationalist skinhead organization. The Hammerskins, like other groups within the militant White nationalist movement, adhere to the White nationalist mantra, the Fourteen Words.[191]

Another important element within this category is the alt-right, a term that first entered national consciousness after the election of President Trump, who found many supporters within its contours. Once seen as a distinct entity, the alt-right, which has always had nebulous boundaries, has today become integrated within the larger White nationalist movement as a whole. In essence, the proliferation of the term *alt-right* and similar labels is an example of efforts to destigmatize and repackage White nationalism. Though the monikers *alt-right* and even *new right,* another term many members under the label *alt-right* have used to rebrand themselves, were created from within the movement as self-identifiers, many individuals who subscribe to White nationalist beliefs prefer labels like *race realist, White identitarian,* or *White racialist* because they normalize racism.[192] The founder of the term *alt-right,* Richard Spencer, prefers the label *identitarian.*

The Proud Boys is an example of an organization that is neither religious nor antigovernment but instead focuses on attempting to rebrand White nationalism as "anti-white guilt."[193] It was founded in 2016 by Vice cofounder Gavin McInnes, a conservative media personality who has explicitly denied the group's ties to White nationalism but does call himself a "xenophobe."[194] Viewing men as a victimized minority, the group itself characterizes members as "Western chauvinists who refuse to apologize for creating the modern world." The Proud Boys claims to be inclusive of "all races, religions, and sexual preferences," and it now operates globally.[195] However, over one hundred incidents of violence have been attributed to the Proud Boys.[196] The group's platform includes Islamophobia, antisemitism, Queerphobia, and misogyny, in addition to a vehemence for antifascist, or Antifa, protesters.[197] Members of the Proud Boys also participated in the Unite the Right rally in Charlottesville in 2017. In 2019, the organization staged a rally in Portland, Oregon. Though they were dwarfed in numbers by antifascist protesters, the Proud Boys declared the event a resounding success because it attracted the support of President Trump on Twitter. In response to the rally, President Trump tweeted that "major consideration is being given to naming ANTIFA an 'ORGANIZATION OF TERROR,'" further declaring, "Portland is being watched very closely."[198] Joe Biggs, who organized the event, responded, "Mission success."[199]

Though they share the Fourteen Word motto of White nationalism as a whole, alt-right or new right groups like the Proud Boys seek to present their White nationalist agenda in an unassuming way. Their ideology allows for the inclusion of members who describe themselves as atheists, agnostics, lapsed Christians, and Christian Identity adherents. They generally view Christianity not as a prerequisite but as a cultural entity that encompasses Whiteness.[200] The individuals behind the alt-right have been successful in propelling the shared concerns, values, and ideals of White nationalism from the outskirts of acceptability into mainstream discourse. The current rebranding of White nationalism has reframed what are essentially racist ideas for new audiences in broadly acceptable and seemingly unthreatening language through a variety of enterprises that include think tanks, online publications, and publishing houses.[201]

CONCLUSION

Securing the existence and future of White people is the foundational principle of White nationalism, and this goal has increasingly taken over a large part of the political far right, save for some segments of antigovernment groups that abstain from prioritizing it or disregard it entirely, like Moorish sovereign citizens and those who view themselves as part of the Washitaw Nation; and incels, whose focus is on misogyny; as well as some tax protesters, survivalists, and preppers. Antiabortionists may similarly be regarded as single-issue activists, but as this chapter has also discussed, their views are shaped by their religion, which is primarily Christianity, which is also implicated in supporting historical White nationalism in the United States.[202] Moreover, White nationalist evangelicalism, Christian Identity, Creativity, Wotanism, and militant expressions of the Church of Jesus Christ of Latter-Day Saints share core precepts of White supremacy, and their adherents often cloak their shared quest to realize a White ethnostate by sanctioning violence under the mantle of religion. Though differences do exist in their tenets—such as whether they believe in the Trinity, a pantheon of gods, or no deity, and whether they believe in the apocalypse, Ragnarok, or that there is no rebirth—what remains constant among them is the attraction of their adherents toward David Lane's Fourteen Words, which is the rallying cry of White nationalists in America today.

Other militant White nationalist groups that interact with each other in support of the Fourteen Words include antigovernment groups, groups that identify as solely religious, groups that are both antigovernment and religious, and groups that are neither antigovernment nor religious, including the amalgamation of the alt-right, the new right, and identitarians, discussed in the introduction. Whatever their organizational affiliation, they collectively hold the mutual ideal of America as a nation advancing the political and social dominance of White people in all facets of life, and they rebuke perspectives that contradict their own, including pluralism and equity. Taken together, they pose a grave threat to the national security, economic stability, social cohesion, and, ultimately, the overall prosperity and position of leadership of the United States.

Because these groups and the individuals who subscribe to them advance religion to justify their political grievances and successfully legitimize themselves to their audiences by situating their actions within the context of their self-proclaimed religious beliefs, it can be difficult for those unfamiliar with Islam, Christianity, or Odinism to tell the difference between the orthodox teachings of these faiths and the way their religious tenets have been appropriated by those who exploit religion to wage war.

Though the purpose of this book is to comparatively examine how concepts within White nationalism and militant Islamism are weaponized for political purposes, it must also be noted that the majority of religious adherents around the world continue to be appalled at how their religious beliefs are misappropriated by terrorists.

Much as Muslims in the United States and around the world denounce terrorism and object to sweeping generalizations that portray Islam as an incubator of terrorism, so, too, do members of Christian communities denounce the racism underpinning White nationalism. For many Christians, Christian Identity and White nationalist evangelicalism are as far removed from what they believe Christianity to be as militant Islamism is from most Muslims' understanding and practice of Islam.[203] Ásatrúers, too, are equally dismayed at how their rites and symbols have been co-opted by terrorists. Ironically, while the vast majority of Muslims, Christians, and Ásatrúers alike claim that those who perpetrate such violence are not holding true to their scriptural doctrines, the subjects of this book levy this same claim back, labeling those in the majority as nominal believers or apostates.

As the next chapter will examine, certain theological concepts in Islam are exploited by militant Islamists in pursuit of political goals in much the same way as the White nationalist groups discussed here exploit concepts of Christianity and Ásatrú. Like their White nationalist counterparts, militant Islamists are waging a war against the United States fueled by the same sense of displacement and victimhood, claiming that they, too, are fighting for survival.

CHAPTER 2

Loyalty and Disavowal

*The Exclusionary Ideology of
Militant Islamists*

On December 2, 2015, recently married couple Syed Rizwan Farook and Tashfeen Malik opened fire during a holiday office party hosted by Farook's employer at the Inland Regional Center in San Bernardino, California, murdering fourteen people and wounding twenty-two others before being killed themselves in a shootout with police.

On the day of the shooting, Tashfeen Malik had posted on Facebook a declaration of allegiance to Islamic State (Dāʿish) on behalf of herself and her husband, referencing Abu Bakr al-Baghdadi, its leader at the time: "We pledge allegiance to *Khalifa bu bkr al bhaghdadi al quraishi.*"[1] It may seem natural to conclude that because Syed Rizwan Farook and Tashfeen Malik declared their loyalty to Islamic State (Dāʿish), they were moved by religion to commit violence; however, authorities question the shooters' knowledge of and allegiance to the organization itself, because their Internet search history included al-Baghdadi's name.[2] They are also thought to have watched videos produced by ash-Shabab (the Youth), al-Qaʿida's militant Islamist affiliate in Somalia, and to have read a treatise on waging war in the defense of Islam by ʿAbdullah ʿAzzam, a twentieth-century Sunni Muslim theologian, influential to the formation of al-Qaʿida. Farook also followed instructions detailing how to make a DIY bomb in al-Qaʿida's online magazine, *Inspire,* a pathway that recalls Timothy McVeigh, who replicated the attacks described in William Pierce's *The Turner Diaries* when he carried out the 1995 Oklahoma City bombing.[3] In any case, Farook and Malik appear to have had no direct affiliation with any one militant Islamist organization but were perhaps incited in part by an underlying ethos of revenge against the United States due to its foreign policy.[4]

It may never be truly known what motivated Farook and Malik that day to cause so much devastation, but as chapter 4 will explore more fully, many American militant Islamists have scant religious knowledge. Furthermore, in many instances they are also new converts, which allows their worldview to be shaped by individuals and organizations seeking to fulfill certain political aims.

Farook and Malik were also encouraged by their neighbor, Enrique Marquez Jr.—a recent convert to Islam, albeit one who disparaged Islam to a congregant of the masjid (the term I use in preference to *mosque*) that he himself rarely attended—perhaps another indication that being born into Muslim families is not an indication of religiosity or religious learning.[5] This may have made it easier for Farook and Malik to latch on to the propaganda of larger militant Islamist organizations such as al-Qaʻida and Islamic State (Dāʻish)—which have their own political agendas of establishing a caliphate and attacking the United States—to legitimate the killing of innocent partygoers that day in 2015.[6]

Focusing on these themes, this chapter will first look at instances of terrorism perpetrated by American militant Islamists in the United States before moving on to give an overview of the global organizations promoting militant Islamism. It will then examine how seven centuries of theology are distorted by militant Islamists to give grounds for violence against the United States and its citizens, including Muslim Americans. It concludes by considering some of the common attitudes and methods shared by White nationalists and militant Islamists.

AMERICAN MILITANT ISLAMISTS AND THE UNITED STATES

Whereas White nationalist organizations have long-standing histories in the United States—if not direct or indirect support by the state, as examined in the previous chapter—American militant Islamism is a post-9/11 phenomenon. This is not to say, however, that Muslim Americans themselves are newcomers: in fact, Muslims were an integral element of the establishment of the United States as many enslaved people were adherents of Islam. The first incidents of known militant Islamism in the United States were in 1993, when the CIA headquarters in Virginia was attacked and the first World Trade Center bombing in New

York occurred, though both crimes were committed by non-Americans. Since the atrocities of September 11, 2001, however, there have been instances of terrorism on U.S. soil carried out by American citizens who sanctify their political violence through Islamist rhetoric.

As the introduction detailed, fewer acts of terrorism have been perpetrated by American militant Islamists than by American White nationalists.[7] And some national security experts, such as Michael German, a former FBI agent who is currently a researcher at New York University's Brennan Center for Justice, point out that incidences of American militant Islamist terrorism are often due to the "manufacturing" of cases by law enforcement agencies.[8] This problem is also detailed in journalist Trevor Aaronson's 2013 book, *The Terror Factory: Inside the FBI's Manufactured War on Terrorism.* The existence of these cases does not of course discount the severity of the violence that American militant Islamists have planned and perpetrated, but it does bring into stark relief the nature of the threat of militant Islamism in contrast to that of violent expressions of White nationalism.

The following cases were carried out by Americans who have been found guilty of violence against their fellow citizens, or who have died at the scene, and who have pronounced their acts of violence in militant Islamist religious terms. As they will evidence, the complex psychological factors at play cannot be known; however, it is clear that most of these actors sanctified their violence with language about protecting innocent Muslims, defending Islam, or both. According to their calculus, the only outlet for their frustration with the American government and their disgust at its foreign policies, which they viewed as purposefully targeting Muslim-majority nations, was to wage war in the name of religion.[9]

According to police reports, Naveed Haq, an American citizen of Pakistani descent who shot six women at the Seattle Jewish Federation in 2006, killing one of them, was angered by the war in Iraq and U.S. military cooperation with Israel.[10]

Carlos Bledsoe, an American convert to Islam who changed his name to Abdulhakim Mujahid Muhammad, opened fire with a rifle in a drive-by shooting on soldiers in front of a military recruiting office in Little Rock, Arkansas, in 2009, killing one soldier and injuring another. His goal was to kill as many U.S. military personnel as possible to avenge the civilian deaths of Muslims at the hands of U.S. Army personnel.[11]

In 2014, American-born Ali Muhammad Brown murdered three men in Washington State to retaliate against the United States for military actions in the Middle East. In the same year, naturalized American citizen Mohammad Youssuf Abdulazeez, also spelled Muhammad Youssef, killed four U.S. Marines and a Navy sailor and wounded two others in shootings at two military facilities in Chattanooga, Tennessee. Though he did post on his blog three days before the shooting a message encouraging readers to follow historic Islamic figures who had fought in holy wars, Abdulazeez's motive is unclear.[12]

In 2014, American Alton Nolen killed one coworker by beheading her and injured another in an attack at his workplace. Prior to the incident, he had been suspended for expressing racist views, yet he told the judge during his trial that he had committed murder because he felt his religious identity was oppressed. He also gave his own interpretation of the Qur'an, stating that no one had guided him in the religion and that he had come his beliefs on his own, mirroring the lack of religious knowledge many self-identified militant Muslim Americans have, even though they wrap their reasonings for violence in religious rhetoric.[13] The FBI has said that Nolen did not have any links to militant Islamist organizations.

In 2016, Ahmad Khan Rahimi, a naturalized American citizen born in Afghanistan, set off two pressure cooker bombs in the Chelsea neighborhood of New York City and one at charity race in Seaside Park, New Jersey. Though one of the bombs in New York City failed to detonate, the other exploded, injuring thirty people. The bomb in New Jersey went off but did not harm anyone due to a last-minute change in the race schedule. A handwritten confession found in a notebook he was carrying during a shootout with police days later was addressed to the U.S. government and expressed his anger over U.S. foreign policy, including what Rahimi considered the slaughter of Muslims in Afghanistan, Iraq, Syria, and Palestine. Additionally, Rahimi praised Nidal Malik Hasan and Anwar al-Aulaqi, both fellow American militant Islamists. The document closes with the following declaration: "Inshallah [God willing] the sounds of bombs will be heard in the streets. Gunshots to your police. Death to your OPPRESSION."[14]

In 2017, Joshua Cummings, a recent convert to Islam, a former U.S. Army soldier, and an Islamic State (Dāʿish) devotee, was arrested and charged with shooting and killing a security guard in Denver. He had been on a terrorism watchlist, and leaders at the local masjid had reported him to the Department of Homeland Security as suspicious after he attended a meeting for recent converts. In another incident of violence in which a lack of identity and religious knowledge was a factor, Corey Johnson, a former neo-Nazi and recent convert to Islam, stabbed three people—two teen brothers and their mother—during a birthday sleepover in 2018. Johnson had been on police's radar for a while for a variety of violent acts, threats, and the expression of both militant White nationalist and militant Islamist views. According to police, Johnson had converted to Islam, watched militant Islamist videos online, and admitted that his religious beliefs had led him to commit the stabbings.[15]

In 2018, Demetrius Pitts, an American Muslim convert, who also has the aliases Abdur Raheem Rafeeq and Salah ad-Deen Osama Waleed, was arrested for planning a bombing in Cleveland, Ohio, during Independence Day of that year. After he put up a post on social media expressing an interest in joining al-Qaʻida, along with other alarming posts between 2015 and 2017, the FBI set up a sting operation to test his willingness to follow through with his threats of violence. An undercover FBI agent, whom Pitts thought was a militant Islamist "brother," recorded conversations in which Pitts made threats against President Trump and the president's family members. Expressing a desire to "destroy the government," Pitts was provided a bus pass to conduct reconnaissance of areas of Cleveland where he could potentially carry out his act of terrorism.[16] He plead guilty to attempting to provide material support to a foreign terrorist organization.

The collective lack of religious knowledge evidenced in this list of recent acts of terrorism, coupled with the many instances of recent conversions, suggest that many American militant Islamists are seeking ideas with which to validate violence. The next section will overview the development of the two most prominent militant Islamist organizations, al-Qaʻida and Islamic State (Dāʻish), highlighting the main figures in each.

MILITANT ISLAMIST ORGANIZATIONS AND THE UNITED STATES

In contrast to the plethora of militant White nationalist groups in the United States, there are currently just two militant Islamist organizations brandishing sacred ideas and values in furtherance of political aims: al-Qaʻida and Islamic State (Dāʻish). The narratives of the groups within these respective ideologies are so parallel that American militant Islamists are prized as propaganda tools by both. Al-Qaʻida and Islamic State (Dāʻish) laud their acts of terrorism as victorious battles in the war against the United States, while militant White nationalists utilize acts of terrorism perpetuated in the name of Islam to validate their Islamophobia.

The previous chapter outlined the universe of American White nationalism. This section will sketch the contours of the development of al-Qaʿida and Islamic State (Dāʿish) to provide context for the waging of war in the name of religion. Just as militant White nationalists veil their goal of establishing a White ethnostate in sacred concepts like the Fourteen Words, so, too, do militant Islamists wrap their animus against the United States' imperialism and their political desire for a caliphate in religious terms.

On the surface, it might be easy to see Islamic State (Dāʿish) and al-Qaʿida as interchangeable organizations, given their usage of religious concepts to further their political goals. Alternatively, they might appear to be rivals, given the attempts by the former to position itself as the dominant global militant Islamist organization by establishing a caliphate, however little support from the *umma* it receives. Both groups also had early support from state actors: Al-Qaʿida was originally supported by the United States and Saudi Arabia, as well as Pakistan; Islamic State (Dāʿish) was supported by Saudi Arabia.[17] But the reality is that their political strategies and their use of theology in pursuit of those strategies differ as well as overlap.[18]

Both organizations employ centuries of Islamic theological concepts interpreted and applied in specific ways to call on Muslims everywhere to reject the countries in which they live and instead devote themselves to redressing political grievances against their homelands. They both declare that true piety can be displayed only via manifestations of violence. They both preach that the proverbial West, spearheaded by the United States, is at war with Islam, in a repeat of the Crusades. They both warn that only a caliphate will provide a safe haven for those regarded as truly pious Muslims. And both lure recruits with the promise of an enthralling adventure in the quest to avenge their fellow Muslims and redress the wrongs of American foreign policy. This fantasy is not often carried out overseas—fewer than three hundred Americans have actually traveled to take part in conflicts in the Middle East, in comparison to the thousands of Europeans who have done so—but the sense of participating in a heroic, global cause appeals to those who take actions domestically.[19]

Though both organizations have come to support the primary goal of establishing a caliphate, their primary political aims initially differed.

In its early years, al-Qaʿida strategized that by targeting the United States, as with the atrocities of 9/11, it would eventually force the country to withdraw its support for what the organization regarded as illegitimate Arab governments, leaving those regimes vulnerable to attack from within.[20] Conversely, Islamic State (Dāʿish) began by directly targeting what it claimed were apostate regimes, applying the principle of *takfir,* discussed below, which anathematizes entities as non-Muslim.[21] These were the governments of Syria and Iraq, under the control of Bashar al-Asad and Haider al-ʿAbadi, respectively, and Hamas and the government of Palestinian Authority president Mahmoud ʿAbbas.

The two organizations also clashed in their perspectives on attacking Shiʿi and other religious minorities. To the chagrin of al-Qaʿida's leadership, Islamic State (Dāʿish) leaders Abu Musʿab az-Zarqawi and Abu Bakr al-Baghdadi favored doing so, effectively seeking to eliminate non-Sunni groups and other perceived enemies. Az-Zarqawi orchestrated the 2006 bombing of one of the holiest sites in Shiʿi Islam, al-Askari Shrine, also known as the Golden Mosque, in Samarra, Iraq.[22] This attack led to many reprisals on both sides, resulting in hundreds of deaths. Al-Baghdadi also targeted the Yazidis (a Kurdish ethnoreligious minoritized group located predominantly in Iraq) as well as rival militant Islamist groups, including Hayat Tahrir ash-Sham (the Organization for the Liberation of the Levant, previously known as Jabhat an-Nusra and Jabhat Fateh ash-Sham). These and other attacks prompted al-Qaʿida leader az-Zawahiri to rebuke Islamic State's (Dāʿish) seemingly indiscriminate use of violence and to call on supporters to reject its claims to a caliphate.[23]

These different stances may be traced in part to the divergent origins of these two organizations. Al-Qaʿida was formed as a result of the proxy war fought by various geopolitical forces in Afghanistan during the Cold War. During the administration of Ronald Reagan, the United States gave money to Pakistan to combat communism under the auspices of Operation Cyclone.[24] Meanwhile, the intelligence agencies of America and Pakistan—the CIA and the Inter-Services Intelligence (ISI), respectively—were providing Afghan nationalist armed forces with weapons.[25] The Soviet Union officially invaded Afghanistan in 1979 and withdrew in 1989, after a decade of war, when American support also dissolved, leaving Afghanistan with a power vacuum that was then filled by multiple factions in the tribal nation vying for power. In many ways, the fighting in this beleaguered nation continues to the present day.

Osama bin Laden, a wealthy and well-connected Saudi businessman, left his country in 1979, after his college graduation, to fight the Soviets in Afghanistan as part of a contingent called the Afghan Arabs; the moniker came from the fact that these Arabs joined Afghan forces to fight against the Soviet invasion of the Muslim-majority nation. Many Muslims around the world, including Afghan Arabs, saw the war between the Afghans and the Soviets as a legitimate holy war, because the Muslim-majority nation of Afghanistan was being oppressed by a foreign occupier. Afghan Arabs who later became prominent within global militant Islamism include not only Bin Laden but also ʿAbdullah ʿAzzam, Ayman az-Zawahiri, and Abu Musʿab az-Zarqawi.

By 1984, Osama bin Laden, along with the Palestinian-born ʿAzzam, a professor at Bin Laden's alma mater, King Abdul Aziz University in Jeddah, Saudi Arabia, and the Egyptian az-Zawahiri, already a leader of another group, al-Jihad al-Islami al-Misri (Egyptian Islamic Jihad), had set up the Maktab Khadamat al-Mujahidin al-ʿArab (Arab Mujahidin Services Bureau), or MAK, to recruit and train fighters. The MAK effectively became al-Qaʿida, headed by Bin Laden and az-Zawahiri, when it merged with az-Zawahiri's al-Jihad al-Islami al-Misri in 1988.

Even though the organization that would become al-Qaʿida was propped up by Saudi funding through Osama bin Laden as the prime benefactor, as well as by American weapons, ʿAzzam and az-Zawahiri would become its ideological influencers. Az-Zawahiri would also go on to become the catalyst for the creation of Islamic State (Dāʿish). Because of the charisma and prolific intellectual output of ʿAzzam and the longevity of az-Zawahiri, al-Qaʿida and Islamic State (Dāʿish) would become powerful propaganda machines and recruiting organizations for terrorists globally.

ʿAzzam supplied much of the theological rationales calling for violence in the name of religion, while az-Zawahiri not only was part of the growth of both al-Qaʿida and Islamic State (Dāʿish) but also gave particular emphasis to the delineation of a true Muslim versus an apostate Muslim, a theme that is prominent in the discourse of militant Islamism. The two figures are separated by important ideological divides. While some ideologues, like az-Zawahiri, prioritized establishing a separate Islamic theopolity because they regarded their own Muslim-majority governments as apostate regimes, ʿAzzam did not regard such governments as illegitimate. Rather, he emphasized pan-Islamism, calling for Muslims everywhere to unite against a common, foreign enemy, as there had been in both his homeland of Palestine and his adopted homeland of Afghanistan.

'Azzam's future attitudes on occupation and the oppressive forces of the United States and Israel were shaped by the fact that he and his family had faced the encroachment of what he regarded as the enemy when the West Bank was taken over by the Israeli military in 1967, forcing them to flee to Jordan. By this point, he was already associated with the Palestinian Muslim Brotherhood, and he would later join the Jordanian Muslim Brotherhood, only to be expelled. He would also become acquainted with Sayyid Qutb, a prominent member of the Muslim Brotherhood.

In 1979, while 'Azzam was teaching at the International Islamic University in Islamabad, Pakistan, the Soviet Union officially invaded Afghanistan. 'Azzam responded by writing the treatise *The Defense of the Muslim Lands: The First Obligation after Faith* (*ad-Difa 'an Aradi al-Muslimin Aham Furud al-A 'yan*), in which he equated defensive war with the other traditional actions associated with practicing Islam, including saying the five daily prayers, fasting during Ramadan, performing acts of charity during Ramadan, and completing the hajj at least once in one's lifetime if one has the means and ability to do so. The notion of war that is made holy has since become central to the propaganda of militant Islamism. Political violence in the quest for a caliphate is justified by being portrayed as a holy war.

Alongside 'Azzam, az-Zawahiri also developed the ideological foundations of al-Qa'ida. Eschewing his wealthy family, az-Zawahiri was influenced by fellow Egyptians Sayyid Qutb and Muhammad 'Abd as-Salam Faraj. According to Faraj, the rulers of Muslim-majority nations are, using Qutb's label, part of the Crusader-Zionist alliance seeking to destroy Muslims.[26] Az-Zawahiri befriended Faraj based on their mutual desire to replace the Egyptian secular political order with a theopolity.[27] Further linking the two is the assassination of Egyptian President Anwar as-Sadat in 1981. Faraj would be executed for his role in masterminding the killing, and az-Zawahiri would go to prison because of his political alliances. Left behind by as-Sadat's assassins was one of Faraj's publications, the influential document *The Neglected Duty* (*al-Farida al-Gha'iba*). In it, Faraj argues the rulers of Egypt during his time should be labeled apostates and overthrown to establish a "true" Islamic theocracy.[28]

Much like the fluctuating alliances within American White nationalism, the history of the development of al-Qa'ida and Islamic State

(Dāʿish) makes evident the fluidity of affiliations and membership among various militant Islamists groups. In addition to helping formulate al-Qaʿida, ʿAzzam would also form the organization Lashkar-e-Taiba (Army of the Pure) in 1987 with help from others, including funding from Osama bin Laden. It remains one of the most active militant Islamist groups today and has as its aim rejoining the disputed regions of Jammu and Kashmir with Pakistan, which were separated after the 1947 partition of India. In another instance of ʿAzzam's influence, an offshoot of al-Qaʿida established in Lebanon in 2009 called themselves the ʿAbdullah ʿAzzam Brigade in tribute to their ideological hero.[29] Another layer of complexity to these connections is shown by persistent doubts regarding the possibility that az-Zawahiri had a role in ʿAzzam's 1989 assassination, despite the logic that ʿAzzam's death enabled him to consolidate his power in al-Qaʿida. Within militant Islamist circles, blame of az-Zawahiri is dismissed and reapportioned to the Mossad, the Israeli intelligence agency.[30] Whatever his involvement, what is clear is that after the assassination of ʿAzzam in 1989 and the death of Osama bin Laden in 2011, it was az-Zawahiri who became al-Qaʿida figurehead, continuing to operate its logistics and messaging as he had done when Bin Laden was providing the financing.[31]

Another significant stage in the development of al-Qaʿida as a global organization was the forming of Jamaʿat at-Tawhid wa-l-Jihad (the Organization of Monotheism and Struggle) in 1999 by Abu Musʿab az-Zarqawi, one of the Afghan Arabs financially supported by Bin Laden. After the organization pledged allegiance to Osama bin Laden and thus al-Qaʿida in 2004, it came to be known as al-Qaʿida in Iraq. Due to regional resentment of the American-led war in Iraq during this time, its membership increased. Years later, the devolution of the Arab uprisings across the Middle East and North Africa, which began in 2011, into civil unrest and civil war also fueled the growth and appeal of many militant organizations, including az-Zarqawi's al-Qaʿida in Iraq. He would not see these events, however, as he was killed in 2006 in a targeted airstrike by U.S. forces.

Though there is some debate regarding the process and timeline by which al-Qaʿida in Iraq came to be called the Islamic State of Iraq after az-Zarqawi's death in 2006, it was only after long-standing al-Qaʿida figurehead az-Zawahiri failed to reach a reconciliation between al-Qaʿida and what is now Islamic State (Dāʿish) that Islamic State (Dāʿish) emerged in 2010, headed by Abu Bakr al-Baghdadi.[32] In his first major speech as its leader, al-Baghdadi proclaimed that Islamic State (Dāʿish) would uphold the true version of Islam, abolish all un-Islamic laws and practices, and protect sincere Muslims against oppression.[33] His primary attestation was that once Islamic State (Dāʿish) applied what he interpreted as shariʿa, corrupt institutions would be no more.[34]

Capitalizing on the legitimacy of the Prophet Muhammad, al-Baghdadi used the signature "al-Husayni al-Qurayshi," meaning descendant of the Prophet's grandson, Husayn, from the Quraysh clan of Mecca, at the end of all of his communiqués. Both Shiʿis and Sunnis regard Imam Husayn as a great martyr, someone who gave up his life to defend Islam and to stand up against tyranny. By asserting a direct lineage to the Prophet Muhammad, al-Baghdadi legitimated his call to arms against the United States and its allies.[35] He likewise gave himself the honorific "Caliph Ibrahim" and declared the establishment of the caliphate.

Since the death of al-Baghdadi in 2019, Islamic State (Dāʿish) has been fragmented and is no longer claiming to be a robust territory, though it did for a time provide governance infrastructure, including utilities and trash collection, in ar-Raqqa, its former capital, and towns in Aleppo province, particularly al-Bab and Manbij, taking advantage of a lack of governance in these areas since the U.S.-led wars in the region and the subsequent Arab uprisings in 2011.[36]

Because of Islamic State's (Dāʿish) deterritorialization, al-Qaʿida's many affiliates throughout the region are now positioning themselves to win the hearts and minds of civilians, jockeying for legitimacy in Muslim-majority countries devastated by war by building wells and providing utilities in war-ridden Yemen, Syria, and Iraq, for example.[37] The future of these militant Islamist organizations remains to be seen, and their futures remain in flux. The names of organizations brandishing Islamist rhetoric to legitimize their political agendas will most likely be recast and their membership and leadership altered, only to be replaced by new groups with different dynamics and overlapping coalitions, potentially resulting in a diffuse network of militant Islamist proxies, each waging war in the name of religion and each pursuing its own discrete political agenda, centered on establishing a caliphate. In any case, the manipulation of centuries of Islamic and Islamist principles to disseminate messages of discord, hate, and violence will remain.

THE PRINCIPLES OF MILITANT ISLAMISM

The two sources of law that all Muslims, including militant Islamists, agree make up the shariʿa, or canonical Islamic law, are the Qurʾan, literally "that which is to be read," and the sunna, literally "a clear and well-trodden path." The Qur'an is the scripture of Islam, believed by Muslims to have been transmitted verbatim from God to the Prophet Muhammad via the angel Gabriel. The sunna is the example of the Prophet Muhammad and includes the hadith, or narrations (a hadith is literally "a piece of information conveyed either in a small or large quantity") of what the Prophet Muhammad said, what he did, and what he tacitly approved and disproved of.

Certain key concepts from these sources have remained relevant throughout centuries of Islamist thought—and have been reconfigured by American militant Islamists to justify violent retribution for political grievances against the United States. These concepts include al-walā' wa-l-barā' (loyalty and disavowal), ṭāghūt/ṭawāghīt (idolatry), takfīr (anathematization), jāhiliyya (immorality and ignorance), farḍ ul-'ayn (individual duty), and al-'amr bi-l-ma'rūf wa-n-nahī 'an al-munkar (enjoining good and preventing wrong). After a brief overview of the development of Islamic schools of jurisprudence, the balance of the chapter will focus on these terms, paying particular attention to important theologians, such as Ibn Taymiyya in the thirteenth century, and significant militant Islamist ideologues, such as al-Maqdisi in the twenty-first century, who have contributed to and developed these concepts.

It is important to make clear that, because their work was developed in specific sociopolitical contexts, it would be a historical fallacy of presentism to label some of the following individuals, such as Ibn Taymiyya, as militant Islamists. Also, while many nonmilitant Muslims look to some of the same ideologues, like Ibn Taymiyya, for deeper religious understanding, militant Islamists revere the works of certain figures more than other Muslims do. For example, while al-Wahhab is not widely recognized as a foundational theologian for most Muslims today and was found to be a heretic by his own family, his legacy is disproportionately revered among militant Islamists.[38] It is through its own specific readings and interpretations of the works of these Islamist ideologues that militant Islamism is able to retain its veneer of religious legitimacy and have broad appeal in its recruitment for the war against the United States.

ISLAMIC SCHOOLS OF JURISPRUDENCE: DIFFERENTIATING *FIQH* FROM FICTION

Because the Prophet Muhammad occupied leadership roles in both the religious community and the state, his death in 632 CE ignited the need to develop not only religious disciplines for instruction, theories, principles, and methods but also systematic approaches and processes to reach juridical rulings. Over the next three hundred years, as Islam spread over a greater geographic area and religious practice melded with new cultures and different languages, the four classic schools of Sunni Islamic jurisprudence (*fiqh*) developed.

Collectively, these schools are called *madhāhib* (singular: *madhhab*), an Arabic word translated as "ways of going." Each is eponymously named after a pioneering jurist of Sunni Islam. They are: the Hanafi school (after Imam Abu Hanifa, 699–767 CE), the Maliki school (after Imam Malik ibn Anas, 711–795 CE), the Shafiʻi school (after Imam Muhammad Idris ash-Shafiʻi, 767–820 CE), and the Hanbali school (after Imam Ahmad ibn Hanbal, 780–855 CE).[39] The distinctions between them are mainly how they apply theological principles to reaching legal decisions on issues pertaining to everyday life, including problems and questions that had not appeared during the Prophet's lifetime.

Over the centuries, the four *madhāhib* came to dominate different regions in the Islamic world. For example, the Hanafi school, known for being the most focused on reason and analogy, is dominant among Sunnis in Central Asia, Egypt, Pakistan, Afghanistan, India, China, Turkey, the Balkans, and the Caucasus. The Maliki school prevails in North Africa, and the Shafiʻi school is prominent in Indonesia, Malaysia, Brunei Darussalam, and Yemen. The Hanbali school, regarded as following the most orthodox form of Islam, is embraced in Saudi Arabia and Qatar, with many adherents in Palestine, Syria, and Iraq.[40]

It is the Hanbali *madhhab* that is most often associated with militant Islamism, because of Wahhabi Islam. Wahhabi Islam, named after Muhammad ibn ʻAbd al-Wahhab, who was from Saudi Arabia, is not a direct *madhhab,* but it draws inspiration from the Hanbali school. Though al-Wahhab's teachings were dismissed during his lifetime in the centers of Islamic learning, such as the famed al-Azhar in Egypt, as simplistic and erroneous to the point of heresy, later permutations of his philosophies continue to influence many militant Islamists. He often draws heavily on Ibn Taymiyya, and for this reason he is seen as an imitator rather than an innovator of Islamism.[41]

An alliance between the as-Saʻud family and al-Wahhab helped to establish Saudi Arabia, and its influence is still clear in Wahhabi Islam's status as the dominant religious movement in the kingdom today.[42] Moreover, the proliferation of Saudi petrodollars, which first enriched the Saudi royal regime in the early to mid-twentieth century, led to the proselytism of Wahhabi Islam not only in *masājid* (the plural of *masjid*) but also in *madāris* (the plural of *madrasa,* a religious school for Islamic instruction), in Muslim-majority nations such as Pakistan and Afghanistan, and in religiopolitical factions like the Taliban. (Many of the students who attend such institutions do so not necessarily out of religious zeal but because they are in search of food and shelter.[43])

Ultimately, Saudi Arabia, as the land that holds the Islamic sacred cities of Mecca and Medina, as well as the vast majority of the world's oil reserves, exported Wahhabi Islam, leading to the conflation of Wahhabi Islam with orthodox Islam. The stringent worldview of Wahhabi Islam explains the destruction of figures, statues, tombs, and shrines in the Islamic world, including the widely publicized destruction of the centuries-old Buddhist statues in Bamiyan, Afghanistan. Osama bin Laden and the majority of the hijackers on the 9/11 airplanes, who were of Saudi Arabian origin, subscribed to Wahhabi Islam.

AL-WALĀ' WA-L-BARĀ': LOYALTY AND DISAVOWAL

Central to the logic by which militant Islamists justify their violent opposition to the United States and other targets is *al-walā' wa-l-barā',* indicating the antagonistic relationship of love and hate, loyalty and disavowal, friendship and enmity. The Arabic word *al-walā'* comes from the root *w-l-a,* indicating a close bond or relationship. Another word with this root is *al-walī,* meaning "protector," "custodian," or "friend." On the other hand, the Arabic word *al-barā'* comes from the root *b-r-',* signifying either "creation" or "distance" and indicating "enmity after admonishing and warning."[44] Meaning loyalty and solidarity to Muslims and disavowal of anything and anyone considered un-Islamic, *al-walā' wa-l-barā'* is the concept foundational to the theology of militant Islamism, which sustains a polarized point of view that divides the world into *dār ul-Islam* (the abode of Islam), *dār ul-kufr* (the abode of unbelief), and *dār ul-ḥarb* (the abode of war), thus allowing for the invocation of *takfīr* (anathematization) of any Muslim or Islamic government perceived as betraying Islamic principles.[45]

The interpretation and application of the concept of *al-walā' wa-l-barā'* has implications for both the religious and political spheres of militant Islamists. Because many understand it to mean the rejection not only of other religions but also of un-Islamic ways of life, *al-walā' wa-l-barā'* has become the basis by which to justify political agendas and war against not only un-Islamic governments, like the United States, but also Muslim governments, institutions, and individuals who are deemed to be deserving of *al-barā'*.

Taqi ad-Din Ahmad ibn 'Abd al-Halim ibn Taymiyya, who is venerated as the Shaykh ul-Islam, is often regarded as the earliest theologian to influence present-day militant Islamist thought, and though he never used *al-walā' wa-l-barā'* to mean enmity between Muslims and non-Muslims, he remains associated with the concept. During his lifetime (1263–1328 CE), the Islamic world was in a state of upheaval, rocked by threats to its very existence in the form of the Christian Crusades, which spanned the eleventh, twelfth, and thirteenth centuries, as well as the Tatar invasion in the thirteenth and fourteenth centuries. For Ibn Taymiyya, whose family were forced to flee from their village in what is now Turkey to Syria, these events shaped his view that war becomes just when it is undertaken as a defensive necessity to protect an Islamic nation.

Ibn Taymiyya wrote extensively on distinguishing between the loyalists of God and the loyalists of Satan, the latter of which included the Mongol/Tatar government. Much as American militant Islamists perceive the U.S. government as an oppressive, illegitimate force, Ibn Taymiyya maintained that the Mongol/Tatar government of his day was unlawful, going so far as to issue a fatwa against their rule.[46] So while Ibn Taymiyya used the phrase *al-walā' wa-l-barā'* in the context of protecting against religious innovations (*bid'a*) rather than in the context of separating Muslims and non-Muslims, militant Islamists often trace the latter application back to him.[47]

Building on Ibn Taymiyya's scholarship, Muhammad ibn 'Abd al-Wahhab sought to unify Muslims divided throughout the Middle East with the concept of *al-walā' wa-l-barā'*. Born in what is now Saudi Arabia, al-Wahhab (1703–92 CE) lived four centuries after Ibn Taymiyya, and, like Ibn Taymiyya, he was a Hanbali jurist. He declared that it is not enough merely to declare oneself a Muslim. Al-Wahhab asserted that belief must be coupled with the practice of "pure" Islam, and he viewed the practices of many Muslims—such as treating graves as shrines, wearing amulets with Qur'anic inscriptions, and following certain Sufi practices—as antithetical to Islam.[48] Because al-Wahhab was dedicated to eradicating religious innovation, mysticism, pre-Islamic practices, saint worship, and Shi'i Islam, he maintained that most Muslims were disavowing their faith by being devoted to un-Islamic rituals and following false gods, like material possessions. Enmity toward all things un-Islamic, *al-walā' wa-l-barā'*, must be unequivocal.[49] His lasting legacy to militant Islamism is his belief that Muslims must not participate in the institutions and societies of non-Muslims.[50] Under his exclusivist view of Islam, al-Wahhab claimed his followers were the only ones sincerely adhering to the principle of *tawḥīd* (absolute monotheism) and categorized everything else as *shirk* (polytheism), the greatest transgression identified by God in the Qur'an. According to this logic, he also asserted the duty to oppose and kill Muslim rulers who do not implement the shari'a.[51]

Centuries later, the Palestinian-Jordanian theorist Abu Muhammad al-Maqdisi (b. 1959) took the concept of *al-walā' wa-l-barā'* beyond the excommunication of Muslims and Islamic governments seen as partaking in un-Islamic practices and called for active fighting against perceived religiopolitical threats to Islam.[52] One of the most significant militant Islamist thinkers alive today, al-Maqdisi was initially influenced by Salafi Islam and advocates of nonviolence.[53] He would later gravitate toward al-Wahhab, befriending al-Qa'ida leader az-Zawahiri and az-Zarqawi, the founder of al-Qa'ida in Iraq. Al-Maqdisi wrote the influential *The Community of Abraham (Millat Ibrahim)* as well as *Clear Evidence of the Disbelief of the Saudi State (al-Kawashif al-Jaliyya fi Kufr ad-Dawla as-Sa'udiyya)*. The former was an indictment of Islamic governments he believed were forsaking Islamic law; the latter was a denunciation of what he considered to be the apostate Saudi regime.[54] Al-Maqdisi's impact on militant Islamism as a whole can be seen in his reconfiguration of *al-walā' wa-l-barā'*, which was steeped in the tradition of Wahhabi Islam, to justify waging war against Muslim rulers. In this he echoes his friend and mentor az-Zawahiri, who argues in his own book on *al-walā' wa-l-barā'* that leaders of Muslim-majority nations who have shown solidarity, or *al-walā'*, to un-Islamic countries rather than to their own people should be subjected to a sort of excommunication, or *al-barā'*.[55]

Stemming from this understanding of *al-walā' wa-l-barā'* are *tawāghīt* (singular: *ṭāghūt*), a multidefinition term referring to the legislators and man-made laws of non-Muslim-majority nations when they are worshiped rather than God, and *takfīr*.

ṬĀGHŪT AND ṬAWĀGHĪT: IDOLS AND MAN-MADE LAWS

Associated with the notion of *al-walā' wa-l-barā'* is the rejection of *ṭāghūt* or *tawāghīt*, which can be translated as idols, forces of disbelief, or powers of evil. The word comes from the root *ṭ-gh-w* and means "to overflow, to transgress, to exceed the limits, to be excessive, to violate established norms, to be tyrannical, tyranny."[56] This word was first applied to the devil and to idols.

As with many principles wielded by present-day militant Islamists, it has taken on a political resonance in addition to its original religious application. Specifically, many militant Islamists view man-made laws that are contrary to God's law—specifically those of the governments of un-Islamic states, which may include the laws of Muslim rulers—as the modern iteration of *ṭāghūt*. *Ṭāghūt* or *ṭawāghīt* can thus be understood to mean anything or anyone that exceeds the limits set by God, including those who rule by any law other than that revealed by God in the Qur'an and the example set by the Prophet Muhammad, who embodies the teachings of the Qur'an. This rendering by militant Islamists of governments that do not conform to their specific beliefs as tyrannical apostates recalls the depiction of the United States as the Whore of Babylon by some White nationalists.

Known for his book entitled *Book of Monotheism (Kitab at-Tawhid)*, al-Wahhab also describes the "five heads," or applications, of the term, citing the Qur'an in his eighteenth-century treatise *The Meaning of Taghut (Ma'ana at-Taghut)*: the devil; the tyrannical and oppressive ruler who changes God's rulings; the ruler who judges according to something other than what God has revealed; the ruler who claims to have knowledge of the Unseen; and the ruler who is worshipped apart from God and is pleased with being worshipped.[57] He also writes that harboring *al-barā'* (enmity) toward *ṭāghūt* is part of one's faith as a Muslim: "No one truly believes until he rejects the *ṭāghūt*."[58]

Centuries later, Sayyid Qutb (1906–66 CE) would use a similar definition, juxtaposing the worship of God to all else. For Qutb, *ṭāghūt* is antithetical to the worship of God, and the two cannot be reconciled. He further emphasizes the tyranny of *ṭāghūt* by equating it with the oppressive rule of Pharaoh in Moses's time as described in the Qur'an: "*Ṭāghūt* is a symbolic representation that denotes all tyrannical forces and oppressive forces that oppress consciousness, feelings and awareness, perceptions, comprehension and knowledge. The *ṭāghūt* is any force that oppresses the right [*haq*] and transgresses the framework laid down by God for His servants. . . . Any principle or system based on, or derived from, other than the principles of shari'a is *ṭāghūt*. Any conception, idea, literature, philosophy not derived from the principles of shari'a is *ṭāghūt*."[59]

According to Qutb, if one does not follow shari'a exactly, as God intended, then one is outside the realm of Islam and cannot be called a

Muslim. His stance, which was supported by other significant ideologues, like al-Maqdisi and Faraj, has direct implications for relations
between Muslims and non-Muslims, including Muslims living in countries governed by non-Muslims, like Muslim Americans in the United
States.[60] According to this ideology, because the vast majority of Muslim Americans do not reject the un-Islamic legislation of America, the
only appropriate course of action is to label them as apostates by means
of *takfīr*.

TAKFĪR: THE EXCOMMUNICATION OF MUSLIMS AND ISLAMIC INSTITUTIONS

The label *takfīr* is applied by militant Islamists to individuals or institutions they deem to be apostates. In particular, it is applied to governments believed to be violating Islamic principles by ruling via American-
style democracy, secularism, and/or liberalism, as well as to individual
Muslims who are seen as imitating non-Muslims in attitudes, lifestyle,
and clothing, though there is debate among militants about whether or
not apostasy has to be expressly intended. Once the term *takfīr* is
applied, war is justified and necessitated.[61]

The root of the Arabic word *takfīr* is *k-f-r*, meaning "to cover," "to
conceal," or "to be ungrateful." Another word that emerges from this
root is kafir, a Qur'anic reference to a specific type of non-Muslim, one
who rejects the existence of God rather than worshipping others in
addition to God. To invoke *takfīr* and thereby declare a Muslim to actually be a non-Muslim and thus worthy of *al-barā'* (enmity) is a very
serious matter and odious to many Muslims around the world.

Two other labels are also used to designate non-Muslims: *murtadd*
and *munāfiq*. *Murtadd* comes from the root *r-d-d*, which means "to
turn back, to retract, to retire, to withdraw from." *Murtadd* is traditionally used for an individual who once was Muslim but has made the
conscious choice to abandon the faith. This is different from *takfīr*, in
that *takfīr* is a label that is applied to delegitimize, whereas *murtadd* is
a label one can apply to oneself to signify that one has renounced the
religion of Islam. The label *munāfiq*, by contrast, signifies a hypocrite
who outwardly pretends to be Muslim but secretly disavows Islam. The
root of this word is *n-f-q*, connoting the underground tunnels that some
creatures, such as lizards, use for camouflage or flight, and suggests the
deceptive nature of hypocrisy.

Militant Islamists apply these terms with slightly different nuances. The accusation of *murtadd* is often levied against Muslim Americans by Islamic State (Dā'ish)—for example, when it urged them not to vote in the 2016 presidential elections, or what it termed "the Murtadd Vote," in an English-language pamphlet released by its media wing, the al-Hayat Media Centre. The label *munāfiq* is in their terms seemingly less severe. In a 2016 article entitled "Kill the Imams of Kufr in the West" in the now defunct online magazine *Dabiq*, published by Islamic State (Dā'ish), the differentiation is made clear: "The person who calls himself a 'Muslim' but unapologetically commits blatant *kufr* [disbelief] is not a *munāfiq* [hypocrite], as some mistakenly claim. Rather, he is a *murtadd* [apostate]."[62] In its attacks on Muslim American imams for preaching the compatibility of Islam and American ideals, accusing them of transgressing the boundaries of hypocrisy into outright apostasy, Islamic State (Dā'ish) is also leveling the claim that Muslim Americans in the United States are, in fact, not actually Muslim.

Because many militant Islamists choose to interpret the Qur'an as promoting the belief that outsiders, including nonmilitant Muslims around the world, will use treachery and every means at their disposal to abolish the religion of Islam, they create a distinct line between themselves and anything or anyone regarded as transgressing the bounds of Islam. The following Qur'anic verse, revealed to the Prophet Muhammad during the Battle of Tabuk, is often used as divine permission to label those who are suspected of being insincere Muslims as disbelievers, under the principle of *takfir*: "They swear by God that they belong with you [believers], but they do not. They are cowardly" (9:56). Compliance with the shari'a in all matters, public and private, becomes a litmus test determining the difference between "true" Muslims and Muslims-in-name-only, who are thus deserving of *takfir*.

Most recently, the label *takfir* has been applied by militant Islamists to other militant Islamists, evidencing both its ubiquity and its haphazard application. Within the ranks of Islamic State (Dā'ish), several members have denounced their own leaders as apostates. Indeed, the organization itself has been fraught with internal tensions over who is actually religious and who is only outwardly appearing to be so through clothing, hairstyle, and habits. Within this extreme application of *takfir*, not calling out someone's seeming apostasy makes one complicit and thus makes one worthy of the label oneself. This use of *takfir* to name a fellow Muslim as an apostate, which is actually prohibited in the Qur'an

(4:94), like its use to label all governments, including those of Muslim-majority states, as apostates, was first put into practice by Helmi Hashimi, an Egyptian juridical authority for Islamic State (Dā'ish) and former police officer.[63]

Al-Wahhab, influenced by Ibn Taymiyya, sought to apply *al-walā' wa-l-barā'* to anyone deemed un-Islamic, and this has heavily impacted the understanding and application of *takfir*.[64] For al-Wahhab, professing one's adherence to Islam by stating the *shahāda*, or testimony of faith ("There is no deity but God and Muhammad is His messenger"), is not enough to qualify one as Muslim, even though its sincere declaration is what differentiates a Muslim from a non-Muslim according to all of the *madhāhib* and the majority of Muslims around the world. In his work, he established ten categories that could void one's claim of being Muslim: "(1) polytheism; (2) using mediators for God; (3) doubting that non-Muslims are disbelievers; (4) judging by non-Islamic laws and believing that these are superior to divine law; (5) hating anything the Prophet practiced; (6) mocking Islam or the Prophet [Muhammad]; (7) using or supporting magic; (8) supporting or helping the nonbelievers against Muslims; (9) believing that someone has the right to stop practicing Islam; (10) turning away from Islam by not studying or practicing it."[65] He also established an additional principle that expands on all of the above: one becomes a disbeliever if one does not declare *takfir* against a disbeliever.[66] Many of his detractors accuse him of indiscriminately using the label of *takfir*, an argument he dismissed as itself being worthy of *takfir*.[67]

It is indicative of the spectrum of interpretation within militant Islamist theology that while some later Islamist ideologues, like Hasan al-Banna, founder of the al-Ikhwan al-Muslimun (the Muslim Brotherhood), would completely reject the political application of *takfir*, other militant Islamists, such as al-Maqdisi, would agree that although the general application of *takfir* is sinful, many Muslim rulers are worthy of the label because they actively attack Islam, as are many Muslims who follow laws contrary to Islamic principles.[68] Al-Maqdisi posits that since all Muslim states are worthy of the pronouncement of *takfir* because they are based on corrupt, un-Islamic systems, warfare against them is legitimate.[69] Significantly, Faraj believed the fight against the "near enemy," or corrupted Islamic governments that deserve the label *takfir*, should take priority over the "far enemy," or un-Islamic governments like the United States, which was the strategy initially pursued by al-Qa'ida's az-Zawahiri until the need to establish a caliphate became imperative because of the rivalry between his organization and Islamic State (Dā'ish).[70]

Once something or someone has been determined as deserving of disavowal, or *al-barā'*, because *ṭawāghīt* or *takfīr* is invoked, the label *jāhiliyya* applies as well.

JĀHILIYYA: IMMORALITY AND IGNORANCE

For many militant Islamists, the hallmark of *jāhiliyya* is the United States and its separation of church and state—the modern political legacy of the Enlightenment that resulted in the division between the sacred and the secular, which is antithetical to Islam's teachings that the head of state be a learned religious leader. The word *jāhiliyya* refers to the immorality of Arabia before the time of the Prophet Muhammad, and it is applied by militant Islamists not only to the United States but also more generally to all societies and institutions that are regarded as disavowing shari'a and thus partaking in immorality.

Sayyid Qutb, who spent two years in the United States during the 1950s, writes extensively on the subject, including in his book *Milestones (Ma'alim fi-t-Tariq)*, where he states that the societies of true Islamic nations and those of *jāhiliyya*, as found in the United States and its Zionist allies, are in stark contrast and will forever be at odds with one another.[71] He defines *jāhiliyya* as the condition of any society "which does not dedicate itself to submission to God alone, in its beliefs and ideas, in its observances of worship, and in its legal regulations."[72] Beyond lambasting the materialism, racism, and sexual promiscuity of what he saw as a debased American culture, Qutb further states that "according to this definition, all the societies existing in the world today are *jahili*." These include, by his count, communist societies, all idolatrous societies, all Jewish and Christian societies, and "'so-called Muslim' societies . . . because their way of life is not based on submission to God alone."[73] By equating Islamic regimes to un-Islamic regimes, he delegitimizes them and gives permission to wage war against them.

By using this standard, put forth by Qutb and other religious scholars and political activists, to ascertain who is insincere in his or her faith, present-day militant Islamists can argue that they are the only true Muslims; as such, they are obliged to spread their concept of Islam to the entire world by sweeping away all governments, religious institutions, and cultures that challenge this divine mission.

The general militant Islamist worldview strongly emphasizes the notion that coexistence with non-Muslims denies a Muslim the bliss of paradise. They seek Qur'anic support for this position through their unusual interpretation of verses such as 4:97: "When the angels take the souls of those who have wronged themselves, they ask them, 'What circumstances were you in?' They reply, 'We were oppressed in this land,' and the angels say, 'But was God's earth not spacious enough for you to migrate to some other place?' These people will have Hell as their refuge, an evil destination." According to the militant Islamist interpretation, this verse means that Muslims who willingly live in a country that is not ruled in accordance with Islamic law, such as Muslim Americans who live in the United States, are destined for hell because they have failed to attempt to migrate for God's sake to a nation ruled by a Muslim ruler, though ironically this same ideology deems many of those rulers worthy of *takfir* themselves.

According to this logic, to live as a Muslim in the United States is to turn one's back on Islam and give up one's claim to be a true Muslim. The only refuge from living in the American land of *jāhiliyya* in this life—and the only refuge from eternal hell in the afterlife—is to fight to establish and live in a caliphate ruled under militant Islamist terms.

FARḌ UL-ʿAYN: INDIVIDUAL DUTY

To combat the dominance of *jāhiliyya* and defend the sanctity and implementation of shariʿa, figures like Muhammad ʿAbd as-Salam Faraj (1954–82 CE) promoted in his influential book *The Neglected Duty* (*al-Farida al-Ghaʾiba*) the idea that war against such entities is *farḍ ul-ʿayn,* or incumbent on each individual Muslim. *Farḍ ul-ʿayn* stands in contrast to *farḍ ul-kifāya,* which is seen as a collective duty, meaning that all Muslims do not have to participate. Building on Faraj's work, al-Qaʿida's ʿAzzam laid out the theological basis for his argument that *farḍ ul-ʿayn* is the personal religious obligation of each Muslim around the world to attack the occupiers of Muslim-majority nations.[74] In *The Defense of the Muslim Lands,* ʿAzzam writes that whereas offensive jihad is not an individual responsibility (*farḍ ul-ʿayn*) but can be carried out only under the leadership of a caliph whose authority is recognized by the majority of Muslims, defensive jihad can and must be carried out when necessitated under the following conditions:

A) If the disbelievers enter a land of the Muslims.

B) If the rows [forces] meet in battle and they begin to approach each other.

C) If the Imam calls a person or a people to march forward, then they must march.

D) If the disbelievers capture and imprison a group of Muslims.[75]

'Azzam's justification of violence, which he defines as an individual mandatory duty to defend one's property and fellow Muslims, just as significant as the five daily prayers, is one that continues to reverberate throughout present-day militant Islamist ideology. Rather than interpreting 'Azzam's words to narrow the application and permissibility of what militant Islamists call jihad, their perception of victimhood gives them grounds to view every confrontation as necessitating jihad.

AL-'AMR BI-L-MA'RŪF WA-N-NAHĪ 'AN AL-MUNKAR: ENJOINING GOOD AND PREVENTING WRONG

The final concept exploited by militant Islamists to justify their war against the United States is one that is upheld by all Muslims, who collectively believe they are commanded by God in the Qur'an to enjoin right and forbid wrong, stipulated in the Qur'anic phrase al-'amr bi-l-ma'rūf wa-n-nahī 'an al-munkar (enjoining good and forbidding evil). Whereas al-ma'rūf, the root of which is 'a-r-f, signifying "to know," means "good," "permissible," "accepted," and "commendable," al-munkar, the root of which is n-k-r, "to not know," is often understood to mean "wrong" or "evil." Related Arabic words using the root n-k-r indicate denial, rejection, and disapproval. Much as they do with the contrasting categories of al-walā' wa-l-barā', many militant Islamists determine what constitutes al-ma'rūf and al-munkar through their selective interpretations and applications of the Qur'an and the hadith. They decry what they see as the spread of al-munkar, or evil, throughout the United States and its allies, including apostate regimes, and believe that al-ma'rūf is their sacred duty to establish a caliphate ruling in accordance with their interpretation of shari'a.

Quoting from Qutb's Under the Shade of the Qur'an (Fi Zilal al-Qur'an), Faraj rebukes those who forego their obligation of jihad, as he understands the concept, claiming that they prefer "cheap comfort" over "noble toil."[76] In his formulation, waging a defensive war to protect an Islamic nation and the Muslims within it is a collective obligation on the entire Muslim community. The oft-repeated phrase al-'amr bi-l-ma'rūf wa-n-nahī 'an al-munkar thus becomes a validation for the call to arms against attacking forces. The non-Muslim attackers become the evildoers, and the Muslims who are defending their lives and properties become the doers of good. In a theological move that recalls how religiously oriented White nationalists justify violence, warfare thus becomes an extension of fulfilling God's command.

CONCLUSION

The context in which the body of Islamist political concepts utilized by many militant Islamists was developed, the Crusades and colonialism, helps explain why many militant Islamist organizations brandish a somewhat contradictory narrative of imminent global conquest juxtaposed with a state of victimhood. Individual militant Islamists also view themselves as victims of the historical oppression of colonialism while simultaneously actively anticipating an ultimate showdown with present-day Crusading forces, from which they envision they will emerge absolutely victorious. To substantiate this dual positioning, invoking both the abject now and the inevitable gloriousness of the future, they draw on particular Islamist figures, past and present, who are either stripped of their social context and nuanced legal opinions or extoled despite having been ostracized for gross misinterpretations of religious concepts during their own lifetimes.

As discussed throughout this chapter, even though the prolific works of Ibn Taymiyya are actually quite nuanced and in many ways adhere strictly to the rules of warfare set down by the Prophet Muhammad himself, militant Islamists decontextualize his teachings, or are illiterate of them, and apply his terminology—such as *al-walā' wa-l-barā'* (loyalty and disavowal)—to legitimize their own political agendas. Other ideologues, like al-Wahhab, who were not widely accepted by Muslims during their lifetimes, are now viewed by militant Islamists as pillars of Islam, even though these ideologues continue to be unaccepted by the majority of Muslims. Contributing to this dissonance is the lack of religious literacy on the part of many militant Islamists, who misuse concepts without understanding them, as well as the influence of nations like Saudi Arabia, which have exported Wahhabism to further their own particular political agendas.

The Crusades and colonialism—both periods of intense anxiety for Muslims, who were not only concerned for their lives and livelihoods but also unsettled by the resulting political and economic disturbances—produced centuries of Islamist scholarship that is now reduced to and refracted into binaries. Subsequently, thinkers retooled jihad to justify waging war against governments they believed were tainted by its legacy, particularly Qutb, who decried colonialism because he believed it led to the secularization of Muslim-majority states. Thus, a distorted view of what *jāhiliyya* (ignorance) means and how it is applied to societies—including Muslim-majority states, which are often considered un-Islamic—has continued to undergird militant Islamist rhetoric and rationales for violence, which is discussed in detail in chapter 5.

The victimization narratives within White nationalism, examined in the previous chapter, also exist within militant Islamism. Both are confirmed through their respective historical understandings. For White nationalists across the spectra of militancy, religious affiliation, or lack thereof, White genocide is a real and present danger. It is evidenced by the demographic shift toward fewer White Americans and more people of color in the United States as well as by changing social norms from conservative, once-traditional structures to feminism, the perceived increase of women's rights and Queer rights, and what is seen as cloying political correctness. All are interpreted as threats to White existence itself—culturally, biologically, and numerically. The status of White people as supreme—something that is believed to be ordained by God, scientifically proven, or a combination thereof—is threatened by White genocide, and violence is justified, even required, to right this wrong. A parallel rendering of militant Islamists would see the true version of Islam and its rightful sincere adherents as having been put on the defense by oppressive Crusaders and then driven to the point of extinction by colonialism. Again, violence is the only appropriate response. In both cases, righteous self-defense in the face of these historical and cultural threats motivates making the United States either a White ethnostate or part of a global caliphate and justifies the call for racial holy war or jihad, as chapters 5 and 6 scrutinize in detail.

Narratives of victimization are also foundational to the conceptual underpinnings of both groups, as seen in the Fourteen Words ("We must secure the existence of our people and a future for white children") and *al-walā' wa-l-barā'*. As chapter 1 detailed, the Fourteen Words encapsulates the palpable fear of a White genocide. Their very blood and soil are in danger. Moreover, the concept of masculinity, traditional gender roles, and the nuclear family unit are seismically shifting as well, threatening the White heteronormative masculine identity that is fundamental to White nationalism. This "with us or against us" mentality, leaving no room for abstainers, also underlines militant Islamism. *Al-walā' wa-l-barā'*, as interpreted by militant Islamists, signals the same Manichean worldview. Muslims who are deemed to be insincere are regarded as apostates, and any questioning of the beliefs, understandings, and applications of the Qur'an and the sunna may also render one an apostate, even if one has professed a belief in Islam. Viewing themselves as vanguards for sincere Muslims, particularly those who live in Muslim-majority nations afflicted by U.S.-led wars, militant Islamists justify their political pursuit of a caliphate, legitimizing their violence by declaring it to be in defense of the innocent lives of others.

While billions of Muslims around the world feel concerned about U.S. acts of aggression in Muslim-majority nations and other legacies of colonialism, the vast majority of them most certainly do not agree with the methodology of militancy. For the Muslim Americans who choose to wage war against the United States, however, this worldview is alluring, as it seems to provide the identity, community, and purpose many of them have long been seeking. As the case of Farook and Malik suggests, first- and second-generation Americans, who struggle with identity and community acceptance regardless of their socioeconomic background and ethnic identity, are often easy targets for such arguments.

There are also White Americans, some of whom identify with the many religions promoting White nationalism, who feel similarly misunderstood because they are conflated with militants. They, like their Muslim American counterparts, may share some of the same sense of the world as people who would commit acts of terrorism. For White people, this could include a sense of disempowerment, an anxiety over a perceived loss of cultural dominance or of the many privileges that, perhaps unbeknownst to them, being White affords. Certainly, as the introduction discussed at length, the myriad factors involved in why the subjects of the book act in the manner they do may never be known. However, it is important to understand how *they* recognize their own motivations for violence, which, in the case of many of the militants, entails the maneuvering of rhetoric to engage in terrorism.

Part 2 of this book will thus discuss the grievances each group holds against the United States. White nationalists, both religious and nonreligious, promote the notion of White genocide to sanction violence. Similarly, to justify their narrative of victimhood, militant Islamists propagate the idea that the current conflict between Islam and the West is a repeat of the Crusades. These separate, but comparable, sets of grievances are exemplified in the locations of Ruby Ridge, Idaho, and Waco, Texas, on the one hand, and Palestine and the Guantánamo Bay detention facility, on the other, the histories of which galvanize the adherents of these respective ideologies. This examination will lay the groundwork for the analysis in part 3 of the book, specifically looking at how these groups employ religious rhetoric to legitimize the usage of violence, which takes on transcendent significance in their attempts to trigger the apocalypse and realize their political aims of a White ethnostate or a caliphate.

PART TWO

Why They Fight

CHAPTER 3

#WhiteGenocide

Grievances of White Nationalists

On April 13, 2014, Frazier Glenn Miller Jr. (also known as Frazier Glenn Cross Jr.) murdered a fourteen-year-old boy and his grandfather outside the Overland Park Jewish Community Center in Overland, Kansas. He also killed a woman who was on her way to visit her mother at a Jewish assisted living facility. Miller mistakenly believed all three of his victims were Jewish.[1] Minutes after his arrest, while handcuffed in the back seat of a police car, Miller shouted, "Heil Hitler! I wish I'd have killed all of you." He then asked the arresting officer, "How many fucking Jews did I kill?"[2] Later, explaining his actions, he said he had wanted to kill as many Jewish people as he could before he died, because he was thought he was dying of emphysema.[3]

Exhibiting the overlapping affiliations and allegiances common in the world of White nationalist organizations within the political far right, Miller was associated with a plethora of groups in which he could exercise his antisemitism. A veteran of the U.S. Army Special Forces and a Wotanist with a long history of violence, Miller was also a member of The Order, as well as a founder and a former leader of the Carolina Knights of the Ku Klux Klan and the White Patriot Party, both paramilitary organizations.

In 1999, Miller wrote an autobiography, *A White Man Speaks Out*, praising martyrdom and its promise of Valhalla, envisioned as an afterlife solely for the White race.[4] In 2010, he ran unsuccessfully for one of the U.S. Senate seats for Missouri. Miller's campaign platform of racism, xenophobia, and nativism signaled the mainstreaming of these themes in the American political far right. His campaign ads lambasted as cowards White people who had let America's government, banks, and media be overrun by Jewish people: "White men have become the biggest cowards ever to walk the earth. The world has never witnessed such yellow cowards. We've sat back and allowed the Jews to take over our government, our banks, and our media. We've allowed tens of millions of mud people to invade our country, steal our jobs and our women, and destroy our children's futures. America is no longer ours. America belongs to the Jews who rule it and to the mud people who multiply in it."[5] His ads urged listeners to go to the website of former Grand Wizard of the Ku Klux Klan David Duke. Six years later, Duke would endorse Donald Trump's successful presidential campaign.

In consonance with so many of his fellow White nationalists, Miller called for RAHOWA, or racial holy war, sometimes referred to as race war. In fact, in 1987, he mailed a "Declaration of War" to supporters, authorities, and news organizations, seeking to start a race war. In this call to arms, he references his Wotanist beliefs, exhorting the "sons of Odin" to fight, proclaiming "it is time" for "the blood of our enemies [to] flood the streets, rivers and fields of the nation, in Holy vengeance and justice."[6] Miller's pronouncement was based on a document of the same name authored in 1984 by Robert Jay Mathews. Mathews was founder of The Order and an acolyte of Richard Girnt Butler, the Christian Identity leader who himself founded the militant group the Aryan Nations. Also calling for a race war, Mathews's "Declaration of War" established a point system for the killing of people of color, who, it claimed, had sacrilegiously usurped White Christian patriarchal authority in the United States.

The following quote by Mathews elucidates how the fear of White racial annihilation resounds within militant White nationalism ideology today: "Throughout this land our children are being coerced into accepting nonwhites for their idols, their companions, and worst of all for their mates. A course which has taken us straight to oblivion. . . . We declare ourselves to be in a full and unrelenting state of war with those forces seeking and consciously promoting the destruction of our Faith and our Race. Therefore, for Blood, Soil and Honor, and for the future of our children, we commit ourselves to battle."[7] Though it was written in the 1980s, Mathews's declaration is a perfect example of how many White nationalists today continue to perceive themselves as victims of a racial and cultural genocide inflicted on them by immigrants and people of color. In his battle cry, he calls on the themes so prevalent in White nationalist propaganda: isolation, alienation, and frustration, in addition to the superiority of the White race. Many who subscribe to this weltanschauung believe that violence is necessary to reestablish the White race as the rightful inheritors of the United States and the God-given stewards of the world.

The conviction that White people are threatened and marginalized—indeed, that they are on the precipice of racial and cultural extinction—shapes White nationalist points of view on other aspects of American life, including the economy, immigration, religious pluralism, and feminism. This chapter will delve into how the anxiety over White genocide—that is, racial and cultural displacement—also affects White nationalists' perception of other groups of Americans, most notably immigrants, Jewish and Muslim Americans, people who identify as women, and Queer Americans, as well as their attitudes toward law enforcement and the government.

#WHITEGENOCIDE

"White genocide" does have a basis in demographic evidence, depending on how the categories are framed, a fact that is sometimes obscured by the shadow of conspiratorial elements within the political far right. The eclipse of White people as America's demographic majority is unquestionably happening: adult non-Hispanic White people, the highly exclusionary category used in U.S. Census Bureau parlance, will lose their majority in the United States by 2050, and White children have already become a minority.[8] People of color will soon become the new demographic majority.[9] America's changing demographics, which have been affected by declining White birth rates and shifts in immigration streams, mean that White nationalists, along with everyday White Americans, are confronting the prospect of a nation that is no longer numerically representative of the power and privilege their White identity affords them.[10]

The result, for White nationalists, is an elongated list of enemies judged to be complicit in White genocide. As recently as the 1980s and 1990s, White nationalism was fairly narrowly focused on the hatred of people of color, or "mud races" (an umbrella term now also sometimes used to refer to Jewish Americans, Queer Americans, and Muslim Americans). Vociferously antisemitic, strong elements of White nationalism fostered the conspiracy theory of the ZOG, or Zionist Occupied

Government, and promulgated the polygenist view of Jewish people having descended from the unholy coupling of Eve and Satan, which resulted in Cain. Today, while antisemitism and the denigration of people of color vehemently continue, the catalogue has expanded to include resentment about the decline of some sectors of the American economy; demonization of immigration; rage at the possibility of losing the Second Amendment right to bear arms; suspicion of a globalist government, which conspiratorial and antisemitic elements within White nationalism believe to be colluding with murky actors to eradicate them; violent hatred of Muslim Americans; disparagement of feminism and the loss of patriarchal roles; and vitriol directed at Queer people.

White nationalists share the anxieties of White cultural displacement with many everyday White Americans who would not subscribe to the beliefs of these groups and who are in no way militant. However, White nationalists exploit the fragility and White anxiety felt by many to promote a narrative of victimhood—instead of advancing a dialogue of privilege—and to recruit for racial holy war and acts of terrorism. White genocide has thus become a shorthand vindicating not only racial animus but also xenophobia, antisemitism, Islamophobia, misogyny, and Queerphobia.

The Economy and White Genocide

Since 2016 and the election of President Donald Trump, economic anxiety has been touted as one factor for the rise of White nationalist terrorism. Such a conclusion is logical when placed in context of the aftermath of the global Great Recession, which is often marked as starting in 2008.[11] The United States has since seen a continual decline in real wages because of the increasing cost of living, a high number of discouraged workers who have completely stopped looking for employment, the conversion of full-time jobs to temporary positions making up the gig economy, and the automation of many jobs, especially in the retail sector, by cost-cutting technology.[12]

However, and perhaps surprisingly for some, the grave concern about the situation of the American economy (even before the novel coronavirus pandemic wreaked global economic havoc) did not fuel White nationalism; rather, White nationalism elevated apprehensions that the economy was performing poorly during this period.[13] That is, the higher the level of a person's fearfulness regarding the demographic and political status of White people being threatened or overtaken, the more likely that person believes American economic strength is compromised. For many White Americans—militant and nonmilitant—the alarm of losing any facet of power by becoming a minoritized group, demographically, culturally, or even politically, exacerbates their impression of economic decline, inciting concerns about the future. The negative feedback cycle is thus fortified: White Americans who are incited by concern over racial demographic shifts are more likely than other Americans to negatively perceive national economic performance and employment rates.[14] This, in turn, creates fear and anxiety of those identified as the Other, who are seen as a threat for limited resources, such as jobs. Such apprehensions are especially held by White Americans who experience lower social mobility and have less social capital than other Americans, and who have had less direct contact with people of color; many are blue-collar workers of all ages who have had difficulty in finding employment because opportunities have withered away since the Great Recession.[15]

The fear of White genocide held by many White Americans not only is sustained by the ramifications of the rise of the majority-minority in the United States but also is shaped by the perception that people of color are taking over jobs that properly belong to White people and are exploiting the welfare system.[16] This line of thinking has endured within White nationalist circles, even though recent studies have affirmed that White people actually benefit more than other racial groups from government poverty-reducing initiatives like the Supplemental Nutrition Assistance Program and the Affordable Care Act, which provide food and healthcare, respectively.[17] These racist suspicions are intensified by the recruitment propaganda created by various White nationalist organizations and conservative media outlets, which exploits abiding themes such as economic collapse, suspension of the U.S. Constitution, impending civil strife, and the creation of citizen detention camps.

Immigration, Racist Religions, and White Genocide

White nationalist evangelicalism, Christian Identity, Creativity, Wotanism, and the Fourteen Words all anathematize immigration, providing validation for claims of White genocide. Even though immigration is a foundational American tradition, White nationalists, many of whom adhere to these racist religions, and all of whom uphold the Fourteen Words in ethos, whether or not they commit terrorism, vilify immigrants. Immigrants of color are particularly scapegoated as orchestrating White genocide. Staving off White genocide by opposing the immigration of people of color amounts to piety within these teachings.[18]

The concept of White genocide was cemented in the canon of White nationalism by icon and Christian Identity adherent turned Wotanist David Lane in his Fourteen Words, "We must secure the existence of our people and a future for white children." Lane regarded immigration by people who are not White, racial integration, interracial relationships, and policies like affirmative action as instigating White genocide, stances that are now central to Wotanist thought.[19] In a treatise entitled the *White Genocide Manifesto*, Lane concluded that the only recourse for the survival of the White race would be establishing "exclusive White homelands" in North America and Europe.[20] For David Lane and other Wotanists, this would in fact be a restitution of a homeland they believe is rightfully theirs based on blood and soil.[21] According to their understanding of history, the first inhabitants of what is now the United States of America were actually Vikings who settled in North America in the eleventh century and named the territory Vinland. Present-day Wotanists assert their indigeneity to establish a neo-Völkisch, or neo-Folkish, claim to the United States as a national heritage rooted in White racial identity.[22] The former Vinland, now the United States, is thus their land—and their land only—as rightful heirs to this Viking lineage.[23]

The focus on reclaiming Vinland as a White ethnostate is why the historical Viking legacy of cultural exchange and economic trade with other cultures, including Muslims and Arabs, is discarded in Wotanist religious imagery, and it is also the source of their delegitimization of any universalist approach to Odinism.[24] It is also at the heart of the Wotanists' detestation of immigrants. From the perspective of Wotanists, just as people of color are disqualified from joining the religion because they do not have the genetic qualifications, so, too, should immigrants of color be barred from entering the United States, ensuring the purity of the White bloodline.

Christian Identity leaders teach that the United States is God's chosen nation and that it is solely reserved for White people. Immigration of people of color is counter to the divine plan for the nation because it threatens White racial purity. In the film *Christian Identity: Identifying God's Chosen*, the narrator explains, "Christian men . . . didn't mind the white Anglo-Saxon Protestant immigrants from Europe. They were *their* people. They *do* mind the Oriental, the Latino, the Africans and others who refuse to accept their culture, their English language, and their Christian God."[25] Maintaining "racial purity" through the separation of races is, within Christian Identity beliefs, an expression of God's will. Even biblical figures are not immune to criticism on this score—a Christian Identity pamphlet entitled *GOD and Lincoln on Negro-White Marriages* contends Hebrews 12:16 states that the Prophet Esau was a "fornicator" because he married "OUTSIDE OF HIS OWN ADAMIC RACE!"[26] Proximity and intimacy between White people and people of color is tantamount to sin.

Commensurate to Christian Identity, Creativity exploits biblical passages to provide religious reasoning for racial segregation and anti-immigration policies. Ben Klassen, the founder of Creativity, was opposed to all forms of racial integration. His writing warns against interracial marriages and relationships because he feared the White race becoming a demographic minority. Recalling the racial superiority argument of eugenics, Klassen states that the current White race has not reached the glory it once held in ancient Rome, even as he expounds on its innate genetic eminence.[27] He argued that White identity must be protected at all costs because White people are inheritors of the genetic legacy of ancient Romans, while immigrants who are not White bring only "disease, poverty, and mongrelization."[28] Like Klassen, adherents of Creativity seek to prevent the immigration of people of color and to expunge all people of color from the United States to maintain the country as a White ethnostate.

Throughout his writings, Klassen expounds the narrative that White lives are being threatened by the immigration—and the simple existence—of people of color. In *The White Man's Bible,* in Credo 18, "The Melting Pot: The Ugly American Dream," he states that "integration spells the Death Knell of the White Race."[29] Within Klassen's worldview, the influx of people of color into the United States means not only that the number of White people will decrease but also that it will become more difficult for the White race to survive, expand, and advance in accordance with the ultimate mission of Creativity. Klassen maintains that immigration will create a society in which "niggers and the scum are proud to be 'Americans' and the Whites are ashamed to be White."[30] Despite being an immigrant himself, Klassen claimed that Emma Lazarus's 1883 poem "The New Colossus," which envisions the Statue of Liberty crying out to the "wretched refuse" of the world, was a Jewish invention meant to subsume the White race. Moreover, he argued that White immigrants were purposefully being kept out of the United States as part of a Jewish conspiracy to "mongrelize" the White race.[31]

Decades later, in 2019, Ken Cuccinelli, the Trump administration's acting director of Citizenship and Immigration Services, also reinterpreted
Lazarus's poem. After reciting the lines, "Give me your tired, your poor,
your huddled masses yearning to breathe free," he added, "who can
stand on their own two feet and who will not become a public charge."
Cuccinelli was defending a new Trump administration policy of denying
food aid to legal migrants.[32] His rhetoric is representative of that of White
people who condone White nationalist rhetoric and beliefs without
directly identifying as White nationalists themselves.

The Department of Homeland Security under the Trump administration, in its ongoing efforts to criminalize immigration and immigrants,
has gone so far as to allude to the Fourteen Words. A recent DHS report
on immigration statistics has a fourteen-word title, "We Must Secure the
Border and Build the Wall to Make America Safe Again," which eerily
mimics the Fourteen Words battle cry. The report's contents enumerate
negative facts about undocumented immigrants, crime, and crossings at
the U.S.-Mexico border.[33] Such xenophobic language and policies are
not novel; what is perhaps new is that the undisguised language of racism of the militant White nationalist sphere is now commonplace in the
political sphere, allowing the former in many ways to be validated by the
latter. Certainly, the prominence of such purposefully incendiary rhetoric in the political realm feeds into the realm of militancy.[34]

In 2019, on the last day of the Gilroy Garlic Festival in Gilroy, California, nineteen-year-old Santino William Legan killed three people and
injured sixteen others with an AK-47-style semiautomatic rifle before he
was killed by Gilroy police officers. Outfitted in camouflage, he had cut
through a fence to get into the park and had opened fire near a stage
where a band was playing. The lead guitarist later told reporters he
heard someone shout to Legan, "Why are you doing this?" "Because
I'm angry," was Legan's reply.[35] Shortly before the terrorist attack,
Legan posted a message on Instagram to the audience he knew he would
attract. The caption under a picture of Smokey Bear next to a sign stating "Fire Danger High Today!" read, "Read *Might Is Right* by Ragnar
Redbeard / Why overcrowd towns and pave more roads to make room
for hordes of mestizos and Silicon Valley white twats."[36]

Might Is Right is a book published in 1890 by an enigmatic author
who used the pen name Ragnar Redbeard. The book covers social Darwinism and White superiority over people of color, degrading Black people specifically and propagating antisemitism and misogyny while decry-
ing religion as irrational. The only way to ensure victory for oneself, it

claims, is to oppress the Other: "Human rights are and wrongs are not determined by Justice, but by Might. . . . You must ride to success (by preference) over the necks of your foeman. Their defeat is your strength. Their downfall is your uplifting."[37] Citing the U.S. Constitution's preamble, Redbeard declares, "To solemnly proclaim that 'all men are created equal' is as stupid and unscientific as to assert that all dogs, cattle, apes, and trees are created equal."[38] Legan, who was of Italian and Iranian descent, identified as White and perhaps sought to target those whom he regarded as inferior in order to safeguard fellow members of the superior White race, a theme threaded throughout White nationalism. Because he was killed, his worldview can only be garnered posthumously via gleaning insight from his social media account. At the very least, his posts announce his opposition to immigration and his commitment to the community of White nationalists and its battle cry of the Fourteen Words.

Gun Control and White Genocide

Gun control is one of the long-standing antigovernment issues at the core of White nationalism because the ideology's rhetoric often equates gun ownership with White identity. From the vantage of the majority of White nationalists, guns not only are needed for protection against a predatory, corrupt government but also are required to restore America to its ideal self, the way the Founding Fathers intended. For many politicians within the far right as well, the right to own and use guns is God-given. Making plain the amalgamation of politics and religion that often contributes to the narrative of White genocide in the United States, the NRA's chief executive officer and executive vice president Wayne LaPierre equated the Bill of Rights with God-given freedoms, unalterable and outside the purview of any government to bestow or curtail.[39] Any reform, including of the Second Amendment, is thus seen as changing God's word.

Moreover, those within the political far right, including White nationalists, consider gun control measures to be one sign of White cultural displacement, of White people becoming strangers in what is supposed to be their country. Hence, any proposed legislation promoting gun control is widely interpreted as an attempted hostile takeover of the U.S. government by the globalist, Jewish elite, or ZOG, intended to eradicate the White race.[40] Any government that conspires against its own citizens to take away the sacred right to bear arms is viewed as despotic. Preventing the curtailment of the Second Amendment is thus a necessary battle.

Collectively, White nationalist evangelicalism, Christian Identity, Creativity, and Wotanism uphold the right of White men to bear arms as divine will, expressed by the Founding Fathers in the U.S. Constitution, which many of them believe to have been inspired by God.[41] To be armed is often understood to be a sacred command.[42] For example, in an article titled "What Would Odin Say about Gun Control?" Stephen McNallen, a prominent Wotanist who founded the Viking Brotherhood, the Asatru Folk Assembly, and then the Asatru Free Assembly, linked the Second Amendment to a command by Odin "to be armed."[43]

Because the Second Amendment is central to the identity of so many within the political far right, including White nationalists, any proposals perceived as threatening the cherished, God-given right to bear arms serve only to increase White nationalists' sense of alienation within a country that they believe they have a sacred duty to govern. The conspiratorial elements within political far right attitudes toward gun control legislation are heightened by gun control measures. Demonstrating how attempts to legislate gun control provoke unwarranted and fantastical accusations, Alex Jones, a well-known political far right radio host and founder of the news website InfoWars, put forward a particularly heinous claim about the 2012 massacre at Sandy Hook Elementary School in Connecticut. He claimed the murders of twenty children and six adult staff members, all of them shot to death, were a hoax.[44]

Antisemitism, Antiglobalism, and White Genocide

Antisemitism is integrated within the White nationalist discourse by many White racist theologies, specifically Christian Identity, Creativity, and Wotanism, and is subscribed to by many within the wider White nationalist sphere, including by those who are not religiously inclined. This underlying attitude encourages the conspiratorial worldview that a Jewish cabal is creating a globalist order to dominate the world and control its resources. Certainly, a corollary of the belief in White genocide and the need for armed self-defense is the proliferation of conspiracy theories about Jewish people, whom most White nationalists classify as not White.

Demonstrating the interconnectedness of the grievances that motivate all White nationalists, those affiliated with Christian Identity have defined the debate on gun ownership as a thinly veiled plot by this Jewish, globalist government to target Christians. In a Christian Identity pamphlet, this topic is portrayed as part of a ZOG conspiracy to eliminate the White race: "You may ask: 'Why have you brought the Jews into this discussion, I thought you were speaking on Gun Control?' The reason, as any thinking person should be able to see, is that Jewish influence in America, is foremost in every effort to destroy White Christian civilization."[45] Similarly, within Creativity, antisemitism is a main factor for the intensity of adherents' fear of losing the right to bear arms. For them, the only people entitled to this constitutional right are members of the White race. In *The Creativity Handbook,* proponents of the Second Amendment are upheld as warriors primed for a racial holy war, spiritually healthy and able to resist "Jewish propaganda."[46]

Despite the undoubted virulence of antisemitism throughout the political far right, there is some disagreement regarding whether Jewish people are to blame for the perceived plight of White racial and cultural genocide. The streams of pro-Zionism within the various factions of the far right include White evangelical Protestants who support Israel (without being militants themselves) and the Christian Reconstructionists and millenarian Christians who understand the restoration of the Temple in Jerusalem as a prerequisite for the coming of Christ. This constituency of the political far right was ecstatic at the Trump administration's decision to move the U.S. embassy in Israel from Tel Aviv to Jerusalem in recognition of Jerusalem as the country's capital. Other White evangelical preachers sound a more alarmist note, among them Christian broadcaster Pat Robertson, who promotes the assertion that the enemies of the U.S government are actively working toward the goal of a supranational globalist government.[47] Richard Spencer, head of the National Policy Institute, has repeatedly invited antisemitic speakers to his events.[48] However, while some leaders of the political far right are unquestionably antisemitic, others regard Jewish people as White.

White nationalist antisemitism has also manifested in the deadliest attack on Jewish people in American history. In 2018, shortly before entering the Tree of Life synagogue in Pittsburgh, in the neighborhood of Squirrel Hill, which has a deeply rooted Jewish community, and killing eleven worshippers during Shabbat services, Robert Bowers posted an ominous message on Gab, the social media network he often frequented to connect with other like-minded users steeped in conspiracism who find traditional networks like Twitter constrictive.[49] Foreshadowing the destruction he would exact, he declared, "HIAS [Hebrew Immigrant Aid Society, a U.S. nonprofit] likes to bring invaders in that kill our people. I can't sit by and watch my people get slaughtered. Screw your optics. I'm going in."[50] For Robert Bowers, the very presence of people who did not share his beliefs, and whom he did not consider White, was a battle in the larger race war. The wording "our people" and "my people" in Bowers's Gab post directly references White people and echoes the Fourteen Words.

Bowers also used Gab to showcase his vitriol. Moreover, his bio line on Gab read, "Jews are the children of Satan."[51] This is another antisemitic point of reference within nationalist thought, which preaches polygeny, or the belief that Jewish people are of the lineage of Eve and Satan, while the White race is descended from Eve and Adam. He posted an image of the Auschwitz concentration camp, which was one of the deadliest in Nazi Germany. Instead of reading, as the original sign did, "Arbeit Macht Frei" (Work Sets You Free), the image he posted read, "Lies Make Money," referencing key antisemitic points in White nationalism, including the negative stereotype that Jewish people are money-hungry financiers. It also refers to Holocaust denial, diminishing the devastating suffering Jewish people experienced. Some White nationalist adherents believe that the Jewish people who died during the Holocaust were not systematically exterminated by Nazis but rather were victims of disease. Others believe the Holocaust was a media ruse set up by Jewish people to manipulate the media. Ultimately, Holocaust denial is used to prop up the need for a White ethnostate and rekindle Nazi Germany's vision.

Bowers's antisemitism led him to decry what he felt was President Trump's hypocrisy, including his campaign slogan, Make America Great Again, which has become a signal for many White nationalists that their views align with those of the president. For Bowers, President Trump was not doing *enough* to support the Fourteen Words. Bowers posted days before the shooting, "There is no #MAGA as long as there is a kike infestation."[52] White nationalists, and militant White nationalists like Robert Bowers, see Jewish people as a direct threat to the existence of White people. During the shooting itself, as he moved through the synagogue murdering innocent people, Bowers screamed at them, "All Jews must die."[53]

Muslim Americans and White Genocide

Islamophobia is a central energizing element of White nationalism in the United States and transnationally. It is also the touchstone by which to measure loyalty to the White nationalist cause of establishing a White ethnostate. Muslim Americans are increasingly the primary targets of White nationalist terrorists, both religious and nonreligious. Their narrative is that the values of Islam are antithetical to the American way of life; Muslims are intent on destroying White Western civilization; and Islam and Muslims are the vanguards of eliminating traditional Christian and White identity through genocide.[54] Several White nationalist groups and several notable figures have found their raison d'être in sustaining this rendering.[55] Muslims are emblematic of White nationalist animosity toward immigrants, people of color, and the proverbial Other. The greater their odium toward Islam and Muslim Americans—as evidenced by attacks on Muslims and *masājid* across the United States, and by support for the anti-shari'a movement—the more patriotic and sincere White nationalists consider themselves.[56]

Before 9/11, Islam and Muslim Americans were not on the radar of White nationalism; the position of the touchstone object of hatred was occupied instead by the globalist ZOG. Much of the White nationalist literature of the twentieth century on Muslims is actually about the Nation of Islam and the mutual antipathy of White nationalists and the Nation of Islam toward Jewish people. Earlier attitudes toward Islam and Muslims even included what could be described as a positive orientation. Ben Klassen did reference Islam, but only to compare it to his own religion, as part of a series of disparaging articles that juxtapose his creed to religions around the world, in an attempt to convert and proselytize his message of White superiority and RAHOWA. Rather than call Islam a threat, as it is commonly perceived in White nationalist circles now, he wrote somewhat admiringly of the religion he referred to as "Mohammedanism," claiming that it held lessons that should be applied by Creativity.[57]

There is one exception to this general early disinterest in Islam, however. Perceptively foreshadowing the rhetoric of current White nationalists, prolific Wotanist author Stubba touches on themes of White genocide and being overrun by Muslims in a 1979 essay calling Islam a "violent and proselytising religion," claiming "a great expansion of Odinism and Odinist activity" is the only solution to the "coming threat of Islam and the mullahs."[58]

Though it seems surprising now, in the beginning of the twentieth-first century, there was concern among some White nationalists and even American academics on the political far right that far right militants and militant Islamists would somehow combine forces based on their mutual antagonism toward the United States and attack.[59] Along these lines, there have also been anomalous instances of White nationalists converting to militant Islamism, such as American Joseph Jeffrey Brice. Brice, who once idolized Timothy McVeigh and was "a self-declared, conservative, rightwing Christian," later became interested in militant Islamism after a homemade bomb nearly killed him in 2010. Another rare case is Leo Felton, who wrote of his experiences in his autobiography *Beige: An Unlikely Trip through America's Racial Obsession*.[60]

Since the election of President Trump, who has embraced aggressive Islamophobic rhetoric and policies, White nationalists have targeted Muslim Americans in a brazenly hostile manner, perceiving fellow Americans through the lens of a clash of civilizations. In 2016, three members of a militant White nationalist group named the Kansas Security Force formed a subgroup that they called the Crusaders, an overt reference to the medieval religiopolitical wars between Christians and Muslims. The FBI infiltrated this group through a confidential source who taped conversations and attended secret planning meetings as the members finalized plans to blow up an apartment complex housing more than one hundred mostly Somali-born Muslim immigrants and a small masjid.[61] Officials seized an array of weapons, ammunition, and explosives components. One of its members spoke of using a silenced .22-caliber weapon to execute residents one by one, and he further proposed using a bow and arrow to kill, instructing his followers that the arrows be dipped in pig's blood first, because Muslims do not eat pork products. This same member discussed the 1995 Oklahoma City bombing, saying he held at his farm supplies of the ammonium nitrate and fuel oil components that revered White nationalist Timothy McVeigh had used. "The only good Muslim is a dead Muslim," he allegedly told his comrades. "If you're a Muslim, I'm going to enjoy shooting you in the head. When we go on operations there's no leaving anyone behind, even if it's a one-year-old. . . . I guarantee if I go on a mission those little fuckers are going bye-bye."[62] The date the Crusaders from Kansas allegedly chose for their proposed massacre was the day after the presidential election, November 9, 2016. This date underlines the role that the election—which featured vituperative Islamophobic attacks on Muslim Americans by Donald Trump, as well as by other Republican presidential candidates—played in the subsequent desire of the members of this group to kill Muslims. In 2019, the three men were each sentenced to at least twenty-five years in prison for conspiring to use a weapon of mass destruction and conspiring against civil rights.[63]

In 2015, Christian Patriot and former Navy SEAL Matt Bracken wrote an essay called "Tet Take Two: Islam's 2016 European Offensive" that went viral. The title of the essay is a reference to the 1968 infiltration of South Vietnam by Vietcong guerrilla fighters, who then launched a surprise offensive. Bracken believes Muslims are carrying out a second Tet Offensive, describing Islam as a "ringworm infection [that] is dead and barren within the ring, but flares up when it parasitically feeds off the healthy, non-Islamic societies around it."[64] Bracken's claim upholds the logic that all Muslim Americans secretly harbor animosity toward the United States. Not one of them is to be trusted. They are all national security threats. The essay was endorsed by the White nationalist organization Oath Keepers. The Oath Keepers are virulently Islamophobic; they have provided security for several March against Sharia rallies organized by Islamophobic groups such as ACT for America, the mission of which is to counteract what is believed to be the imminent implementation of shariʿa in several cities across the United States.[65] ACT for America was founded by Brigitte Gabriel, who herself has written several books purporting that the United States has been infiltrated by militant Islamist sleeper cells—not only throughout all levels of government but also in colleges and universities.[66] Rallies organized by ACT for America have been attended by various White nationalists, including members of the Soldiers of Odin, Arizona Liberty Guard, Proud Boys, Identity Evropa, Texas State Militia, and League of the South, evidencing the primacy of Islamophobia throughout the entirety of White nationalism.[67]

The portrayal of Islam and Muslim Americans as anti-American, unpatriotic, and threatening to the security and sanctity of the White race is also on display in the political realm. Since 2010, 120 anti-shariʿa bills, known as "American Laws for American Courts," have been introduced in forty-two states; thirteen states have enacted this type of legislation.[68] This is despite the fact that shariʿa is actually not a substitute for civil law but rather a set of guidelines. The anti-shariʿa bills demonstrate how ignorance and suspicion have converged to create an environment of insidious Islamophobia in the United States. These incidents of vehement rhetoric portray Muslim Americans as anti-American, one element of classifying them as primary enemies in the ongoing race war to prevent White genocide.

The perception that all Muslim Americans—no matter how seemingly benign—are secretly harboring animus toward White people and other Americans is currently intensifying within White nationalist collective thought. White nationalists believe that to prevent a White genocide, a race war must be waged against its instigators, the main contingent of whom are Muslim Americans. Though examining the full extent of this transnational Islamophobia is outside the parameters of this book, it is worth noting that Muslims are also increasingly being instru-mentalized as primary targets of hate by White nationalists outside of the United States.[69] This narrative, in turn, prompts militant Islamists to recruit to their ranks, as chapter 4 explores.

Feminism, Misogyny, and White Genocide

The Fourteen Words, emphasizing a state of victimhood for White peo-ple, also contains an implicit demand for procreation to safeguard the White race ("a future for white children"). In *Might Is Right,* the book cited by the Gilroy shooter, Redbeard defines a woman solely on the basis of her reproductive function, in language that presaged present-day fears of White genocide due to declining White birth rates: "A woman is primarily a reproductive cell-organism, a womb structurally embastioned by a protective, defensive, osseous framework; and sur-rounded with the attenæ, and blood vessels, necessary for supplying nutriment to the growing ovum or embryo. Sexualism and maternity dominate the lives of all true women."[70]

What is at stake for White nationalists is not only the survival of the White race but also the preservation of White patriarchal cisheteronor-mative culture. The victimhood theme that runs through White nation-alist thought reappears here, in the insistence that while masculinity is superior, it is in crisis. The so-called manosphere, or the online misogy-nist arena, is replete with men who express misogyny together with racism and/or Queerphobia.[71] Incels, men who label themselves "invol-untary celibates," are particularly predisposed to have their own net-works in the digital domain. Subreddits like r/MGTOW (an acronym for "men going their own way") are full of threats of physical violence, while r/Braincels is concerned with people who are Queer and the cor-rectness of the patriarchy.

In just one example of the vituperative intersection of racism, misog-yny, and antifeminism, Daniel McMahon, a thirty-one-year-old White nationalist, was charged with cyberstalking and threatening a Black city council candidate in Charlottesville, Virginia, in 2019. His online posts on various sites were filed with racist, homophobic, and misogynistic lan-guage. On Discord, a gaming chat platform also used by White national-ists for internal communication, he wrote that a "White girl with a nig-ger" was "beastilaty [sic]." On Gab, he wrote, "It's impossible to rape a female Leftist, because they are so slutty they will sleep with everyone."

He had corresponded on Twitter with Robert Bowers, the perpetrator of the antisemitic terrorist attack in Pittsburgh in 2018.[72]

It is important to note that White nationalist women also participate in this discourse. Though not often associated with militancy or positions of leadership in White nationalism, female White nationalists engage online to promote a vision of the White woman as a dutiful, traditional housewife, or "tradwife," who lives to please her husband and raise children, enacting the mission of the Fourteen Words and performing her duty to the White race.

Queer Americans and White Genocide

Legal and social acceptance of Queer people also evokes the White nationalist fear of cultural displacement in many, but not all, instances. While the narrative of White victimhood promoted by the Fourteen Words and racist theologies portrays people of color as threats, paints Jewish Americans as participating in a globalist conspiracy, calls for the complete excision of Muslim Americans from the national landscape, and holds feminism in contempt, some within White nationalism recognize that heterosexuality is no longer the norm for many within its membership base—even if this stance is not wholeheartedly embraced. That is not to say there is not a large contingent of anti-Queer advocates. Presently, many White nationalists within the political far right consider advancements in the civil rights and liberties of Queer people to be an affront to their own rights and liberties. White nationalists frequently link Queer people with pedophilia and consider them a threat to children and society, sometimes characterizing them as mentally ill.

Christian Identity assails Queer Americans, regarding them as contributing to the persecution of truly devout Christians.[73] Its newsletter cites scriptural verses that condemn same-sex sexual relations in particular, including Romans 1:24–28, which describes how "men did shameful things with other men," including abandoning "the natural way to have sex." The verses also state that these men were punished because they did "vile and degrading things." In the same newsletter, Leviticus 18:22 is cited as unmitigatedly condemning sexual relations between members of the same gender: "Do not practice homosexuality, having sex with another man as with a woman. It is a detestable sin."[74] Such attitudes against Queer Americans are evidenced by members of the Aryan Nations, once a pillar of Christian Identity, posting the following defamatory song lyrics online, an inversion of "America, the Beautiful" that claims the atrocities of 9/11 were actually God's punishment of "sodomites":

> O wicked land of sodomites,
> Your World Trade Center is gone.
> With crashing planes and burning flames,
> America, America,
> God's wrath was shown to thee.[75]

While Odinists accept Queer people because their religion, based on the natural world, embraces multiple sexual orientations, Wotanist David Lane characterizes "homosexuality" as "a crime against Nature."[76] Creativity remains relatively silent about Queer Americans, noting only that their existence is the result of the machinations of a globalist government run by Jewish people.[77]

Reluctant acceptance of Queer people by some White nationalists signals a strategic shift to expand their membership base, given increased acceptance of Queer identities among younger Americans.[78] For instance, White nationalists responded to the murder of forty-nine people at Pulse, a Queer nightclub in Orlando, Florida, by militant Islamist Omar Mateen, by fomenting Islamophobia rather than Queerphobia.[79] Additionally, Richard Spencer, president of the White nationalist National Policy Institute and the person credited with coining the term *alt-right,* barred the identitarian Matthew Heimbach, of the Traditionalist Youth Network, from an NPI speaking engagement because of his Queerphobic comments and scheduled Jack Donovan, who is Queer, as a keynote speaker instead.[80] Spencer also took part in an AMA, or "Ask Me Anything," session on Reddit, a popular social media platform for the alt-right. When he received the question, "How do you feel about your large following in the gay community?" rather than balk, Spencer responded, "The gays love me."[81] His satisfaction at the support of a once-derided demographic displays how significant the appearance of tolerance of Queer people is, if not within the legislative sphere of the political far right, then within those on the ground.

It is important to note that the Queer label is far from monolithic. Those in the transgender community, and particularly Black women of color, remain intensely vulnerable to rhetorical and actual violence at the hands of White nationalists and others who endorse transphobia.[82] White nationalist Paul Nehlen, who unsuccessfully ran against former

U.S. Speaker of the House Paul Ryan in the Wisconsin Republican primary in 2016 and vocally supported Robert Bowers's terrorism, called for the trolling of "drag queen story hour" programs run by libraries and bookstores nationwide. On the app Telegram, he promoted the doxing of the drag queens who presented at these events, as well as attendees, via Project Dox Tranny Storytime, while also conflating drag performers with people who identify as transgender or nonbinary.[83] In another post to Telegram, Christopher Cantwell, a Unite the Right rally attendee and White nationalist host of the podcast Radical Agenda, stated, "Assisted suicide is the only help you can give trannies."[84]

Queer people challenge the power that White nationalists draw from cisgendered heteropatriarchy. Because White nationalists view Queer rights, and transgender rights especially, as political correctness run amok, they feel that anyone who does not conform to their conceptualizations of gender identity, gender roles, sexual orientation, and expressions must be disempowered. White nationalist violence against Queer Americans is very often the result of compounding racism, misogyny, and Queerphobia.

ANTIGOVERNMENT RESISTANCE: THE SYMBOLIC POWER OF RUBY RIDGE AND WACO

Though White nationalists view President Trump as an ally in the White House and therefore have lost some of their traditional animus toward the federal government, mistrust of the government at large, especially at the federal level, and wariness of international alliances, treaties, and multinational corporations is the standard position within White nationalism and the political far right. More government, from this point of view, will only impede freedom, liberty, and the fulfillment of White destiny through the imposition of unnecessary regulations. Many White nationalists advocate for the complete dismantling of government bureaucracy, including treaties, taxes, regulations, and the agencies responsible for their oversight.[85] So while White nationalists, and those within the political far right more broadly, may support President Donald Trump, the executive of the government, they also advocate for its dismantling. In fact, President Trump himself has supported this.[86] The religions discussed in this book also allege the Founding Fathers held this view.[87]

For many of the disparate and overlapping segments within the political far right, including White nationalists, their grievances against and mistrust of the government are crystalized in two deadly encounters that occurred between primarily defenseless individuals and the U.S. government in the 1990s. The tragic events at Ruby Ridge, Idaho, and Waco, Texas, caused by the missteps of the U.S. government, are both significant symbols of antigovernment rage and gun rights that are ingrained on these segments' shared historical consciousness. The fallout from both episodes immediately resulted in Timothy McVeigh's devastating Oklahoma City attack in 1995 and the rise of Christian Identity–inspired groups. His act of terrorism continues to reverberate today.

A botched federal reconnaissance mission led to an eleven-day stand-off at Ruby Ridge in August 1992 between Randy Weaver and his family, on one side, and the FBI, the U.S. Marshals Service, and the Bureau of Alcohol, Tobacco, and Firearms, or ATF, on the other. This escalated into a shootout resulting in the deaths of Deputy U.S. Marshal William Francis Degan, Vicki Weaver, Sammy Weaver, and the Weaver dog, Striker. Kevin Harris, a Weaver family friend, was left gravely wounded.

Randy Weaver is a former Green Beret and a U.S. Army combat engineer. He and his wife, Vicki, were ardent Christian Identity adherents and were in contact with members of the Aryan Nations, with Randy attending several of the organization's annual World Congress conferences in the summer despite not being a member himself.[88]

According to their daughter Sara Weaver, who was interviewed decades later, and who also coauthored a book with her father, the reason the Weavers moved their family to the remote woods of Ruby Ridge was to prepare for an apocalypse they believed to be imminent.[89] Their worldview was shaped by the tenets of their faith, which also fostered in them deep skepticism of the federal government and law enforcement. They purposefully chose the location to be near fellow adherents.

The events building up to the 1992 shootout began in 1989, when Randy Weaver sold an illegally sawed-off shotgun unknowingly to a federal informant. The informant had set Weaver up to commit a federal crime so that he could leverage the charge to pressure Weaver to inform on the Aryan Nations, a tactic that continues to be used on both White nationalists and many would-be militant Islamists decades later. Despite the leverage on him, however, Weaver refused to work with the agents, remaining loyal to his biblical antigovernment beliefs. Elaborating on this worldview, Vicki Weaver expressed her religious-based aversion toward the government in two letters she wrote to the U.S. Attorney for Idaho, addressing the office as Servants of the Queen of Babylon. She interpreted the Book of Revelation to prophesy a coming racial holy war between White Anglo-Saxon Christians and the U.S. government. According to the Weavers' religious beliefs, shared by many in the area, engaging with the government was tantamount to making a pact with the devil.

Because of his beliefs, Randy Weaver failed to show up in court after he was arraigned for the gun charge, prompting a bench warrant to be issued for his arrest. It would be this warrant that would bring the federal agents to the secluded cabin where the Weavers were peacefully living with their children, Sara, Sammy, Rachel, and Elisheba.

In May 1992, the Weavers took part in a rare interview conducted by Michael Weland, a local newspaper reporter. Weland quoted Vicki Weaver explaining that her husband's failure to show up for court was due to fear he would "be railroaded through the court and once he was gone [the government] would have come in, kicked us off the property and torn this place apart." She said that the property had been given to them by "Yahweh," which meant they could not leave. Randy Weaver was quoted in the same article stating, "Right now, the only thing they can take away from us is our life. Even if we die, we win. We'll die believing in Yahweh."[90] Their worldview was framed by their Christian Identity beliefs, which equated the government with the servants of evil. They had escaped to the remote hillside of Ruby Ridge to flee this evil and the apocalyptic showdown they believed was imminent. From the perspective of the political far right, the government then colluded to entrap Randy Weaver in an attempt to force him to betray his Aryan Nations brethren, who had taken him in and offered him support. When he refused to denounce his compatriots, the federal government massacred his family to set an example.

The alleged targeting of Randy Weaver to become an FBI informant, and the subsequent government violation of his family—most poignantly the unjust deaths of his wife and son—intensify the mistrust and fear many White nationalists feel toward the U.S. government and what they interpret as the betrayal of true American ideals. The death of Vicki Weaver by a sniper's bullet while she was cradling baby Elisheba exacerbates their conviction that the U.S. government is not to be trusted.

Less than a year later, another incident took place between White nationalists and the federal government. The second standoff, this time in Waco, Texas, did not end with a shootout but instead started with one. What would become the second epicenter of rage for the political far right began with a report that David Koresh, born Vernon Howell, had an illegal weapons cache at the Branch Davidian compound, also known as Mount Carmel, in Waco. The Bureau of Alcohol, Tobacco, and Firearms went to investigate.

In 1990, Vernon Howell changed his name to David Koresh, taking the first name from King David of the Israelites and the last name from King Cyrus, the biblical liberator of the Jewish people. The Branch Davidian compound was not affiliated with Christian Identity but with millennialism, a religious tradition that asserts that Christ's return to earth and the establishment of a divine kingdom are imminent. As a millenarian, Koresh believed that within the pages of the Bible are specific clues about when and how the Second Coming will arrive. Ultimately, Koresh saw himself as the liberator of his people from the government. His mission was to lead them into the final battle that would end the world and take his followers into eternal glory.

During Bible study sessions—which could be as long as twelve hours—Koresh preached a vision of violent confrontation with the government. The members understood that meant they would die. The children were taught this morbid message, too. They used to chant: "We are soldiers in the army. We've got to fight. Some day we have to die. We have to hold up the blood-stained banner. We have to hold it up until we die."[91] While Koresh saw himself as a religious leader, the FBI viewed him as a cult leader and child molester.

Outside the Mount Carmel complex in February 1993, the FBI assembled what has been called one of the largest military forces ever to be gathered against a civilian suspect in American history: ten Bradley tanks, two Abrams tanks, four combat-engineering vehicles, and 668 agents, in addition to six U.S. Customs officers, fifteen U.S. Army personnel, thirteen members of the Texas National Guard, thirty-one Texas Rangers, 131 officers from the Texas Department of Public Safety, seventeen officers from the McLennan County sheriff's office, and eighteen Waco police, for a total of 899 people.[92] Koresh, however, had already been tipped off to this Goliath-like ambush. The resulting gunfire exchange ended with the deaths of six Davidians and four agents, with twenty wounded. A fifty-one-day standoff, from February 28 to April 19, ensued.

When the final standoff between the scores of federal agents and the Davidians began, FBI agents authorized combat engineering vehicles to punch through the compound's walls and inject tear gas, also called CS gas, in hopes of forcing the parents inside the compound to release their children.[93] Less than two dozen children were released, paired in twos as a biblical reference to Noah's Ark, per Koresh's command, but many more mothers and children were still inside the compound. Koresh claimed that the rest of the children were his own, and they remained with him. Koresh himself and at least fifty adults and over twenty children were found dead in the resulting funeral pyre. Every surviving child lost one or both parents.

David Koresh has since become a martyr figure for many within the political far right.[94] The back-to-back events at Ruby Ridge and Waco ignited a maelstrom of mistrust between them and the U.S. federal government. As Timothy McVeigh, the primary perpetrator of the 1995 Oklahoma City bombing, the most devastating terror attack on American soil by an American citizen, said, "What the U.S. government did at Waco and Ruby Ridge was dirty, and I gave dirty back to them at Oklahoma City."[95] He was incensed with how unjustly federal agencies targeted the Weavers in Ruby Ridge. McVeigh also held the government responsible for the deaths at the Branch Davidian compound in Waco, and he even visited Waco to proselytize his antigovernment beliefs.[96]

Ruby Ridge and Waco have become potent symbols for a range of White nationalists, from those who would never engage in violence to those who embrace terrorism as the only proper recourse to right the wrongs of society and nefarious government entities. Randy and Vicki Weaver in particular have become figureheads as fighters in the war against the U.S. federal government. "While many of us have lost loved ones in this war, Mr. Weaver goes down in history as one of our best," reads one comment posted on Stormfront, one of the largest and most well-known White nationalist web forums, which was also cited in the *Spokesman-Review* two decades after the standoff.[97] Likewise, the deaths of children and their mothers in the fire at Mount Carmel in Waco, incited by federal forces, also serve to legitimate the political far right view that the federal government is an abusive, oppressive power that must be dismantled, or kept to a minimum at the very least. Ruby Ridge and Waco both remain potent symbols of how a corrupted government is willing to go to war against its own citizens.

CONCLUSION

The grievances of White nationalists, including White nationalist evangelicals, Christian Identity adherents, Creators, Wotanists, and those who do not identify as religious, are based on these individuals' communal sense of racial and cultural displacement, victimhood, and alienation. The eclipsing of White identity, substantiated by a very real demographic shift, affects White nationalist attitudes on diversity and pluralism. Those who hold this perspective see anything supportive of changing the status quo as a threat to their very existence. This worldview anathematizes multiculturalism and immigration, which are seen as the vehicles of their destruction. Apprehensions about gun rights (the abiding staple of far right politics), the economy, and the role of government stand alongside fears of globalization and a combination of disdain for and feeling threatened by the human rights of Queer people, women, Jewish people, and Muslim Americans.[98]

Their binary understanding of the world—White versus the Other—means that for the White race to exist, all others must perish. Correspondingly, for the White cisheteronormative patriarchy to remain in power, everyone who does not fit into this mold must cease to have rights. As a result, the underlying anxiety over White genocide articulated by the Fourteen Words only further increases racism, antisemitism, and Islamophobia, fueling conspiracy theories. Belief in these conspiracies in turn intensifies the sense of victimization that underlies the Fourteen Words and its call to arms, feeding a vicious cycle of militancy that parallels the way that Islamophobia functions as a recruiting strategy for militant Islamist organizations.

The next chapter focuses on the grievances of militant Islamists and will discuss how the narrative of victimhood of this group is similar in many ways to that of its White nationalist counterparts. Rather than look to sociopolitically constructed notions of race, however, to justify their war against the United States, its state apparatus, and citizens, militant Islamists harness particular interpretations of Islam and of U.S. foreign policy to bolster their claim of self-preservation. This in turn creates the framework that they need to defend themselves against perceived religious oppression, political disenfranchisement, and social immorality.

CHAPTER 4

The Crusades Redux

Grievances of Militant Islamists

On November 5, 2009, just weeks before his scheduled deployment to Afghanistan, U.S. Army psychiatrist Nidal Malik Hasan donned his dress uniform one last time and went to work at the Soldier Readiness Processing Center at Fort Hood, Texas. That day, he killed thirteen people and wounded thirty-two others using a semiautomatic tactical pistol.

Born in Virginia, Hasan majored in biochemistry at Virginia Tech in Blacksburg. After joining the U.S. Army, he was sent to the Uniformed Services University of the Health Sciences in Maryland to study medicine. He graduated in 2001. He then spent the period of time between 2003 and 2009 serving first as an intern, then as a resident, and, finally, as a psychiatry fellow at Walter Reed National Military Medical Center in Washington, DC, before moving to Fort Hood.

It was there, as a U.S. Army psychiatrist, that Hasan listened to the stories of fellow military members, often consulting with his supervisors and Army legal advisers about how to cope with disturbing reports of soldiers' deeds in Afghanistan and Iraq. He became increasingly vocal in his opposition to the American military presence in these Muslim-majority nations, only to receive orders that would upset him deeply: he was to deploy to Afghanistan on November 28, 2009.

During his 2013 trial, in which he—like militant White nationalists Dylann Roof and Frazier Glenn Miller Jr.—represented himself, Hasan gave a brief opening statement, telling the court simply, "I am the shooter." As is the case for the other perpetrators of terrorism scrutinized in this book, his full rationale may never be known, and the multidimensional dynamics that motivated him to commit such an egregious act of violence must be specified within their own contexts. What can be understood, however, is his point of view. Perhaps provoked by the accounts of his patients, Hasan seems to have believed he was defending the lives of innocent civilians in Afghanistan from American military personnel. Instead of calling witnesses or testifying at his trial, he sent a handwritten letter to the *Killeen Daily Herald,* the local newspaper in Fort Hood, several days before the testimony phase of his trial began: it was a manifesto, like those written by many so-called lone wolves. In this letter, Hasan both posed and answered questions, concluding each answer with his signature, printed name, and the acronym "SoA," for "Soldier of Allah," a description he also used on his business cards.

The first self-posed question asked, "What was your motive on November 5?" His response: "I was defending my religion. It is one thing for the United States to say 'We don't want Sharia'h (God's SWT) law to govern us' but its [sic] not acceptable to have a foreign policy that tries to replace Sharia'h law for a more secular form of government. Fledgling Islamic states like Afghanistan need help to better govern their people under Sharia'h law. We are imperfect Muslims trying to establish the perfect religion of All-Mighty God."[1] His testimony here is in line with the "defense of others" reasoning he invoked throughout his trial. Hasan was ultimately found guilty of thirteen counts of premeditated murder and thirty-two counts of attempted premeditated murder and was sentenced to death.

American militant Islamists interpret the foreign policy of the United States as perpetuating the paradigm of the West versus Islam, recalling the medieval Crusades and the oppression of colonialism in the nineteenth-century Middle East—as well as the "clash of civilizations" narrative that is also promoted by White nationalists. They see colonialism as a continuation of the medieval Crusades, maintained by the same Western nations to suppress the growth of Islam as a religion and subdue Muslims from ever becoming a united dominant power. Many of the Islamist thinkers and theologians who are looked to today by militant Islamists for inspiration in the current war against the United States experienced firsthand the disintegration of the cohesive polity of the *umma* either during the Crusades or centuries later during the collapse of the Ottoman Empire. Since the end of the Ottoman Empire, Muslims around the world have lacked a significant territory in which to exercise their collective geopolitical voice.

The Crusades occurred in the eleventh, twelfth, and thirteenth centuries and have remained a prevailing theme within centuries of Islamist discourse. The works of Islamic theologian Ibn Taymiyya, who is venerated by many Muslims, nonmilitants and militant Islamists alike, have been co-opted by terrorists to perpetuate the imagery of the Crusades in the war against the United States and its allies. During the thirteenth and fourteenth centuries, Ibn Taymiyya confronted the remnants of the Christian Crusades amid the throes of conflict between Muslims and Mongols/Tatars in his homeland in what is now Turkey. Islamist thought, militant and nonmilitant, has also been shaped by other prominent religious scholars and political actors who were similarly firsthand witnesses to critical events signaling the political decline of the *umma*.

One such ideologue is Sayyid Qutb, a child of the British occupation of Egypt, which took place seven centuries after the Crusades. The influential twentieth-century Egyptian Islamist ideologue wrote bitterly that colonialism recalled the military expeditions of the Crusades, embedding them in the present day. Because he witnessed the overtaking of his homeland by foreign forces, Qutb understood all ideologies— including capitalism, communism, and pan-Arabism—as having failed to support Islamic identity, jeopardizing Muslim-majority nations. For Qutb, the only systems able to succeed against the ongoing Crusades are institutions that follow a certain interpretation of Islam, among them the caliphate.[2]

Qutb set forth the notion that the Crusader spirit is to be found in the hearts of all Americans and Europeans. Furthermore, he argued that all Muslims are involved in a perpetual struggle against Jewish people everywhere. Ultimately, these forces seek to eliminate Muslims.[3] Equating the fears that many, including White nationalists, have of the billons of Muslims around the world, Qutb upheld the idea that millions of modern-day Americans, along with their Anglo-European counterparts, are bonded together by the sole ambition of eliminating Islam as a religion and as a way of life.[4] His assertion, which continues to resonate for many militant Islamists around the world, is that the United States and its allies are orchestrating a concerted effort to exterminate Islam as a religion and replace it with secularism.[5] The calculated hostilities of the Crusaders, experienced by Ibn Taymiyya and perceived by Qutb, continue to be demonstrated by the past and present antagonism of the United States and allied powers. The religion of Islam and all Muslims are thus on the defensive, and the need for self-preservation is paramount.

From the perspective of most militant Islamists, examples of Qutb's claim of current Crusades against Muslims everywhere include America's role in the establishment of the state of Israel and the recognition of Jerusalem as its capital; the U.S.-led wars in Iraq and Afghanistan; and the lack of U.S. action in regions of the world where Sunni Muslims are being persecuted through systemic ethnoreligious discrimination, like the massacres in Bosnia, the persecution against the Cham in Vietnam, the criminalization and forced detention of the Uighurs in China, and the genocide faced by the Rohingya Muslims in Myanmar.[6] The billions of Muslims around the world who are not militant share consternation over these events; however, they do not agree with the methodology of violence enacted by the terrorists, who self-identify as Muslim.

Equating the United States and its political allies in the present day to the Christian Crusaders and colonizers of the past ensures that in the mindset of many militant Islamists, the Crusades—often used in conjunction with Zionism as a metonym for conflict with the United States—are not relegated to history books but are an active part of collective consciousness.

This chapter will examine the centrality of the Crusader theme, and how militant Islamists argue that the war against oppression and tyranny represented by the Crusades has never really ended, by focusing on three areas: how the motif of the Crusades has been used by militant Islamists to shape antagonism toward the United States, dovetailing with antisemitism; how American foreign policy has been construed by militant Islamists to buttress the abiding belief that the United States seeks the eradication of Islam; and how American policy on Palestine and Guantánamo reinforces Crusader imagery as interpreted by militant Islamists.

COMBATING THE CRUSADES AND COLONIALISM

For many American militant Islamists, like Nidal Malik Hasan, committing violence is a political obligation supported through a warped reading of religious texts. Perhaps because of their lack of religious literacy, the original context and long history of symbolically loaded religious terms like al-walā' wa-l-barā' (loyalty and disavowal) are of no significance for militant Islamists. Based on their nonnormative interpretation of Islam, which centralizes Wahhabi discourse, al-barā' means opposition to non-Muslims for the sake of God, an opposition that is natural, justified, and part of the religion. Moreover, by referencing key terms in the canon of militant Islamist ideology, including *al-walā'* *wa-l-barā'*, militant Islamists can sanctify through religious legitimacy what they perceive to be an inevitable conflict between themselves and the United States.

Reifying the Orientalist discourse within White nationalism, militant Islamists similarly proclaim that the West and Islam are on course for an escalating conflict. According to many American militant Islamists, the war against the United States is a primordial one. Sincere believers who truly obey God are destined to vanquish the Satanic false gods of America. Their worldview simply designates anyone who does not subscribe to their interpretation of Islamic law as an open enemy and a conspirator of Satan.

For many American militant Islamists, the only type of relationship possible between Muslims, whether American citizens or not, and the United States is a combative one. According to them, all Americans are non-Muslim, regardless of the faith with which they self-identify. Reiterating Qutb, the current Crusade is an ongoing fight. Any concession or cessation of violence would result in the oppressive force of the United States subduing those who are considered true Muslims. For them, the Crusades are present and ongoing. A violent response is mandated. Ultimately, they believe that the whole world must come to live under a specific rendition of Islamic law and that the establishment of this world order can be accomplished only through violent means.

Furthermore, most American militant Islamists view the United States as inconsistent and duplicitous when it comes to policies regarding Muslims and Muslim-majority nations. For instance, while many Americans regard religious pluralism as a primary social value worthy of universal acceptance (and might assume that militant Islamists would unilaterally deny such a value), within the scope of the militant Islamist worldview, the principle of religious pluralism itself is a sham, a cover for aggressions against Islam and thus another reason to wage a just war in the name of Islam against the United States. The criticism is not pluralism per se; rather, the objection is to what is regarded to be the hypocritical stance of the U.S. government toward pluralism, in calling for all people to live together while surreptitiously supporting the very regimes that suppress pluralism among their citizens. The ideal of the Islamic state as headed by the Prophet Muhammad contains the concepts of religious, social, and political pluralism as well as the concept of democracy as a government that grants agency to its citizens.[7] What is being objected to, then, is what is regarded as the antagonism of U.S.

foreign policy toward the religion of Islam, in that it supports rulers of *jāhiliyya* who are currently governing Muslim-majority nations.

Moreover, from the standpoint of militant Islamists, the long-standing alliance between the United States and these corrupt Muslim-majority regimes inhibits the establishment of a true caliphate and has prevented sincere Muslims from fully living in their ideal society. Because they maintain U.S. domestic rhetoric is at complete odds with its foreign policy, they also consider the United States to be the leader of the forces of evil in an inevitable "clash of civilizations," a phrase taken from the book of that name by American political scientist Samuel Huntington, the premise of which is also the incompatibility of Islam with Western culture.[8]

The imagery of the Crusades as an ongoing campaign to raze Islam is exploited by militant Islamist organizations for recruitment, religiopolitical legitimacy, and justification of warfare. It leads naturally to the need for a global caliphate, the result of an inherent dichotomy between what are perceived as two disparate world systems.

Long before Islamic State (Dā'ish) was established to combat the crusading United States, al-Qa'ida figurehead Osama bin Laden railed against what he termed the "Judeo-Crusading alliance" in one of the first fatwas, or nonbinding legal opinions, issued by a global militant Islamist organization. His 1996 fatwa, "Declaration of War against the Americans Occupying the Land of the Two Holy Places," made clear the need for violent self-defense. By directly addressing Muslim Americans in the United States and chastising them with verses of the Qur'an for failing to rise up against their government, Bin Laden connected abiding by the U.S. Constitution to abandoning Islam.[9] Highlighting centuries-old themes within militant Islamist thought, he attested that Islam and Muslims were under attack specifically by the United States and its pro-Zionist Western allies. The call to arms had been declared.

The title of the fatwa itself is heavily symbolic. Firstly, it references the two holiest sites in Islam, the Ka'ba in Mecca, which is the site of the annual hajj, and al-Masjid an-Nabawi, or the Prophet's Masjid, in Medina, where the Prophet Muhammed lived and taught after he fled persecution from his birthplace of Mecca. Secondly, it maintains the linkage of the United States to the Crusades by mentioning America as an occupying force, just as the Crusaders are depicted as transgressing the rights and sovereignty of Islamic lands and Muslims centuries ago.

Two years later, bin Laden's rhetoric was no longer confined to declaring grievances and labeling the United States and its allies as enemies. His 1998 fatwa, "World Islamic Front Statement Urging Jihad against Jews and Crusaders," signaled the shift in tone that many militant Islamists would adopt from then on. The statement, which was later co-opted and repeated by five other representatives from various global militant Islamist organizations, urges the killing of "Jews and Crusaders." Such violence is framed, however, not as a desire for bloodshed but rather as a response to a religious imperative to preserve the sanctity of Muslim-majority countries and, by extension, the religion of Islam.

Another way in which militant Islamist organizations take advantage of the theme of the Crusades is by perpetuating the victim narrative, which compels militancy as self-defense. This is in part accomplished by linking the medieval history of the Crusades with the more modern history of colonialism. In 2014, for the formal announcement declaring Islamic State (Dā'ish) a caliphate, albeit one that is not endorsed by many Muslims, an English-language video called "The End of Sykes-Picot" was released.[10] A militant Islamist is shown crossing out what he derides as the "so-called border" between Iraq and Syria. The reference to Sykes-Picot in the announcement of Islamic State (Dā'ish) as a self-declared caliphate is significant because the borders imposed on the Middle East by the 1916 Sykes-Picot Agreement are regarded as a symbol of colonialism, foreign imperialism, Western meddling, and the complicity of Muslim-majority nations.

Named after the two diplomats, Briton Mark Sykes and Frenchman Francois Georges-Picot, who met and signed the document (with the agreement of Russia), the Sykes-Picot Agreement divided the land that had been under Ottoman rule since the early sixteenth century into new countries without regard to actual sectarian, tribal, or ethnic distinctions on the ground. Furthermore, by placing Iraq, Transjordan, and Palestine under British influence and Syria and Lebanon under French influence, the agreement both failed to account for the future growth of Arab nationalism and negated the main promise that Britain had made to the Arabs in the 1910s, that if they rebelled against the Ottomans, the fall of that empire would bring them independence.[11] These imposed divisions continue today: the 2011 Arab popular uprisings—which devolved into civil war in many nations—were arguably an attempt to change the consequences of the state order that began with the Sykes-Picot Agreement in 1916. Though a plethora of religions were represented among the affected populations, the betrayal of Sunni Muslim Arab trust by the main European powers at the time is now brandished as a propaganda tool to recruit terrorists against what are considered to be the current Crusaders, who are viewed as seeking to continue to extirpate Islam and Muslims.

The announcement by Islamic State (Dāʿish) makes full use of the resentment against the Crusades and colonialism to gain followers and to pronounce the organization's legitimacy in continuing the battle against the Crusaders. Through depicting, quite literally, how Islamic State (Dāʿish) is fundamentally juxtaposed to the imposition of Crusader powers, the organization also attempts to certify that it is able to accomplish instituting a fully-fledged, globally recognized caliphate, one that will replace the Crusader-Zionist paradigm.[12] Certainly, Islamic State (Dāʿish) takes advantage of the lamentations of Sunni Muslims, militant and nonmilitant, who were aggrieved that the division of the Middle East by European powers after World War I resulted in the lack of an internationally recognized territory for them.[13]

In more contemporary history, militant Islamists lambast the United States for having installed regimes in Muslim-majority states that deter citizens of these nations from achieving political and cultural saliency. The United States is castigated for supporting the various secular and secularizing regimes—including Gamal ʿAbdel Nasser and Muhammad Anwar as-Sadat in Egypt, Bashar al-Asad's government in Syria, and the Saudi monarchy—that have ruled Muslim-majority nations since the World War II, leaving a legacy of denied or downplayed Islamic traditions. For this reason, militant Islamists believe that unfaithful rulers of Muslim-majority countries, must also be targeted, because they are in actuality enemies of "true" Muslims. As al-Qaʿida leader az-Zawahiri wrote in *The Bitter Harvest (al-Hisad al-Murr)*, governments that do not rule exclusively by his understanding of shariʿa are tantamount to new religions and are thus heresy.[14] Furthermore, tolerance of such apostates within the Muslim community poses a greater menace than do non-Muslim heretics because of their proximity to Islam. In this Manichean worldview, hostility toward Islam and innocent Muslims is everywhere and can be resolved only through violence directed at its source, the Crusader-Zionist alliance.

The rhetoric of many presidents of the United States has only reinforced militant Islamists' perception of the United States as a pro-Zionist, Crusaderist government.[15] For instance, after 9/11, then president George W. Bush declared his intention to "rid the world of evil-doers," cautioning that "this crusade, this war on terrorism, is going to take a while."[16] By recalling the Christian military expeditions to capture the Holy Land from Muslims, this language only strengthened the Islamist quest for a caliphate and justified the use of violence in pursuing that goal. As the introduction discussed at length, President Trump and his administration, with their talk of Islam as a "cancer" and of all Muslims as potentially suspect, have offered particularly potent examples of this rhetoric. In addition to erroneously conflating all Muslims with militant Islamists, President Trump has repeatedly reiterated the clash of civilizations thesis, setting up an opposition between radical Islamic terrorists—whom he understands to be all Muslims, including those Muslims who are American citizens—and the misnomer of "the West," by which he seems to mean White America.

These oppositions, of course, play directly into the hands of militant Islamist propaganda. Ultimately, the historical resonance of the Crusades is exploited by militant Islamists to starkly separate the world between Muslims and non-Muslims. At present, militant Islamists envision themselves as engaged in an unprecedented battle for the survival of the *umma* that is pitting the forces of the Crusaders against the army of true devotees of Islam.[17] War must be waged at all costs to protect the institutions and people practicing Islam.

ANTISEMITISM AND THE CRUSADER-ZIONIST ALLIANCE

Antisemitism features in what many militant Islamists refer to as the Crusader-Zionist alliance. As we have seen, antisemitism is also a prominent theme within the political far right. Interestingly, while American White nationalism imagines a global Zionist conspiracy that seeks to overtake (or has already overtaken) the U.S. government, militant Islamists assert that Jewish people are in league with the United States in the Crusaderist mission to eliminate Islam and truly devout Muslims. For both sets of terrorists, the divide between themselves and what they regard as the subspecies of the Jewish people can never be bridged—not only because of how they choose to interpret their respective sacred texts but also because antisemitism serves as a recruitment tool that will help them achieve their political aims of instituting a governance structure, whether it be a White ethnostate or caliphate.

Much as Christian Identity theology characterizes Jewish people as the offspring of an immoral union between Satan and Eve, militant Islamist theology asserts that Jewish people are degenerate beings. In an attitude recalling the two-seed theory espoused by Christian Identity adherents and Creators, many militant Islamists perceive Jewish people as subhuman. While the Qur'an, which Muslims believe to be the direct word of God, addresses Muslims and Christians alongside Jewish people, and arguably others who have received scripture as well, as People of the Book, antisemitism has been exploited as a political tool within centuries of Islamist thought. It has been particularly pronounced since the nineteenth century, when the major powers of Europe, including Britain and France, began their encroachment on the Middle East. Antisemitism became an expedient political tool for Islamists who sought to retain a vestige of political power despite the collapse of the Ottoman Empire after World War I. It also served as a convenient apparatus to protest colonialism against British and Zionist forces while supporting the Palestinian cause. The antagonism toward Britain and France for carving up the Middle East and signing the Sykes-Picot Agreement would also manifest itself in an alliance between Islamists and Nazi Germany.[18] Militant Islamists disguise their antisemitism, which is strategically leveraged for political expediency, under the pretext of theological grounding, legitimated by God in the Qur'an.[19]

In the present day, a significant source of antisemitism within militant Islamism comes from individuals who have converted from Judaism, including former al-Qaʿida media spokesperson and Muslim American convert Adam Yahiye Gadahn and Yousef al-Khattab, former leader of the militant Islamist organization Revolution Muslim, best known for issuing a threat against the creators of the animated TV sitcom *South Park* after an episode suggested that a figure wearing a bear costume was the Prophet Muhammad.[20] Al-Khattab was born Joseph Leonard Cohen. He came from an Orthodox Jewish family and entered a yeshiva, an Orthodox Jewish religious school, in 1988. He went on to marry a Jewish woman of Moroccan descent and lived in East Jerusalem, the West Bank, Morocco, and New York. He converted to Islam in 1999. Even before he founded Revolution Muslim with fellow Muslim convert Younes Abdullah Muhammad, al-Khattab's antisemitism brought him to the attention of New York authorities in 2002. In 2014, he was sentenced to U.S. federal prison after he used the Internet to incite violence against Jewish people around the world.[21]

With its mission statement of "establishing Islamic law in the U.S., destroying Israel, and taking al-Qaeda's message to the masses," Revolution Muslim had a small membership but ran an influential militant Islamist website (now defunct) that employed gory scenes, including photos of the bodies of deceased Palestinian children, to proselytize antisemitism.[22] The website was also a conduit for antisemitic messages from militant Islamist clerics, including influential American-born al-Qaʿida operative Anwar al-Aulaqi. Reiterating Sayyid Qutb's clarion call against the Crusader spirit embedded within the heart of each Westerner, al-Aulaqi wrote in an antisemitic post on the website that Jewish people "have a hidden agenda" and have infiltrated every government in the world. Messages such as these, especially posted by someone so influential, foster militant Islamists' suspicion of, enmity for, and sense of persecution by Crusaders and their allies, including Jewish people.

Mobilizing its online audience further, the Revolution Muslim website included the following posts: a video encouraging viewers to seek out the leaders of Jewish Federation chapters in the United States and "deal with" them directly at their homes, an implicit call to carry out violence; directions to specific Jewish facilities along with a link to a manual for constructing and using explosive devices; and a poem, written by al-Khattab himself, titled "A Prayer to My God," calling for the destruction of the Jewish people, featuring the plea to "make their fingers and brains stick on cafe walls from impact." In another antisemitic post, al-Khattab posted a video on Revolution Muslim's website in 2008 that ended with gunshots and included detailed information about the headquarters of the Orthodox Jewish sect Chabad-Lubavitch, which oversees Jewish community outreach centers worldwide. The video appeared only weeks after Pakistani terrorists affiliated with Lashkar-e-Taiba massacred 164 people in Mumbai, including six people at that city's Chabad center.[23]

To justify this stance, the Qur'anic verse 5:60 is often referenced, which, according to the particular interpretation of militant Islamists, describes Jewish people as "apes and pigs." Examining the commentary given for this verse alone would warrant an entire book, but suffice it to say that within the worldview of militant Islamists like al-Khattab, the exegesis on whether or not this phrase is a metaphor and to whom it actually applies is irrelevant to al-Khattab and others like him, who only understand the verse as applying to Jewish people everywhere.[24]

Despite being born Jewish, al-Khattab found in antisemitism an outlet to express his anger at the aggression faced by Muslims around the world. He wielded the imagery of the Crusades and the antisemitism inherent in the application of the term Crusader-Zionist alliance as political tools covered in religiosity to promote an epic battle between the two factions. By advocating for warfare, al-Khattab also believed himself to be a holy warrior fighting in the path laid out by God.

U.S. FOREIGN POLICY AS A WAR AGAINST ISLAM

Wade Michael Page, Frazier Glenn Miller Jr., Santino William Legan, Robert Bowers, and other White nationalists whose cases have been examined thus far all committed acts of violence in seeking redress for political grievances—whether to do with gun rights, religion, or race. Though their precise and distinct calculations may never be understood, their own testimony points to their belief that policies of the American government contribute to White genocide. Militant Islamists similarly interpret U.S. actions, though in the international rather than the domestic arena, in ways that fuel the flames of hate against the United States and those they view as its willing pro-Zionist agents.[25] The Crusaders and their Zionist allies, encompassing Muslim-majority governments and Muslim citizens living in those nations and in the United States, are viewed as conspiring to carry out a catalogue of abuses against Muslims around the world.[26] The killing of American military personnel and American civilians is retaliation for these injustices.

Organizations such as al-Qaʿida and Islamic State (Dāʿish) view the foreign policy of the United States as a form of warfare directly aimed at undermining Islam and ensuring that Muslims cease to exist. Within the logic of their worldview, because the religion of Islam as a whole is threatened by the United States' assaults, it is their religious obligation to fight back and construct a caliphate, with the ultimate goal of taking over the United States and its allies. They use this rendering of international events as fodder for propaganda aimed at inciting further conflict as well as enlisting supporters.

Examples of such foreign policy injustices include the displacement of Muslims around the world due to U.S.-led wars in Iraq and Afghanistan; armed drone strikes that kill innocent civilians in Muslim-majority countries; the failure of the United States to intervene early in the Syrian civil war, which resulted in the deaths of hundreds of thousands of Muslims who were fighting against President Bashar al-Asad's forces; and the absence of American intervention in Bosnia and Herzegovina, where the genocide of Muslim civilians took place in Srebrenica and Zepa in the 1990s, and in Myanmar, where Muslims are being ethnically cleansed by a military fueled by ethnoracial Buddhist nationalism.[27]

Moved by these and other perceived injustices by the United States, American militant Islamists see their true allegiance as being to the innocent Muslim victims of U.S.-sponsored violence. Rather than pledge allegiance to their country of citizenship, American militant Islamists like Nidal Malik Hasan, Anwar al-Aulaqi, Faisal Shahzad, and Dzhokhar Tsarnaev pledge to exact retribution against that very nation for perceived aggression against members of the *umma*. These acts of U.S. aggression and their victims, though geographically very distant, are vividly present for American militant Islamists. Born in Pakistan, Faisal Shahzad married a Muslim American from Denver and went on to major in computer science and engineering at the University of Bridgeport in Connecticut. In 2010, a year after obtaining U.S. citizenship, he attempted a car bombing in New York City's Times Square. During his trial, Shahzad called himself a "Muslim soldier," the same appellation used by Hasan. In his statement, Shahzad excoriated what he saw to be the tyranny of the U.S. government. He willingly pleaded guilty for federal terrorism-related crimes, proclaiming he would do so many times over until the United States "stops the occupation of Muslim lands and stops killing the Muslims and stops reporting the Muslims to its government."[28] When the judge pressed him about the possibility of his bomb killing children in Times Square, an area known for being constantly packed with people, Shahzad replied if the bomb had gone off and children had died, it would have been to avenge the innocent Muslims who are killed as part of collateral damage in the many wars waged by the United States in Muslim-majority countries. In his own words, the United States is "terrorizing the Muslim nations and the Muslim people," not the other way around.[29]

These same rationales were later invoked by a more lethal American militant Islamist. In 2013, three years after Shahzad's failed bomb attempt and the same year as Hasan's trial, Dzhokhar Tsarnaev was a nineteen-year-old student attending the University of Massachusetts Dartmouth and living on campus. His older brother, Tamerlan, was a married twenty-six-year-old and an aspiring boxer. Their ethnic Chechen family had settled in the United States in 2002 after fleeing the Caucasus because they were prevented from resettling in war-torn Chechnya. While Dzhokhar was a naturalized American citizen, his brother's status was still pending in 2013.

On April 15, 2013, at the finish line of the 177th Boston Marathon, the two detonated homemade explosives, killing three and wounding 264 others. Four days later, after an intense manhunt and standoff between the Tsarnaevs and police, Tamerlan Tsarnaev was shot and then tackled by three officers who attempted to handcuff him. Dzhokhar

Tsarnaev then drove a car at the group of officers and ran over his brother, which led to fatal injuries. Dzhokhar ultimately hid in a dry-docked boat in Watertown until he was captured by the police. While in hiding, he wrote messages on the inside wall and beam of the boat, including: "'The U.S. Government is killing our innocent civilians'; 'I can't stand to see such evil go unpunished'; 'We Muslims are one body, you hurt one you hurt us all'; 'Now I don't like killing innocent people it is forbidden in Islam but due to said [unintelligible] it is allowed'; 'Stop killing our innocent people and we will stop.'"[30]

The collectively aggrieved worldview shared by Hasan, al-Aulaqi, Shahzad, Tsarnaev, and many other militant Islamists is a political tool of warfare enveloped in religiosity. In a 2016 issue of *Dabiq,* the article "Why We Hate You and Why We Fight You" is a direct message to Americans and other Crusaders and Zionists clearly explaining from the militant Islamist point of view why the war against the United States must be waged. Militant Islamists are redressing not only the deaths of countless innocent Muslims around the world due to U.S.-led wars and drones but also the takeover of Islamic territory and the support of apostate regimes that have dismantled Islamic institutions. The article gives a stark rationale for the enmity between what they view as Islam and true Muslims on one side and the West on the other: "We hate you for invading our lands and fight you to repel you and drive you out. As long as there is an inch of territory left for us to reclaim, jihad will continue to be a personal obligation on every single Muslim."[31] For them, it is a holy war, and their hatred of institutions and individuals they deem to be un-Islamic is based on their specific interpretation of Islam.

This type of propaganda reinforces the view that many militant Islamists have of themselves as defensively responding to the illegitimate, occupying forces of the United States and its pro-Zionist Western allies, which they believe are seeking the military, economic, political, and cultural domination of Muslim-majority nations, including the eradication of the very existence of the religion of Islam.[32] Though the argument may be made that some of these grievances against the foreign policy of the United States are legitimate, militant Islamists abstain from working within the democratic system to advocate for more just policies and better governance. Instead, perhaps because they see themselves as desperate victims of hegemonic forces that seek to annihilate them, they view themselves as compelled to fight back, ultimately sanctifying their political quest with the mantle of religion.

THE PARABLES OF PALESTINE AND GUANTÁNAMO
IN MILITANT ISLAMIST IDEOLOGY

American White nationalists, especially those who are militant, are galvanized by the events of Ruby Ridge and Waco. Though these took place decades ago, simply citing their names readily evokes mistrust of the federal government and the need to protect and defend the White race from the forces colluding against it. Similarly, American militant Islamists are activated by two touchstones of U.S. policy that they view as seeking to expunge Islam and eliminate Muslims: the pro-Zionist Israeli occupation of Palestine and the detention facilities located on the Guantánamo Bay Naval Base in southeastern Cuba. They proclaim both to be part of America's crusade against the Islamic world and use that claim to provoke anti-American sentiment and gain recruits.

From the vantage point of militant Islamists around the world, and especially those in the United States, the issue of Palestine epitomizes the Christian Crusades and functions as a rallying cry against the United States and allied pro-Zionist Western forces. Palestine exemplifies what is perceived to be the United States' blinding bias toward Israel at the expense of the Islamic world, symbolizes America's fervent disregard of the concerns of Muslims, and also reflects the struggle between righteousness and tyranny. In particular, many American militant Islamists exploit the United States' support of Israel's settlements on Palestinian land as evidence of the United States' iniquitous war against Islam as a whole. They also take advantage of the fact that the United States has exhibited its bias toward Israel by recognizing Jerusalem, the city that is simultaneously contested and revered by all Abrahamic faiths, as Israel's capitol and moving the U.S. embassy there from Tel Aviv.[33]

Their sense of a global conspiracy is heightened by the fact that the international political arena refuses to acknowledge the Palestinian case for political independence; even in the largest international arena, the United Nations, Palestine is referred to as the Occupied Palestinian Territory. Over the years, Palestinians have presented their arguments for statehood to such international commissions as the Permanent Mandates Commission of the League of Nations in the 1920s and 1930s, the Anglo-American Committee of Enquiry of 1945–46, the United Nations Special Committee to Investigate Israeli Practices Affecting the Human Rights of the Population of the Occupied Territories from the 1970s onward, the Mitchell Commission in 2001, and the United Nations

Goldstone Commission of 2009. Though a decisive vote by the United Nations Educational, Scientific and Cultural Organisation (UNESCO) in favor of admitting Palestine as a member state in 2011 strengthened Palestine's position at the United Nations, the vote also led the United States to suspend funding for the organization. In 2012, the United Nations General Assembly passed resolution 67/19, upgrading Palestine from "observer entity" to "non-member observer state" status, with only the United States and Israel voting against the motion.

One additional point that militant Islamists use as a propaganda tool is the humanitarian crisis of Palestinians, including the millions of Palestinian refugees.[34] Indeed, nowhere are the grievances against the Crusading colonial powers crystallized more than in the generations of Palestinians who have suffered as a direct result of oppressive policies such as Sykes-Picot, Israeli-government sanctioned settlements, and what is understood to be American Zionism.

After the British ended their League of Nations mandate of direct control over Palestine in 1948, the Jewish state of Israel was born. The 1948 Arab-Israeli War caused the flight of approximately 750,000 Palestinian refugees. This conflict is referred to by Jewish Israelis as the War of Independence and by Palestinians as the *nakba* (catastrophe). The 1967 Israeli conquest of the Gaza Strip, the West Bank, and eastern Jerusalem, as well as the Syrian Golan Heights and the Egyptian Sinai Peninsula, during the Six-Day War is referred to in Arabic as the *naksa* (setback or defeat). The latter also meant that more than one million Palestinians now lived in Israel. Since 1967, Israel has proceeded with building settlements on confiscated Palestinian land, which are accompanied by roads and infrastructure built especially for the settlers, creating a segregated community privileging Israeli Jewish people at the expense of non-Jewish citizens, who are primarily Palestinians, including Muslims, Christians, Druze, adherents of other faiths, and those who do not identify as religious. These settlements have been found to be in flagrant violation of international law by the United Nations Security Council. Furthermore, because Israeli citizenship is bound together with Jewish identity, many of these so-called Arab-Israelis have had their citizenship revoked. Without Israeli citizenship, Palestinians cannot vote in national elections and are not afforded the same right to due process and the same civil rights as Israelis.

The quality of life endured by Palestinians has been characterized by Michael Lynk, a United Nations special rapporteur on the situation of human rights in the Palestinian territories, as "unsustainable, unliveable, and in many ways horrific."[35] Education, employment, and healthcare all suffer due to lack of resources, travel restrictions, Israeli military checkpoints, electricity cuts, and crumbling infrastructure. Access to clean water has become politicized, with Israel accused of exercising "water apartheid" by denying Palestinians the right to this natural resource.[36] The Office of the UN Commissioner for Human Rights describes the situation of Palestinians in Gaza as a "human calamity."[37]

Of the almost seven million Palestinian refugees around the world, about five million live in UN Relief and Work camps in in Jordan, Lebanon, the Syrian Arab Republic, the Gaza Strip, and the West Bank, including East Jerusalem.[38] Many lack basic services, such as electricity and sewage networks. As noncitizens, they are treated as a subclass, often not allowed to own property and barred from formal education. Moreover, though international law accords refugees the right to return, this has been denied by the state of Israel, a position endorsed by the United States. In 2018, President Trump cancelled hundreds of million dollars in aid to Palestinians who live in Gaza and the West Bank, including East Jerusalem, with the aim of drastically reducing the number of people who are classified as refugees and hold the right to return to a future Palestinian state or be compensated. The Palestinian diaspora, particularly in Europe, also faces numerous challenges with regard to identity and belonging.[39]

The dismissal of Palestinian suffering, and by extension, the cries of the Muslim civilian casualties of American-led wars around the world and those whom the United States has refused to support, including the Rohingya in Myanmar and the Uighurs in China, provide many militant Islamists with the precise ammunition they need: namely, the view that the United States is a malignant force in the Islamic world and is allied with pro-Zionist powers to eradicate Islam. Though antisemitism has seen a resurgence in the era of President Trump, his administration has adamantly supported the nation-state of Israel. Certainly, there is no more potent representation of American injustice and perceived American indifference to the suffering of Muslims around the world than the symbiotic relationship between the United States and Israel. For militant Islamists, Palestine is a clarion call to war in retribution for the oppression of the Crusader-Zionist alliance of the United States and its pro-Zionist Western allies, including self-serving governments of Muslim-majority governments, many of which are in the Middle East.

Militant Islamists also consider the detention center in Guantánamo Bay, commonly called Gitmo, to be a symbol of American-led oppression against Islam and true Muslims everywhere. In response to 9/11, what were once migrant detention facilities at the Guantánamo Bay Naval Station were repurposed for the several hundred prisoners of President George W. Bush's War on Terror. His administration controversially claimed that these prisoners were not entitled to certain constitutional protections because they were classified as "enemy combatants." This classification was later dropped, but the prisoners remained incarcerated at Gitmo, with U.S. Supreme Court cases affording them certain limited rights. Throughout President Obama's two terms in office, 197 detainees were repatriated to their home countries, resettled, or transferred, and many of them were released without charge.[40] He was, however, unable to keep his campaign promise of closing Gitmo, as he encountered difficulties in finding alternate places to house the prisoners. As of 2020, there are forty prisoners still detained at the facility. In addition to questions about the length of time detainees have been imprisoned without charge or trial, concerns about the COVID-19 pandemic affecting the prisoners have also been raised by international human rights organizations as well as members of the U.S. Congress.[41] The prison has become synonymous with illegal abuse of executive power, torture, and the West's war against Islam, and it is often touted in militant Islamist propaganda.[42]

Now that the majority of prisoners have been released, and with more attention being given to the lack of a U.S. military response in Syria and to the genocide of Rohingya Muslims in Myanmar, Gitmo is far less visible in militant Islamist propaganda than it once was, but it remains a salient issue. The various media outlets of both al-Qaʿida and Islamic State (Dāʿish) have used the issue of Gitmo as a symbol of the Crusaderist oppression against the *umma* spearheaded by the United States, with varying emphasis.

Al-Qaʿida leadership classifies Gitmo as another U.S. attack on innocent Muslims, equating the detention center to the occupation of Palestine and linking it to two other infamous prisons headed by the U.S. military: the Parwan Detention Facility in Afghanistan, commonly referred to as Bagram prison, and Abu Ghraib in Iraq.[43] It has used reported desecrations of the Qurʾan at Gitmo, such as soldiers urinating on the holy text, within its propaganda as further evidence of the Crusader agenda to desecrate Muslim identity and expunge the practice of Islam.[44] Ayman az-Zawahiri reflected this outrage, declaring in 2003, "Crusader America will pay dearly for any harm done to any of the Muslim prisoners in its holding."[45] A 2010 issue of *Inspire* included an in-depth interview with 'Uthman al-Ghamidi, a former Gitmo detainee, entitled "My Life in Jihad," detailing the physical and psychological abuse he suffered at the hands of American troops. Anwar al-Aulaqi also cited the detention center and the sexual assault of male prisoners there as rationale for taking action against the United States and, by extension, Crusader governments.

The propaganda released by Islamic State (Dā'ish), by contrast, does not focus explicitly on Gitmo, but Islamic State (Dā'ish) alludes to the detention center and related injustices by forcing its own prisoners to wear orange jumpsuits, the clothing Gitmo prisoners were initially forced to wear. Symbolically, Islamic State (Dā'ish) is seemingly avenging the unjust imprisonment, torture, and even deaths of the Muslim prisoners of Gitmo by having their own captives—whose torture and deaths are often filmed for distribution as propaganda—don those distinctive orange jumpsuits.[46]

For militant Islamists, organizationally and individually, the U.S. Naval base and detention center in Guantánamo represent the clash of civilizations and Crusader agenda of the United States, its allies (such as Israel), and what are considered to be apostate governments of Muslim-majority nations: to subdue true Muslims from establishing their particular rendering of global militant Islamism. Many American militant Islamists consider engaging in war against the United States, though it is their nation of citizenship, to be not only justified but also necessitated to ensure their path to political power in this world and paradise in the hereafter.

CONCLUSION

The grievances of American militant Islamists, like the grievances of many American White nationalists, stem from a worldview shaped by an interpretation of religious texts that reinforces a narrative of oppression, political disenfranchisement, and social immorality. The moral authority of victimhood appeals to each group: seeing themselves as having been wronged, they desperately seek to defend their identities against their perceived enemies. These victimhood stories are ironically crystallized by each other: White nationalists endorse Islamophobia, which energizes militant Islamists, while militant Islamists espouse anti-American doctrine, which energizes White nationalists. Each is able to appeal to supporters and broaden its membership base by instrumentalizing the other. Furthermore, each regards certain situations and events—whether in

Palestine and Guantánamo Bay or in Ruby Ridge and Waco—as tyrannical pursuits by the U.S. government and uses these to justify a shared perception that the American government—and by extension, American citizens—are their enemies. Each ideology mirrors the other in virulent antisemitism, and they share the perspective that the present state of the world is in complete dissonance with their values.

Muslims have become an increasingly prominent target at which White nationalists direct their existential angst and very real prejudice, not only in the United States but globally. For many White nationalists in the United States and across the world, Muslims have come to embody the fear of White genocide. Muslims personify and embody many of the threats perceived by White nationalists and the political far right: within the context of the United States, the majority of Muslim Americans were born abroad or are children of immigrants, representing the vast geographic range of the Islamic world, coming from Europe, Central and South Asia, the Middle East, North Africa, and Sub-Saharan Africa; they are often people of color; they visibly display their religious symbols (e.g., by wearing the hijab); and they have a different place of worship (the masjid) and conduct religious services in a different language (the recitation of the Qur'an is in Arabic regardless of the language of the congregants).[47] White nationalists fear a cultural takeover by Muslim Americans, which they seek to forestall not only by carrying out violent attacks but also by supporting myriad initiatives to prevent Muslim Americans from fully and publicly participating in American life as well as making attempts to stoke Islamophobia, including anti-shari'a rallies across the United States.[48]

Militant Islamists, paradoxically, draw strength from Western Islamophobia and anti-Muslim policies. American militant Islamists believe they are acting in the name of Islam, mainly in retaliation for American foreign and domestic policy, in an apocalyptic war against moral corruption, creating a vicious cycle that accelerates the militant Islamist threat. Militant Islamists believe that responding to these tyrannical and oppressive forces with violence is a necessary religious duty—in their view, they must defend Islam against the myriad threats ranged against it.

Many American militant Islamists see the war they are waging against the United States as a defensive struggle against illegitimate, occupying Crusaderist forces. They fully endorse the clash of civilization premise, also beloved by White nationalists, which argues that Islam and the Crusader-Zionist alliance are at war in an inevitable, apocalyptic showdown. The survival of true Muslims is dependent on doing away with secularism and what they term "Christian paganism and Western 'modernism.'"[49] They denounce both secularism, or the separation between church and state, and all religions other than their version of Islam.

Paralleling the trope of White genocide as the primary grievance of American White nationalists is the militant Islamist use of theological term *al-walā' wa-l-barā'*, or loyalty and disavowal. It similarly positions militant Islamists as needing to undertake self-defense in response to an enemy that seeks its eradication. This dichotomous worldview divides the world into supporters and enemies, with no neutral column. In the list of enemies, or those who are deserving of *al- barā'*, are the nations of *jāhiliyya*. Today, the dominant nation of *jāhiliyya* is the United States; followed by the nation of Israel, for conspiring against Muslims and taking over their land in Palestine; and then by the Muslim-majority nations that have forsaken their religious principles to side politically with America. These Muslim-majority governments are widely pilloried as U.S.-led puppet regimes. Not only have they been supported and helped into power by the Crusaders (the United States) and Zionists (Israel) but they also fail to govern by the correct version of the shari'a.[50] These regimes and the citizens who support them are considered *murtadūn,* or apostates, through the principle of *takfīr,* the anathematization of any Muslim who is regarded as having betrayed his or her Islamic beliefs. Because of this stance, no American—including Muslim Americans, who are deemed to be *murtadūn* because they continue to live in the United States—may be given sanctuary.

Islamist ideologues and organizations use all these theological concepts to advance the perception that the Crusader-Zionist alliance spearheaded by the United States is blatantly hostile to sincere Muslims. Most militant Islamists believe that the primary motive of the Crusader-Zionist alliance is to uproot Islam and Muslims around the world and to prohibit the establishment of a true Islamic caliphate; in this view, the United States and its allies desire nothing more than for Islamic institutions and values to be rendered obsolete.[51]

Much as the fear of White genocide leads to an increase in Islamophobia, apprehension about the Crusader-Zionist alliance leads militant Islamists to revile the vast majority of their fellow Americans. And just as White nationalists fear a secret militant Islamist concealed in the heart of every Muslim, militant Islamists are apprehensive about a Crusader spirit lurking in the heart of every American and of every citizen of nations perceived to be allies of the United States. The theologically inspired weltanschauung of *al-walā' wa-l-barā'* leaves militant Islamists no choice but to proceed with war against the United States and its allies until all Muslim-majority lands are free from the occupying forces of the Crusaders and a caliphate, encompassing the United States and Israel and recognized by the entire *umma,* is established. The quest to install a globally recognized caliphate has never been more indispensable.

Building on the respective grievances of these two sets of American terrorists and their shared mindset of victimhood, part 3 will directly compare how both seek to redress their political grievances through declaring racial holy war or jihad, establishing a governance structure, and triggering the Apocalypse. Utilizing a variety of religious and sacred concepts, from the Fourteen Words to dominion to *al-walā' wa-l-barā',* they justify their calls for racial holy war and jihad as the respective— and singular—means of safeguarding and asserting their identity in an inherently disordered world. Destroying the current order and establishing a White ethnostate or global caliphate becomes a religious duty, central to self-preservation from the pernicious evils of those perceived as the Other.

What They Want

PART THREE

What They Want

(RA)HOWA

(Re)Claiming the United States through (Racial) Holy War

On May 26, 2017, hours before the first day of the Islamic holy month of Ramadan was to begin at sunset, thirty-five-year-old Jeremiah Joseph Christian began to shout racial and religious epithets at two Black American teenage girls on a commuter train in Portland, Oregon. One of the girls was visibly Muslim because she was wearing the hijab, a scarf that covers the hair but shows the face, as a symbol of her religious identity. Destinee Magnum, who was sixteen years old at the time of the event, later recounted to news outlets what Christian had yelled at them: "[He] told us to go back to Saudi Arabia and he told us we shouldn't be here, to get out of his country. He was just telling us that we basically weren't anything and that we should just kill ourselves."[1] An affidavit made by Christian shows that he targeted the girls because of their presumed religious identities and skin color, as evidenced by his choice of words, including: "Go home, we need American [sic] here!"; "I don't care if you are ISIS!"; and "Fuck Saudi Arabia!" Christian also raved about "decapitating heads."[2]

Three other passengers leapt to the girls' defense and urged Christian to calm down. Instead, he became only more agitated, stabbing each of these three men in the neck with a folding knife that had been hidden in his pocket.[3] Two of them—Ricky John Best and Taliesin Myrddin Nam-kai-Meche—would ultimately die from their injuries. Christian then grabbed his belongings and a bag that belonged to one of the girls, exited the train, and threatened several people on the platform, brandishing his knife. He threw the girl's bag on the freeway before being arrested a few blocks away.

Jeremiah Joseph Christian identified himself as "White and a Nationalist for Vinland," as well as a "Viking and Patriot," referencing his belief in Wotanism. His forearms were covered in Nordic rune tattoos, further professing his adherence to a distortion of the ancient pagan religion.[4] Christian promoted his message of White nationalism through a variety of outlets. Like Wade Michael Page, he listened to the music of White power bands such as the Swedish metal group Black Circle.[5] He also took part in marches. At a political far right rally in Montavilla, a neighborhood of Portland, in April 2017, he shouted, "Fuck you niggers!," and, draped in an American Revolutionary War flag, he met police officers with a baseball bat.[6]

Online, Christian used social media to espouse views commonly found within White nationalism, including Islamophobia, antisemitism, and calls for the prohibition of gun control.[7] Christian's posts included the meme, "If we're removing statues because of the Civil War, we should be removing mosques because of 9/11"; pictures of himself delivering Nazi salutes while donning the American flag fashioned as a cape; a challenge inviting Nuremberg prosecutor Ben Ferencz to a future debate, with the declaration, "I will defend the Nazis"; and an image of a black T-shirt with a drawing of a handgun above the slogan, "The Second Amendment IS my gun permit. Issue Date: 12/15/1791."[8] He also referenced Vinland, the historical name given to a part of eastern Canada that some Odinists and most Wotanists believe was settled by Vikings in the eleventh century, as a model of a pure, White society and called for the creation of a White homeland in the Pacific Northwest called Cascadia, encompassing the city of Portland, where he lived.[9] This idea, also called the Northwest Territorial Imperative and the White American Bastion, was popularized by some of the most prominent ideologues within the White nationalist movement in the twentieth century, including Richard Girnt Butler, Robert Jay Mathews, and David Lane.[10] It continues to be promoted today by prominent survivalists, including Chuck Baldwin and James Wesley, Rawles. The distinction of course is that ideologues like Butler, Mathews, and Lane have been tied to or have directly committed acts of violence, whereas Rawles and Baldwin have not. Simply believing in Vinland and/or desiring a separate state does not indicate a predilection for perpetrating terrorism.

Like many of his fellow American White nationalists, Christian glorified Timothy McVeigh, using the same designation, "patriot," that

McVeigh used to describe himself: "May all the Gods Bless Timothy McVeigh a TRUE PATRIOT!!!"[11] Christian seemed to see in McVeigh's Christian Identity–inspired antigovernment views a reflection of his own vitriol toward people of color as well as Muslim and Jewish Americans. For Christian, what he perceived to be the war against White genocide mandated the killing of Americans of color and attacking a government understood to eliminates citizens' rights. In a 2017 court appearance, Christian made repeated outbursts to the courtroom to this effect, including, "You've got no safe place!" and "Death to the enemies of America!"[12] In subsequent years in court, he shouted claims of victimhood and self-defense.[13] Christian therefore equated his attempted murder of the two girls and actual killing of the two men with patriotism. Even so, for the reasons that will be discussed in the conclusion, Christian's attack has not been classified by law enforcement as an act of terrorism. He was charged, instead, with aggravated murder, attempted aggravated murder, and intimidation.

Building on earlier chapters detailing the organizational structures and central beliefs of White nationalists and militant Islamists, this chapter analyzes the concept of warfare, whether racial, holy, or both, within the logic of the respective worldviews of American militant White nationalists and American militant Islamists. White nationalists call this struggle a racial holy war, or race war, also known as RAHOWA, while militant Islamists contentiously use the Islamic concept of jihad. For the former, the necessity of RAHOWA is validated by the battle cry of the Fourteen Words as well as by picking and choosing among distorted readings of traditional scriptures. For the latter, the call for holy war is fulfilled by a similar approach of selectively choosing and decontextualizing Qur'anic verses and distorting concepts found throughout centuries of theological and political thought, in addition to what many Muslims around the world would admonish as misapplying lessons from the life of the Prophet Muhammad. Notably, for the majority of Christians and Muslims alike, such militant understandings of these holy texts are tantamount to apostasy.

To understand how religious texts are maneuvered to substantiate views of warfare as self-defense, this chapter will also examine how the Bible and the Qur'an are interpreted, respectively, by White nationalists who self-identify as Christian—particularly Christian Identity adherents, whose numbers have declined in recent years, and White nationalist evangelicals—and by militant Islamists. The theological justifications of racism and militancy have had a formative influence throughout

White nationalism, most directly seen by the adoption of both RAHOWA itself as a term and of the Fourteen Words as the mission statement of White nationalism. These terms, now part of the ideology's vernacular, signal the reliance on warfare as a tool to obtain political goals.

RAHOWA TO PROTECT AGAINST WHITE GENOCIDE AND TO PRESERVE THE UNITED STATES

RAHOWA is a dominant theme across White nationalism, upheld as the sole methodology by which the Fourteen Words can be implemented. In the White nationalist imagination, the "enemy"—made up of people of color, Queer Americans, and Muslim and Jewish Americans, as well as those who would take away the right to bear arms—already knows the power of violence and counts on the complacency or ignorance of White people. An immediate, unwavering, and violent response is thus necessitated to defend the White race from all of the forces that seek its annihilation.[14]

The term RAHOWA has been a central tenet in the canon of White nationalism since it was first coined by Creativity's Ben Klassen. As discussed in chapter 1, despite Klassen's aversion to traditional religions, and his own atheism, he borrowed terms from many faiths when constructing his own system of belief, Creativity. Indeed, Klassen likened RAHOWA to jihad in his writings. Defined by Klassen, RAHOWA is both a racial and religious war stemming from Creativity's main tenet, "My race is my religion." The RAHOWA Klassen envisioned would target what he called the Jewish Occupied Government and the "mud races"—although in the present-day, Muslims have increasingly also become targets, as Islamophobia has become a coalescing force within White nationalism. Within the logic of RAHOWA, violence is the necessary response to perceived cultural and racial dislocation and the primary method to combat White genocide, or the usurpation of the White race by people of color, and the subsequent moral degradation of the United States.[15]

In 2017, self-avowed White nationalist James Jackson traveled from Washington, DC, to New York City to stalk Black men and kill them. He stabbed and killed an elderly man in midtown Manhattan with a "Roman-style sword," admitting to a news outlet later that he wished he had instead killed "a young thug" or "a successful older black man with blondes, . . . people you see in Midtown. These younger guys that put white girls on the wrong path." He later called the death a "practice run" for what he hoped to be many more killings in his aspiration to eliminate Black people by participating in RAHOWA. In his manifesto, Jackson referenced RAHOWA, stating, "The racial world war starts today. . . . Negroes are obviously first on the list for extermination." His intent, as he later told law enforcement, was to "inspire white men to kill black men, to scare black men, and to provoke a race war." He also declared that murder of the innocent Black man was "a call to arms" to the governments of the United States and other nations to pursue a "global policy aimed at the complete extermination of the Negro race." Violence in the name of RAHOWA is, for militant White nationalists like Jackson, seen as the only way to achieve the aims of the Fourteen Words.

However, because of the variations within American White nationalism, across religious affiliations and in terms of engagement in violence, there are differences in how RAHOWA is interpreted by the many groups and individuals within its ecology. Though all agree that "White survival" is the priority, in accordance with the shared belief in the Fourteen Words, debate remains regarding what RAHOWA entails.[16] Some interpret it to mean simply that the White race should be the dominant race, in charge of governance; others understand it to mean that people of all other races should be annihilated; still others conceive of RAHOWA as military participation in a current civil war in which sincere patriots are facing off against illegitimate globalist powers. Ultimately, the purpose of the race war is to defend, expand, and advance the White race.[17]

Furthermore, within the teachings of Christian Identity, Creativity, and Wotanism, the ideal outcome of violence varies. For Christian Identity believers, the purpose of RAHOWA is to transform the United States into a theopolity ruled in Jesus Christ's name with all of its citizens submitting utterly to the lordship of Jesus Christ, in accordance with the true wishes of the Founding Fathers. For adherents of Creativity, RAHOWA's aim is to set up an exclusively White society. For Wotanists, RAHOWA is waged to fight for the White bloodline and homeland.[18] Within all these prominent racist theologies supportive of White nationalism, violence is tantamount to a pious deed because killing will eliminate the supposed threats to the White race, though of course not all believers will carry out acts of violence. Believers of all three religions, understand and teach RAHOWA through the lens of the Fourteen Words, which unites all these elements within White nationalism.

From the vantage point of Christian Identity, RAHOWA is a religious duty required by God to preserve the United States as the White nation bestowed to Manasseh, the son of the Prophet Joseph, and consecrated by the divinely inspired Founding Fathers.[19] War is understood as a necessary precursor to instituting God's law and bringing forth the kingdom of heaven on earth.[20] Before the promised land of a New Jerusalem, prophesied in the Bible as solely meant for White Anglo-Saxons, God's chosen people, can be established, the supremacy of the White race must be enacted. Therefore, all threats to the White race must eliminated, and these include the globalist Jewish elite, who are the result of relations between Satan and Eve; Black and Brown people, who are regarded as subhuman; and Muslims and the religion of Islam, which are viewed with rancor.[21]

Within the weltanschauung of Christian Identity adherents and other Christianist White nationalists, including some White evangelicals, the incentive to implement God's law on earth stems not only from the fear of God's wrath but also from the example of Jesus, who, they believe, advocated violence rather than peace. The Jesus they know is not a benevolent force for mercy, compassion, and love, as he is for nonmilitant Christians, but a vengeful figure that entrusts his believers with a mission to kill to establish religion in his name and abolish all others. While nonmilitant Christians disagree with this understanding and may even be shocked by it, the vision of a militant Jesus and the embracing of stories of vengeance from the Old Testament are central to how many within White nationalism understand the Bible as supporting violence against their perceived enemies.

LITERALISM AND TERROR IN THE NAME OF GOD

Pastor Warren Mike Campbell of the Church at Kaweah in California offers, in a sermon, representative militant Christian justifications for violence in the name of God:

(1) As in Genesis 6:13, the Earth is filled with violence today.

(2) Exodus 20:13 says, "Thou shalt not kill" or commit murder (Exodus 21:12). The positive of the negative command "thou shalt not kill" is the positive command "thou shalt preserve life." We train martially to preserve the life of the innocent.

(3) The Bible instructs all healthy men twenty years and above to be ready when called upon to defend the just cause (Judges 3 and Numbers 32).

(4) I train martially because I owe a debt to our Founding Fathers, who pledged their lives, their fortunes, and their sacred honor in the *holy* cause of liberty.

(5) Martial skills are perishable skills. As Hebrews 2:1 states, it is easy to let that which one has learned slip, so martial skills need to be practiced again and again.[22]

The verses Pastor Campbell cites are in the Old Testament, which is generally thought to contain more endorsements of violence than the New Testament, though both contain passages advocating violence. Most Christians, including those who do not harness religion to promote violence for political aims, believe that the New Testament does not amend or nullify the Old Testament. The Christian Identity theological argument is that if Jesus as the God of the Old Testament condoned violence against those who did not believe in him, then the Jesus of the New Testament supports the same. This view minimizes any differences between the Old and New Testaments as well as lays the groundwork for justifying violence through religion. In support of this worldview, the verses John 10:30, Malachi 3:6, and James 1:17, which declare that God does not change, are often cited to signify the unity between Jesus and God as well as the concordance of the messages of the Old and New Testaments. Indeed, Jesus insists on the continuity of his law: "Don't misunderstand why I have come. I did not come to abolish the law of Moses or the writings of the prophets. No, I came to accomplish their purpose. I tell you the truth, until heaven and earth disappear, not even the smallest detail of God's law will disappear until its purpose is achieved" (Matthew 5:17–18).

In the Christian Identity reading, "the purpose" Jesus alludes to is establishing the United States as a White ethnostate ruled by biblical law and a strict reading of the U.S. Constitution, excising all amendments except the Bill of Rights. Any and all who stand in opposition to this must be executed. Because not even the smallest point of God's law is to be overturned, as stated in Luke 16:17, Jesus commands that those who do not want him as their king should be executed in front of him (Luke 19:26–27). Such aggression is in keeping with the Christian Identity–related understanding of Jesus as seeking violence instead of peace: "Don't imagine that I came to bring peace to the earth! I came not to bring peace, but a sword" (Matthew 10:34). War, conflict, and dissension are meant to further the grander purpose of establishing God's law. Just as, in this view, the slaughter of any who do not submit to God is completely justified in the Bible, the Bible give grounds for RAHOWA against people of color, Jewish and Muslim Americans, Queer people, feminists, endorsers of political correctness, people thought to endorse cancel culture, people who have disabilities, gun control legislators, and others who are deemed enemies.[23] Sacrilege against God is punishable by death. Those who refuse to engage in combat and therefore do not show support for annihilating the enemies of Christianity are cursed

(Jeremiah 48:10). These nominal Christians are akin to those that militant Islamists declare as apostates through *takfīr*, and similarly they must be put to death for not supporting the holy war (Leviticus 24:13–17). In fact, in the Christian Identity interpretation, all Christians must participate in holy violence (Luke 22:36).

Many Christian-related White nationalists consider themselves the true Israelites favored by God in the Bible, in keeping with Christian Identity teaching and the belief within the political far right generally that the United States is the blessed tribe of Manasseh. This perception resembles the view most militant Islamists have that they alone comprise the last bastion of truly sincere Muslims. These White nationalists rely on Old Testament verses that assure the military victory of God's chosen people, favoring verses that depict the Israelites' rapid succession of victories and killing, as in the conquest of the land of Canaan under Joshua: "So Joshua conquered the whole region—the kings and people of the hill country, the Negev, the western foothills, and the mountain slopes. He completely destroyed everyone in the land, leaving no survivors, just as the Lord, the God of Israel, had commanded. Joshua slaughtered them from Kadesh-barnea to Gaza and from the region around the town of Goshen up to Gibeon. Joshua conquered all these kings and their land in a single campaign, for the Lord, the God of Israel, was fighting for his people" (Joshua 10:40–42). God also orders Moses to take vengeance on the Midianites because they have corrupted the Israelites at Peor (Numbers 25:1–18). The people of Moses are further instructed to "destroy every living thing" they encounter in the cities they are conquering, and to do so in the name of God (Deuteronomy 20:16–17). No mercy is to be shown, and all enemies are to be utterly destroyed by the command of God (Deuteronomy 7:1–2). Graphic scenes of violence are depicted, describing the carnage of war and the aftermath of brutality: "I will make my arrows drunk with blood, and my sword will devour flesh—the blood of the slaughtered and the captives, and the heads of the enemy leaders" (Deuteronomy 32:42). God Himself supports such destruction and decimation; those who wage war in his name are doing so with his approval: "When you go out to fight your enemies and you face horses and chariots and an army greater than your own, do not be afraid. The Lord your God, who brought you out of the land of Egypt, is with you!" (Deuteronomy 20:1).

Christianist White nationalists interpret these and similar passages as assurances of their eventual victory and as legitimizations of the war they are waging against the United States. They believe that just as

Joshua conquered because he was commanded to do so by God, it is their destiny to fulfill what they understand to be the will of God and physically extinguish all those they perceive be God's enemies. They believe they will ultimately be victorious: "If you fully obey the Lord your God and carefully keep all his commands that I am giving you today, the Lord your God will set you high above all the nations of the world" (Deuteronomy 28:1). Interpreting the phrase "other people" in the following verse to mean people of color and non-Christians, they solidify their Manichean worldview as well as their sense of destiny to prevail: "But I have promised you, 'You will possess their land because I will give it to you as your possession—a land flowing with milk and honey.' I am the Lord your God, who has set you apart from all other people" (Leviticus 20:24).

Seeking the succor of God in their holy quest to reclaim the United States, militant American Christian White nationalists heed passages in the Old and New Testaments that they believe approve warfare in God's name. The sanctioning of bloodshed and domestic terror against their own nation as directed by God gives them reason to agitate for civil war within the United States, because they believe White Christians are God's chosen people. It is only through engaging in RAHOWA that the kingdom of God will be established as heaven on earth.

Creativity and Wotanism similarly teach that the United States must be reclaimed as a nation for White people, by White people. In one of the three foundational texts of Creativity, *The White Man's Bible,* Ben Klassen reasons that violence is necessary to expunge the unwanted parts of society, such as mud people, who serve only to degrade it. Moreover, Klassen explicitly states that unlike the mainstream interpretation of Christianity, Creativity does not categorize killing as a sin.[24]

While Christian Identity and Creativity promote RAHOWA to either enact the kingdom of heaven on earth or to enable an earthly future in which the White race commands exclusively, Wotanism declares that restoring the United States, referred to as Vinland, to its original racial purity is a religious duty. This divine mandate stems from the Wotanist notion of blood and soil, namely that Whiteness demarcates genetic superiority ("blood") and that only White people can be the rightful inheritors of the United States ("soil").[25] Wotanists' benediction of RAHOWA attracts those who see violence as the only absolution for the woes they perceive as plaguing the United States.

A stark example of this is the Odinist belief that the soul, which circulates in the blood of one's mortal body, must exit through a gaping wound in order to attain the highest level in Valhalla, sometimes referred to as the White Kingdom.[26] It is the slain, or *einherjar,* who have the honor of being escorted to the otherworldly bliss of Valhalla by the Valkyries, envisioned as fair maidens. Violence is revered in Odinism, which traditionally teaches that the greatest honor one can achieve in life is a violent death and martyrdom, a belief that Wotanists also subscribe to, but not all Odinists, or even all Wotanists, engage in violence.

JIHAD AS *JUS AD BELLUM*

Most Muslims understand the word *jihad* as not specifically related to violence—rather, it signifies "struggle" broadly, and "spiritual struggle" more specifically.[27] But the term has also been used as a synonym for defensive or just war *(jus ad bellum)* in the canon of Islamist thought, militant and otherwise. Understood from the worldview of militant Islamists, both in the United States and around the world, jihad is a necessary, violent holy war against all those who would seek to keep the laws of God, as interpreted by them, from being implemented fully, which is why their targets include anyone they perceive as non-Muslim, including some individuals who self-identify as Muslims. Like militant White nationalists, militant Islamists employ historical and theological terms laden with symbolism to support their holy war, promoting the belief that God favors their interpretation of Islam and those they consider to be true Muslims above all while condemning Jewish people and unbelievers, including Muslim Americans and Muslim-majority governments that they label as apostates because they are seen as supporting the United States and Israel.

According to Ibn Taymiyya, the thirteenth-century theologian who continues to be revered for his astute scholarship by Muslims around the world, including militant Islamists, jihad is a necessary component of God-consciousness in worship. In his book *The Religious and Moral Doctrine of Jihad (as-Siyasat ash-Shar'iyya fi Islah ar-Ra'i wa-r-Ra'iyya),* Ibn Taymiyya argues that jihad should permeate every aspect of existence for a true adherent of Islam. His capacious definition of jihad encompasses any act requiring striving and self-control while being mindful of God, implying the utter surrender of one's life and property to God.[28]

Despite the emphasis he places on the concept of jihad in his writings, Ibn Taymiyya circumvents the fact that the Qur'an does not use the word *jihad* in the context of warfare; instead, the Qur'an uses the words *qitāl* and *ḥarb,* depending on context. His argument for doing so can be summed up thus: since the aim of jihad is to establish God's word as the most exalted (Qur'an 9:40) and the purpose of *qitāl* is to abolish discord and establish no other religion but Islam (Qur'an 8:39), jihad means to engage in lawful warfare with all those who stand in the way of securing justice and peace in the name of Islam. Even though Ibn Taymiyya tacitly acknowledges that the Qur'an does not equate jihad with killing or warfare for the purpose of establishing justice or removing oppression, he promotes an understanding of jihad that equates it with the concepts of *qitāl* and *ḥarb*, alongside other meanings, as the underlying basis of worship and daily life, infusing every aspect of what a Muslim should say, do, and believe.

For Ibn Taymiyya, jihad is the most honorable way to conclude one's life. Every living creature must die, because only God is eternal. The outcome of jihad, in the context of warfare, is one of two "blissful outcomes: either victory and triumph or martyrdom and Paradise."[29] Like the Odinist point of view, which upholds dying in battle as the most honorable death, Ibn Taymiyya's view envisions death on the battlefield as the most auspicious way for one's life to end. Whereas most people focus on the temporal nature of this life and its pleasures, Ibn Taymiyya states that martyrs are the ones who achieve true victory both in their earthly existence and in the afterlife, which is eternal, because of their sacrifice.

The influence of Ibn Taymiyya's definition of jihad, which includes warfare in God's name, is evident in the writings of prominent political figures and religious scholars in the subsequent centuries, whose work is often referenced by militant Islamists around the world. For example, in the writings of Hasan al-Banna, founder of al-Ikhwan al-Muslimum (the Muslim Brotherhood), particularly in his *Five Tracts of the Martyr Imam Hasan al-Banna* (*Majmu'at Rasa'il al-Imam ash-Shahid Hasan al-Banna*), jihad is explained as a tool by which peace is guaranteed and God's law is implemented. Jihad is not meant to be a selfish method of gaining personal power or political domination. For al-Banna, as for his fellow Egyptian Sayyid Qutb and for political figures before and after them who have used theology to advance their agendas, fighting in the name of God under the banner of Islam is the most noble of goals, and death in the name of God the highest of achievements. Waging war is not solely a defensive act but a duty to God as part of establishing Islam as the singular and true religion. Proposing that the West poses an intellectual, political, and military threat to Islam and Muslims, jihad as warfare becomes a necessary duty for all true devotees of Islam.[30]

For Abu-l-'ala Mawdudi, participating in such a defensive war is mandated for every Muslim. In his book *Towards Understanding Islam,* Mawdudi writes that warfare against a foreign power is essential for the state and vital to one's faith, as important as the Five Pillars of Islam, the primary actions a Muslim must undertake during his or her life-time.[31] The grave transgression of attacking and fragmenting Muslim-majority states justifies defensive war in response, via the concepts of *ḥākimiyyat Allah,* the belief that nothing is outside the realm of God's sovereignty, and *al-walā' wa-l-barā',* loyalty toward Muslims and disa-vowal of non-Muslims. Given the Qur'anic role of the state to protect and uphold the tenets of Islam as defined by the shari'a, the state must engage in war when it is threatened.

Qutb, who was a prominent member of the Muslim Brotherhood and is revered as a martyr for his death by hanging as a political pris-oner in Egypt, imparted on contemporary militant Islamism an essen-tialist view of the world in which only God has the right to make laws, thereby rejecting the U.S. model of democracy as both a false political notion and a false religion. Qutb's vision of Islamic rule meant that human beings should always remember their subservience to God, thus rendering worldly laws unnecessary and heretic. Furthermore, in his *The Islamic Concept and Its Characteristics (al-Khasa'is at-Tasawwur al-Islami wa-l-Muqawwimatuh),* Qutb argues that only God should be the recipient of human devotion, and thus only God should have the power to establish rules, regulations, laws, and doctrines.[32] In fact, the ultimate purpose of Islam is to free all of mankind from the shackles of servitude to any creature except their Creator, who is God alone.[33] Qutb writes in his famous *Milestones* that the ultimate objective of war in the name of Islam is not to defend Islam but to establish an Islamic home-land where this divine authority may be implemented.[34] Indeed, jihad, as *jus ad bellum,* is the only way to establish Islam as the primary gov-erning force in the world, thus placing God's law above man-made regulations.[35] According to Qutb, all nations must reject man-made leg-islation and institute Islamic rule, governed by an uncompromising interpretation of the shari'a, to establish justice and restore social har-mony. To this end, Qutb directly states that jihad must be physical in nature, and he vociferously criticizes Muslims and others who have defined jihad solely as self-defense or solely in peaceful terms. The phys-ical jihad must begin locally, then move to the national and interna-tional fronts.[36]

MAKING AMERICA GREAT (AGAIN)

Militant Islamists, following and invoking these theological guides, continue to endorse Qutb's formulation of jihad, which acknowledges Ibn Taymiyya's conceptualization of the term and creatively reappropriates Mawdudi's concepts of jihad, *jāhiliyya*, and *ḥākimiyyat Allah* to envision jihad as an offensive endeavor for the sake of spreading Islam. Furthermore, because Qutb did not define who or what is to be understood as an enemy combatant, present-day militant Islamists view as targets all institutions of *jāhiliyya*, including the United States, Israel, and allied Muslim-majority governments, that threaten the practice, establishment, and institutionalization of their particular renderings of Islam and Islamism.

Most militant Islamists believe that the United States and its allies—armed forces and civilians alike—are already waging war against Muslim people and Islam itself, so jihad as *jus ad bellum* is necessitated, because it is a religious duty not only to fight in defense of the faith but also to establish institutions that propagate the militant Islamist interpretation of Islam.

Mirroring this desire to unify church and state, religious White nationalists seek to impose biblical law in the United States. Whereas militant Islamists see themselves as enjoined to punish the United States for its ostensible opposition to Islam, religious White nationalists believe they must redeem the nation from social ills and restore its genuine, divinely intended nature as a land for White people only. The Fourteen Words emphasizes this mission, while scriptures validate this worldview. For the White race to survive and thrive, as intended by God, the United States must be reclaimed. In its present form, as the land of immigrants, political correctness, and everyone deemed non-White, it is a threat to the racial, cultural, and inherent biological supremacy of White people, as well as to God's will. Whereas militant Islamists perceive the United States as perpetually in opposition to their interpretation of Islamic values, religious White nationalists, particularly those affiliated with White nationalist understandings of Christianity, attribute the discrepancy between the current state of the union and how they aspire it to be to the absence of a particular version of Christian law.

On this topic, the revered American of Yemeni descent Anwar al-Aulaqi expounded at length on the incongruity between the Islamic and American ways of life. He depicts the *umma* as in an inexorable conflict with the United States. The only theologically sound course is to strike back.[37] In many of his online sermons, al-Aulaqi goes even further, reiterating Qutb's stance that war to proselytize—rather than simply to defend—is justified because Islam and *jāhiliyya,* exemplified by the United States, will forever be at odds with one another.[38] Jihad as defensive holy war, the ultimate battle of good versus evil, is interpreted by al-Aulaqi—and understood by his eager listeners and followers—to have an expansive, imperative, and global reach. Ultimately, the goal of jihad, like RAHOWA for many White nationalists, is to eliminate any opposition to the rule of the Other.[39]

The social delinquency and political malfeasance manifested by the respective Other demands RAHOWA and jihad. Within the context of militant Islamism, the Other is the immoral United States, its Zionist allies, and governments of Muslim-majority feigning to follow Islam. In a twisted rationale, American citizens, even those who are Muslims, are considered enemies because they support the United States' crimes against Muslims around the world simply by virtue of residing in the country. There is a narrow definition of who is Muslim and who is not, analogous to the constrictive vision of Whiteness many White nationalists have. Within the White nationalist view, the Other includes Muslims and Jewish people, Queer people, people with disabilities, immigrants, feminists, and any government institution supporting these groups. Moreover, those who would take away their gun rights are also seen as the Other. Because the purpose of RAHOWA is to establish a nation that excises these groups and fully embraces the White identity, it also serves as a litmus test of patriotism. According to this calculus, true patriots desire a White ethnostate, one that in many versions is ruled by a certain interpretation of biblical law. By contrast, militant Islamists comprehend engaging in jihad not as a way of restoring the United States to an imagined White utopia of yore but as a reparation for the centuries-old—and in the minds of many, still ongoing—Crusades, manifested in the injustices perpetrated by American foreign policy in Muslim majority lands. Both construct this as a necessary, divinely mandated form of self-defense.

Certainly, in his online sermons, al-Aulaqi not only exploits the limited doctrinal knowledge of (would-be) militant Islamists by taking advantage of religious terminology but also takes advantage of the alienation felt by many Muslims, including Muslim Americans, to prompt them to carry out violent actions against their fellow citizens. For instance, he explicitly lambasts fellow Muslim Americans for still living amicably in the United States, given the social and political delinquency of the United States, and in light of what he understands to be the Qur'an's commandment of violence to combat such dereliction. He cites as evidence Muslim Americans taking part in the U.S. Armed Forces and U.S.-led wars to murder fellow Muslims in Muslim-majority nations and becoming undercover operatives for the FBI to inform on fellow Muslims. The current situation is, he warns, as ominous for Muslim Americans as it was for Muslims in Grenada just prior to the sixteenth-century Inquisition, when Islam was outlawed. American history, he cautions, will repeat itself. Just as Black people were enslaved, so will Muslim Americans be forced into concentration camps. His online speech "Message to the American People" concludes with an ominous warning: "The West will eventually turn against its Muslim citizens."[40]

What is notable about al-Aulaqi's rhetoric is how it capitalizes on the threats many White nationalists have made against Muslim Americans. Politicians in the far right as well as militant White nationalists have indeed threatened Muslim Americans with internment camps, proposing plans that call to mind the trauma suffered by Japanese Americans during World War II. Al-Aulaqi's Manichean worldview is in fact a direct inverse of the propaganda of militant White nationalists. Islam and Muslims everywhere have increasingly been portrayed by White nationalists as the primary enemy perpetrating White genocide, and the battle against them is seen as divinely sanctioned. In his last online video, a speech called "And Make It Known and Clear to Mankind," posted in Arabic in November 2010, al-Aulaqi exhorted his fellow militant Islamists to kill Americans, whom he likened to the devil. Invoking scripturally sanctioned holy warriors, as many white nationalists do in their portrayal of Islam as the satanic civilization to defeat, al-Aulaqi likens the combat of sincerely devout Muslims against the United States to the battle between Moses and Pharaoh. In language similar to that used by White nationalists, al-Aulaqi, like militant Islamists before him, describes the fight ahead as the ultimate "battle between right and injustice."[41]

Like their White nationalist counterparts, militant Islamists take scriptural verses out of context to sanction their use of violence. The verses are decontextualized both from the circumstances in which they were revealed, and thus the particular issues they were meant to address, and from their relationship to other verses, which is how they are traditionally understood.[42] This disregard for centuries-old exegetical principles enables militant Islamists to justify their holy war against the Crusaderist United States and its allies. Though all Muslims look first to the

Qur'an for divine guidance, it is how they interpret and implement its verses that distinguishes militant Islamists from all the other Muslims—just as the interpretation of biblical passages distinguishes Christian Identity adherents and some White evangelicals, particularly White nationalist evangelicals, from Christians who do not condone or carry out violence, and the interpretation of the Eddas distinguishes Wotanists from Ásatrúers.

LITERALISM AND TERROR IN THE NAME OF ALLAH

Notably, militant Islamists do more than interpret the shari'a, specifically the Qur'an and the sunna of the Prophet Muhammad, as advocating violence. They also believe that the exhortation to terrorism is an inherent feature of all three Abrahamic faiths (Judaism, Christianity, and Islam). Within orthodox Islam, anyone who identifies as Muslim believes that the Qur'an is the last of a long succession of books of guidance sent to prophets throughout time, which includes the now-corrupted versions of the Torah and the Bible. Militant Islamists debauch this recognition of previous scripture to chastise nonmilitant Christians for not applying the exhortations to violence found throughout the Old and New Testaments.[43] Arguably, they share the Christian Identity vision of a militant God.

Militants who maintain a literal and decontextualized reading of the Qur'an include Osama bin Laden and Anwar al-Aulaqi, both of whom have cited in different instances the following verse to argue that the primary reason for conflict is to establish their interpretation of God's laws on earth: "And whoever does not judge by what Allah has revealed—then it is those who are the disbelievers" (Qur'an 5:44). Like their White nationalist counterparts, they believe that warfare possesses a singular aim: to render the word of God supreme (a reference to Qur'an 9:40). Reiterating these verses, al-Aulaqi stated that the purpose of fighting is to "eliminate any opposition to the rule of Allah."[44] As chapter 6 will examine, the goal of waging war against the United States is to take over the nation and make it part of a global caliphate, instituting a specific interpretation of God's law.[45]

By way of illustration, American militant Islamists interpret the following Qur'anic verse to mean that the purpose of warfare is to overcome *fitna*, which can be translated from Arabic as "trial" or "persecution": "Fight [*q-t-l*] them until there is no more persecution [*fitna*], and worship is devoted to God. If they cease hostilities, there can be no [further] hostility, except toward aggressors" (Qur'an 2:193). From the perspective of American militant Islamists, *fitna* is manifest in the oppressive policies of the American government and its pro-Zionist allies, including un-Islamic Muslim-majority nations; their wayward citizens; and those who are regarded as apostate Muslims by virtue of their support of these regimes. Furthermore, they believe that those whom they regard as enemies are attempting to destroy Islam and convert Muslims into Christians or Jews, and they use the following Qur'anic verses to support the existence of the clash of civilizations and of the Crusader-Zionist alliance against Islam and Muslims: "They will not stop fighting you [believers] until they make you revoke your faith, if they can" (2:217); and "The Jews and the Christians will never be pleased with you unless you follow their ways" (2:120). According to the militant Islamist interpretation of these verses, non-Muslims share a common hatred of Islam that prompts them to conspire against, subvert, or attack Islam and Muslims at every opportunity. The perceived hostility of non-Muslims and Muslims-in-name-only warrants the avoidance of any fraternity that could tempt militant Islamists to sacrifice their religious principles. Moreover, according to the militant Islamist reading of the following Qur'anic verse, "true" Muslims are admonished not to take anyone other than similarly "true" Muslims as friends: "You who believe, do not take the Jews and Christians as allies. They are allies only to each other. Anyone who takes them as an ally becomes one of them—God does not guide such wrongdoers" (Qur'an 5:51). Militant Islamists also invoke Qur'an 3:118: "You who believe, do not take for your intimates such outsiders as spare no effort to ruin you and want to see you suffer: their hatred is evident from their mouths, but what their hearts conceal is far worse." They also cite the example of Abraham, who disavowed his own community because it worshipped idols and not God (Qur'an 60:4).

On this note, militant Islamists see acts of violence like beheadings and bombings as conscientiously fulfilling what they interpret to be the Qur'anic commandment to "smite the necks" of non-Muslims, which appears in two verses: "When you meet the disbelievers in battle, strike them in the neck, and once they are defeated, bind any captives firmly— later you can release them by grace or by ransom—until the toils of war have ended" (Qur'an 47:4); and "Your Lord revealed to the angels: 'I am with you: give the believers firmness; I shall put terror into the hearts of the disbelievers—strike above their necks and strike all their fingertips'" (Qur'an 8:12). Like their Christian militant White nationalist counterparts, they have a markedly literal way of reading scriptures: in places where mainstream believers understand passages to be metaphorical, both these groups insist on the concrete reading.

Finally, many militant Islamists read verses from the penultimately revealed sura of the Qur'an, at-Tawba, or "The Repentance," as conclusive endorsement of their holy mandate to conquer the United States and establish a global caliphate. They often maintain that, as one of the last chapters to be revealed, the commandments of Sura at-Tawba abrogate everything that came before them, rendering moot previous Qur'anic commandments for peace.[46] Within Sura at-Tawba is what is often referred to as the "Verse of the Sword," which militant Islamists interpret as requiring all humankind to become Muslims or find themselves entrenched in warfare: "When the [four] forbidden months are over, wherever you encounter the idolators, kill them, seize them, besiege them, wait for them at every lookout post; but if they turn [to God], maintain the prayer, and pay the prescribed alms, let them go on their way, for God is most forgiving and merciful" (Qur'an 9:5). They believe the Qur'anic commandment to wage war is then repeated: "Fight [q-t-l] them: God will punish them at your hands, He will disgrace them, He will help you to conquer them, He will heal the believers' feelings" (Qur'an 9:14). Later in the same Qur'anic chapter, another verse rebukes believers who refuse to "go forth" in God's cause, much like the nominal Christians mentioned above: "If you do not go out and fight, God will punish you severely and put others in your place, but you cannot harm Him in any way: God has power over all things" (Qur'an 9:39). Terrorists who misuse religion to pursue their political goals interpret this verse as a chastisement of those who fail to wage holy war under the banner of Islam. Many American militant Islamists therefore believe that killing those who are perceived to be the enemies of Islam is a direct order from God to sincerely devout Muslims.

They also interpret Sura at-Tawba as calling for war (again, q-t-l) against those who do not believe in God: "Fight those of the People of the Book who do not [truly] believe in God and the Last Day, who do not forbid what God and His Messenger have forbidden, who do not obey the rule of justice, until they pay the tax [jizya, a tax on non-Muslims] and agree to submit" (Qur'an 9:29). This Qur'anic verse is also seen as being supported by the following hadith of the Prophet Muhammad: "Allah's Apostle said: I have been ordered (by Allah) to fight against the people until they testify that none has the right to be worshipped but Allah and that Muhammad is Allah's Apostle, and offer the prayers perfectly and give the obligatory charity, so if they perform that, then they save their lives and property from me except for Islamic laws and then their reckoning (accounts) will be done by Allah."[47] This hadith is labeled as ṣaḥīḥ, or sound, which means that it has been accorded the highest category of authenticity as determined by scholars entrusted with verifying the sayings, actions, and preferences of the Prophet Muhammad, known as the science of hadith.[48] Bolstered by these sources of shariʿa, militant Islamists undertake warfare for the purpose of establishing a caliphate and demanding obeisance from the United States and what they regard as its pro-Zionist allies.

CONCLUSION

Regarding themselves to be the sole vanguards of the "true" versions of their respective faiths, American terrorists glorify violence as a regenerative force. In their views, RAHOWA or jihad against the United States is wholly sanctified by the primacy of upholding the Fourteen Words or a particular interpretation of the Qurʾan and sunna of the Prophet Muhammad, respectively. In particular, both militant Christian White nationalists and militant Islamists believe that their scriptures promise them victory over their enemies and a path to reclaiming or claiming power over the United States.

The response of many militant American White nationalists to the feared White genocide—to losing what they regard as their racial, cultural, and demographic superiority—is founded on their interpretations of religious texts related to Christian Identity, White evangelicalism, Creativity, or Odinism, in addition to the Fourteen Words battle cry common to them all. Defending the White race is the highest of aspirations and the most sacred of purposes. Christian White militants do so in the name of God, and their worldview assures them that God intends to establish dominion on earth for the White race; Creators call it racial holy war in defense of the White race; and Wotanists believe that defending blood and soil is the warrior's way that leads to a noble death welcomed by the Valkyries.

Militant Islamists also manipulate scripture to validate the use of violence. They believe that the only solution to what they perceive to be an inherently disordered and un-Islamic world is to wage war so that what they understand to be God's law on earth can be established. Violence in the name of God, under the label of jihad, is thus a religious duty in response to the umbrage they take at American foreign policy.

Religious militant White nationalists and militant Islamists are thus joined in their self-righteous self-regard and in their identification of the United States as a divinely ordained target. Each believes they are the sole delegates of God, who has promised them exclusive rule over the United States and indeed over the world; each is convinced that violence in the name of creating a new social order and avenging political grievances will result in their spiritual triumph. As the next two chapters discuss, believing themselves to be sanctioned by God to (re)claim the United States, both groups are eager to usher in the reign of righteousness.

CHAPTER 6

America the Beautiful

Establishing a White Ethnostate or
Constructing a Caliphate

Pastor John Weaver is a popular White nationalist speaker and a former member of the neo-secessionist Council of Conservative Citizens, the organization that Dylann Roof stated inspired his act of terrorism. In one of his sermons posted online, Weaver reinforces many of the perceptions White nationalists have of the Founding Fathers. Namely, he asserts that because the Founding Fathers clearly intended the United States to be a White ethnostate, it is his listeners' patriotic duty to ensure this vision comes to fruition. It is worth quoting him at length:

> Now, listen carefully to what our Founding Fathers said: 'To secure the Blessings of Liberty to ourselves and our Posterity.' The question must be asked, How many Mexicans? How many Orientals? How many blacks and other races were present and participating in the execution of that document? What is the answer? None. Not one. Yes, there were blacks in the country, but they were slaves. Yes, there were Mexicans and there were Indians out in the Western frontier that had not yet been conquered or purchased, but none were at the founding of this nation.[1]

Weaver reads the "ourselves and our Posterity" language of the preamble of the U.S. Constitution as signaling that the Founding Fathers envisioned the United States as a nation for White Anglo-Saxons only. As he sees it, they rejected cultural pluralism and religious diversity. Weaver's rationalization also echoes the Fourteen Words ("We must secure the existence of our people and a future for white children"). According to Weaver's interpretation, which echoes David Lane exclusive definition of "our people," the Founding Fathers were motivated by biblical ideas of kinism, a formulation that overlaps with the conception of nationhood active in Wotanism and Creativity. Kinism dictates that nations must be developed from familial lines, prioritizing race and heritage much as the concept of "blood and soil" does.[2]

The belief that the Founding Fathers wrote the Constitution to establish the United States—a nation now corrupted by pluralism, globalism, political correctness, and calls for gender and reproductive rights—as a White ethnostate is one that is maintained to varying degrees by many White nationalists, including those who adhere to more mainstream interpretations of Christianity, devotees of Christian Identity, Creativity, and Wotanism, and those who self-identify as nonreligious.

For Weaver, and for White nationalists who hold fast to certain interpretations of Christianity, not only must the United States be a White ethnostate but it also must be ruled according to an interpretation of biblical law. They believe that God inspired the Founding Fathers to write the U.S. Constitution because God chose the United States as the land where he would implement his law. Christian Identity, for example, teaches that the United States is a divine land, the Founding Fathers were true Christians, and the nation's founding documents were inspired by God.[3] Creativity and Wotanism, both of which preach the sociopolitical concept of race as concomitant with religion, have similar conceptions of the United States. Whiteness itself is an identity worthy of worship. Establishing America as a White ethnostate is arguably the equivalent of formulating it into a theopolity within the framework of their respective religions.

Militant Islamists also have the aim of transforming the United States into a theopolity. Their use of the concept of *ḥākimiyyat Allah* (a neologism meaning God's sovereignty), which demands that the laws governing any society must be in accordance with the shariʿa—or in this case, with their particular interpretation of the shariʿa—mirrors many White nationalists' interpretations of religious scriptures to call for a theopolity. The pronouncement by militant Islamists that the United States must become part of the caliphate relies on their own understanding of Qurʾanic mandates.

Moreover, paralleling the White nationalists, who maintain that the federal government of the United States is morally corrupt for perverting the laws of the respective racist religions to which many adhere, militant Islamists perceive American institutions to be morally corrupt due to their state of *jāhiliyya,* a direct result of nonadherence to the militant Islamist interpretation of the shari'a. They, like many of their White nationalist counterparts, have the goal of replacing the dominant sociopolitical and cultural systems of the United States with their own configurations of government.

Previous chapters have discussed the Manichean worldviews of both American White nationalists and American militant Islamists. They share a sense of victimhood and oppression, though their conceptions of "evil" differ. As chapters 3 and 4 discuss in detail, their grievances, while similar, are also distinctive. White nationalists emphasize the domestic policies of the U.S. government and the supposed ascendance of people of color (for them, this includes Jewish and Muslim Americans) as signs of the impending End Times, while militant Islamists focus on the unbelief of Americans, including Muslim Americans, as well as what they see as the unjust nature of U.S. foreign policy.

Accordingly, the focus of this chapter is how White nationalists and militant Islamists interpret the Fourteen Words and religious texts to legitimize their political quest to transform the United States into a White ethnostate or a caliphate through RAHOWA or jihad. This chapter will also examine the shared conviction of White nationalists and militant Islamists that they are the only ones who can right the wrongs of the world.

THE FOURTEEN WORDS AND THE UNITED STATES

Irrespective of religious identity, White nationalists view it as both their destiny and their right to establish the United States as a White ethnostate. Their de facto motto, David Lane's Fourteen Words, is the axis around which the disparate organizations and many individuals revolve in pursuit of this singular aim. The Fourteen Words provides the impetus for the core myth within the discourse of White nationalism, namely that anyone deemed non-White is a genetic and cultural threat and must be eliminated. A White ethnostate thus becomes the primary vehicle by which to achieve the goals of the Fourteen Words.

In his manifesto, David Lane writes, "Let it be understood that the term 'racial integration' is a euphemism for genocide."[4] After putting forth his argument that White people are facing genocide—evidenced by a variety of factors, including racial integration, affirmative action, and what he calls the "Zionist occupation" of governments—he maintains the imperative for a White ethnostate: "In light of these and innumerable crimes against the collective White race, as well as the self-evident policy of genocide. . . . We further demand the formation of exclusive White homelands on the North American continent and in Europe. If denied, then we will seek redress in whatever measures are necessary."[5] From the vantage point of White nationalism, a White ethnostate is the only way to safeguard the only people who deserve to exist.

The United States as the New Jerusalem

Though the First Amendment of the Constitution clearly allows freedom of religion, the twinning of the religious and the political, of church and state, has long been an element of political rhetoric, past and present, within both the larger political far right and its White nationalist subset.[6] Circulating in political far right circles as proof that it is God's will for the United States to be a White ethnostate are literal interpretations of the references to Christianity that appear in early American documents. Of course, Christian Identity adherents are not the only ones who take references to Christianity and broader religious themes in the writings of key U.S. figures as assertions of the Christian heritage of the United States. Other Christians, particularly many White evangelicals, also frequently make the same claim.[7] And both are correct in their observation that since the earliest days of the republic, Christian religious themes have been a touchstone for many American politicians, particularly in the context of the Constitution.[8] But for Christian Identity followers and many Christians on the political far right, the United States' special role in world history as a nation of White people is willed by God himself.[9] God generously bestowed his laws only to his people, the White Anglo-Saxon race "in Israel" (that is, in the United States).[10] Ultimately, the purpose of the government is to implement a wholly Christian way of life in a land known as the New Jerusalem.[11]

For all Christians, the New Jerusalem is a promised utopia that is discussed throughout the Bible, most vividly in Revelation 21.[12] It is described as a holy city that will descend from heaven to the new earth after the first heaven and earth pass away. The only inhabitants of this celestial city will be people who are saved; there will be no crimes or violence, and God will dwell there with his people forever. While most Christians understand the New Jerusalem as a state of grace that will be attained only after the end of time, Christian Identity adherents believe that the United States is destined to become the New Jerusalem.[13]

For instance, one prominent preacher espousing Christian Identity views, Pete Peters, cites the biblical prophecies in the Book of Micah as evidence of this glorious fate: "'Then I, the Lord, will rule from Jerusalem as their king forever.' As for you, Jerusalem, the citadel of God's people, your royal might and power will come back to you again. The kingship will be restored to my precious Jerusalem" (Micah 4:7–8).[14] Christian Identity writers also link the oft-touted theme of the United States as a city on a hill—first stated by Puritan leader John Winthrop in 1630, and frequently evoked by the present-day members of the political far right—to Jesus's Sermon on the Mount.[15]

As biblical evidence, the Book of Isaiah is particularly employed, with its assertions that the Messiah will govern the earth. In these interpretations, the United States is identified with the scriptural Israel. In Isaiah 9:6–7, the future government prophesied by Isaiah is described as resting on Jesus's shoulders, and peace will never end. Similar biblical verses about God's support for Israel, such as Isaiah 43:1–4, are quoted extensively throughout the works of many Christian Identity authors to encourage their White American readers to see themselves as God's chosen, precious people.

For many who seek a White ethnostate and are also influenced by Christian Identity, Dominionism, Reconstructionism, or White nationalist evangelicalism, the manifestation of such an ideal world, one fully submitted to God's law, will be an authoritarian society in which sinful humans will be subjected to harsh laws based on God's will. White Christian women will be helpmates, and their children will become the property of their parents, while those White Christians who contravene God's law by condoning Queerness, interracial relations, usury, and taxation of property will be punished.[16] Secular ordinances of the state, including the tax code and public education, will be expressly forbidden. While White Christians will live under these "biblical" laws in this religious utopia, people of color, people of any other faith, and those who profess having no faith will be excluded or killed. Having made the Bible the law of the land, the White, male elite, as the sole holders of power, will then fend off the globalist world order, which seeks to usurp the sovereignty of the United States and replace the U.S. Constitution.[17] In this battle, the forces of good (White, Christian, Anglo-Saxon, Aryan, "Israelite" Protestants) will be pitted against the armies of Satan. Christian Identity members believe that Jewish people in particular, whom they consider to be the children of Eve and Satan, and the pernicious threat of Islam must be eliminated for the United States to regain its rightful inheritance in their rendering of a Christian nation.

Though Christian Identity is far from traditional Christianity from the perspective of many strands of Christians, many Christians also regard themselves as protectors of what they believe to be the American homeland of God's chosen people, White "Israelites." Evangelicals who support White nationalism, Dominionists, Reconstructionists, and Christian Identity adherents differ in their readings of scriptures. However, they share the belief that only when "life, liberty, and property" are given back to "We the People" (the White race) will the kingdom of heaven be established on earth.[18] White Anglo-Saxons will then be the inheritors of God's kingdom on earth, the mission of the Fourteen Words will be accomplished, and paradise will be regained. Fulfilling this destiny requires complete compliance with biblical authority (which they take to include the U.S. Constitution), as well as the hastening of the apocalypse.

Notably, emphasizing the divinity of the U.S. Constitution, some White nationalists—both religious and not—do not accept *all* of the current U.S. Constitution as legitimate. Rather, they accept only the first ten amendments of the Constitution, the Bill of Rights, because they understand these as protecting states' rights from a tyrannical federal government and supporting a White ethnostate. All amendments that appear after the ratification of the Bill of Rights in 1791 alter the original meaning of the document and are considered by them to be illegal, unconstitutional, and never intended by God.[19] Christian Identity theology specifically espouses that all amendments made after the Bill of Rights are part of the "Jewish anti-Christian conspiracy" to alter the original meaning of the document and are to be expressly invalidated and disobeyed.[20]

Within White nationalism, many insist that the true and legitimate U.S. Constitution intended by the Founding Fathers should not include the following amendments: the Thirteenth Amendment, which prohibits slavery; the Fourteenth Amendment, which extends citizenship rights to all persons born or naturalized in the United States, thereby guaranteeing equal protection of the law to all citizens, including people of color; the Fifteenth Amendment, which ensures citizens the right to vote regardless of "race, color, or previous condition of servitude"; and the Nineteenth Amendment, which ensures citizens the right to vote regardless of sex. Reading the U.S. Constitution minus these amendments supports the White supremacist patriarchal worldview of many American White nationalists, reifying the position of White Anglo-Saxon men as the only "true" citizens of the republic and the "we" of the Fourteen Words. People of color living in America are not considered true citizens; they are merely Fourteenth Amendment "state citizens." In the America these White nationalists envision, one based on their interpretation of the Founding Fathers' model, Christian or not, laws are meant only to protect and benefit the White Anglo-Saxon race.

Christian Identity, the Founding Fathers, and America

In consonance with its belief in Anglo-Israelism and the polygenist origins of mankind, Christian Identity preaches that the United States was divinely ordained by God to be a White ethnostate ruled by biblical law. In fact, adherents believe that God himself inspired many of the Founding Fathers throughout the process of drafting the U.S. Constitutions and Bill of Rights, just as he had guided members of his chosen race of White Anglo-Saxons to compose other significant documents throughout history, including the Magna Carta (England, 1215), the Mayflower Compact (Massachusetts, 1620), the Declaration of Independence (American colonies, 1776), and the Articles of Confederation (United States of America, 1777).[21]

Many prominent Christian Identity ideologues have promoted this view. William Potter Gale, a U.S. Army colonel who went on to become an influential Christian Identity minister in the mid-twentieth century, posited in his booklet *Racial and National Identity* that the Founding Fathers themselves considered the United States to have biblical origins. Repeating Gale's views, Pete Peters, pastor of the LaPorte Church of Christ in Colorado and creator of an Internet and radio ministry called Scriptures for America Worldwide Ministries, extolled the divine origins of the U.S. Constitution and the Founding Fathers' Christian beliefs.[22] These ideas were echoed by Bob Hallstrom, who for many years hosted the *Herald of Truth* radio broadcast out of the Kingdom Identity Ministries in Arkansas.[23] Christian Identity leaders insistently promote what they understand to be the Christian influence of the Founding Fathers.

At the epicenter of their claim is the idealized figure of George Washington, who, before he was elected the first president of the United States in 1789, presided over the Constitutional Convention in 1787. Christian Identity adherents revere Washington as a "man of God" who first received a vision of the fate of the United States while stationed in Valley Forge, Pennsylvania, as leader of the Continental Army.[24] Instilled with a sense of destiny, Washington was clearly aware of the biblical prophecy for what would become the United States under his helm.

In Gale's hands, Washington's political and military legacy were reconfigured to fully display his affiliation with Christian Identity doctrine. According to Gale, Washington nobly declined a royal title not because he wanted a full separation from the tyranny of English monarchical rule but because he recognized that only Jesus Christ could be king. Gale claims that this cognizance was demonstrated in a number of ways. For instance, documents of the time were dated "in the year of our Lord," which means, Gale argues, that Washington, like the other Founding Fathers, fully embraced Jesus as his Lord.[25] In keeping with Christian Identity's antisemitism and overt racism, Washington, like other Founding Fathers, is esteemed by Gale for his alleged stance against racial equality and for having proclaimed America as a solely Christian nation, excising the Judaic tradition from Christianity.[26]

Furthermore, conforming to the conspiratorial elements within the Christian Identity worldview, Gale and others have theorized about the secret Christian origins of common national symbols and the numerological connections between the American colonies and biblical tribes. One emblem of such theories is the Great Seal of the United States, which appears on many federally issued documents, such as passports, as well as on the dollar bill. Called the Seal of Manasseh by Christian Identity adherents, it is upheld as proof that George Washington and the Founding Fathers were made aware by God of the glory of what would become the United States in fulfillment of the prophecy given to the sons of Joseph, Manasseh and Ephraim.

One side of the Great Seal displays an eagle with spread wings. The banner in the eagle's mouth reads *E pluribus unum* (Out of many, one). Some White nationalists, like Kenneth Goff, a Christian Identity minister, survivalist, and KKK affiliate, who also wrote extensively on the religious foundation of the Founding Fathers and the symbols of the United States, believe that *E pluribus unum* is a statement declaring the favors bestowed on Manasseh by God and a nod to the secret knowledge the Founding Fathers had about the White destiny of the United States. On the reverse side of the Great Seal, above the pyramid, are words that repeat the theme of God's blessings bestowed on Joseph's sons: *Annuit cœptis*. Christian Identity ideologue William Potter Gale translated these words as "God shall favor thy beginnings." Completing the imagery of heavenly favor on the United States is the all-seeing eye, interpreted to be that of Jesus Christ, underneath the words.[27]

Gale believed that the eagle of the Great Seal was the same one described in the Book of Revelation (8:13).[28] Other White nationalists, including some Christian Identity believers, view the eagle as symbolic of the Exodus story: after the deliverance of the Israelites, God reveals they were borne on eagle's wings (19:4). Reflecting the complexity of overlapping symbolism, beliefs, and points of view among the network of organizations and religions within American White nationalists discussed in this book, the eagle is also a symbol within White nationalist groups outside of Christian Identity, including Nazis, neo-Nazis, and Wotanists. Each utilizes variations of the original Nazi Party logo, which depicts a powerful eagle clutching a swastika, often replacing the swastika with a Celtic cross.[29]

An element of the conspiratorial mindset within the political far right broadly and White nationalism specifically, numerology also plays a prominent role in analyzing the significance of the Great Seal. Like the numbers 14, 88, and 1488, which are all symbols within transnational White nationalism to varying degrees, the number 13 is unique in its significance to White nationalism within the United States. Because the number 13 represents not only the thirteen colonies and thirteen states but also the thirteen tribes of Israel as understood by some Christian Identity adherents, it also represents the bond between Christian Identity and the divine founding of the United States.[30] Furthermore, the number 13 features heavily in the Great Seal—there are thirteen stars, a shield with thirteen red and white bars, an olive branch with thirteen leaves, a talon clutching thirteen arrows, and thirteen levels to the pyramid—all proof to Christian Identity adherents of God's plan for the nation's founding.[31]

Religious symbolism is transposed onto not only the Great Seal but also the U.S. Constitution, which is understood by many White nationalists as governing the chosen nation of Manasseh. For them, because they believe that the Founding Fathers were inspired by God, the U.S. Constitution is irrevocable, unchangeable, and as divinely inspired as the biblical scriptures.[32] In fact, they claim that the Constitution of the United States *is* a Christian document based on scripture. Though the issue of biblical inerrancy has a long and fierce history of debate among Christians, White nationalist adherents who identify as Christian believe no word of the Old and New Testaments—or of the U.S. Constitution—to be untrue.[33]

The Inerrant Bible and the Divine U.S. Constitution

For a wide array of Christians, including evangelicals, Dominionists, Reconstructionists, and Christian Identity adherents, the purpose of the

Bible is to instruct and to govern, and the separation of church and state is nonexistent.[34] The "dominion mandate," or "dominion covenant," of Genesis 1:26–28 is thus interpreted by many who identify with Christianity to be a direct commandment from God to conquer the world and establish biblical rule over every aspect and institution of human society. Humans were created in God's image, entitling them to rule over the earth and everything on it.[35] Ultimately, they believe that there is no discord between the laws of God and U.S. laws: the Bible contains God's laws for governing nations and governments, so the laws of the United States must be based on the divine and inerrant Bible.[36] For subscribers of Christian Identity, these biblical verses also call for the punishment of those who are viewed as violating what they interpret to be God's law.

Using passages like Matthew 5:19, Christian Identity adherents promulgate the view that it is only through implementing and following God's commands as the sole law that redemption and salvation will be achieved: "So if you ignore the least commandment and teach others to do the same, you will be called the least in the Kingdom of Heaven. But anyone who obeys God's laws and teaches them will be called great in the Kingdom of Heaven."[37]

In fact, they interpret the passages like Romans 13:1–7 and I Peter 2 to mean that the church should rule the state: "Everyone must submit to governing authorities. For all authority comes from God, and those in positions of authority have been placed there by God" (Romans 13:1). This biblical passage has had a complicated history within the context of American political rhetoric. Romans 13:1 has at times been used by politicians and religious leaders, including by those who favored the American Revolution, to defy the state. For them, the only legitimate rule is one that is just.[38] But the verse has also long been utilized to justify enslavement, racial segregation, and the Civil War in the United States and racial oppression around the world, including apartheid in South Africa and Nazism in Germany. In this reading, to question the law of the land is to question God. Famously, the verse has been used by some White nationalist American evangelicals to endorse the Trump administration's political authority.[39] In 2018, then attorney general Jeff Sessions cited the verse to defend the separation of children of undocumented migrants and asylum seekers from their families at the U.S-Mexico border, a policy that resulted in thousands of children being placed in shelters or foster care.[40] Sessions stated, "God ordained [laws] for the purpose of order. . . . Orderly and lawful processes are good in themselves and protect the weak and lawful."[41] This enthusiasm about submission to political authority is in opposition to these groups' typi-cal antigovernment stance. This literal reading of Romans 13:1 posi-tions them to interpret policies that align with their own racist and xenophobic worldviews as a manifestation of God's will while they con-tinue to be fiercely antigovernment when other policies, like gun con-trol, do not accord with their own political goals.

Creativity, Wotanism, and the Founding of America

Creators and Wotanists share the common White nationalist belief that the White race is genetically and culturally superior and consider Amer-ica to be a nation exclusively for White Americans. While the primary goal for followers of Christian Identity, Creativity, and Odinism, includ-ing its Wotanist interpretation, is for the United States to become a White ethnostate, they differ in their attitudes toward the Founding Fathers and their beliefs about the origins of the United States. Creativity, Odinism, and Wotanism also deviate from one another in terms of what they find more contentious—the Founders or the beginning of the nation.

Creativity departs dramatically from Christian Identity in its lack of reverence for the United States as a divinely ordained nation. Religion, according to its founder, Ben Klassen, an uninhibited atheist, was to be scorned—only Whiteness should be worshipped. For this reason, when Klassen established the religion of Creativity, he pronounced the central creed to be "Our race is our religion." Whereas the U.S. Constitution is cherished by many within White nationalism—indeed, as we have seen, the document is revered on par with the Bible—Creativity actually dis-parages it. The Founding Fathers are eviscerated for their failure to defend and support the White race. In actuality, Klassen reserved par-ticular vehemence for the Constitution: "How good is it, and what has it done, not for the Jews and niggers, but for the White Race? Whom is it helping more, the White Race, or the Jews, niggers and the multitudes of the mud race that are invading and flocking in by the millions to destroy this once great land built by the White Man?"[42]

Klassen maintained that the Founding Fathers were enslavers and hypocrites.[43] However, he did not claim they were hypocrites because these signatories of the Declaration of Independence, a document pro-claiming "All men are created equal," owned people; rather, he called them hypocrites because they inserted the "blatant lie" of equality in the declaration, influenced, he claims, by French Jewish people who were inciting their own revolution with the "propaganda" of "Liberty,

Equality, Fraternity."[44] Klassen's disgust at the Founders for allowing what he decries as the "mongrelization of the White Race" is also apparent in other writings in which he accuses later governments of favoring "black and muds and discriminating against Whites, all the while hypocritically preaching equality for all."[45] For Klassen, the failure of the Founding Fathers and successive government administrations to secure and defend the existence of the White race is commensurate with sinning.

Odinists and Wotanists, for their part, are divided on whether to lay claim to any of the Founding Fathers. Thomas Jefferson is co-opted by many as a "proto-Odinist" on the basis of phrases taken from his letters. In one, he wrote that "many Christians worship a demon"; in another, he explained that his design of the University of Virginia would be inspired by "architectural principles that honor Odin, but neither Jehovah nor Jesus." In *Odinism: Past, Present and Future,* Odinist writer Osred claims that Jefferson preferred pre-Christian Odinist laws to Anglo-Saxon laws and fought unsuccessfully to have what Osred calls a "depiction of heathen Odinist leaders who brought the Anglo-Saxons to England" appear on the seal of the United States.[46] Much to the chagrin of such Odinists, the Great Seal, with its plethora of Christian themes, became the symbol of the nation.

The argument about Jefferson aside, most Wotanists, like Creators, and in contrast with Christian Identity adherents, see nothing inherently sacred about the U.S. Constitution or the Founding Fathers. Importantly, David Lane argues against visions of the United States as God's chosen land or the Founding Fathers as divinely inspired by either God or Odin, sometimes referred to as Wotan. Instead, echoing Klassen's antisemitic rebuke of the Founders for their imagined support of French Jewish people, Lane chastises America for being entrenched in Zionism, calling it "the most vile political entity on earth." Lane also derides the Founding Fathers for being "willing accomplices in the Zionist conspiracy."[47] Lane saw the United States as overrun by globalists, which threatened the survival of White identity—so much so that he once wrote about the incompatibility of being American and being White: "You can no more be both White and American than you can stop the motion of the planets. The singular intent of America in all facets is to mix, overrun and exterminate the White race. How can you be what destroys you?"[48]

Despite David Lane's seeming misgivings about the United States, which were reflective of the time period in which he lived, most Wotanists regard the nation as their rightful racial inheritance. Akin to the

White nationalists who seek to claim divine authority for an idealized United States—while, as chapter 3 explored, condemning its current condition—Wotanists and Odinists assert that America was actually first settled by White Vikings. Many of them attribute the actual discovery of the continent to Norse explorer Leif Eriksson, who attempted to establish Norse settlements in an area called Vinland before returning to Greenland around the year 1000. Vinland is a significant symbol within Odinism specifically and within Wotanism and White nationalism more generally. That Eriksson established a pure land for the White race in North America only to have its legacy erased from history is viewed by Odinists and Wotanists as proof of Christianity's false claim to America and as part of a conspiracy to belittle the rightful Odinist inheritance of White America. As evidence, many Wotanists make an elaborate argument for the Norse etymology of the word America. It is not, they assert, derived from Amerigo Vespucci but instead reveals the Viking and Anglo-Saxon roots of the continent.[49]

Resentful of Christianity's takeover of their religious rites centuries ago, Odinists and Wotanists assert not only their proper claim to the United States as an originally Viking, White nation but also their allegiance to a global White Odinist community of Aryans. These Aryans, like Creators, believe their race is their nation and uphold David Lane's Fourteen Words, the mission statement of all White nationalism.[50]

The array of White nationalist organizations may disagree on the importance of individuals like the Founding Fathers and the role of the Bible in the nation's governance, but what they do communally advocate for is a White ethnostate. Within their collective logic, the United States must be a country for White Americans and ruled by White Americans or else it will not survive the genocide brought on by people of color and threatening religions such as Judaism and Islam.

THE INFALLIBLE QUR'AN AND THE DOMINION MANDATE

Like Christianist groups within White nationalism, militant Islamists understand their sacred text to be the ultimate authority in all matters pertaining to both church and state. For each, scriptures provide the objective, absolute authority for humanity and are considered to be the only true guide and the ultimate criterion by which all creatures must be judged and all laws made. Analogous to Christians who believe the Bible to be the inerrant word of God, as discussed above, the majority of Muslims believe that the Qur'an is the direct word of God. It is safe-guarded in *al-Lawḥ al-Maḥfūẓ*, or the Preserved Tablet, in which all things past, present, and future are written, incorruptible for all of time.

For Christians and Muslims around the world, the concept of dominion, found in both the Bible and the Qur'an, advances the concept that human beings, as God-given rulers, have primacy over all other creatures. Though the Qur'an instructs humans that they have been created to represent God on earth, it explicitly states that humans have not been made in God's likeness, because he is incomparable: "Your Lord told the angels, 'I am putting a successor on earth'" (Qur'an 2:30). The term translated in this verse as "successor," "representative," or "viceregent" is *khalīfa*, or "caliph," a concept with deep significance for Muslims everywhere, and for militant Islamists in particular, who have seized on the concept to legitimate their quest for political power. In the Qur'an, the term is used to represent the idea of a just government. In several verses, the word "caliph" denotes the responsibility of all humans, not just prophets or messengers, to establish justice: "It is He who made you successors [*khalīfa*] on the earth and raises some of you above others in rank, to test you through what he gives you" (Qur'an 6:165).[51] Militant Islamists interpret such verses as expressions of a divine mandate for global dominion.

Several other Qur'anic verses make it evident that God favors people above all other creatures, including the one in which God directly teaches Adam the names of everything, an honor not bestowed on any others in his Creation (Qur'an 2:31). This honor is further highlighted in the Qur'an's recounting of how mankind first came to existence. Angels were commanded to bow down to Adam, the first human, thus displaying the superiority of humans over all of Creation: "When We told the angels, 'Bow down before Adam,' they all bowed" (Qur'an 2:34). In Islam, the concept of dominion underlies the purpose of human existence—namely, to create a society that adheres to a certain interpretation of the shari'a in order to worship God properly by obeying his laws. According to both the Christian and the Islamic understandings of dominion, humans are the sole species endowed by God with authority over all creatures and resources. Many Christians and Muslims understand that the role of human beings on earth is to establish and enforce the will of God by placing God at the apex of the state and forming all rules, private and public, in accordance with God's law. From their perspective, secularism, or the separation of religion from public life, is therefore to be disavowed as the antithesis of this ideal form of government and as the source of all modern-day evils. They believe that the

United States must become a theocratic nation, in full accordance with their respective interpretations and applications of God's law.

Curiously, many White nationalists and militant Islamists, as well as nonmilitant Christians and Muslims, attach particular significance to the phrase "In God we trust," which not only is the official motto of the United States, adopted in 1956 and printed on paper money since 1957, but also is found in verse 7:89 of the Qur'an. As the United States' motto, this saying justifies the use of biblical scriptures to establish God's will on earth.[52] In the Qur'an, this phrase signals the authority of the shari'a, based on the Qur'an and the sunna, as God's law on earth.[53]

Militant Islamists read scriptural verses regarding dominion out of their theological contexts, sometimes mixing and matching the concepts and arguments that best support their strategic objectives, much like Christian-oriented White nationalists read the Bible.[54] Viewing temporal, man-made laws as heretical, they declare that following anything other than what they understand to be God's commands is a religious aberration.

The Caliphate and the Golden Age of Islam

Just as White nationalists call for a White ethnostate, in keeping with God's will to establish a White Anglo-Saxon Israelite nation, Islamists advocate for the creation of a global caliphate encompassing the United States. As the introduction discussed at length, simply believing in a future caliphate in no way indicates the promotion of, endorsement of, or carrying out of violence. In fact, the idea of a caliphate has a long and complex history within Muslim theology, one distorted by Islamists. During the Prophet Muhammad's lifetime, to be a Muslim was to be a citizen as well as a believer. Both state and religion were thus embodied in one figure. This seventh-century religiopolitical compact remains one that many Muslims seek to emulate. They do not dispute the significance of a caliph and a caliphate (*khalīfa* and *khilāfa* in Arabic) to the *umma*.

After the death of the Prophet Muhammed in 632 CE, the first four caliphs—his former companions, known as al-Khulafa' ur-Rashidun, the Rightly Guided Caliphs—assumed control of the emerging Islamic empire in Arabia and ruled for the subsequent three decades. The last of these caliphs was 'Ali, one of the Prophet's cousins, whose five-year caliphate was marred by civil war and ended with his assassination in 661. These Rightly Guided Caliphs were political and religious leaders, who ruled with the consent of the majority of Muslims, creating community cohesion throughout the *umma*. The caliphs' piety, implementation of justice, and promotion of equality among economic classes, tribes, and genders inaugurated what would come to be known as the Golden Age of Islam, which would arguably last until the Mongol/Tatar destruction of Baghdad in 1258 CE. This period is not only regarded with nostalgia by all Muslims but also considered a model moment in society, when rulers and citizens alike were God-conscious. Importantly, this mindfulness of God meant that the pillars of justice stood upright, based on God's command in the Qur'an to shun wrong and enjoin good. Muslims, militant and nonmilitant, look back at the utopia of the Islam's Golden Age, and particularly the unified model of religion and the state, with longing not too dissimilar from the anticipation of the prophesied New Jerusalem by Christians, militant and nonmilitant. However, deep divisions arise among Islamists, theologians, ideologues, and militants regarding the interpretation of religious sources and the system of governance by which the caliph should rule.

Pointedly, even though the concept of a caliph and a caliphate can be found in the Qur'an and the sunna of the Prophet Muhammad, the meaning of Qur'anic references to a caliph or a caliphate has been debated in theological circles for centuries. Muslims who do want a caliphate agree that it should combine temporal and religious authority, employing civil as well as ecclesiastical rules to govern, whereas those who identify as Muslim reformists advocate for secular government rather than a caliphate. Complicating matters, because the separation of church and state is nonexistent in Islam, the definition and application of the term *secular* is widely debated.[55] Additionally, Shi'i and Ahmadi Muslims, for example, view the role of the caliph differently than do Sunni Muslims. Of course, there are also a multitude of voices within Sunni Islam on this matter.

Separating themselves from the vast majority of Muslims who envision a caliphate, militant Islamists assert that the only way forward is for governments to embrace their violent, misogynistic ideology, believing it is their version that most closely resembles government during the lifetime of the Prophet Muhammad and the subsequent rule of the four Rightly Guided Caliphs. Militant Islamists also contrast with nonmilitant Muslims and Islamists in the criteria they stipulate for appointing a caliph and in the tactics they envision employing to establish a caliphate. Drawing on themes present throughout the centuries-long canon of Islamist thought, current militant Islamists seek to establish a caliphate through violence. This caliphate would abolish the Crusader-Zionist alliance by taking over the United States, overthrowing apostate leaders of Muslim-majority nations, and eliminating their apostate pro-Zionist supporters as well as all Western institutions. The caliph would then regulate all public and private matters.

The United States of Islam: Constructing a Caliphate

Muslims around the world collectively felt a catastrophic loss of socio-political and religious unity at the abolishment of the Sunni Islamic Caliphate in the 1920s, after the Ottoman Empire ceded control to European powers and crumbled in the aftermath of World War I. This historical moment of the disintegration of the globally recognized Islamic Caliphate impacted many contemporary and future Islamist intellectuals and activists, including Muhammad Rashid Rida, Abu-l-'ala Mawdudi, and Sayyid Qutb. Indeed, since the bitter aftertaste of the dissolution of the Islamic Caliphate represented by the Ottoman Empire became palpable in the subsequent sufferings of colonialism, the desire for a caliphate has become even more relevant to many Islamists, militant and nonmilitant, worldwide.

Born in Ottoman Syria in what is now Lebanon, Muhammad Rashid Rida, known as an Islamist revivalist, shared the fears of the *umma* that the loss of the Ottoman Caliphate meant that the domination of European powers would never abate. His legacy to the canon of militant Islamism is his view that the religion of Islam and a literal territory for Muslims to inhabit were mutually dependent on each other. His political worldview is a consequence of directly observing the historical downfall of the Islamic Empire and the end of the Islamic Caliphate in the twentieth century. He also attributed the decline of Islamic civilization to the abandonment of fundamental Islamic beliefs and as a result championed political Islamism over European colonialism and called for the establishment of a true caliph, who would be uniquely responsible for adapting practices of traditional Islam for application in contemporary societies.[56] Because Rida believed that a physical Islamic state was a necessity for Muslims to defend Islam against foreign domination, he also called for the political independence of Islamic lands, especially those in the Middle East and North Africa—believed to be the cradle of Islam. Today's militant Islamists are heavily influenced by Rida's support of a caliphate in his quest for the unity of the *umma,* to which his later endorsement of Wahhabism can be attributed, though Rida is not explicitly acknowledged, as Ibn Taymiyya and Qutb are, in contemporary militant Islamist literature.[57]

Alongside Rida is another influential figure whose life course was formed by encroaching powers, the Islamist Abu-l-'ala Mawdudi. Mawdudi lived as part of the Muslim minority in Hyderabad, India, during the British Raj and later moved to Pakistan after that nation was founded in 1947. Mawdudi's writings show how his experiences as a religious minority under British colonial rule shaped his stance that a person could not be obedient to two different systems of government simultaneously. "It is impossible," he wrote, "for a Muslim to succeed in his aim of observing the Islamic pattern of life under the authority of a non-Islamic system of government. All rules which he considers wrong, all taxes which he deems unlawful, all matters which he believes to be evil, the civilization and way of life which he regards as wicked, the education system which he views as fatal, . . . all these will be so relentlessly imposed on him, his home and his family, that it will be impossible to avoid them."[58] Much as the views of Ibn Taymiyya and Sayyid Qutb were shaped by their direct experiences with the Crusades and colonialism, respectively, the British colonial power structure shaped Mawdudi's ideology, which dictated that Muslims will be able to fully practice their religious faith only within an Islamic state. This belief prompted him to establish the political party al-Jama'at al-Islamiyya (the Islamic Organization, sometimes referred to as JI) in India in 1941.

Mawdudi not only called for a caliphate, like many political theologians, but also developed the concept of *ḥākimiyyat Allah,* a neologism meaning God's sovereignty, to describe his ideal Islamic state, which he frames as directly in opposition to *jāhiliyya.*[59] His ideal state would be a theodemocratic caliphate, rather than an outright theocracy, in which the citizenry would be restricted to "true" Muslims.[60] Building on the foundation of *al-walā' wa-l-barā',* Mawdudi bases his barometer for who falls in this category on personal and public devotion to the precepts of Islam.[61] In contrast to Christian Identity thinkers, who explicitly exclude women from being true citizens of their New Jerusalem, Islamists like Mawdudi proffer an orthodox Islamic approach, in which women have the right to be financially supported and provided with housing, to own property, and to receive an education.[62] In Mawdudi's theodemocratic caliphate, women would be citizens with voting rights and the right to set up their own associations, albeit with the condition that they observe the segregation of the sexes.[63] However, they would still to be barred from engaging in political life outside the home, such as holding political office.[64]

Within Mawdudi's worldview, systems of government other than the one ruled by God's law, *ḥākimiyyat Allah,* are to be disobeyed.[65] The role of a sincerely Islamic government is to prevent people from offering obedience to "those who are given to excess and who spread corruption in the land instead of doing what is right" (Qur'an 26:151–52). To support this view, Mawdudi cites Qur'anic verses that he understands as commandments by God to avoid obeying selfish rulers who are corrupted by greed and societies in a state of *jāhiliyya:* "When We decide to destroy a town, We command those corrupted by wealth [to reform], but they [persist in their] disobedience; Our sentence is passed, and We destroy them utterly" (Qur'an 17:16). Mawdudi believed his theodemocracy was the only route to ultimately achieving a caliphate; his conception of democracy was built on Islamic ideas of mutual consultation, reliance on consensus among the community of Muslims, and his interpretation of the legacy of the Prophet Muhammad, as well as on his study of contemporary non-Islamist European political philosophers, including Fichte, Hegel, Rousseau, Voltaire, and Montesquieu.[66]

Despite the visible legacy of his work on Islamism and the idea of a theodemocratic caliphate, Mawdudi is not often cited directly by militant Islamists. Because Qutb drew so heavily from his writings, Mawdudi's ideas have been filtered and co-opted by militant Islamists through Qutb.[67] For example, even though Qutb is credited as the source of the clash of civilization trope now used by present-day militant Islamists—their specific rendering of Islam versus the state of *jāhiliyya*—it is actually Mawdudi who conceptualized the term as a modern typological designation. The difference is that whereas Mawdudi defined *jāhiliyya* as anything counter to Islamic culture, morals, or conduct, Qutb applied *jāhiliyya* more broadly to include even Muslim-majority nations.[68] By declaring that all societies are in the state of *jāhiliyya,* Qutb offers a rationale for jihad to build a singular global society under the domain of his conceptualization of shari'a.

Certainly, even though Mawdudi influenced Qutb in many ways, including the latter's position that compliance with the shari'a is a barometer of sincerity in faith, it is Qutb whose name is primarily cited by militant Islamists to legitimate their ideology about the caliphate.[69] Qutb wrote passionately about the ways in which social and political forces fail because they are made by humans. According to Qutb, in an argument that harks back to al-Wahhab, human reliance on political institutions results in ignorance of "divine guidance"; the only legitimate laws are God's laws. Qutb was attracted to the Islamic reform movement, but he saw the problem as one not of modernizing Islam but rather of expunging Western secular ideas and recapturing the purity of early Islam, much as al-Wahhab had sought to do centuries before.[70]

Contemporary militant Islamists agree that reform is impossible and only a purge of Western influences will suffice. It is only under a specific application of the caliphate system that the true Islam will be preserved and only under the shari'a that justice will prevail. For American militant Islamists, warfare to claim the United States as part of the singular Islamic state, and to rule in God's name and under God's name alone, is thus sanctioned by God. According to this logic, militant Islamists justify the killing of whomever they deem to be a non-Muslim in their quest to establish a global caliphate.

Al-Qa'ida and Islamic State (Dā'ish): Competing for a Caliphate

Since Osama bin Laden's death in 2011, the various individuals and organizations related to militant Islamist ideology, including al-Qa'ida and Islamic State (Dā'ish), have supported the goal of a caliphate with the aim of taking over the United States, among other nations considered part of the Zionist-Crusader alliance. (As chapter 4 demonstrated, in addition to non-Muslims, the enemies of militant Islamists also encompass Muslims who are seen as betraying Islam, as well as governments that are deemed to be corrupt puppet regimes installed by the United States and its pro-Zionist Western allies in Muslim-majority countries.) In their view, there is no common ground between being an American and being a true Muslim; rather, it is the religious duty of all Muslims to oppose the pro-Zionist Crusader West and engage in war to restructure countries in crisis and, ultimately, establish the caliphate.[71]

That said, the most notable source of discord between the two groups is the issue of the caliphate. Though al-Qa'ida and Islamic State (Dā'ish) once had markedly different interpretations of the idea of a caliphate, the cofounder of al-Qa'ida, the Egyptian physician turned militant Islamist Ayman az-Zawahiri, has since the death of Bin Laden expounded on the importance of a caliphate. During Bin Laden's lifetime, al-Qa'ida was focused primarily on attacking the United States and related targets because he was concerned that prematurely declaring a caliphate would be untenable given that it would likely be impossible to control the territory seized.[72] Now, although az-Zawahiri concedes that a globally recognized caliphate is not an easy goal, he insists that it is institutionally and symbolically significant to the *umma*.

While the perspective within current al-Qaʿida leadership is shifting over whether al-Qaʿida sincerely wants a physical territory in which to establish an Islamic caliphate, with the ultimate goal of overthrowing the corrupt "apostate" regimes in the Middle East and replacing them with "true" Islamist governments, Islamic State (Dāʿish) has primarily aimed to do just that. Its late leader, Abu Bakr al-Baghdadi, self-styled as Caliph Ibrahim, envisioned himself as the charismatic caliph of the *umma* and also bestowed on himself the name al-Qurayshi, referencing the Prophet Muhammad's tribe, the Quraysh, and thereby indicating his lineage to the Prophet. The status of being related to the Prophet Muhammad confers indubitable religious legitimacy and is therefore coveted by the leadership of militant organizations like Islamic State (Dāʿish), despite most Muslims around the world regarding this ancestry as specious.

To legitimate their claim to establishing the caliphate, Islamic State (Dāʿish) uses a hadith—classified as a *ṣaḥīḥ*, or sound, from the books compiled by Imam al-Bukhari—in which the Prophet Muhammad is reported to have said, "This matter [the caliphate] will remain with the Quraysh [his familial tribe] even if only two of them were still existing."[73]

Islamic State (Dāʿish) makes further claims for the validity of this new formation of a caliphate in its propaganda magazine, *Dabiq*. In the first issue of *Dabiq*, the leadership of Islamic State (Dāʿish) is equated to that of al-Khulafaʾ ur-Rashidun. The article employs the same title, "Amirul-Muʾminin," meaning Commander of the Faithful, that is traditionally used to describe ʿUmar ibn al-Khattab, the second of the Rightly Guided Caliphs, to describe Abu Bakr al-Baghdadi, leader of Islamic State (Dāʿish).[74] Furthermore, the magazine makes the argument that any Muslim who does not pledge allegiance to Islamic State (Dāʿish) is actually not a Muslim, relying on a hadith that calls for striking back at anyone who disrupts the unity of Muslims.[75]

Seeking to legitimize the organization in the eyes of Muslims everywhere, an article in another of its online magazines, *Rumiyah*, attests that the alleged success of Islamic State (Dāʿish) is due to the piety of its leadership and followers. The article also reasons that previous attempts were unsuccessful because of their failure to walk the straight path in God's name:

We would not be exaggerating if we were to say that hundreds of move-ments, parties, and factions have arisen over the course of the past century claiming to be working for the return of the khilafah, the implementation of the Shari'ah, and the establishment of the religion on the earth. However, they all failed to achieve that, despite some of them having reached a stage of either actual consolidation or pseudo-consolidation. Among them were those who even managed to establish some of the rulings of the Shari'ah, but the aforementioned aspirations were never achieved in their entirety except by the Islamic State, and virtue has and always will belong to Allah.[76]

Despite these claims, the installation of an actual *khilāfa* has proven well-nigh impossible for several reasons, including the fact that Islamic State (Dā'ish) does not have the support of Muslims around the world. Indeed, the legitimacy of the self-declared caliphate of Islamic State (Dā'ish) is dubious at best in the context of historical Islamic thought. The Rashidun were appointed as caliphs by consensus rather than by self-proclamation.[77] This is why the phrase "Islamic State" implemented by Islamic State (Dā'ish) is a misleading neologism for many.[78] Interestingly, in a departure from the concept of an Islamic state as promoted by schol-ars like Mawdudi, the group claims that it does not need this support.[79]

Since the alleged death of Abu Bakr al-Baghdadi in 2017, Islamic State (Dā'ish) appears to be fragmented and dissolving into various fac-tions on the ground, much like the plethora of al-Qa'ida affiliates that emerged after bin Laden's death. The lack of physical territory over which to preside, coupled with a dearth of recognition by Muslims to legitimate it, has led to a caliphate that exists perhaps in name but is not a de facto government.

CONCLUSION

Many White nationalists, particularly those who self-identify with Christianity, including White evangelicalism and Christian Identity, believe they must fulfill the Founding Fathers' divinely inspired vision of a White and Christian United States. To reestablish the United States as God's New Jerusalem, the sacredness of the U.S. Constitution and, by extension, the manifest destiny of the United States as a nation of Chris-tian goodness, many White nationalists hark back to an imagined uto-pian era in which Whiteness, religion, and patriotism were synonymous. They seek to fulfill what they understand to be a divine mandate and believe that war must be waged in God's name, for God's cause can be won only by them, his rightful adherents. Their interpretation does not allow for consensus between Christians and non-Christians, only confrontation.

Militant Islamists share the same low regard for the U.S. federal government and make similar claims about the future of the United States as part of a global caliphate. They also invoke an imagined utopian era, the Golden Age of Sunni Islam, especially the time of the Prophet Muhammad and the first four caliphs after him, al-Khulafa' ur-Rashidun, to legitimize their conception of a caliphate. Distorting centuries of complex theological literature to justify the use of aggression against the United States and its citizens in the name of God, militant Islamists seek to establish a global caliphate by inciting war against the United States. Like their White nationalist counterparts, they believe that the United States is a morally corrupt nation in need of redemption, adding that it is in a conspiracy with Israel to demolish Palestine and all things related to Islam.

While they might not acknowledge such similarities, both militant White nationalists and militant Islamists strive to establish in the United States a political order ruled by their respective interpretations of the Fourteen Words or racial theologies. They also share the aim of eradicating what many White nationalists perceive as the globalist power of the Zionist Occupied Government and many militant Islamists regard as the secular rule of *jāhiliyya*. RAHOWA and jihad endorse violence not only against people of color and unbelievers but also against errant believers. The scriptural arguments militant adherents of racist theologies and militant Islamists wield to justify their right to establish a singular, global, theopolitical entity administering what they regard as God's will through his law are possible because both employ strictly literal exegeses of their respective sacred texts. As the violent attacks detailed throughout this book show, these beliefs frequently have fatal consequences.

As the next chapter will examine, these scriptural understandings also lead to attempts to trigger the apocalypse. Their eschatological readings necessitate and validate RAHOWA and jihad in the collective quest to transform the United States into a White ethnostate or a caliphate. The coming battle at the end of time—whether waged as a race war, as many White nationalists believe it will be, between the despotic American government and the nation's true White heirs, as well as between people of color and White people, or waged as a religious holy war, as militant Islamists believe it will be, between the corrupt Crusader-Zionist alliance and its apostate allies on one side and true Muslims on the other—is very much a reality in the minds of these Americans.

CHAPTER 7

Encouraging the End of Days

*The Apocalyptic Rhetoric of
Political Violence*

Based in the Midwestern United States, the Hutaree, a racist, paramilitary, survivalist group was formed around 2006. The members proclaimed themselves soldiers for Christendom. (Their name, Hutaree, is a neologism, though the members claim it means "Christian warrior.")

> We believe that one day, as a prophecy say [*sic*], there will be an Anti-Christ. All Christians must know this and prepare. . . . Jesus warned us to be ready to defend ourselves using the sword and stay alive using equipment. The only thing on earth to save the testimony and those who follow it, are the members of the testimony, til [*sic*] the return of Christ in the clouds. We, the Hutaree, are prepared to defend all those who belong to Christ and save those who aren't. We will spread the word, and fight to keep it, up to the time of the great coming. . . . The Hutaree will one day see its enemy and meet him on the battlefield if so God wills it.[1]

The singular purpose of the Hutaree was to rid America of its unlawful and despotic federal government. Members of the group plotted to kill various police officers and possibly civilians using illegal explosives and firearms. For them, local, state, and federal law enforcement personnel were eradicating Christians to establish a "New World Order" as part of the globalist conspiracy to take over the world. Viewing themselves as part of an armed struggle against the U.S. government, for which they had convinced themselves they had religious sanction, the Hutaree were shown to be clearly preparing for the End Times on their now long-defunct website.

In an online video created to inspire their fellow warriors, members of the Hutaree are shown camouflaged and painted, assault rifles in hand, running through gas attacks and wading through the mud. Two flags with crosses triumphantly ripple in the wind overhead in the final frame while the following White power lyrics blare:

We're sick and tired of trying to explain
That it's a life it's not a game.
The need to be will never wane,
We're warriors, warriors.
Rebel Inside, rebel for life,
Rebel Inside.

These lyrics, much like the White power music of Wade Michael Page, glorify violence. The Hutarees' commitment to battling the wayward U.S. government is on full display in this video. According to the pastor of Thornhill Baptist Church in Hudson, Michigan, who knew members of the Hutaree, they believed that by attacking the federal government they were taking part in an apocalyptic battle against the Antichrist.[2] They, like some others within the constellation of White nationalism, believed that the government was under the influence of the Antichrist, a scriptural signal that the battle of Armageddon at the end of the world had begun.[3] Arrested in police raids in Michigan, Ohio, and Indiana in 2010, nine Hutaree members were charged with attempting to use weapons of mass destruction; they were subsequently acquitted, and in 2012, all charges against them were dismissed. As the Hutaree demonstrates, the worldviews of White nationalists, like those of militant Islamists, are underlain by a narrative of victimhood, one starkly dividing the world between "good" and "evil," "right" and "wrong." The Fourteen Words and al-walā' wa-l-barā', examined in the previous chapters, are operationalized to legitimize conceptualizations of RAHOWA or jihad, respectively. These groups believe that their survival relies on the achievement of their political aims of establishing a White ethnostate or caliphate. To garner support, these American terrorists promote the belief they are destined to triumph as the sole winners in the battle at the End of Days. Within the worldview of many, there will be no Rapture, or being whisked away to heaven along with Jesus Christ; to be saved, they must survive the battle with the Antichrist that will take place before the final showdown of Armageddon. Violence is further imbued with a higher purpose: the pursuit of political ends.

As with each chapter of this book, the purpose of this chapter is to exercise empathy and fully enter into the weltanschauung of the subjects to understand the rationales for hate and violence to accomplish political aims. This chapter will thus focus on the apocalyptic and eschatological visions of various White nationalists and militant Islamists. It concludes with a comparison of the role of Jesus in White nationalist and militant Islamist eschatologies.

APOCALYPSE AND ESCHATOLOGY: DEFINITIONS

Because this chapter focuses on apocalyptic literature that depicts the cataclysmic events prophesied by the various theologies within White nationalism and militant Islamism, paying some attention to terminology is useful from the outset. The word *apocalypse* derives from the Greek verb *apokalupto,* meaning "to uncover, to reveal."[4] Its noun form, *apokalupsis,* appears in the Book of Revelation. According to Christian scripture, John of Patmos received several visions concerning the Last Days and the Second Coming of Christ, which are compiled in the Book of Revelation, which itself is dependent on several Jewish sources, such as the Books of Daniel, Maccabees, and Isaiah.

Complicating the understanding of apocalyptic literature are designations like *millennialism, millenarianism,* and *chilliast.* Though these are often used interchangeably with the term *apocalypticism,* the scholarship of apocalypticism is actually somewhat distinct. Whereas *millennialism, millenarianism,* and *chilliast* are rooted in Christianity and the promise of the thousand-year reign of Jesus Christ described in the Book of Revelation, *apocalypticism* is a more impartial label for events occurring across religions and cultures. In this chapter, the term *apocalypticism* reflects this neutrality: it is an orientation that affirms that one day there will be a dramatic transformation of the cosmos whereby evil will be overcome and the righteous will prevail.[5]

Another related word is *eschatology.* Deriving from the Greek *eschaton,* it means "last, at the last, finally, till the end."[6] Eschatology is thus the branch of theology concerned with final, turbulent events in history, also known as the End Times. Though eschatology can comprise a part of apocalypticism, not all eschatology is apocalyptic. Indeed, some eschatologies envision a peaceful, rather than violent and calamitous, end to the world. However, the groups discussed in this chapter—save for Creativity, which does not envision an afterlife in a different realm, such as heaven or hell—are both apocalyptic and eschatological. Each believes in violent eschatologies that will bring about the apocalypse, which they all believe will ultimately establish their respective visions of an afterlife, resulting in an eternally supreme and triumphant reign.

Finally, it should be noted that many Christians and Muslims believe in these eschatological timelines. Having this belief does not mean that an individual is militant or prone to violence, nor does this understanding of the End Times discount the perspective of those who perpetrate violence in the names of their faiths.

SCRIPTURE AND THE END OF TIMES: ACCELERATING THE APOCALYPSE

White nationalists who identify as Christian have various interpretations of how Armageddon will unfold. Some contend it will be a violent and bloody race war in which the forces of evil (people of color, Jewish people, Muslims, Christians-in-name-only, and/or Queer people) will attempt to destroy the forces of good (White, true Christians), while others view Armageddon as an economic or social collapse that will lead to a takeover by Jewish or Muslim Americans, as representatives of the Antichrist.[7] During these final conflicts, adherence to Christianity will be persecuted, due to the immorality and sin in the world. Utilizing the same scriptures as Christians who would decry it as separate from Christianity entirely, Christian Identity has one of the most detailed depictions of the End Times. Creativity lacks an eschatology per se. Wotanism, which borrows heavily from Odinism, has its own version of the end of the world, culminating in a final battle called Ragnarok. Ragnarok seeks to reconstitute the golden age of the religion's pre-Christian tribal ethos.[8]

For militant Islamists, the binary distinctions between good and evil, the inevitability of victory over those who oppose them, and the urgent need for victory are all suffused with End Times rhetoric as well. Though the Qur'an depicts the end of the world in detail, it does not describe all of the events understood to occur at that time, such as Jesus coming to earth to battle the Antichrist, known as al-Masih ad-Dajjal (the False Messiah). These are instead documented in the ahadith (plural of hadith), the sayings, actions, and preferences of the Prophet Muhammad, recorded centuries after his death in accordance with strict criteria. The most reliable and highly regarded ahadith in Sunni Islam are the compilations by two ninth-century Muslim scholars, Imam Bukhari and Imam Muslim, respectively titled *Sahih Bukhari* and *Sahih Muslim*, each consisting of hundreds of reports. From these and other interpretations of religious texts, militant Islamists have developed a worldview insisting on the destruction of the United States as a necessary part of the impending apocalypse.

Creativity and Its Lack of an Eschatology

Ben Klassen, the founder of Creativity, disregarded belief in God and any concept of an afterlife, or what he referred to "spooks in the sky." However, he also taught that Creativity's rejection of an afterlife does not preclude the virtues of a race war. According to Klassen, Creators do not need to believe in the apocalypse, nor do they need to concern themselves with the Last Judgment. In "Creative Credo Number 59: Life, Death, and Immortality," in his *White Man's Bible,* one of Creativity's foundational texts, Klassen discusses eschatology specifically and rejects it completely. The concept of an eternal afterlife is dismissed as "superstitious Jewish nonsense." He maintains that rather than fearing an afterlife and potential hell that have, Klassen points out, failed to be substantiated through scientific fact, Creators should focus on living a noble life.[9] This entails them making contributions to the "survival, expansion and advancement" of the White race, preferably by perpetrating violence to establish the vision of utopia in this world, which can, according to Klassen, only be instigated by the White race eliminating all others. Klassen's promised land is for those who are deemed to be White only; to attain it, people of color, including Jewish Americans, will first have to be "eradicated," as he describes in *Nature's Eternal Religion.* Klassen's vision of utopia was not a heaven or paradise to be rewarded to the righteous in life after death. He saw it as a mortal world in which material fantasies will be fulfilled, including "movie star" looks, fine clothes, books, good food, high IQs, and an artistic renaissance surpassing even the creativity of the civilizations he most admired, those of ancient Greece and Rome.[10] This vision of White prosperity is the closest that Creativity comes to the beatific afterlife envisioned by the other religions studied here. Creators thus have as much motivation to die in the name of their beliefs as do the others examined in this book.

Odinism, Wotanism, and the Final Battle

Depictions of Ragnarok, the final battle in which the world will be destroyed and reborn, are found both the Poetic Edda and the Prose Edda, believed in by Odinists as well as by Wotanists, who adhere to

David Lane's interpretation of the religion. These Odinist scriptures depict Ragnarok as the final battle in which gods and humans will fight together against other gods, all of whom will be destroyed, except for one couple, who will then repopulate the earth.[11] David Lane exploits this depiction as motivation for Wotanists, who seek the glory of Ragnarok through racial holy war.[12] In Lane's account, when Ragnarok occurs, those who did not fight for the mission of the Fourteen Words will face exacting retribution and an unpleasant demise. Only true warriors— those who martyr themselves for the cause of the Fourteen Words—will forever be glorified in Valhalla, living with the gods.[13] Those who are evil will be sent to Hifhel, a realm of eternal torment, and the rest will enter a place of peace.[14]

White Nationalist Evangelicals

Within the logic of many White nationalists who self-identify as Christian, the vast apocalyptic vision of war presented in the Old and New Testaments specifically mandates the race war they are currently waging in the United States. RAHOWA is a religious duty that must be carried out to reclaim the United States as a White Christian nation so that Jesus the Messiah can return and the kingdom of heaven can be established. Militancy is a prerequisite of the apocalypse, which will result in the inevitable triumph of White people intended by God.

These themes pervade the religious element of the political far right, in part due to the influence of a popular series of novels by a White evangelical minister, Tim LaHaye, who preaches dispensational premillennialism. LaHaye's *Left Behind* series, published throughout the 1990s and 2000s, influenced a wide-ranging audience. LaHaye's books, which have been adapted into films and video games, include scriptural references and apocalyptic visions of the United States and the satanic forces of the New World Order, blended with more mainstream Protestant ideas regarding events like the Rapture and the Great Tribulation.

For many of the White evangelicals who adhere to premillennial dispensational theology, like Tim LaHaye, as well as for those aligned with White nationalism, President Trump's decision to move the U.S. Israeli embassy to Jerusalem and the recognition of Jerusalem as the capital of Israel portend the End Times. The current state of Israel is believed by many modern-day evangelicals, many of whom are Christian Zionists, to have been divinely established according to the mandate detailed in the Book of Numbers 34:1–12 and the Book of Ezekiel 47:13–20. An elemental part of modern-day evangelicalism is that Jerusalem must return to Jewish people, because it is prophesied in the Bible that this will occur before Jesus's return (2 Chronicles 6:5–6).[15] The U.S. recognition of Jerusalem as the capital of Israel validates this version of Christian apocalypticism. They anticipate that, following this restoration of Jerusalem, Jewish people will be converted to Christianity en masse, Jesus will return, and sincere Christians will be raptured to heaven while warfare ravages the earth.

Christian Identity

Christian Identity eschatology is based on references scattered throughout the Old and the New Testaments, including the Book of Revelation. Through the lens of this particular worldview, believers are the central warriors, and even martyrs, in the ultimate battle to bring the kingdom of Christ to earth.[16] Christian Identity members do not believe in a Rapture in which Christians will be swept up from disaster by the returning Christ, which distinguishes them from other Christian-related groups that have a similar apocalyptic bent and view of the literal inerrancy of the Bible. Instead, they believe the events leading up to the apocalypse will include surviving the present-day period of the Great Tribulation.

The Great Tribulation, which they believe is happening at present, features great trials from the satanic forces of the "Whore of Babylon"—for Christian Identity adherents, this may refer to the Zionist Occupied Government, the United Nations, or Islam. In any case, the Great Tribulation requires true Christians to assert their faith against false prophets and the ungodly.[17]

A segment of White nationalists prepares for the challenge of the Great Tribulation by engaging in survivalist, paramilitary, and self-defense training, including practicing weaponry in remote areas on isolated and enclosed compounds. In many instances, they also gather and store large supplies of food, water, and ammunition, anticipating the final strife predicted by Jesus: "Nation will go to war against nation, and kingdom against kingdom. There will be famines and earthquakes in many parts of the world. But all of this is only the first of the birth pains, with more to come. Then you will be arrested, persecuted, and killed. You will be hated all over the world because you are my followers" (Matthew 24:7–9).[18]

Christian and separatist pastor Warren Mike Campbell of the Church at Kaweah advocates training in war camps, much like the militant Islamist camps in Central Asia, the Middle East, and North Africa. In a segment of one of his video sermons, entitled "To Teach Them War," posted on a spinoff of YouTube called GodTube, families are shown undergoing shooting practice and field exercises together at the church-sponsored war training camps.[19] The video is quite similar to one created by Islamic State (Dā'ish) called "Establishment of the Islamic State," in which the late Anwar al-Aulaqi's voice lecturing on the End of Days is dubbed over images of militant Islamists from all over the world training and preparing for battle.

The volatile mix of apocalypticism and antisemitic and Islamophobic conspiracy theories is a perfect formula for producing violent acts aimed at precipitating the end of the world as prophesied in the Bible.[20] Within the framework of Christian Identity's conspiratorial mindset, Christian Identity eschatology prophesizes that the feared New World Order will attempt to gain global dominance, eventually eliminating all nation-states, and will finally establish a totalitarian One World Government linked to a One World Church that will culminate in Satan worship and the emergence of the Antichrist.[21] Only sincere White Christians will survive the Great Tribulation of the End Times and inherit the kingdom of heaven in accordance with Christian Identity, which also teaches that they must establish a White nation ruled by a particular interpretation of biblical guidelines.

Illustrating this understanding is the doctrinal statement of the Kingdom Identity Ministries, a Christian Identity church. According to this statement, it is the ultimate destiny of the truly faithful among the White race, who are the rightful children of Adam and Eve, to live under the peaceful, just guardianship of the kingdom of God on earth, ruled by the Messiah, Jesus Christ.[22] While Christian doctrine largely agrees an ultimate battle between good and evil will occur and that it will result in the final conquest of good and the obliteration of evil, Christian Identity theology adds an additional, racist premise: White Christians, as the chosen race of God, must be physically and spiritually prepared for their role in this inevitable war at the End of Time.[23]

Militant Islamism

Similar to its fellow Abrahamic faith of Christianity, Sunni Islamic tradition contends that the End Times will be filled with trials and suffering for mankind due to rampant sin.[24] Much the same as the Christian eschatology described in the Book of Revelation (20:7–10), these afflictions are believed to include famine, drought, and other natural disasters, as well as an increasing wealth gap between the rich and the poor, and social and moral degeneration. Christian scriptures prophesy the rising of a beast, marked with the number 666, who some believe to be the Antichrist, and a second beast, who will be the false prophet (Revelation 13:1–10, 11–18).[25] Though the beast, the Antichrist, the false prophet, and the evil forces of Gog and Magog will rise up against God, they are doomed to failure. For many Christians, the "mark of the beast" is understood to be 666, the symbol of the Antichrist, whereas for Muslims, the symbol marking the Antichrist, or al-Masih ad-Dajjal, the False Messiah, will be k-f-r, an abbreviation for kafir, one who is not grateful to God, thus an unbeliever. The Qur'an also explains that the beast will emerge as a physical being, serving as warning sign for people to believe in God (Qur'an 27:82).

Ad-Dajjal will appear somewhere in ash-Sham, an area referring to Greater Syria, also known as the Levant. The significance of ash-Sham is harnessed by militant Islamist organizations, like Islamic State (Dāʿish), who use the name to demarcate a territory resonant with symbolism denoting the End Times. Discussed in many ahadith, ash-Sham is considered a significant area for preserving the faith of Islam, particularly during the period of trials. The region is one that holds great import for billions of Muslims around the world who do not engage in violence. Qur'anic depictions of the End Times are understood literally by many nonmilitant Islamists, as well as by all militant Muslims. These foundational sources of Islam, however, have been recast by militant Islamists in ways that justify their terrorism.

One particular hadith classified as ṣaḥīḥ, or sound, by the Prophet Muhammad is often cited by many militant Islamists to reframe their sense of victimhood as evidence of their ultimate triumph in the End Times. They believe that this validates their quest to trigger the End of Days through violence. The hadith reads, "Islam began as something strange and will revert to being strange as it began, so give glad tidings to the strangers."[26] Characterizing Muslims as estranged from the world, militant Islamists harness this hadith to imbue their alienation with a sense that they are on the path of the devout. If they feel estranged, then they must be on the correct course of religious action. If strangeness is a prerequisite for heavenly rewards, then strange they will be.

This hadith is classified as sound, but others that militant Islamists rely on are dubious. Militant Islamists continue to cite alleged prophetic narrations to warrant violence, despite the questionable validity of these texts. One such hadith depicts a conquering Islamic army arising from a location called Aden-Abyan, thought to be in what is now Yemen. (As discussed below, Christian eschatology similarly emphasizes the hill of Megiddo as where the final battle of Armageddon will take place.) The preoccupation with the final battle within the militant Islamist mindset is also evidenced in the name of one of al-Qaʿida's media outlets, al-Malahem Media. Taking its name from the Arabic word for battlefields, *al-malāḥim,* it specifically connotes *al-Malḥama al-Kubra,* or the Battle of Armageddon, the ultimate battle between good and evil, during which the great army led by Jesus and al-Mahdi will defeat al-Masih ad-Dajjal.

Perhaps the most crucial and potent apocalyptic symbol employed by militant Islamists is the black flag inscribed with the *shahāda,* the testimony or witnessing of faith, which states in part, "There is no deity but God," in Arabic. Various organizations around the world throughout history have adopted this flag as their standard to substantiate their claims to exclusive allegiance to what is argued to be the true legacy of the Prophet Muhammad. These include al-Qaʿida, Boko Haram in Nigeria, and Islamic State (Dāʿish) and its affiliates. The black flag sanctions and sanctifies terrorism because it is viewed as "a harbinger of the final battle at the End of Days" and thus wielded in attempts to accelerate the prophesied events resulting in the triumph of Islam.[27] Tamerlan Tsarnaev, one of the perpetrators of the 2013 Boston Marathon bombing, had a video called "The Emergence of Prophesy: The Black Flags from Khorasan" on his YouTube playlist.[28] The video depicts the wars in Iraq and Afghanistan as a sign of the End Times and summons Muslims to wage war against the United States to trigger the apocalypse.[29]

Several versions of a certain unsubstantiated hadith purportedly claim that the army of al-Mahdi will bear a black banner. Al-Mahdi is recognized by the majority of Muslims to be one of Prophet Muhammad's descendants who will fight the Antichrist alongside Jesus the Messiah. One version of the contested hadith is, "If you see the Black Banners coming from Khorasan go to them immediately, even if you must crawl over ice, because indeed amongst them is the Caliph, al-Mahdi."[30] Khorasan, an important region in the pre-Ottoman Islamic Caliphate, was spread across parts of modern-day Iran, Pakistan, Afghanistan, Turkmenistan, and Uzbekistan.

Despite the tenuous nature of this hadith, belief in the apocalypse and the Day of Judgment, when the earthly life of each person will be assessed by God and their eternal life in paradise or hell will begin, is a necessary part of why the message of militant Islamist organizations like Islamic State (Dāʿish) resonates for those who seek identity. The End Times narrative promoted by militant Islamists provides a rationale for their alienation and vindication for their victimhood. Violence is the only recourse for the grievances they view as being perpetrated against them. Following the U.S.-led invasion of Iraq in 2003 and the Arab uprisings that began in December 2010, the crises throughout Muslim-majority nations—from conflicts in the Middle East and North Africa sparked by the civil war in Syria to ongoing wars in countries such as Afghanistan and Somalia—are framed as events building up to the apocalyptic showdown between unbelievers and true Muslims.

Drawing on themes present in Islamic history and centuries-old Islamist ideology, Islamic State (Dā'ish) named one of its online English-language magazines *Dabiq*, a term that has become a metonym in militant Islamist circles for the End Times battle. Some ahadith in *Sahih Muslim* foretell that this may occur in Dabiq—the name of an actual town in northern Syria, near the border with Turkey—where many Muslims, militant and nonmilitant, believe al-Mahdi and Jesus will bring peace and justice to the world.[31] Islamic State (Dā'ish)'s claim to have begun the fulfillment of that prophecy by capturing Dabiq in August 2014 was a powerful engine of the organization's growth. The loss of the town of Dabiq to Turkish-backed Syrian opposition forces in October 2016 was detrimental to their propaganda and theological legitimacy. Soon after, Islamic State (Dā'ish) launched another online magazine, *Rumiyah*. Like that of its predecessor, *Rumiyah*'s title related to End Times prophecies, in this instance by referring to the "Roman" armies that Muslims are fated to fight during the End Times. (Much like the term Crusader, Rome is militant Islamist shorthand for the United States and what they regard as its pro-Zionist alliance.) Although Islamic State (Dā'ish) was not able to maintain control of Dabiq, militant Islamists continue their attempts to trigger the apocalypse and Final Judgment through violence so that salvation may be achieved in the final battle between good and evil.[32]

Both militant Islamists and American militant White nationalists adhering to an array of religions make use of their respective scriptures as eschatological guidebooks not only to navigate troubled times but also to endeavor to activate the End Times. All of them (save Creators) believe this will result in eternal victory and entry to either the kingdom of God, Valhalla, or paradise. The majority believe that they are chosen by God to be the last line of defense to save the sincere and faithful from forces of evil during Armageddon. Serving as the instruments of God's judgment against those who neither repented nor believed while they had the chance, they see their punishment of unbelievers as wholly justified. This battle will be not only a defensive war but also part of a necessary cleansing process that will prove their worthiness of heavenly rewards.[33]

JESUS AND THE END TIMES: UNDERSTANDING HIS ESCHATOLOGICAL ROLES

The self-identified adherents of Christianity and Islam discussed in this book utilize religion to endorse violence in order to achieve their political aims. As we have examined thus far, there are many similarities and differences in terms of their organizational structures, worldviews, and wielding of religious concepts to legitimize, and sometimes carry out, militancy. One of these areas of overlap is the function of Jesus, particularly the integral part he is prophesied to have in the End Times according to the teachings of both religions, despite the overt theological difference of Christianity's embrace of the Trinity and Islam's rejection of it. Examining the role of Jesus offers insight into their shared justifications for violence.

According to the Christian eschatological timeline believed in by many White nationalist evangelicals and Christian Identity adherents (though each group would label the other as un-Christian), it is only after White Christians have conquered their enemies—people of color and non-Christians—that the kingdom of God can be established. The final battle of Armageddon will be terminated by the Second Coming of Jesus Christ, who will destroy the enemy, thereby delivering the White Christian faithful through the gates of the New Jerusalem, the Promised Land, to live forever. Christ's glorious thousand-year reign of justice, peace, and harmony will be ushered in, establishing his kingdom on earth.

A large number understand their theology as foretelling that Jesus Christ, in the Second Coming, will use deadly force to exact revenge for sin in the political, moral, spiritual, and environmental realms. When the Second Coming commences, Christ will order his kingdom, "Just as the weeds are sorted out and burned in the fire, so it will be at the end of the world" (Matthew 13:40). He will separate the righteous on his right from the wicked on his left and send the latter into "the eternal fire" (Matthew 25:41), where they will perish (Revelation 20:14–15). Those who do not share in what these Christian White nationalists regard as the true Christian worldview will be condemned to torture by God's terrifying power.

Like the suspect hadith identifying Aden-Abyan as the location of the final battle, the apocalyptic vision of war within Christian Identity gives a specific location for the final battle of Armageddon. In this conflict, Jesus Christ and his saints will fight against the Antichrist and his armies at the hill of Megiddo in northern Israel.[34]

Many White nationalists, including those who identify as White evangelicals and Christian Identity adherents, believe this final battle is depicted in the Books of Zechariah 14, Joel, Ezekiel 38 and 39, and Revelation 16. They understand it to be Jesus who speaks in Ezekiel 38:16: "You will attack my people Israel, covering their land like a cloud. At that time in the distant future, I will bring you against my land as everyone watches, and my holiness will be displayed by what happens to you, Gog. Then all the nations will know that I am the Lord." The martial vision of a violent, vengeful Jesus battling on the "great day of God Almighty" (Revelation 16:14) is also found in other verses of the Book of Revelation: "He wore a robe dipped in blood, and his title was the Word of God. The armies of heaven . . . followed him on white horses. From his mouth came a sharp sword to strike down the nations. He will rule them with an iron rod. He will release the fierce wrath of God, the Almighty, like juice flowing from a winepress" (Revelation 19:13–15). In accordance with the Manichean worldview of many White nationalists, Jesus is not the feminist, environmentalist, advocate of people experiencing poverty, and supporter of immigrants many Christians believe him to be. Instead, Jesus is a potent force of violence, valorized for his maleficence against his enemies, and this perspective of him is largely based on these White nationalists' understanding of these apocalyptic texts.

In Islamic eschatology, Jesus, who is a prominent religious figure and a revered and human prophet in Islam, takes a slightly different role. He aids al-Mahdi, the Guided One, a direct descendant of the Prophet Muhammad who will consequently be the leader of all Muslims and will fight the Antichrist. Most Muslims believe that to help al-Mahdi against the tyrannical forces of the Antichrist, Jesus the Messiah will descend from heaven, where he is currently waiting, having been lifted by God Himself instead of having been crucified (according to Qur'anic teachings, another person was made to resemble him and crucified in his stead).[35] According to another hadith in *Sahih Muslim,* Jesus will "descend at the white minaret in the eastern side of Damascus wearing two garments lightly dyed with saffron and placing his hands on the wings of two angels."[36] Then Gog and Magog will be released from their caves: "And when the peoples of Gog and Magog are let loose and swarm swiftly from every highland, when the True Promise draws near, the disbelievers' eyes will stare in terror, and they will say, 'Woe to us! We were not aware of this at all. We were wrong'" (Qur'an 21:96–97). Jesus the Messiah will then marry and lead the world in peace and justice.

In a hadith recorded in *Sahih Bukhari,* the Prophet Muhammad states that this time is near: "By Him in Whose Hands my soul is, the son of Mary [Jesus] will shortly descend amongst you people [Muslims] as a just ruler and will break the Cross and kill the pig and abolish the *jizya* [a tax levied on non-Muslims for the protection of the Islamic government]."[37] Just as in Christian eschatology, Muslims also believe the Second Coming of Jesus will usher in a time of prosperity, harmony, and wealth, as described in the following hadith in *Sahih Muslim:* "Then Allah would send rain which no house of clay or [tent of] camels' hairs would keep out and it would wash away the earth until it could appear to be a mirror. Then the earth would be told to bring forth its fruit and restore its blessing and, as a result thereof, there would grow (such a big) pomegranate that a group of persons would be able to eat that, and seek shelter under its skin and the milch cow would give so much milk that a whole party would be able to drink it."[38] This depiction of a peaceful earth as a result of Jesus's reign is akin to the rendering of the New Jerusalem in Revelation 21:2–3, in which John of Patmos recounts his prophetic visions of the holy city "coming down from God out of heaven like a bride beautifully dressed for her husband." He describes the "loud shout from the throne, saying, 'Look, God's home is now among his people! He will live with them, and they will be his people. God himself will be with them.'" For Christians, the reward of the faithful is not only the kingdom of God on earth but also the ultimate bliss of God's company. White nationalist Christians of course add the caveat that this kingdom, and those who enjoy that bliss, will be exclusively White.

Examining Jesus's role in the eschatologies of Christianity and Islam highlights the complex dimensions of comparative analysis between the worldviews of White nationalists—specifically those who identify as Christian—and militant Islamists. Though Christianity and Islam have starkly opposed theological conceptions of Jesus, Jesus as a warrior is co-opted by both sets of militant ideologies. Jesus, whether a deity or a mortal, authenticates their respective narratives of victimhood and the subsequent need for vengeance to right the wrongs of the world. Certainly, the definitive role of Jesus in battling the Antichrist or al-Masih ad-Dajjal provides legitimacy for RAHOWA or conceptualizations of jihad. Envisioning the aid of a martial Jesus strengthens their apocalyptic vision of the world, justifying the violence by which they seek to achieve their respective political aims.

CONCLUSION

The subjects of this book interpret their respective eschatologies to sustain their worldviews, in which diametrically opposed forces struggle over the fate of the world. They believe they are destined to participate in a divinely ordained battle between good and evil, one that will result in victory at the end of time. Many of the adherents of these theologies steadfastly prepare for the final strife prophesied to occur when the world will cease to exist. Others go beyond preparation for the End Times: not content merely to wait, some actively seek to hasten the final battle by fomenting discord and instigating violent conflict.

Though there are a range of eschatological timelines within Christianity and Islam, belief in the apocalypse is a point of commonality. These two groups also share the conviction that those who do not submit to their respective faiths will be tormented and only those who share their particular faith will be rewarded with the bliss of heaven. Most importantly, they envision themselves playing a direct and violent role in God's cause, lifting them from marginalization to a central role as champions of justice and righteousness for their communities.[39] Thus, they have a theological imperative to bring the world to an end to hasten the day when ultimate justice shall prevail. Certainly, the mutual underlying need for belonging revealed in their respective understandings of the apocalypse imbues their acts of political violence with a greater meaning. Indeed, as chapter 8 will discuss, so-called lone wolves seek out stories of martyrdom and heroic feats to uphold the carrying out of bloodshed. In the final analysis, their respective grand narratives provide a sense of identity and belonging, conferring upon mortal political pursuits an immortal purpose.

CHAPTER 8

The Myth of the Lone Wolf

Joining Virtual Packs Online

On June 17, 2015, Dylann Storm Roof, then twenty-one years old, entered the historic Emmanuel African Methodist Episcopal Church in Charleston, South Carolina, under the pretense of attending Bible study. Instead, he killed nine Black churchgoers—six women and three men—with a .45-caliber Glock handgun. According to one of the survivors, Roof explicitly accused his innocent victims of perpetrating White genocide, alluding to the Fourteen Words: "You rape our women, and you're taking over our country. And you have to go."[1]

A complete understanding of why he committed this atrocious act of terrorism may remain forever unknown to any person other than Roof. There are many who share his grievances, possess the same views of racial segregation, and harbor the same racist resentment and derision for people of color, yet they do not all kill. However, his two manifestos, one posted online and one written in prison, his own trial testimony, and information gleaned from his life history all suggest that Roof murdered because he saw himself as taking part in a racial holy war in defense of his race.[2] Fearful of what he perceived as the overtaking of the White race and affronted at calls for gun control, he sought out concepts to justify his racism, latching on to the cause of RAHOWA, which is prolific in the online world of White hate. The title of the manifesto he wrote before the attack, *Last Rhodesian*, posted on an eponymous website, refers to colonialism in the African continent and the notion within White nationalism that White people are equipped to run governments and be in charge whereas Black people are not.

Roof's own words—not only to the worshippers that awful day but also repeated online—demonstrate his full embrace of the White nationalist worldview enshrined in the Fourteen Words: "We must secure the existence of our people and a future for white children." Echoing the themes underpinning the constellation of White nationalism, Roof wrote, "Europe is the homeland of white people"; "niggers are stupid and violent"; and America has a "Jewish problem."[3] Segregation, he wrote, is required as a defensive measure against White genocide to protect the White race from Black people and people of color more generally. Violence is, Roof asserts in the manifesto, the only appropriate response to safeguard Whiteness: "I chose Charleston because it is [the] most historic city in my state, and at one time had the highest ratio of blacks to Whites in the country. We have no skinheads, no real KKK, no one doing [anything] but talking on the internet. Well someone has to have the bravery to take it to the real world, and I guess that has to be me."

Roof committed his acts of terror in a house of worship, as did many of the militant White nationalists discussed in this chapter. In his vision, which he shared with others online, it is only by eliminating the threats to this vision of a glorious, albeit fictional, White past through violence that White genocide will be stopped and Whiteness will be preserved.

Online, Roof utilized social media as a megaphone to voice his contempt of people of color, whom he viewed as subhuman. Posts to his personal website and Facebook page often included pictures displaying common White nationalist symbols of hate.[4] In various photos, Roof flaunts his racism. He is crouching next to the number 1488 drawn in beach sand in one photo.[5] In others, he carries the Confederate battle flag, or sports a T-shirt featuring the number 88 or a jacket covered with the flags of countries Roof regarded as racially segregated utopias, including apartheid-era South Africa and the former British colony Rhodesia, now Zimbabwe, from which he derived his website's domain name, the now defunct lastrhodesian.com.[6]

As examined throughout this book, 14 is shorthand for the Fourteen Words, the sacrosanct belief uniting the disparate elements of White nationalism. Like 14, the number 88 is also deeply rooted within White nationalism. An alphanumeric code for "Heil Hitler," 88 serves as a symbol for The Order, an organization discussed in chapter 1 and associated with a plethora of militant White nationalists, including Timothy McVeigh, Robert Jay Mathews, David Lane, and Wade Michael Page.[7]

Roof took eighty-eight bullets with him when he set out to murder the worshippers who welcomed him just prior to their deaths.

Roof represented himself during his trial, during which he was convicted of thirty-three federal charges, including murder and hate crimes, but not terrorism (because there is no federal statute for domestic terrorism, as the introduction examines). Though acts of domestic terrorism by White people are often attributed to mental illness, Roof pointedly refused a defense based on mental illness.[8] In his final arguments, he explained how racist hatred underlined his terrorism: "I felt like I had to do that, and I still do feel like I had to do it. . . . Anyone who hates anything in their mind has a good reason for it."[9] In 2017, Dylann Roof became the first federal hate crime defendant in the United States to be sentenced to death.

Dylann Roof is only one example of how the Internet amplifies the voice of every individual who has online access, providing a platform to engage in raw and unfiltered discourse, often anonymously, and enabling terrorists to motivate others to commit acts of terrorism. For White nationalists and militant Islamists, their grievances and a collective sense of injustice are already magnified. Online, the pursuit of correcting social and political wrongs is made even more acute, and their self-portraits of victimhood are made all the more bleak. The Other—whether identified solely by skin color or by a confluence of gender identity, sexual orientation, religion, ability, and socioeconomic status—is demonized as an epic adversary. Ultimately, the insular silos of social media in the digital world do not challenge such worldviews but rather reinforce them.

Addressing the online dynamics of American militant White nationalism and American militant Islamism that provide individuals like Dylann Roof with a political narrative to justify terrorism, this chapter will first demythologize the concept of the lone wolf and then examine the utility of the Internet in promulgating messages about identity, crisis, and violence to bolster the ranks of online wolf packs. Whether through the surface Web or the various social media hubs called darknets on the Dark Web, White nationalists and militant Islamists are adept at harnessing the Internet to promote and recruit, as well as to raise awareness, support, and funds, all to further their shared political goal of taking over the United States.[10] The virtual world enables offline organization.[11]

Importantly, this chapter does not approach so-called lone wolves as cherry-picked data points to prove that the Internet compels violence.

Indeed, the topic of whether exposure to content promoting violence compels individuals to carry out acts of violence is tricky to research for a variety of reasons.[12] Rather, this chapter discusses the claustral world of online White nationalist and militant Islamist hate with the clear understanding that behind every act of terrorism, there is a complex set of ungeneralizable psychosocial and political dynamics. The chapter concludes with a discussion of how social media promotes the idealization of such individuals as martyrs, fueling the recruitment and messaging cycle.

LONE WOLVES AND LEADERLESS RESISTANCE

The term *lone wolf* is meant to indicate an individual who does not belong to a structured group but is more often than not influenced by the messaging of a particular group, whether directly or indirectly. Reflecting the lack of concrete definitions across the study of terrorism, there are a variety of definitions of the term within law enforcement. Some U.S. agencies support the notion that this type of offender is a completely unattached individual who operates without any direct outside command or hierarchy, while others, including the U.S. Department of Homeland Security, use the term "lone offender" to define "an individual motivated by one or more extremist ideologies who, operating alone, supports or engages in acts of violence in furtherance of that ideology or ideologies that may involve influence from a larger terrorist organization or a foreign actor."[13] The nuances and discrepancies in these definitions bring to the surface a question that continues to confound national security policymakers and enforcers: How alone is a lone wolf?

The question can be answered by looking at early models of the lone wolf framework and how it has been developed by the subjects of this book. Though the lone wolf model is predominantly associated in modern vernacular with militant Islamists, it was actually initially developed and promoted by a militant White nationalist. Louis Beam, once one of White nationalism's most recognizable faces and a member of both the KKK and the Aryan Nations, first outlined the concept of a lone wolf in his 1983 essay *Leaderless Resistance*.

Beam actually borrowed the template of a "phantom cell" from Colonel Ulius Louis Amoss, a former CIA operative who is credited with coining the phrase "leaderless resistance" in the 1960s. Beam proposed that these phantom cells were the new committees of correspondence, which had fought during the American Revolution. But rather than fight the tyranny of England, the phantom cells would rebuff the tyranny of the American government. Beam favored the phantom cell approach, or what he would call leaderless resistance, over a traditional pyramid framework of leadership with one person at the top and many at the bottom because it would create what he described as "a thousand points of resistance" for waging war against the United States.[14] This leaderless resistance model would also prove beneficial in that it provided immunity against dismantling. Beam believed that connections between each point of resistance would be enforced not by a command structure but by virtue of sharing the same philosophical approach. Because of this commitment, true devotees would take independent actions in due course rather than answering to the orders of a leader.[15]

Embellishing on the idea of leaderless resistance first promulgated by Beam in White nationalist circles, Tom Metzger, a former grand dragon of the California KKK and founder of the group White Aryan Resistance (WAR), which Beam himself would later join, also contributed to what has become the lone wolf model. Like Beam, Metzger published his own essay on the topic, "Laws for the Lone Wolf." A call to arms of sorts, the essay further developed the language of the lone wolf paradigm. Written in the first person, Metzger's manifesto encourages the reader to inhabit the psyche of the lone wolf completely: "I am preparing for the coming War. I am ready when the line is crossed. . . . I am the underground Insurgent fighter and independent. I am in your neighborhoods, schools, police departments, bars, coffee shops, malls, etc. I am, The Lone Wolf!"[16] These ominous words depicting the lone wolf are meant to create a sense of urgency and encourage individuals to take charge of their racial destiny through violence.

The leaderless resistance paradigm, and the idea of the lone wolf in particular, was also heavily aggrandized by Wotanist David Lane, who is revered as a martyr by many White nationalists. Like Beam and Metzger, Lane wrote his own essay about the concept, entitled "Wotan Is Coming." Wotan is the name Lane gives to the lone wolf, referencing the Old High German name for the Norse god Odin and serving as an acronym for "Will of the Aryan Nation." Wotan, loyal to no one except the White race, is a mercenary of sorts; his sole allegiance is to the goal of a White ethnostate. Wotan prioritizes his singular mission at the expense of all else: "Wotan has a totally revolutionary mentality. He has no loyalty to anyone or anything except his cause. Those who do not share his cause are expendable and those who oppose his cause are targets. . . . No one, not wife, brother, parent or friend, knows the identity or actions of Wotan."[17] By emphasizing the resoluteness and anonymity of Wotan, Lane reinvigorated the idea that the lone wolf could be anyone, anywhere, at any time.

Though prominent and influential American militant White nationalists like Beam, Metzger, and Lane promoted the lone wolf strategy as a vehicle for political violence, not everyone within American White nationalist circles agreed.[18] Creativity's founder, Ben Klassen was skeptical of any nonhierarchical approach to RAHOWA. Klassen preferred a single, monolithic organization instead of the thousand points of resistance model first posited by Beam.[19] Matt Hale, regarded by some, but not all, Creators as Klassen's legitimate successor, veered slightly from Klassen's dissent. He had already taken unconventional stances: after Klassen's death, Hale renamed the organization the World Church of the Creator, which then had to be changed due trademark infringement, ultimately resulting in Creativity separating into two branches, the Creativity Alliance and the Creativity Movement.[20] Hale supported a partial acceptance of leaderless resistance on his show, *White Revolution,* seeking a compromise between Beam, Metzger, and Lane on one side and Klassen on the other. Favoring neither a model of completely solitary individuals nor a top-down management style, Hale proposed an organization of small cells, made up of groups of Creators who would plan and initiate their own violent acts.[21]

Though developed by militant White nationalists, the lone wolf concept would also be promulgated within militant Islamism by Syrian al-Qaʿida associate and prolific writer Mustafa Setmariam Nasar, widely known as Abu Musʿab as-Suri. In 2004, as-Suri published a sixteen-hundred-page tome in Arabic on leaderless resistance, called *The Call for a Global Islamic Resistance (Daʿwat al-Muqawama al-Islamiyya al-ʿAlamiyya).* Just as Beam's essay defines leaderless resistance, as-Suri's magnum opus calls for militant Islamists to establish solitary cells without connecting directly to the larger organization of al-Qaʿida, theorizing that the group's propaganda will naturally produce lone wolves. Similar to how Beam repudiates a pyramidal model of militancy, as-Suri particularly calls for *"nizām, lā tanzīm"* (system, not organization).[22] Much as the "thousand points of resistance" have become predominant within White nationalism, the paradigm of *nizām, lā tanzīm* has flourished within militant Islamism.

Though they revolutionized the concepts within present-day terrorism, from leaderless resistance and Wotan to as-Suri's *nizām, lā tanzīm,* none of these ideologues could completely foresee how technology would transform communications between points of resistance or systems. The Internet has allowed what were once fringe concepts, considered nonsensical to many, to proliferate into the mainstream and even become normalized in public consciousness.[23]

RECRUITING LONE WOLVES ONLINE TO JOIN OFFLINE WOLF PACKS

The ideologies of White nationalism and militant Islamism were developed over centuries and are now dispersed in seconds.[24] During the late 1990s, when the Internet came into broad public use, websites spread the worldviews of militant White nationalists and militant Islamists, promoting war against the United States. Then interactive chatrooms were added, followed by the video- and picture-sharing platforms of YouTube, Instagram, and WhatsApp, in addition to social media sites such as Facebook, Twitter, and Gab, and message boards like 4chan, 8chan's /pol/ and k/, 8kun, and Reddit's r/The_Donald, r/Europe, and r/New Right, where racist hate-filled memes abound, as well as apps like Dawn, created by Islamic State (Dāʿish), that keep supporters apprised of developments.[25] Members of these groups have responded flexibly to efforts to restrict their access to the Internet. When militant Islamists were kicked off messaging platforms like Telegram and Riot and had their communication restricted by Twitter, they began using a series of open-source messaging services, like RocketChat, Yahoo Together, Viber, and Discord, as well as the blockchain messaging app BCM (Because Communication Matters).[26] Fundraising and video sites, online radio, and the Dark Web also serve as platforms of hate. Communicating online through these myriad venues has sparked quickly changing shorthand, including symbols, memes, and hashtags, that delineates insiders from outsiders. Examples include antisemitic punctuation, or triple parentheses, demarcating Jewish names with "echoes," like (((this))); memes co-opting the image of Pepe the Frog; and hashtags like #WhiteGenocide and #SpeakFreely; and three stars next to one's Twitter handle to signal support of QAnon. Anonymity in particular is a compelling component of communication in the digital age. Whether occurring before a global audience on the surface Web or for a select few on the Dark Web, the faceless interactions these individuals have online serve only to create more anger, in what social psychologists refer to as the online disinhibition effect.[27]

An early pioneer of efforts to harness technology to recruit and promote White nationalist propaganda was Creativity adherent Tom Metzger, whose media savvy was apparent at the dawn of the Internet era. A contemporary of Louis Beam and a prolific producer of hate programming, Metzger hosted a television show called *Race and Reason*. Broadcasting to over sixty cities on public access television, it aired interviews with White nationalist ideologues, such as William Pierce and Ben Klassen.[28] Metzger viewed public access much as the plethora of online platforms are seen today, as a technological promised land, a censorship-free zone to reach the masses.[29] In a precursor to the uninterrupted nature of the Internet, he set up twenty-four-hour phone hotlines in eight highly populated cities, including Los Angeles, Sacramento, and San Francisco, readying listeners for RAHOWA. Callers listened to prerecorded White nationalist propaganda deploring the moral morass of the United States and legitimizing violence in the political quest for a White ethnostate: "The flabby and disgusting state of white creatures who call themselves men is a disgrace to the memory of our white ancestors. If white men were strong, idealistic, and bold, this nation [the United States] wouldn't have turned into the slime pit it is now. You have reached WAR, White Aryan Resistance."[30] In the 1990s, presciently harnessing what was then the newest computer technology, Metzger, alongside his son, John, developed a nationwide computer-run program specifically designed to target young people.[31]

What the instrumentalization of technology by those who support, call for, or perpetrate violence against the United States teaches us is that while the methods of proselytizing and communicating hate may change, the act itself will not. Indeed, legislating this type of behavior has proven woefully futile, particularly because of debates around the First Amendment rights to freedom of speech and freedom of association. The Global Internet Forum to Counter Terrorism—a consortium of technology giants that includes Facebook, Microsoft, Twitter, and YouTube, founded in 2017—attempted to ban material promoting terrorism, including photos, videos, comments, and tweets, on the surface Web, which only drove many White nationalist and militant Islamist groups and individuals deeper underground to the Dark Web. Because it provides ultimate anonymity, secrecy, and communicator-controlled access, the Dark Web has become the preferred space for communication via encrypted communication tools.[32] While the move to the Dark Web also makes it more difficult for these organizations to attract new followers, it also makes it more difficult for tech companies and government agencies to track and monitor their communications.[33]

Moreover, technology not only facilitates congregating in the virtual world but has also been used to coordinate actions offline—including mass demonstrations and rallies like the Unite the Right rally in 2017 and the violent actions promoted by sites like the *Daily Stormer*.[34] Spearheaded by founder Andrew Anglin, the *Daily Stormer* is one of the most popular White nationalist websites, and its online activities including deploying a particularly aggressive "troll army" against those with whom Anglin disagrees.

One striking example of how lone wolves are not actually alone but rather exist in wolf packs is that of Tanya Gersh, a Montana real estate agent who is also Jewish and a resident of the same town as Sherry Spencer, the mother of prominent White nationalist Richard Spencer. After Gersh and Sherry Spencer became embroiled in a conflict over real estate, Richard Spencer and subsequently Andrew Anglin accused Gersh of exploiting Sherry Spencer. The online wolf pack made up of the *Daily Stormer*'s troll army sprang into offline action, doxing Gersh and her family. As a form of retaliation, the *Daily Stormer* repeatedly posted Gersh's contact details—including her phone number, home address, and social media account information. Gersh received an avalanche of antisemitic messages, many of them alluding to the gas chambers and crematoriums of the Holocaust, as well as doctored photos of her at these sites.[35] Taylor Dumpson, another victim of Anglin's troll army, had a similarly traumatic experience. After Dumpson's 2017 election as the first Black student-government president who identifies as a woman at American University in Washington, DC, Anglin published her photo online and instructed his readers to "send her some words of support." Among other threatening messages, bananas were found hanging from nooses on campus, referencing the lynching of Black Americans throughout U.S. history and insinuating that the same could be done to Dumpson. She was harassed to such an extent, she later stated, that she had to be treated for posttraumatic stress disorder and ultimately resigned from her hard-earned position.[36]

By organizing these and other offline activities to prepare for the race war that they believe is coming, Anglin and his troll army have built "an invisible empire" of White nationalists around the world. Anglin labeled in-person meetings "book clubs." Highlighting the misogyny and glorification of White heteronormative masculine violence within White nationalism as a whole, Anglin describes these so-called book clubs as "a bit like *Fight Club*," the cult 1999 film referencing the themes of masculinity and acting out against the world to discover one's personal power.[37] Anglin envisions these book clubs, of which there are already dozens, as brotherhoods of militants whose online communication

facilitates offline meetings through affiliate chapters.[38] Social media enables the organization of in-person meetings with an immediacy that
renders them almost impossible to police. It also facilitates the posting
of propaganda to social media sites immediately after a current event,
attracting more attention. Certainly, rapidity of communication, access
to a vast number of potential or actual readers or viewers, and anonymity make the Internet indispensable. Though the technology used by
terrorists will continue to change—as it did even within Tom Metzger's
lifetime—it will continue to empower individuals who might not otherwise be able to find like-minded individuals with whom they can share
their grievances and plan actions to address them. Particularly for disaf-
fected people who crave social ties yet do not have real-world relationships and for those who already feel like they don't belong in the real
world, the virtual world can be too enticing to resist.

LONE WOLVES AND THE LONGING TO BELONG

The Internet provides a means for terrorists to cultivate social networks,
allowing them to meet like-minded individuals they otherwise would
not encounter and supplying them with something they long for: a sense
of community. In one of his online manifestos, last modified the day of
the shootings, Dylann Roof stated that what he called his racial awakening had been initiated online. He cited both the 2012 death of Trayvon Martin, an unarmed Black teenager from Florida who was fatally
shot by George Zimmerman, a member of the neighborhood watch, in
what Zimmerman claimed was self-defense; and the Council of Conservative Citizens, a prosegregation White nationalist political organization whose worldview overlaps with Christian Identity theology.[39]

Martin's murder and the subsequent acquittal of Zimmerman sparked
the #BlackLivesMatter movement, a protest against the gross inequity
and institutionalized racism directed at Black Americans in all aspects of
society, including the criminalization of Black boys and men.[40] According to Roof's interpretation of the killing of Martin, however, Zimmerman was blatantly in the right. It was during the Zimmerman court case
that Roof was searching online for similar crimes and came across the
website for the Council of Conservative Citizens. What he found
cemented his belief that "something was very wrong" with society,
exhibited by the lack of media attention on Black-on-White crimes. In
his manifesto and online writings, Roof rationalized that it was not
crimes *against* Black people that should be prosecuted but crimes perpe-

trated *by* Black people against members of the White race. Incongru-
ously, he disparages Black people for thinking about race, while maintaining that White people do not think about race enough.[41] Roof goes
on to describe himself, since learning about these issues online, as "completely racially aware" and a "White nationalist."[42] In another twist of
logic, Roof appropriates the term *racial awareness,* which is similar to
racial consciousness. Racial consciousness is a progressive term denoting
that one is cognizant of the impact of skin color on a person's privilege—
the opportunities, advantages, and benefits available to them—while
also rejecting the premise of eugenics and racism. However, by claiming
racial awareness, Roof is indicating that the biological and cultural differences between races are, in fact, a hardened reality and is sanctioning
violence against Black people to save the White race.

The organization that Roof claimed prompted this racial awareness,
the Council of Conservative Citizens, was founded in 1985. The Council of Conservative Citizens succeeded the White Citizens' Councils,
which were formed to oppose the 1954 Supreme Court decision *Brown
v. Board of Education,* the landmark case that attempted to integrate
the American public school system.[43] (Supreme Court Justice Thurgood
Marshall once called the White Citizens' Councils the "uptown Klan."[44])
Similar to its predecessor, the Council of Conservative Citizens seeks to
severely restrict immigration, abolish affirmative action, and dismantle
what it calls the "imperial judiciary."[45] Displaying the White nationalism so prominent within the political far right, the Council of Conservative Citizens vocally endorses the idea that the superiority of the
White race is God's will. Its website once openly declared racial integration to be a sin, because God created racism: "God is the author of
racism. God is the One who divided mankind into different types. Mixing the races is rebelliousness against God."[46]

Though the Council of Conservative Citizens had never heard of
Roof before his crime, the organization not only was a significant force
in his self-described White nationalist awakening but also offered carefully worded support for him after he committed his act of terrorism. In
a statement responding to Roof's claim that he had been inspired by
the organization, Earl Holt, president of the Council of Conservative
Citizens, agreed with the White nationalist principles that Roof himself
claimed had motivated his murder of nine innocent worshippers: "In his
manifesto, Roof outlines other grievances felt by many whites. Again,
we utterly condemn Roof's despicable killings, but they do not detract
in the slightest from the legitimacy of some of the positions he has

expressed."[47] These words eerily mirror President Donald Trump's equivocation in response to the deadly White nationalist violence on display at the Unite the Right rally in 2017, when he said that there were "good people on both sides." Both statements demonstrate the normalization of racism in the American public sphere and the perpetuation of systemic racism in the halls of power. Other prominent White nationalists, including identitarian Richard Spencer, weighed in to endorse Roof's attacks by signaling support for the racist America that Roof envisioned in his manifesto.[48] Roof was not a lone wolf but rather part of the collective wolf pack sharing the ideas and vision of White nationalism's most powerful figures.

Roof not only found validation of his racist hate online but also roused others to take action in the race war with his act of White nationalist terrorism. James Harris Jackson, who planned and then brazenly carried out the murder of a Black man in New York City in 2017 for the sole reason of the man's skin color, studied Dylann Roof's manifesto online.[49] Benjamin T. S. McDowell was another devotee who cited Roof as inspiration.[50] Like many others, including Wade Michael Page, McDowell was so eager to belong to the White nationalist cause that he covered his body in tattoos to prove his fealty. McDowell had first come to the attention of federal authorities in 2017 for posting a largely incoherent rant on Facebook disparaging the lack of violence in today's White nationalist movement. He was then caught in a sting set up by an FBI special agent posing as a fixer for the Christian Identity organization the Aryan Nations. When the undercover agent met with McDowell under the pretense of selling him a firearm, McDowell expressed the desire to make the purchase to emulate his hero, Roof: "If I could do something on a fucking big scale and write on the fucking building or whatever, 'In the spirit of Dylann Roof.'"[51]

The Internet provides a platform for those seeking an outlet to justify their violence by providing a narrative of fear of, anxiety about, and anger toward the Other. The many social media sites also give the perpetrators of terrorism a global audience, enhancing their sense of power and belonging. Dylann Roof never met Earl Holt or Benjamin T. S. McDowell. All Roof had to do was enter the realm of White nationalist discourse online to encounter the hate-filled messages of the Council of Conservative Citizens and others. And all McDowell had to do was read heroic accounts of Roof's vicious rampage and racist rhetoric to validate his desire to take similar dramatic action.

Within the militant Islamist cosmos, the same dynamics of seeking out narratives online to sanction real-world violence prevail. Perhaps the most important contemporary militant Islamist on the Internet is Anwar al-Aulaqi, who is linked to many terrorist attacks and is revered as a martyr by militant Islamists. As a young, educated, American-born Muslim, al-Aulaqi was well versed in religious concepts and well-spoken in both Arabic and English. This fluency allowed him to convincingly brandish Islamic theological concepts, such as *al-walā' wa-l-barā'*, to justify war against non-Muslims and "hypocrite" Muslims in his call for the *umma* "to be separated into *mu'min* [believers] and *munāfiq* [hypocrites]" as a test of allegiance to God.[52]

Born in Las Cruces, New Mexico, in 1971 to Yemeni parents, Anwar al-Aulaqi earned degrees in engineering at Colorado State University and in education leadership at San Diego State University. Although it may seem incomprehensible in retrospect, al-Aulaqi became a prominent Muslim American figure advocating for peace after the September 11, 2001, attacks. He was even touted by the *New York Times* as the epitome of a "new generation of Muslim leaders capable of merging East and West."[53] As with the other supporters and perpetrators of terrorism discussed throughout this book, the psychological factors that molded al-Aulaqi into one of the preeminent militant Islamist figures of the twenty-first century after his initial condemnation of the 9/11 horrors are still unclear.

Al-Aulaqi's online presence and even his correspondence have often been cited by American militant Islamists who committed acts of terrorism in the United States. These individuals include the husband and wife duo of Syed Rizwan Farook and Tashfeen Malik; Nidal Malik Hasan, the American-born perpetrator of the 2009 Fort Hood shootings in Texas; Faisal Shahzad, the Pakistani American who attempted to bomb Times Square in 2010; Tamerlan and Dzhokhar Tsarnaev, two brothers of Chechen descent, one of them a naturalized U.S. citizen, who orchestrated the Boston Marathon bombings in 2013; and Omar Mateen, an American citizen by birth, who carried out a mass shooting in Orlando in 2016.[54]

The case of Nidal Malik Hasan, which was discussed in chapter 4, is a particularly powerful example of both how al-Aulaqi's rhetoric has served to justify a narrative of violence for would-be militants and how the resulting acts of terrorism burnish al-Aulaqi's reputation—encouraging future acts of terror. Hasan purportedly shared a close bond with al-Aulaqi, describing him as a "teacher and mentor and friend."[55] The affection seemed to be reciprocal: al-Aulaqi displayed an affinity for Hasan, whose transformation into a militant Islamist mirrored his own. After the Fort Hood shootings, al-Aulaqi lauded Hasan as "a hero" in a video posted on his website. The video, with Arabic subtitles, entitled "A Message to the American People," was taken offline by the Internet host company shortly after it was put up.[56] In it, al-Aulaqi sits professorially at a desk. In the background hangs a flag emblazoned with the *shahāda,* or declaration of Islamic faith, *lā 'ilāha 'ill Allāh* ("There is no deity but God"), giving a veneer of religious legitimacy. Speaking in English with an affected accent, al-Aulaqi commends Hasan for committing murder as retribution for American-led wars in Muslim-majority nations.[57] In his address, al-Aulaqi reiterates that Hasan carried out his actions because of the United States' blatant hostility against Islam and Muslims, Arguing that the defense of "true" Muslims from outside oppression is wholly necessitated.[58] Recounting his own conflict of identity as a Muslim and as an American, al-Aulaqi concludes his speech by declaring that the two identities are irreconcilable. Warfare against the United States is religiously binding upon himself and all able Muslim Americans who consider themselves sincere.

Made famous while alive because of how adeptly he digitally proselytized to countless impressionable and alienated youth to wage war against the United States, al-Aulaqi continues to live online even after his death. In the echo chambers of the Internet, al-Aulaqi's prolific posthumous presence in videos and references in militant Islamist publications ensures that he remains a key figure today, though he was killed in a drone attack in Yemen by CIA-led U.S. special operatives in 2011. In fact, among the maze of available online sources, al-Aulaqi retains a global audience in part because of his perceived martyrdom by the U.S. government.[59] The cherished figure of the late al-Aulaqi, whose name and images are now co-opted by many militant Islamist organizations, supersedes any organizational affiliation. As in militant White nationalism, lone wolves in militant Islamism are not truly alone. Broadly, the individuals who choose to redress their grievances through terrorism find and attract a community that shares their victimization, resentment, and anger.

OPEN-SOURCE HATE ONLINE

White nationalists and militant Islamists have revolutionized the concept of warfare through the development of the misnamed lone wolf model, the latter group essentially building on the concept of leaderless resistance put forth by the former. Collectively, they have also spearheaded the use of technology and mass communication to spread their message of hate, share their narratives of victimhood, and recruit followers to the cause of a White ethnostate or a caliphate. In addition to utilizing radio and print marketing, they mobilize the Internet as a formidable tool for recruitment and messaging though online media outlets, including video series, websites, blogs, and podcasts.

The Andrew Show, a popular YouTube series hosted by preteen Andrew Pendergraft, the grandson of Thomas Robb, the modern-day Ku Klux Klan's national director, is one example. Pendergraft's online videos use pop culture references to advise against race-mixing and promote White nationalist beliefs. Other influential websites include KKK leader Don Black's Stormfront, one of the first popular websites among militant White nationalists, frequented by the likes of Wade Michael Page, who immersed himself in the world of hate online; Richard Spencer's Radix Journal; Steve Bannon's Breitbart.com; the Occidental Observer, founded by Kevin MacDonald, a retired psychology professor; the Daily Stormer, a news and commentary website founded by Andrew Anglin; Counter-Currents, an online blog and podcast founded by Greg Johnson; the identitarian Traditionalist Youth Network website, founded by Matthew Parrott and Matthew Heimbach; and the antisemitic blog The Right Stuff, whose founder Mike Enoch was forced out once it was revealed that his legal last name was Peinovich and that his wife had a Jewish background.[60]

Similarly, there are several media entities affiliated with Islamic State (Dā'ish), including Amaq News Agency, Halummu, and Mutarjim, as well as Nashir News, Fursan ar-Rafa, and Invasion Brigades. A variety of militant Islamist organizations also have affiliated online magazines. Parallel to White nationalist literature online, militant Islamist motivational literature attaches spiritual consequences to violence.[61] Earlier publications affiliated with al-Qa'ida, such as Voice of Jihad (Sawt al-Jihad) and The Pinnacle (Dhurwat as-Sanam), have been replaced by more appealing English-language publications.[62] These are the magazines Inspire, first published in 2010 and managed by Americans Samir Khan and Anwar al-Aulaqi, both of whom were killed in an American-led drone strike in Yemen in 2011; One Ummah, started in 2019; and Islamic State (Dā'ish)'s Voice of Hind, which premiered in 2020; as well as Rumiyah, released in 2016 and regarded as the successor to its former magazine, Dabiq, first published on the Dark Web in 2014.

Some of these, like Rumiyah and Dabiq, are now defunct, while others are still published sporadically. All of these magazines are published in both Arabic and in English, heightening their appeal and accessibility to American militant Islamists. Within each issue are articles packaged with glossy graphics expounding on scripture and advocating attacks for political purposes, in addition to practical combat advice and military know-how with clear-cut directions.[63]

The first issue of *Inspire* began with a letter from the editor explaining the title of the magazine as a reference to a Qur'anic verse. In the verse, set during the Battle of Badr of 624 CE, the first major conflict between Muslims and the Meccan polytheists, the Prophet Muhammad is explicitly addressed by his title of Prophet and commanded by God to "inspire [*ḥarriḍ*] the believers to fight" (8:65). The word *ḥarriḍ* stems from the root *ḥ-r-ḍ*, which means "a person or a being that is perishing" and can also mean "to exhort" or "to urge." According to the editor, the magazine's message is that readers face an ultimatum between enacting violence, as they are being inspired to do, or perishing.

Dabiq and its successor *Rumiyyah* have symbolic titles as well. Serving as major outlets for Islamic State (Dāʿish) propaganda, both iterations are sophisticated recruiting tools advancing political goals in the guise of religiosity. Each issue promotes the self-declared caliphate and places contemporary events within Islamic eschatology to sanctify the organization's call to arms. After Islamic State (Dāʿish) failed to capture the town of Dabiq, in northern Syria, a location central to its eschatological logic, the magazine was renamed *Rumiyah*, or Rome. This title change reveals how the group adapts its messaging to fit the context and trying to appeal to followers, though the actual state of the organization is in flux. Astutely, the title *Rumiyah* situates the group's current fight in a longer historical context, since militant Islamists sometimes depict the United States as a continuation of the ancient Roman Empire, against which the early Muslims fought.

Both publications contain exhortations to commit acts of violence as well as clear instructions on how readers can carry these out. *Inspire* has a how-to section called Open Source Jihad; in *Rumiyah*, the how-to column is named Just Terror, focusing on less sophisticated attacks than those proposed by *Inspire*. Open Source Jihad includes articles with titles like "Make a Bomb in the Kitchen of Your Mom," "Destroying Buildings," "Making Acetone Peroxide," "Training with the Handgun," "Remote Control Detonation," "The Convoy of Martyrs: Rise Up and Board with Us," "It Is Your Freedom to Ignite a Firebomb," "Qualities of an Urban Assassin," "Torching Parked Vehicles," "Causing Road Accidents," "Car Bombs inside America," "Breaching Security Barriers,"

"Making the Hidden Bomb," "Designing a Timed Hand Grenade," "Assassination Field Tactics," "Professional Assassinations," and "Home Assassinations: Parcel Bomb, Magnet Car Bomb, Door-Trap Bomb."[64] Titles within *Rumiyah*'s Just Terror section include "Knife Attacks," "Vehicle Attacks," "Arson Attacks," and "Hostage Taking."[65]

Investigators of the 2013 Boston Marathon bombings found that the Tsarnaev brothers had taken direct instructions from *Inspire* for making pressure-cooker bombs with low-explosive powder from fireworks and shrapnel.[66] Other downloads by the Tsarnaevs included a digital copy of a book titled *The Slicing Sword,* which calls on Muslims not to offer allegiance to governments that "invade Muslim lands." The book's forward was written by Anwar al-Aulaqi. The Tsarnaevs' case demonstrates the complexity of factors at work in the lone wolf model, particularly its cyclical nature, created by the megaphone of online platforms: in additional to perhaps unknowable psychological and personal motivations, their act of terrorism was the result of a culmination of exhortations, specific instructions, and need for validation, which are all perhaps now serving as inspiration for others.

THE FOURTEEN WORDS, TREATISES OF TERROR, AND TRANSNATIONAL WHITE NATIONALISM

An important subgenre within the online worlds of White nationalists is the online manifesto, written to inspire others to commit acts of terror and to justify the writer's own planned or impending violence. Despite the many parallels between White nationalists and militant Islamists examined throughout this book, American White nationalists are particularly likely to write manifestos citing other White nationalists as inspiration and leveraging social media to gain a global audience for their performative violence. American militant Islamists who have committed acts of terrorism have neither referenced other militants in the same way nor utilized social media to post their rationales for violence with the aim of motivating others to do the same.[67] Undoubtedly, some texts written by Islamist ideologues, both militant and nonmilitant, which are now available online decades or even centuries after they were written, such as those discussed in chapter 2, have found collective resonance with militant Islamists around the world. Certainly, militant Islamists have exploited social media for communication, organization, and recruitment, as discussed earlier in this chapter. However, American militant Islamists have not deployed manifestos online in the same way as their White nationalist counterparts, especially those who are also American. The ones who wrote what are faintly congruous to White nationalist diatribes did not post them online. Nidal Malik Hasan and Dzhokhar Tsarnaev both wrote out their explanations for their attacks—in Hasan's case, in a letter, and in Tsarnaev's case, in pencil on the boat he was hiding in before being captured.[68]

Recent American manifesto writers who perpetrated acts of terrorism include Dylann Roof, who posted his manifesto as a website called *The Last Rhodesian* (2015), in reference to colonial Africa; Robert Bowers, who shot and killed eleven worshippers at the Tree of Life synagogue in Pittsburgh in 2018 and posted what is akin to a manifesto to Gab, a political far right social media forum that uses the same format as Twitter; John Earnest, who killed one worshipper and injured three people at the Chabad of Poway synagogue in Poway, California, in 2019 and posted his manifesto, *An Open Letter* (2019), to 8chan, a message board that attracts people who align with the political far right; and Patrick Wood Crusius, the twenty-one-year-old who murdered twenty-three people and injured twenty-four at a Walmart store in El Paso, Texas, in 2019 and posted his manifesto, *The Inconvenient Truth* (2019), to 8chan shortly before the attack.

Manifestos have long been a mainstay in the canon of White nationalist literature. Preaching the sanctity of Whiteness and the need for land, whether a physical nation-state or an idealized concept of soil, to be exclusively inhabited by the White race, the authors of these public declarations are often lauded as martyrs by adherents who subscribe to the notion of Whiteness as biologically and culturally superior. Manifestos can provide a lineage of thought as well as a reference guide, and because they often reach across group membership, they evidence the binding force of transnational White nationalism that stretches beyond the scope of religious affiliation. In many ways, manifestos have become gospel in many American and European White nationalist circles, having significantly impacted present-day White nationalist ideology, transcending the disparate religious and nonreligious affiliations within transnational White nationalism today, which include White nationalist evangelical Protestantism, Christian Identity, Cosmotheism, Creativity, Wotanism, pantheism, atheism, and agnosticism.

The idea behind the Fourteen Words—that the imminent extinction of the White race necessitates violence in the quest to establish a White ethnostate—is threaded throughout White nationalist manifestos both past and present. Certainly, from the United States to Germany and Norway to Australia, the notion of White identity as biologically and culturally superior to all other skin colors, and thus worthy of protecting through warfare, inciting the call for a White ethnostate, has been central to generations of manifestos. The authors of these foundational manifestos reference one another, demonstrating the transnational nature of White nationalism today. What is immutable, from the authors' shared perspective, is the abiding genetic and cultural superiority of the White race, especially White Northern and Western Europeans.

The authors of these historic tracts include Madison Grant, an American eugenicist who wrote *The Passing of the Great Race* (1916); Adolf Hitler, with his *Mein Kampf* (1925); Frenchman Jean Raspail, author of the influential book *The Camp of the Saints* (1973), which declares that White Western culture is on the precipice of being overtaken by hordes of immigrants from the east and the south; William Pierce, founder of the White nationalist religion of Cosmotheism and author, under the pseudonym Andrew Macdonald, of *The Turner Diaries* (1978), a fictional manifesto of sorts that inspired both the real-life organization The Order and Timothy McVeigh, perpetrator of the 1995 bombing of the Alfred P. Murrah Federal Building in Oklahoma City, the deadliest terrorist attack by an American citizen on U.S. soil; and, of course, David Lane, who wrote the *White Genocide Manifesto* (1988) while he was imprisoned.

Madison Grant's 1916 manifesto, *The Passing of the Great Race* is grounded in the pseudoscience of eugenics—namely, the claim that the White race is biologically superior. In his work, Grant expounded on the decline of what he called the Nordic people, which he claimed was due to miscegenation and immigration of inferior races, including Alpine and Mediterranean peoples. His thesis, which argued for a particular aesthetic of White skin, blond hair, and blue eyes to be considered superior to all others, appealed to many prominent politicians of the time. He wrote that

> mistaken regard for what are believed to be divine laws and a sentimental belief in the sanctity of human life tend to prevent both the elimination of defective infants and the sterilisation of such adults as are themselves of no value to the community. The laws of nature require the obliteration of the unfit and human life is valuable only when it is of use to the community or race.[69]

Grant's views on race and his Nordic thesis shaped the exclusionary American immigration policies of the twentieth century—namely, the Immigration Act of 1924, which created quotas on people entering the United States, effectively barring migrants from the Middle East and

Asia and limiting those from Eastern and Southern Europe and the African continent. The purpose of the act was to "preserve the ideal of U.S. [racial] homogeneity" by creating structural barriers to immigration.[70] What this meant in practice was that for decades after, the United States would primarily allow entry to those who held Nordic identities, according to Grant's eugenic criteria, and deny admission to others, including Alpines, Mediterraneans, and Eastern and Southern Europeans.

Grant's call to fend off racial suicide and build a monoracial society would later influence Adolf Hitler's own manifesto, *Mein Kampf*. Hitler wrote to Grant to express his admiration for Grant's writing, declaring *The Passing of the Great Race* his "Bible."[71] Indeed, Hitler wrote of his reverence for restrictive U.S. immigration policies:

> There is at present one State where at least feeble attempts of a better conception [of immigration and citizenship laws] are noticeable. This is of course not our German model republic, but the American Union [the United States] where one endeavors to consult reason at least partially. The American Union, by principally refusing immigration to elements in poor health, and even simply excluding certain races from naturalization, acknowledges by slow beginnings an attitude which is peculiar to the national State conception. The *folkish State* divides its inhabitants into three classes: State citizens, State subjects, and aliens.[72]

Hitler also wrote that the decline of previous empires had been due to their failure to preserve White identity and propagate.

For any White society to be successful in what White nationalists would declare to be cultural and biological dominance, people of different skin colors must be separated and treated differently, in accordance with "the laws of nature [that are] happenings of the urge of self-preservation and propagation of species and race."[73] Interaction between the races, as Hitler writes later, is the cause of the destruction of the White race. Only "pure blood" contains the superior natural instincts that will determine White survival:

> The blood-mixing, however, with the lowering of the racial level caused by it, is the sole cause of dying-off of old cultures; for the people do not perish by lost wars, but by the loss of that force of resistance which is contained only in the pure blood. All that is not race in this world is trash.[74]

Hitler's writings would in turn lay the groundwork for David Lane's Fourteen Words. Certainly, the concept of White genocide and the underlying assumption of scientific and cultural superiority of the White race in Hitler's *Mein Kampf* is summarized in Lane's phrase, "We must secure the existence of our people and a future for white children."

Another influential book, written in 1973 as an apocalyptic manifesto of sorts, is Jean Raspail's dystopian novel *The Camp of the Saints*. It fictionalizes the concept of White genocide caused by immigration as a violent story culminating in Black and Brown people literally trampling to death the people who welcome them to their shores. In the epigraph, Raspail compares refugees seeking safe haven to Gog and Magog, repeating the White nationalist binary view of us versus them. The title of the book comes from the biblical verses of Apocalypse 20:7–9, which Raspail interprets as depicting refugees (Gog and Magog) siding with Satan to surround "the camp of the saints" and attack them. The underlying reference given the themes of the book is that the camp of the saints "and the beloved city" are inhabited by members of the White race and divinely meant for Whiteness only.[75] White nationalists, from French politician Marine Le Pen to Breitbart editor Steve Bannon and Stephen Miller, senior advisor to President Trump, have all cited this book.[76]

In that same decade, what some have called the bible of White nationalism, *The Turner Diaries*, was published. Written in 1978 by White nationalist figurehead William Luther Pierce under the pen name Andrew Macdonald, the book is a fictional account of the diary entries of Earl Turner, who fears demographic change based on skin color and then commits violence in order to rectify this through RAHOWA. As Pierce's manifesto of sorts, it lays the groundwork for future militant activists, among them Timothy McVeigh. As chapter 1 described, *The Turner Diaries* seems to have provided McVeigh with the recipe for the bomb he used to kill 168 people; a page from the book was found inside his car at the time of his arrest.[77] The book features vivid descriptions of targeted racist mass murders, including the Day of the Rope, an event during which race traitors, or White people deemed to have "defile[d]" or "betray[ed]" the White race—for example, "White women who were married to or living with Blacks, with Jews, or other non-White males"—are hanged in the streets.[78] David Lane's tract, the *White Genocide Manifesto*, proposed a solution to the onslaught of immigrants and Others through "the formation of exclusive White homelands on the North American continent and in Europe . . . by whatever measures are necessary."[79] In this widely circulated and revered text, Lane introduced two foundational concepts that are now integral to White nationalism, including the term *White genocide* and the Fourteen Words, the battle cry of White nationalists.

Though Madison Grant, Adolf Hitler, Jean Raspail, William Pierce, and David Lane have varying religious affiliations and nationalities, what unites their writings is the thread of proclaiming Whiteness as biologically and culturally superior in addition to declaring that Whiteness is threatened by immigrants and people of color, all of which necessitates violence. These ideas are now encapsulated within the Fourteen Words. The writings of these men would shape the views of other White nationalists in the next century who may have varying religious affiliations but, as their own manifestos evidence, all perpetrated their acts of terrorism to defend and safeguard Whiteness.

Certainly, in the twenty-first century, the individuals, both White nationalists and militant Islamists, mistakenly perceived as lone wolves because they commit violence unaccompanied are not "lone" at all. Moreover, the White nationalists who carry out these crimes are imitating and echoing one another across nationalities and religious affiliations. They are also seeking to impress one another, including through the victims they choose to target. Their actions have been accelerated, via their online manifestos, by the expediency of social media.

The transnational nature of militant White nationalism emphasizes how not alone these individuals are. American White nationalists have directly cited influential terrorists outside of the United States. These include the Norwegian Anders Behring Breivik (now known as Fjotolf Hansen), whose online manifesto, entitled *2083: A European Declaration of Independence* (2011) and published under the name Andrew Berwick, explains why he killed seventy-seven people and injured hundreds more in 2011; and Brenton Tarrant, the perpetrator of mass shootings in New Zealand at two different *masājid* in 2019 that killed fifty-one worshippers and wounded dozens more, who posted a document called *The Great Replacement* (2019) and livestreamed the attacks on Facebook.[80] The fact that Brenton Tarrant cited Anders Breivik and Dylann Roof and was then himself referenced by John Earnest and Patrick Crusius displays how these terrorists are not acting alone but rather are inflicting violence within the framework of a larger, connected narrative encapsulated within the Fourteen Words.

Breivik claimed that he carried out his murders to publicize his manifesto, which railed against what he perceived to be the Islamicization of Europe. In the manifesto, which was initially posted to Stormfront, Breivik referred to himself a "Justiciar Knight Commander," leading a "refounded" Knights Templar, a reference to the Crusades, the eleventh- to thirteenth-century war in which global geopolitics saw European

Christian forces warring against the Islamic Empire. He declared that the purpose of this reinstated organization, and indeed, the violence he would carry out only hours after posting his manifesto, is to "seize political and military control of Western European countries and implement a cultural conservative political agenda."[81] Violence is the only way to reclaim what he calls "Western European countries" from Muslims and establish a White ethnostate. Though the targets of his bombing and shooting campaigns were not all Muslims, his vitriol for immigration and Islam, as well as what he calls "cultural Marxism," was made clear through his writings.

In 2019, the Australian Brenton Tarrant, who self-identifies as an "ethno-nationalist," uploaded his manifesto, *The Great Replacement,* the title of which references White genocide, to Scribd, an online library. He then carried out two terrorist attacks at different *masājid,* next to each other, killing fifty-one worshippers who had gathered for Friday prayers in Christchurch, New Zealand, and injuring dozens more, all of which was livestreamed on Facebook. In his manifesto, he justified these atrocities by citing falling birth rates within the White population and mass immigration into countries he believed should be for White people only, such as the United States, European nations, Australia, and New Zealand.

He claims to have had brief contact with Anders Breivik, whom he refers to as "Knight Justiciar Breivik," stating that he got Breivik's blessing and received "true inspiration" from him, in addition to reading "the writings of Dylan Roof [*sic*] and many others."[82] Openly stating the "anti-Islamic motivation to the attacks," Tarrant plays on White nationalist tropes harking back to the Crusades, which also featured in Breivik's manifesto.[83] Tarrant describes Muslims as "the most despised group of invaders in the West. . . . They are also one of the strongest groups, with high fertility, high in group preference and a will to conquer."[84] This language references not only the common Islamophobic theme of Muslims as virulently violent but also the centrality of the depiction of Muslims and Islam as the true threats to the White race and Whiteness in White nationalism around the world.

Tarrant's language reflects the Nazi cry of blood and soil that is also referenced in Wotanist writing and that has become a war chant of White nationalists, irrespective of religious affiliation. Referencing the colonized lands of Australia and New Zealand, which were taken from the area's Indigenous people, including the Māori, as "our lands," Tarrant states these areas are exclusively for the White race, much like the American White nationalist claim that the United States is a nation solely for

White people. All others must be removed: "Our lands are not their home, they can return to their own lands or found their homelands elsewhere. But they will not occupy our soil."

Tarrant's citation of Breivik and Roof is only one example of how individuals who on the surface seem to be lone wolves acting alone in different parts of the world are, in fact, part of a transnational ideological network, or virtual den, that is connected through social media. The case of the American John Earnest is another.

In 2019, on the last day of Passover—one of the holiest of Jewish holidays, celebrating the Jewish people's deliverance from enslavement—which in that year fell on Shabbat, John Earnest walked into the Chabad of Poway synagogue in Poway, California, and killed one worshipper and wounded three others, including the rabbi. Shortly beforehand, he posted his manifesto, *An Open Letter,* online. Whereas Breivik posted to Stormfront and Tarrant to Scribd, Earnest posted to 8chan, an imageboard-style forum that, like Gab, attracts users whose speech would otherwise be restricted on sites like 4chan.

Earnest also directly cites Tarrant, who had committed his act of terror just a few weeks prior, as inspiration, writing, "I remember a specific moment in time after Brenton Tarrant's sacrifice that something just clicked in my mind. 'If I won't defend my race, how can I expect others to do the same?'" He explained that Tarrant's rampage served as a model for his own: "Tarrant was a catalyst for me personally. He showed me that it could be done. And that it needed to be done. 'WHY WON'T SOMEBODY DO SOMETHING? WHY WON'T SOMEBODY DO SOMETHING? WHY DON'T I DO SOMETHING?'—the most powerful words in his entire manifesto."[85] Earnest, who had been posting on the online message board for a year and a half, included links to the livestream of the massacre he perpetrated, in addition to his manifesto, in another imitation of and tribute to Tarrant, who had done the same.

His fellow American Patrick Crusius, also known as Patrick Wood Brown, was similarly motivated by Tarrant's manifesto, *The Great Replacement.* Though they never directly came into contact, Crusius points to Tarrant as inspiring him to carry out terrorism.[86] Crusius published a PDF of his own screed, called *The Inconvenient Truth,* on 8chan, the same platform used by Earnest, shortly before killing twenty-two people—eight Mexican nationals and two Americans with dual citizenship with Mexico—and injuring twenty-four others at a Walmart in El Paso, Texas.[87] In Crusius's writing, the repetition of Tarrant's themes is resoundingly clear. Immigration is equated to an "invasion."

From the perspective of Crusius, the murderous rampage in Texas was only one battle in the broader racial holy war, signaling "just the beginning of the fight for America and Europe. I am honored to head the fight to reclaim my country from destruction."[88]

On the surface, John Earnest and Patrick Crusius acted alone and targeted different demographics—the former went after Jewish people, and the latter sought to kill Latinx Americans and immigrants. However, the centuries of White nationalist writings directly referencing one another and expounding on the threats posed by immigrants and people of color to Whiteness demonstrate otherwise. Earnest and Crusius perpetrated acts of terrorism against those they believed to be a threat to Whiteness; their respective targets share the identity of explicit non-Whiteness. They may have carried out their acts of violence as single individuals, drawing on Tarrant's manifesto specifically, but their actions are shaped by the long lineage of White nationalist literature. The transnational nature of White nationalism, and its militant expression especially, is exemplified in the repeated declaration that all White people must participate in RAHOWA to protect White identity, no matter what their nationality or religious affiliation, and irrespective of the specific demographics of the victims themselves. In the current theater of RAHOWA, when White people everywhere must band together to defend themselves against the onslaught of White genocide, all those regarded as non-White are legitimate targets.

MARTYRDOM AND THE INTERNET

The online sanctification of individuals who are regarded as having died as a result of participating in a holy war, whether militant White nationalist or militant Islamist, plays a role in sustaining violence. These deaths are used as recruitment opportunities, in turn generating more proclaimed martyrs in a cycle that is ouroboros-like in its continuity. Militancy is lauded and co-opted as a heroic example for new would-be militants, who are ultimately exploited by propagandists seeking martyrs for their respective causes.

These stories of martyrdom can also become part of larger political narratives, as evidenced by the sieges at Ruby Ridge and Waco or the ongoing conflicts over Palestine and Guantánamo Bay. In these renderings, it is often emphasized that these martyrs were killed by U.S. law enforcement agencies or military. Death at the hands of such agents is lauded as the highest spiritual attainment for many militants, demonstrating their true devotion and thereby reinforcing their commitment to the cause. Prominent martyrs in this category include Timothy McVeigh, who was executed by lethal injection at the U.S. penitentiary in Terre Haute, Indiana, in 2001, and Anwar al-Aulaqi, who, in Yemen in 2011, was the first American citizen ever to be killed extrajudicially via drone strike by the American government.[89] But martyr status is not restricted to individuals directly killed by the U.S. government.

Martyr status can also be extended to figures who had less dramatic deaths. Among White nationalists, such martyrs include David Lane, who died in prison in 2007. On Stormfront, Tom Metzger, former KKK grand dragon and prolific propagandist of White nationalism, accused the government of "murdering" Lane by transferring him to the federal penitentiary shortly before his death, using the opportunity to stoke the conspiratorial elements within the political far right: "We probably will never know what they did to him at Terre Haute. I assume it was pretty rough treatment. Never Forgive. Never Forget."[90] Likewise, Robert LaVoy Finicum, a neighbor of Ammon and Cliven Bundy, the militant Mormon ranchers, was killed in 2016 during a traffic stop in a clash with state police and FBI agents. In response, the Bundys posted on Facebook: "One of liberty's finest patriots is fallen. He will not go silent into eternity."[91]

With his Islamophobic manifesto, *The Great Replacement,* having been translated into different languages, Brenton Tarrant has likewise been sanctified; he is referred to as Saint Tarrant by White nationalists around the word online. One Telegram channel has been named in his honor, with users posting messages like "Glory to Tarrant! Eternal glory for opening our eyes to the future that is preparing us."[92]

Mirroring this pattern, many of the individuals who are drawn on by militant Islamists to support their understanding of Islam are venerated as martyrs. Martyrdom in Islam is a significant theological concept that has been exploited as a recruitment tool.[93] That list includes Hassan al-Banna, who was assassinated in Egypt in 1949; Sayyid Qutb, who was executed by hanging in Egyptian prison in 1966; and Osama bin Laden, who was killed by a team of U.S. Navy SEALs in Pakistan in 2011. After their deaths in 2015, both perpetrators of the San Bernardino attack, Syed Rizwan Farook and Tashfeen Malik, were eulogized as propaganda tools in *Dabiq,* which portrayed them as martyrs in the holy war to establish the caliphate: "How much more deserving of Allah's blessing are a husband and wife who march out together to fight the crusaders in defense of the Khilafah!" The martyrdom imagery also included photographs of the attack's aftermath, specifically Farook's bullet-riddled body, and the article ended by expressing hope that the San Bernardino attack would "awaken" Muslims across the United States, Europe, and Australia. By lauding Farook and Malik's attack as answering the call to "terrorize crusaders in their very strongholds," Islamic State (Dā'ish) drew on powerful symbolism to motivate other like-minded militants.[94] In laying claim to Farook and Malik posthumously, it also sent the message to would-be lone wolves that the community and acceptance that many long for may be achieved through successful acts of terror—even (and perhaps especially) when those are fatal to the attacker.

As propagandists on both sides have found, the promise of paradise or Valhalla and the welcome of angels, maidens, or Valkyries prove alluring enticements for sacrificing one's life for the cause. The recruits who kill and die with the promise of those rewards are then memorialized and sacralized online, drawing in other prospective militants. Lone wolves, who are never actually solitary in their seeking out narratives to legitimize their political aims, encounter the stories of these and other martyrs online, presented as heroes and defenders of their faiths or sacred beliefs.

CONCLUSION

Online platforms provide a longed-for sense of community for many White nationalists and militant Islamists, including those who share the beliefs but would not commit violence, those who support acts of violence but who would not engage in it themselves, and those who do carry out such deeds. Their ideologies, tactics, and goals do not exist in a vacuum. Terrorists who are falsely perceived as lone wolves are never completely devoid of support. An individual may carry out an act of violence alone and thus be viewed as a lone wolf, but there is no independent lone wolf per se, because each joins a virtual pack online that shares his (or her) worldviews and sociopolitical goals.[95]

The virtual world not only provides a like-minded community wherein individuals can reciprocally air frustrations but also allows those who are seeking a narrative to justify a desire to carry out violence to find their viewpoints encouraged and their grievances echoed. Online, the feedback loop is often amplified by algorithms that reinforce—rather than challenge—these insular echo chambers, in what is referred to as algorithmic confounding, incubating hateful worldviews.[96] Social media, in particular, nurtures the creation of transnational networks, providing an interactive space for recruitment, education, and socialization.[97] Technology also provides opportunities for direct communication in real time and for offline interactions.

Despite the focus on online radicalization by criminal justice agencies, policing the digital realm will not actually counter terrorism for the simple reason there is no single profile of a terrorist. A multitude of factors of vulnerability must converge for a person to transition from merely reading terrorist material or even making incendiary remarks online to engaging in violence in the real world. It is perhaps this unknowability that makes the dangers lurking in the digital world and in the real world so menacing.

Tech companies have attempted to prevent the dissemination of online terrorist content and communication, particularly after Brenton Tarrant livestreamed the killing of so many Muslims in New Zealand live on Facebook and the footage was restreamed around the world.[98] Doing so, however, will require a collaborative and sustained relationship between tech companies, governments, and civil society actors that share a comprehensive and common vision of pluralism, equity, and justice and that enact a comprehensive approach that goes beyond redirecting sites.[99] While the Big Tech companies are complicit, if not actively involved, in racism in the United States and violence, including genocide, around the world, particularly the criminalization and surveillance of people of color in coordination with American federal government agencies, the prospects of combating transnational White nationalism and militant Islamism are dim.[100] Certainly, just as White nationalists and militant Islamists reinforce each other's respective aims of a White ethnostate or global caliphate, algorithms often amplify feedback loops of homegrown hate online.

PART FOUR

What Can Be Done

Securing the Homeland

Counterterrorism and the Need for
Holistic Justice

Over the course of this book, we have seen why White nationalism is as great a threat as militant Islamism, if not more so, to the sociopolitical, economic, and security interests of the United States. Though they have different visions for the United States, both White nationalists and militant Islamists broadly share a sense of alienation in a world gone awry, a narrative of victimhood and disenfranchisement, and a self-perception of righteousness. American militant White nationalists want to reclaim the United States as a White ethnostate. For them, the soil of the United States once was Vinland, the biblical Manasseh, or the fulfillment of the Founding Fathers' collective intent, which they must now reclaim. Mirroring these White nationalists, most American militant Islamists similarly seek to claim the United States as part of a caliphate, a global state ruled by their violent interpretation of shariʿa.

Both ideologies also demand violence to fulfill their visions of the United States as a theopolity, often in an attempt to instigate the apocalypse. Their aggregate endorsement and carrying out of acts of terrorism is legitimized by their belief in a racial holy war defined by the Fourteen Words ("We must secure the existence of our people and a future for white children"), in many instances underscored by understandings of Christianity, Creativity, or Wotanism, or a particular application of jihad under the banner of Islam, respectively.

Moreover, White nationalism is deeply entrenched in the history of the United States, a history that has established Whiteness as the identity

249

marker of power, exclusive yet dominant. However, even though Muslims, especially Black Muslims, have a long history in the United States, first brought over as enslaved human beings before the nation's founding, American militant Islamism is a post-9/11 phenomenon. In the decades since the September 11 attacks, the utilization of social media to communicate, propagate, proselytize, and organize online and offline have accelerated the transnational reach of White nationalism and militant Islamism.

Despite sharing so many parallels, or perhaps because of the multitude of similarities, White nationalists and militant Islamists reflexively instrumentalize each other as their primary target, reifying their claims for the necessity of violence. From the positionality of the former, all Muslims, irrespective of their generational ancestry in the United States, are exemplars of the Other. Through the lens of the latter, White nationalists, especially the militant variety, are construed as present-day Crusaders. Specifically, Islamophobia is employed by White nationalists to gain recruits and to buttress current rhetoric endorsing racial holy war (RAHOWA); this same narrative is then absorbed and recycled by militant Islamists to bolster their narrative of victimhood and demands for violence.

Given the dire nature of militant White nationalism, in addition to militant Islamism perpetrated by American citizens, the first half of this conclusion will contend that the current U.S. approach to counterterrorism is myopic and thus undermines American security interests, ultimately rendering it ineffective. This is because it magnifies the dichotomy between Muslim Americans and their fellow citizens, seemingly absolving militant White nationalists while condemning innocent Muslim Americans. Failing to address the very real threat of White nationalism and instead targeting Muslim Americans by virtue of their religious affiliation results in federal resources not being properly apportioned. Worse, a culture of fear of what is seemingly the Other is perpetuated, pitting Muslim Americans against other Americans, as well as against each other. These American counterterrorism strategies corrode the civil liberties and the economic and social security of all Americans.[1] Ironically, the reductive "us versus them" narrative perpetuated by American terrorists who wage war by instilling fear in the national psyche to degrade the American social fabric is duplicated in the simplistic paradigm of current U.S. domestic counterterrorism efforts, which fail to address the nature and scope of legitimate homeland security threats. Only by recalibrating America's counterterrorism approach to address the deficiencies of the current strategy—which perpetuates Islamophobia and overlooks White nationalism—can the situation be remedied.

The second half of this conclusion will therefore advance a new approach to counterterrorism, a holistic justice approach, one based on the principles of anti-oppression and empathy, in order to effectively secure the homeland for all Americans, irrespective of creed or color. The holistic justice approach I am proposing can be defined as a framework for redressing the systemic inequities that undergird the current paradigm of domestic counterterrorism within the United States. These inequities include both structural Islamophobia, "a type of racism that targets expressions of Muslimness or perceived Muslimness,"[2] stigmatizing an entire swathe of innocent American citizens; and institutionalized White privilege, the systemic cultural reality that being White confers an array of inherent systemic advantages, which are often taken for granted by White people themselves.[3]

Holistic justice moves beyond antiracism to anti-oppression in order to address militant White nationalism and end the disproportionate vilification of Muslim Americans, and other marginalized groups, by current counterterrorism efforts. The additional component of empathy is necessary for both White people and people of color to understand their own histories and those of others, particularly within the context of the American story. Such a process creates opportunities to recognize the dynamics of institutional oppression and White privilege, both of which are also embedded within the U.S. Constitution, perpetuating the structures that have minimized the threat of White nationalism and criminalized people of color within the counterterrorism paradigm.

Specifically, I define *holistic justice* as the visibility, amplification, and empowerment of all people, in accordance to their needs, so that each person—particularly those who are multiply minoritized, including because of religion, skin color, heritage, citizenship, gender identity and expression, sexual orientation, socioeconomic status, age, and ability—may have the same rights, resources, protection, benefits, and opportunities afforded to those in positions of power. There can be no freedom and justice for all if one group of people is excluded from the equation. Whereas oppressive power is the minoritization of the many for the privilege of a few, holistic justice demands equity for all.

Such an approach to counterterrorism calls on White liberals in particular, as well as on Muslim Americans, to bear the onus of enacting this change. By virtue of their Whiteness, the former are in a position of privilege to leverage institutional change. Muslim Americans are in a unique position, too, as a result of their pluralistic makeup. By allying with those minoritized across identities, they are in a position to organize at a grassroots level. These two demographics, though on the surface dissimilar, are integral to addressing the breadth of injustice buttressing the inequities in counterterrorism strategy today. It is only by both addressing these from the top-down at the institutional level, as only White people can do, and uniting the marginalized from the bottom-up, as only Muslim Americans can do, that the gospel of hate of White nationalists and militant Islamists can be undermined.

TERRORIZING MUSLIMS: WHY CURRENT U.S. COUNTERTERRORISM EFFORTS ARE NOT EFFECTIVE

In the words of eminent statesman and former enslaved person Frederick Douglass, "When men oppress their fellow men, the oppressor ever finds in the character of the oppressed, a full justification."[4] Though Douglass was addressing the institutionalized oppression of slavery, his timely words apply to the structural Islamophobia that has become the defining feature of American counterterrorism policies today.

Since 2015, American domestic counterterrorism has increasingly been oriented around countering violent extremism (CVE) and preventing violent extremism (PVE).[5] Both CVE and PVE, which primarily target Muslim Americans, are predicated on what is often referred to as the "conveyor belt" theory of terrorism, or the notion that outward expressions of religiosity, such as praying five times a day—one of the primary duties of every Muslim—is an indicator of potential terrorism. The fallacy of this logic, which criminalizes the exercising of First Amendment rights, has been solidly refuted by research.[6] In fact, practicing one's faith as a Muslim is shown to be a determining factor in *not* becoming a terrorist.[7] Nevertheless, this erroneous line of reasoning has led to the current CVE and PVE approaches, resulting in the overt and covert surveillance of entire communities of Muslims, including the use of informants, which has fostered mistrust and discord between and within several key demographics: between Muslim Americans and government agencies, including law enforcement; between Muslim Americans and other Americans, because the former's patriotism, loyalty, and belonging are questioned; and, between members of Muslim American communities, who are in many instances faced with the ultimatum of either spying on fellow Muslims or being targeted by the FBI.

Not only is the conveyor belt theory misguided as an approach to countering terrorism, but it actually makes matters worse by providing recruitment propaganda for both transnational White nationalist and militant Islamist organizations, ultimately unifying disparate groups and individuals. The former utilize the approach to consolidate rampant Islamophobia, because it justifies their rationale for why the United States must be a White ethnostate.[8] The latter perceive the American counterterrorism approach as another manifestation of the current Crusaderist persecution of Muslims, even despite their ironic disavowal of the Muslim-ness of the Muslim Americans who live in the United States.

While it has been repeatedly stated in previous chapters that the complete confluence of factors that lead an individual to commit terrorism is unknowable, the current CVE and PVE policies serve only to enhance the oppression and injustice of structural Islamophobia by dismantling Muslim Americans' sense of belonging. This is done by placing entire communities of Muslim Americans under surveillance and leveraging the fear of deportation or other forms of manipulation to coerce them to inform on one another. The erroneous good Muslim versus bad Muslim trope has devolved into the falsity that all Muslim Americans secretly harbor animosity toward their own nation.[9]

Domestically, the targeting and surveillance of Muslim Americans is a needless waste of resources. The current strategy serves only to separate Muslim Americans from their sense of civic allegiance. Muslim Americans are essentially forced to see themselves as the Other through constant surveillance, monitoring, and exposure to propaganda in which they are overwhelmingly characterized as criminals or potential criminals. The highlighting of structural Islamophobia within the context of U.S. counterterrorism is not to erase the history of Islamic civilizations that have failed to live up to the stated ideals of Islam's sacred texts, nor is it to dismiss the terrorism of militant Islamist individuals and organizations. Rather, the purpose is to disassemble the detrimental myth that all Muslims are inherently militant and somehow foreign to their own country, unable to be both American and Muslim—a delusion that has come to frame much of the War on Terror and the American approach to counterterrorism.

By singling out the religion of Islam as promoting violence, and often reducing it to a cult rather than a global faith with more than one billion adherents, this myth dangerously and erroneously accuses Muslim Americans of collectively bearing overt or secret enmity toward their own homeland. Many Muslim Americans find that, despite their great diversity and despite the fact that they make up only a minute fraction of the American population, they are somehow viewed with the same disparagement and outright hostility as those who have actually committed acts of terrorism. Unlike nonmilitant White Americans, who have never been condemned by their fellow Americans as a homogenous entity for the violence perpetrated by militant White nationalists, innocent Muslim Americans are repeatedly blamed for the violent acts of militant Islamists—if not in the court of law, then through the media and in the court of public opinion. The perceptions of Islam as ideologically opposed to American democratic values and of Muslim Americans as harboring aggression (secretly or otherwise) against their fellow American citizens are ubiquitous and often taken for granted in the post-9/11 landscape. As theories about stereotype threat state, this collective criminalization of Muslims for the actions of very few individuals risks forcing them to confirm these negative generalizations.[10] Beyond the domestic scope, U.S. foreign counterterrorism policy has had a devastating impact on many Muslim-majority nations, particularly the many Muslim civilian casualties of American-led drone strikes. Under the command of President Obama, the United States not only surveilled Muslim Americans in greater scope than ever before but also unleashed drone strikes across a swathe of Muslim-majority countries, killing thousands of innocent Muslims. Although weaponized drones are often touted as a lower-cost, lower-risk means of waging war, they have become a powerful recruiting tool for American and international militant Islamists. These policies serve only to threaten the lives of Americans who become targets for vengeful domestic and international militant Islamists.[11]

Militant Islamist organizations online and around the world exploit the lethal results of American foreign policy as a focal point on which individuals may hinge their need for valor, fragmented identity, weak sense of belonging, and even mental health issues. In avenging these faraway deaths through acts of terrorism, American militant Islamists seek to restore their own sense of self. Unequivocally, this logic is not an excuse for their actions. By their own admission, and as this book has examined at length, the American militant Islamists perpetrating acts of violence within the United States do so in pursuit of political aims. What this logic nevertheless highlights is how the results of American foreign policy decisions—from wars in Iraq and Afghanistan to drones strikes in Muslim-majority nations—provide a cover of legitimacy to American militant Islamists who seek a justification for attacking the United States.

Drones are also a driver of anti-American sentiment among nonmilitant civilian populations, particularly because of the rates at which they kill noncombatants. In the minds of many Muslims around the world, the deaths of innocent civilians are directly linked to the morass that has engulfed Afghanistan, Iraq, Libya, Syria, and many other countries. Undoubtedly, there are constantly evolving social, economic, geographical, political, and military factors at play. Drone strikes especially antagonize already aggrieved populations, creating resentment not only toward the United States but also toward their own governments, which are often perceived as colluding with the United States rather than prioritizing the interests of the local citizens. The killing of civilians creates further tension in the already fragile relationships between the United States and its much-needed partners in Muslim-majority nations.[12]

The United States must not only cease drone strikes but also consistently work to repair civilian infrastructure, such as damage to hospitals, schools, and roads, as well as make reparations to civilians themselves in the regions where drone strikes have been carried out. The security of American citizens and the lives of equally valuable people around the world can be safeguarded by fulfilling promises of aid and nation-building and providing basic services to local populations, as well as addressing local needs and concerns as articulated by the people themselves. If the United States fails to repair public trust through practicing transparency with citizens at home and dismantling anti-American sentiment abroad, it will continue to play into militant Islamist propaganda and continue to be viewed as an occupying Crusader nation.

A FEDERAL STATUTE CRIMINALIZING DOMESTIC TERRORISM: TO BE OR NOT TO BE

In the current American legal system, for a White nationalist who perpetrates an act of politically motivated violence to be classified as a terrorist, that individual must be affiliated with a militant Islamist organization. In other words, there is no federal criminal statute for domestic terrorism, and there is no way to prosecute militant White nationalists as terrorists on a national level.[13] While there are arguably legal means to prosecute a White nationalist terrorist crime as such, there is a glaring exception: these acts of violence are not prosecutable if they are carried out using firearms, as most are. Moreover, there is no list of proscribed White nationalist organizations, as there is for militant Islamist organizations, which would make it a crime to provide material support to certain groups.[14]

For the U.S. counterterrorism strategy to be effective, then, it would seem necessary to enact a federal statute defining what constitutes an act of domestic terrorism that includes the crimes of White nationalists, in the same way that the federal criminal statute of terrorism is applied to militant Islamists. The excuse generally given for not doing so—that militant Islamism is fundamentally foreign, whereas militant White nationalism is domestic—is no longer viable. Many militant White nationalists are now taking inspiration from and communicating with individuals and groups in countries outside of the United States, particularly in Europe and Australia. Ideally, if all citizens who commit acts of terror, regardless of ideology and political affiliation, are considered terrorists under the U.S. law code and able to be prosecuted as such, then violent acts perpetrated in the name of militant Islamism and militant White nationalism would be able to be equally prosecuted and sentenced.[15]

More realistically, however, as the history of the surveillance practices of federal law enforcement agencies has shown, broadening the label of domestic terrorism to include all forms of political violence, regardless of creed, color, or political ideology, will only compound the current injustices within the counterterrorism paradigm. Advocates of movements like Black Lives Matter (who have been labeled as Black identity extremists), #Not1More Deportation, and Critical Resistance, as well as Latinx and Indigenous Americans, all of whom are also currently surveilled in the name of national security, would be denounced, criminalized, and prosecuted under this type of legislation.[16] Expanded prosecutorial powers could very well be leveraged against minoritized communities should federal prosecutors have the ability to charge a greater array of crimes as domestic terrorism, as some proposed legislation entails.[17] Clearly, some other approach to the problem is called for.

"TO ESTABLISH JUSTICE": MOVING BEYOND ANTIRACISM TO ANTI-OPPRESSION

The history of the United States is a study of the contradictions between the ideals of America and the policies of its government. The application of the term *justice* itself reflects the inconsistencies between American aspirations and policies. The preamble of the Constitution, the supreme law of the United States, declares that "We the People" intend "to form a more perfect union" and "to establish justice." Even if we set aside the exclusion of generations of Americans of color from "We the People," the goal of establishing justice rings as hypocritical in light of the embeddedness of structural oppression in American history and law.[18] America's struggle has always been to embrace the full aspirational weight of its founding principles, from the "We the People" of the Constitution to the "created equal" of the Declaration of Independence. The holistic justice framework I propose here is founded on an anti-oppression and empathy-based counterterrorism paradigm, which begins by encouraging all Americans to understand not only how laws and practices in the United States have focused on keeping the United States White for centuries but also how systemic oppression impacts quality of life and opportunities today. Though systemic racism is the central axis on which other types of discrimination and power differentials occur, the framework of how we understand the interplay between a nation's mindset, laws, and institutions that have justified discrimination based on skin color, must be expanded to include other forms of oppression, across the spectrum of identities, for holistic justice to be realized and for true solidarity to be achieved across minoritized identities.

Expanding the lens from an antiracist perspective to an anti-oppression perspective thus includes the learning of subaltern histories, which are often excluded or dismissed from primary and secondary education. Though there is only one race—the human race—it is vital to understand how the concept of race is a sociopolitical construct exploited for power. This includes encouraging the many communities of color and the heterogeneous groups within them to learn their own racial histories and those of others as subjects of systemic oppression in the United States; and placing a particular onus on White people to learn these histories and to grasp the full scope of how Whiteness has been wielded as a tool to justify this oppression and privilege in the United States, especially when compounded with other forces of discrimination, such as ableism, ageism, misogyny, the stigma of poverty, and Queerphobia, to name a few.

Essentially, all Americans must learn how people have historically been oppressed or privileged due to their sociopolitically constructed racial identities and other identities, with an emphasis on how these intersectional identities impact outcomes in institutions such as the media, health care, education, and criminal justice, as well as access to housing, clean air and drinking water, safe and reliable public transportation, and nurturing public spaces.[19] This educational framework requires religious adherents, particularly Muslims, Christians, and Odinists, to learn about their histories of respect for difference and interfaith movement, not from an apologist stance but from one of cultivating empathy across seemingly intractable divides.

WHITE LIBERAL COMPLICITY AND
COUNTERTERRORISM

Structural Islamophobia and institutionalized White privilege within the context of counterterrorism are mutually reinforcing. White privilege—the myriad unearned material, psychological, and legal advantages that accrue to White people by virtue of their skin color—creates a White racist lens by which militant White nationalism is excluded from the scope of U.S. domestic counterterrorism efforts.[20] Though White fragility—what Whiteness studies scholar Robin DiAngelo calls a state of racial stress that triggers "the outward display of emotions such as anger, fear, and guilt, and behaviors such as argumentation, silence, and leaving the stress-inducing situation"—has hindered many White people from recognizing their unearned privileged position within society, it is White people who arguably have the most agency to make significant change, making their consistent and continual participation all the more imperative.[21] It is also White people who have created the institutions of oppression across systems that result in the minoritizing of people deemed to be non-White in the United States.

Whiteness is imbued with inherent institutional power not fully recognized by many White liberals. Such is the nature of privilege. However, the White nationalist narrative of simultaneous White superiority and White victimization can be countered by White people.[22] They therefore bear the burden of addressing the systemic injustices that are now maintained in the current counterterrorism paradigm, from Islamophobia and the marginalization of communities of color to the ongoing blind spot of White nationalism. Colorblindness must give way to racial consciousness, as well as to awareness of other forms of identity that are not privileged—not just based on skin color and the more known aspects of pluralism, such as gender, religion, sexual orientation, and national origin, but also other aspects of identities, including linguistic diversity, geographic diversity, and socioeconomic diversity.[23]

The sincerity, efficacy, and commitment specifically of White people who believe themselves to be allies in recognizing White privilege and addressing institutional inequities and thereby empowering communities of color has long been debated in American political, social, and academic realms.[24] For instance, Derrick Bell, an American legal scholar and a founding critical race theorist, advanced what he called "interest convergence theory," which posits that "the interest of blacks in achieving racial equality will be accommodated only when it converges with the interests of whites."[25] After stating that the Fourteenth Amendment is not enough to grant racial equality, Bell concludes, "Racial remedies may instead be the outward manifestations of unspoken and perhaps subconscious judicial conclusions that the remedies, if granted, will secure, advance, or at least not harm societal interests deemed important by middle and upper class whites."[26] A similar argument could be made regarding the interests of minoritized communities in achieving holistic justice within counterterrorism. In his 1963 *Letter from a Birmingham Jail*, Martin Luther King Jr. called out White moderates, expressing his grave disappointment that the White moderate was, in fact, the "great stumbling block in the stride toward freedom," more so than the "Ku Klux Klaner."[27] Malcom X would voice this same position on White people, not out of disparagement at unmet expectations, but out of outrage at what he decried as their blatant hypocrisy:

> Politically the American Negro is nothing but a football and the white liberals control this mentally dead ball through tricks of tokenism: false promises of integration and civil rights. In this profitable game of deceiving and exploiting the political politician of the American Negro, those white liberals have the willing cooperation of the Negro civil rights leaders. These "leaders" sell out our people for just a few crumbs of token recognition and token gains. These "leaders" are satisfied with token victories and token progress because they themselves are nothing but token leaders.[28]

It was not only Black leaders who were condemning White Americans for their complicity in creating and perpetuating systemic racism. In 1967, President Lyndon B. Johnson appointed the National Advisory Commission on Civil Disorders to investigate the source of the race protests that permeated the American landscape during that decade, from Newark, Minneapolis, and Cincinnati to Milwaukee, Tampa, and Detroit. The group would come to be known as the Kerner Commission, named after its chairperson, Otto Kerner, the Democratic governor of Illinois. On February 29, 1968, the report was published, and it eventually sold over two million copies. Mirroring the words of Martin Luther King Jr. and Malcolm X, the report provides a damning indictment of White Americans because they perpetuate the oppression of Black people "and every minority group," both unwittingly and systemically:

> What white Americans have never fully understood—but what the Negro can never forget—is that white society is deeply implicated in the ghetto. White institutions created it, white institutions maintain it, and white society condones it. It is time now to turn with all the purpose at our command to the major unfinished business of this nation. It is time to adopt strategies for

action that will produce quick and visible progress. It is time to make good the promises of American democracy to all citizens—urban and rural, white and black, Spanish-surname, American Indian, and every minority group.[29]

Weeks later, on April 4, 1968, the Reverend Martin Luther King Jr., who described the report as a "physician's warning of approaching death, with a prescription for life," would be assassinated, generating a new wave of riots.[30] His murder was preceded by the 1965 assassination of Malcolm X, who by then was el-Hajj Malik el-Shabazz. Before their deaths—both were murdered at the age of thirty-nine—they had been moving closer toward each other in their views on civil and human rights.[31] Presidential hopeful and Kerner Commission supporter Robert F. Kennedy was also assassinated in 1968, making way for Richard M. Nixon to become the president a few months later, after which the report, its findings, and, significantly, its recommendations, were largely removed from public consciousness and political will.

The country would have to wait until the next century to have the opportunity for another president to talk about race in a meaningful way. Hope seemed to come alive with the presidency of Barack Hussein Obama, whose father was a Black Kenyan and whose mother was a White American. Many felt the possibility that the legacy of institutional slavery, Jim Crow laws, and segregation could be healed through his presidency, lauding a post-racial America that would finally realize the American Dream of hard work and in which intellect would triumph over discrimination. As a candidate, he spoke poignantly of his own heritage and background; when he was president, however, some segments of White America felt that he represented Black America too much, as the increase of White nationalist groups during this time attests. On the other hand, some Americans without melanin privilege felt that he never spoke about race as frankly as they wanted him to. The argument has even been made that his failure to address race head-on and matter-of-factly contributed to his being succeeded by Donald Trump.[32] Other Black American thinkers have argued that the election of Donald Trump was not a simple reflexive reaction to the presidency of Barack Obama but rather the result of a desire among White voters to completely obliterate the values and agenda of the nation's first Black president.[33]

In any case, the election of onetime reality show personality and businessman Donald Trump to the presidency of the United States brought into stark relief the structural racism that has undergirded America since its founding. Regarded by many avowed White nationalists, including

David Duke, former Grand Wizard of the KKK, as a like-minded ally, Trump has offered racist rhetoric and policies to affirm their belief. From echoing conspiracy theories to denigrating people of color, the values of the Trump administration reflect the White nationalist agenda, discussed in the previous chapters. The hosting of the Presidential Social Media Summit in 2019 at the White House that included some of the staunchest figures on the political far right in the digital world declared President Trump's endorsement of their views. His slogan, Make America Great Again, invokes an America steeped in colorblindness, or a nation that refuses to respect the breadth and depth of the pluralism of its citizens.[34] It calls for a return to a time when White privilege was not yet a term and when White people did not have to confront their complicity in upholding institutions of oppression; the "again" in the term signals a Rockwellian America that never truly existed. Donald Trump's voting constituency was primarily made up of White high-wage earners without college degrees and White evangelical Protestants. Many voted for Donald Trump's presidency because they were fueled by White anxiety and a disconnect from the travails of poverty, which, although experienced disproportionately by Black and Brown Americans, are also experienced by White Americans.[35]

Since the 2016 election, however, the concept of nationalism, and particularly White nationalism, as concomitant with a true version of patriotism, and exclusively for White people, has risen to prominence.[36] This is evidenced by the increased popularity of political far right parties in Europe and autocratic regimes, which share a racist platform of Islamophobia, antisemitism, anti-immigration, and a proprietary claim on Whiteness. In the present age, the political rise of White nationalism is twinned with violence in the name of self-defense of White culture. Perpetrators of this violence, from the shootings in Christchurch, New Zealand, to the sprees of killings across Europe and the United States, repeatedly decry the White genocide they perceive as taking place. Even in nations that do not have a White majority, a destructive form of nationalism is taking root. For instance, Indian nationalism has become synonymous with a patriotic identity of an India excised of its Muslim citizens. In many nations, nativism in its most base sense is taking hold in political spheres; exclusionary nationalism, undergirded by hate of the Other, is coming to be equated with patriotism.

This is not to argue that militant nationalists, or those who kill in the name of racial holy war, are akin to political supporters who exercise their right to vote. The point is that divisive identity politics, based on racism, xenophobia, and Othering, have never gone away and are, indeed, exploited by the elite to maintain power. This is true in the United States as well as in many nations without a White majority elite. Within the context of the United States, Donald Trump is certainly not the first commander in chief to verbalize, support, and enact racist policies. What marks a significant change from past presidential administrations is the normalization of White identity politics and fascistic approach to governance. Although the phrase *white identity politics* does not explicitly denote animosity toward people of color, it does indicate a sense of solidarity among White Americans who are anxious about the diminishing status of Whiteness.[37]

The holistic justice approach to counterterrorism seeks to change the narrative of victimhood cultivated by White nationalists by acknowledging that though they do not experience racism, they may undergo disenfranchisement across other categories of identities, thereby offering empathy for and recognition of their grievances. Though White nationalists focus exclusively on the racial component of identity, White privilege and disadvantage are not mutually exclusive. Illustrating this point is the fact that many White Americans experience economic disenfranchisement today because of increasing wealth inequality, though it is Americans of color who suffer the most from the racial wealth gap. This acknowledgment is especially crucial within the context of this book and the justice-based counterterrorism approach because studies show that poverty is linked with a sense of victimhood, which is more strongly correlated with White anxiety and American White nationalism than with American militant Islamism.[38] There is a symbiotic relationship between White anxiety, poverty experienced by White people, and racism, because White people who are experiencing poverty are also more likely to feel discriminated against, fueling the need for retaliation.[39]

The insistence by White nationalists that White genocide is taking place—indicated by the rising number of immigrants and the increasing percentage of Americans of color—emphasizes their perception that White people are endangered. Seeing themselves on the brink of racial and cultural extinction, they perceive any attempt to address the power inequalities experienced by oppressed groups as unfair to White people.[40] Co-opting the language of the political left, White nationalists thus understand themselves as victims of "reverse racism," meaning racism perpetrated by people of color against White people. From the perspective of White nationalists, a definition of racism as solely perpetuated by White people and institutions against people of color is simply a double standard, one that only increases the urgency of what they view as their fight for White survival, emblematized in the Fourteen Words. This narrative of victimhood legitimizes their use of violence, and because they often portray themselves as victims and targets of racism, White identity is framed as a burden instead of a boon.

According to many scholarly definitions of racism, however, so-called reverse racism cannot exist because racism is rooted in a power imbalance that favors White people, who are embedded within societal structures that maintain White privilege.[41] By this definition, White people cannot be victims of racism because Whiteness has been a signifier of power and institutional control since the founding of the United States.[42] White people can experience prejudice, or prejudgment, and even discrimination, bias, and individual racism, but they cannot be subjects of structural racism. White Americans must recognize that while they may be disadvantaged at the junctures of other identities, the sociopolitical construct of race is not one of them.[43]

The complicity of White liberals who claim solidarity with Black and Brown people yet fail to exercise their privilege to support them is tantamount to sustaining systems of oppression. Rather than leverage their power for the greater good to uplift people of color who are criminalized within the current counterterrorism paradigm, dismantle this system of oppression, and restructure it to achieve holistic justice, White political moderates bask in their privilege.

In the anti-oppression, empathy-based approach to counterterrorism that I propose, White people must stand for holistic justice by amplifying and empowering the voices of the marginalized, oppressed, and historically underrepresented, not by speaking up for them, or over them, but by acknowledging the history and condition of all people based on the color of their skin; namely how Whiteness is instrumentalized as a tool of power and how race is a social and historical construct that is weaponized against Black and Brown people so that Whiteness can retain its privilege of power.[44]

Serving as an alternative to the reductive, simplistic narratives of White supremacy and hatred promoted by White nationalists, this approach offers a sincere starting point to address the inequities facing the plethora of groups within the United States today. It does so by fostering the values that truly make America great: respect for multiculturalism, endorsement of pluralism, and support for complex dialogue within democracy.

THE NECESSITY OF EMPATHY

Cultural competency, religious literacy, and socioeconomic equity are all predicated on one factor: empathy. By being aware of and acknowledging one's own assumptions and judgments with regard to culture, religion, race, and wealth, one is able to enter into the worldview of another person more completely. It is only when the perspective of the Other is considered and understood that the path to reconciliation can be found. It is only by advancing holistic justice, calling out with sincere patriotism for America to live up the ideals of "We the People," written by White Founding Fathers and now demanded by Americans of all colors, that economic and social stability can be fostered and the homeland secured.

Without empathy, there can be no peace, nor will the vulnerable be protected against the exploitation, marginalization, and oppression of the powerful; in short, it is only through connecting with one another, with each acknowledging the humanness of all, that holistic justice will be achieved. Despite the digital connections we all share and our human capacity for connection, we, as a species, are more divided than ever. Empathy affords us all the opportunity for self-reflection, for mutual recognition, and for reconciliation.

In the context of counterterrorism, empathy calls for shifting away from views of Muslim Americans as a singular entity espousing violence, White Christians as evangelical supporters of racism, and Odinists as militant advocates of blood and soil in order to work toward a recognition of the breadth and depth of expressions and experiences within and among Americans.

Reclaiming Islam's Integral Role to the United States

Each community of color in the United States—including Black Americans, Brown Americans, Indigenous Americans, Asian Americans, and Latinx Americans, and combinations thereof—has its own distinct struggle with prejudice, discrimination, and systemic racism in the American experience.[45] A multitude of laws have contributed to racial inequity. To take just a few examples, Black Americans were subjected to centuries of enslavement, Black Codes, Jim Crow laws, and segregation; the many Indigenous Nations living on the land that became the United States were forced by the 1819 Civilization Fund Act to send their children to live and attend classes at boarding schools, where many faced all forms of abuse; tens of thousands of Japanese Americans were forced into internment camps during World War II, losing their livelihoods and properties in the process; Latinx Americans have also been subjected to lynchings in American history, and they face stricter voter ID laws, as well as harsher immigration enforcement in the wake of anti-immigration sentiment.[46]

Muslim Americans, who may or may not also identify with communities of color, face Islamophobia. Like Americans across religious and sociopolitically constructed racial lines, Muslim Americans grapple with the challenges of relations with local and federal law enforcement and the need for criminal justice reform.[47] Since 9/11, America's national security paradigm has increasingly resulted in many of its own citizens being surveilled, monitored, and ostracized, all in the name of national security.

Though the histories of each community of color are unique within the story of the United States, their shared experience of injustice and systemic oppression can provide a platform for solidarity. Black Muslim Americans face a particular form of discrimination, as they are marginalized both by Islamophobia, as a result of their religious identity, and by racism, as a result of their skin color.[48] Moreover, Black Muslims are often discriminated against by other Muslims, in spite of clear Qur'anic teachings of unity and harmony (Qur'an 30:22 and 49:13). Intrafaith experiences and worship services are very often divided along ethnic lines.[49] But when Muslim Americans embrace their incredible diversity as a demographic, with adherents who identify as White, Asian, Latinx, and Black, and combinations thereof, they can recognize their common oppression with minoritized groups as a collective force. The spectrum of Whiteness and Blackness are like bookends. Colorism is as problematic within communities as racism is against them. People with melanin privilege are in a singular position to strive toward holistic justice by standing with—and uplifting—the most marginalized within these communities—those who are facing political oppression, economic exploitation, and social degradation.

As this conclusion has thus far advanced, a reconceptualized counterterrorism framework based on holistic justice is an essential antidote to structural Islamophobia and American militant Islamism, which are, in part, incited by the false belief within the current U.S. counterterrorism paradigm that Islam is adversarial and antithetical to the West. The overarching clash of civilizations trope of "Islam versus the West" not only erroneously presupposes that two monoliths of "Islam" and "the West" actually exist, but also fallaciously mischaracterizes the relationship between the two supposed entities, providing fodder for both transnational White nationalists and militant Islamists.

The confusion is deepened by the fact that militant Islamists call themselves Muslim and use the same textual foundations that billions of Muslims around the world, including the almost four million Muslim Americans, rely on. The resulting perception among many non-Muslims that all Muslims are truly militant at heart—a common refrain at anti-shari'a rallies across the United States—has unfortunately shaped American counterterrorism policies.

Muslim Americans are linked in the public imagination not only with terrorism but also with danger and suspicion in general.[50] Even people who are perceived as Muslim, regardless of their actual religious affiliation—particularly Sikh American men, because of their turbans and beards—are frequently assaulted verbally or physically, demonstrating the embeddedness of Islamophobia in America. Muslims across America and throughout the world have witnessed Islam become synonymous with terrorism and their own identities become homogenized and stigmatized. Just as Islam is perceived as a rigid monolith espousing violence, Muslim Americans are more often than not regarded as Muslim only; often, the intersectionality of their many identities is overlooked.[51] This is especially true of Muslim women who are visibly Muslim because they choose to wear the hijab, a scarf that covers the hair and often the neck while keeping the face visible. It is only through realigning the current American counterterrorism approach toward holistic justice that the multiplicity of intersecting identities of Muslim Americans will be acknowledged, their many modes of religious expression will be understood, and their cultural diversity will be respected. In turn, recognizing these elements will disassemble the detrimental myth that all Muslims are actually inherently militant and somehow foreign to their own country while enabling the acknowledgment of the heterogenous experiences of Muslim Americans.

Significantly, though Islam is often portrayed as an insidious threat to the American way of life, what is erased, forgotten, unheard, or silenced is the incontrovertible fact that for as long as America has been a nation, there have been Muslim Americans. Black Muslims were some of the first people to come to the land that would become the United States, arriving unwillingly as slaves as early as the 1500s. Even though it was crime for slaves to read, some Muslim American slaves kept a copy of the Qur'an to recite, and their education was often exploited by their owners.[52] The legacy of these Black Muslims is extraordinary: they not only provided the labor that built America in its formative years but also fought alongside colonists in the Revolutionary War and served in the Union Army in the Civil War, conflicts in which they were noted for their valor and determination.[53] They were integral to the founding and development of the United States.

Furthermore, the roots of Islam in the United States are as old as the nation itself. The Judeo-Christian lineage that is so often touted by those on the political far right as being part and parcel of America and as having shaped the Founding Fathers' conceptions of the United States actually includes Islam. The Qur'an, which has been housed in American public libraries since at least 1683, constantly brings attention to Islam's connection to the Jewish and Christian faiths because Islam views the Qur'an as the final successor to the Torah and Bible. Members of the political far right, especially militant White nationalists, and militant Islamists ignore this basic precept of Muslim faith—a willful or simply uneducated omission that religious literacy seeks to address. It was one of America's Founding Fathers, John Adams, who owned and read copies of the Qur'an, who insisted that the United States was "not in any sense founded upon the Christian religion" and therefore has "no character of enmity against the laws, religion and tranquility of Mussulmen."[54] Indeed, there are many parallels between the ideals of the American Constitution, however flawed in practice, and the lessons of the Qur'an and the example of the Prophet Muhammad. The First Amendment allows for freedom of religious expression; so, too, does the Qur'an: "There is no compulsion in religion. . . . To you be your way, and to me mine."[55] Diversity is part of God's doing: "Another of His Signs is the creation of the heavens and the earth, and the diversity of your languages and colors" (Qur'an 30:22).[56] Reinforcing the notion that the concept of race is illusory, this verse is a reminder to humanity of its shared lineage and a call to all people to connect with one another out of love, seeking to understand each other—not to abstain from interconnection due to fear, bigotry, or hate. And just as the Constitution guarantees equal rights to all, regardless of religion, the Qur'an does not guarantee salvation and heaven explicitly to Muslims, or to any group, but instead addresses the "Children of Adam" throughout, instructing that those who are righteous shall be rewarded, because only God truly knows the heart and intentions of every person. Islam thus teaches that salvation is not reserved for a particular group of people, but for any who believe in God, perform good deeds with good intentions, and hold themselves accountable to the impending Last Day.[57]

Islam has throughout its history frequently been expressed as pluralistic, multicultural, and a bastion of justice and freedom. There are many examples of respect for humanity and holistic justice throughout

Islam's global history, including the fertile coexistence of Islam, Judaism, and Christianity in medieval Spain; the Ottoman Empire, and especially Baghdad, from the seventh to the thirteenth centuries, what is now termed the Golden Age of Islam; and the courage of Muslims in Albania, who harbored Jewish refugees during World War II.[58] Far from being threats to American values, Muslim Americans today are inheritors of the legacy of pluralism, cultural sensitivity, and connectivity that made these historical communities so dynamic and productive—values that are central to American identity and spirit as well.[59]

Reclaiming Jesus from White Nationalism

Whereas Islam and Muslim Americans are popularly seen as completely foreign to the United States, Christianity is generally viewed as innate to America. As this book has examined, the Christianist White nationalist justification of violence has been built on centuries-old racist tensions that are cloaked in religious and sacred expression. For its part, American Christianity in various forms has had a contentious history from the outset, having been used to justify centuries of slavery, Jim Crow segregation, eugenics, White nationalism, structural racism, prejudice, discrimination, and groups like the Ku Klux Klan, while also being called on to validate abolition, integration, equality, justice, and diversity.[60]

But the current resurgence in White nationalist evocations of Christianity has sparked an existential debate among American Black and White evangelicals, and Christian communities generally, on what it means to be Christian in an era when White Christendom is no longer the norm and political leaders espouse xenophobia, discrimination, prejudice, and misogyny. Throughout the duration of his first term in office, President Trump's nativist rhetoric and White ethnonationalist policies caused consternation within various Christian denominations and among Christian people of color.

Intrafaith engagement in response to Trump's presidency has resulted in a movement called Reclaiming Jesus, as well as a revival of the Reverend Dr. Martin Luther King Jr.'s Poor People's Campaign, which he had been formulating at the time of his assassination in 1968. Reclaiming Jesus and the Poor People's Campaign counter the White nationalist promotion of Jesus as a White warrior god and Christianity as a religion espousing holy war with a vision of Jesus as a figure of peace and of Christianity as grounds for antiracist practice.

Utilizing the same Christian precept of the *imago dei* that is exploited by White nationalists, who claim they alone are made in God's likeness, the prominent Christians behind Reclaiming Jesus argue that Christianity denies racist bigotry. If one believes that Jesus was a light-skinned White man, the oppression of people with more of a specific type of melanin by centuries of enslavers was justified. Frederick Douglass wrote, eloquently as ever, of the dichotomy between the Christianity he practiced and that which was practiced by the enslaver: "The man who wields the blood-clotted cowskin during the week fills the pulpit on Sunday and claims to be a minister of the meek and lowly Jesus."[61] According to Douglass, the "infernal business" of the violent subjugation of Black people was only reinforced by "the pulpit," to which "the dealer gives his blood-stained gold," receiving in exchange the cover of "the garb of Christianity."[62] However, in omnipresent hope, Douglass asserted the antislavery message of the Christianity in which he believed: "The glorious principle, of love to God and love to man; which makes its followers do unto others as the themselves would be done by."[63] The National Association of Evangelicals also issued a statement directed toward churches and pastors to "combat attitudes and systems that perpetuate racism."[64]

This Christian argument is that all humans are made in God's likeness; the *imago dei* "confers a divinely decreed dignity, worth, and God-given equality to all," which makes racial bigotry "a brutal denial of the image of God." Twenty-three prominent Christian leaders, among them Bishop Michael Curry, presiding bishop of the Episcopal Church; Richard Rohr, Catholic priest and famed spiritual writer; and Jim Wallis, an evangelical and founder of *Sojourners* magazine, issued this statement in *Reclaiming Jesus: A Confession of Faith in a Time of Crisis* as part of a declaration denouncing the utilization of religion to promote a White nationalist political agenda.[65]

The rhetoric, propaganda, and rationales for violence of self-styled Christian holy warriors who see themselves as fighting for White identity are disavowed as "public sin" by the Christians of Reclaiming Jesus. The movement also rejects as theological heresy misogyny, attacks on immigrants and refugees, lying for political gain, authoritarian rule, and "America first"-style xenophobic nationalism.

A 2020 revitalization of King's Poor People's Campaign, describing itself as "a national call for moral revival," led by two Protestant ministers, William Barber II and Liz Theoharis, similarly seeks to "confront the interlocking evils of systemic racism, poverty, ecological devastation, militarism and the war economy, and the distorted moral narrative of religious nationalism."[66] Citing the Old Testament, the New Testament, and even the Qur'an (4:135), as well as the Declaration of Independence and the U.S. Constitution, this movement strives to realize the equality endowed by God in scriptures and recognized by the legal founding documents of the United States, despite some instances of hypocrisy in these sources. Seeking to reassert Christian values regarding caring for the most vulnerable in American society, Reclaiming Jesus and the Poor People's Campaign are working to dismantle the theological racism that has justified the labeling of Indigenous Americans as heathens, supported the institution of slavery, and continues to uphold Whiteness as a sign of the favor of God.[67]

Reclaiming Runes from Racists

Like Muslims and Christians around the world, nonmilitant Odinists, who call themselves Ásatrúers, are also now struggling to separate their religion and its symbols, such as runes, and concepts like blood and soil, from the violence and racism of the militant activists. Ásatrúers also contest the centrality of the concept of blood and soil, which many White nationalists adopt to justify their claim to racial superiority.[68] The number of American militant Wotanists is disproportionately high in relation to the number of Odinists in the United States compared to the number of militant Islamists in relation to Muslim Americans, for example, though there are far fewer American Ásatrúers than Muslim Americans.

Ásatrú has recently seen a revival in the lands where it was practiced a millennium ago. It is the fastest growing religion in Iceland, and both Iceland and Denmark have built their first temples, or *hofs,* in hundreds of years. The White nationalist organization Asatru Folk Assembly established a *hof* in Brownsville, California, in 2015, and another in Murdock, Minnesota, in 2020.[69] But the relationship that many practitioners have to the principle of blood and soil is complicated. Many, like Hilmar Örn Hilmarsson, the high priest of the Association of Ásatrúers in Iceland, focus on the faith's environmentalism and reject any claims that it is inherently racist.[70] But other prominent figures, such as Stephen McNallen of the Asatru Folk Assembly, which established the Óðinshof in California, view Ásatrú as a religion that specifically upholds racial ties to White European ancestry. McNallen has written extensively, and controversially, on eugenics.[71] A diluted version of this adherence to blood and soil is also present within the rules of the Association of Ásatrúers: though anyone can practice its faith, only Icelandic citizens or people who have a domicile in Iceland can become members.

Hilmarsson's predecessor, Sveinbjörn Beinteinsson, cut all formal ties with foreign congregations in the 1980s because of alarm at the nativist and nationalist reading of the religion. According to Hilmarsson, the sacred text of the Eddas are not meant to be literal but instead to serve as metaphors about the changing course of life and the nature of human psychology.[72] Rejecting what he calls modern inventions, Hilmarsson preaches Ásatrú as a religion whose position is fundamentally different from that of the Abrahamic faiths, in that it is not "one truth for many people" but "many truths for one person." The fluidity of gender identity within the pantheon of Norse gods is one such example of this: the Eddas depict the god Thor impersonating the goddess Freyja and marrying a king to recover his hammer, Mjölnir, because the king had demanded her hand in marriage in exchange for it.

While many Muslim Americans seek for Islam to be recognized as integral to the founding and flourishing of the United States, and many Christian Americans look to disentangle Christianity from those who endorse racial oppression and injustice, Ásatrúers are attempting to rescue their religious traditions from the racism of Wotanists by asserting the environmentalism, inclusivity, and gender fluidity of their faith.[73]

In the United States, nonmilitant Odinists have organized to publicly denounce racist readings of their religion and to reclaim the symbolic value of their runes and rituals. These groups include Heathens United against Racism, the Asatru Community, the Troth, and Alliance for Inclusive Heathenry. In August 2016, forty-three pagan organizations signed Declaration 127, a public renunciation of any form of Ásatrú or Odinism that promotes hatred or discrimination.[74] Since then, more than 180 organizations in dozens of countries have signed the declaration. In 2017, a declaration titled "The Shieldwall," referencing a traditional Viking formation of fighters protecting themselves with shields on the battlefield, was issued by a coalition of Ásatrú groups and individuals calling for a global alliance against racism and nationalism.[75]

E PLURIBUS UNUM: RECOGNIZING OUR COMMON HUMANITY

Ours is a crucial period for the homeland security, economic prosperity, and social stability of the United States. The distances across identities, including religious, socioeconomic, and political strata, have never seemed more expansive. The United States has always been replete with contradictions—simultaneously calling for liberty while taking away the freedom of its citizens, espousing equity while minoritizing Black and Brown Americans, professing justice while institutionalizing asymmetrical oppression—and, at present, the United States is teetering on the precipice of choice between light and dark, constructive and destructive, to empower all equitably or to bestow benefits upon only the few. For the religiously minded, God will judge; for the atheistic or agnostic, history is the ultimate arbiter. It is both a moral imperative and in our collective self-interest to make the choice to benefit from holistic justice, which is for all, rather than to wreak mutually assured destruction by collectively disavowing one another. In the final analysis, it is only by fully recognizing our common humanity that we will be able to strive toward mutual peace and prosperity on this planet we all share.

Notes

INTRODUCTION

1. Despite the symbolism of Charlottesville in the American vernacular for organized White nationalist violence, the Unite the Right rally was actually not the first such protest the city had witnessed. In May 2017, just three months prior, Richard Spencer, president of the National Policy Institute, a White nationalist think tank, led a rally of torch-wielding protesters at the same Confederate monument.

2. Jason Hanna, Kaylee Hartung, Devon M. Sayers, and Steve Almasy, "Virginia Governor to White Nationalists: 'Go Home, Shame on You,'" *CNN*, posted August 12, 2017, updated August 13, 2017, www.cnn.com/2017/08/12 /us/charlottesville-white-nationalists-rally/index.html; Jonah Engel Bromwich and Alan Blinder, "What We Know about James Alex Fields, Driver Charged in Charlottesville Killing," *New York Times*, August 13, 2017, www.nytimes .com/2017/08/13/us/james-alex-fields-charlottesville-driver-.html; Charlie Savage and Rebecca R. Ruiz, "Sessions Emerges as Forceful Figure in Condemning Charlottesville Violence," *New York Times*, August 14, 2017, www.nytimes .com/2017/08/14/us/politics/domestic-terrorism-sessions.html.

3. Ian Shapira, "Inside Jason Kessler's Hate-Fueled Rise," *Washington Post*, August 11, 2018, www.washingtonpost.com/local/inside-jason-kesslers-hate-fueled-rise/2018/08/11/335eaf42-999e-11e8-b60b-1c897f17e185_story.html.

4. Hanna, Hartung, Sayers, and Almasy, "Virginia Governor to White Nationalists." For more on the role of development of political correctness and cancel culture within the political far right, see Moira Weigel, "Political Correctness: How the Right Invented a Phantom Enemy," *Guardian* (UK), November 30, 2016, www.theguardian.com/us-news/2016/nov/30/political-correctness-how-the-right-invented-phantom-enemy-donald-trump, Accessed June 17, 2020; Ed Kilgore, "'Political Incorrectness' Is Just 'Political Correctness' for Conservatives,"

Intelligencer (blog), *New York Magazine,* July 17, 2018, https://nymag.com /intelligencer/2018/07/anti-pc-is-political-correctness-for-the-right.html; Chi Luu, "Cancel Culture Is Chaotic Good," *JSTOR Daily* (blog), December 18, 2019, https://daily.jstor.org/cancel-culture-is-chaotic-good; Brandon Tensley, "Cancel Culture is About Power—Who Has It and Who Wants to Be Heard," *CNN,* July 10, 2020, www.msn.com/en-us/news/us/cancel-culture-is-about-power-who-has-it-and-who-wants-to-be-heard/ar-BB16AMo5; and Ryan Lizza, "Americans Tune In to 'Cancel Culture'—and Don't Like What They See," *Politico,* July 22, 2020, www.politico.com/news/2020/07/22/americans-cancel-culture-377412.

5. "Deconstructing the Symbols and Slogans Spotted in Charlottesville," *Washington Post,* August 18, 2017, www.washingtonpost.com/graphics/2017 /local/charlottesville-videos/?utm_term=.79827638793a.

6. Aja Romero, "Richard Spencer Is an Infamous White Nationalist. Twitter Says He's Not Part of a Hate Group," *Vox,* September 5, 2018, www.vox .com/2018/9/4/17816936/why-wont-twitter-ban-richard-spencer-hate-groups . The mission statement of the National Policy Institute reinforces the themes of White nationalism, describing itself as an "independent organization dedicated to the heritage, identity, and future of people of European descent in the United States." "About," National Policy Institute, accessed June 29, 2020, https:// nationalpolicy.institute/whoarewe.

7. Ben Klassen, *The White Man's Bible* (Lighthouse Point, FL: Church of the Creator, 1981), 11.

8. Sophie Bjork-James and Jeff Maskovsky, "When White Nationalism Became Popular: Populism Rising," *Anthropology News,* May 18, 2017, www .anthropology-news.org/index.php/2017/05/18/when-white-nationalism-became-popular. For an overview of the notion of White identity throughout American political history, see Alexander Saxton, *The Rise and Fall of the White Republic: Class Politics and Mass Culture in Nineteenth Century America* (London: Verso, 2010).

9. In his seminal work, *Orientalism,* first published in 1978, Edward Said, founder of postcolonial studies, argued that the ontological and epistemological disparities between Islam and the West that resulted in negative perceptions of the Islamic world were an extension of colonial European power dynamics.

10. Kate Manne, *Down Girl: The Logic of Misogyny* (Oxford: Oxford University Press, 2017). For an understanding of the role of misogyny in militancy in South and Southeast Asia, see Katherine E. Brown, David Duriesmith, Farhana Rahman, and Jacqui True, "Conflicting Identities: The Nexus Between Masculinities, Femininities, and Violent Extremism in Asia," UN Women, March 25, 2020, www.unwomen.org/en/digital-library/publications/2020/03 /conflicting-identities-the-nexus-between-masculinities-femininities-and-violent-extremism-in-asia.

11. See Kathleen M. Blee, "Becoming a Racist: Women in Contemporary Ku Klux Klan and Neo-Nazi Groups," in *The Populist Radical Right: A Reader,* ed. Cas Mudde (New York: Routledge, 2017), 258–76; Kathleen M. Blee, *Women of the Klan: Racism and Gender in the 1920s* (Berkeley: University of California Press, 1991); Seyward Darby, *Sisters in Hate: American Women on the Front Lines of White Nationalism* (Boston: Little, Brown, 2020); Jessica Davis, *Women*

in Modern Terrorism: From Liberation Wars to Global Jihad and the Islamic State (Lanham, MD: Rowman and Littlefield, 2017); Beverley Milton-Edwards and Sumiya Attia, "Female Terrorists and Their Role in Jihadi Groups," Brookings Institute, May 9, 2017, www.brookings.edu/opinions/female-terrorists-and-their-role-in-jihadi-groups; Lydia Khalil, "Behind the Veil: Women in Jihad after the Caliphate," Lowy Institute, June, 25, 2019, www.lowyinstitute.org/publications /behind-veil-women-jihad-after-caliphate; Center on Extremism, "When Women Are the Enemy: The Intersection of Misogyny and White Supremacy," Anti-Defamation League, 2018, www.adl.org/resources/reports/when-women-are-the-enemy-the-intersection-of-misogyny-and-white-supremacy; Aja Romano, "How the Alt-Right's Sexism Lures Men into White Supremacy," *Vox*, April 26, 2018, www.vox.com/culture/2016/12/14/13576192/alt-right-sexism-recruitment; Elle Reeve, "She Went from a Liberal Non-Voter to Burning Books with White Supremacists. Here's Why She Finally Left the Movement," *CNN*, October 31, 2019, www.cnn.com/2019/10/30/us/white-supremacist-woman-reeve/index.html; Alia E. Dastagir, "Mass Shootings and Misogyny: The Violent Ideology We Can't Ignore," *USA Today*, August 6, 2019, www.usatoday.com/story/news/nation /2019/08/06/shooting-ohio-dayton-el-paso-texas-shooter-gilroy-california /1924532001; Nina Burleigh, "Hatred of Women Is Jihadism's First Pillar," *Newsweek*, January 10, 2016, www.newsweek.com/hatred-first-pillar-jihadism-413710; and Sara Posner, *Unholy: Why White Evangelicals Worship at the Altar of Donald Trump* (New York: Penguin Random House, 2020). For more on the role of White women in maintaining White supremacy, see Elizabeth Gillespie McRae, *Mothers of Massive Resistance: White Women and the Politics of White Supremacy* (Oxford: Oxford University Press, 2018).

12. This book focuses on Sunni Islam, but for Shi'i responses to various Sunni militant Islamist actors and the interaction between them, see Christopher Anzalone, "In the Shadow of the Islamic State: Shi'i Responses to Sunni Jihadist Narratives in a Turbulent Middle East," in *Jihadism Transformed: Al-Qaeda and Islamic State's Global Battle of Ideas,* ed. Simon Staffell and Akil N. Awan (Oxford: Oxford University Press, 2016), 157–82. For a study of terrorism committed in the name of Shi'i Islam, see Matthew Levitt, *Hezbollah: The Global Footprint of Lebanon's Party of God* (Washington, DC: Georgetown University Press, 2015).

13. Joe Ilardi Gaetano, "Redefining the Issues: The Future of Terrorism Research and the Search for Empathy," in *Research on Terrorism: Trends, Achievements and Failures,* ed. Andrew Silke (London: Frank Cass, 2004), 214–28.

14. United States Government Accountability Office, "Countering Violent Extremism: Actions Needed to Define Strategy and Assess Progress of Federal Efforts (GAO-17-300),", April 2017, www.gao.gov/assets/690/683984.pdf; David Neiwert, "Far-Right Extremists Have Hatched Far More Terror Plots Than Anyone Else in Recent Years," *Reveal*, June 22, 2017, www.revealnews.org/article /home-is-where-the-hate-is; Janet Reitman, "U.S. Law Enforcement Failed to See the Threat of White Nationalism. Now They Don't Know How to Stop It," *New York Times*, November 3, 2018, www.nytimes.com/2018/11/03/magazine/FBI-charlottesville-white-nationalism-far-right.html; Peter Bergen, Albert Ford, Alyssa

Sims, and David Sterman, "Part IV. What Is the Threat to the United States Today?" New America, www.newamerica.org/in-depth/terrorism-in-america/what-threat-united-states-today; Anti-Defamation League, "Murder and Extremism in the United States in 2016: An Anti-Defamation League Report," 2017, www.adl.org/combating-hate/domestic-extremism-terrorism/c/murder-and-extremism-2016.html; David Neiwert, "Charlottesville Underscores How Homegrown Hate Is Going Unchecked," *Reveal,* last updated August 14, 2017, www.revealnews.org/article/home-is-where-the-hate-is. For a database of domestic terrorism plots and attacks, see David Neiwert, Darren Ankrom, Esther Kaplan, and Scott Pham, "Homegrown Terror: Explore Nine Years of Domestic Terrorism Plots and Attacks," *Reveal,* June 22, 2017, https://apps.revealnews.org/homegrown-terror. Another database, listing only acts of violence classified as antigovernment, compiled by J.J. MacNab, a fellow at the Program on Extremism at the George Washington University Center for Cyber and Homeland Security, can be found at "Anti-Government Extremist Violence and Plots: 2000 to 2018," last updated March 24, 2018, www.seditionists.com/antigovviolence.pdf.

15. United States Department of Homeland Security, "Rightwing Extremism: Current Economic and Political Climate Fueling Resurgence in Radicalization and Recruitment," Office of Intelligence and Analysis Assessment, April 7, 2009, p. 7, available at www.fas.org/irp/eprint/rightwing.pdf.

16. Heidi Beirich, "Inside the DHS: Former Top Analyst Says Agency Bowed to Political Pressure," *Intelligence Report,* Southern Poverty Law Center, 2011 Summer Issue, June 17, 2011, www.splcenter.org/get-informed/intelligence-report/browse-all-issues/2011/summer/inside-the-dhs-former-top-analyst-says-agency-bowed.

The Southern Poverty Law Center, often referred to by its acronym, SPLC, is an organization whose mission is "fighting hate and bigotry and seeking justice for the most vulnerable members of our society." However, it is not without controversy. It has been accused of casting too broad a net when identifying hate groups, though the organization claims to use a definition that is similar to that used by the FBI to define hate crimes. Creating maps of active hate groups in the United States, as determined by the SPLC, is a central feature of the organization's work. See Jessica Prol Smith, "The Southern Poverty Law Center Is a Hate-Based Scam That Nearly Caused Me to Be Murdered," *USA Today,* August 18, 2019, www.usatoday.com/story/opinion/2019/08/17/southern-poverty-law-center-hate-groups-scam-column/2022301001; David Montgomery, "The State of Hate," *Washington Post Magazine,* November 8, 2018, www.washingtonpost.com/news/magazine/wp/2018/11/08/feature/is-the-southern-poverty-law-center-judging-hate-fairly; and "Southern Poverty Law Center Brands Some Peaceful Groups as 'Hate Groups,'" *Fox News,* July 14, 2017, www.foxnews.com/us/2017/07/14/southern-poverty-law-center-brands-some-peaceful-groups-as-hate-groups.html. On the origins of the Southern Poverty Law Center, see Elinor Langer, *A Hundred Little Hitlers: The Death of a Black Man, the Trial of a White Racist, and the Rise of the Neo-Nazi Movement in America* (New York: Metropolitan Books, 2003), 330–55.

17. Ron Nixon, "Homeland Security Looked Past Antigovernment Movement, Ex-Analyst Says," *New York Times,* January 8, 2016, www.nytimes

.com/2016/01/09/us/politics/homeland-security-looked-past-militia-movement-ex-analyst-says.html.

18. Jennifer Hansler, "DHS Shifts Focus of Funding to Counter Violent Extremism," *CNN*, July 4, 2017, www.cnn.com/2017/07/01/politics/cve-funding-changes/index.html; FBI, "White Supremist Extremism Poses Persistent Threat of Lethal Violence," Joint Intelligence Bulletin, May 10, 2017, available at www.documentcloud.org/documents/3924852-White-Supremacist-Extremism-JIB.html.

19. Neiwert, Ankrom, Kaplan, and Pham, "Homegrown Terror."

20. United States Government Accountability Office, "Countering Violent Extremism."

21. Charles Kurzman, "Muslim-American Involvement with Violent Extremism, 2001–2019," Triangle Center on Terrorism and Homeland Security, January 21, 2020, p. 2, available at https://drive.google.com/file/d/1JmL7MjWCSwV2j YEu1fEUdVtCUXE3pA46/view.

22. For a discussion of White privilege, see Frances E. Kendall, *Understanding White Privilege: Creating Pathways to Authentic Relationships across Race* (New York: Routledge, 2013).

23. Kimberly A. Powell, "Framing Islam/Creating Fear: An Analysis of U.S. Media Coverage of Terrorism from 2011–2016," *Religions* 9, no. 9 (2018): 257, https://doi.org/10.3390/rel9090257; Erin M. Kearns, Allison E. Betus, and Anthony F. Lemieux, "Why Do Some Terrorist Attacks Receive More Media Attention Than Others?" *Justice Quarterly* 36, no. 6 (2019): 985–1022, https://doi.org/10.1080/07418825.2018.1524507; Charles Kurzman, *The Missing Martyrs: Why There Are So Few Muslim Terrorists* (Oxford: Oxford University Press, 2018).

24. Andrew Dunn, "Resolution Denouncing Neo-Nazis Dies in Tennessee Legislature for Second Time," *CNN*, April 5, 2018, www.cnn.com/2018/04/04 /politics/tennessee-legislature-white-nationalist-resolution/index.html.

25. Confronting Violent White Supremacy (Part II): Adequacy of the Federal Response, Hearing before the Subcommittee on Civil Rights and Civil Liberties of the Committee on Oversight and Reform of the House of Representatives, 116th Congress, First Session, June 4, 2019, Serial no. 116–32, p. 4, www.govinfo.gov /content/pkg/CHRG-116hhrg36828/pdf/CHRG-116hhrg36828.pdf.

26. Zolan Kanno-Youngs, "Homeland Security Dept. Affirms Threat of White Supremacy after Years of Prodding," *New York Times*, October 1, 2019, www.nytimes.com/2019/10/01/us/politics/white-supremacy-homeland-security .html; "White Supremacists Double Down on Propaganda in 2019," Center on Extremism, Anti-Defamation League, February 2020, www.adl.org/media/14038 /download.

27. Hannah Allam, "FBI Announces That Racist Violence Is Now Equal Priority to Foreign Terrorism," *NPR*, February 10, 2020, www.npr.org/2020/02/10 /804616715/fbi-announces-that-racist-violence-is-now-equal-priority-to-foreign-terrorism; Christopher Wray, "Statement before the House Judiciary Committee," FBI, February 5, 2020, www.fbi.gov/news/testimony/fbi-oversight-020520; Christopher Wray, "FBI Oversight Hearing," C-SPAN, February 5, 2020, www .c-span.org/video/?468923–1/fbi-director-wray-testifies-oversight-hearing.

28. Associated Press, "In a First, U.S. Slaps Sanctions on Russian White Supremacists," *Politico,* April 6, 2020, www.politico.com/news/2020/04/06/russia-white-supremicist-sanctions-169275; Daniel Byman, "The U.S. Government Is Finally Getting Tough on White Nationalist Terrorism," *Foreign Policy,* April 6, 2020, https://foreignpolicy.com/2020/04/06/the-u-s-government-is-finally-getting-tough-on-white-nationalist-terrorism; Charlie Savage, Adam Goldman, and Eric Schmitt, "U.S. Will Give Terrorist Label to White Supremacist Group for First Time," *New York Times,* April 6, 2020, www.nytimes.com/2020/04/06/us/politics/terrorist-label-white-supremacy-Russian-Imperial-Movement.html.

29. Devlin Barrett, "FBI Faces Skepticism over Its Efforts against Domestic Terrorism," *Washington Post,* August 15, 2019, www.washingtonpost.com/national-security/fbi-faces-skepticism-over-its-anti-domestic-terror-efforts/2019/08/04/c9c928bc-b6e0-11e9-b3b4-2bb69e8c4e39_story.html; Donald J. Trump, "National Strategy for Counterterrorism of the United States of America," White House, October 2018, p. 10, www.whitehouse.gov/wp-content/uploads/2018/10/NSCT.pdf.

30. For an exposé of this symbiosis, see Stuart Stevens, *It Was All a Lie: How the Republican Party Became Donald Trump* (New York: Knopf, 2020). For an examination of how the media amplified and normalized Donald Trump's racist, conspiratorial worldview, see Brian Stelter, *Hoax: Donald Trump, Fox News, and the Dangerous Distortion of Truth* (New York: One Signal Publishers, 2020).

31. *Breitbart,* an online platform for the alt-right whose executive chairman is Steve Bannon, once chief advisor and strategist to President Trump, emphasizes the intellectual roots of the alt-right and says of its constituency only that it is made up of "mostly white, mostly male middle-American radicals, who are unapologetically embracing a new identity politics that prioritizes the interests of their own demographic." Allum Bokhari and Milo Yiannopoulos, "An Establishment Conservative's Guide to the Alt-Right," *Breitbart,* March 29, 2016, www.breitbart.com/tech/2016/03/29/an-establishment-conservatives-guide-to-the-alt-right. The National Policy Institute has a mission statement that echoes the concept of Anglo-Israelism (see chapter 1), in which it describes itself as an "independent organization dedicated to the heritage, identity, and future of people of European descent in the United States." "About," National Policy Institute. For some examples of how people whom I call White nationalists prefer to self-identify, see Joe Sterling, "White Nationalism, a Term Once on the Fringes, Now Front and Center," *CNN,* November 17, 2016, www.cnn.com/2016/11/16/politics/what-is-white-nationalism-trnd/index.html; Rebel Redneck 59, "What is White Racialism?" *Stormfront,* March, 25, 2011, 4:48 a.m., www.stormfront.org/forum/t789365; and Richard Spencer, "'Vikings' and the Pagan-Christian Synthesis," *Radix Journal,* December 2, 2014, www.radixjournal.com/journal/vikings-pagan-christian-synthesis..

32. One influential advisor to President Trump is Stephen Miller, who has been a guiding force in the administration's anti-immigration policies. See Jean Guerrero, *Hatemonger: Stephen Miller, Donald Trump, and the White Nationalist Agenda* (New York, NY: HarperCollins, 2020). One example of how attacks on minoritized groups have increased during Trump's presidency are

assaults against Muslim Americans, which in 2016 surpassed the previous peak, reached in 2001 after the September 11 terrorist attacks, which then triggered virulent Islamophobia across the nation. See Katayoun Kishi, "Assaults against Muslims in U.S. Surpass 2001 Level," Fact Tank, Pew Research Center, November 15, 2017, www.pewresearch.org/fact-tank/2017/11/15/assaults-against-muslims-in-u-s-surpass-2001-level. For more on President Donald Trump's conspiracy theories, see Peter Nicholas, "Trump Needs Conspiracy Theories," *Atlantic*, November 29, 2019, www.theatlantic.com/politics/archive/2019/11/trump-conspiracy-theories-ukraine/602728; and Jeremy Venook, "20 Conspiracy Theories Trump Has Pushed before and during His Presidency," Center for American Progress, May 19, 2020, www.americanprogressaction.org/issues/democracy/news/2020/05/19/177746/20-conspiracy-theories-trump-pushed-presidency.

33. "Foreword: America Burns," *One Ummah*, no. 2 (June 2020): 7; Robert Windrem, "ISIS, Al Qaeda Use Trump to Rally Jihadis," *NBC News*, May 19, 2017, www.nbcnews.com/storyline/isis-uncovered/isis-al-qaeda-use-trump-rally-jihadis-n762201; Frank Gardner, "George Floyd Death: Al-Qaeda Tries to Exploit US Unrest," *BBC*, June 11, 2020, www.bbc.com/news/world-us-canada-52999812.

34. Aileen Graef, "Trump: 'I Am Not a Racist,'" *CNN*, January 15, 2018, www.cnn.com/2018/01/14/politics/donald-trump-racist/index.html; Ian Haney López, *Dog Whistle Politics: How Coded Racial Appeals Have Reinvented Racism and Wrecked the Middle Class* (Oxford: Oxford University Press, 2015).

35. William Cummings, "'I Am a Nationalist': Trump's Embrace of Controversial Label Sparks Uproar," *USA Today*, November 12, 2018, www.usatoday.com/story/news/politics/2018/10/24/trump-says-hes-nationalist-what-means-why-its-controversial/1748521002.

36. Maric C. Baca, "Who Was Who at Trump's Social Media Summit," *Washington Post*, July 11, 2019, www.washingtonpost.com/technology/2019/07/11/who-was-who-trumps-social-media-summit.

37. Donald Trump (@RealDonaldTrump), "So interesting to see 'Progressive' Democrat Congresswomen," Twitter, July 24, 2019, 2:27 p.m., https://twitter.com/realDonaldTrump/status/1150381394234941448.

38. Glenn Kessler, "A Look at Trump's Birther Statement," *Washington Post*, April 28, 2011, www.washingtonpost.com/blogs/fact-checker/post/a-look-at-trumps-birther-statements/2011/04/27/AFeOYb1E_blog.html; Chris Moody and Kristen Holmes, "Donald Trump's History of Suggesting Obama Is a Muslim," *CNN*, September 18, 2015, www.cnn.com/2015/09/18/politics/trump-obama-muslim-birther/index.html.

39. Emma Grey Ellis, "That Racist Kamala Harris Birther Conspiracy Is Nothing New," *Wired*, August 19, 2020, www.wired.com/story/kamala-harris-racist-conspiracy-theories.

40. Donald Trump (@RealDonaldTrump), "....horrible BLM chant, 'Pigs In A Blanket, Fry 'Em Like Bacon'. Maybe our GREAT Police, who have been neutralized and scorned by a mayor who hates & disrespects them, won't let this symbol of hate be affixed to New York's greatest street. Spend this money

fighting crime instead!," Twitter, July 1, 2020, 3:48 p.m., https://twitter.com /realDonaldTrump/status/1278324681477689349.

41. Donald Trump (@RealDonaldTrump), "This is a battle to save the Heritage, History, and Greatness of our Country! #MAGA2020," Twitter, June 30, 2020, 1:00 a.m., https://twitter.com/realdonaldtrump/status/1278101078165372929.

42. Associated Press, "County Democratic Chairman Compared MAGA Hats to KKK Hoods," July 23, 2019, https://apnews.com/82ce58a5167f4005bbb9991 64caa9677; Naomi Shaven, "The Confederate Flag Is a Racist Symbol. Just Ask the KKK," *New Republic*, July 1, 2015, https://newrepublic.com/article/122216 /confederate-flag-still-flying-today-because-kkk; Reuters, "Nancy Pelosi Says Trump Wants to Make America White Again—Video," *Guardian* (UK), July 9, 2019, www.theguardian.com/global/video/2019/jul/09/nancy-pelosi-says-trump-wants-to-make-america-white-again-video; Robert A. Stribley, "The MAGA Hat Rorschach Test," *Medium*, February 5, 2019, https://medium.com/s/story/the-maga-hat-rorschach-test-41f466364cfc; Justin Wise, "Trump on Confederate Flag: It's 'Freedom of Speech,'" *The Hill*, July 7, 2020, https://thehill.com /homenews/administration/506320-trump-on-confederate-flag-its-freedom-of-speech. For academic studies researching the Confederate flag as a symbol of racism, see Christopher A. Cooper and H. Gibbs Knotts, "Region, Race and Support for the South Carolina Confederate Flag," Social Science Quarterly 87, no. 1 (2006): 142–54, https://doi.org/10.1111/j.0038-4941.2006.00373.x; Joyce Erhlinger et al., "How Exposure to the Confederate Flag Affects Willingness to Vote for Barack Obama," *Political Psychology* 32, no. 1 (2011): 131–46, https:// doi.org/10.1111/j.1467-9221.2010.00797.x; Jessica Halliday Hardie and Karolyn Tyson, "Other People's Racism: Race, Rednecks and Riots in a Southern High School," Sociology of Education 86, no. 1 (2013): 83-102, https:// doi.org/10.1177/0038040712456554; Lori Holyfield, Matthew Ryan Moltz, and Mindy S. Bradley, "Race Discourse and the U.S. Confederate Flag," Race, Ethnicity and Education 12, no. 4 (2009): 517–37, https://doi.org/10.1080 /13613320903364481; Scott L. Moeschberger, "Heritage or Hatred: The Confederate Battle Flag and Current Race Relations in the U.S.A.," in Symbols that Bind: The Semiotics of Peace and Conflict, Symbols that Divide, Peace Psychology, ed. Scott L. Moeschberger and Rebekah A. Philips De Zalia, (Cham, Switzerland: Springer International, 2014), 207–18; Hemant Shah and Seungahn Nah, "Long Ago and Far Away: How U.S. Newspapers Construct Racial Oppression," Journalism 5, no. 3 (2004): 259–78, https://doi.org/10.1177/1464884904041659; Logan Strother, Spencer Piston, and Thomas Ogorzalek, "Pride or Prejudice? Racial Prejudice, Southern Heritage, and White Support for the Confederate Flag," Du Bois Review: Social Science Research on Race 14, no. 1 (2017): 295–323, https://doi.org/10.1017/S1742058X17000017; Gerald R. Webster and Jonathan I. Lieb, "Black, White or Green? The Confederate Battle Emblem and the 2001 Mississippi State Flag Referendum," Southeastern Geographer 52, no. 3 (2012): 299–326, https://doi.org/10.1353/sgo.2012.0029; Gerald R. Webster and Jonathan I. Lieb, "Political Culture, Religion and the Confederate Battle Flag Debate in Alabama," Journal of Cultural Geography 20, no. 1 (2002): 1–26, https://doi.org/10.1080/08873630209478279; Gerald R Webster and Jonathan I. Lieb, "Whose South Is It Anyway? Race and the Confederate Battle Flag in South

Carolina," Political Geography 20, no. 3 (2001): 271–99, https://doi.org/10.1016/S0962-6298(00)00065-2; Laura R. Woliver, Angela D. Ledford, and Chris J. Dolan, "The South Carolina Confederate Flag: The Politics of Race and Citizenship," Politics & Policy 29, no. 4 (2001): 708–30, https://doi.org/10.1111/j.1747-1346.2001.tb00612.x.

43. Donald Trump (@RealDonaldTrump), ". . ..If the Democrats are successful in removing the President from office (which they will never be), it will cause a Civil War like fracture in this Nation from which our Country will never heal.' Pastor Robert Jeffress, @FoxNews," Twitter, September 29, 2019, 3:11 a.m., https://twitter.com/realDonaldTrump/status/1178477539653771264.

44. Joseph Goldstein, "Alt-Right Gathering Exults in Trump Election with Nazi-Era Salute," New York Times, November 20, 2016, www.nytimes.com/2016/11/21/us/alt-right-salutes-donald-trump.html; Sarah Posner and David Neiwert, "How Trump Took Hate Groups Mainstream," Mother Jones, October 14, 2016, www.motherjones.com/politics/2016/10/donald-trump-hate-groups-neo-nazi-white-supremacist-racism; Eyes on the Right, "Greg Johnson Says Donald Trump Could Lead to the 'Salvation of the White Race' in America," Angry White Men (blog), May 26, 2016, https://angrywhitemen.org/2016/05/26/greg-johnson-says-donald-trump-could-lead-to-the-salvation-of-the-white-race-in-north-america.

45. Donald Trump (@RealDonaldTrump), "Thank you to the great people of The Villages. The Radical Left Do Nothing Democrats will Fall in the Fall. Corrupt Joe is shot. See you soon!!!" Twitter, June 28, 2020, 7:39 a.m., https://twitter.com/realDonaldTrump/status/1277204969561755649, post has been deleted; Benjamin Swasey, "Trump Retweets Video of Apparent Supporter Saying 'White Power,'" NPR, June 28, 2020, www.npr.org/sections/live-updates-protests-for-racial-justice/2020/06/28/884392576/trump-retweets-video-of-apparent-supporter-saying-white-power.

46. Daniel Kreiss, Regina G. Lawrence, and Shannon C. McGregor, "Political Identity Ownership: Symbolic Contests to Represent Members of the Public," Social Media + Society, April 2020, https://doi.org/10.1177/2056305120926495.

47. "Remarks by President Trump at South Dakota's 2020 Mount Rushmore Fireworks Celebration—Keystone, South Dakota," White House, July 4, 2020, www.whitehouse.gov/briefings-statements/remarks-president-trump-south-dakotas-2020-mount-rushmore-fireworks-celebration-keystone-south-dakota.

48. "Remarks by President Trump on Infrastructure," White House, August 15, 2017, www.whitehouse.gov/briefings-statements/remarks-president-trump-infrastructure.

49. Oath Keepers (@Oathkeepers), "Here's the money quote from that thread," Twitter, September 29, 2019, 7:59 a.m., https://twitter.com/oathkeepers/status/1178549790847590400.

50. An example of the rise of antisemitic violence during Donald Trump's presidency is the number of bomb threats made against Jewish community centers in the United States, and around the world, in 2017. See Matt Ferner, "Jewish Leaders Frustrated by Lack of Progress in Bomb Threat Probe," Huffington Post, March 9, 2017, www.huffingtonpost.com/entry/jcc-letter-to-jeff-sessions_us_58c06be4e4b0ed7182698e84?yxwfb5g65qyjbgldi.

51. Mitch Berbrier, "Making Minorities: Cultural Space, Stigma Transformation Frames, and the Categorical Status Claims of Deaf, Gay, and White Supremacist Activists in Late Twentieth Century America," *Sociological Forum* 17, no. 4 (2002): 553–91. For an overview of the history of the concept of the Deep State, see Mike Lofgren, *The Deep State: The Fall of the Constitution and the Rise of a Shadow Government* (New York: Penguin Books, 2016); and David Rohde, *In Deep: The FBI, the CIA, and the Truth about America's "Deep State"* (New York: W.W. Norton, 2020).

52. The number of recognized Islamophobic hate groups in the United States, which tripled over the course of 2016, during President Trump's campaign, to the highest numbers since 9/11, also lends credence this type of propaganda. See "Anti-Muslim Activities in the United States: Violence, Threats, and Discrimination at the Local Level," New America, accessed September 8, 2020, www.newamerica.org/in-depth/anti-muslim-activity; and "Hate Groups Increase for Second Consecutive Year As Trump Electrifies Radical Right," Southern Poverty Law Center, February 15, 2017, www.splcenter.org/news/2017/02/15/hate-groups-increase-second-consecutive-year-trump-electrifies-radical-right.

53. López, *Dog Whistle Politics*, 3–4.

54. Robin Wright, "President Trump's Surprisingly Warm Welcome in the Middle East," *New Yorker*, November 10, 2016, www.newyorker.com/news/news-desk/president-trumps-surprisingly-warm-welcome-in-the-middle-east.

55. Muhammad al-Maqdisi (@lmaqdese), Twitter, November 9, 2016, 1:50 p.m., twitter.com/lmaqdese/status/796278971675643904.

56. Barack Obama, "Remarks by the President at Cairo University, 6-04-09," White House, Office of the Press Secretary, June 4, 2009, https://obamawhitehouse.archives.gov/the-press-office/remarks-president-cairo-university-6-04-09.

57. John S. Rozel and Edward P. Mulvey, "The Link between Mental Illness and Firearm Violence: Implications for Social Policy and Clinical Practice," *Annual Review of Clinical Psychology* 13 (2017): 445–69; J.R. Meloy, A.G. Hempel, B.T. Gray, K. Mohandie, A. Shiva, and T.C. Richards, "A Comparative Analysis of North American Adolescent and Adult Mass Murderers," *Behavioral Sciences and the Law* 22, no. 3 (2004): 291–309; James L. Knoll IV and George D. Annas, "Mass Shootings and Mental Illness," in *Gun Violence and Mental Illness,* ed. Liza H. Gold and Robert I. Simon (Arlington, VA: American Psychiatric Publishing, 2016), 81–104; Jeffrey W. Swanson, E. Elizabeth McGinty, Seena Fazel, and Vicki M. Mays, "Mental Illness and Reduction of Gun Violence and Suicide: Bringing Epidemiologic Research to Policy," *Annals of Epidemiology* 25, no. 5 (2015): 366–76.

58. Faiza Patel, "Rethinking Radicalization," Brennan Center for Justice, March 8, 2011, p. 19-28, www.brennancenter.org/sites/default/files/legacy/RethinkingRadicalization.pdf.

59. Karen Armstrong, *Fields of Blood: Religion and the History of Violence* (New York: Anchor, 2015); William T. Cavanaugh, *The Myth of Religious Violence: Secular Ideology and the Roots of Modern Conflict* (Oxford: Oxford University Press, 2009).

60. Cavanaugh, *Myth of Religious Violence,* 58; Jeroen Gunning and Richard Jackson, "What's So 'Religious' about 'Religious Terrorism'?" *Critical Studies on Terrorism* 4, no. 3 (2011): 369–88, https://doi.org/10.1080/175391 53.2011.623405.

61. Karen Armstrong, "The Myth of Religious Violence," *Guardian* (UK), September 25, 2014, www.theguardian.com/world/2014/sep/25/-sp-karen-armstrong-religious-violence-myth-secular.

62. Daniel Dubuisson, *The Western Construction of Religion: Myths, Knowledge, and Ideology,* translated by William Sayers (Baltimore, MD: John Hopkins University Press, 2003).

63. Sam Gill, "The Academic Study of Religion," *Journal of the American Academy of Religion* 62, no. 4 (1994): 965.

64. Bruce Lincoln and Cristiano Grottanelli, *Gods and Demons, Priests and Scholars: Critical Explorations in the History of Religions* (Chicago: University of Chicago Press, 2012), 123.

65. Jonathan Z. Smith, *Imagining Religion: From Babylon to Jonestown* (Chicago: University of Chicago Press, 1982), xiii.

66. Mark Juergensmeyer and Mona Kanwal Sheikh, "Introduction: The Challenge of Entering Religious Minds," in *Entering Religious Minds: The Social Study of Worldviews,* ed. Mark Juergensmeyer and Mona Kanwal Sheikh (New York: Routledge, 2020), 4-5; Sara Kamali, "Interviewing White Ethno(-Religious) Nationalists: Reflections on Fieldwork," in *Entering Religious Minds: The Social Study of Worldviews,* ed. Mark Juergensmeyer and Mona Kanwal Sheikh (New York: Routledge, 2020), 93–98.

67. Andrew Silke, "An Introduction to Terrorism Research," in *Research on Terrorism: Trends, Achievements and Failures,* ed. Andrew Silke (London: Frank Cass, 2004), 1–29.

68. Bruce Hoffman, *Inside Terrorism* (New York: Columbia University Press, 1998), 15.

69. Hoffman, *Inside Terrorism,* 31.

70. Charlie Savage, "A Hate Crime? How the Charlottesville Car Attack May Become a Federal Case," *New York Times,* August 13, 2017, www.nytimes.com/2017/08/13/us/politics/charlottesville-sessions-justice-department.html.

71. This is an amendment of 18 U.S.C., which relates to "crimes and criminal procedure." See Uniting and Strengthening America by Providing Appropriate Tools Required to Intercept and Obstruct Terrorism (USA Patriot Act) Act of 2001, Pub. L. No. 107–52, 115 Stat. 2721 (2001). 8 U.S.C. § 2331 (2001), p. 274. The full act can be read at www.sec.gov/about/offices/ocie/aml/patriotact2001.pdf. According to the act, domestic terrorism refers to activities that "(A) involve acts dangerous to human life that are a violation of the criminal laws of the United States or of any State; (B) appear to be intended (i) to intimidate or coerce a civilian population; (ii) to influence the policy of a government by intimidation or coercion; or (iii) to affect the conduct of a government by mass destruction, assassination, or kidnapping; and (C) occur primarily within the territorial jurisdiction of the United States."

72. Federal Bureau of Investigation, "Terrorism 2002–2005," U.S. Department of Justice, n.d., accessed March 6, 2011, p. iv, www.fbi.gov/stats-services /publications/terrorism-2002-2005; Greg Myre, "Why the Government Can't Bring Terrorism Charges in Charlottesville," *NPR*, August 14, 2017, www.npr .org/2017/08/14/543462676/why-the-govt-cant-bring-terrorism-charges-in-charlottesville.

73. Sara Kamali, "Our Shooting Double Standard: How Do We Decide Which Madmen Are Terrorists?" *Salon*, May 11, 2014, www.salon.com/2014/05/11 /our_shooting_double_standard_how_do_we_decide_which_madmen_are_terrorists; Al Letson, "Trial and Terror," *Reveal* (podcast), produced by Katherine Mieszkowski and Stan Alcorn, June 24, 2017, www.revealnews.org/episodes/trial-and-terror; Daniel Koehler, *Right-Wing Terrorism in the Twenty-First Century: The "National Socialist Underground" and the History of Terror from the Far-Right in Germany* (New York: Routledge, 2017), 57–59; Helen Taylor, "Domestic Terrorism and Hate Crimes: Legal Definitions and Media Framing of Mass Shootings in the United States," *Journal of Policing, Intelligence and Counter Terrorism* 14, no. 3 (2019): 227–44, https://doi.org/10.1080/18335330.2019.1667012.

74. Trevor Aaronson, "Terrorism's Double Standard: Violent Far-Right Extremists are Rarely Prosecuted as Terrorists," *Intercept*, March 23, 2019, https://theintercept.com/2019/03/23/domestic-terrorism-fbi-prosecutions/; Mary B. McCord, "It's Time for Congress to Make Domestic Terrorism a Federal Crime," *Lawfare*, December 5, 2018, www.lawfareblog.com/its-time-congress-make-domestic-terrorism-federal-crime.

75. U.S. Department of Homeland Security, "Domestic Terrorism and Homegrown Violent Extremism Lexicon," Office of Intelligence and Analysis, November 10, 2011, 1, http://info.publicintelligence.net/DHS-ExtremismLexicon .pdf.

76. U.S. Department of Homeland Security, "Domestic Terrorism and Homegrown Violent Extremism Lexicon."

77. Grace Davie, "The Evolution of the Sociology of Religion: Theme and Variations," in *Handbook of the Sociology of Religion*, ed. Michele Dillon (Cambridge: Cambridge University Press, 2003), 73; John L. Esposito, *The Islamic Threat: Myth or Reality?* (London: Oxford University Press, 1999), 6; Sara Diamond, *Roads to Dominion: Right-Wing Movements and Political Power in the United States* (New York: Guilford Press, 1995), 5.

78. John McWhorter, "The Big Problem with Calling It 'Radical Islam,'" *CNN*, July 11, 2016, www.cnn.com/2016/06/14/opinions/dont-call-it-radical-islam-john-mcwhorter/index.html.

79. *Oxford English Dictionary*, s.v. "activism," accessed August 30, 2017, https://en.oxforddictionaries.com/definition/activism; Mark Juergensmeyer, "Entering the Mindset of Violent Religious Activists," *Religions* 6, no. 3 (2015): 852–59, https://doi.org/10.3390/rel6030852; Mark Juergensmeyer, *Terror in the Mind of God: The Global Rise of Religious Violence*, 4th ed. (Oakland: University of California Press, 2017).

80. Federal Bureau of Investigation, "COINTELPRO Black Extremist Parts 1–23," FBI Records: The Vault, accessed August 15, 2020, https://vault.fbi.gov /cointel-pro/cointel-pro-black-extremists, especially part 1, p. 3; Federal Bureau

of Investigation, "COINTELPRO White Hate Groups Parts 1–14," FBI Records: The Vault, accessed August 15, 2020, https://vault.fbi.gov/cointel-pro /White%20Hate%20Groups/white-hate-groups-part-01-of-14/view, especially part 1, p. 4.

81. Allen Brown, Will Parrish, and Alice Speri, "Leaked Documents Reveal Counterterrorism Tactics Used at Standing Rock to 'Defeat Pipeline Insurgencies,'" *Intercept*, May 27, 2017, https://theintercept.com/2017/05/27/leaked-documents-reveal-security-firms-counterterrorism-tactics-at-standing-rock-to-defeat-pipeline-insurgencies; Mark Morales and Laura Ly, "Released NYPD Emails Show Extensive Surveillance of Black Lives Matter Protestors," *CNN*, January 18, 2019, www.cnn.com/2019/01/18/us/nypd-black-lives-matter-surveillance /index.html.

82. Investigative journalist Trevor Aaronson examined this troubling phenomenon with regard to militant Islamist terrorist cases in his 2013 book, *The Terror Factory: Inside the FBI's Manufactured War on Terrorism* (Brooklyn: Ig Publishing, 2013). See also Sara Kamali, "Informants, Provocateurs, and Entrapment: Examining the Histories of the FBI's PATCON and the NYPD's Muslim Surveillance Program," *Surveillance and Society* 15, no. 1 (2017): 68–78, https://doi.org/10.24908/ss.v15i1.5254; Neiwert, "Charlottesville Underscores"; and Al Letson, "Trial and Terror."

83. Cas Mudde, *Populist Radical Right Parties in Europe* (Cambridge: Cambridge University Press, 2007), 11–12; Arie Perliger, "Challengers from the Sidelines: Understanding America's Violent Far-Right," Combating Terrorism Center at West Point, November 2012, p. 13, https://ctc.usma.edu/wp-content /uploads/2013/01/ChallengersFromtheSidelines.pdf.

84. Betty A. Dobratz and Stephanie L. Shanks-Meile, *White Power, White Pride! The White Separatist Movement in the United States* (New York: Twayne Publishers, 1997), 35. For proposed typologies, see Jeffrey Kaplan, "Right Wing Violence in North America," *Terrorism and Political Violence* 7, no. 1 (1995): 46–47; and Daryl Johnson, *Right Wing Resurgence: How a Domestic Terrorism Threat Is Being Ignored* (Lanham, MD: Rowman and Littlefield, 2012), 49.

85. Katie Reilly, "Student Who Attended Charlottesville White Supremacist Rally Leaves Boston University After Backlash," *Time*, August 17, 2017, https:// time.com/4905939/nicholas-fuentes-white-supremacist-rally-charlottesville; Charles Tanner and Devin Burghart, *From Alt-Right to Groyper: White Nationalists Rebrand for 2020 and Beyond*, Institute for Research and Education on Human Rights, 2020, www.irehr.org/reports/alt-right-to-groyper.

86. Jane Coaston, "Why Alt-Right Trolls Shouted Down Donald Trump Jr.," *Vox*, November 11, 2019, www.vox.com/policy-and-politics/2019/11/11 /20948317/alt-right-donald-trump-jr-conservative-tpusa-yaf-racism-antisemitism; Patrick Casey, "Groyper Leadership Summit: 'Why The Dissident Right is Winning,'" YouTube video, 23:45, January 8, 2020, www.youtube.com/watch?v= GPGSJ_PSZgk; Donald Trump (@RealDonaldTrump), "The Radical Left is in total command & control of Facebook, Instagram, Twitter and Google. The Administration is working to remedy this illegal situation. Stay tuned, and send names & events. Thank you Michelle!" Twitter, May 16, 2020, 4:56 a.m., https://twitter.com/realDonaldTrump/status/1261626674686447621; Zachary

Petrizzo, "White nationalist Groypers are taking Trump's retweet as an endorsement," Daily Dot, May 17, 2020, www.dailydot.com/debug/trump-nicholas-fuentes-groypers-retweet; Roger Sollenberger, "Trump's Properties: A Playground for White Nationalists, Groypers and Other Far-Right Loons," Salon, July 30, 2020, www.salon.com/2020/07/30/trumps-properties-a-playground-for-white-nationalists-groypers-and-other-far-right-loons.

87. Jared Holt, "Nick Fuentes Denies Being a White Nationalist by Explaining That He's a White Nationalist," Right Wing Watch, May 8, 2018, www.rightwingwatch.org/post/nick-fuentes-denies-being-a-white-nationalist-by-explaining-that-hes-a-white-nationalist; The Public Space, episode 5, "The State of Identity: Richard Spencer and Nick Fuentes," featuring Jean-François Gariépy, Richard Spencer, and Nick Fuentes, May 2, 2018.

88. George Hawley, email to author, July 14, 2017; Cas Mudde, "Stop Using the Term 'Alt-Right'!" Huffington Post, August 25, 2016, www.huffingtonpost.com/cas-mudde/stop-using-the-term-alt-r_b_11705870.html; George Orwell, "Notes on Nationalism," Orwell Foundation, 1945, www.orwellfoundation.com/the-orwell-foundation/orwell/essays-and-other-works/notes-on-nationalism; Southern Poverty Law Center, "White Nationalist," n.d., accessed August 30, 2017, www.splcenter.org/fighting-hate/extremist-files/ideology/white-nationalist.

89. Kathleen Belew, Bring the War Home: The White Power Movement and Paramilitary America (Cambridge, MA: Harvard University Press, 2018), ix.

90. Jennifer Harvey, "Race and Reparations: The Material Logics of White Supremacy," in Disrupting White Supremacy from Within, eds. Jennifer Harvey, Karin A. Case, and Robin Hawley Gorsline (Cleveland: Pilgrim Press, 2004), 96–97; Jorge J.E. Gracia, "Race and Ethnicity," in The Oxford Handbook of Philosophy and Race, ed. Naomi Zack (Oxford: Oxford University Press, 2017), 180–90; Michael Yudell, Dorothy Roberts, Rob Desalle, and Sarah Tishkoff, "Taking Race out of Human Genetics," Science 351, no. 6273 (February 5, 2015): 564–65; Dorothy E. Roberts, Fatal Invention: How Science, Politics, and Big Business Re-create Race in the Twenty-First Century (New York: New Press, 2011); Sally Haslanger, "Tracing the Sociopolitical Reality of Race," in What Is Race? Four Philosophical Views, by Joshua Glasgow, Sally Haslanger, Chike Jeffers, and Quayshawn Spencer (New York: Oxford University Press, 2019), 4–37; David R. Williams, "Racial Bias in Health Care and Health: Challenges and Opportunities," JAMA 314, no. 6 (2015): 555–56.

91. Jeffry R. Halverson, H. Lloyd Goodall, and Steven R. Corman, Master Narratives of Islamist Extremism (New York: Palgrave McMillan, 2011), 6.

92. Noah Feldman, After Jihad: America and the Struggle for Islamic Democracy (New York: Farrar, Strauss and Giroux, 2003), 42; Olivier Roy, The Failure of Political Islam (Cambridge, MA: Harvard University Press, 1994); Graham E. Fuller, The Future of Political Islam (New York: Palgrave, 2003), 47; Abby Ohlheiser, "The Associated Press's Definition of 'Islamist,'" Slate, April 5, 2013, www.slate.com/blogs/the_slatest/2013/04/05/_islamist_definition_changed_in_the_ap_stylebook_two_days_after_illegal.html.

93. For more on how militant Islamists and Islamists differ in their ideologies, see Fawaz A. Gerges, The Far Enemy: Why Jihad Went Global (Cam-

bridge: Cambridge University Press, 2005), 117; and Meghnad Desai, *Rethinking Islamism: The Ideology of the New Terror* (London: I.B. Tauris, 2007), 23–27.

94. "The Gods That Failed," *Economist,* September 11, 2003, www.economist.com/node/2035097.

95. Ugandan academic Mahmood Mamdani argues that political Islam was born of the colonial period and that militant Islamism, in particular, resulted from the Cold War. See Mahmood Mamdani, *Good Muslim, Bad Muslim: America, the Cold War, and the Roots of Terror* (New York: Pantheon Books, 2004).

96. Feldman, *After Jihad*; Roy, *Failure of Political Islam.*

97. Fuller, *Future of Political Islam.*

98. Ohlheiser, "Associated Press's Definition of 'Islamist.'"

99. Shiraz Maher, *Salafi-Jihadism: The History of an Idea* (New York: Oxford University Press, 2016), 16.

100. Shireen Khan Burki, "Haram or Halal? Islamists' Use of Suicide Attacks as 'Jihad,'" *Terrorism and Political Violence* 23, no. 4 (2011): 584.

101. "What We Believe," Black Lives Matter, accessed August 1, 2020, https://blacklivesmatter.com/what-we-believe.

102. For more on the history of the racialization of Blackness from a philosophical standpoint, see Achille Mbembe, *Critique of Black Reason*, translated by Laurent Dubois (Durham: Duke University Press, 2017). For more on the many arguments for capitalizing *Black*, see Robert S. Wachal, "The Capitalization of *Black* and *Native American,*" *American Speech* 75, no. 4 (2000): 364–65, muse.jhu.edu/article/2793; Kwame Anthony Appiah, "The Case for Capitalizing the *B* in Black," *Atlantic*, June 18, 2020, www.theatlantic.com/ideas/archive/2020/06/time-to-capitalize-blackand-white/613159; John Eligon, "A Debate Over Identity and Race Asks, Are African-Americans 'Black' or 'black'?" *New York Times*, June 26, 2020, www.nytimes.com/2020/06/26/us/black-african-american-style-debate.html; "NABJ Statement on Capitalizing Black and other Racial Identifiers," National Association of Black Journalists, June 11, 2020, www.nabj.org/news/news.asp?id=512370; Dean Baquet and Phil Corbett, "Uppercasing 'Black,'" *New York Times*, June 30, 2020, www.nytco.com/press/uppercasing-black; Merrill Perlman, "Black and White: Why Capitalization Matters," *Analysis* (blog), *Columbia Journalism Review,* June 23, 2015, www.cjr.org/analysis/language_corner_1.php; David Bauder, "AP Says It Will Capitalize Black But Not White," Associated Press, July 20, 2020, https://apnews.com/7e36c00c5afo436abc09e051261ffff1f; Lori Tharps, "The Case for Black With a Capital B," *New York Times*, November 18, 2014, www.nytimes.com/2014/11/19/opinion/the-case-for-black-with-a-capital-b.html; Luke Visconti, "Why Capitalizing the B in Black Still Matters for Cultural Competence and Accurate Representation," DiversityInc, August 18, 2020, www.diversityinc.com/why-the-b-in-black-is-capitalized-at-diversityinc; Aly Colón, "Black, black, or African American?" *Poynter*, October 14, 2003, www.poynter.org/reporting-editing/2003/black-black-or-african-american; Ann Thúy Nguyễn and Maya Pendleton, "Recongizing Race in Language: Why We Capitalze 'Black' and 'White,'" Center for the Study of Social Policy, March 23,

2020, https://cssp.org/2020/03/recognizing-race-in-language-why-we-capital-ize-black-and-white; and Kristen Hare, "Many Newsrooms are Now Capital-izing the B in Black. Here Are Some of The People Who Made That Happen," *Poynter,* June 30, 2020, www.poynter.org/reporting-editing/2020/many-newsrooms-are-now-capitalizing-the-b-in-black-here-are-some-of-the-people-who-made-that-happen.

103. Nell Irvin Painter, "Why 'White' Should Be Capitalized, Too," *Wash-ington Post,* July 22, 2020, www.washingtonpost.com/opinions/2020/07/22/why-white-should-be-capitalized; Eve L. Ewing, "I'm a Black Scholar Who Studies Race. Here's Why I Capitalize 'White,'" *Zora, Medium,* July 1, 2020, https://zora.medium.com/im-a-black-scholar-who-studies-race-here-s-why-i-capitalize-white-f94883aa2dd3; J.T. Cramer, "Why The Times Is Capitalizing the 'B' in Black," *Los Angeles Times,* June 16, 2020, www.latimes.com/about/readers-representative/story/2020-06-16/why-the-times-is-capitalizing-the-b-in-black; WashPostPR, "The Washington Post Announces Writing Style Changes for Racial and Ethnic Identifiers," *WashPost PR Blog,* July 29, 2020, www.washingtonpost.com/pr/2020/07/29/washington-post-announces-writ-ing-style-changes-racial-ethnic-identifiers.

104. Sally Haslanger, *Resisting Reality: Social Construction and Social Cri-tique* (New York: Oxford University Press, 2012), 311n1.

105. "Queer: Terminology," Stylebook, NLGJA: The Association of LGBTQ Journalists, accessed September 8, 2020, www.nlgja.org/stylebook/queer; Jonathan Rauch, "It's Time to Drop the 'LGBT' from 'LGBTQ,'" *Atlantic,* January/February 2019, www.theatlantic.com/magazine/archive/2019/01/dont-call-me-lgbtq/576388; Mimi Marinucci, *Feminism Is Queer: The Intimate Con-nection between Queer and Feminist Theory,* London: Zed Books, 2016.

106. Michael Yellow Bird, "What We Want to Be Called: Indigenous Peo-ples' Perspectives on Racial and Ethnic Identity Labels," *American Indian Quarterly* 23, no. 2 (1999): 1–21.

107. Stephen Nuño-Pérez and Gwen Aviles, "Is 'Latinx' Elitist? Some Push Back at the Word's Growing Use," *NBC News,* March 7, 2019, www.nbcnews.com/news/latino/latinx-elitist-some-push-back-word-s-growing-use-n957036; Claudia Amezcua, "Does Latinx Turn Its Back on Latino, Chicano and Hispanic Identity?" *KGW News,* April 30, 2019, www.kgw.com/article/news/does-latinx-turn-its-back-on-latinoa-chicano-hispanic-identity/283-e9aaeb46-7ea0-4667-9c6b-e7f065f236a6; GENIAL, "Is it Hispanic, Chicano/Chicana, Latino/Latina, or Latinx?" Exploratorium, 2017, www.exploratorium.edu/sites/default/files/Genial_2017_Terms_of_Usage.pdf; John McWhorter, "Why *Lat-inx* Can't Catch On," *Atlantic,* December 23, 2019, www.theatlantic.com/ideas/archive/2019/12/why-latinx-cant-catch-on/603943; Rachel Hatzipana-gos, "'Latinx': An Offense to the Spanish Language or a Nod to Inclusion?" *Washington Post,* September 14, 2018, www.washingtonpost.com/news/post-nation/wp/2018/09/14/latinx-an-offense-to-the-spanish-language-or-a-nod-to-inclusion; Luis Noe-Bustamante, Lauren Mora, and Mark Hugo Lopez, "About One-in-Four U.S. Hispanics Have Heard of Latinx, but Just 3% Use It," *Pew Research Center,* August 11, 2020, www.pewresearch.org/hispanic/2020/08/11/about-one-in-four-u-s-hispanics-have-heard-of-latinx-but-just-3-use-it.

108. To keep the Arabic orthography and phonetics as representative as possible, I diverged from the *IJMES* standard on two fronts. Firstly, I assimilated the definite article *al-* when it is followed by any of the letters referred to in Arabic as "sun" letters (versus "moon" letters, which are left unassimilated). So, for example, I have used as-Salaf as-Salihin instead of al-Salaf al-Salihin. This change in the *al-* to include the "sun" letters does not indicate a *shadda*, or doubling of the consonant; rather, the purpose is for pronunciation guidance only.

Secondly, the *IJMES* guide states that if a word is found in *Merriam-Webster's Collegiate Dictionary,* then the word should be spelled as it is appears there and anglicized plurals of the word may be used. However, I have retained Arabic plurals to enhance cultural competency.

Examples of the departure from the *IJMES* guide in this regard include *masjid* and *madrasa,* both of which are found in *Merriam-Webster's.* Instead of using their anglicized plurals, *masjids* and *madrasas,* I employ the plural forms *masājid* and *madāris.* I recognize that there are many languages that Muslims speak, so this is not to prioritize Arabic over this panoply of languages but rather to signal cultural competency within the context these words are discussed. Another complication does arise when *Merriam-Webster's* includes the correct Arabic plural albeit without diacritics. This is the case for *hadith,* the plural of which is given as *ahadith,* so I use this plural form, without diacritics.

For the most part, however, I do apply the *IJMES* standard. It generally calls for the removal of diacritical marks from titles of books and many proper nouns. Thus, when I refer to the classification of hadith—the sayings, actions, and preferences of the Prophet Muhammad—as *ṣaḥīḥ,* or sound, meaning that they have a reliable chain of transmission between narrators of unimpeachable character, I use the full diacritics and italics as required. Yet, when the same term appears in the title of a compilation of texts by renowned religious scholars Imam Bukhari and Imam Muslim, the word is spelled *Sahih.* For more on the principles by which a hadith is evaluated, see Ibn al-Ṣalāḥ al-Shahrazūrī, *An Introduction to the Science of the Ḥadīth,* trans. Eerik Dickinson (Reading, UK: Garnet Publishing, 2006).

Furthermore, while I refrained from using diacritics on many proper nouns, for personal names, I dropped the initial hamza (ʾ) but retained it and the letter ʿayn (ʿ) if appropriate. I also retained the transliterated spellings for the names of people in many instances unless their names have accepted English spellings. For American citizens, like Anwar al-Aulaqi, I have used the English spellings they themselves use or used.

CHAPTER I. THE FOURTEEN WORDS

1. "Military, Music Marked Temple Suspect's Path to Wisconsin," *CNN,* August 7, 2012, http://edition.cnn.com/2012/08/06/us/wisconsin-shooting-suspect/index.html.

2. For more on how symbols of the militant Christian Right have changed to become less abrasive, see Serge F. Kovaleski, Julie Turkewitz, Joseph Goldstein,

and Dan Barry, "An Alt-Right Makeover Shrouds the Swastikas," *New York Times,* December 10, 2016, www.nytimes.com/2016/12/10/us/alt-right-national-socialist-movement-white-supremacy.html .

3. The number 838 corresponds to the eighth, third, and eighth letters of the alphabet—*H, C, H*—in reference to the Hammerskins' pictorial logo "Hail the Crossed Hammers," which the organization's website calls a symbol of its strength, pride, and solidarity. See "Our History," Hammerskin Nation, accessed September 2, 2017, www.hammerskins.net, website no longer active.

4. "Our History," Hammerskin Nation.

5. Robert T. Wood, "Indigenous, Nonracist Origins of the American Skin-head Subculture," *Youth and Society* 31, no. 2 (December 1999): 131–51; Marilyn Elias, "Sikh Temple Killer Wade Michael Page Radicalized in Army," *Intelligence Report,* Southern Poverty Law Center, 2012 Winter Issue, November 11, 2012, www.splcenter.org/fighting-hate/intelligence-report/2012/sikh-temple-killer-wade-michael-page-radicalized-army.

6. Matt Pearce, "Sikh Temple Gunman Played in White Supremacist Rock Band Called End Apathy," *Los Angeles Times,* August 6, 2012, http://articles.latimes.com/2012/aug/06/nation/la-na-nn-sikh-temple-gunman-end-apathy-20120806.

7. "Our History," Hammerskin Nation. It is important to note that there are also antiracist skinheads, typified by the group SHARP (Skinheads against Racial Prejudice).

8. Charlie Spiering, "2010: Suspected Sikh Shooter Wade Michael Page Frus-trated with 'Sick Society,'" *Washington Examiner,* August 6, 2012, http://washingtonexaminer.com/2010-suspected-sikh-shooter-wade-michael-page-frustrated-with-sick-society/article/2504100.

9. For how the Bible was used to justify the enslavement of Black people, see, for example, Josiah Priest, *Slavery, As It Relates to the Negro, or African Race: Examined in the Light Of Circumstances, History and the Holy Scripture* (Louis-ville: W. S. Brown, 1849); and Noel Rae, *The Great Stain: Witnessing American Slavery* (New York: Overlook Press, 2018). The following museum exhibits are also instructive: *The Yoke of Bondage: Christianity and African Slavery in the United States,* Harvard Divinity School's Andover-Harvard Theological Library, Cambridge, MA, December 5, 2018, to March 15, 2019, https://library.harvard.edu/events/yoke-bondage-christianity-and-african-slavery-united-states; and *The Slave Bible: Let the Story Be Told,* Museum of the Bible, Washington, DC, November 28, 2018, to September 1, 2019, www.museumofthebible.org/exhibits/slave-bible.

10. For an in-depth examination of how White supremacy in particular is intertwined with White Christianity, see Robert P. Jones, *White Too Long: The Legacy of White Supremacy in American Christianity* (New York: Simon & Schuster, 2020). See also Alan Cross, *When Heaven and Earth Collide: Racism, Southern Evangelicals, and the Better Way of Jesus* (Montgomery, AL: NewSouth Books, 2014).

11. Kristin Kobes Du Mez, *Jesus and John Wayne: How White Evangelicals Corrupted a Faith and Fractured a Nation* (New York: Liveright, 2020).

12. "What Is an Evangelical?" National Association of Evangelicals, accessed August 18, 2020, www.nae.net/what-is-an-evangelical.

13. George M. Marsden, *Understanding Fundamentalism and Evangelicalism* (Grand Rapids, MI: W. B. Eerdmans, 1991), 4–5.

14. Andrew L. Whitehead, Samuel L. Perry, and Joseph O. Baker, "Make America Christian Again: Christian Nationalism and Voting for Donald Trump in the 2016 Presidential Election," *Sociology of Religion* 79, no. 2 (2018): 147–71, https://doi.org/10.1093/socrel/srx070; John Fea, *Believe Me: The Evangelical Road to Donald Trump* (Grand Rapids, MI: Eerdmans, 2018); John Fea, *Was America Founded as a Christian Nation? A Historical Introduction* (Louisville, KY: Westminster John Knox Press, 2011); Katherine Stewart, *The Power Worshippers: Inside the Dangerous Rise of Religious Nationalism* (New York: Bloomsbury, 2020); Andrew L. Whitehead and Samuel L. Perry, *Taking America Back for God: Christian Nationalism in the United States* (New York, NY: Oxford University Press, 2020).

15. For an excellent take on this, see Robert P. Jones, *The End of White Christian America* (New York: Simon and Schuster, 2016). See also Andrew L. Whitehead and Samuel L. Perry, *Taking Back America for God: Christian Nationalism in the United States* (Oxford: Oxford University Press, 2020); Alex Vandermaas-Peeler, Daniel Cox, Molly Fisch-Friedman, Rob Griffin, and Robert P. Jones, "American Democracy in Crisis: The Challenges of Voter Knowledge, Participation, and Polarization," Public Religion Research Institute, July 17, 2018, www.prri.org/research/american-democracy-in-crisis-voters-midterms-trump-election-2018; Michael Lipka, "Evangelicals Increasingly Say It's Becoming Harder for Them in America," *FactTank*, Pew Research Center, July 14, 2016, www.pewresearch.org/fact-tank/2016/07/14/evangelicals-increasingly-say-its-becoming-harder-for-them-in-america; "U.S. Muslims Concerned about Their Place in Society, but Continue to Believe in the American Dream," Pew Research Center, July 26, 2017, www.pewforum.org/2017/07/26/findings-from-pew-research-centers-2017-survey-of-us-muslims; Janelle S. Wong, *Immigrants, Evangelicals, and Politics in an Era of Demographic Change* (New York: Russell Sage Foundation, 2018); Stephen Mansfield, *Choosing Donald Trump: God, Anger, Hope, and Why Christian Conservatives Supported Him* (Grand Rapids, MI: Baker Books, 2017); and Thomas S. Kidd, *Who Is an Evangelical? The History of a Movement in Crisis* (New Haven, CT: Yale University Press 2019).

16. For exhaustive histories of evangelicalism in the United States, see Frances FitzGerald, *The Evangelicals: The Struggle to Shape America* (New York: Simon and Schuster, 2017); Sam Haselby, *The Origins of American Religious Nationalism* (New York: Oxford University Press, 2015); William C. Martin, *With God on Our Side: The Rise of the Religious Right in America* (New York: Broadway Books, 1996); and Mark A. Noll, David W. Bebbington, and George M. Marsden, *Evangelicals: Who They Have Been, Are Now, and Could Be* (Grand Rapids, MI: William B. Eerdmans, 2019).

17. Campbell Robertson, "A Quiet Exodus: Why Black Worshipers Are Leaving White Evangelical Churches," *New York Times*, March 9, 2018, www.nytimes.com/2018/03/09/us/blacks-evangelical-churches.html; Jemar Tisby,

The Color of Compromise: The Truth about the American Church's Complicity in Racism (Grand Rapids, MI: Zondervan, 2019).

18. The statistic of 81 percent of White evangelicals voting for Donald Trump in the 2016 U.S. presidential election has been much publicized. Another number worth mentioning is the 60 percent of White Catholics who voted for Trump, who comprised 23 percent of the electorate. Many Latter-day Saints also voted for Trump, though the data does not differentiate White adherents from adherents of color. These members as a whole make up 1 percent of the electorate, and 61 percent voted for Trump. While still a large portion of the electorate, Latter-day Saints supported past Republican presidential candidates in greater numbers, with 80 percent voting for George W. Bush in 2004 and 78 percent for Mitt Romney in 2012. See Daniel Cox, "White Christians Side with Trump," Public Religion Research Institute, November 9, 2016, www.prri.org /spotlight/religion-vote-presidential-election-2004-2016; Robert P. Jones, "The High Correlation between Percentage of White Christians, Support for Trump in Key States," Public Religion Research Institute, November 17, 2016, www .prri.org/spotlight/trump-triumphed-white-christian-states; "Religious Land-scape Study," Pew Research Center, 2014, www.pewforum.org/religious-landscape-study; and Alec Tyson and Shiva Maniam, "Behind Trump's Victory: Divisions by Race, Gender, and Education," *FactTank,* Pew Research, November 9, 2016, www.pewresearch.org/fact-tank/2016/11/09/behind-trumps-victory-divisions-by-race-gender-education.

19. Kidd, *Who Is an Evangelical?;* Ann M. Oberhauser, Daniel Krier, and Abdi M. Kusow, "Political Moderation and Polarization in the Heartland: Eco-nomics, Rurality, and Social Identity in the 2016 U.S. Presidential Election," *Sociological Quarterly* 60, no. 2 (2019): 224–44, https://doi.org/10.1080/0038 0253.2019.1580543; Sean McElwee and Jason McDaniel, "Economic Anxiety Didn't Make People Vote Trump, Racism Did," *Nation,* May 8, 2017, www .thenation.com/article/archive/economic-anxiety-didnt-make-people-vote-trump-racism-did.

20. Geoffrey C. Layman and Laura S. Hussey, "George W. Bush and the Evangelicals: Religious Commitment and Partisan Change among Evangelical Protestants, 1960–2004," in *A Matter of Faith: Religion in the 2004 Presiden-tial Election,* ed. David E. Campbell (Washington, DC: Brookings Institution, 2007), 180–98; Richard M. Harley, "The Evangelical Vote and the Presidency," *Christian Science Monitor,* June 25, 1980, www.csmonitor.com/1980/0625 /062555.html; Ashley Jardina, "In-Group Love and Out-Group Hate: White Racial Attitudes in Contemporary U.S. Elections," *Political Behavior*, March 3, 2020, https://doi.org/10.1007/s11109-020-09600-x.

21. Diana C. Mutz, "Status Threat, Not Economic Hardship, Explains the 2016 Presidential Vote," *PNAS* 115, no. 19 (May 8, 2018): E4330–39, https:// doi.org/10.1073/pnas.1718155115.

22. For more on the recent split within American evangelism, see Harry Bruinius, "Amid Evangelical Decline, Growing Split between Young Christians and Church Elders," *Christian Science Monitor,* October 10, 2017, www .csmonitor.com/USA/Politics/2017/1010/Amid-Evangelical-decline-growing-split-between-young-Christians-and-church-elders. The Red Letter Christian

movement is one center for this Christian rejection of White supremacy and White nationalism; see the Red Letter Christians' website, www .redletterchristians.org.

Historically, the sociopolitical construct of race and institutionalized racism have caused division within predominantly White denominations. For example, just prior to the U.S. Civil War, Presbyterians and Methodists split over the question of the institution of slavery, and they did not reunite until the twentieth century.

23. Mark Galli, "Trump Should Be Removed from Office," *Christianity Today*, December 19, 2019, www.christianitytoday.com/ct/2019/december-web-only/trump-should-be-removed-from-office.html.

24. Franklin Graham, "My Response to Christianity Today: Christianity Today released an editorial stating that President Trump should be removed from office—and they invoked my father's name," Facebook, December 19, 2019, www.facebook.com/FranklinGraham/posts/my-response-to-christianity-todaychristianity-today-released-an-editorial-statin/2925457574177071.

25. Melissa Barnhardt, "Nearly 200 Evangelical Leaders Slam *Christianity Today* for Questioning Their Christian Witness," *Christian Post*, December 22, 2019, www.christianpost.com/news/nearly-200-evangelical-leaders-slam-christianity-today-for-questioning-their-christian-witness.html.

26. Kelly J. Baker, *Gospel According to the Klan: The KKK's Appeal to Protestant America, 1915–1930* (Lawrence: University Press of Kansas, 2011); Kyle Haselden, *The Racial Problem in Christian Perspective* (New York: Harper, 1959); Cathy Meeks, *Living into God's Dream: Dismantling Racism in America* (New York: Morehouse Publishing, 2016).

27. R. J. Rushdoony, "Is America a Christian Nation?" *Chalcedon*, July 1, 1998, https://chalcedon.edu/magazine/is-america-a-christian-nation; Sara Diamond, *Roads to Dominion: Right-Wing Movements and Political Power in the United States* (New York: Guilford Press, 1995).

28. Prominent thinkers in this tradition include Rousas John Rushdoony and Gary North, both of whom advocated for a complete transformation of American society into a conservative Christian theocracy.

29. Ammon Bundy, "Dear Friends," YouTube video, 19:27, January 1, 2016, www.youtube.com/watch?v=M7MomG6HUyk. In 2017, U.S. District Judge Gloria M. Navarro declared a mistrial in *United States v. Cliven Bundy, et al.*, the court case of the federal government against Cliven Bundy, two of his sons, Ammon and Ryan, and their associate, Ryan Payne, throwing out charges of assault, threats against the government, firearms offenses, obstruction, and a range of other offenses. This decision was hailed by White nationalists, who view Cliven Bundy as a hero for standing up to the oppressive overreach of the federal government. In 2018, the case was dismissed, with prejudice, by Judge Navarro; see Sam Levin, "Stunning Victory for Bundy Family as All Charges Dismissed in 2014 Standoff Case," *Guardian* (UK), January 8, 2018, www.theguardian.com /us-news/2018/jan/08/bundy-family-charges-dropped-nevada-armed-standoff.

In 2020, federal prosecutors sought to appeal for a retrial of the 2014 case, *USA v. Cliven Bundy, et al.*, No. 18-10287, but the dismissal of the case was upheld. See Bundy brief, United States of America v. Cliven D. Bundy, Ryan C.

Bundy, Ammon E. Bundy, and Ryan W. Payne, United States Court of Appeals for the Ninth Circuit, case no. 18-10287, March 20, 2019, available at www .documentcloud.org/documents/6931642-BUNDY-Brief.html; and opinion, United States of America v. Cliven D. Bundy, Ryan C. Bundy, Ammon E. Bundy, Ryan W. Payne, United States Court of Appeals for the Ninth Circuit, case no. 18-10287, August 6, 2020, https://cdn.ca9.uscourts.gov/datastore/opinions/2020 /08/06/18-10287.pdf.

Though never issuing a statement about Cliven Bundy, the Church of Jesus Christ of Latter-day Saints has condemned the actions of Ammon Bundy. The statement reads in full: "While the disagreement occurring in Oregon about the use of federal lands is not a Church matter, Church leaders strongly condemn the armed seizure of the facility and are deeply troubled by the reports that those who have seized the facility suggest that they are doing so based on scriptural principles. This armed occupation can in no way be justified on a scriptural basis. We are privileged to live in a nation where conflicts with government or private groups can—and should—be settled using peaceful means, according to the laws of the land." "Church Responds to Inquiries Regarding Oregon Armed Occupation," *Newsroom,* Church of Jesus Christ of Latter-Day Saints, January 4, 2016, https://newsroom.churchofjesuschrist.org/article/church-responds-to-inquiries-regarding-oregon-armed-occupation.

30. Leah Sottile, "Cliven Bundy's Fight against the Feds Has Roots in Interpretation of Mormon Scripture," *Washington Post,* December 7, 2017, www .washingtonpost.com/national/cliven-bundys-fight-against-the-feds-has-roots-in-interpretation-of-mormon-scripture/2017/12/07/0ef8fea6-d93b-11e7-a841-2066faf731ef_story.html.

31. "Article of Faith 12," Church of Jesus Christ of Latter-day Saints, accessed September 11, 2020, www.churchofjesuschrist.org/study/friend/2015/11/article-of-faith-12. In response to the Charlottesville rally, the Church of Jesus Christ of Latter-day Saints explicitly denounced White nationalists as "not in harmony with the teachings of the Church." The full statement reads as follows: "It has been called to our attention that there are some among the various pro-white and white supremacy communities who assert that the Church is neutral toward or in support of their views. Nothing could be further from the truth. In the New Testament, Jesus said: 'Thou shalt love the Lord thy God with all thy heart, and with all thy soul, and with all thy mind. This is the first and great commandment. And the second is like unto it, Thou shalt love thy neighbour as thyself' (Matthew 22:37–39). The Book of Mormon teaches 'all are alike unto God' (2 Nephi 26:33). White supremacist attitudes are morally wrong and sinful, and we condemn them. Church members who promote or pursue a 'white culture' or white supremacy agenda are not in harmony with the teachings of the Church." "Church Releases Statement Condemning White Supremacist Attitudes," Church of Jesus Christ of Latter-Day Saints, August 15, 2017, https://newsroom .churchofjesuschrist.org/article/church-statement-charlottesville-virginia.

32. The tenth of the Thirteen Articles of Faith of the LDS Church states that "Zion (the New Jerusalem) will be built upon the American continent." "The Articles of Faith," Church of Jesus Christ of Latter-day Saints, www.lds.org /scriptures/pgp/a-of-f/1.1-13.

33. Reed D. Slack, "The Mormon Belief of an Inspired Constitution," *Journal of Church and State* 36, no. 1 (1994): 35–56, www.jstor.org/stable/23919344; Dallin H. Oaks, "The Divinely Inspired Constitution," Church of Jesus Christ of Latter-Day Saints, February 1992, www.churchofjesuschrist.org/study/ensign/1992/02/the-divinely-inspired-constitution.

34. "The White Horse Prophecy: Preface," Ogdenkraut.com, accessed August 20, 2020, http://ogdenkraut.com/?page_id=316; Lyman Kirkland, "Church Statement on 'White Horse Prophecy' and Political Neutrality," Church of Jesus Christ of Latter-day Saints, January 6, 2010, https://newsroom.churchofjesuschrist.org/blog/church-statement-on-white-horse-prophecy-and-political-neutrality. For an examination of the White Horse Prophecy as it relates to apocalypticism, see Christopher James Blythe, *Terrible Revolution: Latter-day Saints and the American Apocalypse* (New York: Oxford University Press, 2020).

35. Don L. Penrod, "Edwin Rushton as the Source of the White Horse Prophecy," *Brigham Young University Studies* 49, no. 3 (2010): 75–131, www.jstor.org/stable/43044811.

36. Ezra Taft Benson, "Our Divine Constitution," Church of Jesus Christ of Latter-Day Saints, speech given October 1987, accessed September 2, 2017, www.lds.org/general-conference/1987/10/our-divine-constitution?lang=eng; Max Perry Mueller, *Race and the Making of the Mormon People* (Chapel Hill: University of North Carolina Press, 2017).

37. Leah Sottile, "Cliven Bundy's Fight against the Feds Has Roots in Interpretation of Mormon Scripture," *Washington Post,* December 7, 2017, www.washingtonpost.com/national/cliven-bundys-fight-against-the-feds-has-roots-in-interpretation-of-mormon-scripture/2017/12/07/0ef8fea6-d93b-11e7-a841-2066faf731ef_story.html.

38. "Articles of Faith," Church of Jesus Christ of Latter-Day Saints.

39. Sottile, "Cliven Bundy's Fight."

40. Matthew L. Harris, ed., *Thunder from the Right: Ezra Taft Benson in Mormonism and Politics* (Chicago: University of Illinois Press, 2019); D. Michael Quinn, "Ezra Taft Benson and Mormon Political Conflicts," *Dialogue: A Journal of Mormon Thought* 26, no. 2 (1993): 12, doi:10.2307/45228582; Matthew L. Harris, *Watchman on the Tower: Ezra Taft Benson and the Making of the Mormon Right* (Salt Lake City: University of Utah Press, 2020); Keith Dunn, "Ezra Taft Benson on The John Birch Society," YouTube video, 8:52, August 3, 2011, www.youtube.com/watch?v=XTvdUcLLZ5E.

41. Dan Hernandez and Joseph Langdon, "Federal Rangers Face Off against Armed Protestors in Nevada 'Range War,'" *Guardian* (UK), April 13, 2014, www.theguardian.com/world/2014/apr/13/nevada-bundy-cattle-ranch-armed-protesters.

42. Kathy Leodler and Paul Leodler, *Report of Investigation Regarding Representative Matt Shea Washington State House of Representatives,* Rampart Group, December 1, 2019, p. 11, available at www.documentcloud.org/documents/6589242-Shea-WA-House-Report.html.

43. K. Leodler and P. Leodler, "Report of Investigation Regarding Representative Matt Shea," 10.

44. "Biblical Basis for War," *Spokesman-Review,* October 25, 2018, www
.spokesman.com/documents/2018/oct/25/biblical-basis-war.

45. Matthew Shea, "MY INITIAL RESPONSE: Like we are seeing with our
President this is a sham investigation meant to silence those of us who stand up
against attempts to disarm and destroy our great country," Facebook, December 19, 2019, www.facebook.com/mattsheawa/posts/10220865721578991.

46. When news of his involvement with White nationalism surfaced, Shea
refused to resign, equating the investigation into his militant ties with Trump's
impeachment by the House of Representatives in 2019, which he also saw as
unfair: "MY INITIAL RESPONSE: Like we are seeing with our President this is
a sham investigation meant to silence those of us who stand up against attempts
to disarm and destroy our great country. I will not back down, I will not give
in, I will not resign. Stand strong fellow Patriots." Shea, "MY INITIAL
RESPONSE." In 2020, Shea decided not to seek reelection.

For an in-depth and focused discussion of the Oath Keepers, see Sam Jackson, *Oath Keepers: Patriotism and the Edge of Violence in a Right-Wing Antigovernment Group* (New York: Columbia University Press, 2020).

47. Eugenics was also used by the Nazi government in Germany to justify its
mass killings, abortion programs, and attempts to create what was envisioned
as an Aryan master race; see Henry P. David, Jochen Fleischhacker, and Charlotte Horn, "Abortion and Eugenics in Nazi Germany," *Population and Development Review* 14, no. 1 (1988): 81–112. In the United States, eugenics became
a singularly powerful force and was, in essence, legalized in the 1896 Supreme
Court case *Plessy v. Ferguson,* which maintained racial exclusion in public
spaces under the "separate but equal" clause; see Tufuku Zuberi, *Thicker than
Blood: How Racial Statistics Lie* (Minneapolis: University of Minnesota Press,
2001), 59.

48. Leonard Zeskind, *The "Christian Identity" Movement: Analyzing Its
Theological Rationalization for Racist and Anti-Semitic Violence"* (Atlanta,
GA: Division of Church and Society of the National Council of the Churches of
Christ in the U.S.A., 1986), 11. See also Zuberi, *Thicker than Blood,* 66. For an
in-depth discussion on eugenics and racism, see Daniel J. Kevles, *In the Name
of Eugenics: Genetics and the Uses of Human Heredity* (New York: Knopf,
1985); Saul Dubow, *Scientific Racism in Modern South Africa* (Cambridge:
Cambridge University Press, 1995); Stefan Kühl, *The Nazi Connection: Eugen-
ics, American Racism, and German National Socialism* (New York: Oxford
University Press, 1994); Nancy Leys Stepan, *The Hour of Eugenics: Race, Gen-
der, and Nation in Latin America* (Ithaca, NY: Cornell University Press, 1991);
Richard Soloway, *Demography and Degeneration: Eugenics and the Declining
Birthrate in Twentieth-Century Britain* (Chapel Hill: University of North Caro-
lina Press, 1990); and W.E.B. DuBois, *Black Reconstruction in America: An
Essay toward a History of the Part which Black Folk Played in the Attempt to
Reconstruct Democracy in America, 1860–1880* (New York: Oxford University
Press, 2007); and Dorothy Roberts, *Fatal Invention: How Science, Politics, and
Big Business Recreate Race in the Twenty-First Century* (New York: New Press,
2012).

49. M.K. Hallimore, *God's Great Race* (Harrison, AR: Kingdom Identity Ministries, n.d.), 2.

50. "Kingdom Identity Ministries Doctrinal Statement of Beliefs," Kingdom Identity Ministries, accessed August 27, 2011, www.kingidentity.com/doctrine .htm.

51. Bob Hallstrom, *Judeo-Christianity: A Study* (Boise, ID: Gospel Ministry Publications, 1993), 75–76.

52. Hallstrom, *Judeo-Christianity,* 1.

53. Hallstrom, *Judeo-Christianity,* 2.

54. Hallstrom, *Judeo-Christianity,* 3.

55. Leslie Pearson Rees, *Ye Have Been Hid: Finding the Lost Tribes of Israel* (Salt Lake City: Digital Legend, 2011); Philip Neal, *Two Nations that Changed the World: America and Britain; Their Biblical Origin and Prophetic Destiny* (Hollister, CA: York Publishing, 2014), 30.

56. Angela L. Apple and Beth A. Messner, "Paranoia and Paradox: The Apocalyptic Rhetoric of Christian Identity," *Western Journal of Communication* 65, no. 2 (2001): 222.

57. Michael Barkun, *Religion and the Racist Right: The Origins of the Christian Identity Movement* (Chapel Hill: University of North Carolina Press, 1994), 30.

58. In tribute to its owner, American industrialist and founder of the Ford Motor Company, Henry Ford, the *Dearborn Independent* was also called the *Ford International Weekly.*

59. Michael Barkun, "Essay: The Christian Identity Movement," *Intelligence Files,* Southern Poverty Law Center, accessed August 26, 2011, www .splcenter.org/get-informed/intelligence-files/ideology/christian-identity/the-christian-identity-movement (article no longer available).

60. James Coates, *Armed and Dangerous: The Rise of the Survivalist Right* (New York: Hill and Wang, 1987), 90.

61. "Kingdom Identity Ministries Doctrinal Statement of Beliefs," Kingdom Identity Ministries.

62. Wesley A. Swift, *God, Man, Nations, and the Races* (Kernville, CA: Church of Jesus Christ Christian, 1970), 3, 42.

63. Daniel Levitas, *The Terrorist Next Door: The Militia Movement and the Radical Right* (New York: St. Martin's Press, 2002), 2, 10, 24; Bertrand L. Comparet, *The Cain-Satanic Seed Line* (Hayden Lake, ID: Kingdom Identity Ministries, n.d.).

64. Zeskind, *"Christian Identity" Movement,* 40.

65. William Potter Gale, *Racial and National Identity* (Mountain City, TN: Sacred Truth Ministries, 2002), 2–5.

66. Bertrand L. Comparet, *Your Heritage: An Identification of the True Israel through Biblical and Historical Sources* (Harrison, AR: Kingdom Identity Ministries, n.d.), 34.

67. Comparet, *Cain-Satanic Seed Line,* 28–29, italics in the original.

68. Comparet, *Cain-Satanic Seed Line,* 31–32.

69. Comparet, *Your Heritage,* 2, 57.

70. Comparet, *Cain-Satanic Seed Line,* 4–5. Mainstream Jewish and Christian theologians understand the word *Adam* to be derived from the Hebrew *adamah,* meaning *earth.* Genesis 2:7 seems to make this connection explicit: "Then the Lord God formed the man [*adam*] from the dust of the ground [*adamah*]." See W. D. Davies, *Christian Engagements with Judaism* (Harrisburg, PA: Trinity Press International, 1999), 88.

71. George Michael, *Theology of Hate: A History of the World Church of the Creator* (Gainesville: University Press of Florida, 2009), viii.

72. Whaler, "Quote from: 'Yo Mama,'" *Info Underground,* April 17, 2011, http://theinfounderground.com/smf/index.php?topic=14248.10;wap2.

73. Race & Reason, "Race & Reason 309: Ben Klassen," YouTube video, 28:10, December 30, 2015, www.youtube.com/watch?v=DkEOVPQY-lo& spfreload=1.

74. Ben Klassen, *The White Man's Bible* (Lighthouse Point, FL: Church of the Creator, 1981), 11.

75. Ben Klassen, *A Revolution of Values through Religion* (Otto, NC: Church of the Creator, 1991), 99; Ben Klassen, *RAHOWA! This Planet Is All Ours!* (Otto, NC: Church of the Creator, 1987), 170.

76. Pierce also began a pantheistic religion he called Cosmotheism in the 1970s, blending "Darwinian evolutionary theory with ideas from ancient Teutonic legend" and synthesizing "the scientific with the mystical in its construction of reality"; see Brad Whitsel, "The Turner Diaries and Cosmotheism: William Pierce's Theology," *Nova Religio: The Journal of Alternative and Emergent Religions* 1, no. 2 (April 1998): 186. Cosmotheism shares many parallels with but also has some differences from Ben Klassen's Church of the Creator, which is now called Creativity; see Jeffrey Kaplan, "William Pierce," in *Encyclopedia of White Power: A Sourcebook on the Radical Racist Right,* ed. Jeffrey Kaplan (Walnut Creek, CA: AltaMira Press, 2000), 248.

77. Klassen, *RAHOWA!,* 137; Michael, *Theology of Hate,* 18–19.

78. Klassen, *RAHOWA!,* 191.

79. Ben Klassen, *The Klassen Letters,* vol. 2 (Otto, NC: Church of the Creator, 1988), 9. "P.M." stands for *pontifex maximus,* the title Klassen gave himself as head of his church, referring to the Latin title of the pope, which Klassen argues the Catholic Church took from the Roman state religion.

80. Race & Reason, "Race & Reason 309: Ben Klassen."

81. David A. Kaplan, "Is the Klan Entitled to Public Access?" *New York Times,* July 31, 1988, www.nytimes.com/1988/07/31/arts/tv-view-is-the-klan-entitled-to-public-access.html; Race & Reason, "Race and Reason 309: Ben Klassen," italics in the original.

82. Under Matt Hale's leadership, Creators cooperated with a variety of other militant White nationalists, religious and otherwise, but William Pierce was not impressed. See Mark Pitcavage, "With Hate in Their Hearts: The State of White Supremacy in the United States," *Anti-Defamation League,* July 2015, p. 7, www.adl.org/sites/default/files/documents/state-of-white-supremacy-united-states-2015.pdf. In his final speech at National Alliance leadership conference in April 2002, Pierce said of Creativity, then called the World Church of

the Creator: "The Alliance has no interest at all in the so-called movement. We're not interested in uniting with the movement, and we're not interested in competing with the movement for members. If anything, we should be grateful that the movement is out there to soak up a lot of the freaks and weaklings who otherwise might find their way into the Alliance and make problems for us. In this regard, I was sorry to note Aryan Nations and the [World] Church of the Creator have, for all practical purposes, died in the last few weeks. I hope one or two replacement groups spring up to draw away from us the defectives." CreativityAlliance, "William Pierce Talks about 'World' Church of the Creator," YouTube video, 3:58, July 7, 2011, www.youtube.com/watch?v=1jDco AwdL2Q.

83. Andrew Macdonald, *The Turner Diaries* (Arlington, VA: Alliance National Vanguard Books, 1978), 1, 102, 195–96.

84. Ben Klassen, *Building a Whiter and Brighter World* (Otto, NC: Church of the Creator, 1986), 11.

85. Klassen, *Building a Whiter and Brighter World,* 10–11; Race & Reason, "Race & Reason 309: Ben Klassen."

86. Klassen, *RAHOWA!,* 131–36.

87. George Michael, "RAHOWA! A History of the World Church of the Creator," *Terrorism and Political Violence* 18, no. 4 (2006): 561–83, 577–78.

88. Stephen A. McNallen, *An Odinist Anthology* (Breckenridge, TX: Asatru Free Assembly, 1983), 68.

89. Stephen Flowers, "Revival of Germanic Religion in Contemporary Anglo-Saxon American Culture," *Mankind Quarterly* 21, no. 3 (1981): 279–94.

90. Committee for the Restoration of the Odinic Rite, *This Is Odinisim* (Gorleston, England: Committee for the Restoration of the Odinic Rite, n.d.), 1.

91. Britt-Mari Näsström, *Freyja: The Great Goddess of the North* (Lund: University of Lund, 1995), 12.

92. "Through Odin's Eyes," *Sunwheel* (Toronto: Odinist Movement), no. 19 (October 1974): 2.

93. George Michael, "David Lane and the Fourteen Words," *Totalitarian Movements and Political Religions* 1, no. 1 (2009): 59n58.

94. Committee for the Restoration of the Odinic Rite, *This Is Odinisim,* 5.

95. Anthony Winterbourne, *When the Norns Have Spoken: Time and Fate in Germanic Paganism* (Madison, NJ: Fairleigh Dickinson University Press, 2004), 12.

96. Mattias Gardell, "David Lane," in *Encyclopedia of White Power: A Sourcebook on the Radical Racist Right,* ed. Jeffrey Kaplan (Walnut Creek, CA: AltaMira Press, 2000), 167.

97. Nicholas Goodrick-Clarke, *Black Sun: Aryan Cults, Esoteric Nazism, and the Politics of Identity* (New York: New York University Press, 2002), 275.

98. "Through Odin's Eyes," *Sunwheel,* 2. See also Mattias Gardell, *Gods of the Blood: The Pagan Revival and White Separatism* (Durham, NC: Duke University Press, 2003).

99. Michael, "David Lane and the Fourteen Words," 60n86.

100. Michael, "David Lane and the Fourteen Words," 60n86. McNallen also appeals to more widely held ideas about the mind-body connection to support Odinist claims about racial superiority: "The idea of metagenetics may be threatening to many who have been taught there are no differences between the branches of humanity. But in reflecting, it is plain that metagenetics is in keeping with the most modern way of seeing the world. A holistic view of the human entity requires that mind, matter, and spirit are not separate things but represent a spectrum or continuum. It should not be surprising, then, that genetics is seen as a factor in spiritual or psychic matters." McNallen, *An Odinist Anthology,* 25.

101. McNallen, *An Odinist Anthology,* 23–24.

102. Carrie B. Dohe, *Jung's Wandering Archetype: Race and Religion in Analytical Psychology* (London: Routledge, 2016), 223.

103. "New Brand of Racist Odinist Religion on the March," *Intelligence Report,* Southern Poverty Law Center, 1998 Winter Issue, March 15, 1998, www.splcenter.org/fighting-hate/intelligence-report/1998/new-brand-racist-odinist-religion-march.

104. Stubba, *This Is Odinism and Other Essays* (Melbourne: Renewal Publications, 2016), 77–78.

105. Michael Barkun, "Millennialism on the Radical Right in America," in *The Oxford Handbook of Millennialism,* ed. Catherine Wessinger (Oxford: Oxford University Press, 2011), 655.

106. Meghann Myers, "A Soldier Just Got Authorization to Wear a Beard Because of His Norse Pagan Faith," *Army Times,* April 25, 2018, www.armytimes.com/news/your-army/2018/04/25/this-soldier-just-got-authorization-to-wear-a-beard-because-of-his-norse-pagan-faith. Some Odinists state that there is no religious requirement to grow a beard, as there is for Sikhs, for example, who were also granted the accommodation.

107. "Many Americans Mix Multiple Faiths," Pew Research Center, December 9, 2009, www.pewforum.org/2009/12/09/many-americans-mix-multiple-faiths; Michael Lipka and Claire Gecewicz, "More Americans Now Say They're Spiritual but Not Religious," *FactTank,* Pew Research Center, September 6, 2017, www.pewresearch.org/fact-tank/2017/09/06/more-americans-now-say-theyre-spiritual-but-not-religious; "In U.S., Decline of Christianity Continues at Rapid Pace," Religion & Public Life, Pew Research Center, October 17, 2019, www.pewforum.org/2019/10/17/in-u-s-decline-of-christianity-continues-at-rapid-pace; "Why America's 'Nones' Don't Identify with a Religion," *FactTank,* Pew Research Center, August 8, 2018, www.pewresearch.org/fact-tank/2018/08/08/why-americas-nones-dont-identify-with-a-religion; Ronald F. Inglehart, "Giving Up on God: The Global Decline of Religion," *Foreign Affairs,* September/October 2020, www.foreignaffairs.com/articles/world/2020-08-11/religion-giving-god; Michael Shermer, "Silent No More," *Scientific American* 318, no. 4 (April 2018): 77, https://doi.org/10.1038/scientificamerican0418-77.

108. Will Carless, "White Supremacists Are Killing in the Name of an Ancient Nordic Religion," *Reveal,* May 25, 2017, www.pri.org/stories/2017-05-25/white-supremacists-are-killing-name-ancient-nordic-religion. See also Gardell, *Gods of the Blood.*

109. Committee for the Restoration of the Odinic Rite, *This Is Odinisim,* 1.

110. McNallen, *Odinist Anthology,* 4.

111. Sæbjørg Walaker Nordeiade, "Thor's Hammer in Norway: A Symbol of Reaction against the Christian Cross?" in *Old Norse Religion in Long-Term Perspectives: Origins, Changes, and Interactions,* ed. Andres Andren (Lund: Nordic Academic Press, 2006), 218.

112. Odinist Fellowship, *An Introduction to Odinism* (Crystal River, FL: Giallherhorn Book Service, a Division of the Odinist Fellowship, 1980), 2.

113. Asatru Free Church Committee, *The Religion of Odin: A Handbook* (Red Wing, MN: Viking House, 1978), 18–19; Karla O. Poewe, *New Religions and the Nazis* (New York: Routledge, 2006), 173.

114. Committee for the Restoration of the Odinic Rite, *This Is Odinisim,* 3.

115. Pitcavage, "Hate in Their Hearts," 15–16.

116. Michael, *Theology of Hate,* 52. For a biography of Else Christensen, see Osred, *Odinism: Present, Past and Future* (Melbourne: Renewal Publications, 2011), 203–5.

117. Klassen, *RAHOWA!,* 194.

118. Klassen, *RAHOWA!,* 187.

119. Klassen, *RAHOWA!,* 192.

120. Klassen, *RAHOWA!,* 188.

121. Committee for the Restoration of the Odinic Rite, *This Is Odinisim,* 3; David Lane, *Deceived, Damned, and Defiant: The Revolutionary Writings of David Lane* (St. Maries, ID: 14 Word Press, 1999), 135.

122. Lane, *Deceived, Damned, and Defiant,* 273.

123. Kathleen Belew, *Bring the War Home: The White Power Movement and Paramilitary America* (Cambridge, MA: Harvard University Press, 2018).

124. Preppers and survivalists both seek to prepare for what they believe are imminent catastrophic events, such as a global economic collapse or natural disasters. Though the terms are often used interchangeably, the term *prepper* is more associated with an apolitical outlook, while *survivalist* has a stronger connotation of conspiracy-mindedness. Moreover, though this discussion is limited to the scope of the political far right, there are many on the political far left who are antigovernment, such as antifascists. Some of these groups may use the same tactics as their counterparts on the political far right, albeit for different reasons. For examples of antigovernment violence from the political far left, see Mark Berman, "Texas Man Charged with Trying to Bomb a Confederate Statue in Houston," *Washington Post,* August 21, 2017, www.washingtonpost.com/news/post-nation/wp/2017/08/21/texas-man-charged-with-trying-to-bomb-a-confederate-statue-in-houston; Robert Patrick, "Two in Ferguson-Related Bomb Plot Sentenced to Seven Years in Prison," *St. Louis Post-Dispatch,* September 3, 2015, www.stltoday.com/news/local/crime-and-courts/two-in-ferguson-related-bomb-plot-sentenced-to-years-in/article_e853a196-d5c5-51c6-a9f0-580062329865.html; and David Ariosto, "Five Arrested in Alleged Plot to Blow Up Cleveland-Area Bridge," *CNN,* May 1, 2012, www.cnn.com/2012/05/01/justice/ohio-bridge-arrests/index.html.

125. Michael T. Miller, "Black Judaism(s) and Hebrew Israelites," *Religion Compass* 13, no. 11, (2019), https://doi.org/10.1111/rec3.12346; Jacob S.

Dorman, *Chosen People: The Rise of American Black Israelite Religions* (Oxford: Oxford University Press, 2013).

126. Jan-Willem van Prooijen, André P.M. Krouwel, and Thomas V. Pollet, "Political Extremism Predicts Belief in Conspiracy Theories," *Social Psychological and Personality Science* 6, no. 5 (July 2015): 570–78, https://doi.org/10.1177/1948550614567356; Joseph E. Uscinski and Joseph M. Parent, *American Conspiracy Theories* (New York: Oxford University Press, 2014), 105–29; Whitney Phillips and Ryan M. Milner, *You Are Here: A Field Guide for Navigating Polarized Speech, Conspiracy Theories, and Our Polluted Media Landscape*, Cambridge, MA: MIT Press, 2021.

127. Joseph E. Uscinski, "What Is a Conspiracy Theory?" in *Conspiracy Theories and the People Who Believe in Them,* ed. Joseph E. Uscinski (New York: Oxford University Press, 2018), 48.

128. Federal Bureau of Investigation, Intelligence Division, *Anti-Government Identity Based, and Fringe Political Conspiracy Theories Very Likely Motivate Some Domestic Extremists to Commit Criminal, Sometimes Violent Activity,* May 30, 2019, p. 2, available at www.justsecurity.org/wp-content/uploads/2019/08/420379775-fbi-conspiracy-theories-domestic-extremism.pdf.

129. Ben Zimmer, "The Origins of the 'Globalist' Slur," *Atlantic,* March 14, 2018, www.theatlantic.com/politics/archive/2018/03/the-origins-of-the-globalist-slur/555479. In 2020, the *Atlantic* published "Shadowland," an immersive series of articles examining different facets of conspiracy theories. See Ellen Cushing, editorial director, "Shadowland," *Atlantic,* accessed September 11, 2020, www.theatlantic.com/shadowland.

130. Ashler Stockler, "White Nationalist Propaganda Has Doubled Nationwide over the Last Year: Report," *Newsweek,* February 12, 2020, www.newsweek.com/white-nationalism-campus-anti-defamation-league-1487037.

131. Stockler, "White Nationalist Propaganda."

132. "President Trump: 'We Have Rejected Globalism and Embraced Patriotism,'" Economy & Jobs, White House, August 7, 2020, www.whitehouse.gov/articles/president-trump-we-have-rejected-globalism-and-embraced-patriotism.

133. Donald Trump (@RealDonaldTrump), "The deep state, or whoever, over at the FDA is making it very difficult for drug companies to get people in order to test the vaccines and therapeutics." Twitter, 4:49 a.m., August 22, 2020, https://twitter.com/realDonaldTrump/status/1297138862108663808. For more on the intersection of political affiliation and belief in conspiracy theories related to the COVID-19 pandemic, see Uscinski et al., "Why Do People Believe COVID-19 Conspiracy Theories?" in "COVID-19 and Misinformation," special issue, *Harvard Kennedy School Misinformation Review* 1 (April 28, 2020), https://doi.org/10.37016/mr-2020-015.

134. Blyth Crawford and Florence Keen, "The Hanau Terrorist Attack: How Race Hate and Conspiracy Theories are Fueling Global Far-Right Violence," *CTC Sentinel* 13, no. 3 (2020): 18, https://ctc.usma.edu/hanau-terrorist-attack-race-hate-conspiracy-theories-fueling-global-far-right-violence; Aoife Gallagher,

Jacob Davey, and Mackenzie Hart, *Key Trends in QAnon Activity since 2017* (London: Institute for Strategic Dialogue, 2020), www.isdglobal.org/wp-content/uploads/2020/07/The-Genesis-of-a-Conspiracy-Theory.pdf.

135. Eric Hananoki, "An Ongoing List of How the Republicans Have Built Up the QAnon Conspiracy Theory," Media Matters for America, August 19, 2020, www.mediamatters.org/qanon-conspiracy-theory/ongoing-list-how-republicans-have-built-qanon-conspiracy-theory.

136. Donald Trump (@RealDonaldTrump), "Congratulations to future Republican Star Marjorie Taylor Greene on a big Congressional primary win in Georgia against a very tough and smart opponent," Twitter, August 12, 2020, 5:29a.m.,https://twitter.com/realDonaldTrump/status/1293525010523578375,

137. Kevin Liptack, "Trump Embraces QAnon Conspiracy Because 'They Like Me,'" *CNN*, August 19, 2020, www.cnn.com/2020/08/19/politics/donald-trump-qanon/index.html.

138. Baldwin, who once promoted his antigovernment worldview through his radio show on the Christian Patriot Network, gave, as rationale for the move, themes that motivate the political far right as a whole: "We're talking about citizens' militias, federal government's encroachment on individual rights, New World Order, United Nations, gun control, it's all related." Thomas Halpern et al., *Beyond the Bombing: The Militia Menace Grows* (New York: Anti-Defamation League, 1995), 11, available at www.adl.org/sites/default/files/documents/assets/pdf/combating-hate/adl-report-1995-beyond-the-boming-the-militia-menace-grows-an-update-of-armed-and-dangerous.pdf.

In Baldwin's words, "I would rather die fighting for Freedom with liberty-loving patriots by my side than be shuttled off to some FEMA [Federal Emergency Management Agency] camp." Timothy N. Baldwin, *Freedom for a Change* (Orlando: Agrapha Publishing, 2010), 450–51. Chuck Baldwin also wrote an article praising the Confederacy; see Chuck Baldwin, "The Confederate Flag Needs to Be Raised, Not Lowered," VDare.com, July 9, 2015, http://archive.is/JtvkA.

139. "What Is the Three Percenters?" Three Percenters, accessed September 11, 2020, www.thethreepercenters.org/about-us; Federal Bureau of Investigation, Counterterrorism Analysis Section, "Sovereign Citizens: A Growing Domestic Threat to Law Enforcement," *FBI Law Enforcement Bulletin*, September 1, 2011, https://leb.fbi.gov/articles/featured-articles/sovereign-citizens-a-growing-domestic-threat-to-law-enforcement.

140. Robin L. Einhorn, *American Taxation, American Slavery* (Chicago: University of Chicago Press, 2006), 6-7. In this book, Einhorn argues that the aversion to taxes does not stem from an antigovernment mistrust but rather from slaveholding elites who "knew only one thing about democracy: that it threatened slavery" (6–7). See also Romain Huret, *American Tax Resisters* (Cambridge: Harvard University Press, 2014).

141. Bruce Hoffman, *Inside Terrorism* (New York: Columbia University Press, 1999), 113.

142. White House Office of the Press Secretary, "Remarks by the President at the National Defense University," White House, May 23, 2013, https://

obamawhitehouse.archives.gov/the-press-office/2013/05/23/remarks-president-national-defense-university.

143. Andrea Canning and Lee Ferran, "Exclusive: Stack's Daughter Retracts 'Hero' Statement," *ABC News,* February 22, 2010, http://abcnews.go.com/GMA/joe-stacks-daughter-samantha-bell-calls-dad-hero/story?id=9903329.

144. Joe Weisenthal, "The Insane Manifesto of Austin Texas Crash Pilot Joseph Andrew Stack," *Business Insider,* February 18, 2010, www.businessinsider.com/joseph-andrew-stacks-insane-manifesto-2010-2.

145. J. J. MacNab, *Seditionists: Inside the Explosive World of Anti-Government Extremism in America* (London: Palgrave Macmillan, 2015).

146. Martin Durham, *White Rage: The Extreme Right and American Politics* (New York: Routledge, 2007), 51.

147. Also see Matt Kennard, *Irregular Army: How the U.S. Military Recruited Neo-Nazis, Gang Members, and Criminals to Fight the War on Terror* (London: Verso Books, 2012).

148. Federal Bureau of Investigation, Counterterrorism Division. *Ghost Skins: The Fascist Path to Stealth*. October 17, 2006, p. 1, available at www.documentcloud.org/documents/402522-doc-27-ghost-skins.html.

149. Kelly Weill, "Inside the New Push to Expose America's White Supremacist Cops," *Daily Beast,* June 29, 2020, www.thedailybeast.com/inside-the-new-push-to-expose-americas-white-supremacist-cops; Maddy Crowell and Sylvia Varnham O'Regan, "Extremist Cops: How US Law Enforcement is Failing to Police Itself," *Guardian* (UK), December 13, 2019, www.theguardian.com/us-news/2019/dec/13/how-us-law-enforcement-is-failing-to-police-itself. The phenomenon of Ghost Skins is not relegated to the United States, and can be found in other countries as well. See, for example, Katrin Bennhold, "As Neo-Nazis Seed Military Ranks, Germany Confronts 'an Enemy Within,'" *New York Times,* July 3, 2020, www.nytimes.com/2020/07/03/world/europe/germany-military-neo-nazis-ksk.html.

150. Federal Bureau of Investigation, Counterterrorism Division, *FBI Intelligence Assessment: White Supremacist Recruitment of Military Personnel Since 9/11,* July 7, 2008, p. 3, available at www.documentcloud.org/documents/402528-doc-33-fbi-whitesuprec.html.

151. Heidi L. Beirich, "Written Testimony of Heidi L. Beirich, Ph.D., Co-Founder, Global Project against Hate and Extremism, before the Congress of the United States House of Representatives Armed Services Committee Military Personnel Subcommittee Regarding 'Alarming Incidents of White Supremacy in the Military—How to Stop It?'" February 11, 2020, www.congress.gov/116/meeting/house/110495/witnesses/HHRG-116-AS02-Wstate-BeirichH-20200211.pdf.

152. For more on these efforts in the military, see David Holthouse, "Several High Profile Racist Extremists Serve in the U.S. Military," *Intelligence Report,* Southern Poverty Law Center, 2006 Summer Issue, August 11, 2006, www.splcenter.org/fighting-hate/intelligence-report/2006/several-high-profile-racist-extremists-serve-us-military; and Samuel Vincent Jones, "Law Enforcement and White Power: An FBI Report Unraveled," *Thurgood Marshall Law Review* 41, no. 1 (2015): 99–104.

153. Jessica Schulberg, Travis Waldron, and Doha Madani, "A Couple Dozen Neo-Nazis Got the Red Carpet Treatment from DC Law Enforcement," *Huffington Post,* August 12, 2018, updated August 13, 2018, www.huffingtonpost.com /entry/protesters-outnumber-nazis-unite-the-right-ii-washington-dc_us_ 5b7042efe4b0bdd0620a179a; Sam Levin, "California Police Worked with Neo-Nazis to Pursue 'Anti-Racist' Activists, Documents Show," *Guardian* (UK), February 9, 2018, www.theguardian.com/world/2018/feb/09/california-police-white-supremacists-counter-protest.

154. Jackson Landers, "A Leaked Message Board Shows What White Supremacists Think of the Police," *Rewire.News,* March 9, 2018, https:// rewire.news/article/2018/03/09/leaked-message-board-shows-white-supremacists-think-police.

155. Hector Tobar, "Deputies in 'Neo-Nazi' Gang, Judge Found: Sheriff's Department: Many at Lynwood Office Have Engaged in Racially Motivated Violence against Blacks and Latinos, Jurist Wrote," *Los Angeles Times,* October 12, 1991, http://articles.latimes.com/1991-10-12/local/me-107_1_deputy-county; Anne-Marie O'Connor and Tina Daunt, "The Secret Society among Lawmen," *Los Angeles Times,* March 24, 1999, http://articles.latimes.com/1999/mar/24 /news/mn-20461; Robert Faturechi, "L.A. County Sheriff's Department Intends to Fire Seven Deputies," *Los Angeles Times,* February 6, 2013, http://articles .latimes.com/2013/feb/06/local/la-me-jump-out-boys-20130207; Maya Lau, "After Decades of Problems, New Allegations Surface of a Secret Clique within L.A. County Sheriff's Department," *Los Angeles Times,* July 10, 2018, www .latimes.com/local/lanow/la-me-compton-sheriff-shooting-20180710-story .html; Maya Lau, "L.A. Sheriff Watchdogs Alarmed about New Claims of Secret Deputy Clique at Compton Station," *Los Angeles Times,* July 13, 2018, www .latimes.com/local/lanow/la-me-sheriff-tattoo-compton-investigation-20180713-story.html.

156. Leo Shane III, "One in Four Troops Sees White Nationalism in the Ranks," *MilitaryTimes,* October 23, 2017, www.militarytimes.com/news /pentagon-congress/2017/10/23/military-times-poll-one-in-four-troops-sees-white-nationalism-in-the-ranks. A ProPublica and Frontline investigation also found that numerous Marines were members of neo-Nazi groups; see A. C. Thompson, "An Alarming Tip about a Neo-Nazi Marine, Then an Uncertain Response," ProPublica, May 22, 2018, www.propublica.org/article/an-alarming-tip-about-a-neo-nazi-marine-then-an-uncertain-response.

157. After pleading guilty to twenty-nine hate crimes, James Alex Fields Jr. was sentenced to life in prison in 2019. He was also charged for state hate crimes and sentenced to life in prison plus 419 years. In 2017, he drove a car into a crowd of counterprotesters, killing Heather Heyer and injuring dozens. During the Unite the Right rally, he was dressed as a Vanguard America member and carried a shield with the group's logo, forming a barrier around the statue of the Confederate general Robert E. Lee with other members of the organization. "Ohio Man Pleads Guilty to 29 Federal Hate Crimes for August 2017 Car Attack at Rally in Charlottesville," United States Department of Justice, March 27, 2019, www.justice.gov/opa/pr/ohio-man-pleads-guilty-29-federal-hate-crimes-august-2017-car-attack-rally-charlottesville; Justin Wm.

Moyer and Lindsey Bever, "Vanguard America, a White Supremacist Group, Denies Charlottesville Ramming Suspect was a Member," August 15, 2017, *Washington Post*, www.washingtonpost.com/local/vanguard-america-a-white-supremacist-group-denies-charlottesville-attacker-was-a-member/2017/08/15/2ec897c6-810e-11e7-8072-73e1718c524d_story.html.

158. John Hudson, "Soldiers in Anti-Obama Plot Wanted to 'Give Government Back to the People,'" *Atlantic,* August 28, 2012, www.theatlantic.com/national/archive/2012/08/us-soldiers-anti-obama-plot-wanted-give-government-back-people/324206; "'Anarchists' Accused of Murder; Broader Plot against Government," *CNN*, August 28, 2012, www.cnn.com/2012/08/28/justice/georgia-soldiers-plot/index.html.

159. Authorities found some of his correspondence located in his "Deletions" subfolder, under the "Recoverable Items" folder. He also seems to have sent himself a draft of the letter he sent to Covington. United States of America vs Christopher Paul Hasson, Motion for detention pending trial, United States Of America v. Christopher Paul Hasson, United States District Court for the District Of Maryland, case no. GLS-19-63, https://int.nyt.com/data/documenthelper/625-us-v-hasson/be7a4841596aba86cce4/optimized/full.pdf, p. 2, 4.

160. Tim Jackman, "Self-Proclaimed White Nationalist Accused of Planning Mass Killing Expected to Plead Guilty," *Washington Post,* October 2, 2019, www.washingtonpost.com/crime-law/2019/10/02/self-proclaimed-white-nationalist-who-planned-mass-killing-expected-plead-guilty.

161. Michael Levenson, "Former Coast Guard Lieutenant Is Sentenced to 13 Years in Prison on Gun and Drug Charges," *New York Times,* January 31, 2020, www.nytimes.com/2020/01/31/us/christopher-hasson-coast-guard-terrorism.html.

162. Stephen Losey, "Airman Accused of White Nationalist Ties Loses Stripe after Investigation—But Still in the Air Force," *AirForce Times,* November 12, 2109, www.airforcetimes.com/news/your-air-force/2019/11/12/airman-accused-of-white-nationalist-ties-loses-stripe-after-investigation-but-still-in-the-air-force; Stephen Losey, "The Air Force Is Moving to Discharge Airman Investigated for White Nationalist Ties," *AirForceTimes,* December 17, 2019, www.airforcetimes.com/news/your-air-force/2019/12/17/the-air-force-is-moving-to-discharge-airman-investigated-for-white-nationalist-ties.

163. Chris Schiano and Freddy Martinez, "Neo-Nazi Hipsters Identity Evropa Exposed in Discord Chat Leak," Unicorn Riot, March 6, 2019, https://unicornriot.ninja/2019/neo-nazi-hipsters-identity-evropa-exposed-in-discord-chat-leak.

164. "White Nationalist 'Ravensblood Kindred' Features Haralson County Jailer and Active Duty National Guardsman," Atlanta Antifa, April 9, 2019, updated May 21, 2019, https://atlantaantifa.org/2019/04/09/white-nationalist-ravensblood-kindred-features-haralson-county-jailer-and-active-duty-national-guardsman.

165. National Defense Authorization Act for Fiscal Year 2020, Pub. L. No. 116-92, S. 1790, 116th Cong., https://rules.house.gov/sites/democrats.rules.house.gov/files/CRPT-116hrpt333.pdf, p. 370.

166. Elaine Frantz Parsons, *Ku-Klux: The Birth of the Klan during Reconstruction* (Chapel Hill: University of North Carolina Press, 2015), 9.

167. Michael S. Rosenwald, "The Ku Klux Klan Was Dead: The First Hollywood Blockbuster Revived It," *Washington Post,* August 12, 2017, www .washingtonpost.com/news/retropolis/wp/2017/07/08/the-ku-klux-klan-had-been-destroyed-then-the-first-hollywood-blockbuster-revived-it.

168. Durham, *White Rage,* 45.

169. Baker, *Gospel According to the Klan,* 38–39, 64–65.

170. For an understanding of what fascism is, see Jason Stanley, *How Fascism Works: The Politics of Us and Them* (New York: Random House, 2018). For the applicability of the term *facist* to the presidency of Donald Trump, see Masha Gessen, *Surviving Autocracy,* New York: Riverhead Books, 2020; and Masha Gessen, "Donald Trump's Fascist Performance," *New Yorker,* June 3, 2020, www.newyorker.com/news/our-columnists/donald-trumps-fascist-performance.

171. "Anti-Semitism: Neo-Nazism," Jewish Virtual Library: A Project of AICE, accessed September 2, 2017, www.jewishvirtuallibrary.org/neo-nazism-2.

172. Serge F. Kovaleski, Julie Turkewitz, Joseph Goldstein, and Dan Barry, "An Alt-Right Makeover Shrouds the Swastikas," *New York Times,* December 10, 2016, www.nytimes.com/2016/12/10/us/alt-right-national-socialist-movement-white-supremacy.html.

173. Coates, *Armed and Dangerous,* 49.

174. Federal Bureau of Investigation, "Project Megiddo," in *Millennial Violence: Past, Present, Future,* ed. Jeffrey Kaplan (Portland, OR: F. Cass, 2002), 7.

175. Mattias Gardell, "The Order," in *Encyclopedia of White Power: A Sourcebook on the Radical Racist Right,* ed. Jeffrey Kaplan (Walnut Creek, CA: AltaMira Press, 2000), 233.

176. Evidence linking Timothy McVeigh to Elohim City, collected by the Associated Press, includes hotel receipts, a speeding ticket, prisoner interviews, informant reports, and phone records. See Deborah Hastings, "Elohim City on Extremists' Underground Railroad," *Los Angeles Times,* February 23, 1997, http://articles.latimes.com/1997-02-23/news/mn-31595_1_elohim-city.

177. Joel Dyer, *Harvest of Rage: Why Oklahoma City Is Only the Beginning* (Boulder, CO: Westview Press, 1998), 223.

178. Federal Bureau of Investigation, "Project Megiddo," 32.

179. For an overview of neo-Confederates, see Euan Hague, Edward H. Sebesta, and Heidi Beirich, *Neo-Confederacy: A Critical Introduction* (Austin: University of Texas Press, 2008). For a study of American secessionist movements, see Richard Kreitner, *Break It Up: Secession, Division, and the Secret History of America's Imperfect Union* (New York: Little, Brown, 2020).

180. Michael Hill, "What Is the League of the South?" League of the South, accessed September 1, 2017, http://dixienet.org/rights/2013/what_is_League_of_the_South.php.

181. Janet Smith, "League of the South: 'What Would It Take to Get You to Fight?'" *Hatewatch* (blog), Southern Poverty Law Center, August 4, 2011,

www.splcenter.org/blog/2011/08/04/league-of-the-south-what-would-it-take-to-get-you-to-fight.

182. Joe Arpaio, who was convicted of defying a court order to stop the racial profiling of Latinxs (American citizens as well as undocumented Americans and undocumented immigrants), was noted for his harsh and often inhumane treatment of prisoners in his jail, which was often referred to as Tent City. Tent City was described by Arpaio himself as a "concentration camp." See Fernanda Santos, "Outdoor Jail, a Vestige of Joe Arpaio's Tenure, Is Closing," *New York Times*, April 4, 2017, www.nytimes.com/2017/04/04/us/arpaio-tent-city-maricopa-sheriff-penzone.html; and Jesse Taylor, "Sheriff Joe Arpaio: 'Tent City' Concentration Camp," YouTube video, 2:15, June 1, 2012, www.youtube.com/watch?v=1fj3mRGQoow. Evidencing the convergence of groups on the political far right, and most especially White nationalism, Arpaio was pardoned by President Trump in 2017 before he was due to be sentenced, granting a boon to Constitutional Sheriffs everywhere, who, despite their stance against the apparatus of the federal government, had found an ally at the top level of the White House.

183. Religious themes are often present in the rhetoric of Richard Mack, a prominent Constitutional Sheriff. He has stated that "the Constitution only protects the rights endowed by God in the Bible." David Neiwert, "Richard Mack, Enemy of Federal Power, Now Attacking Same-Sex Marriage," *Hatewatch* (blog), Southern Poverty Law Center, January 7, 2014, www.splcenter.org/hatewatch/2014/01/07/richard-mack-enemy-federal-power-now-attacking-same-sex-marriage. Journalist Ashley Powers reported that Mack was influenced by "Salt Lake City police chief and author W. Cleon Skousen, who believed that the Founders were God's disciples and the Constitution a Christian document. As a young officer, Mack had attended one of Skousen's workshops. 'That man spoke with the power of angels,' he told me." Powers, "The Renegade Sheriffs," *New Yorker*, April 30, 2018, www.newyorker.com/magazine/2018/04/30/the-renegade-sheriffs. For more on the Constitutional Sheriffs and Peace Officers Association and other key players within the Constitutional Sheriffs movement, see Julia Harte and R. Jeffrey Smith, "'The Army to Set Our Nation Free,'" Center for Public Integrity, April 18, 2016, updated May 24, 2016, www.publicintegrity.org/2016/04/18/19568/army-set-our-nation-free; and Robert L. Tsai, "The Troubling Sheriff's Movement that Joe Arpaio Supports," *Politico*, September 1, 2017, www.politico.com/magazine/story/2017/09/01/joe-arpaio-pardon-sheriffs-movement-215566.

184. Ben Cameron, "The Constitutional Republic," *Identity: A Christian Church Publication* 6, no. 1 (n.d.), available at www.seditionists.com/identity_6_1.pdf.

185. Levitas, *Terrorist Next Door*, 2, 10, 24.

186. For firsthand accounts of the violence targeting abortion providers, see David S. Cohen and Krysten Connon, *Living in the Crosshairs: The Untold Stories of Anti-Abortion Terrorism* (New York: Oxford University Press, 2015).

187. Jennifer L. Jefferis, *Armed for Life: The Army of God and Anti-Abortion Terror in the United States* (Santa Barbara, California: Praeger, 2011), 13–14.

188. Mark Juergensmeyer, *Terror in the Mind of God: The Global Rise of Religious Violence,* 4th ed. (Oakland: University of California Press, 2017), 20–40.

189. Army of God, "Sword of the Lord," no date, accessed September 1, 2017, https://www.armyofgod.com.

190. Eric Rudolph, "Full Text of Eric Rudolph's Confession," NPR, April 14, 2005, accessed September 1, 2017, www.npr.org/templates/story/story.php?storyId=4600480.

191. "Our History," Hammerskin Nation.

192. Joe Sterling, "White Nationalism, a Term Once on the Fringes, Now Front and Center," *CNN,* November 17, 2016, www.cnn.com/2016/11/16/politics/what-is-white-nationalism-trnd/index.html; Rebel Redneck 59, "What is White Racialism?" Stormfront, March 25, 2011, www.stormfront.org/forum/t789365; Andrew Marantz, "The Alt-Right Branding War Has Torn the Movement in Two," *New Yorker,* July 6, 2017, www.newyorker.com/news/newsdesk/the-alt-right-branding-war-has-torn-the-movement-in-two.

193. Alexandra Minna Stern, *Proud Boys and the White Ethnostate: How the Alt-Right Is Warping the American Imagination* (Boston: Beacon Press, 2019).

194. Simon Houpt, "Everything inside Gavin McInnes," *Globe and Mail* (Toronto), August 18, 2017, updated November 12, 2017, www.theglobeandmail.com/arts/television/gavin-mcinnes-path-to-the-far-rightfrontier/article36024918.

195. Proud Boy (website), www.proudboysusa.com; "Proud Boys Founder on Whether He Feels Responsible for Its Controversial Behavior," ABC News, video, December 12, 2018, https://abcnews.go.com/Nightline/video/proud-boys-founder-feels-responsible-controversial-behavior-59766444.

196. Skutner, "Proud Boys Incidents 2016–2019," ArcGIS web map, last modified October 30, 2019, www.arcgis.com/home/webmap/viewer.html?webmap=46c5dd159e984d59b636229a55561807&extent=-146.5001,22.4863,-45.4259,57.7828.

197. Garrett Epps, "The Proud Boys' Real Target," *Atlantic,* August 23, 2019, www.theatlantic.com/ideas/archive/2019/08/meaning-street-protests-portland/596686.

198. Donald Trump (@RealDonaldTrump), "Major consideration is being given to naming ANTIFA an 'ORGANIZATION OF TERROR,'" Twitter, August 17, 2019, 7:04 a.m., https://twitter.com/realdonaldtrump/status/1162726857231544320.

199. "Portland Protests: 13 Arrested as Police Declare Civil Disturbance," *Oregonian,* August 17, 2019, updated August 18, 2019, www.oregonlive.com/portland/2019/08/portland-protests-antifa-right-wing-groups-set-to-face-off-downtown-live-updates.html.

200. Richard Spencer, "'Vikings' and the Pagan-Christian Synthesis," *Radix Journal,* December 2, 2014, www.radixjournal.com/journal/vikings-pagan-christian-synthesis.

201. Sophie Bjork-James and Jeff Maskovsky, "When White Nationalism Became Popular," *Populism Rising* 58, no. 3 (2017): 86–91; Cas Mudde, "Stop Using the Term 'Alt-Right'!" *Huffington Post,* August 25, 2016, www

.huffingtonpost.com/cas-mudde/stop-using-the-term-alt-r_b_11705870.html; George Hawley, email to author, July 14, 2017.

202. Julie Ingersoll, "Religiously Motivated Violence in the Abortion Debate," in *The Oxford Handbook of Religion and Violence,* ed. Mark Juergensmeyer, Margo Kitts, and Michael Jerryson (New York: Oxford University Press, 2013), 315–23.

203. "Southern Baptists Condemn 'Alt-Right White Supremacy,'" *Time,* June 15, 2017, http://time.com/4819638/southern-baptists-condemn-alt-right-white-supremacy. *Incels* is a term for "involuntary celibate" and is a group made up of mostly men who have come to view women generally and feminism in particular as the cause of their inability to find a sexual or romantic partner. See Sylvia Jaki, Tom De Smedt, Maja Gwóźdź, Rudresh Panchal, Alexander Rossa, and Guy De Pauw, "Online Hatred of Women in the Incels.me Forum: Linguistic Analysis and Automatic Detection," *Journal of Language Aggression and Conflict* 7, no. 2 (2019): 240–68, https://doi.org/10.1075/jlac.00026.jak.

CHAPTER 2. LOYALTY AND DISAVOWAL

1. Affidavit of Enrique Marquez, U.S. Department of Justice, December 17, 2015, www.justice.gov/opa/file/800606/download.

2. Megan Christie, Rhonda Schwartz, Josh Margolin, and Brian Ross, "Christmas Party May Have Triggered San Bernardino Terror Attack: Police," ABC News, November 30, 2016, https://abcnews.go.com/US/christmas-party-triggered-san-bernardino-terror-attack-police/story?id=43884973.

3. William Finnegan, "Last Days," *New Yorker,* February 22, 2016, www.newyorker.com/magazine/2016/02/22/preparing-for-apocalypse-in-san-bernardino.

4. Margaret Sullivan, "Systemic Change Needed after Faulty Times Article," *New York Times,* December 18, 2015, https://publiceditor.blogs.nytimes.com/2015/12/18/new-york-times-san-bernardino-correction-margaret-sullivan-public-editor.

5. Scott Glover, Lorenza Brascia, and Evan Perez, "Enrique Marquez: San Bernardino Killer and I Plotted in 2012," *CNN,* December 10, 2015, www.cnn.com/2015/12/08/us/san-bernardino-investigation-neighbor/index.html.

6. See Lorenzo Vidino and Seamus Hughes, *ISIS in America: From Retweets to Raqqa* (Washington, DC: George Washington University Program on Extremism, December 2015), https://extremism.gwu.edu/sites/g/files/zaxdzs2191/f/downloads/ISIS%20in%20America%20-%20Full%20Report.pdf; Lorne L. Dawson and Amarnath Amarasingam, "Talking to Foreign Fighters: Insights into the Motivations for Hijrah to Syria and Iraq," *Studies in Conflict and Terrorism* 40, no. 3 (2017): 191–210.

7. "Murder and Extremism in the United States in 2018," Center on Extremism, Anti-Defamation League, January 2019, www.adl.org/murder-and-extremism-2018#the-perpetrators; Charles Kurzman, "Muslim-American Involvement with Violent Extremism, 2001–2019," Triangle Center on Terrorism and Homeland Security, January 21, 2020, available at https://drive.google.com/file/d/1JmL7MjWCSwV2jYEu1fEUdVtCUXE3pA46/view.

8. Eric Lichtblau, "F.B.I. Steps Up Use of Stings in ISIS Cases," *New York Times,* June 7, 2016, www.nytimes.com/2016/06/08/us/fbi-isis-terrorism-stings .html; Peter Aldhous, "How the FBI Invents Terror Plots to Catch Wannabe Jihadis," *Buzzfeed News,* November 17, 2015, www.buzzfeednews.com/article /peteraldhous/fbi-entrapment#.cfrO1AoWN.

9. Criminal complaint, United States of America v. Enrique Marquez Jr., United States District Court, Central District of California, December 17, 2015, available at, www.justice.gov/usao-cdca/file/1066121/download; plea agreement, United States of America v. Enrique Marquez Jr., United States District Court, Central District of California, case no. CR 15-93-JGB, February 14, 2017, available at www.justice.gov/opa/press-release/file/939261/download.

10. Curt Woodward, "Seattle Suspect Allegedly Ambushed Girl," *Washington Post,* July 29, 2006, www.washingtonpost.com/wp-dyn/content/article/2006 /07/29/AR2006072901032.html.

11. Richard Serrano, "Federal Government Isn't Touching Arkansas Terrorism Case," *Los Angeles Times,* July 11, 2011, www.latimes.com/world/la-xpm-2011-jul-11-la-na-little-rock-death-20110710-story.html.

12. Yasmin Khorram, Ben Brumfield, and Scott Zamost, "Chattanooga Shooter Changed after Mideast Visit, Friend Says," *CNN,* September 15, 2015, www.cnn.com/2015/07/17/us/tennessee-shooter-mohammad-youssuf-abdulazeez /index.html.

13. Caroline Vandergriff, "Jurors Hear Interviews with Alton Nolen Explaining Why He Beheaded Co-worker," *Fox 25 News,* September 20, 2017, http:// okcfox.com/news/local/jurors-hear-interviews-with-alton-nolen-explaining- why-he-beheaded-co-worker.

14. Arrest warrant, United States of America v. Ahmad Khan Rahami, United States District Court, Southern District of New York, case no. 16 MAG 6009, September 20, 2016, available at www.justice.gov/opa/file/894491 /download.

15. Steve Almasy and Chuck Johnson, "Florida Teen Held in Killing Was Being Investigated by FBI over Possible ISIS Interest," *CNN,* March 15, 2018, www.cnn.com/2018/03/14/us/florida-teen-fatal-stabbing-muslim/index.html.

16. "Ohio Man Pleads Guilty to Plotting July 4th Attack in Cleveland as Part of Plot to Provide Support to Al Qaeda," Office of Public Affairs, U.S. Department of Justice, November 5, 2019, www.justice.gov/opa/pr/ohio-man-pleads- guilty-plotting-july-4th-attack-cleveland-part-plot-provide-support-al-qaeda.

17. Daniel Byman, "How States Exploit Jihadist Foreign Fighters," *Studies in Conflict and Terrorism* 41, no. 12 (2018): 931–45, https://doi.org/10.1080/1 057610X.2017.1361281.

18. Tricia Bacon and Elizabeth Grimm Arsenault, "Al Qaeda and the Islamic State's Break: Strategic Strife or Lackluster Leadership?" *Studies in Conflict and Terrorism* 42, no. 3 (2019): 229–63, https://doi.org/10.1080/1057610X .2017.1373895.

19. Alexander Meleagrou-Hitchens, Seamus Hughes, Mennett Clifford, *The Travelers: American Jihadists in Syria and Iraq* (Washington, DC: Program on Extremism, George Washington University, February 2018), p. x, https:// extremism.gwu.edu/sites/g/files/zaxdzs2191/f/TravelersAmericanJihadistsin

SyriaandIraq.pdf; Richard Barrett, *Beyond the Caliphate: Foreign Fighters and the Threat of Returnees* (New York: Soufan Center, October 2017), 11, http://thesoufancenter.org/wp-content/uploads/2017/11/Beyond-the-Caliphate-Foreign-Fighters-and-the-Threat-of-Returnees-TSC-Report-October-2017-v3.pdf.

20. Daniel Byman and Jennifer Williams, "ISIS vs. Al Qaeda: Jihadism's Global Civil War," National Interest, February 24, 2015, http://nationalinterest.org/feature/isis-vs-al-qaeda-jihadism's-global-civil-war-12304.

21. Ruthie Blum, "New ISIS Announcement: Victory in Palestine Near—First over Hamas and PA and 'Infidels,' Then the Jews," *Algemeiner,* May 2, 2016, www.algemeiner.com/2016/05/02/new-isis-announcement-victory-in-palestine-near-first-over-hamas-and-pa-infidels-then-the-jews.

22. "Zawahiri's Letter to Zarqawi (English Translation)," Combatting Terrorism Center at West Point, accessed September 4, 2017, https://ctc.usma.edu/v2/wp-content/uploads/2013/10/Zawahiris-Letter-to-Zarqawi-Translation.pdf.

23. Daniel L. Byman, "Comparing Al Qaeda and ISIS: Different Goals, Different Targets," Brookings, April 29, 2015, www.brookings.edu/research/testimony/2015/04/29-terrorism-in-africa-byman; "Zawahiri's Letter to Zarqawi," Combatting Terrorism Center at West Point; Jeff Stein, "Ayman al-Zawahiri: How a CIA Drone Strike Nearly Killed the Head of Al-Qaeda," *Newsweek,* April 21, 2017, www.newsweek.com/ayman-al-zawahiri-cia-donald-trump-drone-strike-osama-bin-laden-pakistan-587732.

24. Lawrence Wright, "The Double Game: The Unintended Consequences of America Funding Pakistan," *New Yorker,* May 16, 2011, www.newyorker.com/magazine/2011/05/16/the-double-game.

25. Ahmed Rashid, *Taliban: Militant Islam, Oil, and Fundamentalism in Central Asia* (New Haven, CT: Yale University Press, 2000); Michael Moran, "Bin Laden Comes Home to Roost: His CIA Ties Are Only the Beginning of a Woeful Story," *NBC,* August 24, 1988, www.nbcnews.com/id/3340101/t/bin-laden-comes-home-roost/#.WZNW24qQyCQ; Ahmed Rashid, "Osama Bin Laden: How the U.S. Helped Midwife a Terrorist," Interactive Media Lab at the University of Florida, September 13, 2001, http://iml.jou.ufl.edu/projects/fall01/Easton/webstuff%5Cwhoisosama.html; National Commission on Terrorist Attacks upon the United States, The *9/11 Commission Report: The Official Report of the 9/11 Commission and Related Publications* (New York : Norton, 2004), 56; "Mapping Militant Organizations: Al Qaeda," Stanford University, accessed September 4, 2017, http://web.stanford.edu/group/mappingmilitants/cgi-bin/groups/view/21#note97.

26. Muhammad 'Abd as-Salam Faraj, *The Neglected Duty: The Creed of Sadat's Assassins and Islamic Resurgence in the Middle East,* trans. Johannes J. G. Jansen (New York: Macmillan, 1986), foreword, 8.

27. Fawaz A. Gerges, *The Far Enemy: Why Jihad Went Global* (Cambridge: Cambridge University Press, 2005), 12.

28. Faraj, *Neglected Duty,* foreword, vii, 172–75.

29. Rashid, *Taliban,* 131.

30. Aryn Baker, "Who Killed Abdullah Azzam?" *Time,* June 18, 2009, http://content.time.com/time/specials/packages/printout/0,29239,1902809_1902810_1905173,00.html.

31. Aubrey Immelman and Kathryn Kuhlmann, "'Bin Laden's Brain': The Abrasively Negativistic Personality of Dr. Ayman al-Zawahiri" (paper presented at the Twenty-Sixth Annual Scientific Meeting of the International Society of Political Psychology, Boston, July 6–9, 2003).

32. For more on the development of Islamic State (Dā'ish) during the time of az-Zarqawi, see Joby Warrick, *Black Flags: The Rise of ISIS* (New York: Anchor Books, 2016).

33. "ISIS Spokesman Declares Caliphate, Rebrands Group as 'Islamic State,'" SITE Intelligence Group, June 29, 2014, https://news.siteintelgroup .com/Jihadist-News/isis-spokesman-declares-caliphate-rebrands-group-as-islamic-state.html.

34. "ISIS Spokesman Declares Caliphate," SITE Intelligence Group.

35. Al-Baghdadi was highly conscious of the symbolic value of such gestures. He also attempted to sanctify his position as Amir ul-Mu'minin (Leader of the Believers) and express his supposed piety by founding Islamic State (Dā'ish) during the Islamic holy month of Ramadan, on the first day of the month in 1435 AH (June 29, 2014).

36. Charles Caris and Samuel Reynolds, *ISIS Governance in Syria, Middle East Security Report* 22 (Washington, DC: Institute for the Study of War, 2014), 4.

37. Alyssa Martino, "Water Scarcity Is Helping Radicalize the Middle East," *Vice,* April 25, 2015, www.vice.com/en_us/article/exq45z/is-water-scarcity-radicalizing-the-middle-east-235; Marcus DuBois King, "The Weaponization of Water in Syria and Iraq," *Washington Quarterly* 38, no. 4 (2015): 153–69.

38. Michael Crawford, *Ibn 'Abd al-Wahhab,* Makers of the Muslim World (London: Oneworld Publications, 2014).

39. In addition to the four main schools of Sunni jurisprudence, there is also the Shi'i school of jurisprudence, which differs greatly in its sources, interpretation, and application of Islamic law. For these reasons, the case studies in this book are limited to those that identify with Sunni Islam.

40. Toni Johnson and Muhammad Aly Sergie, "Islam: Governing under Sharia," Council on Foreign Relations, July 25, 2014, www.cfr.org/religion /islam-governing-under-sharia/p8034.

41. Samira Haj, *Reconfiguring Islamic Tradition: Reform, Rationality, and Modernity* (Stanford, CA: Stanford University Press, 2009), 31.

42. Andrew McGregor, "'Jihad and the Rifle Alone': Abdullah 'Azzam and the Islamist Revolution," *Journal of Conflict Studies* 23, no. 2 (Fall 2003), https://journals.lib.unb.ca/index.php/jcs/article/view/219/377#56.

43. Julten Abdelhalim, *Indian Muslims and Citizenship: Spaces for Jihād in Everyday Life* (Oxford: Routledge, 2015), 99; Zia Ur Rehman, "Pakistani Madrassas: An Indispensable Institution, A Worry for the State," *TRT World,* May 20, 2019, www.trtworld.com/magazine/pakistani-madrassas-an-indispensable-institution-a-worry-for-the-state-26787; Chris Kraul, "Dollars to Help Pupils in Pakistan," *Los Angeles Times,* April 14, 2003, www.latimes.com/archives /la-xpm-2003-apr-14-fg-schools14-story.html; Sabrina Tavernise, "Pakistan's Islamic Schools Fill Void, but Fuel Militancy," *New York Times,* May 3, 2009, www.nytimes.com/2009/05/04/world/asia/04schools.html; Nellie Peyton, "Tradition or Trafficking? Guinea-Bissau Children Suffer in Senegal's Islamic Schools,"

Reuters, March 5, 2019, www.reuters.com/article/us-bissau-education-trafficking/tradition-or-trafficking-guinea-bissau-children-suffer-in-senegals-islamic-schools-idUSKCN1QN054; International Crisis Group, *Pakistan: Madrasas, Extremism and the Military,* ICG Asia Report no. 36., July 29, 2002, available at www.refworld.org/docid/3de778624.html.

44. ʿAbd al-Raḥmān ibn Muʿallā Luwayḥiq, *Religious Extremism in the Lives of Contemporary Muslims,* trans. Jamaal al-Din M. Zarabozo (Denver: Al-Basheer Company for Publications and Translations, 2001), 184; Muḥammad ibn Saʿīd ibn Sālim Qaḥṭānī, *Al-Walaʾ waʾl-baraʾ: According to the ʿAqeedah of the Salaf,* trans. Omar Johnstone (London: Al-Firdous, 1999), 90.

45. Rohan Guanaratna and Mohamed Feisal Bin Mohamed Hassan, "Terrorist Rehabilitation: The Singapore Experience," in *Terrorist Rehabilitation and Counter-Radicalisation: New Approaches to Counter-Terrorism,* ed. Rohan Gunaratna, Jolene Jerard, and Lawrence Rubin (London: Routledge, 2011), 41.

46. Uriya Shavit, *Sharīʿa and Muslim Minorities: The Wasaṭī and Salafī Approaches to Fiqh al-Aqalliyyāt al-Muslima* (Oxford: Oxford University Press, 2015), 58; Ibn Taymiyyah, *The Friends of Allah and the Friends of the Shatyan,* trans. Abu Rumaysah (Birmingham: Daar us-Sunnah Publishers, 2005), 39–84.

47. Shavit, *Sharīʿa and Muslim Minorities,* 58; Joas Wagemakers, "The Transformation of a Radical Concept: *Al-walaʾ wa-l-baraʾ* in the Ideology of Abu Muhammad al-Maqdisi," in *Global Salafism: Islam's New Religious Movement,* ed. Roel Meijer (New York: Columbia University Press, 2009), 87; Ibn Taymiyyah, *Friends of Allah,* 60, 63–64. Ibn Taymiyya, *Majmuʿ al-Fataawa,* vol. 28 (Dar al-Kutub al-Islami: Riyadh, 1991), 32; Qaḥṭānī, *Al-Walaʾ waʾl-baraʾ,* 17.

48. Mohamed Bin Ali, *The Roots of Religious Extremism: Understanding the Salafi Doctrine of al-Walaʾ Wal Baraʾ* (London: Imperial College Press, 2016), 132.

49. Bin Ali, *Roots of Religious Extremism,* 137.

50. Bin Ali, *Roots of Religious Extremism,* 138.

51. Yahya M. Michot, "Ibn Taymiyya (1263–1328)," in *The Princeton Encyclopedia of Islamic Political Thought,* ed. Gerhard Böwering, Patricia Crone, and Mahan Mirza (Princeton, NJ: Princeton University Press, 2013), 239.

52. Joas Wagemakers, "Framing the 'Threat to Islam': *Al-Walaʾ wa al-Baraʾ* in Salafi Discourse," *Arab Studies Quarterly* 30, no. 4 (Fall 2008): 13.

53. Joas Wagemakers, *A Quietist Jihadi: The Ideology and Influence of Abu Muhammad al-Maqdisi* (Cambridge: Cambridge University Press, 2012), 239.

54. Daniel Lav, *Radical Islam and the Revival of Medieval Theology* (New York: Cambridge University Press, 2012), 168.

55. Raymond Ibrahim, ed. and trans., *The Al Qaeda Reader* (New York: Broadway Books, 2007), 92–93.

56. As-Saʿīd Muḥammad Badawī and M.A.S. Abdel Haleem, *Arabic-English Dictionary of Qurʾanic Usage* (Leiden: Brill, 2008), 565.

57. Muhammad Ibn Abd al-Wahhab and Muhammad bin ʿAbdir-Rahmaan Al-Khumayyis, *Explanation of "The Meaning of Taghoot," of the Imaam and Mujaddid Muhammad bin ʿAbdil-Wahhaab,* trans. Ismaʿeel Alarcon (n.p.:

Al-Ibaanah Book Publishing, 2003), 9-13, available at http://tawheednyc.com
/aqeedah/tawheed/Taghoot.pdf.

58. Qaḥṭānī, *Al-Walaʾ waʾl-baraʾ*, 17.

59. Sayed Khatab, *The Power of Sovereignty: The Political and Ideological Philosophy of Sayyid Qutb,* Routledge Studies in Political Islam (New York: Routledge, 2006), 49; Sayyid Qutb, *In the Shade of the Quʾan (Fī Ẓilāl al-Qurʾan)*, trans. M. A. Salahi and A. A. Shamis (Leicester: Islamic Foundation, 1999), 1330–31; Sayyid Qutb, *Milestones* (Indianapolis: American Trust Publications, 1993), 108.

60. Wagemakers, *Quietist Jihadi,* 67; Ellis Goldberg, "Smashing Idols and the State: The Protestant Ethic and Egyptian Sunni Radicalism," *Comparative Studies in Society and History* 33, no. 1 (January 1991): 22.

61. Olivier Roy, *Afghanistan: From Holy War to Civil War* (Princeton, NJ: Darwin Press, 1995), 37.

62. Katie Zavadski, "ISIS Targets American Imams for Believing Muslims Can Thrive in U.S.," *Daily Beast,* April 14, 2016, www.thedailybeast.com/isis-targets-american-imams-for-believing-muslims-can-thrive-in-us.

63. Hashimi is believed to have been jailed for ties to Anwar as-Sadat's assassination in 1981.

64. Crawford, *Ibn ʿAbd al-Wahhab,* 61–71.

65. Devin R. Springer, James L. Regens, and David N. Edger, *Islamic Radicalism and Global Jihad* (Washington, DC: Georgetown University Press, 2009), 130.

66. Crawford, *Ibn ʿAbd al-Wahhab,* 61–63.

67. Crawford, *Ibn ʿAbd al-Wahhab,* 63.

68. Gudrun Krämer, *Hasan al-Banna,* Makers of the Muslim World (Oxford: Oneworld Publications, 2010), 103; Goldberg, "Smashing Idols and the State," 22; Wagemakers, *Quietist Jihadi,* 70–71.

69. Wagemakers, *Quietist Jihadi,* 70.

70. Giles Kepel, *Muslim Extremism in Egypt: The Prophet and Pharaoh* (Berkeley: University of California Press, 2003), 203.

71. Khatab, *Power of Sovereignty,* 7; Sayed Khatab, *The Political Thought of Sayyid Qutb: The Theory of Jahiliyya,* Routledge Studies in Political Islam (New York: Routledge, 2006).

72. Qutb, *Milestones,* 66.

73. Qutb, *Milestones,* 66.

74. Thomas Hegghammer, "ʿAbdallāh ʿAzzām and Palestine," *Welt des Islams* 53 (2013): 353–87.

75. ʿAbdullah ʿAzzam, *Defence of the Muslim Lands,* 2nd English ed. (London: Azzam Publications, 2002), 4.

76. Faraj, *Neglected Duty,* foreword, 30.

CHAPTER 3. #WHITEGENOCIDE

1. "Frazier Glenn Miller," Southern Poverty Law Center, accessed September 4, 2017, www.splcenter.org/fighting-hate/extremist-files/individual/frazier-glenn-miller.

2. Judy L. Thomas, "F. Glenn Miller Jr. Talks for the First Time about the Killings at Jewish Centers," *Kansas City Star,* November 15, 2014, www.kansascity.com/news/local/crime/article3955528.html.

3. Thomas, "F. Glenn Miller Jr. Talks."

4. Frazier Glenn Miller Jr., "A White Man Speaks Out," 1999, available at www.solargeneral.org/wp-content/uploads/library/A-White-Man-Speaks-Out.pdf.

5. "Frazier Glenn Miller," Southern Poverty Law Center.

6. Frazier Glenn Miller, "Declaration of War," *Springfield News-Leader,* April 6, 1987, www.news-leader.com/story/news/local/ozarks/2014/04/14/archive-april-6–1987-letter-from-frazier-glenn-miller/7708641.

7. Robert Jay Mathews, "Declaration of War," November 25, 1984, accessed September 5, 2017, www.mourningtheancient.com/mathews2.htm.

8. Jeffrey S. Passel and D'Vera Cohn, "U.S. Population Projections: 2005–2050," Pew Hispanic Center, February 11, 2008, p. 1, www.pewhispanic.org/2008/02/11/us-population-projections-2005-2050; Mark Potok, "For the Radical Right, Obama Victory Brings Fury and Fear," Southern Poverty Law Center, November 7, 2012, www.splcenter.org/blog/2012/11/07/for-the-radical-right-obama-victory-brings-fury-and-fear; Dowell Myers and Morris Levy, "Racial Population Projections and Reactions to Alternative News Accounts of Growing Diversity," *Annals of the American Academy of Political and Social Science* 677, no. 1 (2018): 215–28.

9. Robert P. Jones, *The End of White Christian America* (New York: Simon and Schuster), 2016; James A. Piazza, "What Drives Far-Right Terrorism in the United States?" Sustainable Security, September 12, 2017, https://sustainablesecurity.org/2017/09/12/what-drives-far-right-terrorism-in-the-united-states; Christina Silva, "White Nationalists Are Right: America Is Becoming Less White," *Newsweek,* August 16, 2017, www.newsweek.com/white-nationalists-are-right-america-becoming-less-white-651541.

10. Amanda Taub, "'White Nationalism' Explained," *New York Times,* November 21, 2016, www.nytimes.com/2016/11/22/world/americas/white-nationalism-explained.html; Gretchen Livingston, "Hispanic Women No Longer Account for the Majority of Immigrant Births in the U.S.," Pew Research Center, August 8, 2019, www.pewresearch.org/fact-tank/2019/08/08/hispanic-women-no-longer-account-for-the-majority-of-immigrant-births-in-the-u-s.

11. Susann Rohwedder, "Well Being 417: Effects of the Financial Crisis," American Life Panel, RAND, accessed August 29, 2018, available at https://alpdata.rand.org/index.php?page=data&p=showsurvey&syid=417; Michael Hirsh, "Why Trump and Sanders Were Inevitable," *Politico,* February 28, 2016, www.politico.com/magazine/story/2016/02/why-donald-trump-and-bernie-sanders-were-inevitable-213685.

12. Darrell M. West, *The Future of Work: Robots, AI, and Automation* (Washington, DC: Brookings Institution Press, 2019).

13. Jonathan T. Rothwell and Pablo Diego-Rosell, "Explaining Nationalist Political Views: The Case of Donald Trump," November 2, 2016, available at https://papers.ssrn.com/sol3/papers.cfm?abstract_id=2822059; Diana C. Mutz, "Status Threat, Not Economic Hardship, Explains the 2016 Presidential Vote," *PNAS* 115, no. 19 (May 8, 2018): E4330–39, https://doi.org/10.1073/pnas

.17181551115; "2016 Pilot Study," American National Election Studies, accessed August 29, 2018, http://electionstudies.org/project/anes-2016-pilot-study. For an interesting study on how the Republican Party has become a party of plutocratic populists, meaning that people who are not socioeconomically privileged, of any skin color, are actually voting against their interests when supporting its economic policies, see Jacob S. Hacker and Paul Pierson, *Let Them Eat Tweets: How the Right Rules in the Age of Extreme Inequality* (New York: Liveright Publishing Corporation, 2020).

14. Mutz, "Status Threat"; Michael Tesler, "Economic Anxiety Isn't Driving Racial Resentment. Racial Resentment Is Driving Economic Anxiety," *Washington Post,* August 22, 2016, www.washingtonpost.com/news/monkey-cage/wp/2016/08/22/economic-anxiety-isnt-driving-racial-resentment-racial-resentment-is-driving-economic-anxiety; Michael Tesler, *Post-Racial or Most-Racial? Race and Politics in the Obama Era* (Chicago: University of Chicago Press, 2016); Geoffrey Evans and Mark Pickup, "Reversing the Causal Arrow: The Political Conditioning of Economic Perceptions in the 2000–2004 U.S. Presidential Election Cycle," *Journal of Politics* 72, no. 4 (2010): 1236–51; Sean McElwee and Jason McDaniel, "Economic Anxiety Didn't Make People Vote Trump, Racism Did," *Nation,* May 8, 2017, www.thenation.com/article/economic-anxiety-didnt-make-people-vote-trump-racism-did.

15. Rothwell and Diego-Rosell, "Explaining Nationalist Political Views." For a compelling study on how interacting with people outside of one's racial group lessens prejudice, see psychology scholar Gordon Allport's seminal work on the subject: Gordon W. Allport, *The Nature of Prejudice,* abridged ed. (Garden City, NY: Doubleday, 1958).

16. Simon Jackman and Lynn Vavreck, "Replication Materials for 'The 2008 Cooperative Campaign Analysis Project (CCAP),'" ISPS Data Archive, 2016, http://hdl.handle.net/10079/99eeff2d-d275-47ef-afb7-29fd3881063f; Daniel Cox, Rachel Lienesch, and Robert P. Jones, "Beyond Economics: Fears of Cultural Displacement Pushed the White Working Class to Trump," Public Religion Research Institute, May 9, 2017, www.prri.org/research/white-working-class-atti-tudes-economy-trade-immigration-election-donald-trump.

17. Ben Klassen, *The White Man's Bible* (Lighthouse Point, FL: Church of the Creator, 1981), 10–11, 20, italics in the original; Isaac Shapiro, Danilo Trisi, and Raheem Chaudhry, "Poverty Reduction Programs Help Adults Lacking College Degrees the Most," Center on Budget and Policy Priorities, February 16, 2017, www.cbpp.org/research/poverty-and-inequality/poverty-reduction-programs-help-adults-lacking-college-degrees-the.

18. Tom Anderson, *His Example: Tom Anderson's Christmas Essay* (Belmont, MA: American Opinion, n.d.); Federal Bureau of Investigation, "Christian Identity Movement," April 28, 1989, available at https://vault.fbi.gov/Christian%20Identity%20Movement%20/Christian%20Identity%20Movement%20Part%201%20of%201.

19. David Lane, *Deceived, Damned, and Defiant: The Revolutionary Writings of David Lane* (St. Maries, ID: 14 Word Press, 1999), 3.

20. David Lane, *White Genocide Manifesto* (St. Maries, ID: 14 Word Press, 1988).

21. Lane, *Deceived, Damned, and Defiant,* 4.

22. Jennifer Snook, Thad Horrell, and Kristen Horton, "Heathens in the United States: The Return to 'Tribes' in the Construction of a Peoplehood," in *Cosmopolitanism, Nationalism, and Modern Paganism,* ed. Kathryn Rountree (New York: Palgrave Macmillan, 2017), 58.

23. Collin Cleary, "Ásatrú and the Political," *Counter-Currents Publishing* (blog), accessed August 31, 2018, www.counter-currents.com/2012/10/asatru-and-the-political.

24. Christina Anderson, "'Allah Is Found on Viking Funeral Clothes," *New York Times,* October 14, 2017, www.nytimes.com/2017/10/14/world/europe/vikings-allah-sweden.html; "Unearthed Treasure Proves Early East-West Trade," *Spiegel Online,* September 7, 2010, www.spiegel.de/international/germany/arabian-coins-unearthed-treasure-proves-early-east-west-trade-route-a-716001.html.

25. SFAGodSaveAmerica, "Christian Identity: Identifying God's Chosen," YouTube video, 54:09, January 21, 2013, www.youtube.com/watch?v=9ph7zKSblzo.

26. *GOD and Lincoln on Negro-White Marriages* (Phoenix: America's Promise, n.d.), 6, italics in the original.

27. Klassen, "Creative Credo #22, 'The Magnificent White Race,'" in *The White Man's Bible,* 132–38.

28. Klassen, "Creative Credo #32, 'We Shall be Masters of Our Own Manifest Destiny': Winning of the West: Prototype for Winning of the World," in *The White Man's Bible,* 191–93.

29. Klassen, "Creative Credo #18: 'The Melting Pot': The Ugly American Dream," in *The White Man's Bible,* 108–9.

30. Klassen, "Creative Credo #18," in *The White Man's Bible,* 108–9.

31. Klassen, "Creative Credo #41: The Jewish Program for the Mongrelization of the White Race," in *The White Man's Bible,* 273–81.

32. "Trump Official Revises Statue of Liberty Poem to Defend against Immigrant Rule Change," *BBC,* August 14, 2019, www.bbc.com/news/world-us-canada-49323324.

33. U.S. Department of Homeland Security, "We Must Secure the Border and Build the Wall to Make America Safe Again," February 15, 2018, www.dhs.gov/news/2018/02/15/we-must-secure-border-and-build-wall-make-america-safe-again#.

34. Griffin Sims Edwards and Stephen Rushin, "The Effect of President Trump's Election on Hate Crimes," *SSRN,* January 14, 2018, https://doi.org//10.2139/ssrn.3102652.

35. Laura Newberry, Jaclyn Cosgrove, and Richard Winton, "At Least 3 Dead, 15 Injured in Gilroy Garlic Festival," *Los Angeles Times,* July 28, 2019, www.latimes.com/california/story/2019-07-28/reports-of-shooting-at-gilroy-garlic-festival.

36. Ellyn Santiago, "Santino William Legan: Gilroy Garlic Festival Shooter's Instagram Page," *Heavy.com,* July 31, 2019, https://heavy.com/news/2019/07/santino-william-legan-gilroy-shooters-instagram.

37. Ragnar Redbeard, *Might Is Right, or Survival of the Fittest* (St. Maries, ID: Fourteen Word Press, 1999), 12.

38. Redbeard, *Might Is Right*, 66.

39. Wayne LaPierre, speech for the National Rifle Association at the 56th Annual Weatherby Foundation International Hunting and Conservation Awards in Reno, Nevada, January 22, 2013. The speech is no longer available on the NRA website, but it can be viewed at PBS NewsHour, "NRA Leader Wayne LaPierre Responds to Obama's Inaugural Address," YouTube video, 12:20, January 22, 2013, www.youtube.com/watch?v=qGDqFMP7sYQ. In 2020, LaPierre was accused of financial malfeasance by the New York Attorney General's office for abusing his position to spend NRA funds for personal use.

40. U.S. Department of Homeland Security, "Rightwing Extremism: Current Economic and Political Climate Fueling Resurgence in Radicalization and Recruitment," Office of Intelligence and Analysis Assessment, April 7, 2009, 3, www.fas.org/irp/eprint/rightwing.pdf.

41. Eliza Griswold, "Gods, Guns, and Country: The Evangelical Right over Firearms," April 19, 2019, *New Yorker,* www.newyorker.com/news/on-religion /god-guns-and-country-the-evangelical-fight-over-firearms; Kate Shellnut, "Packing in the Pews: The Connection between God and Guns," *Christianity Today,* November 8, 2017, www.christianitytoday.com/news/2017/november/god-gun-control-white-evangelicals-texas-church-shooting.html.

42. Gordon Mohr, *Firearms and Freedom! Gun Control Means People Control!* (Little Rock, AR: Crusade for Christ, n.d.), 43.

43. Stephen A. McNallen, "What Would Odin Say about Gun Control?" accessed September 4, 2017, available at www.oocities.org/odinistlibrary /OLArticles/Articles/odinguncontrol.htm; Stephen McNallen, "What Stephen McNallen Really Thinks about Race!" YouTube video, 12:37, March 3, 2017, www.youtube.com/watch?v=ewUuNO636ag.

44. Alex Jones Channel, "Alex Jones Final Statement on Sandy Hook," YouTube video, 20:22, November 18, 2016, www.youtube.com/watch?v= MwudDfz1yAk.

45. Mohr, *Firearms and Freedom!,* 45–46, italics in the original.

46. *The Creativity Alliance Handbook: A Guide for Members, Supporters and Applicants,* 3rd ed. (Oaklands Park, SA, Australia: Creativity Alliance, 2013), 57.

47. Tom W. Smith, "The Religious Right and Anti-Semitism," *Review of Religious Research* 40, no. 3 (1999): 244–58, www.jstor.org/stable/3512370; Pat Robertson, *The New World Order* (Dallas: Word Publishing, 1991). Pat Robertson's best-selling book led to accusations of antisemitism, which he denied. For more on the antisemitism charge and Robertson's response, see Gustav Neibuhr, "*Pat Robertston [sic]Says He Intended No Anti-Semitism in Book He Wrote Four Years Ago,*" *New York Times,* March 4, 1995, www .nytimes.com/1995/03/04/us/pat-robertston-says-he-intended-no-anti-semitism-in-book-he-wrote-four-years-ago.html.

48. "Alternative Right," Southern Poverty Law Center, accessed September 4, 2017, www.splcenter.org/fighting-hate/extremist-files/ideology/alternative-right.

49. FBI Phoenix Field Office, *Anti-government, Identity Based, and Fringe Political Conspiracy Theories Very Likely Motivate Some Domestic Extremists to Commit Criminal, Sometimes Violent Activity,* Federal Bureau of Investigation, intelligence bulletin, May 30, 2019, available at www.justsecurity.org/wp-content/uploads/2019/08/420379775-fbi-conspiracy-theories-domestic-extremism.pdf.

50. "Additional Charges Filed in Tree of Life Synagogue Shooting: Robert Bowers Charged with 63 Counts Including Hate Crimes Resulting in Death," U.S. Department of Justice, Office of Public Affairs, January 29, 2019, www.justice.gov/opa/pr/additional-charges-filed-tree-life-synagogue-shooting.

51. "Additional Charges Filed," U.S. Department of Justice, Office of Public Affairs.

52. Andrew Marantz, "The Pittsburgh Shooting and the Dark, Specific Logic of Online Hatred," *New Yorker,* October 29, 2018, www.newyorker.com/news/daily-comment/the-pittsburgh-shooting-and-the-dark-specific-logic-of-online-hatred.

53. Alex Dobuzinskis, "U.S. to Seek Death Penalty for Accused Pittsburgh Synagogue Shooter," *Reuters,* August 26, 2019, www.reuters.com/article/us-pennsylvania-shooting-idUSKCN1VG27B.

54. Jillian Rayfield, "Bryan Fischer: Muslim Immigration to the US Is a 'Toxic Cancer,'" *Talking Points Memo,* April 7, 2011, http://talkingpointsmemo.com/muckraker/bryan-fischer-muslim-immigration-to-the-u-s-is-a-toxic-cancer.

55. Lucas Nolan, "Milo on Breitbart News Daily: Islam Has 'Contempt and Loathing' for Gays," *Breitbart,* June 14, 2016, www.breitbart.com/milo/2016/06/14/milo-breitbart-news-daily-islam-contempt-gays.

56. Rayfield, "Bryan Fischer."

57. Ben Klassen, *Nature's Eternal Religion in Two Books* (Lighthouse Point, FL: Church of the Creator, 1973).

58. Stubba, "The Menace of the Mullahs," in *This Is Odinism and Other Essays by Stubba: Original Writings Published 1974–1993, with Notes by Osred* (Melbourne: Renewal Publications, 2016), 101.

59. See George Michael, *The Enemy of My Enemy: The Alarming Convergence of Militant Islam and the Extreme Right* (Lawrence: University Press of Kansas, 2006). There is also a contingent of political far right academics who posit that militant Islamism is rooted in Nazism, seemingly in attempts to advance the Islamo-fascist argument, much as Pamela Geller does with her anti-shari'a ACT movement. There are other Islamophobic polemics, including David Patterson, *A Genealogy of Evil: Anti-Semitism from Nazism to Islamic Jihad* (Cambridge: Cambridge University Press, 2011); Jeffrey Herf, *Nazi Propaganda for the Arab World* (New Haven, CT: Yale University Press, 2009); and Paul Berman, *Terror and Liberalism* (New York: Norton, 2003). Richard Wolin, a professor of history and political science at the Graduate Center of the City University of New York, described the connection Herf draws between European fascism and contemporary political Islam as "both needlessly inflammatory and historically inaccurate." Richard Wolin, "Herf's Misuses of History," *Chronicle of Higher Education,* November 22, 2009, www.chronicle.com/article/Herfs-Misuse-of-History/49195.

60. Leo V. Oladimu, *Beige: An Unlikely Trip through America's Racial Obsession* (self-published, 2014).

61. Criminal complaint, United States of America v. Curtis Wayne Allen, Patrick Eugene Stein, and Gavin Wayne Wright, United States District Court, District of Kansas (Wichita Docket), case no. 16-M-6151-GEB, October 14, 2016, available at www.justice.gov/opa/file/903106/download.

62. Criminal complaint, United States of America v. Curtis Wayne Allen, Patrick Eugene Stein, and Gavin Wayne Wright, p. 8.

63. Jacey Fortin, "Three Men Sentenced in Plot to Bomb Somali Immigrants in Kansas," *New York Times,* January 26, 2019, www.nytimes.com/2019/01/26 /us/kansas-militia-trial-sentencing.html.

64. Matthew Bracken, "Tet, Take Two: Islam's 2016 European Offensive," LinkedIn, November 30, 2015, www.linkedin.com/pulse/tet-take-two-islams-2016-european-offensive-sepp-corwin-benedikt.

65. "'Alt-Right' Declares Flame War on Oath Keepers," *Hatewatch,* Southern Poverty Law Center, June 15, 2017, www.splcenter.org/hatewatch/2017 /06/15/alt-right-declares-flame-war-oath-keepers.

66. Laurie Goodstein, "Drawing U.S. Crowds with Anti-Islam Message," *N ew York Times,* March 7, 2011, www.nytimes.com/2011/03/08/us/08gabriel .html.

67. "Live-Blog: ACT for America's 'March against Sharia' Rallies," *Hatewatch,* Southern Poverty Law Center, June 10, 2017, www.splcenter.org/hatewatch/2017 /06/10/live-blog-act-americas-march-against-sharia-rallies.

68. Swathi Shanmugasundaram, "Anti-Sharia Law Bills in the United States," *Hatewatch,* Southern Poverty Law Center, August 8, 2016, www .splcenter.org/hatewatch/2017/08/08/anti-sharia-law-bills-united-states.

69. Al Jazeera English, "Islamophobia Inc, Al Jazeera Investigations," YouTube video, 48:28, May 14, 2018, www.youtube.com/watch?v=-G9G79oImG4; Enes Bayrakli and Farid Hafez, "European Islamophobia Report 2018," Foundation for Political, Economic and Social Research, 2019, www.islamophobiaeurope .com/wp-content/uploads/2019/09/EIR_2018.pdf.

70. Redbeard, *Might Is Right,* 167.

71. Tracie Farrell, Miriam Fernandez, Jakub Novotny, and Harith Alani, "Exploring Misogyny across the Manosphere in Reddit," in *WebSci 19: Proceedings of the 10th ACM Conference on Web Science,* edited by the Association for Computing Machinery (New York: Association for Computing Machinery, 2019), 87–96.

72. Molly Conger (@socialistdogmom), "there are a lot of things about 2018 i could not have predicted. a mass murderer joking about my body hair a few weeks before he killed 11 people in a synagogue is one of those things," Twitter, December 30, 2018, 8:52 a.m., https://twitter.com/socialistdogmom/status /1079782480822128640.

73. Charles LiMandri, "The Tyranny of Made-Up Sexual Identities," *Wanderer Online Daily,* July 13, 2016, http://thewandererpress.com/catholic/news /frontpage/the-tyranny-of-made-up-sexual-identities.

74. *Aryan Nations Youth Action Corps Quarterly* (Hayden Lake, ID: Aryan Nations Teutonic Unity), no. 1 (1996): 6.

75. Philip Herbst, "God References," in *Talking Terrorism: A Dictionary of the Loaded Language of Political Violence* (Westport, CT: Greenwood Press, 2003), 80.

76. David Lane, *88 Precepts* (St. Maries, ID: 14 Word Press, 1990).

77. *Creativity Alliance Handbook,* 57.

78. Greg Johnson, "Gay Panic on the Alt Right," *Counter-Currents* (blog), March 18, 2016, www.counter-currents.com/2016/03/gay-panic-on-the-alt-right, italics in the original.

79. Rose Falvey, "Some White Nationalists Continue to Court the LGBT Community," *Hatewatch,* Southern Poverty Law Center, August 18, 2016, www.splcenter.org/hatewatch/2016/08/18/some-white-nationalists-continue-court-lgbt-community.

80. Falvey, "Some White Nationalists Continue to Court the LGBT Community."

81. 2SweetMeBro, "How do you feel about your large following in the gay community?" comment on _RichardBSpencer, "Ask Me Anything," Reddit, August 10, 2016, www.reddit.com/r/altright/comments/4x3fm2/richard_spencerask_me_anything, link no longer active, content available at http://archive.is/26c95#selection-23385.0-23385.17.

82. Cassie Miller, "White Nationalist Threats against Transgender People Are Escalating," Southern Poverty Law Center, June 26, 2019, www.splcenter.org/hatewatch/2019/06/26/white-nationalist-threats-against-transgender-people-are-escalating; Human Rights Campaign Foundation, "A National Epidemic: Fatal Anti-Transgender Violence in the United States in 2019," 2019, www.hrc.org/resources/a-national-epidemic-fatal-anti-trans-violence-in-the-united-states-in-2019.

83. "Goy Talk LIVE—Dino Returns w/ Paul Nehlen & Patrick Little," *Vanguard Streaming Network Podcast,* April 18, 2019, https://tgstat.com/channel/@Uncle_Paul1488/951.

84. Christopher Cantwell (@followchris), "Assisted suicide is the only help you can give trannies," Telegram post, June 8, 2019, https://t.me/s/followchris/127.

85. *The Sunwheel* (Toronto: Odinist Movement), no. 7 (April 1973): 1–2; Lane, *88 Precepts.*

86. "President Donald J. Trump Has Delivered Record Breaking Results for the American People in His First Three Years in Office," White House, fact sheet, December 31, 2019, www.whitehouse.gov/briefings-statements/president-donald-j-trump-delivered-record-breaking-results-american-people-first-three-years-office; Charles S. Clark, "Deconstructing the Deep State," *Government Executive,* accessed August 23, 2020, www.govexec.com/feature/gov-exec-deconstructing-deep-state; Nathalie Baptiste, "The Trump Administration Has Figured Out How to Get Rid of Federal Workers without Firing Them," *Mother Jones,* October 7, 2019, www.motherjones.com/politics/2019/10/the-trump-administration-has-figured-out-how-to-get-rid-of-federal-workers-without-firing-them; Chris Mills Rodrigo, "Trump Moving to Dismantle OPM: Report," *The Hill,* April 10, 2019, https://thehill.com/homenews/administration/438240-trump-moving-to-dismantle-opm-report.

87. *Creativity Alliance Handbook.*

88. "Ruby Ridge Investigation Day 1 Part 1," *C-SPAN,* 1:02:02–1:02:44, September 6, 1995, www.c-span.org/video/?66973-1/ruby-ridge-investigation-day-1-part-1.

89. PBS, *American Experience: Ruby Ridge,* August 24, 2017, accessed September 5, 2017, www.pbs.org/wgbh/americanexperience/films/ruby-ridge.

90. Mike Weland, "Fugitive: No Surrender," *Coeur D'Ailene Press,* May 3, 1992.

91. "Child Survivors Recall Waco 10 Years On," *ABC News,* April 17, 2003, http://abcnews.go.com/Primetime/story?id=131981.

92. Malcolm Gladwell, "Sacred and Profane: How Not to Negotiate with Believers," *New Yorker,* March 31, 2014, www.newyorker.com/magazine/2014/03/31/sacred-and-profane-4.

93. Lane Crothers, *Rage on the Right: The American Militia Movement from Ruby Ridge to Homeland Security* (Lanham, MD: Rowman and Littlefield, 2003), 109.

94. Michael Barkun, "Appropriated Martyrs: The Branch Davidians and the Radical Right," *Terrorism And Political Violence* 19, no. 1 (2007): 117–24.

95. "McVeigh's Own Words," *ABC PrimeTime,* March 29, 2001, http://abcnews.go.com/Primetime/story?id=132158.

96. Tom Alibrandi and Bill Wassmuth, *Hate Is My Neighbor* (Moscow, ID: University of Idaho Press, 1999), 208; Daniel Levitas, *The Terrorist Next Door: The Militia Movement and the Radical Right* (New York: St. Martin's Press, 2002), 304.

97. "Ruby Ridge Carved Niche in History," *Spokesman-Review* (Spokane, WA), August 19, 2012, www.spokesman.com/stories/2012/aug/19/ruby-ridge-carved-niche-history.

98. In *Gods of the Blood,* Mattias Gardell writes, "The process of globalization is thus interpreted as a process of homogenization, by means of which the New World Order will destroy all the world's distinct races and cultures. This fear is shared by racial and religious nationalists worldwide and has led to an amazing array of cooperative efforts across racial, religious, and national borders." *Gods of the Blood: The Pagan Revival and White Separatism* (Durham, NC: Duke University Press, 2003), 68.

CHAPTER 4. THE CRUSADES REDUX

1. Nidal Malik Hasan, "Hasan Letter," *Killeen Daily Herald,* August 18 2013, http://kdhnews.com/military/hasan_trial/hasan-letter/pdf_b530a86a-068a-11e3-8136-001a4bcf6878.html. SWT is the anglicized Arabic acronym for *Subhana wa ta'ala,* or "Glorified and exalted is He." These words are spoken after referring to God.

2. For an understanding of Qutb, see James Toth, *Sayyid Qutb: The Life and Legacy of a Radical Islamic Intellectual* (New York: Oxford University Press, 2013).

3. Sayyid Qutb, *Milestones* (Indianapolis, IN: American Trust Publications, 1993), 94–96; Ronald L. Nettler, *Past Trials and Present Tribulations: A Muslim*

Fundamentalist's View of the Jews (Oxford: Pergamon Press, 1987), foreword, x, 72–85, 303; William E. Shepard, *Sayyid Qutb and Islamic Activism: A Translation and Critical Analysis of Social Justice in Islam* (Leiden: Brill, 1996), 287–88.

4. Shepard, *Sayyid Qutb and Islamic Activism,* 287–88.

5. Paul Berman, "The Philosopher of Islamic Terror," *New York Times,* March 23, 2003, www.nytimes.com/2003/03/23/magazine/the-philosopher-of-islamic-terror.html.

6. Muhammad Haniff Hassan, "Jihadi Ideology: An Overview," in *Conflict, Community, and Criminality in Southeast Asia and Australia: Assessments From the Field; A Report of the CSIS Transnational Threats Project,* ed. Arnaud De Borchgrave, Thomas Sanderson, and David Gordon (Washington, DC: Center for Strategic and International Studies, 2009), 77; David Zeidan, "A Comparative Study of Selected Themes in Christian and Islamic Fundamentalist Discourses," *British Journal of Middle Eastern Studies* 30, no. 1 (2003): 43–80.

7. Muhammad Khalid Masud, "The Scope of Pluralism in Islamic Moral Traditions," in *Islamic Political Ethics: Civil Society, Pluralism, and Conflict,* ed. Sohail H. Hashmi (Princeton, NJ: Princeton University Press, 2002), 135–47.

8. The phrase "clash of civilizations" was first coined by Bernard Lewis, a British historian controversial for his orientalist views, in the article "Islamic Revival in Turkey," *International Affairs* 28, no. 1 (1952): 48. It was then made famous in an article and a book by another controversial academic, American political scientist Samuel Huntington, whom critics have criticized as xenophobic. See Samuel P. Huntington, "The Clash of Civilizations?" *Foreign Affairs* 72, no. 3 (1993): 22–49; and Samuel P. Huntington, *The Clash of Civilizations and the Remaking of World Order* (New York: Simon and Schuster, 1996).

9. Osama bin Laden, "Declaration of War against the Americans Occupying the Land of the Two Holy Places," *Al Quds Al Arabi,* August 1996, available at https://is.muni.cz/el/1423/jaro2010/MVZ448/OBL___AQ__Fatwa_1996.pdf.

10. Abu Bakr al-Baghdadi, "READ: Full English Translation of ISIS 'Caliph' Abu Bakr al-Baghdadi's New Speech," *Heavy,* December 28, 2015, http://heavy.com/news/2015/12/new-isis-islamic-state-news-pictures-videos-so-wait-indeed-we-along-with-you-are-waiting-abu-bakr-al-baghdadi-speech-english-translation.

11. Tarek Osman, "Why Border Lines Drawn with a Ruler in WW1 Still Rock the Middle East," *BBC,* December 14, 2013, www.bbc.co.uk/news/world-middle-east-25299553. Despite the focus of militants on Sykes-Picot, there is an argument to be made that the agreements made at the 1920 San Remo conference—attended by leaders from Britain, France, Italy, and Japan—are ultimately responsible for the internal borders we know today.

12. Sam Prince, "READ: ISIS Releases Statement on 100th Anniversary of Sykes-Picot Agreement," *Heavy,* May 28, 2016, http://heavy.com/news/2016/05/isis-islamic-state-statement-sykes-picot-agreement-100-one-hundred-year-anniversary-read-al-naba-online-magazine-newspaper-pdf-download, link no longer active.

13. Shepard, *Sayyid Qutb and Islamic Activism,* 286–87. For more on the Crusades as a master narrative, see Jeffry R. Halverson, H. Lloyd Goodall, and

Steven R. Corman, *Master Narratives of Islamist Extremism* (New York: Palgrave McMillan, 2011), 121.

14. Ayman al-Zawahiri, *Al-Hisad al-Murr: Al-Ikhwan al-Muslimun fi Sittin Aman* (Amman: Dar al-Bayariq, 1999).

15. David Aaron, *In Their Own Words: Voices of Jihad* (Santa Monica, CA: RAND Corporation, 2008), 219, available at www.rand.org/content/dam/rand /pubs/monographs/2008/RAND_MG602.pdf.

16. Manuel Perez-Rivas, "Bush Vows to Rid the World of 'Evil-Doers,'" *CNN,* September 16, 2001, http://edition.cnn.com/2001/US/09/16/gen.bush .terrorism.

17. "It Will Be a Fire That Burns: The Cross and Its People in Raqqah," *Rumiyah,* no. 12 (August 2017): 33.

18. Gudrun Krämer, "Anti-Semitism in the Muslim World: A Critical Review," *Die Welt des Islams,* New Series, 46, no. 3 (2006): 243–76.

19. Current Islamophobes and ex-Muslims have picked up on this by decontextualizing source material, such as the work of American political far right author Andrew Bostom, in which he compares shari'a to totalitarianism and includes forewords by ex-Muslim Ibn Warraq. See Andrew G. Bostom, *The Legacy of Islamic Antisemitism: From Sacred Texts to Solemn History* (Amherst, NY: Prometheus Books, 2008).

20. Dave Itzkoff, "'South Park' Episode Altered after Muslim Group's Warning," *New York Times,* April 22, 2010, www.nytimes.com/2010/04/23/arts /television/23park.html.

21. Mary Habeck, "Attacking America: Al Qaeda's Grand Strategy in Its War with the World," Foreign Policy Research Institute, February 18, 2014, www.fpri.org/article/2014/02/attacking-america-al-qaedas-grand-strategy-in-its-war-with-the-world.

22. Heidi Beirich and Brian Levin, "Grown at Home," *Intelligence Report,* Southern Poverty Law Center, 2011 Fall Issue, August 24, 2011, www.splcenter .org/fighting-hate/intelligence-report/2015/grown-home%E2%80%82.

23. Beirich and Levin, "Grown at Home."

24. The exegetical context of the verse describes some Jews being transformed into apes and swine—a transformation that may be interpreted physically, spiritually, or both—because they failed to live according to the covenant God made with them in the period before the Prophet Muhammad.

25. Gilles Kepel, Jean-Pierre Milelli, and Pascale Ghazaleh, *Al Qaeda in Its Own Words* (Cambridge, MA: Belknap Press of Harvard University Press, 2008), 55; Osama bin Laden, *Messages to the World: The Statements of Osama Bin Laden,* ed. Bruce B. Lawrence (London: Verso, 2005), 160.

26. Kepel, Milelli, and Ghazaleh, *Al Qaeda in Its Own Words,* 47.

27. In December 2012, judges at the United Nations Tribunal at the Hague convicted a former senior commander of the Bosnian Serb Army, Zdravko Tolimir, for genocide in Srebrenica and Zepa during the Bosnian War (1992–95). Though genocide convictions for this war have been issued only for crimes committed in Srebrenica, human rights groups and victims argue that genocide also occurred in northern and eastern Bosnia, where Serbian forces began their

ethnic cleansing campaign in 1992, expelling thousands of non-Serbs. Others were imprisoned, tortured, raped, and burned alive in their homes.

28. Plea agreement, United States of America v. Faisal Shahzad, United States District Court, Southern District of New York, case no. 10-CR-541 (MGC), June 21, 2010, available at https://online.wsj.com/public/resources/documents /061shap.pdf.

29. J. M. Berger, *Jihad Joe: Americans Who Go to War in the Name of Islam* (Washington, DC: Potomac Books, 2011), 161.

30. Indictment, United States of America v. Dzhokhar A. Tsarnaev a/k/a "Jahar Tsarni," United States District Court, District of Massachusetts, case no. 1:13-cr-10200-GAO, June 27, 2013, www.justice.gov/sites/default/files/usao-ma/legacy/2013/06/27/Indictment1.pdf.

31. "Why We Hate You and Why We Fight You," *Dabiq,* no. 15, "Break the Cross" (July 2016): 33.

32. Aaron, *In Their Own Words*, 16–17.

33. Ayman az-Zawahiri has cited the move to Jerusalem as evidence that "appeasement" has failed Palestinians and as encouragement for Muslims to carry out "jihad" against the United States. "Al-Qaida Leader Calls for Jihad on Eve of US Embassy Moving to Jerusalem," *Guardian* (UK), May 13, 2018, www.theguardian.com/world/2018/may/14/al-qaida-leader-jihad-us-embassy-move-jerusalem.

34. United Nations Office for the Coordination of Humanitarian Affairs, Occupied Palestinian Territory, *Humanitarian Pooled Fund: Annual Report 2015* (East Jerusalem: United Nations Office for the Coordination of Humanitarian Affairs, 2015), https://docs.unocha.org/sites/dms/Documents/oPt%20 HPF%20Annual%20Report%202015%20(final).pdf.

35. Human Rights Council, "Report of the Special Rapporteur on the Situation of Human Rights in the Palestinian Territories Occupied since 1967," 37th session, February 26–March 23, 2018, p. 6, available at www.ohchr.org/EN/HR Bodies/HRC/RegularSessions/Session37/Documents/A_HRC_37_75_EN.docx.

36. Human Rights Council, "Report of the Special Rapporteur," 6.

37. Human Rights Council, "Report of the Special Rapporteur," 6.

38. Mariam Salim Hammoud, "Educational Obstacles Faced by Palestinian Refugees in Lebanon," *Contemporary Review of the Middle East* 4, no. 2 (2017): 127–48.

39. Abbas Shiblak, ed., *The Palestinian Diaspora in Europe: Challenges of Dual Identity and Adaptation,* Refugee and Diaspora Studies 2 (Jerusalem: Institute for Jerusalem Studies and Shaml, 2005), available at www.rsc.ox .ac.uk/files/files-1/palestinian-diaspora-europe-2005.pdf.

40. "Guantánamo by the Numbers," Human Rights First, March 23, 2017, p. 1, www.humanrightsfirst.org/sites/default/files/gtmo-by-the-numbers.pdf; "The Guantánamo Docket," *New York Times,* accessed August 23, 2020, www.nytimes.com/interactive/projects/guantanamo/timeline.

41. "Warren, Reed, Colleagues Seek Information on DoD Efforts to Prevent COVID-19 Outbreaks at Guantanamo Bay Prison," Elizabeth Warren (website), May 28, 2020, www.warren.senate.gov/oversight/letters/warren-reed-

colleagues-seek-information-on-dod-efforts-to-prevent-covid-19-outbreaks-at-guantanamo-bay-prison.

42. Thérèse Postel, "How Guantanamo Bay's Existence Helps Al-Qaeda Recruit More Terrorists," *Atlantic,* April 12, 2013, www.theatlantic.com /international/archive/2013/04/how-guantanamo-bays-existence-helps-al-qaeda-recruit-more-terrorists/274956.

43. Kepel, Milelli, and Ghazaleh, *Al Qaeda in Its Own Words,* 70. Both the Bagram and Abu Ghraib prisons were closed in 2014.

44. "Pentagon Details Mishandling of Quran," *NBC News,* June 4, 2005, www.nbcnews.com/id/8090656/ns/us_news-security/t/pentagon-details-mis-handling-quran; "Terrorism: Compilation of Al-Qa'ida Senior Leadership and Affiliates Propaganda Messaging on Guantanamo," U.S. Office of the Special Counsel, accessed July 1, 2020, available at https://admin.govexec.com/media /gbc/docs/pdfs_edit/open_source_propoganda_gtmo_jan2015.pdf.

45. Cody M. Poplin and Sebastian Brady, "Is Guantanamo Really a Major Recruiting Tool for Jihadists?" *Lawfare* (blog), June 3, 2015, www.lawfareblog .com/guantanamo-really-major-recruiting-tool-jihadists.

46. "Al Qaeda and ISIS Use of Guantanamo Bay Prison in Propaganda and Materials," Human Rights First, September 2017, www.humanrightsfirst.org /sites/default/files/AQ-ISIS-Propaganda-Use-of-Gitmo-Issue-Brief.pdf.

47. "Demographic Portrait of Muslim Americans," in *U.S. Muslims Concerned about Their Place in Society but Continue to Believe in the American Dream: Findings from Pew Research Center's 2017 Survey of U.S. Muslims* Pew Research Center, July 26, 2017, 30–49, www.pewforum.org/2017/07/26/demographic-portrait-of-muslim-americans.

48. Abigail Hauslohner and Justin Wm. Moyer, "Anti-Sharia Demonstrators Hold Rallies in Cities Across the Country," *Washington Post,* June 10, 2017, www.washingtonpost.com/national/anti-sharia-marches-planned-for-numer-ous-cities-across-the-country-saturday/2017/06/10/40faf61e-4d6f-11e7-a186-60c031eab644_story.html; Elsadig Elsheikh, Basima Sisemore, and Natalia Ramirez Lee, "Legalizing Othering: The United States of Islamophobia," Haas Institute, September 2017, https://haasinstitute.berkeley.edu/sites/default/files /haas_institute_legalizing_othering_the_united_states_of_islamophobia.pdf.

49. "The Fitrah of Mankind and the Near-Extinction of the Western Woman," *Dabiq,* no. 15, "Break the Cross" (July 2016): 20, available at http://clarionproject .org/wp-content/uploads/islamic-state-magazine-dabiq-fifteen-breaking-the-cross. pdf. *Fiṭra* is the Arabic word for the natural inclination to God-consciousness that is imbued within each person by God. This is another concept distorted by militant Islamists that is not in accordance with how the majority of Muslims interpret, understand, or practice their faith (Qur'an 30:30).

50. Samantha Mahood and Halim Rane, "Islamist Narratives in ISIS Recruitment Propaganda," *Journal of International Communication* 23, no. 1 (2017): 15-35, https://doi.org/10.1080/13216597.2016.1263231; Tyler Welch, "Theology, Heroism, Justice, and Fear: An Analysis of ISIS Propaganda Magazines *Dabiq* and *Rumiyah,*" *Dynamics of Asymmetric Conflict* 11, no. 3 (2018): 186–98, https://doi.org/10.1080/17467586.2018.1517943.

51. Sayyid Qutb, *Social Justice in Islam [Adalah al-ijtima iyah fi al-Islam]*, translated by Hamid Algar (New York: Islamic Publications International, 2000), 268–70.

CHAPTER 5. (RA)HOWA

1. News reports also give his name as Jeremy Joseph Christian. Nicole Chavez, "Accused Portland Robber Reveals Himself: In His Own Words," *CNN*, June 7, 2017, www.cnn.com/2017/06/07/us/jeremy-joseph-christian-portland-stabbing/index.html.

2. The affidavit can be viewed at http://media.oregonlive.com/portland_impact/other/PCAFFIDAVIT2JEREMYCHRISTIAN.tif-2.compressed.pdf.

3. Maxine Bernstein, "MAX Attack Unfolded Quickly: Extremist Cut Three in Neck, Police Say," *Oregon Live*, June 2, 2017, www.oregonlive.com/portland/index.ssf/2017/05/horrific_scene_unfolds_on_max.html.

4. Nate Hanson, "Portland Suspect in Courtroom Rant: 'You Call It Terrorism. I Call It Patriotism!'" *USA Today*, May 30, 2017, www.usatoday.com/story/news/nation-now/2017/05/30/portland-train-stabbing-suspect/353963001; Lizzy Acker, "Jeremy Christian's Vocabulary and Related Ideas, Explained," *Oregonian*, June 10, 2017, www.oregonlive.com/portland/index.ssf/2017/06/jeremy_christians_vocabulary_a.html; Lizzy Acker, "Who Is Jeremy Christian? Facebook Shows a Man with Nebulous Political Affiliations Who Hated Circumcision and Hillary Clinton," *Oregonian*, June 2, 2017, www.oregonlive.com/portland/index.ssf/2017/05/who_is_jeremy_christian_facebo.html; Corey Pein, "The Man Accused of MAX Double Murder Is a Portland White Supremacist Who Delivered Nazi Salutes and Racial Slurs at a 'Free Speech' Rally Last Month," *Willamette Week*, May 27, 2017, www.wweek.com/news/2017/05/27/the-man-accused-of-max-double-murder-is-a-portland-white-supremacist-who-delivered-nazi-salutes-and-racial-slurs-at-a-free-speech-rally-last-month.

5. Lizzy Acker, "Jeremy Christian's Vocabulary and Related Ideas, Explained," *Oregonian*, June 11, 2017, www.oregonlive.com/portland/index.ssf/2017/06/jeremy_christians_vocabulary_a.html; Kirsten Dyck, *Reichsrock: The International Web of White-Power and Neo-Nazi Hate Music* (New Brunswick, NJ: Rutgers University Press, 2017), 63.

6. Doug Brown, "Suspect in Portland Hate Crime Murders Is a Known White Supremacist," *Portland Mercury*, May 27, 2017, www.portlandmercury.com/blogtown/2017/05/27/19041594/suspect-in-portland-hate-crime-murders-is-a-known-white-supremacist; Pein, "Man Accused of MAX Double Murder."

7. Amy B. Wang, "'Brave and Selfless' Oregon Stabbing Victims Hailed as Heroes for Standing Up to Racist Rants," *Washington Post*, May 28, 2017, www.washingtonpost.com/news/post-nation/wp/2017/05/28/brave-and-self-less-oregon-stabbing-victims-hailed-as-heroes.

8. Stephen Piggott, "Portland Stabbings: Man Arrested for Double Murder after Allegedly Threatening Woman Has Racist Views, Praised Timothy McVeigh," *Hatewatch*, Southern Poverty Law Center, May 27, 2017, www.splcenter.org/hatewatch/2017/05/27/portland-stabbings-man-arrested-double-

murder-after-allegedly-threatening-muslim-women-has; Jason Wilson, "Suspect in Portland Double Murder Posted White Supremacist Material Online," *Guardian* (UK), May 28, 2017, www.theguardian.com/us-news/2017/may/27 /portland-double-murder-white-supremacist-muslim-hate-speech; Julia Reinstein, "Here's What We Know about the Suspect in the Portland Train Stabbing Attack," BuzzFeed, May 27, 2017, www.buzzfeed.com/juliareinstein/portland-suspect.

9. Acker, "Jeremy Christian's Vocabulary."

10. Jack Jenkins, "Expert: The Key to Understanding the Alleged Portland Killer? His White Supremacy," ThinkProgress, May 31, 2017, https://archive. thinkprogress.org/portland-killer-white-supremacy-7a7a8738e8c5/; Kevin Flynn, *The Silent Brotherhood: Inside America's Racist Underground* (New York: Free Press, 1989), 72–99.

11. Piggott, "Portland Stabbings."

12. "Portland Stabbing: Jeremy Joseph Christian Appears in Court," *BBC News,* May 30, 2017, www.bbc.com/news/world-us-canada-40096993.

13. Fox 12 Staff, "MAX Stabbing Suspect Accused of Aggravated Murder Has Another Outburst in Court," *Fox 12 Oregon,* April 26, 2019, www.kptv .com/news/max-stabbing-suspect-accused-of-aggravated-murder-has-another-outburst/article_a607cfd2-685c-11e9-b625-3f8dd6f1ccac.html.

14. Janet Smith, "League of the South: 'What Would It Take to Get You to Fight?'" *Hatewatch* (blog), Southern Poverty Law Center, August 4, 2011, www.splcenter.org/blog/2011/08/04/league-of-the-south-what-would-it-take-to-get-you-to-fight.

15. John Grady, *George Washington's Vision and Prophecy for America* (Eureka Springs, AR: Christian Research, 1979).

16. Ben Klassen, *RAHOWA! This Planet Is All Ours!* (Otto, NC: Church of the Creator, 1987), 165, italics in the original.

17. Sara Diamond, *Roads to Dominion: Right-Wing Movements and Political Power in the United States* (New York: Guilford Press, 1995), 266; Vincent Coppola, *Dragons of God: A Journey through Far-Right America* (Atlanta: Longstreet Press, 1996), 76–77; "Ruby Ridge," *American Experience,* PBS, aired August 24, 2017, www.pbs.org/wgbh/americanexperience/films/ruby-ridge.

18. Jonathan White, "Political Eschatology: A Theology of Antigovernmental Extremism," *American Behavioral Scientist* 44, no. 6 (2001): 937–56.

19. Lord Wolfram, "Richard Butler: Race and Reason 1," YouTube video, 9:36, January 28, 2011, www.youtube.com/watch?v=zmDziUWblKE.

20. Lyman Tower Sargent, *Extremism in America: A Reader* (New York: New York University Press, 1995), 147.

21. Alice Beck Kehoe, *Militant Christianity: An Anthropological History* (New York: Palgrave Macmillan, 2012).

22. Thechurchatkaweah, "To Teach Them War Preview—Ministry Videos," GodTube video, 6:05, 2012, www.godtube.com/watch/?v=DG7ZLWNX.

23. For White nationalist enmity toward people with disabilities, see Andrew Harnish, "Ableism and the Trump Phenomenon," *Disability and Society* 32, no. 3 (2017): 423–28, https://doi.org/10.1080/09687599.2017.1288684.

24. Ben Klassen, *The White Man's Bible* (Lighthouse Point, FL: Church of the Creator, 1981), 557, italics in the original.

25. Committee for the Restoration of the Odinic Rite, *This Is Odinisim* (Gorleston, England: RPD Lito Printers, n.d.), 11.

26. *Teachings of the Odin Brotherhood* (Portland, OR: Thule Publications, n.d.), xxi.

27. One well-known hadith, judged to be *ṣaḥīḥ* by al-Albani, states that "the best jihad is to speak a word of justice to an oppressive ruler." *Sunan Abu Dawud,* book 39, no. 1603, "Battles, Chapter: Command and Prohibition," https://sunnah.com/abudawud/39/54.

28. Ibn Taymīyah and Aḥmad ibn 'Abd al-Ḥalīm, *The Religious and Moral Doctrine of Jihaad, Taken from the Book* Al-Sīyāsah al-Shar'īyah fī Iṣlāḥ al-Rā'ī wa al-Ra'īyah, *Governance According to Allaah's Law in Reforming the Ruler and His Flock* (Birmingham, UK: Maktabah al-Ansaar, 2001), 27–28.

29. Taymīyah and 'Abd al-Ḥalīm, *Religious and Moral Doctrine of Jihaad,* 27–28.

30. Ḥasan Bannā, *Five Tracts of Ḥasan Al-Bannā' (1906–1949): A Selection from the Majmū'at rasā'il al-Imām al-shahīd Ḥasan al-Bannā'*, ed. and trans. Charles Wendell (Berkeley: University of California Press, 1978), 151.

31. Syed Abul 'Ala Maudoodi, *Towards Understanding Islam* (Leicester: The Islamic Foundation, 1980), 94.

32. Sayyid Qutb, *The Islamic Concept and Its Characteristics* (Indianapolis: American Trust Publications, 1991), 72.

33. Qutb, *Islamic Concept,* 72; Sayyid Qutb, *Milestones* (Indianapolis, IN: American Trust Publications, 1993), 108.

34. Qutb, *Milestones,* 59.

35. Qutb, *Islamic Concept,* 72.

36. Qutb, *Milestones,* 55; Jon Armajani, *Modern Islamist Movements: History, Religion, and Politics* (Oxford, UK: Wiley-Blackwell, 2012), 60–61.

37. Anwar al-Awlaki, "Yemeni-American Jihadi Cleric Anwar Al-Awlaki in First Interview with Al-Qaeda Media Calls on Muslim U.S. Servicemen to Kill Fellow Soldiers and Says: 'My Message to the Muslims . . . Is That We Should Participate in This Jihad against America,'" Middle East Research Institute, Special Dispatch 2970, May 23, 2010, text and video available at www.memri.org/reports/yemeni-american-jihadi-cleric-anwar-al-awlaki-first-interview-al-qaeda-media-calls-muslim-us.

38. Sayed Khatab, *The Power of Sovereignty: The Political and Ideological Philosophy of Sayyid Qutb* (London: Routledge, Taylor and Francis, 2006), 7.

39. Umair Raza, "Purpose of Fighting—Anwar Al Awlaki," YouTube video, May 5, 2012, www.youtube.com/watch?v=PwUxUbwyTgA, no longer available.

40. Anwar al-Aulaqi, "Message to the American People," YouTube video, March 16, 2010, www.youtube.com/watch?v=7Rg57CcDBco, no longer available.

41. "Anwar Nasser Aulaqi," Federal Bureau of Investigation, November 26, 2010, http://nsarchive.gwu.edu/NSAEBB/NSAEBB529-Anwar-al-Awlaki-File /documents/18)%20FBI%20notes%20Awlaki%20video%20calling%20 for%20killing%20American%20Nov%202010.pdf; Anwar al-Awlaki, "Anwar al-Awlaki's Last Broadcast Message," *Telegraph* (UK), September 30, 2011,

www.telegraph.co.uk/news/worldnews/al-qaeda/8798703/Anwar-al-Awlakis-last-broadcast-message.html.

42. For an in-depth discussion of this concept, see Mohamed Bin Ali, *The Roots of Religious Extremism: Understanding the Salafi Doctrine of al-Wala' wal Bara'* (London: Imperial College Press, 2016).

43. "By the Sword," *Dabiq*, no. 15, "Break the Cross" (July 2016): 78–80.

44. Umair Raza, "Purpose of Fighting—Anwar Al Awlaki," YouTube video, May 5, 2012, www.youtube.com/watch?v=PwUxUbwyTgA, no longer available.

45. Umair Raza, "Purpose of Fighting."

46. Most nonmilitant Muslims disagree with this application. Indeed, because the Qur'an is not organized chronologically, the issue of abrogation in the context of the Qur'an is its own subset of exegetical science in the canon of Qur'anic studies.

47. *Sahih al-Bukhari*, book 2, hadith 18, "Book of Belief," https://sunnah.com/bukhari/2/18.

48. For an in-depth examination of what the science of hadith entails, see Ibn al-Ṣalāḥ al-Shahrazūrī, *An Introduction to the Science of the Ḥadīth*, trans. Eerik Dickinson (Reading, UK: Garnet Publishing, 2006).

CHAPTER 6. AMERICA THE BEAUTIFUL

1. Silas Von Lindt, "Rushdoony: Equality Is a Marxist Facade [Christian Kinism]," YouTube video, 1:12, December 2, 2012, www.youtube.com/watch?v=MRhE2VvBxWc.

2. In addition to the theologies prominent within White nationalism—Christian Identity, Creativity, and Wotanism—discussed in this book, kinism is another racist theology of note. See Matt Slick, "What Is Kinism? Is It Biblical?" Christian Apologetics and Research Ministry, accessed October 13, 2018, https://carm.org/what-is-kinism; "Kinism: A Racist and Anti-Semitic Religious Movement," Anti-Defamation League, 2013, www.adl.org/sites/default/files/documents/assets/pdf/combating-hate/Kinism-Racist-and-Anti-Semitic-Religionfinal2.pdf.

3. David Lane, "White Genocide Manifesto," DavidLane1488.com, www.davidlane1488.com/whitegenocide.html.

4. Lane, "White Genocide Manifesto."

5. Juan F. Perea, "Los Olvidados: On the Making of Invisible People; The Framers' Plan for a White America," in *Critical White Studies: Looking behind the Mirror*, ed. Richard Delgado and Jean Stefancic (Philadelphia: Temple University Press, 1997), 258–62.

6. Andrew Romano, "America's Holy Writ," *Daily Beast*, October 17, 2010, www.thedailybeast.com/newsweek/2010/10/17/how-tea-partiers-get-the-constitution-wrong.html; Mark David Hall, "Did America Have a Christian Founding?" Heritage Foundation, June 7, 2011, www.heritage.org/political-process/report/did-america-have-christian-founding#_ftnref7. This view was most formally promulgated by President Ronald Reagan in a 1983 resolution proclaiming it the Year of the Bible, officially linking the Founding Fathers, the U.S. Constitution, and Christianity. The ceremonial congressional resolution's text

cites the ways in which the Bible has been integral to the United States: "Whereas the Bible, the Word of God, has made a unique contribution in shaping the United States as a distinctive and blessed nation and people; . . . Whereas Biblical teachings inspired concepts of civil government that are contained in our Declaration of Independence and the Constitution of the United States." Pub. L. No. 97–280, 96 Stat. 1211 (October 4, 1982), www.gpo.gov/fdsys/pkg/STAT-UTE-96/pdf/STATUTE-96-Pg1211.pdf. In 1999, John Ashcroft, who was then a U.S. Senator from Missouri and would later go on to serve as attorney general under President George W. Bush, commented on what he saw to be the Christian heritage of the United States in terms that more closely echo Christian Identity language. In a speech at Bob Jones University in South Carolina, where he received an honorary degree, Ashcroft made a claim for the influence of Christianity on America's history: "America is different. We have no king but Jesus. When you have no king but Jesus, you release the eternal, you release the highest and best, you release virtue, you release potential. Unique among the nations, America recognized the source of our character as being godly and eternal, not being civic and temporal." John Ashcroft, "Bush Transition Office Releases Ashcroft's Remarks at Bob Jones University," *CNN*, January 12, 2001, www.cnn.com/2001/ALLPOLITICS/stories/01/12/ashcroft.bobjones/index.html.

7. John Fea, *Was America Founded as a Christian Nation? A Historical Introduction* (Louisville, KY: Westminster John Knox Press, 2011).

8. See, for instance, Jeffry H. Morrison, *John Witherspoon and the Founding of the American Republic* (Notre Dame: University of Notre Dame Press, 2005); Garrett Ward Sheldon, *The Political Philosophy of James Madison* (Baltimore: Johns Hopkins University Press, 2001); Mark David Hall, *The Political and Legal Philosophy of James Wilson: 1742–1798* (Columbia: University of Missouri Press, 1997); and Daniel L. Dreisbach and Mark David Hall, eds., *Faith and the Founders of the American Republic* (Oxford: Oxford University Press, 2014), chapters 2, 7, and 8.

9. William Potter Gale, *Racial and National Identity* (Mountain City, TN: Sacred Truth Ministries, 2002), 1.

10. Gale, *Racial and National Identity,* 21–24; Bertrand L. Comparet, *Your Heritage: An Identification of the True Israel through Biblical and Historical Sources* (Harrison, AR: Kingdom Identity Ministries, n.d.), 36–37.

11. Gale, *Racial and National Identity,* 12–13, original capitalization.

12. Other New Testament mentions of the New Jerusalem include Matthew 5:18 and 24:35; Galatians 4:26; and Hebrews 11:10, 12:22–24, and 13:14. Old Testament references to the New Jerusalem can be found in Isaiah 65:17–25 and 66:22.

13. "The Essential Unity of Church and State . . . or Faith and Race . . . ," *Calling Our Nation* no. 80 (1996): 4.

14. Pete Peters, *Scriptures for America* (Laporte, CO: Laporte Church of Christ, n.d.), 30.

15. Molly Worthen, "The Chalcedon Problem: Rousas John Rushdoony and the Origins of Christian Reconstructionism," *Church History* 77, no. 2 (2008): 423–24; Rousas John Rushdoony, *The Politics of Guilt and Pity* (Fairfax, VA: Thoburn Press, 1978).

16. Chip Berlet and Margaret Quigley, "Theocracy and White Supremacy: Behind the Culture War to Restore Traditional Values," in *Eyes Right! Challenging the Right Wing Backlash* (Boston: South End Press, 1995), 17.

17. Lane Crothers, "The Cultural Foundations of the Militia Movement," *New Political Science* 24, no. 2 (2002): 221–34.

18. In their strict constructionist reading of America's founding documents, many White nationalists insist that the phrase "life, liberty, and the pursuit of happiness" in the Declaration of Independence is illegitimate and should be replaced by "life, liberty, and property," the Lockean formulation used in the 1774 Declaration of Colonial Rights. Property looms large in the antigovernment stance of many White nationalists because one of their grievances is the belief the government wants to encroach upon their land.

19. Federal Bureau of Investigation, "Christian Identity Movement," April 28, 1989, available at https://vault.fbi.gov/Christian%20Identity%20Movement%20/Christian%20Identity%20Movement%20Part%201%200f%201.

20. Federal Bureau of Investigation, "Christian Identity Movement."

21. Federal Bureau of Investigation, "Christian Identity Movement."

22. Pete Peters, *Scriptures for America* (Laporte, CO: Laporte Church of Christ, n.d.), 30.

23. Peters also taught baptismal regeneration, like many Christian Identity church leaders. For Bob Hallstrom's radio show, see Robert L. Hilliard and Michael C. Keith, *Waves of Rancor: Tuning into the Radical Right* (New York: Routledge, 2015), 128. Even though his radio show was broadcast by Kingdom Identity Ministries, known for proselytizing Christian Identity, Hallstrom did not accept the two-seed theory. See Charles H. Roberts, *Race over Grace: The Racialist Religion of the Christian Identity Movement* (New York: iUniverse, 2003), 104.

24. John Grady, *George Washington's Vision and Prophecy for America* (Eureka Springs, AR: Christian Research, 1979), n.p.

25. Gale, *Racial and National Identity*, 21, original capitalization. For historical analysis of the many faiths of the Founding Fathers, see Denise A. Spellberg, *Thomas Jefferson's Qur'an: Islam and the Founders* (New York: Vintage, 2014); and David L. Holmes, *The Faiths of the Founding Fathers* (Oxford: Oxford University Press, 2006).

26. M.K. Hallimore, *God's Great Race* (Harrison, AR: Kingdom Identity Ministries, n.d.), 1; Bob Hallstrom, *Judeo-Christianity: A Study* (Boise, ID : Gospel Ministry Publications, 1993), 76.

27. Gale, *Racial and National Identity*, 20.

28. Gale, *Racial and National Identity*, 20.

29. "Nazi Eagle," Anti-Defamation League, accessed September 5, 2017, www.adl.org/education/references/hate-symbols/nazi-eagle. The eagle has been used for centuries to represent strength and honor across cultures. Not just a symbol utilized within Wotanism, the eagle is also regarded as the most sacred of birds within traditional Odinism; its cry is thought to herald the birth of a hero. In the Poetic Edda, the eagle appears perched on top of Yggdrasil, the tree of life, around which all existence hinges, and it is thus symbolic of the realms of uppermost consciousness.

30. According to this logic, there are actually thirteen tribes of Israel rather than the twelve tribes listed in Deuteronomy and Judges. Christian Identity teachings replace the tribe of Joseph with tribes named for his two sons, Ephraim and Manasseh, respectively identifying them with Great Britain and the United States. Kenneth Goff, *America: Zion of God* (Boring, OR: Christian Patriot Association, 1980), 5–8.

31. Though Gale, Goff, and many Christian Identity followers insist that the Founding Fathers were divinely inspired to incorporate Christian themes into national symbols, such as the official seal of the United States, the historical record is more complicated. On July 4, 1776, the day the Continental Congress approved the final version of the Declaration of Independence, Benjamin Franklin, Thomas Jefferson, and John Adams were appointed to jointly design an official seal for the United States of America. Though these statesmen were theologically liberal themselves, at Franklin's suggestion, they proposed an image from the biblical story of the parting of the Red Sea and Israel's deliverance from Pharaoh, in which the Israelites were protected by God by a pillar of fire by night and a pillar of cloud by day (Exodus 13:21), to symbolize deliverance from the tyranny of British rule. Their proposal was tabled, and the final image selected in 1782 was of an eagle with spread wings.

32. Gale, *Racial and National Identity*, 21–22.

33. Roberts, *Race over Grace*, 49.

34. Gale, *Racial and National Identity*, 21–24, original capitalization; Everett Sileven, *From Sovereignty to Slavery* (Louisville, NE: Fundamentalist Publications, 1983), 28; "Americans Have Positive Views about Religion's Role in Society, But Want It Out of Politics," Pew Research Center, November 15, 2019, p. 18, www.pewforum.org/2019/11/15/americans-have-positive-views-about-religions-role-in-society-but-want-it-out-of-politics.

35. The themes of Genesis 1:26 are reiterated in Genesis 9:1–6.

36. Michelle Goldberg, *Kingdom Coming: The Rise of Christian Nationalism* (New York: W.W. Norton, 2007).

37. Debra Downey, "Following God's Laws," Kinsman Redeemer, December 17, 2012, http://kinsmanredeemer.com/following-gods-laws.

38. James P. Byrd, *Sacred Scripture, Sacred War: The Bible and the American Revolution* (Oxford: Oxford University Press, 2013), 123.

39. Specifically, in 2018, U.S. Attorney General Jeff Sessions cited this passage to legitimize the Trump administration's policy of separating immigrant children from their parents at the Mexican border by emphasizing the primacy of unconditional obedience to the government. See also Winsome Munro, "Romans 13:1–7: Apartheid's Last Biblical Refuge," *Biblical Theology Bulletin: A Journal of Bible and Theology* 20, no. 4 (1990): 161–68.

40. Katie Shepherd, "Up to 5 Migrant Children are Still Separated from Their Families Every Day, New Government Data Shows," American Immigration Council, June 26, 2019, https://immigrationimpact.com/2019/06/26/migrant-children-still-separated/#.XgcbKRdKhPN.

41. Colleen Long, "WATCH: Sessions Cites Bible to Defend Separating Immigrant Families," *PBS NewsHour,* June 14, 2018, www.pbs.org/newshour/politics/watch-live-attorney-general-jeff-sessions-talks-about-immigration.

42. Ben Klassen, *The White Man's Bible* (Lighthouse Point, FL: Church of the Creator, 1981).

43. Klassen, *White Man's Bible,* 570.

44. Klassen, *White Man's Bible,* 254–55.

45. Klassen, *White Man's Bible,* 423.

46. Osred, *Odinism: Present, Past and Future* (Melbourne: Renewal Publications, 2011), 159. The last of these claims seems to have some basis in the historical record. Jefferson is recorded as having advocated for the inclusion of "Hengist and Horsa, the Saxon chiefs from whom we claim the honor of being descended, and whose political principles and form of government we have assumed" on the seal. Russell Martin, "Seal of the United States," *Thomas Jefferson Encyclopedia,* June 19, 1989, www.monticello.org/site/research-and-collections/seal-united-states#footnote3_kn7sqx4.

47. David Lane, *Deceived, Damned, and Defiant: The Revolutionary Writings of David Lane* (St. Maries, ID: 14 Word Press, 1999), 56; George Michael, "David Lane and the Fourteen Words," *Totalitarian Movements and Political Religions* 10, no. 1 (2009): 43–61, www.tandfonline.com/doi/pdf/10.1080/14690760903067986.

48. Mattias Gardell, *Gods of the Blood: The Pagan Revival and White Separatism* (Durham, NC: Duke University Press, 2003), 193.

49. The Norse etymology of the word America—and with it the claim that they are rightful inheritors of the land—can be explained as follows: "'America' is a phonetic derivation of an ancient Norse compound word, 'omme-rike'; this combination means 'the remotest land,' a term used to describe the great land mass which the Icelandic Sagas break down into Helluland (Stoneland), Markland (Woodland), and Vinland (Wineland). . . . This name, 'omme-rike,' was in common usage by Scandinavians and Icelanders long before Columbus's 'discovery' of 'America,' for the colonization of the remote continent, with its food and lumber resources, were repeatedly attempted. Stemming from Norse usage, the term 'omme-rike' may also have been common amongst the European, especially English, fisherman who made frequent voyages to the continent's fisheries, whose whereabouts they kept secret for reasons of exploitation monopoly." "Did the Norse Name America?" *The Sunwheel* (Toronto: Odinist Movement), no. 22 (February 1975): 2.

50. "Welcome to the Vinland Folk Resistance: (HOME OF THE VINLAND FOLK PATRIOTS)," *Vinland Folk Resistance* (blog), March 24, 2007, http://vinlandfolkresistance.blogspot.com/2007/03/welcome-to-vinland-folk-resistance.html.

51. See Qur'an 6:133, 7:47, 7:57, 7:96, 7:128–29, 10:14, 10:73, 11:57, 24:55, 27:62, 38:26, and 39:35.

52. Robert P. Jones, *The End of White Christian America* (New York: Simon and Schuster, 2016), 211.

53. See Qur'an 4:65, 4:105, 5:44–45, 5:47–50, and 24:51.

54. The expression "a Tablet Preserved" comes from the Qur'an's description of its own incorruptibility: "Nay, but it is a glorious Qur'an. [Inscribed] in a Tablet Preserved!" (85:22).

55. Yahia H. Zoubir, "Reformist Islamist Thinkers in the Maghreb: Toward an Islamic Age of Enlightenment?" in *Reformist Voice of Islam:*

Mediating Islam and Modernity, ed. Shireen T. Hunter (London: Routledge, 2009), 143.

56. Mahmoud Haddad, "Arab Religious Nationalism in the Colonial Era: Rereading Rashid Rida's Ideas on the Caliphate," *Journal of the American Oriental Society* 117, no. 2 (1997): 253.

57. Henri Lauzière, *The Making of Salafism: Islamic Reform in the Twentieth Century* (New York: Columbia University Press, 2016), 60–94.

58. Richard Bonney, *Jihād: From Qur'ān to Bin Laden* (New York: Palgrave Macmillan, 2004), 204.

59. Jan-Peter Hartung, *A System of Life: Mawdudi and the Ideologisation of Islam* (Oxford: Oxford University Press, 2014), 65.

60. Bonney, *Jihād,* 207.

61. Abū al-Aʿlā Maudūdī, *Let Us Be Muslims,* trans. Khurram Murad (Leicester: Islamic Foundation, 1982), 115.

62. Syed Abul ʿAla Maudoodi, *Ḥuqūq al-zaujain* [The rights of women] (Lahore: Islamic Publications, 1966); Syed Abul ʿAla Maudoodi, *Selected Speeches and Writings of Maulana Maududi* (Karachi: International Islamic Publishers, 1981), 136–38; Syed Abul ʿAla Maudoodi and Khurshid Ahmad, *Islāmī Riyāsat* (Lāhaur: Islāmik Pablīkeshanz, 1967), 506–13.

63. Syed Abul ʿAla Maudoodi and Ashʿari, *Purdah and the Status of Woman in Islam* (Lahore: Islamic Publications, 1998), 152–61.

64. Hartung, *System of Life,* 147–48. For a challenge to this neopatriarchal view, see Margot Badran, *Feminism in Islam: Secular and Religious Convergences* (Oxford: Oneworld Publications, 2009), 311–17.

65. See Roy Jackson, *Mawlana Mawdudi and Political Islam: Authority and the Islamic State* (London: Routledge, 2011).

66. Irfan Ahmed, "Mawdudi, Abu al-Aʿla (1903–79)," in *The Princeton Encyclopedia of Islamic Political Thought,* ed. Gerhard Böwering (Princeton, NJ: Princeton University Press, 2013), 112–15.

67. Sayed Khatab, *The Power of Sovereignty: The Political and Ideological Philosophy of Sayyid Qutb,* Routledge Studies in Political Islam (New York: Routledge, 2006); Asyraf Hf. A.B. Rahman and Nooraihan Ali, "The Influence of Al-Mawdudi and the Jamaʿat Al Islami Movement on Sayyid Qutb Writings," *World Journal of Islamic History and Civilization* 2, no. 4 (2012): 232–36; Irfan Ahmad, "Genealogy of the Islamic State: Reflections on Maududi's Political Thought and Islamism," *Journal of the Royal Anthropological Institute* 15, no. 1 (2009): S145–62.

68. William E. Shepard, "Sayyid Qutb's Doctrine of Jāhiliyya," *International Journal of Middle East Studies* 35, no. 4 (2003): 521–45; Sayed Khatab, "'Hakimiyyah' and 'Jahiliyyah' in the Thought of Sayyid Qutb," *Middle Eastern Studies* 38, no. 3 (2002): 145–70; Hartung, *System of Life,* 65.

69. Youssef H. Aboul-Enein, *Militant Islamist Ideology: Understanding the Global Threat* (Annapolis, MD: Naval Institute Press, 2010), 130.

70. Hassan Hassan, "The Sectarianism of the Islamic State: Ideological Roots and Political Context," Carnegie Endowment for International Peace, June 13, 2016, http://carnegieendowment.org/2016/06/13/sectarianism-of-islamic-state-ideological-roots-and-political-context-pub-63746.

71. Bassam Tibi, *Political Islam, World Politics and Europe: From Jihadist to Institutional Islamism* (New York: Routledge, 2014), 101–29.

72. "Letter from Osama bin Laden to Abu Basir," Office of the Director of National of National Intelligence, 2016, www.dni.gov/files/documents/ubl2016/english/Letter%20to%20Abu%20Basir.pdf.

73. *Sahih Bukhari*, vol. 9, book 89, number 254, available at www.sahih-bukhari.com/Pages/Bukhari_9_89.php.

74. "From Hijrah to Khilafah," *Dabiq*, no. 1, "The Return of the Khilafah" (July 2014): 40, available at https://clarionproject.org/docs/isis-isil-islamic-state-magazine-Issue-1-the-return-of-khilafah.pdf.

75. The hadith, titled "Decision about one who tries to disrupt the unity of the Muslims," reads in full: "It has been narrated on the authority of ʿArfaja who said: I have heard the Messenger of Allah (may peace be upon him) say: Different evils will make their appearance in the near future. Anyone who tries to disrupt the affairs of this Umma while they are united you should strike him with the sword whoever he be. (If remonstrance does not prevail with him and he does not desist from his disruptive activities, he is to be killed.)" *Sahih Muslim*, book 20, number 4565, http://hadithcollection.com/sahihmuslim/148-Sahih%20Muslim%20Book%2020.%20On%20Government/12977-sahih-muslim-book-020-hadith-number-4565.html.

76. "Establishing the Islamic State: Between the Prophetic Methodology and the Paths of the Deviants," *Rumiyah*, no. 7 (March 2017): 7–9.

77. David S. Sorenson, "Confronting the 'Islamic State': Priming Strategic Communications: Countering the Appeal of ISIS," *Parameters* 44, no. 3 (Autumn 2014): 25–36.

78. Hasan Turabi, "Principles of Governance, Freedom, and Responsibility in Islam," *American Journal of Islamic Social Sciences* 4, no. 1 (1987): 1–11.

79. Al-Hayat Media Center, "The Islamic State Is a True Imamah," *Dabiq*, no. 1, "The Return of the Khilafah" (2014): 27–29. For a transcript of the speech in which Abu Bakr al-Baghdadi announced the establishment of Islamic State (Dāʿish) in 2014, see "A Message to the Mujahidin and the Muslim Ummah in the Month of Ramadan from Amirul-Muʾminin Abu Bakr Al-Husayni Al-Qurashi Al-Baghdadi," Al-Hayat Media Center, July 1, 2014, https://scholarship.tricolib.brynmawr.edu/bitstream/handle/10066/14241/ABB20140701.pdf. For an academic consideration of these questions, see Christina Hartmann, "Who Does (Not) Belong to the Jihadis' Umma? A Comparison of IS's and al-Qaida's Use of Takfīr to Exclude People from the Muslim Community," *Journal for Decradicalization*, no. 13 (2017): 213–42.

CHAPTER 7. ENCOURAGING THE END OF DAYS

1. Michael Barkun, *A Culture of Conspiracy: Apocalyptic Visions in Contemporary America* (Berkeley: University of California Press, 2013), 199.

2. Niraj Warikoo, "Many Believe in End of Times: Arrests of Hutaree Renew Interest in End of Times, Spur Controversy," *Detroit Free Press*, April 11, 2010; Niraj Warikoo, "Is Judgment Day Here? Some Michiganders Believe It," *Detroit Free Press*, May 21, 2011.

3. For more on White power music, see Pete Simi and Robert Futrell, *American Swastika: Inside the White Power Movement's Hidden Spaces of Hate* (Lanham, MD: Rowman and Littlefield, 2010), 61–85.

4. R.J. Coggins and Michael A. Knibb, *The First and Second Books of Esdras* (Cambridge: Cambridge University Press, 1979), 105.

5. Frances L. Flannery, *Understanding Apocalyptic Terrorism: Countering the Radical Mindset* (London: Routledge, 2016), 2–3.

6. "Eschatos," Bible Hub, accessed September 5, 2017, http://biblehub.com /greek/2078.htm.

7. Federal Bureau of Investigation, "Christian Identity Movement," April 28, 1989, p. 6, available at https://vault.fbi.gov/Christian%20Identity%20 Movement%20/Christian%20Identity%20Movement%20Part%201%20 of%201.

8. Jeffrey Kaplan, *Radical Religion in America: Millenarian Movements from the Far Right to the Children of Noah* (Syracuse, NY: Syracuse University Press, 1997), 85.

9. Ben Klassen, *The White Man's Bible* (Lighthouse Point, FL: Church of the Creator, 1981), 543–61.

10. Michael Barkun, "Millennialism on the Radical Right in America," in *The Oxford Handbook of Millennialism,* ed. Catherine Wessinger (Oxford: Oxford University Press, 2011), 656; Ben Klassen, *Nature's Eternal Religion in Two Books* (Lighthouse Point, FL: Church of the Creator, 1973), 504.

11. Tore Bjørgo and Noemi Gal-Or, "Right-Wing and Reactionary Terrorism," in *World Terrorism: An Encyclopedia of Political Violence from Ancient Times to the Post-9/11 Era,* 2nd ed., vol. 1, ed. James Ciment (Armonk, NY: M.E. Sharpe, 2011), 34.

12. David Lane, *Deceived, Damned, and Defiant: The Revolutionary Writings of David Lane* (St. Maries, ID: 14 Word Press, 1999), 220.

13. Jeff Kaplan, "Odinism," in *Encyclopedia of White Power: A Sourcebook on the Radical Racist Right,* ed. Jeffrey Kaplan (Walnut Creek, CA: AltaMira Press, 2000), 232.

14. Dawn Perlmutter, *Investigating Religious Terrorism and Ritualistic Crimes* (Boca Raton, FL: CRC Press, 2004), 64.

15. See also Ezekiel 37:2, 47:13–20; Joel 3:2; Amos 9:14–15; Luke 2:25; Luke 21:24; Acts 15:14–16; and Exodus 23:31.

16. Howard L. Bushart, John R. Craig, and Myra Edwards Barnes, *Soldiers of God: White Supremacists and Their Holy War for America* (New York: Kensington Books, 1998).

17. Federal Bureau of Investigation, "Christian Identity Movement," 9.

18. Federal Bureau of Investigation, "Christian Identity Movement," 6.

19. Thechurchatkaweah, "To Teach Them War Preview—Ministry Videos," GodTube video, 6:05, 2012, www.godtube.com/watch/?v=DG7ZLWNX.

20. Federal Bureau of Investigation, "Christian Identity Movement," 6.

21. See Richard Abanes, *American Militias: Rebellion, Racism and Religion* (Downers Grove, IL: InterVarsity Press, 1996), 210–11; Greg R. Broderick, "The Lunatic Fringes," Radical Religious Right Pages, accessed January 25, 2012, www.qrd.org/qrd/www/RRR/lunatic.html; "John Birch Society," Politi-

cal Research Associates, accessed January 25, 2012, www.publiceye.org /tooclose/jbs.html; Pat Robertson, *The New World Order* (Dallas: Word Publishing, 1991), xii, 6, 8–9.

22. "Kingdom Identity Ministries Doctrinal Statement of Beliefs," Kingdom Identity Ministries, accessed August 27, 2011, www.kingidentity.com/doctrine .htm.

23. Federal Bureau of Investigation, "Christian Identity Movement," 6.

24. *Sahih Bukhari,* no. 7060, book 92, hadith 12, "The Book of Afflictions and the End of the World," https://sunnah.com/bukhari/92/12; Charles Selengut, *Sacred Fury: Understanding Religious Violence,* 3rd ed. (Lanham, MD: Rowman and Littlefield, 2017), 83–117.

25. Chip Berlet and Matthew Nemiroff Lyons, *Right-Wing Populism in America: Too Close for Comfort* (New York: Guilford Press, 2000), 206.

26. *Sahih Muslim,* no. 145, "The Book of Faith," https://sunnah.com/muslim/1.

27. William F. McCants, *The ISIS Apocalypse: The History, Strategy, and Doomsday Vision of the Islamic State* (New York: St. Martin's Press, 2015), 20, 22.

28. Michael Crowley, "Khorasan: Behind the Mysterious Name of the Newest Terrorist Threat," *Time,* September 25, 2014, http://time.com/3430960 /obama-isis-khorasan-terrorism.

29. Sam232690, "The Emergence of Prophecy: The Black Flags from Khorasan," YouTube video, July 4, 2012, www.youtube.com/watch?v=uJknGtKV34I, no longer available.

30. Mustazah Bahari and Muhammad Haniff Hassan, "The Black Flag Myth: An Analysis from Hadith Studies," *Counter Terrorist Trends and Analysis* 6, no. 8 (September 2014): 15–20.

31. *Sahih Muslim,* no. 2897, book 54, hadith 44, "The Book of Tribulations and Portents of the Last Hour," https://sunnah.com/muslim/54/44. For more discussion on the significance of al-Amaq, see David Cook, *Studies in Muslim Apocalyptic* (Princeton, NJ: Darwin Press, 2002), 49–91.

32. For a discussion of twentieth-century secular totalitarian movements that exhibited patterns of thinking similar to those of religious eschatological movements, see Norman Cohn, *The Pursuit of the Millennium: Revolutionary Millenarians and Mystical Anarchists of the Middle Ages* (New York: Oxford University Press, 1970).

33. Federal Bureau of Investigation, "Christian Identity Movement," 6.

34. Federal Bureau of Investigation, "Christian Identity Movement," 3.

35. Qur'an 4:157.

36. *Sahih Muslim,* no. 2397a, book 54, hadith 136, "The Book of Tribulations and Portents of the Last Hour," https://sunnah.com/urn/270150.

37. *Sahih Bukhari,* no. 2222, book 34, hadith 169, "The Book of Sales and Trade," https://sunnah.com/bukhari/34/169.

38. *Sahih Muslim,* no. 2397a, book 54, hadith 136, "The Book of Tribulations and Portents of the Last Hour," https://sunnah.com/urn/270150.

39. Simon Staffell and Akil N. Awan, "The Impact of Evolving Jihadist Narratives on Radicalisation in the West," in *Jihadism Transformed: Al-Qaeda and Islamic State's Global Battle of Ideas,* ed. Akil N. Awan (New York: Oxford University Press, 2016), 198.

CHAPTER 8. THE MYTH OF THE LONE WOLF

1. Karen Workman and Andrea Kannapell, "The Charleston Shooting: What Happened," *New York Times,* June 18, 2015, www.nytimes.com/2015/06/18/us/the-charleston-shooting-what-happened.html.

2. Kevin Sack and Alan Blinder, "No Regrets from Dylann Roof in Jailhouse Manifesto," *New York Times,* January 5, 2017, www.nytimes.com/2017/01/05/us/no-regrets-from-dylann-roof-in-jailhouse-manifesto.html.

3. Dylann Roof, *Last Rhodesian,* accessed June 20, 2015, lastrhodesian.com/data/documents/rtf88.txt (website no longer available).

4. Rachel Kaadzi Ghansah, "A Most American Terrorist: The Making of Dylann Roof," *GQ,* August 21, 2017, www.gq.com/story/dylann-roof-making-of-an-american-terrorist.

5. Elizabeth Chuck, "Racist Website Appears to Belong to Charleston Church Shooter Dylann Roof," *NBC News,* June 20, 2015, www.nbcnews.com/storyline/charleston-church-shooting/racist-website-appears-belong-charleston-church-shooter-dylann-roof-n379021. The beach was on Sullivan's Island, South Carolina, where hundreds of thousands of enslaved Africans were forcibly brought between 1700 and 1775; see Ghansah, "A Most American Terrorist."

6. Several news organizations discussed or displayed the photos, including the *Telegraph* (UK) and *NBC News.* See Rob Crilly, "Charleston Church Massacre: Things We Learned from Shooter Dylann Roof's Racist Manifesto," *Telegraph* (UK), June 21, 2015, www.telegraph.co.uk/news/worldnews/northamerica/usa/11689037/Charleston-church-massacre-Things-we-learned-from-shooter-Dylann-Roofs-racist-manifesto.html; and Chuck, "Racist Website."

7. Peter Bergen, Albert Ford, Alyssa Sims, and David Sterman, "Terrorism in America After 9/11," *New America,* September 7, 2016, www.newamerica.org/in-depth/terrorism-in-america.

8. Jesse J. Norris, "Why Dylann Roof Is a Terrorist under Federal Law, and Why It Matters," *Harvard Journal on Legislation* 54 (2007): 501–41.

9. Glenn Smith, Jennifer Berry Hawes, and Abigail Darlington, "Dylann Roof Sentenced to Death for Emanuel AME Church Massacre," *Post and Courier,* March 26, 2017, www.postandcourier.com/church_shooting/they-don-t-know-what-real-hatred-looks-like-dylann/article_3c24cc44-d729-11e6-9e5d-2f037e89bddc.html.

10. Joanna Paraszczuk, "The Frequently Asked Questions of Aspiring Jihadists," *Atlantic,* November 12, 2014, www.theatlantic.com/international/archive/2014/11/the-frequently-asked-questions-of-aspiring-jihadists/382678.

11. Studies show that there is no singular profile of lone wolves. Researchers at the International Center for the Study of Terrorism at Pennsylvania State University published a report in 2013 entitled *Bombing Alone: Tracing the Motivations and Antecedent Behaviors of Lone-Actor Terrorism,* which profiled 119 lone wolf actors from a wide variety of ideological and faith backgrounds. They found that "right-wing offenders" are more likely to be unemployed, less educated, and have more criminal convictions than their militant Islamist counterparts. The former are also more likely to make statements publicly or to reveal their intentions to close associates before acting. See Paul Gill, "Seven Findings

on Lone Actor Terrorists," International Center for the Study of Terrorism, Pennsylvania State University, February 6, 2013, http://sites.psu.edu/icst/2013 /02/06/seven-findings-on-lone-actor-terrorists. Another study, published in 2015, that looked at European militant Islamists in particular, found that they were more likely to be militarized through social networks at home than they were to be militarized online. See Jack Moore, "What Makes an ISIS Foreign Fighter? Disadvantaged Background and Poor Education," *Newsweek,* August 7, 2017, www.newsweek.com/what-makes-isis-foreign-fighter-disadvantage-poor-education-brotherhood-643254. See also Christopher Hewitt, *Understanding Terrorism in America: From the Klan to Al-Qaeda* (London: Routledge, 2003), 78; and Bruce Hoffman, *Al Qaeda, Trends in Terrorism and Future Potentialities: An Assessment* (Santa Monica, CA: RAND, 2003), 17.

12. Maura Conway, "Determining the Role of the Internet in Violent Extremism and Terrorism: Six Suggestions for Progressing Research," *Studies in Conflict and Terrorism* 40, no. 1 (2017): 77–98.

13. United States Department of Homeland Security, "Domestic Terrorism and Homegrown Violent Extremism Lexicon," Office of Intelligence and Analysis, November 10, 2011, p. 2, available at https://info.publicintelligence.net /DHS-ExtremismLexicon.pdf; Fred Burton and Scott Stewart, "The 'Lone Wolf' Disconnect," Stratfor Worldview, January 30, 2008, www.stratfor.com/weekly /lone_wolf_disconnect; Ramón Spaaij, "The Enigma of Lone Wolf Terrorism: An Assessment," *Studies in Conflict and Terrorism* 33, no. 9 (2010): 854–70.

14. Louis Beam, "Leaderless Resistance," *The Seditionist,* no. 12 (February 1992): 3. The essay, originally written in 1983, is available at www.researchgate .net/publication/233097025_%27Leaderless_resistance%27.

15. Paul Joosse, "Leaderless Resistance and Ideological Inclusion: The Case of the Earth Liberation Front," *Terrorism and Political Violence* 19 (2007): 353.

16. Tom Metzger, "Laws for the Lone Wolf," Stormfront, accessed February 30, 2017, www.stormfront.org/forum/t454864.

17. Jeffrey Kaplan, "Leaderless Resistance," *Terrorism and Political Violence* 9, no. 3 (1997): 89.

18. Jeffrey Kaplan, "Ku Klux Klan," in *Encyclopedia of White Power: A Sourcebook on the Radical Racist Right,* ed. Jeffrey Kaplan (Walnut Creek, CA: AltaMira Press, 2000), 164; "Documentary Clip with George Burdi and Tom Metzger," Internet Archive, 9:58, December 17, 2013, https://archive.org /details/DocumentaryClipWithGeorgeBurdiAndTomMetzger.

19. Ben Klassen, *Building a Whiter and Brighter World* (Otto, NC: Church of the Creator, 1986), 106–19; George Michael, "RAHOWA! A History of the World Church of the Creator," *Terrorism and Political Violence* 18, no. 4 (2006): 567.

20. In 2005, Hale was sentenced to forty years in federal prison for conspiring to murder a federal judge who had ruled against him in the trademark case.

21. Matt Hale, "White Revolution, Show 19: Leaderless Resistance / Organization of the Church / Taking Action against the Travesty Going On in Our Country Today," Rev. Matt Hale Archive, accessed September 4, 2017, https:// reverendmatthalearchive.wordpress.com/video/shows/white-revolution/white-revolution-no-19.

22. "The Call for a Global Islamic Resistance," Counterterrorismblog.org, accessed September 4, 2017, available at https://archive.org/details/The-call-for-a-global-Islamic-resistance.

23. Dylan Matthews, "The Alt-Right Is More Than Warmed-Over White Supremacy. It's That, But Way Way Weirder," *Vox,* August 25, 2016, www.vox.com/2016/4/18/11434098/alt-right-explained.

24. Michael C. Keith and Robert L. Hilliard, *Waves of Rancor: Tuning into the Radical Right,* Media, Communication, and Culture in America (New York: Routledge, 2015). On the KKK's use of radio in the 1920s, see Felix Harcourt, *Ku Klux Kulture: America and the Klan in the 1920s* (Chicago: University of Chicago Press, 2017), 142–59.

25. Greg Miller, "Islamist Militants Turned to Less-Governed Social-Media Platform," *Washington Post,* October 15, 2015, www.washingtonpost.com/world/national-security/islamist-militants-turn-to-less-governed-social-media-platform/2015/10/29/265dbaea-7e53-11e5-beba-927fd8634498_story.html; Alina Selyukh, "Feeling Sidelined by Mainstream Social Media, Far-Right Users Jump to Gab," *NPR,* May 21, 2017, www.npr.org/sections/alltechconsidered/2017/05/21/529005840/feeling-sidelined-by-mainstream-social-media-far-right-users-jump-to-gab; Mia Bloom, Hicham Tiflati, and John Horgan, "Navigating ISIS's Preferred Platform: Telegram," *Terrorism and Political Violence* 31, no. 6 (2019): 1242-54, https://doi.org/10.1080/09546553.2017.1339695; Lauren Williams, "Islamic State Propaganda and the Mainstream Media," Lowy Institute for International Policy, February 29, 2016, www.lowyinstitute.org/publications/islamic-state-propaganda-and-mainstream-media; Ryan Scrivens and Amarnath Amarasingam, "Haters Gonna 'Like': Exploring Canadian Far-Right Extremism on Facebook," in *Digital Extremisms,* Palgrave Studies in Cybercrime and Cyber-security, ed. Mark Littler and Benjamin Lee (Cham, Switzerland: Palgrave Macmillan, 2020), 63-89; Barbara Perry and Patrik Olsson, "Cyberhate: The Globalization of Hate," *Information & Communications Technology Law* 18, no. 2 (2009): 185–99, https://doi.org/10.1080/13600830902814984; Maura Conway, Ryan Scrivens, and Logan Macnair, *Right-Wing Extremists' Persistent Online Presence: History and Contemporary Trends,* ICCT Policy Brief (The Hague: International Center for Counter-Terrorism, November 2019), https://icct.nl/wp-content/uploads/2019/11/Right-Wing-Extremists-Persistent-Online-Presence.pdf.

26. Rita Katz, "ISIS Is Now Harder to Track Online—But That's Good News," *Wired,* December 16, 2019, www.wired.com/story/opinion-isis-is-now-harder-to-track-onlinebut-thats-good-news; David Gilbert, "ISIS Is Experimenting with This New Blockchain Messaging App," *Vice News,* December 13, 2019, www.vice.com/en_us/article/v744yy/isis-is-experimenting-with-this-new-blockchain-messaging-app; Rita Katz, "A Growing Frontier for Terrorist Groups: Unsuspecting Chat Apps," *Wired,* January 9, 2019, www.wired.com/story/terrorist-groups-prey-on-unsuspecting-chat-apps.

27. John Suler, "The Online Disinhibition Effect," *CyberPsychology & Behavior* 7, no. 3 (2004): 321–26; John Suler, *Psychology of the Digital Age: Humans Become Electric* (New York: Cambridge University Press, 2016).

28. Bill Duryea and Brad Snyder, "They Preach Hate on Public Access TV," *St. Petersburg Times,* July 12, 1993, p. 1A.

29. Duryea and Snyder, "They Preach Hate on Public Access TV."

30. "Documentary Clip with George Burdi and Tom Metzger."

31. "Documentary Clip with George Burdi and Tom Metzger"; David S. Hoffman, *The Web of Hate: Extremists Exploit the Internet* (New York: Anti-Defamation League, 1996), www.adl.org/sites/default/files/documents/assets /pdf/combating-hate/ADL-Report-1996-Web-of-Hate-Extremists-exploit-the-Internet.pdf.

32. Gabriel Weimann, "Going Dark: Terrorism on the Dark Web," *Studies in Conflict and Terrorism* 39, no. 3 (2016): 197–98; "Jihad Trending: A Comprehensive Analysis of Online Extremism and How to Counter It (Executive Summary)," Quilliam, May 13, 2014, www.quilliaminternational.com/jihad-trending-a-comprehensive-analysis-of-online-extremism-and-how-to-counter-it-executive-summary.

33. In 2015, several militant Islamists posted online an e-book titled *How to Survive in the West: A Mujahid Guide*. This was the latest in a series of e-books compiled by supporters of and recruiters for the Islamic State (Dāʿish). This e-book's chapter titles include: "Hiding the Extremist Identity," "Earning Money," "Internet Privacy," "Training," "Bomb-Making," "Transporting Weapons," and "What Happens When You Are Spied on and Get Raided." See "The 'Dark Web' and Jihad: A Preliminary Review of Jihadis' Perspective on the Underside of the World Wide Web," *Jihad and Terrorism Threat Monitor,* Middle East Media Research Institute, May 21, 2014, www.memri.org/jttm/dark-web-and-jihad-preliminary-review-jihadis-perspective-underside-world-wide-web. One of the techniques discussed in the guidebook is the use of Tor, a Dark Web network, when searching for and researching topics related to militant Islamism online.

34. In the following study, social media was found to be a causal link between online hate speech and real-life violence: Karsten Müller and Carlo Schwarz, "Fanning the Flames of Hate: Social Media and Hate Crime," *SSRN,* February 19, 2018, https://papers.ssrn.com/sol3/papers.cfm?abstract_id=3082972.

35. Criminal complaint, Tanya Gersh v. Andrew Anglin, United States District Court, District of Montana (Missoula), case no. CV 17-50-M-DLC-JCL, April 18, 2017, available at www.splcenter.org/sites/default/files/documents /whitefish_complaint_finalstamped.pdf; order on motion to dismiss, Tanya Gersh v. Andrew Anglin, United States District Court, District of Montana (Missoula), case no. CV 17-50-M-DLC-JCL, November 14, 2018, available at www.splcenter.org/sites/default/files/documents/order_on_motion_to_dismiss .pdf; Mallory Simon and Sara Sidner, "An Avalanche of Hate: How a Montana Mom Became the Target of a Neo-Nazi Troll Storm," *CNN,* July 11, 2017, www.cnn.com/2017/07/10/us/avalanche-of-hate-daily-stormer-lawsuit/index. html. On August 8, 2019, Anglin was ordered to pay more than $14 million in damages to Gersh. Order, Tanya Gersh v. Andrew Anglin, United States District Court, District of Montana (Missoula), case no. CV 17-50-M-DLC-JCL, August 8, 2019, available at www.splcenter.org/sites/default/files/0214._08-08-2019_order_adopting_findings_and_recommendations_and_granting_201_ motion_for_default_judgment._signed_b.pdf.

36. "Student Government President Taylor Dumpson Resigns," *The Eagle,* January 26, 2018, www.theeagleonline.com/article/2018/01/american-university-

student-government-president-taylor-dumpson-resigns; Sarah Lorimer, "Former AU Student Government President Sues over 'Troll Storm' after Bananas Incident," *Washington Post*, May 2, 2018, www.washingtonpost.com/news/gradepoint/wp/2018/05/02/former-au-student-government-president-sues-over-troll-storm-after-bananas-incident .

37. Andrew Anglin, "Register NOW for the IRL Troll Army AKA the Stormer Book Club," *Daily Stormer*, August 3, 2016, https://dstormer6em3i4km.onion.link/register-now-for-the-irl-troll-army-aka-the-stormer-book-club.

38. Andrew Anglin, "Attention All Stormer Book Clubs: This Is Important," *Daily Stormer*, June 2, 2017, https://dstormer6em3i4km.onion.link/attention-all-stormer-book-clubs-this-is-important.

39. Frances Robles, "Dylann Roof Photos and a Manifesto Are Posted on Website," *New York Times*, June 20, 2015. Roof's manifesto is very similar to a post on the *Daily Stormer*, the popular White nationalist website founded by Andrew Anglin. Dylann Roof's manifesto also decries Latinx and Jews, though his belief that Jewish people are White distinguishes his ideology from racist theologies like Christian Identity that pronouncedly demarcate between White people and Jews. He also notes his "great respect for the East Asian races" because of what he understands to be their racism.

40. Michelle Alexander, *The New Jim Crow: Mass Incarceration in the Age of Colorblindness* (New York: New Press, 2010).

41. Roof, *Last Rhodesian.*

42. Roof, *Last Rhodesian.*

43. "Statement of Principles," Council of Conservative Citizens, accessed September 4, 2017, http://conservative-headlines.org/statement-of-principles.

44. Curtis Giovanni Flowers v. State Of Mississippi, 139 S. Ct. 2228 (2019), www.supremecourt.gov/DocketPDF/17/17-9572/77684/20181227104135863_17-9572%20Amicus%20Brief%20of%20NAACP%20LDF.pdf, p. 19.

45. "Statement of Principles," Council of Conservative Citizens; David M. O'Brien, "'The Imperial Judiciary': Of Paper Tigers and Socio-Legal Indicators," *History Teacher* 19, no. 1 (1985): 33–88, https://doi.org/10.2307/493615.

46. "Council of Conservative Citizens," Southern Poverty Law Center, accessed September 4, 2017, www.splcenter.org/fighting-hate/extremist-files/group/council-conservative-citizens.

47. "White Supremacist Cited in Dylann Roof's Alleged Manifesto Donated to Major GOP Campaigns," *Vice*, June 22, 2015, https://news.vice.com/article/white-supremacist-cited-in-dylann-roofs-alleged-manifesto-donated-to-major-gop-campaigns.

48. Richard Spencer, "Dylann Roof and Political Violence," *Radix Journal*, June 23, 2015, accessed June 30, 2015, page no longer available.

49. Jan Ransom, "White Supremacist Who Killed Black Man to Incite Race War Sentenced to Life in Prison," *New York Times*, February 13, 2019, www.nytimes.com/2019/02/13/nyregion/james-harris-jackson-timothy-caughman.html.

50. Criminal complaint, United States of America v. Benjamin Thomas Samuel McDowell, United States District Court, District of South Carolina, case no. 4:17-MJ-00037-MCRI, February 16, 2017, available at https://assets.documentcloud.org/documents/3462816/Benjamin-McDowell.pdf.

51. Criminal complaint, United States of America v. Benjamin Thomas Samuel McDowell. Despite these statements—including his evocation of the fourteen-word battle cry of White nationalists—McDowell, like Dylann Roof, was not charged with a terrorism-related crime but rather for possession of a firearm and ammunition by a prohibited person.

52. Anwar al-Aulaqi, "Full Text of 'Allah Is Preparing Us for Victory,'" transcribed by Amatu and ed. Mujahid fe Sabeelillah, accessed September 3, 2017, http://archive.org/stream/AllahIsPreparingUsForVictory-AnwarAlAwlaki/AllahIsPreparingUsForVictory_djvu.txt. See also AnwarAlAwlakiAudio, "Anwar Al-Awlaki—Allah Is Preparing Us for Victory—1/1," YouTube video, October 30, 2010, www.youtube.com/watch?v=br2fOposRkg, no longer available.

53. Laurie Goodstein, "A Nation Challenged: The American Muslims; Influential American Muslims Temper Their Tone," New York Times, October 19, 2001, www.nytimes.com/2001/10/19/us/nation-challenged-american-muslims-influential-american-muslims-temper-their.html.

54. Scott Shane, "The Lessons of Anwar al-Awlaki," New York Times Magazine, August 18, 2013, www.nytimes.com/2015/08/30/magazine/the-lessons-of-anwar-al-awlaki.html; "A Muslim Reported Omar Mateen to the FBI Well before Orlando Shooting," NPR, June 26, 2016, www.npr.org/2016/06/22/483046567 /a-muslim-reported-omar-mateen-to-the-fbi-well-before-the-orlando-shooting.

55. Nidal Malik Hasan, "Hasan Letter," Killeen Daily Herald, August 18, 2013, http://kdhnews.com/military/hasan_trial/hasan-letter/pdf_b530a86a-068a-11e3-8136-001a4bcf6878.html.

56. Scott Shane and Mark Mazzetti, "Times Sq. Bomb Suspect Is Linked to Militant Cleric," New York Times, May 6, 2010, www.nytimes.com/2010/05/07 /world/middleeast/07awlaki-.html.

57. Chris Heffelfinger, Radical Islam in America: Salafism's Journey from Arabia to the West (Lincoln, NE: Potomac Books, 2011), 128.

58. Anwar al-Aulaqi, "A Message to the American People," YouTube video, March 17, 2010, www.youtube.com/watch?v=rXIRqmS_oLc, no longer available. Excerpts of this video are available at "RAW DATA: Partial Transcript of Radical Cleric's Tape," Fox News, March 18, 2010, www.foxnews.com /politics/2010/03/18/raw-data-partial-transcript-radical-clerics-tape.html.

59. In 2017, YouTube took the dramatic step of removing the vast majority of Anwar al-Aulaqi's videos from its platform; it remains to be seen how this will affect the dispersal of his videos or his posthumous reputation. See Scott Shane, "In 'Watershed Moment,' YouTube Blocks Extremist Cleric's Message," New York Times, November 12, 2017, www.nytimes.com/2017/11/12/us /politics/youtube-terrorism-anwar-al-awlaki.html.

60. Jason Wilson, "Activists Claim to Unveil Leader of 'Alt-Right' Website the Right Stuff," Guardian (UK), January 17, 2017, www.theguardian.com /world/2017/jan/17/right-stuff-alt-right-site-mike-enoch-revealed.

61. Anthony F. Lemieux, Jarrett M. Brachman, Jason Levitt, and Jay Wood, "Inspire Magazine: A Critical Analysis of Its Significance and Potential Impact through the Lens of the Information, Motivation, and Behavioral Skills Model," Terrorism and Political Violence 26, no. 2 (2014): 363–66, https://doi.org/10.1 080/09546553.2013.828604.

62. Radoslava Haršányová and Marek Hrušovský, "Current Trends in Jihadist Online Magazines," Centre for European and North Atlantic Affairs, January 22, 2017, p. 1, www.irsec-hub.org/publications/264.

63. Lemieux, Brachman, Levitt, and Wood, "*Inspire* Magazine," 27; Michael Zekulin, "From *Inspire* to *Rumiyah*: Does Instructional Content in Online Jihadist Magazines Lead to Attacks?" *Behavioral Sciences of Terrorism and Political Aggression,* January 7, 2020, https://doi.org/10.1080/19434472.2019.1707848.

64. Alastair Reed and Haroro J. Ingram, *Exploring the Role of Instructional Material in AQAP's Inspire and ISIS's* Rumiyah, (The Hague: Europol, May 26, 2017), 7, https://icct.nl/wp-content/uploads/2017/06/reeda_ingramh_instructionalmaterial.pdf.

65. Reed and Ingram, *Exploring the Role of Instructional Material,* 8.

66. Criminal complaint, United States of America v. Dzhokhar A. Tsarnaev a/k/a "Jahar Tsarni," United States District Court, District of Massachusetts, case no. 1:13-MJ-02106-MBB, April 21, 2013, available at www.documentcloud.org/documents/690349-tsarnaevaffidavit.html.

67. Fawaz E. Gerges, "Op-Ed: The Three Manifestos That Paved the Way for Islamic State," *Los Angeles Times,* April 16, 2016, www.latimes.com/opinion/op-ed/la-oe-0417-gerges-islamic-state-theorists-20160417-story.html.

68. Prior to his death sentence being overturned in 2020, American militant Islamist Dzhokhar Tsarnaev plead guilty to all thirty counts against him, which included conspiracy and deadly use of a weapon of mass destruction. In 2020, a federal appeal court overturned the death penalty for Dzhokhar Tsarnaev. The case will go back to the lower court for additional hearings, though this does not mean Tsarnaev will have an opportunity to get out of prison. See Maria Sacchetti and Mark Berman, "Death Sentence Overturned for Boston Marathon Bomber," *Washington Post,* July 31, 2020, www.washingtonpost.com/national/boston-marathon-bomber-death-sentence-overturned/2020/07/31/f2a21818-d366-11ea-9038-af089b63ac21_story.html.

69. Madison Grant, *The Passing of the Great Race: or, The Racial Basis of European History* (New York: Charles Scribner's Sons, 1918), 49.

70. "The Immigration Act of 1924 (The Johnson-Reed Act)," Office of the Historian, U.S. State Department, accessed August 24, 2020, https://history.state.gov/milestones/1921-1936/immigration-act.

71. Edwin Black, *War against the Weak: Eugenics and America's Campaign to Create a Master Race* (Washington, DC: Dialog Press, 2012), 259.

72. Adolf Hitler, *Mein Kampf* (New York: Reynal and Hitchcock, 1939), 658.

73. Hitler, *Mein Kampf,* 388.

74. Hitler, *Mein Kampf,* 406.

75. Jean Raspail, *The Camp of the Saints,* trans. Norman Shapiro (New York: Charles Scribner's Sons, 1975).

76. Stephen Miller, a senior adviser to President Trump known for shaping the administration's xenophobic immigration policies, has been lauded by White nationalists for his Islamophobic and anti-immigrant agenda. The revelation in late 2019 of hundreds of his emails evidenced his promotion of White nationalist literature, racist immigration stories, and an obsession over the loss of Confederate symbols. See Michael Edison Hayden, "Emails Confirm Miller's

Twin Obsessions: Immigrants and Crime," *HateWatch,* Southern Poverty Law Center, November 25, 2019, www.splcenter.org/hatewatch/2019/11/25/emails-confirm-millers-twin-obsessions-immigrants-and-crime; Paul Blumenthal and J.M. Rieger, "This Stunningly Racist French Novel Is How Steve Bannon Explains the World," *HuffPost,* March 4, 2017, updated March 6, 2017, www .huffingtonpost.co.uk/entry/steve-bannon-camp-of-the-saints-immigration_ n_58b75206e4b0284854b3dc03; Lulu Garcia-Navarro, "Steven Miller and 'The Camp of the Saints,' a White Nationalist Reference," *NPR,* November 19, 2019, www.npr.org/2019/11/19/780552636/stephen-miller-and-the-camp-of-the-saints-a-white-nationalist-reference; and Marine Le Pen (@MLP_officiel), "Le livre qui m'a beaucoup marquée," Twitter, April 5, 2018, 6:39 p.m., https://twitter.com/mlp_officiel/status/981934318326046720.

77. Joel Dyer, *Harvest of Rage: Why Oklahoma City Is Only the Beginning* (Boulder, CO: Westview Press, 1998), 223.

78. William L. Pierce, *The Turner Diaries* (Hillsboro, WV: National Vanguard Books, 1995), 161.

79. David Lane, *White Genocide Manifesto* (St. Maries, ID: 14 Word Press, 1988).

80. In 2020, Brenton Tarrant was sentenced to life without parole after pleading guilty to the murder of fifty-one people, the attempted murder of forty people, and one charge of terrorism, marking the first terrorism conviction in New Zealand's history. "Christchurch Mosque Attack: Brenton Tarrant Sentenced to Life without Parole," *BBC News,* August 27, 2020, www.bbc.com /news/world-asia-53919624.

81. Andrew Berwick, *2083: A European Declaration of Independence* (London: 2011), p. 831, available at https://info.publicintelligence.net/AndersBehringBreivikManifesto.pdf.

82. Brenton Tarrant, *The Great Replacement,* March 2019, p. 24, available at www.ilfoglio.it/userUpload/The_Great_Replacementconvertito.pdf, no longer available.

83. Tarrant, *Great Replacement,* 18.

84. Tarrant, *Great Replacement,* 29.

85. Michael Davis, "The Anti-Jewish Manifesto of John T. Earnest, the San Diego Synagogue Shooter," Middle East Media Research Institute, May 15, 2019, www.memri.org/reports/anti-jewish-manifesto-john-t-earnest-san-diego-synagogue-shooter; Michael Davis, "The Manifesto Posted on 8chan by Alleged El Paso Shooter Minutes before Attack," Middle East Media Research Institute, August 6, 2019, www.memri.org/reports/manifesto-posted-8chan-alleged-el-paso-shooter-minutes-attack.

86. Patrick Crusius, "Patrick Crusius Manifesto: The Inconvenient Truth," Grabacijas, August 5, 2019, https://grabancijas.com/patrick-crusius-manifesto-the-inconvenient-truth. The manifesto can also be found at "Walmart Shooter Manifesto," Drudge Report, August 3, 2019, https://drudgereport.com/flashtx .htm.

87. 8chan owner, Patrick Watkins, denied that it was Patrick Crusius who uploaded the manifesto, stating it was a different, albeit unknown, user. Law enforcement officials have since stated otherwise. See Oscar Gonzales and

Queenie Wong, "Instagram Denies 8chan Owner's Claim about El Paso Shooting Manifesto," CNET, August 9, 2019, www.cnet.com/news/8chan-owner-says-el-paso-shooter-didnt-post-manifesto.

88. Crusius, "Patrick Crusius Manifesto."

89. It is noteworthy that the conspiratorial elements of both ideologies also create theories that neither of these individuals were true martyrs but rather undercover agents. See Catherine Herridge, "Enemy or Asset? FBI Documents Show Radical Cleric Awlaki Communicated with Federal Agent in '03," *Fox News*, October 1, 2014, www.foxnews.com/politics/2014/10/01/enemy-or-asset-fbi-documents-show-radical-cleric-awlaki-communicated-with.html; and Geoffrey Fattah, "Nichols Says Bombing Was FBI Op," *Deseret News*, February 22, 2007, www.deseretnews.com/article/660197443/Nichols-says-bombing-was-FBI-op.html.

90. "Terrorist, '14 Words' Author, Dies in Prison," *Intelligence Report: 2007*, Southern Poverty Law Center, 2007 Fall Issue, October 1, 2007, www.splcenter.org/fighting-hate/intelligence-report/2007/terrorist-14-words-author-dies-prison.

91. Bundy Ranch, "The resolve for principled liberty must go on," Facebook, January 26, 2016, www.facebook.com/bundyranch/photos/a.624209630989182.1073741827.623383454405133/951182274958581.

92. Lizzie Dearden, "Revered as a Saint by Online Extremists, How Christchurch Shooter Inspired Copycat Terrorists around the World," *Independent* (UK), August 24, 2019, www.independent.co.uk/news/world/australasia/brenton-tarrant-christchurch-shooter-attack-el-paso-norway-poway-a9076926.html.

93. "The Arabic term for martyr is *shahīd,* from the root *sh-h-d,* meaning 'to witness', 'be witness', 'to experience personally' and 'to give testimony.'" See Hans Wehr and J. Milton Cowan, *A Dictionary of Modern Written Arabic* (Ithaca, NY: Spoken Language Services, 1976), 571. This is the same root as *shahāda,* which means to witness or testify that "there is no deity but God and Muhammad is His (final) messenger." A *shahīd* is literally a witness who dies in testimony of his or her faith, because he or she is upholding the values of Islam: peace, patience, fortitude, and stopping oppression.

94. Richard Winton, "San Bernardino Shooters Praised by Islamic State Magazine," *Los Angeles Times,* January 20, 2016, www.latimes.com/local/lanow/la-me-ln-islamic-state-magazine-san-bernardino-terrorists-20160120-story.html.

95. Eli Lee, "What Is 'Lone Wolf' Terrorism in the Digital Age?" Political Research Associates, November 21, 2015, www.politicalresearch.org/2015/11/21/what-is-lone-wolf-terrorism-in-the-digital-age/#sthash.P1QLABL2.dpbs; Timothy G. Baysinger, "Right-Wing Group Characteristics and Ideology," *Homeland Security Affairs* 2, article 3 (July 2006), www.hsaj.org/articles/166; Testimony of Dale Watson before the Senate Select Committee on Intelligence, Washington, DC, February 6, 2002, available at https://archives.fbi.gov/archives/news/testimony/the-terrorist-threat-confronting-the-united-states; Bart Schuurman, Lasse Lindekilde, Stefan Malthaner, Francis O'Connor, Paul Gill, and Noémie Bouhana, "End of the Lone Wolf: The Typology that Should

Not Have Been," *Studies in Conflict and Terrorism* 42, no. 8 (2018): 771–78, https://doi.org/10.1080/1057610X.2017.1419554.

96. Allison J.B. Chaney, Brandon M. Stewart, and Barbara E. Engelhardt, "How Algorithmic Confounding in Recommendation Systems Increases Homogeneity and Decreases Utility," in *RecSys '18: Proceedings of the 12th ACM Conference on Recommender Systems,* ed. Sole Pera and Michael Ekstrand (New York: Association for Computing Machinery, September 2018), 224–32, https://dl.acm.org/doi/10.1145/3240323.3240370.

97. Milton John Kleim Jr., "Internet Recruiting," in *Encyclopedia of White Power: A Sourcebook on the Radical Racist Right,* ed. Jeffrey Kaplan (Walnut Creek, CA: Altamira Press, 2000), 143.

98. In response to Brenton Tarrant's acts of terrorism, the Christchurch Call to Action Summit in 2019 brought together heads of governments with leaders from Big Tech companies like Facebook, Microsoft, and Google to commit to eliminating terrorist content online, taking into account the freedom of expression; see Christchurch Call to Eliminate Terrorist and Violent Extremist Content Online (website), www.christchurchcall.com/call.html. Another example of a tech company attempting to address terrorism is Moonshot CVE (www.moonshotcve.com), a startup founded in 2015. See also Ruha Benjamin, *Race after Technology: Abolitionist Tools for the New Jim Code* (Cambridge: Polity, 2019). However, even as tech companies are being called on to address terrorism, they are also being targeted for fueling it, in addition to other forms of violence, including surveillance, detentions, and deportations of activists, immigrants, and people of color. See Empower LLC, *Who's Behind ICE? The Tech and Data Companies Fueling Deportations*, National Immigration Project of the National Lawyers Guild, Immigrant Defense Project, and Mijente, October 23, 2018, https://mijente.net/wp-content/uploads/2018/10/WHO'S-BEHIND-ICE_-The-Tech-and-Data-Companies-Fueling-Deportations-_v1.pdf.

99. Bobby Allyn, "Big Tech Companies In Need Of A Fundamental Change To Deal With Racial Injustice," *NPR,* June 18, 2020, www.npr.org/2020/06/18/880513732/big-tech-companies-in-need-of-a-fundamental-change-to-deal-with-racial-injustice; Jaron Schneider, "Big Tech Had a Chance to Take Major Steps against Systemic Racism, But It Failed," Digital Trends, June 5, 2020, www.digitaltrends.com/opinion/big-tech-systemic-racism-failure-black-lives-matter; Alexandra Stevenson, "Facebook Admits It Was Used to Incite Violence in Myanmar," *New York Times,* November 6, 2018, www.nytimes.com/2018/11/06/technology/myanmar-facebook.html; "Extremists Are Using Facebook to Organize for Civil War amid Coronavirus," Tech Transparency Project, April 22, 2020, www.techtransparencyproject.org/articles/extremists-are-using-facebook-to-organize-for-civil-war-amid-coronavirus.

100. Alexandra Stevenson, "Facebook Admits It Was Used to Incite Violence in Myanmar," *New York Times,* November 6, 2018, www.nytimes.com/2018/11/06/technology/myanmar-facebook.html; "Banning More Dangerous Organizations from Facebook in Myanmar," Facebook, February 5, 2019, https://about.fb.com/news/2019/02/dangerous-organizations-in-myanmar; National Immigration Project of the National Lawyers Guild, Immigrant Defense Project, and Mijente, *Who's Behind ICE? The Tech and Data Companies*

Fueling Deportation, 2018, https://mijente.net/wp-content/uploads/2018/10
/WHO%E2%80%99S-BEHIND-ICE_-The-Tech-and-Data-Companies-Fue-
ling-Deportations-_v1.pdf.

CONCLUSION

1. Faiza Patel, Andrew Lindsay, Sophia DenUyl, "Countering Violent
Extremism in the Trump Era," Brennan Center for Justice, New York University School of Law, June 15, 2018, www.brennancenter.org/analysis/countering-
violent-extremism-trump-era.

2. All Party Parliamentary Group on British Muslims, *Islamophobia Defined:
The Inquiry into a Working Definition of Islamophobia,* November 2018, 11,
https://static1.squarespace.com/static/599c3d2febbd1a90cffdd8a9/t/5bfd1ea3352f
531a6170ceee/1543315109493/Islamophobia+Defined.pdf.

3. Daniel Cox, Rachel Lienesch, and Robert P. Jones, "Who Sees Discrimination? Attitudes on Sexual Orientation, Gender Identity, Race, and Immigration
Status: Findings from PRRI's American Values Atlas," PRRI, June 21, 2017,
www.prri.org/research/americans-views-discrimination-immigrants-blacks-
lgbt-sex-marriage-immigration-reform. For a discussion of unconscious racism,
see Kristin J. Anderson, *Benign Bigotry: The Psychology of Subtle Prejudice*
(Cambridge: Cambridge University Press, 2010).

4. Frederick Douglass, *Frederick Douglass: Selected Speeches and Writings,*
ed. Philip S. Foner, abridged and adapted Yuval Taylor (Chicago: Lawrence Hill
Books, 1999), 287.

5. Los Angeles Interagency Coordination Group, *The Los Angeles Frame-
work for Countering Violent Extremism,* Department of Homeland Security,
February 2015, www.dhs.gov/sites/default/files/publications/Los%20Angeles%
20Framework%20for%20CVE-Full%20Report.pdf; American-Arab Anti-
Discrimination Committee, *Mapping Countering Violent Extremism (CVE)
Programs,* October 2017, www.adc.org/wp-content/uploads/2017/10/Mapping-
CVE.pdf.

6. M. Steven Fish, *Are Muslims Distinctive? A Look at the Evidence* (New
York: Oxford University Press, 2011), 35–37.

7. For a review of relevant debates and research in the context of CVE policy,
see Faiza Patel and Meghan Koushik, "Countering Violent Extremism," Brennan
Center for Justice, New York University School of Law, March 2017; Hisham
Hellyer, "Observance of Islam Is a Way to Defeat Extremism," *National,* February 25, 2016, www.thenational.ae/opinion/observance-of-islam-is-a-way-to-
defeat-extremism-1.205220.

8. Matthew Lyons, "Fragmented Nationalism: Right-Wing Responses to
September 11 in Historical Context," in *We Have Not Been Moved: Resisting
Racism and Militarism in Twenty-First Century America,* ed. Elizabeth Mar-
tínez, Matt Meyer Sutherland, Mandy Carter, Cornel West, Sonia Sanchez, and
Alice Walker (Oakland: PM Press, 2012), 301–30.

9. For more on the Good Muslim versus Bad Muslim trope, see Mahmood
Mamdani, *Good Muslim, Bad Muslim: America, the Cold War, and the Roots
of Terror* (New York: Pantheon Books, 2004).

10. Claude M. Steel, *Whistling Vivaldi: How Stereotypes Affect Us and What We Can Do* (New York: W. W. Norton, 2011).

11. "Survivor of 2013 Syria Attack Pleads for Action," *Amanpour, CNN,* April 6, 2017, http://edition.cnn.com/videos/world/2017/04/06/intv-amanpour-kassem-eid-syria-chemical-attack.cnn.

12. International Human Rights and Conflict Resolution Clinic (Stanford Law School) and Global Justice Clinic (NYU School of Law), *Living under Drones: Death, Injury, and Trauma to Civilians from U.S. Drone Practices in Pakistan,* September 2012, p. 74, https://law.stanford.edu/wp-content/uploads/sites/default/files/publication/313671/doc/slspublic/Stanford_NYU_LIVING_UNDER_DRONES.pdf.

13. Robert Chesney, "Should We Create a Federal Crime of 'Domestic Terrorism'?" Lawfare, August 8, 2019, www.lawfareblog.com/should-we-create-federal-crime-domestic-terrorism.

14. Chesney, "Should We Create a Federal Crime of 'Domestic Terrorism'?"

15. In August 2019, the FBI Agents Association, which represents more than fourteen thousand active and former bureau agents, called on Congress to make domestic terrorism a federal crime. Meanwhile, during the same time period, Representative Adam Schiff (D-CA), the chairman of the House Intelligence Committee, proposed the Confronting the Threat of Domestic Terrorism Act. The legislation would expand the types of crimes that federal prosecutors could charge as domestic terrorism if the attorney general certified that an act was intended to intimidate a civilian population or influence government policy.

16. In 2020, several members of Congress wrote to Chad F. Wolf, the acting secretary of the Department of Homeland Security, expressing concern over the use of drones to surveil protesters of the Black Lives Matter movement. See the U.S. House of Representatives Committee on Oversight and Reform, 116th Congress, letter to Chad F. Wolf, June 5, 2020, https://oversight.house.gov/sites/democrats.oversight.house.gov/files/2020-06-05.CBM%20et.%20al%20to%20Wolf-%20DHS%20re%20Peaceful%20Protestors_0.pdf.

17. Confronting the Threat of Domestic Terrorism Act, H.R. 4193, 116th Cong. (2019), www.congress.gov/bill/116th-congress/house-bill/4192/text.

18. Yoni Appelbaum, "The Banality of White Nationalism," *Atlantic,* November 26, 2017, www.theatlantic.com/politics/archive/2017/11/the-banality-of-white-nationalism/546749; Alan M. Kraut, "Nativism, An American Perennial," Center for Migration Studies, February 8, 2016, https://doi.org/10.14240/cmsesy020816; Tali Mendelberg, *The Race Card: Campaign Strategy, Implicit Messages, and the Norm of Equality* (Princeton, NJ: Princeton University Press, 2001); Steve Phillips, *Brown Is the New White: How the Demographic Revolution Has Created a New American Majority* (New York: New Press, 2016), 51–52; Reginald Horsman, *Race and Manifest Destiny: The Origins of American Racial Anglo-Saxonism* (Cambridge, MA: Harvard University Press, 1981); Ibram X. Kendi, *Stamped from the Beginning: The Definitive History of Racist Ideas in America* (New York: Nation Books, 2016).

19. The term *intersectionality* comes from legal scholar Kimberlé Crenshaw, who argued that the discrimination and oppression faced by women must be

seen through lenses in addition to gender, such as ethnicity, class, and sexuality. See Kimberlé Crenshaw, "Demarginalizing the Intersection of Race and Sex: A Black Feminist Critique of Antidiscrimination Doctrine, Feminist Theory, and Antiracist Politics," *University of Chicago Legal Forum*, no. 1 (1989): 139–67. For more on social justice as the telos of intersectionality, see Aída Hurtado, "Intersectional Understanding of Inequality," in *The Oxford Handbook of Social Psychology and Social Justice*, ed. Phillip. L. Hammack (New York: Oxford University Press, 2018), 157–72. For more on the intersectionality of sexual orientation and race, see Margot Canaday, *The Straight State: Sexuality and Citizenship in Twentieth-Century America* (Princeton, NJ: Princeton University Press, 2009); and Kevin S. Amidon, "Beyond the Straight State: On the Borderlands of Sexuality, Ethnicity, and Nation in the United States and in Europe," in *Crossing Boundaries: Ethnicity, Race, and National Belonging in a Transnational World,* ed. Brian D. Behnken and Simon Wendt (Lanham, MD: Lexington Books, 2013), 301–19.

20. David Gillborn, "The White Working Class, Racism and Respectability: Victims, Degenerates and Interest-Convergence," *British Journal of Educational Studies* 58, no. 1 (March 2010): 5; Richard Delgado and Jean Stefancic, *Critical Race Theory* (New York: New York University Press, 2001).

21. Robin DiAngelo, "White Fragility," *International Journal of Critical Pedagogy* 3, no. 3 (2011): 54. In her later work, DiAngelo also defines White fragility as the process by which White people "consider a challenge to [their] racial worldview as a challenge to [their] very identities as a good, moral people. Thus, [they] perceive any attempt to connect [them] to the system of racism as an unsettling and unfair moral offense. The smallest amount of racial stress is intolerable—the mere suggestion that being white has meaning often triggers a range of defensive responses. These include emotions such as anger, fear, and guilt and behaviors such as argumentation, silence, and withdrawal from the stress-inducing situation. These responses work to reinstate white equilibrium as they repel the challenge, return [their] racial comfort, and maintain [their] dominance with the white racial hierarchy. . . . Though white fragility is triggered by discomfort and anxiety, it is born of superiority and entitlement. White fragility is not weakness per se. In fact, it is a powerful means of white racial control and the protection of white advantage." Robin J. DiAngelo, *White Fragility: Why It's So Hard for White People to Talk about Racism* (Boston: Beacon Press, 2018), 2. Her definition of White fragility is validated in the work of academic and philosopher George Yancy, *Backlash: What Happens When We Talk Honestly about Racism in America* (New York: Rowman and Littlefield, 2018).

22. Corey Kopitzke, "Security Council Resolution 2178 (2014): An Ineffective Response to the Foreign Terrorist Fighter Phenomenon," *Indiana Journal of Global Legal Studies* 24, no. 1 (2017): 309–41; Daveed Gartenstein-Ross and Nathaniel Barr, "Fixing How We Fight the Islamic State's Narrative," Texas National Security Network, January 4, 2016, available at http://warontherocks .com/2016/01/fixing-how-we-fight-the-islamic-states-narrative.

23. Anya Kamenetz, "How Socioeconomic Diversity in Schools Helps All Students," KQED News, March 16, 2017, https://ww2.kqed.org/mindshift /2017/03/16/how-socioeconomic-diversity-in-schools-helps-all-students.

24. For a discussion on how to engage in a constructive discussion on race, see Derald Wing Sue, *Race Talk and the Conspiracy of Silence: Understanding and Facilitating Difficult Dialogues on Race* (Hoboken, NJ: Wiley, 2015); Kevin Munger, "Tweetment Effects on the Tweeted: Experimentally Reducing Racist Harassment," *Political Behavior* 39, no. 3 (2017): 629–49; Reni Eddo-Lodge, *Why I'm No Longer Talking to White People about Race* (London: Bloomsbury Circus, 2017); and J. J. Yanco, *Misremembering Dr. King: Revisiting the Legacy of Martin Luther King Jr.* (Bloomington: Indiana University Press, 2014), 71–78. For a look at one woman's experience with White privilege and Whiteness, see Debby Irving, *Waking Up White: And Finding Myself in the Story of Race* (Cambridge, MA: Elephant Room Press, 2014). For a White Christian perspective, see Jennifer Harvey, Karin A. Case, and Robin Hawley Gorsline, *Disrupting White Supremacy from Within: White People on What We Need to Do* (Cleveland: Pilgrim Press, 2004). For the experience of a White person with White privilege who is also marginalized because of poverty, see Jim Grimsley, *How I Shed My Skin: Unlearning the Racist Lessons of a Southern Childhood* (Chapel Hill, NC: Algonquin Books of Chapel Hill, 2015). On dismantling structural racism, see Christopher Emdin, *For White Folks Who Teach in the Hood—and the Rest of Y'all Too: Reality Pedagogy and Urban Education* (Boston: Beacon Press, 2016); and Joseph R. Barndt, *Understanding and Dismantling Racism: The Twenty-First Century Challenge to White America* (Minneapolis: Fortress Press, 2007), 255–62.

25. Derrick A. Bell, "Brown v. Board of Education and the Interest-Convergence Dilemma," *Harvard Law Review* 93, no. 3 (1980): 523.

26. Derrick A. Bell, "Brown v. Board of Education and the Interest-Convergence Dilemma," *Harvard Law Review* 93, no. 3 (1980): 523.

27. Martin Luther King Jr., *Letter from a Birmingham Jail*, April 16, 1963, https://kinginstitute.stanford.edu/king-papers/documents/letter-birmingham-jail.

28. Malcolm X, 1963 speech transcript, Digital History, www.digitalhistory.uh.edu/disp_textbook.cfm?smtid=3&psid=3619.

29. National Criminal Justice Reference Service, *Report of the National Advisory Commission on Civil Disorders* (Washington, DC: National Institute of Justice, United States Department of Justice, February 20, 1981), www.ncjrs.gov/pdffiles1/Digitization/8073NCJRS.pdf, p. 1-2. The report has also been published as a book: U.S. Riot Commission, *Report of the National Advisory Commission on Civil Disorders* (New York: Bantam Books, 1968); and National Advisory Commission on Civil Disorders, *The Kerner Report,* James Madison Library in American Politics (Princeton, NJ: Princeton University Press, 2016).

30. James Sellman, "Kerner Report," in *Africana: The Encyclopedia of the African and African American Experience,* ed. Anthony Appiah and Henry Louis Gates (New York: Basic Civitas Books, 1999), 151.

31. Peniel E. Joseph, *The Sword and the Shield: The Revolutionary Lives of Malcom X and Martin Luther King Jr.* (New York: Basic Books, 2020).

32. Jennifer Senior, "The Paradox of the First Black President," *New York Magazine,* October 7, 2015, http://nymag.com/daily/intelligencer/2015/10

/paradox-of-the-first-black-president.html; Michael Eric Dyson, "Is Obama to Blame for Trump—and the Revival for White Supremacist Hate?" *Washington Post,* August 18, 2017, www.washingtonpost.com/outlook/is-obama-to-blame-for-trump—and-the-revival-of-white-supremacist-hate/2017/08/17/f0939fbe-836f-11e7-b359-15a3617c767b_story.html.

33. Ta-Nehisi Coates, *We Were Eight Years in Power: An American Tragedy* (New York: One World, 2017).

34. For a history of the America First concept, see Sarah Churchwell, *Behold, America: The Entangled History of "America First" and "the American Dream"* (New York: Basic Books, 2018).

35. Thomas B. Edsall, "We Aren't Seeing White Support for Trump for What It Is," Portside, September 1, 2019, https://portside.org/node/20888.

36. Weiyi Cai and Simone Landon, "Attacks by White Extremists Are Growing. So Are Their Connections," *New York Times,* April 3, 2019, www.nytimes.com/interactive/2019/04/03/world/white-extremist-terrorism-christchurch.html.

37. Ashley Jardina, *White Identity Politics* (Cambridge: Cambridge University Press, 2019); Maria Abascal, "Contraction as a Response to Group Threat: Demographic Decline and Whites's Classification of People Who Are Ambiguously White," *American Sociological Review* 85, no. 2 (April 2020): 298–322.

38. Don Gonyea, "Majority of White Americans Say They Believe Whites Face Discrimination," *NPR,* October 24, 2017, www.npr.org/2017/10/24/559604836/majority-of-white-americans-think-theyre-discriminated-against.

39. "Discrimination in America: Experiences and Views of White Americans," *NPR,* Robert Wood Johnson Foundation, Harvard T. H. Chan School of Public Health, November 2017, p. 15, www.rwjf.org/content/dam/farm/reports/surveys_and_polls/2017/rwjf441554. See also Peggy McIntosh, "White Privilege and Male Privilege: A Personal Account of Coming to See Correspondences through Work in Women's Studies," 1998, available at www.collegeart.org/pdf/diversity/white-privilege-and-male-privilege.pdf. For a similar analysis, albeit through the lens of misogyny within White supremacy, see "When Women Are the Enemy: The Intersection of Misogyny and White Supremacy," Center on Extremism, Anti-Defamation League, 2018, www.adl.org/resources/reports/when-women-are-the-enemy-the-intersection-of-misogyny-and-white-supremacy#white-men-adopt-a-victomhood-narrative.

40. Mitch Berbrier, "The Victim Ideology of White Supremacists and White Separatists in the United States," *Sociological Focus* 33, no. 2 (2000): 175–91.

41. DiAngelo, *White Fragility,* 21, 19.

42. Nell Irvin Painter, *The History of White People* (New York: W. W. Norton, 2010).

43. See McIntosh, "White Privilege and Male Privilege."

44. Painter, *History of White People;* Carol Anderson, *White Rage: The Unspoken Truth of Our Racial Divide* (New York: Bloomsbury, 2017); Jonathan M. Metzl, *Dying of Whiteness: How the Politics of Racial Resentment Is Killing America's Heartland* (New York: Basic Books, 2019); Nancy Isenberg, *White Trash: The 400-Year Untold History of Class in America* (New York: Penguin Books, 2017).

45. It is important to note that there is broad diversity within those labeled as BIPOC or "people of color." These terms are also not universally accepted. See Tolani Shoneye, "As a Black Woman, I Hate the Term 'People of Colour,'" *Independent* (UK), April 22, 2018, www.independent.co.uk/voices/black-women-people-of-colour-racism-beyonce-coachella-black-lives-matter-a8316561.html.The effects of structural racism on communities of color are broad and well attested. Studies have linked the social experience of race to poor health outcomes, chronic stress, higher instances of type 2 diabetes, cardiovascular diseases, and maternal and infant mortality, among other ills. Indeed, life expectancy itself has been shown to be tied to race: Black and Latinx Americans die, on average, roughly three and a half years earlier than White Americans. Being a person of color is also linked to economic insecurity, employment and housing discrimination, and fewer opportunities for economic mobility. See Tené T. Lewis, Courtney D. Cogburn, and David R. Williams, "Self-Reported Experiences of Discrimination and Health: Scientific Advances, Ongoing Controversies, and Emerging Issues," *Annual Review of Clinical Psychology* 11, no. 1 (2015): 407–40; R. E. Montenegro, "My Name Is Not 'Interpreter,'" *JAMA* 315, no. 19 (2016): 2071–72; Marian F. MacDorman and T. J. Mathews, "Understanding Racial and Ethnic Disparities in U.S. Infant Mortality Rates," *NCHS Data Brief* 74 (September 2011): 1–8; "Most Recent Asthma Data," Centers for Disease Control and Prevention, last updated March 25, 2019, www.cdc.gov/asthma/most_recent_data.htm; Laura Smart Richman and Charles Jonassaint, "The Effects of Race-Related Stress on Cortisol Reactivity in the Laboratory: Implications of the Duke Lacrosse Scandal," *Annals of Behavioral Medicine* 35, no. 1 (2008): 105–10; U.S. Department of Health and Human Services, Centers for Disease Control and Prevention, "Deaths: Final Data for 2015," *National Vital Statistic Report* 66, no. 6 (November 27, 2017), 2; and Angela Hanks, Danyelle Solomon, and Christian E. Weller, *Systematic Inequality: How America's Structural Racism Helped Create the Black-White Wealth Gap*, Center for American Progress, February 21, 2018, www .americanprogress.org/issues/race/reports/2018/02/21/447051/systematic-ine-quality. For an in-depth exploration of the hierarchies of oppression, particularly related to racism, see Isabel Wilkerson, *Caste: The Origins of Our Discontents* (New York: Random House, 2020).

46. For an understanding of how the United States was also built on the eradication of Indigenous Americans, see Jeffrey Ostler, *Surviving Genocide, Native Nations and the United States from the American Revolution to Bleeding Kansas* (New Haven, CT: Yale University Press, 2019); and Mary Annette Pember, "Death by Civilization," *Atlantic*, March 8, 2019, www.theatlantic .com/education/archive/2019/03/traumatic-legacy-indian-boarding-schools /584293. For an untangling of the myths at the heart of the American origin story as currently taught in most schools, see Jared Yates Sexton, *American Rule: How a Nation Conquered the World but Failed Its People* (New York: Dutton, 2020); Paul Ortiz, *An African American and Latinx History of the United States* (Boston: Beacon Press, 2018); and the classic subaltern history book, Howard Zinn, *A People's History of the United States* (New York: HarperCollins, 1980).

47. For two excellent works on the need for criminal justice reform in America, see James Forman, *Locking Up Our Own: Crime and Punishment in Black America* (New York: Farrar, Straus and Giroux, 2017); and Michelle Alexander, *The New Jim Crow: Mass Incarceration in the Age of Colorblindness* (New York: New Press, 2010). For an insightful examination of the need for criminal justice reform at the intersection of mental health, see Christine Montross, *Waiting for an Echo: The Madness of American Incarceration* (New York: Penguin Press, 2020).

48. Khaled A. Beydoun, "Islamophobia: Toward a Legal Definition and Framework," *Columbia Law Review Online* 116 (November 1, 2016): 108–25, https://columbialawreview.org/content/islamophobia-toward-a-legal-definition-and-framework.

49. In fact, Latinx Americans are the fastest growing segment of the Muslim American population. See "Demographic Portrait of Muslim Americans," in *U.S. Muslims Concerned about Their Place in Society, but Continue to Believe in the American Dream: Findings from the Pew Research Center's 2017 Survey of U.S. Muslims,* Pew Research Center, July 26, 2017, 30–49, www.pewforum.org/2017/07/26/demographic-portrait-of-muslim-americans; and Emma Green, "Muslim Americans Are United by Trump—and Divided by Race," *Atlantic,* March 11, 2017, www.theatlantic.com/politics/archive/2017/03/muslim-americans-race/519282.

50. Peter Beinart, "The Right's Islamophobia Has Nothing to Do with National Security," *Atlantic,* November 30, 2017, www.theatlantic.com/politics/archive/2017/11/the-new-islamophobia/547130. For an in-depth discussion of the history of Islamophobia in the United States, see K. A. Beydoun, *American Islamophobia: Understanding the Roots and Rise of Fear* (Oakland: University of California Press, 2018).

51. For more on the lived experiences at this simultaneity of identities, see Sylvia Chan-Malik, *Being Muslim: A Cultural History of Women of Color in American Islam* (New York: New York University Press, 2018).

52. Edward E. Curtis, *Muslims in America: A Short History* (Oxford: Oxford University Press, 2009), 17.

53. Some of their stories have been documented by the National Museum of African American History and Culture at the Smithsonian. See also S. A. Diouf, *Servants of Allah: African Muslims Enslaved in the Americas* (New York: New York University Press, 2013); and Richard Brent Turner, *Islam in the African-American Experience* (Bloomington: Indiana University Press, 1997). On Black Americans as pioneers in the early 1800s, see Anna-Lisa Cox, *The Bone and Sinew of the Land: America's Forgotten Black Pioneers and the Struggle for Equality* (New York: PublicAffairs, 2018).

54. "The Barbary Treaties 1786–1816: Treaty of Peace and Friendship, Signed at Tripoli November 4, 1796," Avalon Project, 2008, article 11, http://avalon.law.yale.edu/18th_century/bar1796t.asp.

55. Qur'an 2:256 and 109:6.

56. See also Qur'an 49:13.

57. Qur'an 2:62 and 18:110.

58. Wilfried Murad Hoffman, "Religious Pluralism and Islam in a Polarised World," in *Islam and Global Dialogue: Religious Pluralism and the Pursuit of*

Peace, ed. Roger Boase (Burlington, VT: Ashgate Publishing Company, 2005), 235–45; Norman H. Gershman, *Besa: Muslims Who Saved Jews during World War II* (Syracuse, NY: Syracuse University Press, 2008). For further reading on these instances of religious tolerance, see Stefano Carboni, ed., *Venice and the Islamic World: 828–1797* (New Haven, CT: Yale University Press, 2007); Yahya Emerick, *The Life and Work of Muhammad* (Indianapolis: Alpha Books, 2002); Mark Graham, *How Islam Created the Modern World* (Beltsville, MD: Amana Publications, 2006); and Michael Hamilton Morgan, *Lost History: The Enduring Legacy of Muslim Scientists, Thinkers, and Artists* (Washington, DC: National Geographic, 2008).

59. An incredible resource for understanding why the arguments of militant Islamists are theologically invalid is "Open Letter to Dr. Ibrahim Awwad al-Badri, Alias ʿAbu Bakr al-Bagdadi,'" September 19, 2014, www.lettertobaghdadi.com.

60. Kelly J. Baker, *Gospel According to the Klan: The KKK's Appeal to Protestant America, 1915–1930* (Lawrence: University Press of Kansas, 2011); Kyle Haselden, *The Racial Problem in Christian Perspective* (New York: Harper, 1959); Cathy Meeks, *Living into God's Dream: Dismantling Racism in America* (New York: Morehouse Publishing, 2016).

61. Frederick Douglass, *Narrative of the Life of Frederick Douglass, an American Slave* (Boston: Anti-Slavery Office, No. 25 Cornhill, 1845), electronic edition, 1999, University of North Carolina at Chapel Hill digitization project, *Documenting the American South, Beginnings to 1920,* https://docsouth.unc.edu/neh/douglass/douglass.html, p. 119.

62. Douglass, *Narrative of the Life of Frederick Douglass,* 120.

63. D. H. Dilbeck and Frederick Douglass, *America's Prophet* (Chapel Hill: University of North Carolina Press, 2018), 66.

64. "NAE Addresses Racial Turmoil, Calls for Action," National Association of Evangelicals, May 29, 2020, www.nae.net/nae-addresses-racial-turmoil-calls-for-action.

65. "A Confession of Faith in a Time of Crisis," Reclaiming Jesus, access date August 24, 2020, http://reclaimingjesus.org.

66. "About the Poor People's Campaign: A National Call for Moral Revival," Poor People's Campaign, accessed August 24, 2020, www.poorpeoplescampaign.org.

67. Mark A. Noll, *God and Race in American Politics: A Short History* (Princeton, NJ: Princeton University Press, 2010); Paul Harvey, *Freedom's Coming: Religious Culture and the Shaping of the South from the Civil War through the Civil Rights Era* (Chapel Hill, NC: University of North Carolina, 2007); Roy Harvey Pearce, *Savagism and Civilization: A Study of the Indian and the American Mind* (Berkeley: University of California Press, 1988); George E. Tinker, *Missionary Conquest: The Gospel and Native American Cultural Genocide* (Minneapolis, MN: Augsburg Fortress Publishing, 1993).

68. Sigal Samuel, "What to Do When Racists Try to Hijack Your Religion," *Atlantic,* November 2, 2017, www.theatlantic.com/international/archive/2017/11/asatru-heathenry-racism/543864.

69. Kimberly Winston, "Thor and His Followers Come to the Northern California Hills," *Washington Post,* October 16, 2015, www.washingtonpost

.com/national/religion/thor-and-his-followers-come-to-the-northern-california-hills/2015/10/16/e6c89eec-7441-11e5-ba14-318f8e87a2fc_story.html.

70. Magnus Sveinn Helgason, "Heathens against Hate: Exclusive Interview with the High Priest of the Icelandic Pagan Association," *Icelandic Magazine,* July 25, 2015, https://icelandmag.is/article/heathens-against-hate-exclusive-interview-high-priest-icelandic-pagan-association.

71. Stephen A. McNallen, *Asatru: A Native European Spirituality* (Browns-ville, CA: Runestone Press, 2015); Winston, "Thor and His Followers."

72. "Iceland to Build First Temple to Norse Gods since Viking Age," *Guardian* (UK), February 2, 2015, www.theguardian.com/world/2015/feb/02/iceland-temple-norse-gods-1000-years.

73. Samuel, "What to Do"; "Odins Auge," *Nornirs Aett* (blog), accessed September 24, 2018, www.nornirsaett.de/ueber-odins-auge-ariosophieprojekt; Eldaring (website), https://eldaring.de.

74. "Declaration 127," *Huginn's Heathen Hof* (blog), accessed September 24, 2018, http://declaration127.com.

75. "Shieldwall: A Public Call to Action," Asatru Community, accessed September 24, 2018, www.theasatrucommunity.org/shieldwall.

Selected Bibliography

Aaron, David. *In Their Own Words: Voices of Jihad.* Santa Monica, CA: RAND Corporation, 2008. Available at www.rand.org/content/dam/rand/pubs /monographs/2008/RAND_MG602.pdf.

Abanes, Richard. *American Militias: Rebellion, Racism and Religion.* Downers Grove, IL: InterVarsity Press, 1996.

Abascal, Maria. "Contraction as a Response to Group Threat: Demographic Decline and Whites' Classification of People Who Are Ambiguously White." *American Sociological Review* 85, no. 2 (April 2020): 298–322.

Abdelhalim, Julten. *Indian Muslims and Citizenship: Spaces for Jihād in Everyday Life.* Oxford: Routledge, 2015.

Aboul-Enein, Youssef H. *Militant Islamist Ideology: Understanding the Global Threat.* Annapolis, MD: Naval Institute Press, 2010.

Ahmad, Irfan. "Genealogy of the Islamic State: Reflections on Maududi's Political Thought and Islamism." *Journal of the Royal Anthropological Institute* 15, no. 1 (2009): S145–62.

———. "Mawdudi, Abu al-A'la (1903–79)." In *The Princeton Encyclopedia of Islamic Political Thought,* ed. Gerhard Böwering, 112–15. Princeton, NJ: Princeton University Press, 2013.

Ahmed, Mufti M. Mukarram. *Encyclopaedia of Islam.* New Delhi: Anmol Publications, 2007.

Aho, James. *Far-Right Fantasy: A Sociology of American Religion and Politics.* New York: Routledge, 2016.

Alexander, Michelle. *The New Jim Crow: Mass Incarceration in the Age of Colorblindness.* New York: New Press, 2010.

Alibrandi, Tom, and Bill Wassmuth. *Hate Is My Neighbor.* Moscow, ID: University of Idaho Press, 1999.

Alkhateeb, Faris. *Lost Islamic History: Reclaiming Muslim Civilisation from the Past*. New York: Oxford University Press, 2014.

Allport, Gordon W. *The Nature of Prejudice*. Abridged ed. Garden City, NY: Doubleday, 1958.

Amidon, Kevin S. "Beyond the Straight State: On the Borderlands of Sexuality, Ethnicity, and Nation in the United States and in Europe." In *Crossing Boundaries: Ethnicity, Race, and National Belonging in a Transnational World*, edited by Brian D. Behnken and Simon Wendt, 301–19. Lanham, MD: Lexington Books, 2013.

Amin, ElSayed M.A. *Reclaiming Jihad: A Qur'anic Critique of Terrorism*. Leicester, England: Islamic Foundation, 2014.

Anderson, Carol. *White Rage: The Unspoken Truth of Our Racial Divide*. New York: Bloomsbury, 2017.

Anderson, Kristin J. *Benign Bigotry: The Psychology of Subtle Prejudice*. Cambridge: Cambridge University Press, 2010.

Anderson, Tom. *His Example: Tom Anderson's Christmas Essay*. Belmont, MA: American Opinion, n.d.

Anzalone, Christopher. "In the Shadow of the Islamic State: Shi'i Responses to Sunni Jihadist Narratives in a Turbulent Middle East." In *Jihadism Transformed: Al-Qaeda and Islamic State's Global Battle of Ideas*, edited by Simon Staffell and Akil N. Awan, 157–82. Oxford: Oxford University Press, 2016.

Apple, Angela L., and Beth A. Messner. "Paranoia and Paradox: The Apocalyptic Rhetoric of Christian Identity." *Western Journal of Communication* 65, no. 2 (2001): 206–27.

Armajani, Jon. *Modern Islamist Movements: History, Religion, and Politics*. Oxford: Wiley-Blackwell, 2012.

Aronson, Trevor. *The Terror Factory: Inside the FBI's Manufactured War on Terrorism*. Brooklyn: Ig Publishing, 2013.

Asatru Free Church Committee. *The Religion of Odin: A Handbook*. Red Wing, MN: Viking House, 1978.

Azzam, Abdullah. *Defence of the Muslim Lands*. 2nd English ed. London: Azzam Publications, 2002.

Bacon, Tricia, and Elizabeth Grimm Arsenault. "Al Qaeda and the Islamic State's Break: Strategic Strife or Lackluster Leadership?" *Studies in Conflict and Terrorism* 42, no. 3 (2019): 229–63. https://doi.org/10.1080/10576 10X.2017.1373895.

Badawī, Al-Sa'īd Muḥammad, and M. A. S. Abdel Haleem. *Arabic-English Dictionary of Qur'anic Usage*. Leiden: Brill, 2008.

Badran, Margot. *Feminism in Islam: Secular and Religious Convergences*. Oxford: Oneworld Publications, 2009.

Bahari, Mustazah, and Muhammad Haniff Hassan. "The Black Flag Myth: An Analysis from Hadith Studies." *Counter Terrorist Trends and Analysis* 6, no. 8 (September 2014): 15–20.

Baker, Kelly J. *Gospel According to the Klan: The KKK's Appeal to Protestant America, 1915–1930*. Lawrence: University Press of Kansas, 2011.

Baldwin, Timothy N. *Freedom for a Change*. Orlando, FL: Agrapha Publishing, 2010.

Balko, Radley. *Rise of the Warrior Cop: The Militarization of America's Police Forces.* New York: Public Affairs, 2014.

Bannā, Ḥasan. *Five Tracts of Ḥasan Al-Bannā' (1906–1949): A Selection from the Majmu'at rasa'il al-Imam al-shahid Hasan al-Banna'.* Translated by Charles Wendell. Berkeley: University of California Press, 1978.

Barkun, Michael. "Appropriated Martyrs: The Branch Davidians and the Radical Right." *Terrorism and Political Violence* 19, no. 1 (2007): 117–24.

———. *A Culture of Conspiracy: Apocalyptic Visions in Contemporary America.* Berkeley: University of California Press, 2013.

———. "Millennialism on the Radical Right in America." In *The Oxford Handbook of Millennialism,* edited by Catherine Wessinger, 649–66. Oxford: Oxford University Press, 2011.

———. *Religion and the Racist Right: The Origins of the Christian Identity Movement.* Chapel Hill: University of North Carolina Press, 1994.

Barndt, Joseph R. *Understanding and Dismantling Racism: The Twenty-First Century Challenge to White America.* Minneapolis: Fortress Press, 2007.

Barrett, Richard. *Beyond the Caliphate: Foreign Fighters and the Threat of Returnees.* New York: Soufan Center, October 2017. http://thesoufancenter .org/wp-content/uploads/2017/11/Beyond-the-Caliphate-Foreign-Fighters-and-the-Threat-of-Returnees-TSC-Report-October-2017-v3.pdf.

Baysinger, Timothy G. "Right-Wing Group Characteristics and Ideology." *Homeland Security Affairs* 2, article 3 (July 2006).

Beam, Louis. "Leaderless Resistance." *Seditionist,* no. 12 (February 1992): 1–7.

Beirich, Heidi L. "Written Testimony of Heidi L. Beirich, Ph.D., Co-Founder, Global Project against Hate and Extremism, before the Congress of the United States House of Representatives Armed Services Committee Military Personnel Subcommittee Regarding 'Alarming Incidents of White Supremacy in the Military—How to Stop It?'" February 11, 2020. www.congress.gov/116 /meeting/house/110495/witnesses/HHRG-116-AS02-Wstate-BeirichH-20200211.pdf.

Belew, Kathleen. *Bring the War Home: The White Power Movement and Paramilitary America.* Cambridge, MA: Harvard University Press, 2018.

Bell, Derrick A. "Brown v. Board of Education and the Interest-Convergence Dilemma." *Harvard Law Review* 93, no. 3 (1980): 518–33.

Benjamin, Ruha. *Race after Technology: Abolitionist Tools for the New Jim Code.* Cambridge: Polity, 2019.

Berbrier, Mitch. "Making Minorities: Cultural Space, Stigma Transformation Frames, and the Categorical Status Claims of Deaf, Gay, and White Supremacist Activists in Late Twentieth Century America." *Sociological Forum* 17, no. 4 (2002): 553–91.

———. "The Victim Ideology of White Supremacists and White Separatists in the United States." *Sociological Focus* 33, no. 2 (2000): 175–91.

Berger, J. M. *Jihad Joe: Americans Who Go to War in the Name of Islam.* Washington, DC: Potomac Books, 2011.

Berlet, Chip, ed. *Eyes Right! Challenging the Right Wing Backlash.* Boston: South End Press, 1995.

Berlet, Chip, and Matthew Nemiroff Lyons. *Right-Wing Populism in America: Too Close for Comfort*. New York: Guilford Press, 2000.

Berlet, Chip, and Margaret Quigley. "Theocracy and White Supremacy: Behind the Culture War to Restore Traditional Values." In *Eyes Right! Challenging the Right Wing Backlash,* edited by Chip Berlet, 1–43. Boston: South End Press, 1995.

Berman, Paul. *Terror and Liberalism*. New York: Norton, 2003.

Bettiza, Gregorio, and Christopher Phillips. "Obama Nation? U.S. Foreign Policy One Year On: Obama's Middle East Policy; Time to Decide." IDEAS Reports, ed. Nicholas Kitchen, SR003. London School of Economics and Political Science, 2010.

Beydoun, Khaled A. *American Islamophobia: Understanding the Roots and Rise of Fear*. Oakland: University of California Press, 2018.

———. "Islamophobia: Toward a Legal Definition and Framework." *Columbia Law Review Online* 116 (November 1, 2016): 108-125. https://columbialawreview.org/content/islamophobia-toward-a-legal-definition-and-framework.

Billy, Jason O. "Confronting Racists at the Bar: Matthew Hale, Moral Character, and Regulating the Marketplace of Ideas." *Harvard BlackLetter Law Journal* 22 (Spring 2006): 25–51.

Bin Ali, Mohamed. *The Roots of Religious Extremism: Understanding the Salafi Doctrine of Al-Wala' wal Bara'*. London: Imperial College Press, 2016.

Bin Laden, Osama. *Messages to the World: The Statements of Osama Bin Laden*. Edited by Bruce B. Lawrence. London: Verso, 2005.

Bjørgo, Tore, and Noemi Gal-Or. "Right-Wing and Reactionary Terrorism." In *World Terrorism: An Encyclopedia of Political Violence from Ancient Times to the Post-9/11 Era,* 2nd ed., vol. 1, edited by James Ciment, 33–34. Armonk, NY: M. E. Sharpe, 2011.

Bjork-James, Sophie, and Jeff Maskovsky. "When White Nationalism Became Popular." *Populism Rising* 58, no. 3 (2017): 86–91.

Blee, Kathleen M. "Becoming a Racist: Women in Contemporary Ku Klux Klan and Neo-Nazi Groups." In *The Populist Radical Right: A Reader,* edited by Cas Mudde, 258–76. New York: Routledge, 2017.

———. *Women of the Klan: Racism and Gender in the 1920s*. Berkeley: University of California Press, 1991.

Bloom, Mia, Hicham Tiflati, and John Horgan. "Navigating ISIS's Preferred Platform: Telegram," *Terrorism and Political Violence* 31, no. 6 (2019): 1242–54. https://doi.org/10.1080/09546553.2017.1339695.

Blythe, Christopher James. *Terrible Revolution: Latter-day Saints and the American Apocalypse*. New York: Oxford University Press, 2020.

Bonney, Richard. *Jihād: From Qur'ān to Bin Laden*. New York: Palgrave Macmillan, 2004.

Bostom, Andrew G. *The Legacy of Islamic Antisemitism: From Sacred Texts to Solemn History*. Amherst, NY: Prometheus Books, 2008.

Brisard, Jean-Charles. *Zarqawi: The New Face of Al-Qaeda*. New York: Other Press, 2005.

Broockman, D., and J. Kalla. "Durably Reducing Transphobia: A Field Experiment on Door-to-Door Canvassing." *Science* 352, no. 6282 (2016): 220–24.

Bulut, Elif. "Pride and Prejudice: The Context of Reception for Muslims in the United States." *Contemporary Social Science* 11, no. 4 (2016): 304–14.

Burki, Shireen Khan. "Haram or Halal? Islamists' Use of Suicide Attacks as 'Jihad.'" *Terrorism and Political Violence* 23, no. 4 (2011): 582–681.

Burton, Fred, and Scott Stewart. "The 'Lone Wolf' Disconnect." Stratfor Worldview, January 30, 2008. https://worldview.stratfor.com/article/lone-wolf-disconnect.

Bushart, Howard L., John R. Craig, and Myra Edwards Barnes. *Soldiers of God: White Supremacists and Their Holy War for America*. New York: Kensington Books, 1998.

Byman, Daniel L. "Comparing Al Qaeda and ISIS: Different Goals, Different Targets." Brookings, April 29, 2015. www.brookings.edu/research/testimony/2015/04/29-terrorism-in-africa-byman.

———. "How States Exploit Jihadist Foreign Fighters." *Studies in Conflict and Terrorism* 41, no. 12 (2018): 931-45. https://doi.org/10.1080/1057610X.2017.1361281.

Byrd, James P. *Sacred Scripture, Sacred War: The Bible and the American Revolution*. Oxford: Oxford University Press, 2013.

Cameron, Ben. "The Constitutional Republic." *Identity: A Christian Church Publication* 6, no. 1 (n.d.). Available at www.seditionists.com/identity_6_1.pdf.

Campo, Juan. "People of the Book." In *Encyclopedia of Islam,* edited by Juan Campo, 548–49. New York: Facts on File, 2009.

Canaday, Margot. *The Straight State: Sexuality and Citizenship in Twentieth-Century America*. Princeton, NJ: Princeton University Press, 2009.

Carboni, Stefano, ed. *Venice and the Islamic World, 828–1797*. New Haven, CT: Yale University Press, 2007.

Cavanaugh, William T. *The Myth of Religious Violence: Secular Ideology and the Roots of Modern Conflict*. Oxford: Oxford University Press, 2009.

Chalmers, David M. *Hooded Americanism: The History of the Ku Klux Klan*. New York: Franklin Watts, 1965.

Chan-Malik, Sylvia. *Being Muslim: A Cultural History of Women of Color in American Islam.* New York: New York University Press, 2018.

Chaney, Allison J. B., Brandon M. Stewart, and Barbara E. Engelhardt. "How Algorithmic Confounding in Recommendation Systems Increases Homogeneity and Decreases Utility." In *RecSys '18: Proceedings of the 12th ACM Conference on Recommender Systems,* edited by Sole Pera and Michael Ekstrand, 224–32. New York: Association for Computing Machinery, September 2018. https://dl.acm.org/doi/10.1145/3240323.3240370.

Chittick, William C. *Divine Love: Islamic Literature and the Path to God*. New Haven, CT: Yale University Press, 2013.

Churchwell, Sarah. *Behold, America: The Entangled History of "America First" and "the American Dream."* New York: Basic Books, 2018.

Coates, James. *Armed and Dangerous: The Rise of the Survivalist Right*. New York: Hill and Wang, 1987.

Coates, Ta-Nehisi. *We Were Eight Years in Power: An American Tragedy.* New York: One World, 2017.

Coggins, R. J., and Michael A. Knibb. *The First and Second Books of Esdras.* Cambridge: Cambridge University Press, 1979.

Cohen, David S., and Krysten Connon. *Living in the Crosshairs: The Untold Stories of Anti-Abortion Terrorism.* New York: Oxford University Press, 2015.

Cohn, Norman. *The Pursuit of the Millennium: Revolutionary Millenarians and Mystical Anarchists of the Middle Ages.* New York: Oxford University Press, 1970.

Committee for the Restoration of the Odinic Rite. *This Is Odinisim.* Gorleston, England: Committee for the Restoration of the Odinic Rite, n.d.

Comparet, Bertrand L. *The Book of Esther.* San Diego, CA: Your Heritage, n.d.

———. *The Cain-Satanic Seed Line.* Hayden Lake, ID: Kingdom Identity Ministries, n.d.

———. *Your Heritage: An Identification of the True Israel through Biblical and Historical Sources.* Harrison, AR: Kingdom Identity Ministries, n.d.

Conway, Maura. "Determining the Role of the Internet in Violent Extremism and Terrorism: Six Suggestions for Progressing Research." *Studies in Conflict and Terrorism* 40, no. 1 (2017): 77–98.

Conway, Maura, Ryan Scrivens, and Logan Macnair. *Right-Wing Extremists' Persistent Online Presence: History and Contemporary Trends.* ICCT Policy Brief. The Hague: International Center for Counter-Terrorism, November 2019. https://icct.nl/wp-content/uploads/2019/11/Right-Wing-Extremists-Persistent-Online-Presence.pdf.

Cook, David. *Studies in Muslim Apocalyptic.* Princeton, NJ: Darwin Press, 2002.

Cooper, Christopher A., and H. Gibbs Knotts. "Region, Race and Support for the South Carolina Confederate Flag." *Social Science Quarterly* 87, no. 1 (2006): 142–54. https://doi.org/10.1111/j.0038-4941.2006.00373.x

Coppola, Vincent. *Dragons of God: A Journey Through Far-Right America.* Atlanta: Longstreet Press, 1996.

Cox, Anna-Lisa. *The Bone and Sinew of the Land: America's Forgotten Black Pioneers and the Struggle for Equality.* New York: PublicAffairs, 2018.

Cox, Daniel. "White Christians Side with Trump." Public Religion Research Institute, November 9, 2016. www.prri.org/spotlight/religion-vote-presidential-election-2004-2016.

Cox, Daniel, Rachel Lienesch, and Robert P. Jones. "Beyond Economics: Fears of Cultural Displacement Pushed the White Working Class to Trump." Public Religion Research Institute, May 9, 2017. www.prri.org/research/white-working-class-attitudes-economy-trade-immigration-election-donald-trump.

Crawford, Blyth, and Florence Keen. "The Hanau Terrorist Attack: How Race Hate and Conspiracy Theories are Fueling Global Far-Right Violence." *CTC Sentinel* 13, no. 3 (2020): 1–8. https://ctc.usma.edu/hanau-terrorist-attack-race-hate-conspiracy-theories-fueling-global-far-right-violence.

Crawford, Michael. *Ibn 'Abd al-Wahhab.* Makers of the Muslim World. London: Oneworld Publications, 2014.

The Creativity Alliance Handbook: A Guide for Members, Supporters and Applicants. 3rd ed. Oaklands Park, SA, Australia: Creativity Alliance, 2013.

Crenshaw, Kimberlé. "Demarginalizing the Intersection of Race and Sex: A Black Feminist Critique of Antidiscrimination Doctrine, Feminist Theory, and Antiracist Politics." *University of Chicago Legal Forum,* no. 1 (1989): 139–67.

Cross, Alan. *When Heaven and Earth Collide: Racism, Southern Evangelicals, and the Better Way of Jesus.* Montgomery, AL: NewSouth Books, 2014.

Crothers, Lane. "The Cultural Foundations of the Militia Movement." *New Political Science* 24, no. 2 (2002): 221–34.

———. *Rage on the Right: The American Militia Movement from Ruby Ridge to Homeland Security.* Lanham, MD: Rowman and Littlefield, 2003.

Curtis, Edward E. *Muslims in America: A Short History.* Oxford: Oxford University Press, 2009.

Curtis, Thomas. *The London Encyclopaedia, or Universal Dictionary of Science, Art, Literature, and Practical Mechanics.* Vol. 16. London: Thomas Tegg, 1829.

Darby, Seyward. *Sisters in Hate: American Women on the Front Lines of White Nationalism.* Boston: Little, Brown, 2020.

David, Henry P., Jochen Fleischhacker, and Charlotte Horn. "Abortion and Eugenics in Nazi Germany." *Population and Development Review* 14, no. 1 (1988): 81–112.

Davie, Grace. "The Evolution of the Sociology of Religion: Theme and Variations." In *Handbook of the Sociology of Religion,* edited by Michele Dillon, 61–78. Cambridge: Cambridge University Press 2003.

Davies, W.D. *Christian Engagements with Judaism.* Harrisburg, PA: Trinity Press International, 1999.

Davis, Jessica. *Women in Modern Terrorism: From Liberation Wars to Global Jihad and the Islamic State.* Lanham, MD: Rowman and Littlefield, 2017.

Dawson, Lorne L., and Amarnath Amarasingam. "Talking to Foreign Fighters: Insights into the Motivations for Hijrah to Syria and Iraq," *Studies in Conflict and Terrorism* 40, no. 3 (2017): 191–210.

De Borchgrave, Arnaud, Thomas Sanderson, and David Gordon. *Conflict, Community, and Criminality in Southeast Asia and Australia: Assessments from the Field; A Report of the CSIS Transnational Threats Project.* Washington, DC: Center for Strategic and International Studies, 2009.

Delgado, Richard, and Jean Stefancic. *Critical Race Theory.* New York: New York University Press, 2001.

Desai, Meghnad. *Rethinking Islamism: The Ideology of the New Terror.* London: I.B. Tauris, 2007.

Diamond, Sara. *Roads to Dominion: Right-Wing Movements and Political Power in the United States.* New York: Guilford Press, 1995.

DiAngelo, Robin J. "White Fragility." *International Journal of Critical Pedagogy* 3, no. 3 (2011): 54–70.

———. *White Fragility: Why It's So Hard for White People to Talk about Racism.* Boston: Beacon Press, 2018.

Dilbeck, D.H., and Frederick Douglass. *America's Prophet.* Chapel Hill: University of North Carolina Press, 2018.

Dilipraj, E. "Terror in the Deep and Dark Web." *Air Power Journal* 9, no. 3 (2014): 120–40.

Diouf, S. A. *Servants of Allah: African Muslims Enslaved in the Americas.* New York: New York University Press, 2013.

Dobratz, Betty A., and Stephanie L. Shanks-Meile. *White Power, White Pride! The White Separatist Movement in the United States.* New York: Twayne Publishers, 1997.

Dohe, Carrie B. *Jung's Wandering Archetype: Race and Religion in Analytical Psychology.* London: Routledge, 2016.

Dorman, Jacob S. *Chosen People: The Rise of American Black Israelite Religions.* Oxford: Oxford University Press, 2013.

Douglass, Frederick. *Frederick Douglass: Selected Speeches and Writings.* Edited by Philip S. Foner, abridged and adapted by Yuval Taylor. Chicago: Lawrence Hill Books, 1999.

———. *Narrative of the Life of Frederick Douglass, an American Slave.* Boston: Anti-Slavery Office, No. 25 Cornhill, 1845. Electronic edition, 1999. University of North Carolina at Chapel Hill digitization project, *Documenting the American South, Beginnings to 1920.* https://docsouth.unc.edu/neh/douglass/douglass.html.

Dreisbach, Daniel L., and Mark David Hall, eds. *Faith and the Founders of the American Republic.* Oxford: Oxford University Press, 2014.

DuBois, W. E. B. *Black Reconstruction in America: An Essay toward a History of the Part Which Black Folk Played in the Attempt to Reconstruct Democracy in America, 1860–1880.* New York: Oxford University Press, 2007.

Dubow, Saul. *Scientific Racism in Modern South Africa.* Cambridge: Cambridge University Press, 1995.

Dubuisson, Daniel. *The Western Construction of Religion: Myths, Knowledge, and Ideology.* Translated by William Sayers. Baltimore, MD: John Hopkins University Press, 2003.

Du Mez, Kristin Kobes. *Jesus and John Wayne: How White Evangelicals Corrupted a Faith and Fractured a Nation.* New York: Liveright, 2020.

Durham, Martin. *The Christian Right, the Far Right and the Boundaries of American Conservativism.* Manchester: Manchester University Press, 2000.

———. *White Rage: The Extreme Right and American Politics.* New York: Routledge, 2007.

Dyck, Kirsten. *Reichsrock: The International Web of White-Power and Neo-Nazi Hate Music.* New Brunswick, NJ: Rutgers University Press, 2017.

Dyer, Joel. *Harvest of Rage: Why Oklahoma City Is Only the Beginning.* Boulder, CO: Westview Press, 1998.

Dykes, Justin Perle. "Homeland Security and Rhetoric: A Guide to Understanding Adam Gadahn's Domestic Terrorist Recruitment Machine." Master's thesis, San Diego State University, 2011.

Eddo-Lodge, Reni. *Why I'm No Longer Talking to White People about Race.* London: Bloomsbury Circus, 2017.

Edwards, Griffin Sims, and Stephen Rushin. "The Effect of President Trump's Election on Hate Crimes." *SSRN,* January 14, 2018. https://doi.org//10.2139/ssrn.3102652.

Ehrlinger, Joyce, E. Ashby Plant, Richard P. Eibach, Corey J. Columb, Joanna L. Goplen, Jonathan W. Kunstman, and David A. Butz. "How Exposure to the Confederate Flag Affects Willingness to Vote for Barack Obama." *Political Psychology* 32, no. 1 (2011): 131-46. https://doi.org/10.1111/j.1467-9221.2010.00797.x.

Einhorn, Robin L. *American Taxation, American Slavery.* Chicago: University of Chicago Press, 2006.

Emdin, Christopher. *For White Folks Who Teach in the Hood—and the Rest of Y'all Too: Reality Pedagogy and Urban Education.* Boston: Beacon Press, 2016.

Emerick, Yahya. *The Life and Work of Muhammad.* Indianapolis: Alpha Books, 2002.

Empower LLC. *Who's Behind ICE? The Tech and Data Companies Fueling Deportations.* National Immigration Project of the National Lawyers Guild, Immigrant Defense Project, and Mijente, October 23, 2018. https://mijente.net/wp-content/uploads/2018/10/WHO'S-BEHIND-ICE_-The-Tech-and-Data-Companies-Fueling-Deportations-_v1.pdf.

Espinosa, Gaston, Harold Morales, and Juan Galvan. "Latino Muslims in the United States: Reversion, Politics, and Islamidad." *Journal of Race, Ethnicity, and Religion* 8, no. 1 (2017): 1–48.

Esposito, John L. *The Islamic Threat: Myth or Reality?* London: Oxford University Press, 1999.

Evans, Geoffrey, and Mark Pickup. "Reversing the Causal Arrow: The Political Conditioning of Economic Perceptions in the 2000–2004 U.S. Presidential Election Cycle." *Journal of Politics* 72, no. 4 (2010): 1236–51.

Evans, J. R. *Emigrants: Why the English Sailed to the New World.* London: Weidenfeld and Nicolson, 2017.

Eyal, Tay, Mary Steffel, and Nicholas Epley. "Perspective Mistaking: Accurately Understanding the Mind of Another Requires Getting Perspective, Not Taking Perspective." *Journal of Personality and Social Psychology* 114, no. 4 (2018): 547–71.

Fait, Stefano. "Apocalypticism." In *Religion and Violence: An Encyclopedia of Faith and Conflict,* edited by Jeffrey Ian Ross, 49–57. Armonk, NY: M. E. Sharpe, 2011.

Falk, Armin, Andreas Kuhn, and Josef Zweimüller. "Unemployment and Right-Wing Extremist Crime." *Scandinavian Journal of Economics* 113, no. 2 (June 2011): 260–85.

Faraj, Muhammad 'Abd as-Salam. *The Neglected Duty: The Creed of Sadat's Assassins and Islamic Resurgence in the Middle East.* Translated by Johannes J. G. Jansen. New York: Macmillan, 1986.

Farrell, Tracie, Miriam Fernandez, Jakub Novotny, and Harith Alani. "Exploring Misogyny across the Manosphere in Reddit." In *WebSci '19: Proceedings of the 10th ACM Conference on Web Science,* edited by the Association for Computing Machinery, 87–96. New York: Association for Computing Machinery, 2019.

Fea, John. *Believe Me: The Evangelical Road to Donald Trump.* Grand Rapids, MI: Eerdmans, 2018.

———. *Was America Founded as a Christian Nation? A Historical Introduction.* Louisville, KY: Westminster John Knox Press, 2011.

Federal Bureau of Investigation. "COINTELPRO Black Extremist Parts 1–23." FBI Records: The Vault, accessed August 15, 2020. https://vault.fbi.gov/cointel-pro/cointel-pro-black-extremists.

———. "COINTELPRO White Hate Groups Parts 1–14." FBI Records: The Vault, accessed August 15, 2020. https://vault.fbi.gov/cointel-pro/White%20Hate%20Groups/white-hate-groups-part-01-of-14/view.

———. "Project Megiddo." In *Millennial Violence: Past, Present, Future,* edited by Jeffrey Kaplan, 28–52. Portland, OR: F. Cass, 2002.

———. "Terrorism 2002–2005." U.S. Department of Justice, n.d., accessed March 6, 2011. www.fbi.gov/stats-services/publications/terrorism-2002-2005.

Federal Bureau of Investigation, Counterterrorism Division. *Counterterrorism Policy Directive and Policy Guide.* April 1, 2015. Available at www.documentcloud.org/documents/3423189-CT-Excerpt.html#document/p50/a336267.

———. *FBI Intelligence Assessment: White Supremacist Recruitment of Military Personnel since 9/11.* July 7, 2008. Available at www.documentcloud.org/documents/402528-doc-33-fbi-whitesuprec.html.

———. *Ghost Skins: The Fascist Path to Stealth.* October 17, 2006, Available at www.documentcloud.org/documents/402522-doc-27-ghost-skins.html.

———. "Sovereign Citizens: A Growing Domestic Threat to Law Enforcement," *FBI Law Enforcement Bulletin,* September 1, 2011, https://leb.fbi.gov/articles/featured-articles/sovereign-citizens-a-growing-domestic-threat-to-law-enforcement.

Federal Bureau of Investigation, Intelligence Division. *Anti-Government Identity Based, and Fringe Political Conspiracy Theories Very Likely Motivate Some Domestic Extremists to Commit Criminal, Sometimes Violent Activity.* May 30, 2019. Available at www.justsecurity.org/wp-content/uploads/2019/08/420379775-fbi-conspiracy-theories-domestic-extremism.pdf.

Feldman, Noah. *After Jihad: America and the Struggle for Islamic Democracy.* New York: Farrar, Strauss and Giroux, 2003.

Figueira, Daurius. *Salafi Jihadi Discourse of Sunni Islam in the Twenty-First Century: The Discourse of Abu Muhammad Al-Maqdisi and Anwar Al-Awlaki.* Bloomington, IN: iUniverse, 2011.

Fish, M. Steven. *Are Muslims Distinctive? A Look at the Evidence.* New York: Oxford University Press, 2011.

FitzGerald, Frances. *The Evangelicals: The Struggle to Shape America.* New York: Simon and Schuster, 2017.

Flannery, Frances L. *Understanding Apocalyptic Terrorism: Countering the Radical Mindset.* London: Routledge, 2016.

Flowers, Stephen. "Revival of Germanic Religion in Contemporary Anglo-Saxon American Culture." *Mankind Quarterly* 21, no. 3 (1981): 279–94.

Flynn, Kevin. *The Silent Brotherhood: Inside America's Racist Underground.* New York: Free Press, 1989.

Forman, James. *Locking Up Our Own: Crime and Punishment in Black America.* New York: Farrar, Straus and Giroux, 2017.

Foucault, Michel. *Archeology of Knowledge and the Discourse on Language.* New York: Pantheon, 1972.

Francis, Matthew D. M. "Why the 'Sacred' Is a Better Resource than 'Religion' for Understanding Terrorism." *Terrorism and Political Violence* 28, no. 5 (2015): 912–27.

Francis, Matthew, and Amanda van Eck Duymaer van Twist. "Religious Literacy, Radicalisation and Extremism." In *Religious Literacy in Policy and Practice,* edited by Matthew Francis and Adam Dinham, 113–35. Bristol: Policy Press, 2015.

Fuller, Graham E. *The Future of Political Islam.* New York: Palgrave, 2003.

Gaetano, Joe Ilardi. "Redefining the Issues: The Future of Terrorism Research and the Search for Empathy." In *Research on Terrorism: Trends, Achievements and Failures,* edited by Andrew Silke, 214–28. London: Frank Cass, 2004.

Gale, William Potter. *Racial and National Identity.* Mountain City, TN: Sacred Truth Ministries, 2002.

Galinsky, A.D., and G. Ku. "The Effects of Perspective-Taking on Prejudice: The Moderating Role of Self-Evaluation." *Personality and Social Psychology Bulletin* 30 (2004): 594–604.

Gallagher, Aoife, Jacob Davey, and Mackenzie Hart. *Key Trends in QAnon Activity since 2017.* London: Institute for Strategic Dialogue, 2020. www.isdglobal.org/wp-content/uploads/2020/07/The-Genesis-of-a-Conspiracy-Theory.pdf.

Gardell, Mattias. "David Lane." In *Encyclopedia of White Power: A Sourcebook on the Radical Racist Right,* edited by Jeffrey Kaplan, 167–69. Walnut Creek, CA: AltaMira Press, 2000.

———. *Gods of the Blood: The Pagan Revival and White Separatism.* Durham, NC: Duke University Press, 2003.

———. "The Order." In *Encyclopedia of White Power: A Sourcebook on the Radical Racist Right,* edited by Jeffrey Kaplan, 233–35. Walnut Creek, CA: AltaMira Press, 2000.

———. "Robert J. Matthews." In *Encyclopedia of White Power: A Sourcebook on the Radical Racist Right,* edited by Jeffrey Kaplan, 199–201. Walnut Creek, CA: AltaMira Press, 2000.

Gartenstein-Ross, Daveed, and Nathaniel Barr. "Fixing How We Fight the Islamic State's Narrative." Texas National Security Network, January 4, 2016. Available at https://warontherocks.com/2016/01/fixing-how-we-fight-the-islamic-states-narrative.

Gerges, Fawaz A. *The Far Enemy: Why Jihad Went Global.* Cambridge: Cambridge University Press, 2005.

Gershman, Norman H. *Besa: Muslims Who Saved Jews during World War II.* Syracuse, NY: Syracuse University Press, 2008.

Gessen, Masha. *Surviving Autocracy.* New York: Riverhead Books, 2020.

Gill, Paul. "Seven Findings on Lone Actor Terrorists." International Center for the Study of Terrorism, February 6, 2013. https://sites.psu.edu/icst/2013/02/06/seven-findings-on-lone-actor-terrorists.

Gill, Paul, John Horgan, and Paige Deckert. "Bombing Alone: Tracing the Motivations and Antecedent Behaviors of Lone-Actor Terrorists." *Journal of*

Forensic Sciences 59, no. 2 (2014): 425–35. https://doi.org/10.1111/1556-4029.12312.

Gill, Sam. "The Academic Study of Religion." *Journal of the American Academy of Religion* 62, no. 4 (1994): 965–75.

Gillborn, David. "The White Working Class, Racism and Respectability: Victims, Degenerates and Interest-Convergence." *British Journal of Educational Studies* 58, no. 1 (March 2010): 3–25.

GOD and Lincoln on Negro-White Marriages. Phoenix: America's Promise, n.d.

Goff, Kenneth. *America: Zion of God.* Boring, OR: Christian Patriot Association, 1980.

Goldberg, Ellis. "Smashing Idols and the State: The Protestant Ethic and Egyptian Sunni Radicalism." *Comparative Studies in Society and History* 33, no. 1 (January 1991): 3–35.

Goldberg, Michelle. *Kingdom Coming: The Rise of Christian Nationalism.* New York: W. W. Norton, 2007.

Goodrick-Clarke, Nicholas. *Black Sun: Aryan Cults, Esoteric Nazism, and the Politics of Identity.* New York: New York University Press, 2002.

Gracia, Jorge J. E. "Race and Ethnicity." In *The Oxford Handbook of Philosophy and Race,* edited by Naomi Zack, 180–90. Oxford: Oxford University Press, 2017.

Grady, John. *George Washington's Vision and Prophecy for America.* Eureka Springs, AR: Christian Research, 1979.

Graham, John R. "The End of the Great White Male." In *Critical White Studies: Looking behind the Mirror,* edited by Richard Delgado and Jean Stefancic, 3–5. Philadelphia: Temple University Press, 1997.

Graham, Mark. *How Islam Created the Modern World.* Beltsville, MD: Amana Publications, 2006.

Grant, Madison. *The Passing of the Great Race; or, The Racial Basis of European History.* New York: Charles Scribner's Sons, 1918.

Grimsley, Jim. *How I Shed My Skin: Unlearning the Racist Lessons of a Southern Childhood.* Chapel Hill, NC: Algonquin Books of Chapel Hill, 2015.

Guanaratna, Rohan, and Mohamed Feisal Bin Mohamed Hassan. "Terrorist Rehabilitation: The Singapore Experience." In *Terrorist Rehabilitation and Counter-Radicalisation: New Approaches to Counter-Terrorism,* edited by Rohan Gunaratna, Jolene Jerard, and Lawrence Rubin, 36–58. London: Routledge, 2011.

Guerrero, Jean. *Hatemonger: Stephen Miller, Donald Trump, and the White Nationalist Agenda.* New York, NY: HarperCollins, 2020.

Gunning, Jeroen, and Richard Jackson. "What's So 'Religious' about 'Religious Terrorism'?" *Critical Studies on Terrorism* 4, no. 3 (2011): 369–88. https://doi.org/10.1080/17539153.2011.623405.

Habeck, Mary. "Attacking America: Al Qaeda's Grand Strategy in Its War with the World." Foreign Policy Research Institute, February 18, 2014. www.fpri.org/article/2014/02/attacking-america-al-qaedas-grand-strategy-in-its-war-with-the-world.

Hacker, Jacob S., and Paul Pierson. *Let Them Eat Tweets: How the Right Rules in the Age of Extreme Inequality*. New York: Liveright Publishing Corporation, 2020.

Haddad, Mahmoud. "Arab Religious Nationalism in the Colonial Era: Rereading Rashid Rida's Ideas on the Caliphate." *Journal of the American Oriental Society* 117, no. 2 (1997): 253–77.

Hague, Euan, Edward H. Sebesta, and Heidi Beirich. *Neo-Confederacy: A Critical Introduction*. Austin: University of Texas Press, 2008.

Haj, Samira. *Reconfiguring Islamic Tradition: Reform, Rationality, and Modernity*. Stanford, CA: Stanford University Press, 2009.

Hall, Mark David. *The Political and Legal Philosophy of James Wilson: 1742–1798*. Columbia: University of Missouri Press, 1997.

Hall, Stuart. "Ethnicity: Identity, and Difference." *Radical America* 23, no. 4 (1989): 9–20.

Hallimore, M.K. *God's Great Race*. Harrison, AR: Kingdom Identity Ministries, n.d.

Hallstrom, Bob. *Judeo-Christianity: A Study*. Boise, ID: Gospel Ministry Publications, 1993.

Halpern, Thomas, David Rosenberg, Irwin Suall, David Cantor, Lori Linzer, and Rebecca Kaufman. *Beyond the Bombing: The Militia Menace Grows*. New York: Anti-Defamation League, 1995. Available at www.adl.org/sites/defaultfiles/documents/assets/pdf/combating-hate/adl-report-1995-beyond-the-boming-the-militia-menace-grows-an-update-of-armed-and-dangerous.pdf.

Halverson, Jeffry R., H. Lloyd Goodall, and Steven R. Corman. *Master Narratives of Islamist Extremism*. New York: Palgrave McMillan, 2011.

Ham, Mordecai F. *A Need of the Anglo Israel Truth*. Springdale, AZ: Truth in History Publications, 2002.

Hammoud, Mariam Salim. "Educational Obstacles Faced by Palestinian Refugees in Lebanon." *Contemporary Review of the Middle East* 4, no. 2 (2017): 127–48.

Harcourt, Felix. *Ku Klux Kulture: America and the Klan in the 1920s*. Chicago: University of Chicago Press, 2017.

Hardie, Jessica Halliday, and Karolyn Tyson. "Other People's Racism: Race, Rednecks and Riots in a Southern High School." Sociology of Education 86, no. 1 (2013): 83-102. https://doi.org/10.1177/0038040712456554.

Harnish, Andrew. "Ableism and the Trump Phenomenon." *Disability and Society* 32, no. 3 (2017): 423–28. https://doi.org/10.1080/09687599.2017.1288684.

Harris, Matthew L., ed. *Thunder from the Right: Ezra Taft Benson in Mormonism and Politics*. Chicago: University of Illinois Press, 2019.

———. *Watchman on the Tower: Ezra Taft Benson and the Making of the Mormon Right*. Salt Lake City: University of Utah Press, 2020.

Haršányová, Radoslava, and Marek Hrušovský. "Current Trends in Jihadist On-line Magazines." Centre for European and North Atlantic Affairs, January 22, 2017. www.irsec-hub.org/publications/264.

Hartmann, Christina. "Who Does (Not) Belong to the Jihadis' Umma? A Comparison of IS's and al-Qaida's Use of Takfīr to Exclude People from the Muslim Community." *Journal for Decradicalization*, no. 13 (2017): 213–42.

Hartung, Jan-Peter. *A System of Life: Mawdudi and the Ideologisation of Islam*. Oxford: Oxford University Press, 2014.

Harvey, Jennifer. "Race and Reparations: The Material Logics of White Supremacy." In *Disrupting White Supremacy from Within*, edited by Jennifer Harvey, Karin A. Case, and Robin Hawley Gorsline, 91–122. Cleveland: Pilgrim Press, 2004.

Harvey, Jennifer, Karin A. Case, and Robin Hawley Gorsline. *Disrupting White Supremacy from Within: White People on What We Need to Do*. Cleveland: Pilgrim Press, 2004.

Harvey, Paul. *Freedom's Coming: Religious Culture and the Shaping of the South from the Civil War through the Civil Rights Era*. Chapel Hill, NC: University of North Carolina, 2007.

Haselby, Sam. *The Origins of American Religious Nationalism*. New York: Oxford University Press, 2015.

Haselden, Kyle. *The Racial Problem in Christian Perspective*. New York: Harper, 1959.

Haslanger, Sally. *Resisting Reality: Social Construction and Social Critique*. New York: Oxford University Press, 2012.

———. "Tracing the Sociopolitical Reality of Race." In *What Is Race? Four Philosophical Views*, by Joshua Glasgow, Sally Haslanger, Chike Jeffers, and Quayshawn Spencer, 4–37. New York: Oxford University Press, 2019.

Hassan, Hassan. "The Sectarianism of the Islamic State: Ideological Roots and Political Context." Carnegie Endowment for International Peace, June 13, 2016. https://carnegieendowment.org/2016/06/13/sectarianism-of-islamic-state-ideological-roots-and-political-context-pub-63746.

Hassan, Muhammad Haniff. "Jihadi Ideology: An Overview." In *Conflict, Community, and Criminality in Southeast Asia and Australia: Assessments from the Field; A Report of the CSIS Transnational Threats Project*, edited by Arnaud de Borchgrave, Thomas Sanderson, and David Gordon, 76–83. Washington, DC: Center for Strategic and International Studies, 2009.

al-Hassani, Salim T.S., ed. *1001 Inventions: The Enduring Legacy of Muslim Civilization; Official Companion to the 1001 Inventions Exhibition*. 3rd ed. Washington, DC: National Geographic, 2012.

Hatina, Meir. "Redeeming Sunni Islam: Al-Qaʿida's Polemic against the Muslim Brethren." *British Journal of Middle Eastern Studies* 39, no. 1 (2012): 101–13.

Hawley, George. *Making Sense of the Alt-Right*. New York: Columbia University Press, 2017.

Hayes, Kevin J. "How Thomas Jefferson Read the Qurʾan." *Early American Literature* 39, no. 2 (2004): 247–61.

Hegghammer, Thomas. "ʿAbdallāh ʿAzzām and Palestine." *Welt des Islams* 53 (2013): 353–87.

Heffelfinger, Chris. *Radical Islam in America: Salafism's Journey from Arabia to the West*. Lincoln, NE: Potomac Books, 2011.

Hemmer, Nicole. *Messengers of the Right: Conservative Media and the Transformation of American Politics.* Philadelphia: University of Pennsylvania Press, 2016.

Herbst, Philip. "God References." In *Talking Terrorism: A Dictionary of the Loaded Language of Political Violence,* 78–80. Westport, CT: Greenwood Press, 2003.

Herf, Jeffrey. *Nazi Propaganda for the Arab World.* New Haven, CT: Yale University Press, 2009.

Hertie School of Governance. *The Governance Report 2013.* Oxford: Oxford University Press, 2013.

Hewitt, Christopher. *Understanding Terrorism in America: From the Klan to Al-Qaeda.* London: Routledge, 2003.

Hilliard, Robert L., and Michael C. Keith. *Waves of Rancor: Tuning into the Radical Right.* New York: Routledge, 2015.

Hirsch-Hoefler, Sivan, and Cas Mudde. "'Ecoterrorism': Terrorist Threat or Political Ploy?" *Studies in Conflict and Terrorism* 37, no. 7 (2014): 586–603.

Hitler, Adolf. *Mein Kampf.* New York: Reynal and Hitchcock, 1939.

Hoffman, Bruce. *Al Qaeda, Trends in Terrorism and Future Potentialities: An Assessment.* Santa Monica, CA: RAND, 2003.

———. *Inside Terrorism.* New York: Columbia University Press, 1998.

Hoffman, David S. *The Web of Hate: Extremists Exploit the Internet.* New York: Anti-Defamation League, 1996. www.adl.org/sites/default/files/documents /assets/pdf/combating-hate/ADL-Report-1996-Web-of-Hate-Extremists-exploit-the-Internet.pdf.

Hoffman, Wilfried Murad. "Religious Pluralism and Islam in a Polarised World." In *Islam and Global Dialogue: Religious Pluralism and the Pursuit of Peace,* edited by Roger Boase, 235–45, Burlington, VT: Ashgate Publishing Company, 2005.

Hollander, Lee M., trans. *The Poetic Edda.* Austin: University of Texas Press, 1962.

Holmes, David L. *The Faiths of the Founding Fathers.* Oxford: Oxford University Press, 2006.

Holyfield, Lori, Matthew Ryan Moltz, and Mindy S. Bradley. "Race Discourse and the U.S. Confederate Flag." Race, Ethnicity and Education 12, no. 4 (2009): 517–37. https://doi.org/10.1080/13613320903364481.

Hoppe, Leslie J. *The Holy City: Jerusalem in the Theology of the Old Testament.* Collegeville, MN: Order of St. Benedict, 2000.

Horsman, Reginald. *Race and Manifest Destiny: The Origins of American Racial Anglo-Saxonism.* Cambridge, MA: Harvard University Press, 1981.

Hourani, Albert. *Arabic Thought in the Liberal Age, 1798–1939.* Cambridge: Cambridge University Press, 1983.

———. *A History of the Arab Peoples.* New York: Warner Books, 1991.

Houtsma, M. Th., T. W. Arnold, R. Basset, and R. Hartman, eds. *The Encyclopædia of Islam: A Dictionary of the Geography, Ethnography and Biography of the Muhammadan Peoples.* 4 vols. London: Luzac, 1913–38.

Huntington, Samuel P. "The Clash of Civilizations?" *Foreign Affairs* 72, no. 3 (1993): 22–49.

———. *The Clash of Civilizations and the Remaking of World Order.* New York: Simon and Schuster, 1996.

Huret, Romain. *American Tax Resisters.* Cambridge, MA: Harvard University Press, 2014.

Hurtado, Aída. "Intersectional Understanding of Inequality." In *The Oxford Handbook of Social Psychology and Social Justice,* edited by Phillip. L. Hammack, 157–72. New York: Oxford University Press, 2018.

Ibn Taymiyya. *The Friends of Allah and the Friends of the Shaytan.* Translated by Abu Rumaysah. Birmingham: Daar us-Sunnah Publishers, 2005.

———. *Majmu ʿal-Fataawa.* Vol. 28. Dar al-Kutub al-Islami: Riyadh, 1991.

———. *The Religious and Moral Doctrine of Jihaad, Taken from the Book* Al-Siyasah al-Sharʿiyah fi Islah al-Raʿi wa al-Raʿiyah, *Governance According to Allaah's Law in Reforming the Ruler and His Flock.* Translated by Aḥmad ibn ʿAbd al-Ḥalīm. Birmingham, UK: Maktabah al-Ansaar, 2001.

Ibrahim, Raymond, ed. and trans. *The Al Qaeda Reader.* New York: Broadway Books, 2007.

Ingersoll, Julie. "Religiously Motivated Violence in the Abortion Debate." In *The Oxford Handbook of Religion and Violence,* ed. Mark Juergensmeyer, Margo Kitts, and Michael Jerryson, 315–23. New York: Oxford University Press, 2013.

Inglehart, Ronald F. "Giving Up on God: The Global Decline of Religion." *Foreign Affairs,* September/October 2020. www.foreignaffairs.com/articles /world/2020-08-11/religion-giving-god.

International Crisis Group. *Pakistan: Madrasas, Extremism and the Military.* ICG Asia Report no. 36. July 29, 2002. Available at www.refworld.org /docid/3de778624.html.

International Human Rights and Conflict Resolution Clinic (Stanford Law School) and Global Justice Clinic (NYU School of Law). *Living under Drones: Death, Injury, and Trauma to Civilians from U.S. Drone Practices in Pakistan.* September 2012. https://law.stanford.edu/wp-content/uploads /sites/default/files/publication/313671/doc/slspublic/Stanford_NYU_LIV-ING_UNDER_DRONES.pdf.

Irving, Debby. *Waking Up White: And Finding Myself in the Story of Race.* Cambridge, MA: Elephant Room Press, 2014.

Isenberg, Nancy. *White Trash: The 400-Year Untold History of Class in America.* New York: Penguin Books, 2017.

Jackson, Roy. *Mawlana Mawdudi and Political Islam: Authority and the Islamic State.* London: Routledge, 2011.

Jackson, Sam. *Oath Keepers: Patriotism and the Edge of Violence in a Right-Wing Antigovernment Group.* New York: Columbia University Press, 2020.

Jaki, Sylvia, Tom De Smedt, Maja Gwóźdź, Rudresh Panchal, Alexander Rossa, and Guy De Pauw. "Online Hatred of Women in the Incels.me Forum: Linguistic Analysis and Automatic Detection." *Journal of Language Aggression and Conflict* 7, no. 2 (2019): 240–68. https://doi.org/10.1075/jlac.00026.jak.

Jardina, Ashley. "In-Group Love and Out-Group Hate: White Racial Attitudes in Contemporary U.S. Elections." *Political Behavior,* March 3, 2020. https:// doi.org/10.1007/s11109-020-09600-x.

————. *White Identity Politics*. Cambridge: Cambridge University Press, 2019.

Jefferis, Jennifer L. *Armed for Life: The Army of God and Anti-Abortion Terror in the United States*. Santa Barbara, CA: Praeger, 2011.

Johnson, Daryl. *Right Wing Resurgence: How a Domestic Terrorism Threat Is Being Ignored*. Lanham, MD: Rowman and Littlefield, 2012.

Johnson, Toni, and Muhammad Aly Sergie. "Islam: Governing under Sharia." Council on Foreign Relations, July 25, 2014. www.cfr.org/backgrounder/islam-governing-under-sharia.

Jones, Robert P. *The End of White Christian America*. New York: Simon and Schuster, 2016.

————. "The High Correlation between Percentage of White Christians, Support for Trump in Key States." Public Religion Research Institute, November 17, 2016. www.prri.org/spotlight/trump-triumphed-white-christian-states.

————. *White Too Long: The Legacy of White Supremacy in American Christianity*. New York: Simon & Schuster, 2020.

Jones, Samuel Vincent. "Law Enforcement and White Power: An FBI Report Unraveled." *Thurgood Marshall Law Review* 41, no. 1 (2015): 99–104.

Joosse, Paul. "Leaderless Resistance and Ideological Inclusion: The Case of the Earth Liberation Front." *Terrorism and Political Violence* 19 (2007): 351–68.

Joseph, Peniel E. *The Sword and the Shield: The Revolutionary Lives of Malcom X and Martin Luther King Jr*. New York: Basic Books, 2020.

Juergensmeyer, Mark. "Entering the Mindset of Violent Religious Activists." *Religions* 6, no. 3 (2015): 852–59. https://doi.org/10.3390/rel6030852.

————. *Terror in the Mind of God: The Global Rise of Religious Violence*. 4th ed. Oakland: University of California Press, 2017.

Juergensmeyer, Mark, and Mona Kanwal Sheikh. "Introduction: The Challenge of Entering Religious Minds." In *Entering Religious Minds: The Social Study of Worldviews*, edited by Mark Juergensmeyer and Mona Kanwal Sheikh, 1–8. New York: Routledge, 2020.

Kamali, Sara. "Informants, Provocateurs, and Entrapment: Examining the Histories of the FBI's PATCON and the NYPD's Muslim Surveillance Program." *Surveillance and Society* 15, no. 1 (2017): 68–78. https://doi.org/10.24908/ss.v15i1.5254.

————. "Interviewing White Ethno(-Religious) Nationalists: Reflections on Fieldwork." In *Entering Religious Minds: The Social Study of Worldviews*, edited by Mark Juergensmeyer and Mona Kanwal Sheikh, 93–98. New York: Routledge, 2020.

Kaplan, Jeffrey. "Church of the Creator." In *Encyclopedia of White Power: A Sourcebook on the Radical Racist Right*, edited by Jeffrey Kaplan, 54–57. Walnut Creek, CA: AltaMira Press, 2000.

————. "Ku Klux Klan." In *Encyclopedia of White Power: A Sourcebook on the Radical Racist Right*, edited by Jeffrey Kaplan, 163–66. Walnut Creek, CA: AltaMira Press, 2000.

————. "Leaderless Resistance." *Terrorism and Political Violence* 9, no. 3 (1997): 80–95.

———. "Odinism." In *Encyclopedia of White Power: A Sourcebook on the Radical Racist Right,* edited by Jeffrey Kaplan, 229–32. Walnut Creek, CA: AltaMira Press, 2000.

———. *Radical Religion in America: Millenarian Movements from the Far Right to the Children of Noah.* Syracuse, NY: Syracuse University Press, 1997.

———. "The Reconstruction of the Asatru and Odinist Traditions." In *Magical Religion and Modern Witchcraft,* edited by James R. Lewis, 193–236. Albany: State University of New York Press, 1996.

———. "Right Wing Violence in North America." *Terrorism and Political Violence* 7, no. 1 (1995): 44–95.

———. "William Pierce." In *Encyclopedia of White Power: A Sourcebook on the Radical Racist Right,* edited by Jeffrey Kaplan, 244–50. Walnut Creek, CA: AltaMira Press, 2000.

———. "Zionist Occupation Government (ZOG)." In *Encyclopedia of White Power: A Sourcebook on the Radical Racist Right,* edited by Jeffrey Kaplan, 367–72. Walnut Creek, CA: AltaMira Press, 2000.

Kaufmann, Eric P. "The Decline of the WASP in the United States and Canada." In *Rethinking Ethnicity: Majority Groups and Dominant Minorities,* edited by Eric P. Kaufmann, 54–73. New York: Routledge, 2004.

———. *The Rise and Fall of Anglo-America.* Cambridge, MA: Harvard University Press, 2004.

Kaul, Inge. "Global Public Goods: A Concept for Framing the Post-2015 Agenda?" German Development Institute, February 2013. www.die-gdi.de /discussion-paper/article/global-public-goods-a-concept-for-framing-the-post-2015-agenda.

Kearns, Erin M., Allison E. Betus, and Anthony F. Lemieux. "Why Do Some Terrorist Attacks Receive More Media Attention Than Others?" *Justice Quarterly* 36, no. 6 (2019): 985–1022.

Keaten, James A., and Charles Soukup. "Dialogue and Religious Otherness: Toward a Model of Pluralistic Interfaith Dialogue." *Journal of International and Intercultural Communication* 2, no. 2 (2009): 168–87.

Keefer, Philip, and Norman Loayza, eds. *Terrorism, Economic Development, and Political Openness.* Cambridge: Cambridge University Press, 2008.

Kehoe, Alice Beck. *Militant Christianity: An Anthropological History.* New York: Palgrave Macmillan, 2012.

Kendall, Frances E. *Understanding White Privilege: Creating Pathways to Authentic Relationships across Race.* New York: Routledge, 2013.

Kendi, Ibram X. *Stamped from the Beginning: The Definitive History of Racist Ideas in America.* New York: Nation Books, 2016.

Kennard, Matt. *Irregular Army: How the U.S. Military Recruited Neo-Nazis, Gang Members and Criminals to Fight the War on Terror.* London: Verso Books, 2012.

Kepel, Gilles. *Muslim Extremism in Egypt: The Prophet and Pharaoh.* Berkeley: University of California Press, 2003.

Kepel, Gilles, Jean-Pierre Milelli, and Pascale Ghazaleh. *Al Qaeda in Its Own Words.* Cambridge, MA: Belknap Press of Harvard University Press, 2008.

Kevles, Daniel J. *In the Name of Eugenics: Genetics and the Uses of Human Heredity.* New York: Knopf, 1985.

Khatab, Sayed. "'Hakimiyyah' and 'Jahiliyyah' in the Thought of Sayyid Qutb." *Middle Eastern Studies* 38, no. 3 (2002): 145–70.

———. *The Political Thought of Sayyid Qutb: The Theory of Jahiliyya.* Routledge Studies in Political Islam. New York: Routledge, 2006.

———. *The Power of Sovereignty: The Political and Ideological Philosophy of Sayyid Qutb.* Routledge Studies in Political Islam. New York: Routledge, 2006.

Khouri, Rami G. "Work to Be Done in a Post–Bin Laden World." *Washington Report on Middle East Affairs* 30, no. 5 (July 2011): 14–15.

Khurshid, Ahmad, and Zafar Ishaq Ansar. *Mawlana Mawdudi: An Introduction to His Life and Thought.* Leicester, England: Islamic Foundation, 1979.

Kidd, Thomas S. *Who Is an Evangelical? The History of a Movement in Crisis.* New Haven, CT: Yale University Press, 2019.

King, Marcus DuBois. "The Weaponization of Water in Syria and Iraq." *Washington Quarterly* 38, no. 4 (2015): 153–69.

Klassen, Ben. *Building a Whiter and Brighter World.* Otto, NC: Church of the Creator, 1986.

———. *The Klassen Letters.* Vol. 2. Otto, NC: Church of the Creator, 1988.

———. *The Little White Book: Fundamentals of the White Racial Religion Creativity for Daily Reading and Affirmation of the White Faith.* Otto, NC: Church of the Creator, 1991.

———. *Nature's Eternal Religion in Two Books.* Lighthouse Point, FL: Church of the Creator, 1973.

———. *RAHOWA! This Planet Is All Ours!* Otto, NC: Church of the Creator, 1987.

———. *A Revolution of Values through Religion.* Otto, NC: Church of the Creator, 1991.

———. "Selling the Church Property." In *Trials, Tribulations, and Triumphs: A History of the Church of the Creator During Its 10-Year Domicile in the State of North Carolina, Coordinated with Biographical Details during the Same Period,* chapter 45. Niceville, FL: Church of the Creator, 1993.

———. *The White Man's Bible.* Lighthouse Point, FL: Church of the Creator, 1981.

Kleim, Milton John, Jr. "Internet Recruiting." In *Encyclopedia of White Power: A Sourcebook on the Radical Racist Right,* edited by Jeffrey Kaplan, 141–44. Walnut Creek, CA: AltaMira Press, 2000.

Knoll, James L., IV, and George D. Annas. "Mass Shootings and Mental Illness." In *Gun Violence and Mental Illness,* edited by Liza H. Gold and Robert I. Simon, 81–104. Arlington, VA: American Psychiatric Publishing, 2016.

Koehler, Daniel. *Right-Wing Terrorism in the Twenty-First Century: The "National Socialist Underground" and the History of Terror from the Far-Right in Germany.* New York: Routledge, 2017.

Kopitzke, Corey. "Security Council Resolution 2178 (2014): An Ineffective Response to the Foreign Terrorist Fighter Phenomenon." *Indiana Journal of Global Legal Studies* 24, no. 1 (2017): 309–41.

Krämer, Gudrun. "Anti-Semitism in the Muslim World: A Critical Review." *Die Welt des Islams,* New Series, 46, no. 3 (2006): 243–76.

———. *Hasan al-Banna.* Makers of the Muslim World. Oxford: Oneworld Publications, 2010.

Kreiss, Daniel, Regina G. Lawrence, and Shannon C. McGregor. "Political Identity Ownership: Symbolic Contests to Represent Members of the Public." *Social Media + Society,* April 2020. https://doi.org/10.1177/2056305120926495.

Kreitner, Richard. *Break It Up: Secession, Division, and the Secret History of America's Imperfect Union.* New York: Little, Brown, 2020.

Krueger, Alan B. *What Makes a Terrorist: Economics and the Roots of Terrorism.* Princeton, NJ: Princeton University Press, 2007.

Kühl, Stefan. *The Nazi Connection: Eugenics, American Racism, and German National Socialism.* New York: Oxford University Press, 1994.

Kurzman, Charles. *The Missing Martyrs: Why There Are So Few Muslim Terrorists.* Oxford: Oxford University Press, 2018.

———. "Muslim-American Involvement with Violent Extremism, 2001–2019." Triangle Center on Terrorism and Homeland Security, January 21, 2020. Available at https://drive.google.com/file/d/1JmL7MjWCSwV2jYEu1fEUdVt CUXE3pA46/view.

———. "Muslim-American Terrorism: Declining Further." Triangle Center on Terrorism and Homeland Security, February 1, 2013. https://sites.duke.edu/tcths /files/2013/06/Kurzman_Muslim-American_Terrorism_February_1_2013 .pdf.

———. "Terrorism Cases Involving Muslim-Americans, 2014." Triangle Center on Terrorism and Homeland Security, February 9, 2015. https://sites .duke.edu/tcths/files/2013/06/Kurzman_Terrorism_Cases_Involving_Muslim-Americans_2014.pdf.

Lamont, Michèle, and Annette Lareau. "Cultural Capital: Allusions, Gaps and Glissandos in Recent Theoretical Developments." *Sociological Theory* 6, no. 2 (1988): 153–68.

Lane, David. *88 Precepts.* St. Maries, ID: 14 Word Press, 1990.

———. *Deceived, Damned, and Defiant: The Revolutionary Writings of David Lane.* St. Maries, ID: 14 Word Press, 1999.

———. "Untitled Speech before Aryan Youth Assembly Given by Mrs. David Lane on April 20, 1996." *Focus Fourteen,* no. 605, n.d., p. 1–4.

———. *White Genocide Manifesto.* St. Maries, ID: 14 Word Press, 1988.

Langer, Elinor. *A Hundred Little Hitlers: The Death of a Black Man, the Trial of a White Racist, and the Rise of the Neo-Nazi Movement in America.* New York: Metropolitan Books, 2003.

Lauzière, Henri. *The Making of Salafism: Islamic Reform in the Twentieth Century.* New York: Columbia University Press, 2016.

Lav, Daniel. *Radical Islam and the Revival of Medieval Theology.* New York: Cambridge University Press, 2012.

Layman, Geoffrey C., and Laura S. Hussey. "George W. Bush and the Evangelicals: Religious Commitment and Partisan Change among Evangelical Protestants, 1960–2004." In *A Matter of Faith: Religion in the 2004 Presi-*

dential Election, edited by David E. Campbell, 180–98, Washington, DC: Brookings Institution, 2007.

Lean, Nathan Chapman. *Understanding Islam and the West: Critical Skills for Students.* London: Rowman and Littlefield, 2018.

Lee, Eli. "What Is 'Lone Wolf' Terrorism in the Digital Age?" Political Research Associates, November 21, 2015. www.politicalresearch.org/2015/11/21/what-lone-wolf-terrorism-digital-age.

Lemieux, Anthony F., Jarrett M. Brachman, Jason Levitt, and Jay Wood. "*Inspire* Magazine: A Critical Analysis of Its Significance and Potential Impact through the Lens of the Information, Motivation, and Behavioral Skills Model." *Terrorism and Political Violence* 26, no. 2 (2014): 354-71. https://doi.org/10.1080/09546553.2013.828604.

Lenski, Gerhard. *The Religious Factor.* Garden City, NJ: Doubleday, 1961.

Leodler, Kathy, and Paul Leodler. *Report of Investigation Regarding Representative Matt Shea Washington State House of Representatives.* Rampart Group, December 1, 2019. Available at www.documentcloud.org/documents/6589242-Shea-WA-House-Report.html.

Levin, Brian. *Special Status Report: Hate Crime in the United States, Twenty State Compilation of Official Data.* San Bernardino: Center for the Study of Hate and Extremism, California State University, 2016.

Levitas, Daniel. *The Terrorist Next Door: The Militia Movement and the Radical Right.* New York: St. Martin's Press, 2002.

Levitt, Matthew. *Hezbollah: The Global Footprint of Lebanon's Party of God.* Washington, DC: Georgetown University Press, 2015.

Lewis, Bernard. "Islamic Revival in Turkey." *International Affairs* 28, no. 1 (1952): 38–48.

Lewis, Carol W. "The Clash between Security and Liberty in the U.S. Response to Terror." *Public Administration Review* 65, no. 1 (January–February 2005): 18–30.

Lewis, Tené T., Courtney D. Cogburn, and David R. Williams. "Self-Reported Experiences of Discrimination and Health: Scientific Advances, Ongoing Controversies, and Emerging Issues." *Annual Review of Clinical Psychology* 11, no. 1 (2015): 407–40.

Lincoln, Bruce, and Cristiano Grottanelli. *Gods and Demons, Priests and Scholars: Critical Explorations in the History of Religions.* Chicago: University of Chicago Press, 2012.

Lofgren, Mike. *The Deep State: The Fall of the Constitution and the Rise of a Shadow Government.* New York: Penguin Books, 2016.

———. *The Party Is Over: How Republicans Went Crazy, Democrats Became Useless, and the Middle Class Got Shafted.* New York: Penguin Books, 2013.

López, Ian Haney. *Dog Whistle Politics: How Coded Racial Appeals Have Reinvented Racism and Wrecked the Middle Class.* Oxford: Oxford University Press, 2015.

Lukianoff, Greg, and Jonathan Haidt. *The Coddling of the American Mind: How Good Intentions and Bad Ideas Are Setting Up a Generation for Failure.* New York: Penguin, 2018.

Luwayḥiq, ʿAbd al-Raḥmān ibn Muʿallā. *Religious Extremism in the Lives of Contemporary Muslims.* Translated by Jamaal al-Din M. Zarabozo. Denver: Al-Basheer Company for Publications and Translations, 2001.

Lyons, Jonathan. *The House of Wisdom: How the Arabs Transformed Western Civilization.* New York: Bloomsbury Press, 2009.

Lyons, Matthew. "Fragmented Nationalism: Right-Wing Responses to September 11 in Historical Context." In *We Have Not Been Moved: Resisting Racism and Militarism in Twenty-First Century America,* edited by Elizabeth Martínez, Matt Meyer Sutherland, Mandy Carter, Cornel West, Sonia Sanchez, and Alice Walker, 301–30. Oakland: PM Press, 2012.

Macdonald, Andrew. *Hunter: A Novel.* Hillsboro, WV: National Vanguard Books, 1989.

———. *The Turner Diaries.* Arlington, VA: Alliance National Vanguard Books, 1978.

MacDorman, Marian F., and T. J. Mathews. "Understanding Racial and Ethnic Disparities in U.S. Infant Mortality Rates." *NCHS Data Brief* 74 (September 2011): 1–8.

MacNab, J. J. *Seditionists: Inside the Explosive World of Anti-Government Extremism in America.* London: Palgrave Macmillan, 2015.

Maher, Shiraz. *Salafi-Jihadism: The History of an Idea.* New York: Oxford University Press, 2016.

Mahmood, Saba. *Politics of Piety: The Islamic Revival and the Feminist Subject.* Princeton, NJ: Princeton University Press, 2011.

Mahood, Samantha, and Halim Rane. "Islamist Narratives in ISIS Recruitment Propaganda." *Journal of International Communication* 23, no. 1 (2017): 15–35. https://doi.org/10.1080/13216597.2016.1263231.

Mamdani, Mahmood. *Good Muslim, Bad Muslim: America, the Cold War, and the Roots of Terror.* New York: Pantheon Books, 2004.

Manne, Kate. *Down Girl: The Logic of Misogyny.* Oxford: Oxford University Press, 2017.

Mansfield, Stephen. *Choosing Donald Trump: God, Anger, Hope, and Why Christian Conservatives Supported Him.* Grand Rapids, MI: Baker Books, 2017.

Marinucci, Mimi. *Feminism Is Queer: The Intimate Connection between Queer and Feminist Theory.* London: Zed Books, 2016.

Marsden, George M. *Understanding Fundamentalism and Evangelicalism.* Grand Rapids, MI: W. B. Eerdmans, 1991.

Martin, William C. *With God on Our Side: The Rise of the Religious Right in America.* New York: Broadway Books, 1996.

Masters, Jonathan. "Targeted Killings." Council on Foreign Relations, May 23, 2013. www.cfr.org/backgrounder/targeted-killings.

Masud, Muhammad Khalid. "The Scope of Pluralism in Islamic Moral Traditions." In *Islamic Political Ethics: Civil Society, Pluralism, and Conflict,* edited by Sohail H. Hashmi, 135–47. Princeton, NJ: Princeton University Press, 2002.

Maudoodi, Syed Abul ʿAla. *Ḥuqūq al-zaujain* [The rights of women]. Lahore: Islamic Publications, 1966.

———. *Selected Speeches and Writings of Maulana Maududi*. Karachi: International Islamic Publishers, 1981.

———. *Towards Understanding Islam*. Leicester, England: Islamic Foundation, 1980.

Maudoodi, Syed Abul 'Ala, and al-Ash'ari. *Purdah and the Status of Woman in Islam*. Lahore: Islamic Publications, 1998.

Maudoodi, Syed Abul 'Ala, and Khurshid Ahmad. *Islāmī Riyāsat*. Lahore: Islāmik Pablīkeshanz, 1967.

Maudūdī, Abū al-A'lā. *Let Us Be Muslims*. Translated by Khurram Murad. Leicester: Islamic Foundation, 1982.

Mbembe, Achillle. *Critique of Black Reason*. Translated by Laurent Dubois. Durham: Duke University Press, 2017.

McCants, William F. *The ISIS Apocalypse: The History, Strategy, and Doomsday Vision of the Islamic State*. New York: St. Martin's Press, 2015.

McGregor, Andrew. "'Jihad and the Rifle Alone': 'Abdullah 'Azzam and the Islamist Revolution." *Journal of Conflict Studies* 23, no. 2 (Fall 2003). https://journals.lib.unb.ca/index.php/jcs/article/view/219/377#56.

McNallen, Stephen A. *Asatru: A Native European Spirituality*. Brownsville, CA: Runestone Press, 2015.

———. *An Odinist Anthology*. Breckenridge, TX: Asatru Free Assembly, 1983.

McRae, Elizabeth Gillespie. *Mothers of Massive Resistance: White Women and the Politics of White Supremacy*. Oxford: Oxford University Press, 2018.

Meeks, Cathy. *Living into God's Dream: Dismantling Racism in America*. New York: Morehouse Publishing, 2016.

Meleagrou-Hitchens, Alexander, Seamus Hughes, and Mennett Clifford. *The Travelers: American Jihadists in Syria and Iraq*. Washington, DC: Program on Extremism, George Washington University, February 2018. https://extremism.gwu.edu/sites/g/files/zaxdzs2191/f/TravelersAmericanJihadistsin-SyriaandIraq.pdf.

Meloy, J.R., A.G. Hempel, B.T. Gray, K. Mohandie, A. Shiva, and T.C. Richards. "A Comparative Analysis of North American Adolescent and Adult Mass Murderers." *Behavioral Sciences and the Law* 22, no. 3 (2004): 291–309.

Mendelberg, Tali. *The Race Card: Campaign Strategy, Implicit Messages, and the Norm of Equality*. Princeton, NJ: Princeton University Press, 2001.

Metzl, Jonathan M. *Dying of Whiteness: How the Politics of Racial Resentment Is Killing America's Heartland*. New York: Basic Books, 2019.

Michael, George. "David Lane and the Fourteen Words." *Totalitarian Movements and Political Religions* 10, no. 1 (2009): 43–61.

———. *The Enemy of My Enemy: The Alarming Convergence of Militant Islam and the Extreme Right*. Lawrence: University Press of Kansas, 2006.

———. "RAHOWA! A History of the World Church of the Creator." *Terrorism and Political Violence* 18, no. 4 (2006): 561–83.

———. *Theology of Hate: A History of the World Church of the Creator*. Gainesville: University Press of Florida, 2009.

Michot, Yahya M. "Ibn Taymiyya (1263–1328)." In *The Princeton Encyclopedia of Islamic Political Thought*, edited by Gerhard Böwering, Patricia

Crone, and Mahan Mirza, 239–41. Princeton, NJ: Princeton University Press, 2013.

Miller, Frazier Glenn, Jr. "A White Man Speaks Out." 1999. Available at www .solargeneral.org/wp-content/uploads/library/A-White-Man-Speaks-Out.pdf.

Miller, Michael T. "Black Judaism(s) and Hebrew Israelites." *Religion Compass* 13, no. 11, (2019). https://doi.org/10.1111/rec3.12346.

Moeschberger, Scott L. "Heritage or Hatred: The Confederate Battle Flag and Current Race Relations in the U.S.A." In Symbols that Bind: The Semiotics of Peace and Conflict, Symbols that Divide, Peace Psychology, edited by Scott L. Moeschberger and Rebekah A. Philips De Zalia, 207–18. Cham, Switzerland: Springer International, 2014.

Mohr, Gordon. *Firearms and Freedom! Gun Control Means People Control!* Little Rock, AR: Crusade for Christ, n.d.

———. *The Hitler Cult!* Bay St. Louis, MI: self-published, n.d.

Montenegro, R. E. "My Name Is Not 'Interpreter.'" *JAMA* 315, no. 19 (2016): 2071–72.

Montross, Christine. *Waiting for an Echo: The Madness of American Incarceration.* New York: Penguin Press, 2020.

Moore, Diane L. *Overcoming Religious Illiteracy: A Cultural Studies Approach to the Study of Religion in Secondary Education.* New York: Palgrave Macmillan, 2007

Morgan, Michael Hamilton. *Lost History: The Enduring Legacy of Muslim Scientists, Thinkers, and Artists.* Washington, DC: National Geographic, 2008.

Morrison, Jeffry H. *John Witherspoon and the Founding of the American Republic.* Notre Dame: University of Notre Dame Press, 2005.

Mudde, Cas, ed. *The Populist Radical Right: A Reader.* New York: Routledge, 2017.

———. *Populist Radical Right Parties in Europe.* Cambridge: Cambridge University Press, 2007.

Mueller, Max Perry. *Race and the Making of the Mormon People.* Chapel Hill: University of North Carolina Press, 2017.

Müller, Karsten, and Carlo Schwarz. "Fanning the Flames of Hate: Social Media and Hate Crime." *SSRN,* February 19, 2018. https://papers.ssrn.com /sol3/papers.cfm?abstract_id=3082972.

Munger, Kevin. "Tweetment Effects on the Tweeted: Experimentally Reducing Racist Harassment." *Political Behavior* 39, no. 3 (2017): 629–49.

Munro, Winsome. "Romans 13:1–7: Apartheid's Last Biblical Refuge." *Biblical Theology Bulletin: A Journal of Bible and Theology* 20, no. 4 (1990): 161–68.

Murphy, G. Ronald. *Tree of Salvation: Yggdrasil and the Cross in the North.* New York: Oxford University Press, 2013.

Mutz, Diana C. "Status Threat, Not Economic Hardship, Explains the 2016 Presidential Vote." *PNAS* 115, no. 19 (May 8, 2018): E4330–39. https://doi .org/10.1073/pnas.1718155115.

Myers, Dowell, and Morris Levy. "Racial Population Projections and Reactions to Alternative News Accounts of Growing Diversity." *Annals of the American Academy of Political and Social Science* 677, no. 1 (2018): 215–28.

Nasr, Seyyed Vali Reza. *Mawdudi and the Making of Islamic Revivalism.* New York: Oxford University Press, 1996.

Näsström, Britt-Mari. *Freyja: The Great Goddess of the North.* Lund: University of Lund, 1995.

National Advisory Commission on Civil Disorders. *The Kerner Report.* James Madison Library in American Politics. Princeton, NJ: Princeton University Press, 2016.

National Commission on Terrorist Attacks upon the United States. *The 9/11 Commission Report: The Official Report of the 9/11 Commission and Related Publications.* New York: Norton, 2004.

National Consortium for the Study of Terrorism and Responses to Terrorism. "Profiles of Individual Radicalization in the United States: Preliminary Findings." Research brief. January 2015.

National Criminal Justice Reference Service. *Report of the National Advisory Commission on Civil Disorders.* Washington, DC: National Institute of Justice, United States Department of Justice, February 20, 1981. www.ncjrs .gov/pdffiles1/Digitization/8073NCJRS.pdf.

Neal, Philip. *Two Nations that Changed the World: America and Britain; Their Biblical Origin and Prophetic Destiny.* Hollister, CA: York Publishing, 2014.

Nesbit, Jeffrey Asher. *Poison Tea: How Big Oil and Big Tobacco Invented the Tea Party and Captured the GOP.* New York: Thomas Dunne Books, 2016.

Nettler, Ronald L. *Past Trials and Present Tribulations: A Muslim Fundamentalist's View of the Jews.* Oxford: Pergamon Press, 1987.

Noe-Bustamante, Luis, Lauren Mora, and Mark Hugo Lopez. "About One-in-Four U.S. Hispanics Have Heard of Latinx, but Just 3% Use It." Pew Research Center, August 11, 2020. www.pewresearch.org/hispanic/2020 /08/11/about-one-in-four-u-s-hispanics-have-heard-of-latinx-but-just-3-use-it.

Noll, Mark A. *God and Race in American Politics: A Short History.* Princeton, NJ: Princeton University Press, 2010.

Noll, Mark A., David W. Bebbington, and George M. Marsden. *Evangelicals: Who They Have Been, Are Now, and Could Be.* Grand Rapids, MI: William B. Eerdmans, 2019.

Noll, Richard. *The Aryan Christ: The Secret Life of Carl Jung.* New York: Random House, 1997.

Nordeiade, Sæbjørg Walaker. "Thor's Hammer in Norway: A Symbol of Reaction against the Christian Cross?" In *Old Norse Religion in Long-Term Perspectives: Origins, Changes, and Interactions,* edited by Andres Andren, 218–23. Lund: Nordic Academic Press, 2006.

Norris, Jesse J. "Why Dylann Roof Is a Terrorist under Federal Law, and Why It Matters." *Harvard Journal on Legislation* 54 (2007): 501–41

Norton, Michael I., and Samuel R. Sommers. "Whites See Racism as a Zero-Sum Game That They Are Now Losing." *Perspectives on Psychological Science* 6, no. 3 (2011): 215–18.

Oberhauser, Ann M., Daniel Krier, and Abdi M. Kusow. "Political Moderation and Polarization in the Heartland: Economics, Rurality, and Social Identity in the 2016 U.S. Presidential Election." *Sociological Quarterly* 60, no. 2 (2019): 224–44. https://doi.org/10.1080/00380253.2019.1580543.

O'Brien, David M. "'The Imperial Judiciary': Of Paper Tigers and Socio-Legal Indicators." *History Teacher* 19, no. 1 (1985): 33–88. https://doi.org/10.2307/493615.

Odinist Fellowship. *An Introduction to Odinism.* Crystal River, FL: Giallher-horn Book Service, a Division of the Odinist Fellowship, 1980.

Oladimu, Leo V. *Beige: An Unlikely Trip through America's Racial Obsession.* Self-published, 2014.

Orsi, Robert A. *Between Heaven and Earth: The Religious Worlds People Make and the Scholars Who Study Them.* Princeton, NJ: Princeton University Press, 2005.

Ortiz, Paul. *An African American and Latinx History of the United States.* Boston: Beacon Press, 2018.

Osred. *Odinism: Present, Past and Future.* Melbourne: Renewal Publications, 2011.

Ostler, Jeffrey. *Surviving Genocide, Native Nations and the United States from the American Revolution to Bleeding Kansas.* New Haven, CT: Yale University Press, 2019.

Painter, Nell Irvin. *The History of White People.* New York: W.W. Norton, 2010.

Parsons, Elaine Frantz. *Ku-Klux: The Birth of the Klan during Reconstruction.* Chapel Hill: University of North Carolina Press, 2015.

Patterson, David. *A Genealogy of Evil: Anti-Semitism from Nazism to Islamic Jihad.* Cambridge: Cambridge University Press, 2011.

Pearce, Roy Harvey. *Savagism and Civilization: A Study of the Indian and the American Mind.* Berkeley: University of California Press, 1988.

Penrod, Don L. "Edwin Rushton as the Source of the White Horse Prophecy." *Brigham Young University Studies* 49, no. 3 (2010): 75–131. www.jstor.org/stable/43044811.

Perea, Juan F. "Los Olvidados: On the Making of Invisible People; The Framers' Plan for a White America." In *Critical White Studies: Looking behind the Mirror,* edited by Richard Delgado and Jean Stefancic, 258–62. Philadelphia: Temple University Press, 1997.

Perliger, Arie. "Challengers from the Sidelines: Understanding America's Violent Far-Right." Combating Terrorism Center at West Point, November 2012. https://ctc.usma.edu/wp-content/uploads/2013/01/ChallengersFromtheSide-lines.pdf.

Perlmutter, Dawn. *Investigating Religious Terrorism and Ritualistic Crimes.* Boca Raton, FL: CRC Press, 2004.

Perry, Barbara, and Patrik Olsson. "Cyberhate: The Globalization of Hate." *Information & Communications Technology Law* 18, no. 2 (2009): 185–99. https://doi.org/10.1080/13600830902814984.

Peters, Pete. *Authority: Resistance or Obedience.* Laporte, CO: Laporte Church of Christ, 1980.

———. *Scriptures for America.* Laporte, CO: Laporte Church of Christ, n.d.

Phillips, Steve. *Brown Is the New White: How the Demographic Revolution Has Created a New American Majority.* New York: New Press, 2016.

Phillips, Whitney, and Ryan M. Milner. *You Are Here: A Field Guide for Navigating Polarized Speech, Conspiracy Theories, and Our Polluted Media Landscape.* Cambridge, MA: MIT Press, 2021.

Pierce, William L. *The Turner Diaries.* Hillsboro, WV: National Vanguard Books, 1995.

Poewe, Karla O. *New Religions and the Nazis.* New York: Routledge, 2006.

Posłuszna, Elżbieta. *Environmental and Animal Rights Extremism, Terrorism, and National Security.* London: Elsevier, 2015.

Posner, Sara. *Unholy: Why White Evangelicals Worship at the Altar of Donald Trump.* New York: Penguin Random House, 2020.

Potter, Will. *Green Is the New Red: An Insider's Account of a Social Movement under Siege.* San Francisco: City Lights Bookstore, 2011.

Powell, Kimberly A. "Framing Islam/Creating Fear: An Analysis of U.S. Media Coverage of Terrorism from 2011–2016." *Religions* 9, no. 9 (2018): 257. https://doi.org/10.3390/rel9090257.

Priest, Josiah. *Slavery, As It Relates to the Negro, or African Race: Examined in the Light of Circumstances, History and the Holy Scripture.* Louisville: W. S. Brown, 1849.

Prothero, Stephen R. *Religious Literacy: What Every American Needs to Know—and Doesn't.* San Francisco: HarperSanFrancisco, 2007.

Qahṭānī, Muḥammad ibn Saʿīd ibn Sālim. *Al-Walaʾ waʾl-baraʾ: According to the ʿAqeedah of the Salaf.* Translated by Omar Johnstone. London: Al-Firdous, 1999.

Quinn, D. Michael. "Ezra Taft Benson and Mormon Political Conflicts." *Dialogue: A Journal of Mormon Thought* 26, no. 2 (1993): 1–87. doi:10.2307/45228582.

Qutb, Sayyid. *In the Shade of the Qurʾan: Fi Zilal al-Qurʾan.* Translated by M. A. Salahi and A. A. Shamis. Leicester: Islamic Foundation, 1999.

———. *The Islamic Concept and Its Characteristics.* Indianapolis, IN: American Trust Publications, 1991.

———. *Milestones.* Indianapolis, IN: American Trust Publications, 1993.

———. *Social Justice in Islam [Adalah al-ijtima iyah fi al-Islam].* Translated by Hamid Algar. New York: Islamic Publications International, 2000.

Rabinataj, Sayed Aliakbar, and Rmezan Mahdavi Azadboni. "Religion and Politics: Social Justice as the Quranic Aim." *International Proceedings of Economics Development and Research* 5 (2011): 8–10.

Rae, Noel. *The Great Stain: Witnessing American Slavery.* New York: Overlook Press, 2018.

Rahman, Asyraf Hf. A.B., and Nooraihan Ali. "The Influence of Al-Mawdudi and the Jamaʾat Al Islami Movement on Sayyid Qutb Writings." *World Journal of Islamic History and Civilization* 2, no. 4 (2012): 232–36.

Rashid, Ahmed. *Descent into Chaos.* New York: Penguin Group, 2009.

———. *Taliban: Militant Islam, Oil and Fundamentalism in Central Asia.* New Haven, CT: Yale University Press, 2000.

Raspail, Jean. *The Camp of the Saints.* Translated by Norman Shapiro. New York: Charles Scribner's Sons, 1975.

Redbeard, Ragnar. *Might Is Right, or Survival of the Fittest.* St. Maries, ID: Fourteen Word Press, 1999. Reprint of the 1910 edition, published in London.

Reed, Alastair, and Haroro J. Ingram. *Exploring the Role of Instructional Material in AQAP's Inspire and ISIS's Rumiyah.* The Hague: Europol, May 26, 2017. https://icct.nl/wp-content/uploads/2017/06/reeda_ingramh_instructionalmaterial.pdf.

Rees, Leslie Pearson. *Ye Have Been Hid: Finding the Lost Tribes of Israel.* Salt Lake City: Digital Legend, 2011.

Richman, Laura Smart, and Charles Jonassaint. "The Effects of Race-Related Stress on Cortisol Reactivity in the Laboratory: Implications of the Duke Lacrosse Scandal." *Annals of Behavioral Medicine* 35, no. 1 (2008): 105–10.

Roberts, Charles H. *Race over Grace: The Racialist Religion of the Christian Identity Movement.* New York: iUniverse, 2003.

Roberts, Dorothy E. *Fatal Invention: How Science, Politics, and Big Business Re-create Race in the Twenty-First Century.* New York: New Press, 2011.

Robertson, Pat. *The New World Order.* Dallas: Word Publishing, 1991.

Robinson, Greg. *A Tragedy of Democracy: Japanese Confinement in North America.* New York: Columbia University Press, 2009.

Rohde, David. *In Deep: The FBI, the CIA, and the Truth about America's "Deep State."* New York: W.W. Norton, 2020.

Roy, Olivier. *Afghanistan: From Holy War to Civil War.* Princeton, NJ: Darwin Press, 1995.

———. *The Failure of Political Islam.* Cambridge, MA: Harvard University Press, 1994.

Rozel, John S., and Edward P. Mulvey. "The Link between Mental Illness and Firearm Violence: Implications for Social Policy and Clinical Practice." *Annual Review of Clinical Psychology* 13 (2017): 445–69.

Rudin, A. James. *The Baptizing of America: The Religious Right's Plan for the Rest of Us.* New York: Thunder's Mouth Press, 2006.

Rushdoony, Rousas John. *The Politics of Guilt and Pity.* Fairfax, VA: Thoburn Press, 1978.

Sargent, Lyman Tower. *Extremism in America: A Reader.* New York: New York University Press, 1995.

Saxton, Alexander. *The Rise and Fall of the White Republic: Class Politics and Mass Culture in Nineteenth Century America.* London: Verso, 2010.

Schuurman, Bart, Lasse Lindekilde, Stefan Malthaner, Francis O'Connor, Paul Gill, and Noémie Bouhana. "End of the Lone Wolf: The Typology that Should Not Have Been." *Studies in Conflict and Terrorism* 42, no. 8 (2018): 771–78. https://doi.org/10.1080/1057610X.2017.1419554.

Scrivens, Ryan, and Amarnath Amarasingam. "Haters Gonna 'Like': Exploring Canadian Far-Right Extremism on Facebook." In *Digital Extremisms,* Palgrave Studies in Cybercrime and Cybersecurity, ed. Mark Littler and Benjamin Lee, 63-89. Cham, Switzerland: Palgrave Macmillan, 2020.

See, Sylvene. "Returning Foreign Terrorist Fighters: A Catalyst for Recidivism among Disengaged Terrorists." *Counter Terrorist Trends and Analyses* 10, no. 6 (2018): 7–15.

Selengut, Charles. *Sacred Fury: Understanding Religious Violence.* 3rd ed. Lanham, MD: Rowman and Littlefield, 2017.

Sellman, James. "Kerner Report." In *Africana: The Encyclopedia of the African and African American Experience,* edited by Anthony Appiah and Henry Louis Gates, 450–51. New York: Basic Civitas Books, 1999.

Sexton, Jared Yates. *American Rule: How a Nation Conquered the World but Failed Its People.* New York: Dutton, 2020.

Shah, Hemant, and Seungahn Nah. "Long Ago and Far Away: How U.S. Newspapers Construct Racial Oppression." Journalism 5, no. 3 (2004): 259–78. https://doi.org/10.1177/1464884904041659.

Shah, Niaz A. *Islam and the Law of Armed Conflict: Essential Readings.* Northampton, MA: Edward Elgar Publishing, 2015.

al-Shahrazūrī, Ibn al-Ṣalāḥ. *An Introduction to the Science of the Ḥadīth.* Translated by Eerik Dickinson. Reading, UK: Garnet Publishing, 2006.

Shavit, Uriya. *Sharīʿa and Muslim Minorities: The Wasaṭī and Salafī Approaches to Fiqh al-Aqalliyyāt al-Muslima.* Oxford: Oxford University Press, 2015.

Sheldon, Garrett Ward. *The Political Philosophy of James Madison.* Baltimore: Johns Hopkins University Press, 2001.

Shepard, William E. *Sayyid Qutb and Islamic Activism: A Translation and Critical Analysis of Social Justice in Islam.* Leiden: Brill, 1996.

———. "Sayyid Qutb's Doctrine of Jāhiliyya." *International Journal of Middle East Studies* 35, no. 4 (2003): 521–45.

Shermer, Michael. "Silent No More." *Scientific American* 318, no. 4 (April 2018): 77. https://doi.org/10.1038/scientificamerican0418-77.

Shiblak, Abbas, ed. *The Palestinian Diaspora in Europe: Challenges of Dual Identity and Adaptation.* Refugee and Diaspora Studies 2. Jerusalem: Institute for Jerusalem Studies and Shaml, 2005. Available at www.rsc.ox.ac.uk /files/files-1/palestinian-diaspora-europe-2005.pdf.

Sileven, Everett. *From Sovereignty to Slavery.* Louisville, NE: Fundamentalist Publications, 1983.

Silke, Andrew. "An Introduction to Terrorism Research." In *Research on Terrorism: Trends, Achievements and Failures,* edited by Andrew Silke, 1–29. London: Frank Cass, 2004.

Simi, Pete, and Robert Futrell. *American Swastika: Inside the White Power Movement's Hidden Spaces of Hate.* Lanham, MD: Rowman and Littlefield, 2010.

Simi, Pete, Steven Windisch, and Karyn Sporer. "Recruitment and Radicalization among US Far Right Terrorists." National Consortium for the Study of Terrorism and Responses to Terrorism, 2016. www.start.umd.edu/pubs /START_RecruitmentRadicalizationAmongUSFarRightTerrorists_Nov2016 .pdf.

Simpson, William Gayley. *Which Way Western Man?* 2nd ed. Hillsboro, WV: National Vanguard Books, 2003.

Singh, Jakeet. "Religious Agency and the Limits of Intersectionality." *Hypatia* 30, no. 4 (2015): 657–74.

Slack, Reed D. "The Mormon Belief of an Inspired Constitution." *Journal of Church and State* 36, no. 1 (1994): 35–56. www.jstor.org/stable/23919344.

Smith, Jonathan Z. *Imagining Religion: From Babylon to Jonestown*. Chicago: University of Chicago Press, 1982.

Smith, Tom W. "The Religious Right and Anti-Semitism." *Review of Religious Research* 40, no. 3 (1999): 244–58. www.jstor.org/stable/3512370.

Snook, Jennifer, Thad Horrell, and Kristen Horton. "Heathens in the United States: The Return to 'Tribes' in the Construction of a Peoplehood." In *Cosmopolitanism, Nationalism, and Modern Paganism*, edited by Kathryn Rountree. New York: Palgrave Macmillan, 2017.

Soloway, Richard. *Demography and Degeneration: Eugenics and the Declining Birthrate in Twentieth-Century Britain*. Chapel Hill: University of North Carolina Press, 1990.

Sorenson, David S. "Confronting the 'Islamic State': Priming Strategic Communications; Countering the Appeal of ISIS." *Parameters* 44, no. 3 (Autumn 2014): 25–36.

Spaaij, Ramón. "The Enigma of Lone Wolf Terrorism: An Assessment." *Studies in Conflict and Terrorism* 33, no. 9 (2010): 854–70.

Spellberg, Denise A. *Thomas Jefferson's Qur'an: Islam and the Founders*. New York: Vintage, 2014.

Spencer, Richard. "'Vikings' and the Pagan-Christian Synthesis." *Radix Journal*, December 2, 2014. www.radixjournal.com/journal/vikings-pagan-christian-synthesis.

Springer, Devin R., James L. Regens, and David N. Edger. *Islamic Radicalism and Global Jihad*. Washington, DC: Georgetown University Press, 2009.

Staffell, Simon, and Akil N. Awan. "The Impact of Evolving Jihadist Narratives on Radicalisation in the West." In *Jihadism Transformed: Al-Qaeda and Islamic State's Global Battle of Ideas*, edited by Akil N. Awan, 183–99. New York: Oxford University Press, 2016.

Stanley, Jason. *How Fascism Works: The Politics of Us and Them*. New York: Random House, 2018.

Steel, Claude M. *Whistling Vivaldi: How Stereotypes Affect Us and What We Can Do*. New York: W. W. Norton, 2011.

Stelter, Brian. *Hoax: Donald Trump, Fox News, and the Dangerous Distortion of Truth*. New York: One Signal Publishers, 2020.

Stepan, Nancy Leys. *The Hour of Eugenics: Race, Gender, and Nation in Latin America*. Ithaca, NY: Cornell University Press, 1991.

Stern, Alexandra Minna. *Proud Boys and the White Ethnostate: How the Alt-Right Is Warping the American Imagination*. Boston: Beacon Press, 2019.

Stevens, Stuart. *It Was All a Lie: How the Republican Party Became Donald Trump*. New York: Knopf, 2020.

Stewart, Katherine. *The Power Worshippers: Inside the Dangerous Rise of Religious Nationalism*. New York: Bloomsbury, 2020.

Strother, Logan, Spencer Piston, and Thomas Ogorzalek. "Pride or Prejudice? Racial Prejudice, Southern Heritage, and White Support for the Confederate Flag." *Du Bois Review: Social Science Research on Race* 14, no. 1 (2017): 295–323. https://doi.org/10.1017/S1742058X17000017.

Stubba. *This Is Odinism and Other Essays by Stubba: Original Writings Published 1974–1993, with Notes by Osred*. Melbourne: Renewal Publications, 2016.

Sue, Derald Wing. *Race Talk and the Conspiracy of Silence: Understanding and Facilitating Difficult Dialogues on Race*. Hoboken, NJ: Wiley, 2015.

Suler, John. "The Online Disinhibition Effect." *CyberPsychology and Behavior* 7, no. 3 (2004): 321–26.

———. *Psychology of the Digital Age: Humans Become Electric*. New York: Cambridge University Press, 2016.

Swanson, Jeffrey W., E. Elizabeth McGinty, Seena Fazel, and Vicki M. Mays. "Mental Illness and Reduction of Gun Violence and Suicide: Bringing Epidemiologic Research to Policy." *Annals of Epidemiology* 25, no. 5 (2015): 366–76.

Swift, Wesley A. *God, Man, Nations, and the Races*. Kernville, CA: Church of Jesus Christ Christian, 1970.

al-Tabari. *Annals of the Prophets and Kings: Part 1* [Ta'rikh al-rusul wa-l-muluk]. Translated by M. J. de Goeje. 3rd ed. London: Brill, 2010.

Tanner, Charles, and Devin Burghart. *From Alt-Right to Groyper: White Nationalists Rebrand for 2020 and Beyond*. Institute for Research and Education on Human Rights, 2020. www.irehr.org/reports/alt-right-to-groyper.

Taylor, Helen. "Domestic Terrorism and Hate Crimes: Legal Definitions and Media Framing of Mass Shootings in the United States." *Journal of Policing, Intelligence and Counter Terrorism* 14, no. 3 (2019): 227–44. https://doi.org/10.1080/18335330.2019.1667012.

Teachings of the Odin Brotherhood. Portland, OR: Thule Publications, n.d.

Tesler, Michael. *Post-Racial or Most-Racial? Race and Politics in the Obama Era*. Chicago: University of Chicago Press, 2016.

"This Is Not Our War: A Letter from United States Citizens to Friends in Europe." *Le Monde*, April 9, 2002. In *Rights versus Public Safety after 9/11: America in the Age of Terrorism*, edited by Amita Etzioni and Jason H. Marsh, 123–30. Lanham, MD: Rowman and Littlefield, 2003.

"Through Odin's Eyes." *Sunwheel* (Toronto: Odinist Movement), no. 19 (October 1974).

Tibi, Bassam. *Political Islam, World Politics and Europe: From Jihadist to Institutional Islamism*. New York: Routledge, 2014.

Tinker, George E. *Missionary Conquest: The Gospel and Native American Cultural Genocide*. Minneapolis, MN: Augsburg Fortress Publishing, 1993.

Tisby, Jemar. *The Color of Compromise: The Truth about the American Church's Complicity in Racism*. Grand Rapids, MI: Zondervan, 2019.

Todd, A. R., G. V. Bodenhausen, J. A. Richeson, and A. D. Galinsky. "Perspective Taking Combats Automatic Expressions of Racial Bias." *Journal of Personality and Social Psychology* 100, no. 6 (2011): 1027–42.

Toth, James. *Sayyid Qutb: The Life and Legacy of a Radical Islamic Intellectual*. New York: Oxford University Press, 2013.

Turabi, Hasan. "Principles of Governance, Freedom, and Responsibility in Islam." *American Journal of Islamic Social Sciences* 4, no. 1 (1987): 1–11.

Turner, Richard Brent. *Islam in the African-American Experience.* Bloomington: Indiana University Press, 1997.

United Nations Office for the Coordination of Humanitarian Affairs, Occupied Palestinian Territory. *Humanitarian Pooled Fund: Annual Report 2015.* East Jerusalem: United Nations Office for the Coordination of Humanitarian Affairs, 2015. https://docs.unocha.org/sites/dms/Documents/oPt%20 HPF%20Annual%20Report%202015%20(final).pdf.

Uscinski, Joseph E. "What Is a Conspiracy Theory?" In *Conspiracy Theories and the People Who Believe in Them,* ed. Joseph E. Uscinski, 47–52. New York: Oxford University Press, 2018.

Uscinski, Joseph E., Adam M. Enders, Casey A. Klofstad, Michelle I. Seelig, John, R. Funchion, Caleb Everett, Stephan Wuchty, Kamal Premaratne, and Manohar, N Murthi. "Why Do People Believe COVID-19 Conspiracy Theories?" In "COVID-19 and Misinformation," special issue, *Harvard Kennedy School Misinformation Review* 1 (April 28, 2020). https://doi.org/10.37016 /mr-2020-015.

Uscinski, Joseph E., and Joseph M. Parent. *American Conspiracy Theories.* New York: Oxford University Press, 2014.

U.S. Department of Homeland Security. "Domestic Terrorism and Homegrown Violent Extremism Lexicon." Office of Intelligence and Analysis, November 10, 2011. Available at http://info.publicintelligence.net/DHS-Extremism Lexicon.pdf.

———. "Rightwing Extremism: Current Economic and Political Climate Fueling Resurgence in Radicalization and Recruitment." Office of Intelligence and Analysis, April 7, 2009. Available at www.fas.org/irp/eprint/rightwing.pdf.

U.S. Department of Justice. "Lawfulness of a Lethal Operation Directed against a U.S. Citizen Who Is a Senior Operational Leader of Al Qa'ida or An Associated Force." November 8, 2011.

U.S. Government Accountability Office. "Countering Violent Extremism: Actions Needed to Define Strategy and Assess Progress of Federal Efforts (GAO-17-300)." April 2017. www.gao.gov/assets/690/683984.pdf.

U.S. Riot Commission. *Report of the National Advisory Commission on Civil Disorders.* New York: Bantam Books, 1968.

van Prooijen, Jan-Willem, André P.M. Krouwel, and Thomas V. Pollet. "Political Extremism Predicts Belief in Conspiracy Theories." *Social Psychological and Personality Science* 6, no. 5 (July 2015): 570–78. https://doi.org/10.1177 /1948550614567356.

Vescio, T.K., G.B. Sechrist, and M.P. Paolucci. "Perspective Taking and Prejudice Reduction: The Mediational Role of Empathy Arousal and Situational Attributions." *European Journal of Social Psychology* 33 (2003): 455–72.

Vidino, Lorenzo, and Seamus Hughes. *ISIS in America: From Retweets to Raqqa.* Washington, DC: George Washington University Program on Extremism, December 2015. https://extremism.gwu.edu/sites/g/files/zaxdzs2191/f /downloads/ISIS%20in%20America%20-%20Full%20Report.pdf.

Wachal, Robert S. "The Capitalization of *Black* and *Native American.*" *American Speech* 75, no. 4 (2000): 364–65. muse.jhu.edu/article/2793.

Wagemakers, Joas. "Framing the 'Threat to Islam': Al-Wala' wa al-Bara' in Salafi Discourse." *Arab Studies Quarterly* 30, no. 4 (Fall 2008): 1–22.

———. "Invoking Zarqawi: Abu Muhammad al-Maqdisi's Jihad Deficit." *CTC Sentinel* 2, no. 6 (June 2009).

———. *A Quietist Jihadi: The Ideology and Influence of Abu Muhammad al-Maqdisi.* Cambridge: Cambridge University Press, 2012.

———. "The Transformation of a Radical Concept: *Al-wala' wa-l-bara'* in the Ideology of Abu Muhammad al-Maqdisi." In *Global Salafism: Islam's New Religious Movement,* edited by Roel Meijer, 81–106. New York: Columbia University Press, 2009.

al-Wahhab, Muhammad Ibn Abd, and Muhammad bin 'Abdir-Rahmaan Al-Khumayyis. *Explanation of the "Meaning of Taghoot," of the Imaam and the Mujaddid Muhammad bin 'Abdil-Wahhaab.* Translated by Isma'eel Alarcon. N.p.: Al-Ibaanah Book Publishing, 2003. Available at http://tawheednyc.com/aqeedah/tawheed/Taghoot.pdf.

Warrick, Joby. *Black Flags: The Rise of ISIS.* New York: Anchor Books, 2016.

Weber, Beverly M. "Gender, Race, Religion, Faith? Rethinking Intersectionality in German Feminisms." *European Journal of Women's Studies* 22, no. 1 (2015): 22–36.

Webster, Gerald R., and Jonathan I. Lieb. "Black, White or Green? The Confederate Battle Emblem and the 2001 Mississippi State Flag Referendum." *Southeastern Geographer* 52, no. 3 (2012): 299–326. https://doi.org/10.1353/sgo.2012.0029.

———. "Political Culture, Religion and the Confederate Battle Flag Debate in Alabama." *Journal of Cultural Geography* 20, no. 1 (2002): 1–26. https://doi.org/10.1080/08873630209478279.

———. "Whose South Is It Anyway? Race and the Confederate Battle Flag in South Carolina." *Political Geography* 20, no. 3 (2001): 271–99. https://doi.org/10.1016/S0962-6298(00)00065-2.

Weimann, Gabriel. "Going Dark: Terrorism on the Dark Web." *Studies in Conflict and Terrorism* 39, no. 3 (2016): 195–206.

Welch, Tyler. "Theology, Heroism, Justice, and Fear: An Analysis of ISIS Propaganda Magazines *Dabiq* and *Rumiyah*." *Dynamics of Asymmetric Conflict* 11, no. 3 (2018): 186–98. https://doi.org/10.1080/17467586.2018.1517943.

Wellman, David T. *Portraits of White Racism.* 2nd ed. Cambridge: Cambridge University Press, 1993.

Wertheimer, L.K. *Faith Ed: Teaching about Religion in an Age of Intolerance.* Boston: Beacon Press, 2015.

West, Darrell M. *The Future of Work: Robots, AI, and Automation.* Washington, DC: Brookings Institution Press, 2019.

White, Jonathan. "Political Eschatology: A Theology of Antigovernmental Extremism." *American Behavioral Scientist* 44, no. 6 (2001): 937–56.

Whitehead, Andrew L., and Samuel L. Perry. *Taking Back America for God: Christian Nationalism in the United States.* Oxford: Oxford University Press, 2020.

Whitehead, Andrew L., Samuel L. Perry, and Joseph O. Baker. "Make America Christian Again: Christian Nationalism and Voting for Donald Trump in the

2016 Presidential Election." *Sociology of Religion* 79, no. 2 (2018): 147–71. https://doi.org/10.1093/socrel/srx070.

Whitsel, Brad. "The Turner Diaries and Cosmotheism: William Pierce's Theology." *Nova Religio: The Journal of Alternative and Emergent Religions* 1, no. 2 (April 1998): 183–97.

Wilkerson, Isabel. *Caste: The Origins of Our Discontents*. New York: Random House, 2020.

Williams, David R. "Racial Bias in Health Care and Health: Challenges and Opportunities." *JAMA* 314, no. 6 (2015): 555–56.

Williams, Lauren. "Islamic State Propaganda and the Mainstream Media." Lowy Institute for International Policy, February 29, 2016. www.lowyinstitute.org/publications/islamic-state-propaganda-and-mainstream-media.

Winterbourne, Anthony. *When the Norns Have Spoken: Time and Fate in Germanic Paganism*. Madison, NJ: Fairleigh Dickinson University Press, 2004.

Wood, Robert T. "Indigenous, Nonracist Origins of the American Skinhead Subculture." *Youth and Society* 31, no. 2 (December 1999): 131–51.

Wong, Janelle S. *Immigrants, Evangelicals, and Politics in an Era of Demographic Change*. New York: Russell Sage Foundation, 2018.

Woliver, Laura R., Angela D. Ledford, and Chris J. Dolan. "The South Carolina Confederate Flag: The Politics of Race and Citizenship." *Politics & Policy* 29, no. 4 (2001): 708–30. https://doi.org/10.1111/j.1747-1346.2001.tb00612.x.

Worthen, Molly. "The Chalcedon Problem: Rousas John Rushdoony and the Origins of Christian Reconstructionism." *Church History* 77, no. 2 (2008): 399–437.

Wray, Christopher. "Statement before the House Judiciary Committee." FBI, February 5, 2020. www.fbi.gov/news/testimony/fbi-oversight-020520.

Yanco, J. J. *Misremembering Dr. King: Revisiting the Legacy of Martin Luther King Jr.* Bloomington: Indiana University Press, 2014.

Yancy, George. *Backlash: What Happens When We Talk Honestly about Racism in America*. New York: Rowman and Littlefield, 2018.

Yellow Bird, Michael. "What We Want to Be Called: Indigenous Peoples' Perspectives on Racial and Ethnic Identity Labels." *American Indian Quarterly* 23, no. 2 (1999): 1–21.

Yudell, Michael, Dorothy Roberts, Rob Desalle, and Sarah Tishkoff. "Taking Race out of Human Genetics." *Science* 351, no. 6273 (February 5, 2015): 564–65.

Zakaria, Rafiq. *Indian Muslims: Where Have They Gone Wrong?* Mumbai: Ramads Bhatkal, 2004.

al-Zawahiri, Ayman. *Al-Hisad al-Murr: Al-Ikhwan al-Muslimun fi Sittin Aman*. Amman: Dar al-Bayariq, 1999.

Zeidan, David. "A Comparative Study of Selected Themes in Christian and Islamic Fundamentalist Discourses." *British Journal of Middle Eastern Studies* 30, no. 1 (2003): 43–80.

Zekulin, Michael. "From *Inspire* to *Rumiyah*: Does Instructional Content in Online Jihadist Magazines Lead to Attacks?" *Behavioral Sciences of Terrorism and Political Aggression*, January 7, 2020. https://doi.org/10.1080/19434472.2019.1707848.

Zeskind, Leonard. *The "Christian Identity" Movement: Analyzing Its Theological Rationalization for Racist and Anti-Semitic Violence*. Atlanta, GA: Division of Church and Society of the National Council of the Churches of Christ in the U.S.A., 1986.

Zia-Ul-Haq, Muhammed. "Religious Diversity: An Islamic Perspective." *Islamic Studies* 49, no. 4 (2010): 493–519.

Zinn, Howard. *A People's History of the United States*. New York: HarperCollins, 1980.

Zoubir, Yahia H. "Reformist Islamist Thinkers in the Maghreb: Toward an Islamic Age of Enlightenment?" In *Reformist Voice of Islam: Mediating Islam and Modernity*, ed. Shireen T. Hunter. London: Routledge, 2009.

Zuberi, Tufuku. *Thicker than Blood: How Racial Statistics Lie*. Minneapolis: University of Minnesota Press, 2001.

Index

13, as symbol, 189, 334n30
14, as symbol, 40, 189
88, as symbol, 189, 220–21
666, as symbol, 212
838, as symbol, 40, 290n3
1488, as symbol, 189, 220

Aaronson, Trevor, *The Terror Factory: Inside the FBI's Manufactured War on Terrorism*, 85
al-'Abadi, Haider, 89
'Abbas, Mahmoud, 89
Abdulazeez, Mohammad Youssuf (also spelled Muhammad Youssef), 86
'Abdullah 'Azzam Brigade, 92
ableism, and Trump's presidency, 13
Abrahamic tradition: antisemitic exclusion of Jewish people from, 51; Islam as part of, 267–68; militant Islamist belief in terrorism as inherent feature of, 176; pluralism and holistic justice among religions of, 267–68
Abu Ghraib prison (Iraq), 154
Abu Hanifa, Imam, 95
ACT for America, 127, 320n59
activism, as alternate term for terrorism, and criminalization of political activism, 21–22
Adams, John, 267, 334n31
affirmative action, 229
Affordable Care Act (ACA), 117

Afghan Arabs, 90, 92. *See also* Maktab Khadamat al-Mujahidin al-'Arab (Arab Mujahidin Services Bureau, MAK)
Afghanistan: origins of al-Qa'ida in, 89–90, 91; Parwan Detention Facility (Bagram prison), 154; Soviet invasion of, 89–90, 91; U.S.-led war in, 3, 14, 86, 138–39, 140, 148, 213, 214; and Wahhabi Islam, 96
African American, as term, 28. *See also* Black Americans
African continent, and the exclusionary Immigration Act (1924), 237–38
ahadith. *See* sunna
Ahmadi Muslims, 196
algorithmic confounding (insularity as reinforcing worldviews), 221, 245, 246
alienation in a world gone awry, sense of: Ghost Skins and, 70; gun control issue and, 122
Alliance for Inclusive Heathenry, 271
alt-right: coined as term by Richard Spencer, 2; Proud Boys, 2, 79–80, 127; religion and, 80; self-identification of, 278n31; support for Trump from, 79; as term, as effort to destigmatize White nationalism, 79, 80; as threat to the U.S., 81. *See also* White nationalism
America, etymology of the term, 193, 335n49
America First, 24

American Identity Movement (Identity Evropa), 2, 72, 127

American Nazi Party, 60

American Redoubt, 67

American Revolution: biblical passage used to support, 190; Black Muslims fighting in, 266–67; as influence on White nationalists, 69; phantom cells and, 222–23

American White evangelicalism: overview, 43; and assertion of the Christian heritage of the United States, 184; distinguished from White nationalist evangelicalism, 44; and evangelicalism, defined, 43; pro-Zionism of, 123, 209–10; rejection of label "evangelical" and White nationalism among, 45, 292–93n22; trend toward White nationalism among, 44–46; Trump detractors among, 45; Trump supporters among, 43, 44–45, 292n18; used to justify oppression, 46, 268–69. See also evangelicals; White nationalist evangelicalism

Amoss, Colonel Ulius Louis, 222

al-ʿamr bi-l-maʿrūf wa-n-nahī ʿan al-munkar (enjoining good and forbidding evil), 105–6

Anglin, Andrew, 227–28, 233, 344n39

Anglo-Israelism (British-Israelism), 51–53, 187

Anglo-Saxon Federation of America, 52

antiabortion activists, 77–78, 80; "A Christian Manifesto" (Schaeffer), 77–78

the Antichrist/al-Masih ad-Dajjal, 204, 205, 207, 211–12, 213, 216, 217; "666" as symbol of, 212; k-f-r as symbol of, 212. See also apocalyptic rhetoric of political violence

antifascists (Antifa), 79–80, 301n124

antigovernment activism (political far right): overview, 63, 81, 131–32; apocalyptic rhetoric and, 204–5; the Bundys and armed confrontations, 46–49, 244, 293–94n29; Constitutional Sheriffs, 63, 76–77, 308nn182–183; militias and paramilitary groups, 2, 63, 69, 113, 204, 210; Patriot movement (e.g. American Redoubt), 67; and symbolic power of the Ruby Ridge standoff and shootout, 131–33, 135; and symbolic power of the Waco siege, 132, 133–35; tax protesters, 68–69, 303n140; terrorist attacks related to, 135; Trump viewed as White nationalist ally and, 131; violence upheld as sole remedy by, 49; White genocide beliefs and, 131–35. See also antigovernment/religious organizations; conspiracy theorists and theories; Ghost Skins; gun control issue

antigovernment/religious organizations: overview as subset of White nationalists, 64, 74, 81; antiabortion activists, 77–78, 80; Constitutional Sheriffs, 63, 76–77, 308nn182–183; neo-Confederates, 2, 63, 67, 76. See also Order, The

anti-immigration (immigrants of color) and the political far right: apocalyptic manifesto (Raspail novel), 239; biblical passage used to justify separation of immigrant families, 190–91, 334n39; Constitutional Sheriffs and, 76–77, 308n182; as the "enemy" of RAHOWA, 174; Adolf Hitler and, 238; Immigration Act (1924) based on eugenics, 237–38; Islamophobia and, 156; manifestos espousing, 219–20, 228–30, 237–40, 241–43, 344n39; terrorist attacks based on, 7, 120–21, 240, 242–43; Trump administration policies of, 120, 190–91, 239, 334n4, 346–47n76; Trump's attacks, 12–13; White genocide beliefs and, 117–21; White nationalist narrative of, 41. See also minoritized communities

anti-oppression, holistic justice and expansion from antiracism to, 251, 256–57

antiracism: holistic justice and expanding to anti-oppression from, 251, 256–57; reclaiming Christianity in support of, 268–70; reclaiming Odinism in support of, 270–71

antisemitism and militant Islamism: overview, 145–46; converts from Judaism as source of, 146, 147; the Crusader-Zionist alliance and, 139, 145–47, 156; as political tool, 146, 147; the Qurʾan and, 146, 147, 325n24; as recruitment tool, 145; social media and, 146–47. See also Crusader-Zionist alliance, militant Islamist conception of

antisemitism and White nationalism: Bible denigration, claims of, 51; Christian Identity and, 51–53, 56–57, 122–23, 188, 344n39; Creativity and, 56, 57, 119, 123, 191–92; doxing and harassment based in, 227; exclusion of Jewish people from the Abrahamic tradition, 51; Holocaust denial, 74, 124; as increasing under Trump, 13, 153, 281n50; and the international rise of nationalism, 261–62; Internet shorthand for, 225; Jesus "was Jewish," 56–57; Jesus "was not Jewish," 54; Jewish people becoming antisemitic, 233; "killing of Christ," 51; manifestos espousing, 220, 242, 243, 344n39; and "mud people" as term, 115–16; neo-Nazis and focus on, 73–74; non-Whiteness of Jewish people, 51, 344n39; Pepe the Frog co-opted as symbol of, 24; as recruitment tool, 145; stereotypes of physical characteristics, 54; terrorist acts based on, 85, 113–14, 123–24, 147, 162, 163, 236, 242, 243; "two-seed theory" (polygenism), 51, 54, 115–16, 124, 145, 185; the White ethnostate and, 185, 186; White genocide beliefs and, 119, 122–24; Wotanism and, 192. *See also* globalism (White nationalist antisemitic conspiracy theory); Nazi Germany

apocalyptic rhetoric of political violence: overview as point of commonality within Christianity and Islam, 205–6, 218; the Antichrist/al-Masih ad-Dajjal, 204, 205, 207, 211–12, 213, 216, 217; antigovernment activists and, 204–5; anti-immigration manifesto (Raspail novel), 239; Armageddon, battle of, 205, 207, 212–13, 214, 215–16; belonging and identity and, 218; Christian Identity and, 207, 210–11, 215–16; Creativity and lack of, 206, 207, 208; definition of apocalypse, 206; definition of apocalypticism, 206; definition of eschatology, 206–7; globalism conspiracy theory and, 204, 209, 211; Great Tribulation, 209, 210, 211; Islamism (militant) and, 205–6, 207–8, 211–15, 216–18; Islamophobia and, 210, 211; Jesus and, 207, 213, 215–17; moving the U.S. embassy to Jerusalem viewed as sign of, 123, 209–10; QAnon messaging and, 66; Rapture, 205, 209, 210; and training for war, 210–11; and victimhood narratives, 205, 212, 213–14, 217; violence not always present in believers in eschatologies, 206, 207, 212; and violent acts aimed at precipitating the end of the world, 211, 212, 214–15, 218; White nationalist evangelicals and, 204–6, 207,

209–10, 211–12, 214–16, 217–18; Wotanism/Odinism and (Ragnarok), 58, 207, 208–9

Arab popular uprisings (beginning in 2011), 92, 93, 143, 214

Arizona Liberty Guard, 127

Armageddon, battle of, 205, 207, 212–13, 214, 215–16. *See also* apocalyptic rhetoric of political violence

Armstrong, Karen, 16

Army of God, 77–78

Arpaio, Joe, 76–77, 208n182

Articles of Confederation (1777), 187

Aryan Nations, 68, 114, 129–30, 132–33, 230, 298–99n82

Aryans: Odinist/Wotanist allegiance to global community of, 193; stereotype of, 62

al-Asad, Bashar, 89, 144, 148

Asatru Alliance, *Vor Trú*, 61

Ásatrú, antiracist organizing within, 270–71

Ásatrú, as term, 57

Asatru Community, 271

Ásatrúers (nonmilitant Odinists): appalled by the misappropriation of religion by terrorists, 81; "blood and soil," contestation of centrality of, 270–71; Declaration 127 (public renunciation of hatred and discrimination), 271; Edda literature, 58, 176, 179, 208–9, 271, 333n29; eugenics and, 270; Norse myth and, 58; reclaiming runes from racists, 270–71; "The Shieldwall" declaration, 271; violence not condoned by, 57–58, 176

Ásatrúers, Association of (Iceland), 270–71

Asatru Folk Assembly, 72, 122, 270

Asatru Free Assembly, 122; *An Odinist Anthology* (McNallen), 59, 300n100

Ashcroft, John, 331–32n6

Asian Americans: evangelicals, 43; systemic racism and, 264

Asian continent: and the exclusionary Immigration Act (1924), 237–38; Dylann Roof's appreciation for, 344n39

al-Askari Shrine (Golden Mosque), 89

Associated Press, 26

Association of Ásatrúers (Iceland), 270–71

atheists and agnostics and the political far right: and the alt-right, 80; holistic justice and, 272; manifestos as transcending religious and nonreligious affiliations, 236; and neo-Nazis, 72–73, 74; and Unite the Right demonstration (2017), 2

Atlanta, Georgia. *See* Rudolph, Eric
al-Aulaqi, Anwar: antisemitism of, 147; and
the clash of civilizations narrative, 3;
condemnation of 9/11 attacks by, 231;
death of, 232, 244; on the incongruity
between the Islamic and American ways
of life, 173–75; as influence, 86; and
Inspire online magazine, 233; and literal
and decontextualized reading of the
Qur'an, 176; "And Make it Known and
Clear to Mankind" (speech on video),
175; martyrdom narrative and, 231,
232, 244; "A Message to the American
People" (speech online), 175, 232; online
presence of, 230–32; removal of videos
by YouTube, 345n59; retribution against
the U.S., advocacy of, 148–49, 150, 155;
The Slicing Sword (forward by al-Aulaqi),
235; and training for battle, 211
Austin, Texas. *See* Stack, Joseph
Australasian Indigenous people, 241
Australia. *See* Tarrant, Brenton
autocratic regimes, 261
al-Azhar, 95
'Azzam, 'Abdullah, 83, 90–91, 92; *The
Defense of the Muslim Lands: The First
Obligation after Faith (ad-Difa 'an
Aradi al-Muslimin Aham Furud
al-A'yan)*, 91, 104–5

al-Baghdadi, Abu Bakr: and attacks on Shi'i
and other religious minorities, 89; death
of, 93, 202; Farook/Malik allegiance to,
83; as leader of Islamic State (Dā'ish),
92–93; signatures/honorifics (al-Husayni
al-Qurayshi, Caliph Ibrahim, and Amir
ul-Mu'minin), 93, 201, 313n35
Baldwin, Chuck, 67, 162, 303n138
al-Banna, Hasan, 102, 244; *Five Tracts of
the Martyr Imam Hasan al-Banna
(Majmu'at Rasa'il al-Imam ash-Shahid
Hasan al-Banna)*, 171
Bannon, Steve, 233, 239, 278n31
Barber, William, II, 269–70
Beach, Henry "Mike," 77
Beam, Louis, *Leaderless Resistance*,
222–23, 224
Beck, Glenn, 47
Beinteinsson, Sveinbjörn, 271
Belew, Kathleen, 25
Bell, Derrick, interest convergence theory,
258–59
belonging: apocalyptic rhetoric of political
violence and, 218; counterterrorism

policies as dismantling Muslim
Americans' sense of, 253; so-called lone
wolves brought into community of, 108,
228–32, 240–43, 245
Benson, Ezra Taft, 48
Berg, Alan, murder of, 59, 75
Berwick, Andrew. *See* Breivik, Anders
Behring
Best, Ricky John, 161–62
Bible: "Adam," etymology of, 54, 298n70;
antiabortion terrorism justified via, 78;
antisemitism justified via, 51; and the
apocalypse/eschatology, 206, 209–10,
211–12, 215–16, 217, 239; and the
Great Seal of the U.S., 334n31;
inerrancy of, 189–91, 203, 334n39; "In
God we trust," 195; New Jerusalem,
184–85, 217; and Old Testament vs.
New Testament, 167, 168, 169;
orthodox Islam view of, 176, 267;
polygenism and, 50, 51–52, 54, 298n70;
and Queerphobia, 129; RAHOWA
validated by selective readings of, 163,
166–69, 176, 179; and reclaiming Jesus
from White nationalism, 270;
segregation of skin colors justified via,
119; translation used in text, 31–32;
tribes of Israel, 51–52, 57, 189, 334n30;
the White ethnostate and the law of,
173, 182, 185–86, 189–91, 334n39
Biggs, Joe, 80
Big Tech and efforts to combat terrorist
content, 225, 226, 246, 345n59,
349n98
Bin Laden, Osama: against "Judeo-Crusading alliance" (fatwa), 142; death of, 92,
200, 202, 244; "Declaration of War
against the Americans Occupying the
Land of the Two Holy Places" (fatwa),
142; and Lashkar-e-Taiba (Army of the
Pure), 92; and literal and decontextualized reading of the Qur'an, 176;
martyrdom narrative and, 244; on the
premature declaration of a caliphate,
200–201; and al-Qa'ida, 90, 92; and the
Soviet invasion of Afghanistan/Afghan
Arabs, 90, 92; and Wahhabi Islam, 96;
"World Islamic Front Statement Urging
Jihad against Jews and Crusaders"
(fatwa), 142–43
BIPOC. *See* Black (people), capitalization of
and use of term; Black Americans;
Blackness; Brown (people), capitalization of and use of term; Brownness;

Indigenous peoples; Latinx people; minoritized communities; people of color
birtherism, 10, 65
Birth of a Nation (1915 film, D. W. Griffith), 73
Black Americans: Black Muslim Americans, 84, 250, 265, 266–67; life expectancy and health issues of, 355n45. *See also* Black evangelicals; Black Lives Matter movement; Blackness; enslaved people; people of color; racism; systemic racism
Black Circle (White power band), 162
Black, Don, 73, 233
Black evangelicals, 43, 44–45, 268
Black Hebrew Israelism, 63
Black Lives Matter movement: claims of "reverse racism" by, 71; demonstrations against systemic racism by, 12; founding of, 28, 228; surveillance and criminalization of, 22, 256, 351n16; Trump's attacks on, 11, 12, 279–80n40. *See also* minoritized communities
Blackness, 28, 29, 265, 287n102
Bledsoe, Carlos (aka Abdulhakim Mujahid Muhammad), 85
Boko Haram (Nigeria), 213
Bosnian War (1992–95), 140, 148, 325–26n27
Bostom, Andrew, 325n19
Boston Marathon attack. *See* Tsarnaev, Dzhokhar; Tsarnaev, Tamerlan
Boston Tea Party (1773), 68
Bowers, Robert, 123–24, 129, 131, 148; manifesto of, 236
Bracken, Matt, "Tet Take Two: Eslam's 2016 European Offensive," 126–27
Branch Davidians, 133–35
Bray, Reverend Michael, 78
Breivik, Anders Behring (aka Fjotolf Hansen aka Andrew Berwick): *2083: A European Declaration of Independence,* 240–41; as influence, 240, 241, 242; terrorist attack by, 240–41
Brice, Joseph Jeffrey, 125–26
British-Israelism, 278n31
British-Israelism (Anglo-Israelism), 51–53, 187
British Israel World Federation, 52
Brown (people), capitalization of and use of term, 29
Brown, Ali Muhammad, 85–86
Brownness, 39
Brown, Patrick Wood. *See* Crusius, Patrick

Brüder Schweigen. *See* Order, The
Buddhist nationalism and state-sponsored genocide of Rohingya Muslims (Myanmar), 3, 140, 148, 153, 154
Buddhist statues, destruction of, 96
Bukhari, Imam, 201, 207
Bundy, Ammon, 46–48, 49, 244, 293–94n29
Bundy, Cliven, 46, 48, 49, 244, 293–94n29
Bundy, Ryan, 46, 293–94n29
Bush, George W.: and "crusade" of War on Terror, 144–45; and evangelicals, 45, 331–32n6; and Guantánamo Bay detention center, 154; and Latter-day Saints, 292n18; and U.S.-led wars in Iraq and Afghanistan, 14
Butler, Richard Girnt, 114, 162

caliphate: overview, 182–83; as answer to the ongoing Crusader-Zionist alliance, 139, 141, 142, 143, 144–45, 148, 157–58, 196–97, 200, 203; colonialism and the need for, 197–98; debate on the nature of, 196; democracy and pluralism as supported by, 141, 198–99; Dominionism and, 194–95; equality and justice in, 195–96; the Golden Age of Islam (c. 632–1258 CE), 195–96, 203, 267–68; Islamic Caliphate (Ottoman Empire), dissolution of (1920s), 197; Islamic State (Dāʿish) and claim to, 27–28, 143, 144, 201–2; as the only safe haven for truly pious Muslims, 88; and physical territory, need for, 197, 200–201; al-Qaʿida and, 200–201; Qutb and the purge of Western influences, 199–200; and the Rightly Guided Caliphs (al-Khulafaʾ ur-Rashidun), 195–96, 201, 202, 203; secular government calls by reformists, 196; shariʿa cited as mandate for, 178–79, 331n46; temporal and religious authority embodied in one figure, 195–96; theodemocratic (Mawdudi), 198–99, 202; violence in quest for, as holy war, 91, 172, 196–97, 200, 203; violence not a part of traditional caliphate, 195–96. *See also* caliphate, territory and
caliphate, territory and: apocalyptic rhetoric and, 212; the Crusader-Zionist alliance and lack of, 138, 144, 197; deterritorialization of Islamic State (Dāʿish), 93, 202; lack of, and the need for the

caliphate, territory and *(continued)*
   caliphate, 197, 200–201; al-Qaʻida and
   relationship with, 200–201
Cameron, William, 51, 52
Campbell, Pastor Warren Mike, 166–67;
   "To Teach Them War," 211
cancel culture, 13, 39, 167, 273n4
Cantwell, Christopher, 131
Carolina Knights of the Ku Klux Klan, 113
Carter, Jimmy, 45
Cascadia, 162
Cavanaugh, William, 16
Celtic cross, 40
Center for Investigative Reporting, 6
Chabad-Lubavitch (Jewish sect), 147
Chabad of Poway synagogue. *See* Earnest,
   John
Chamberlain, Houston Stewart, 50
Cham people, 140
Charleston, South Carolina. *See* Roof,
   Dylann Storm
Charlottesvillle, Virginia. *See* Unite the
   Right demonstration (2017)
Chattanooga, Tennessee. *See* Abdulazeez,
   Mohammad Youssuf
Chicanos/as. *See* Latinx people
chilliast, 206. *See also* apocalyptic rhetoric
   of political violence
China, 140
Christchurch Call to Action Summit (2019),
   349n98
Christensen, Else, 61–62
Christian Crusades. *See* Crusades
Christian Identity: overview, 50; Anglo-
   Israelism (British-Israelism), 51–53;
   antisemitic doctrines, 51–53, 56–57,
   122–23, 188, 344n39; Constitutional
   Sheriffs and, 77; Creativity distinguished
   from, 55, 56–57; decline of, 60; eugenics
   and, 50, 62; and the Founding
   Fathers/U.S. Constitution, 182, 186–89,
   191, 202, 333n23, 334nn30–31;
   founding of, 51, 114; and the Great Seal
   of the U.S., 188–89, 334n31; and gun
   control issue, 122; immigrants of color
   as vilified in, 117–19; and the inerrancy
   of the Bible, 189–91, 334n39; the Ku
   Klux Klan as affiliated with, 63, 72, 73;
   Timothy McVeigh as linked to, 75,
   307n176; militant Islamists as sharing
   vision of militant God, 176; and The
   Order, 75; and Queerphobia, 129–30;
   racial superiority doctrine (polygenism),
   50–51, 52–54, 56–57, 145, 185, 187;

and RAHOWA, meaning of, 165–66,
   167–68, 169, 176, 179; tribes of Israel,
   51–52, 57, 189, 334n30; two-seed
   theory (polygenism), 51, 145, 185; and
   Unite the Right demonstration (2017),
   2; and violence, justification of, 167–68,
   169; war training of members, 210–11;
   and the White ethnostate, 62, 118–19,
   182, 184–87, 198. *See also* Christian
   Identity literature
Christian Identity literature: *The Cain-
   Satanic Seed Line* (Comparet), 54; *GOD
   and Lincoln on Negro-White Marriages*,
   119; *God, Man, Nations, and the Races*
   (Swift), 53; *Identification of the British
   Nation with Lost Israel* (Hine), 52;
   Lectures on Our Israelitish Origins
   (Wilson), 51–52; "The Protocols of the
   Elders of Zion," 52; *Racial and
   National Identity* (Gale), 53, 187,
   188–89; *Your Heritage: An Identification of the True Israel through Biblical
   and Historical Sources* (Comparet), 54
Christianity and Christians: antiabortion
   terrorism and, 77–78, 80; Creativity and
   opposition to, 56–57; as disagreeing
   with the misappropriation of religion by
   terrorists, 81, 163, 166, 176; *imago dei*,
   269; the Ku Klux Klan as affiliated with,
   63; militant Islamists chastising
   nonmilitant Christians, 176; Odinism
   and Wotanism and rejection of, 57,
   60–61; used to justify oppression, 46,
   268–69; used to validate social justice
   and antiracism, 46, 268–70. *See also*
   American White evangelicalism;
   evangelicals; Jesus; Latter-day Saints
   (LDS), Church of Jesus Christ of; White
   nationalist evangelicalism; White nationalist religions
Christianity Today, 45
Christian, Jeremiah Joseph, 161–63
Christian Patriot Network, 303n138
Church of Jesus Christ Christian, 53
Church of the Creator. *See* Creativity
Church of the RAHOWA. *See* Creativity
CIA: bombing of Virginia headquarters of
   (1993), 84–85; and the Soviet invasion
   of Afghanistan, 89
cisheteronormativity. *See* patriarchal
   cisheteronormativity
Citizens for Constitutional Freedom, 47
citizenship: equated with White identity, 10;
   Palestinian people and lack of, 152, 153

Civilization Fund Act (1819), 264

civil liberties, American militant Islamists and loss of, overview, 3–4

civil rights movement, White liberal allies of, interest convergence and, 259–60

Civil War (1861–65): Black Muslims fighting in, 266–67; and divisions between predominantly White religious groups, 292–93n22; as influence on White nationalists, 69; neo-Confederates and calls for new secession, 76

civil war: agitation for, 169; Trump's references to, 11, 281n43

clash of civilizations narrative (Islam vs. the West): exploited by White nationalists to perpetuate Islamophobia, 3, 156, 265; militant Islamism advocated via, 3, 138, 141, 156–57, 177, 265; militant Islamism and conception of the U.S. as leader in, 142; as Orientalist, 3, 141, 274n9, 324n8; as term, 142, 199, 324n8; Trump and, 145; and the U.S. counterterrorism paradigm, 265. See also Crusader-Zionist alliance, militant Islamist conception of

class, and the Republican Party as plutocratic populists, 316–17n13

coded language: "civil war" threat, 11–12; dog whistles, 10; globalism, 65; for RAHOWA, 11

Cohen, Joseph Leonard. See al-Khattab, Yousef

Cold War, and militant Islamism, 287n95

colonialism: as a continuation of medieval Crusades, 138, 139, 143–44; and the caliphate, need for, 197–98; as context for development of militant Islamist foundational concepts, 106–8; and the Islamic Caliphate (Ottoman Empire), dissolution of (1920s), 197; Islamism as arising from, 287n95; Orientalism as extension of, 274n9; and the victimhood narrative of militant Islamists, 3; and White nationalist claims for White ethnostate, 219–20, 241–42

colorblindness, 258, 261

colorism within communities of color, 265

Columbus, Christopher, 335n49

Comparet, Bertrand, 51, 52–53; The Cain-Satanic Seed Line, 54; Your Heritage: An Identification of the True Israel through Biblical and Historical Sources, 54

Confederate flag, 11, 76, 220

Confederate monument removals: calls for, Trump lambasting, 12. See also Unite the Right demonstration (2017, Charlottesville, Virginia)

Conger, Molly, 321n72

conspiracy theorists and theories: as antigovernment activists, 63, 64; and apocalyptic rhetoric of political violence, 210, 211; birtherism attacks by Trump, 10, 65; definition of conspiracy theories, 64; disinformation and, 67; and the Great Seal of the U.S., 188–89, 333n29; and gun control, 122; the Internet as controlled by the "Radical Left," 285n86; and martyrdom narrative, 244, 348n89; normalization under Trump administration, 9, 65, 66–67, 285n86, 302n133, 303n136; normalization within the political far right, 66; QAnon, 66–67, 225, 303n136. See also globalism (White nationalist antisemitic conspiracy theory)

Constitutional Convention (1787), 187–88

Constitutional Sheriffs, 63, 76–77, 308nn182–183

Constitutional Sheriffs and Peace Officers Association, 76–77

Constitution Party, 67

Cosmotheism, 54, 55, 56, 237, 298n76

Council of Conservative Citizens, 181, 228, 229, 230

counterterrorism: Big Tech and efforts to ban terrorist content online, 225, 226, 246, 345n59, 349n98; civic allegiance of Muslim Americans questioned by, 253; coercion of Muslim Americans to inform on each other, 175, 252, 253; conveyor belt theory, 15, 252–53; criminalization of all Muslim Americans for violent acts of the very few, 253–54; current approach to, as undermining U.S. security interests, 250, 252–55; dismantling and defunding of White nationalism programs under Obama administration, 6; dismantling and defunding of White nationalism programs under Trump administration, 8–9; focus on countering violent extremism (CVE) and preventing violent extremism (PVE), 252, 253; holistic justice as altering the paradigm of, 251–52, 258–59, 263, 264, 265–66; and Muslim-majority nations as U.S. allies, effects on, 254–55; as recruitment tool

counterterrorism *(continued)*
for militant Islamists, 252–53, 254; as recruitment tool for White nationalists, 252–53; sense of belonging of Muslim American dismantled by, 253; structural Islamophobia as defining feature of, 252–54, 265–66; targeting and surveillance of Muslim Americans, 252–53; targeting and surveillance of other minoritized groups, 256, 351n16; White privilege and the exclusion of White nationalism from programs for, 8, 258. *See also* drone strikes; FBI; federal statute criminalizing domestic terrorism, lack of; holistic justice

COVID-19 pandemic: and Guantánamo prisoners, 154; Trump and conspiracy theories about, 65

Covington, Harold, 71

Creativity: overview, 54; antisemitism and, 56, 57, 119, 123, 191–92; apocalypse/ eschatology as nonexistent in, 206, 207, 208; as borrowing from other religions, 55–56, 164; Christian Identity distinguished from, 55, 56–57; Cosmotheism as merged with, 54, 55, 56; "Creators" as name for adherents of, 54; eugenics and, 56, 119; and the Founding Fathers/U.S. Constitution, 182, 191–92; and gun control issue, 122; and hierarchical leadership vs. small cells, 224; immigrants of color as vilified in, 117–18, 119; and kinism, 182; logo of, 55; nontheistic framework of, 55, 62, 191; other names for, 54; "our race is our religion" doctrine, 56, 164, 191; William Pierce on, 298–99n82; Queerphobia of, 130; RAHOWA attributed to, 54, 56; and RAHOWA, meaning of, 164, 165, 169, 179, 208, 224; and Unite the Right demonstration (2017), 2; and violence, justification of, 56, 169; and the White ethnostate, 62, 119, 182, 208. *See also* Creativity literature; Klassen, Ben

Creativity Alliance, 54, 224

Creativity literature: *Building a Whiter and Brighter World,* 57; *The Creativity Handbook,* 123; *Nature's Eternal Religion,* 55, 208; *Racial Loyalty,* 55; *RAHOWA,* 55, 164; *Salubrious Living,* 55; *The White Man's Bible,* 55, 119, 169, 208

Creativity Movement, 54, 224

Crenshaw, Kimberlé, intersectionality, 351–52n19

Critical Resistance, 256

Cross, Frazier Glenn, Jr. *See* Miller, Frazier Glenn, Jr.

Crusaders (Kansas Security Force), 126

Crusader-Zionist alliance, militant Islamist conception of: overview, 138–40, 155–58; antisemitism and, 139, 145–47, 156; apocalyptic rhetoric of political violence and, 214; belief that the Crusader spirit is embedded within the heart of all Westerners, 139, 147, 157; the caliphate as inhibited by, 142; the caliphate as the answer to, 139, 141, 142, 143, 144–45, 148, 157–58, 196–97, 200, 203; colonialism and, 138, 139, 143–44; counterterrorism strategy of structural Islamophobia and, 253; definition of, 140; enmity of, ideologues on, 139–40, 142–43, 146–47; eradication of Islam and replacement with secularism construed as the goal of, 139–40, 144, 156–58; the Guantánamo Bay detention center and, 151, 153–55; Ibn Taymiyya's works co-opted to perpetuate imagery of, 139; and jihad, 150, 173, 174, 175–76, 177–79, 326n33; the Palestinian question and, 151–53; Qur'anic verse used to support the existence of, 177; recruitment of terrorists based on, 142, 143–44, 151; religiopolitical legitimacy as based on, 142, 143; as representative of present-day U.S.-led wars in Muslim-majority nations, 140, 148, 150, 153; as representative of rhetoric by U.S. presidents, 144–45; as representative of U.S. foreign policy, 140, 141–42, 148–50, 151–55, 325–26nn27,33; and territory, lack of Muslim, 138, 144, 197; the victimhood narrative and, 143, 150; violence as mandated response to, 141, 142–43, 144–45, 147, 150, 156

Crusades (medieval): overview, 97; colonialism as continuation of, 138, 139, 143–44; as context for development of militant Islamist foundational concepts, 106–8; as Islamist theme for centuries, 138–39; militant Islamist belief in U.S. intention to repeat, 88; and the victimhood narrative of militant Islamists, 3; White nationalist terrorist attacks in the name of, 240–41

Crusius, Patrick (aka Patrick Wood Brown), 7, 240, 242–43; *The Inconvenient Truth,* 236, 242–43, 347–48n87
Cuccinelli, Ken, 120
Cullors, Patrisse, 28
Cummings, Joshua, 86
Curry, Bishop Michael, 269

Dark Web, 13–14, 221, 225, 226, 343n33
dār ul-ḥarb, 96
dār ul-Islam, 96
Darwinian evolutionary theory, 298n76
ad-Dawla al-Islamiyya. *See* Islamic State (Dāʿish)
Dearborn Independent, 52, 297n58
Declaration 127 (2016), 271
Declaration of Colonial Rights (1774), 333n18
Declaration of Independence (1776), 187, 191–92, 257, 270, 333n18
"Deep State," 66, 67; Trump as normalizing fears of, 13, 65, 302n133
defamiliarization, 17
Degan, William Francis, 132
democracy: the caliphate as supporting, 141, 198–99; as false political notion and false religion, 172; Islamic history of, 267–68
demographic changes as basis of White genocide beliefs, 115, 128, 262
Denmark, Ásatrú religion and, 270–71
DiAngelo, Robin, *White Fragility: Why It's So Hard for White People to Talk about Racism,* 258, 352n21
disabilities, people with, 13, 167, 174, 257. *See also* minoritized communities
discrimination: Black Muslim Americans' experience of, 265; White people as subjects of, 263. *See also* racism; systemic racism
Dobson, James, 33
dog whistles, 10, 41
domestic terrorism: definition of, 20–22, 283n71; homegrown violent extremism as term vs., 21; potential for the criminalization of minoritized groups as terrorists, 7, 22, 246, 256, 351n16; systemic racism and assumption that the term applies to Muslims but not White nationalists, 20. *See also* counterterrorism; federal statute criminalizing domestic terrorism, lack of; holistic justice; Islamism (militant); lone wolf myth; White nationalism

Dominionism: Christianity and, 46, 185–86, 189–90, 194–95; Islam and, 194–95
Donovan, Jack, 130
Douglass, Frederick, 252, 269
drone strikes: al-Aulaqi killed extrajudicially by, and martyrdom narrative, 232, 233, 244; cessation of, and reparations to civilians by the U.S., 255; civilian fatalities and anti-American sentiment in Muslim-majority nations, 254–55; Obama administration and, 14, 232, 233, 244, 254; as recruitment tool for militant Islamists, 254; and U.S. foreign policy viewed as form of warfare, 148, 150
drone surveillance, 351n16
Duke, David, 2, 114, 260–61
Dumpson, Taylor, 227

eagle, as symbol, 188–89, 333n29, 334n31
Earnest, John, 236, 240, 242, 243; *An Open Letter,* 236, 242
economy: global Great Recession, 116, 117; Republican Party policies as plutocratic populists, 316–17n13; White genocide beliefs and anxiety about, 116–17. *See also* poverty
Egypt, government viewed as apostate by militant Islamists, 91, 144
Egyptian Islamic Jihad (al-Jihad al-Islami al-Misri), 90
Einhorn, Robin L., 303n140
El Paso, Texas. *See* Crusius, Patrick
Emmanuel African Methodist Episcopal Church (Charleston, SC). *See* Roof, Dylann Storm
empathy: achieving through epistemic worldview analysis, 17–19. *See also* holistic justice, empathy as necessary to
End Apathy, 40
End Times. *See* apocalyptic rhetoric of political violence
England: common law and Constitutional Sheriffs, 77; origins of Christian Identity in, 51; and skinhead culture, 40, 78–79. *See also* Great Britain
Enoch, Mike, *The Right Stuff,* 233
enslaved people: Black Muslims as, 84, 250, 266; and systemic racism, 264; White supremacist image of Jesus and justification of enslavement, 269
environmentalism: Ásatrúers and, 270, 271; and reclaiming Jesus from White nationalism, 270
Eriksson, Leif, 193

eschatology, definition of, 206–7. *See also* apocalyptic rhetoric of political violence

eugenics: overview, 50, 237; Ásatrúers (nonmilitant Odinists) and, 70; Christian Identity and, 50, 62; Creativity and, 56, 119; and exclusionary Immigration Act (1924), 237–38; hierarchy among Whites, 50, 62, 237–38; Nazi Germany and, 296n47; *Plessy v. Ferguson* ("separate but equal") as legalizing, 296n47

Europeans: eugenics and the hierarchy among Whites, 50, 62, 237–38; Nordic thesis, 237–38; rise of the political far right among, 261; White Northern and Western, as epitome of Whiteness, 237. *See also* transnational White nationalism

evangelicals: Asian evangelicals, 43; Black evangelicals, 43, 44–45, 268; defined, 43; and the inerrancy of the Bible, 189–90; Latinx evangelicals, 43; pro-Zionist, 123, 209–10; and Trump's base of support, 43. *See also* American White evangelicalism; White nationalist evangelicalism

extremism, as term, 21

Falwell, Jerry, 44

Falwell, Jerry, Jr., 44

Family Research Council, 44

Faraj, Muhammad ʿAbd as-Salam, 91, 102, 105–6; *The Neglected Duty (al-Farida al-Ghaʾiba)*, 91, 104

farḍ ul-ʿayn (individual duty), 104–5

Farook, Syed Rizwan and Tashfeen Malik, 83–84, 108, 231, 244–45

Fateh al-Sham, 89

fatwa, 97, 142–43

FBI (Federal Bureau of Investigation): and American militant Islamists, 87; COINTELPRO program of, 22; on conspiracy theories, 64; entrapment and coercion by, 22; *Ghost Skins: The Fascist Path to Stealth,* 70; labeling murders acts of domestic terrorism, 39; on militant White nationalism as greatest, most persistent terror threat, 6, 8; and minimizing of White nationalist violence as national security issue, 8; Muslim American informants to, 175; PATCON program of, 22; Ruby Ridge standoff and shootout, 132–33, 135, 151, 243; and surveillance of political activity by people of color, 22; terror

attack on Muslim Americans revealed as conspiracy by, 126; Waco siege, 132, 133–35, 151, 243; *White Supremacist Recruitment of Military Personnel since 9/11,* 70

FBI Agents Association, 351n15

FDA (Food and Drug Administration), 65, 302n133

FEAR (Forever Enduring, Always Ready), 71

federal laws: military budget, and removal of White nationalist screening, 72; systemic racism enforced by, 264–65

federal statute criminalizing domestic terrorism, lack of: overview, 7, 255–56; calls for, 351n15; crimes must be prosecuted under existing criminal statutes, 20–21; and distinction between "domestic terrorism" and "homegrown violent extremism," 21; examples of violence not classified as terrorism, 163, 221, 345n51; and PATRIOT Act definition of domestic terrorism, 20, 285n86; potential to criminalize minoritized groups, if enacted, 7, 22, 246, 256, 351n16; proposed legislation, 351n15; and transnational White nationalism, growth of, 256

Feldman, Noah, 26

Felton, Leo, *Beige: An Unlikely Trip through American's Racial Obsession,* 126

feminists, as "enemy" in RAHOWA, 167, 174. *See also* misogyny and antifeminism

Fichte, Johann Gottlieb, 199

Fields, James Alex, Jr., 1, 305–6n157

Finicum, Robert LaVoy, 46, 244

fitna, 176–77

fiṭra, 327n49

Floyd, George, 28

Focus on the Family, 44

Food and Drug Administration (FDA), 65, 302n133

Ford, Henry, 52, 297n58

Fort Hood, Texas. *See* Hasan, Nidal Malik

Forth, Tasman (aka Mills, Alexander Rud), 61

Founding Fathers: alleged to hold antigovernment views, 131; believed to have intended a White ethnostate, 165–66, 181–82, 202; Christian Identity and, 182, 186–89, 191, 202, 333n23, 334nn30–31; Christian influence of,

184, 187–89, 331–32n6; Creativity and, 182, 191–92; and gun control issue, 121, 122; and Islam, 267; Wotanism/ Odinism and, 182, 191, 192–93. *See also* U.S. Constitution

Fourteen Words: "14" as symbol of, 40, 220; overview, 41–42, 240; and apocalyptic rhetoric of political violence, 209; as appealing to a wide range of racist religions and organizations, 42; blood and soil and, 58–59; "existence," 42; the Hammerskins and, 79; Adolf Hitler as influence on, 238; Hitler's writings as laying the groundwork for, 238; immigrants of color as vilified in, 117–18; Ben Klassen as presaging, 56; David Lane as writer of, 40, 41–42, 53, 118, 239; manifestos and, 220, 236–37; "must secure," 42; "our people," 42; as RAHOWA battle cry, 163, 164, 165, 173, 179, 205, 239; Wesley Swift as presaging, 53; text of, 42, 118; transnational White nationalism and, 236–37, 240; Trump and allusions to, 11, 120; victimhood narrative and, 136; "White children," 42; and the White ethnostate, 62, 181–82, 183, 236–37, 239; and women's servitude as vessels of reproduction, 42, 128

France, and the division of the Middle East after WWI, 143–44, 146, 324n11

Franklin, Benjamin, 334n31

Fuentes, Nick, 23–24

Fuller, Graham, 26

fundamentalism, as term, 21

Gabriel (angel), 94

Gabriel, Brigitte, 127

Gadahn, Adam Yahiye, 146

Gale, William Potter, 51, 52–53, 334n31; *Identity* (newsletter), 53; and Posse Comitatus, 77; *Racial and National Identity*, 53, 187, 188–89

Galli, Mark, 45

Galton, Sir Francis, 50

Gardell, Mattias, *Gods of the Blood*, 323n98

Gariépy, Jean-François, 24

Garza, Alicia, 28

Geller, Pamela, 320n59

gender fluidity, Ásatrú religion and, 271

gender. *See* misogyny and anti-feminism; patriarchal cisheteronormativity; Queer people

genocide: Big Tech and complicity in, 246; Bosnian War, 148, 325–26n27; of Indigenous peoples, 30; of the Rohingya (Myanmar), 3, 140, 148, 153, 154

Georges-Picot, Francois, 143

German, Michael, 85

German nationalism (19th c.), 58. *See also* Nazi Germany

Gersh, Tanya, 227

al-Ghamidi, Uthman, 154–55

Ghost Skins: as antigovernment activists, 63; definition of, 69–70; *Ghost Skins: The Fascist Path to Stealth* (FBI), 70; recruitment and training, 70–71; separation from the military for participation in, 72; statistics on White nationalism incidents in the military, 71; terrorist incidents by, 71–72 (*see also* FEAR [Forever Enduring, Always Ready]; Hasan, Nidal Malik; Hasson, Christopher; Hopper, Dillon Ulysses; Miller, Frazier Glenn, Jr.; Page, Wade Michael; Reeves, Cory); as transnational phenomenon, 304n149; U.S. Senate and deprioritization of screening for, 72; *White Supremacist Recruitment of Military Personnel since 9/11* (FBI), 70

Gill, Sam, 16

Gilroy, CA. *See* Legan, Santino William

Gitmo. *See* Guantánamo Bay prison

Global Internet Forum to Counter Terrorism, 226

globalism (White nationalist antisemitic conspiracy theory): antisemitism of, 64–65, 122–23, 145, 319n47; and apocalypticism, 204, 209, 211; definition of, 64; gun control issue and, 121; as political far right theme, 64, 204, 303n138, 323n98; Queer people believed to be the result of, 130; RAHOWA and, 165, 166, 203; shared by both White nationalists and militant Islamists, 203, 323n98; Trump reference to, 65; the White ethnostate as fending off, 185, 192; White genocide beliefs and, 116, 121, 122–24, 204

Gobineau, Arthur de, 50

Goff, Kenneth, 188, 334n31

Gog and Magog, 212, 216–17, 239

Golden Age of Islam (c. 632–1258 CE), 195–96, 203, 267–68

Golden Mosque (Samarra, Iraq), 89

Gomez, Dave, 8

Google, 349n98

government anti-poverty programs: racist beliefs about, 117; Trump administration and, 120

Graham, Billy, 44, 45

Graham, Franklin, 44, 45

Grant, Madison, 50; *The Passing of the Great Race*, 237–38

Great Britain: and the antisemitic Anglo-Israelism theory, 51; and the division of the Middle East after WWI, 143–44, 146, 152, 324n11. *See also* England

Great Recession (2008), 116, 117

Great Tribulation, 209, 210, 211. *See also* apocalyptic rhetoric of political violence

Greece, White nationalism harking back to ancient, 208

Greene, Marjorie Taylor, 66

Grim Reapers (gang), 70–71

Grottanelli, Cristiano, 16–17

Groyper Army, 24, 285n86

Guantánamo Bay prison (Gitmo): George W. Bush administration and establishment of, 154; COVID-19 pandemic and, 154; the Crusader-Zionist alliance and, 151, 153–55; desecrations of the Qur'an at, 154; and martyrdom narratives, 243; Obama administration and, 154; prisoners as "enemy combatants," 154; as propaganda focus of militant Islamist groups, 154–55; sexual assault of male prisoners, 155; U.S. Supreme court and limited rights of prisoners, 154

gun control issue: conspiracy theories and, 122; regulators of guns, as "enemy" in RAHOWA, 164, 167, 174; terrorist attacks and, 162; White genocide beliefs about, 121–22

hadith, 94. *See also* sunna

ḥākimiyyat Allah (nothing is outside the realm of God's sovereignty), 172, 173, 182, 198–99

Haleem, Muhammad Abdel, 31

Hale, Matt, 54, 224, 298–99n82, 341n20; *White Revolution* (video series), 224

Hallstrom, Bob, 187, 333n23

Hamas, 26, 89

Hammerskin Nation, 40, 63, 79, 290n3

Hammond, Dwight, Jr., 46–47

Hammond, Steven, 46–47

Hanafi school (*madhhab*), 95

Hanbali school (*madhhab*), 95, 97

Hansen, Fjotolf. *See* Breivik, Anders Behring

Haq, Naveed, 85

ḥarb, as term in lieu of jihad, 27, 170–71

Harris, Kamala, 10

Harris, Kevin, 132

Hasan, Nidal Malik, 86, 137–38, 140, 149, 150, 231–32, 236

Hashimi, Helmi, 101–2

Haslanger, Sally, 29

Hasson, Christopher, 71–72, 306n159

Hayat Tahrir ash-Sham (aka Jabhat an-Nusra or Jabhat Fateh ash-Sham), 89

Heathens United against Racism, 271

Hegel, Georg Wilhelm Friedrich, 199

Heimbach, Matthew, 130, 233

Herf, Jeffrey, 320n59

Herzegovina, 148

heteronormativity. *See* patriarchal cisheteronormativity

Heyer, Heather, 1, 305–6n157

Hezbollah, 26

Hill, Michael, 76

Hill, Paul Jennings, 77–78

Hilmarsson, Hilmar Örn, 270, 271

Hine, Edward, 51; *Identification of the British Nation with Lost Israel*, 52

Hispanic people. *See* Latinx people

Hitler, Adolf: admiration for restrictive U.S. immigration policies, 238; *Mein Kampf*, 237, 238; the number 88 as code for "Heil Hitler), 220; Odinism and, 60. *See also* Nazi Germany

Hoffman, Bruce, 20

holistic justice: overview, 251–52; altering the counterterrorism paradigm and, 251–52, 258–59, 263, 264, 265–66; and American values, 263; beyond antiracism to anti-oppression, 251, 256–57; definition of, 251; education framework for intersectional identities, 257, 258, 351–52n19; and minoritized communities, amplification of, 251; Muslim Americans allying with minoritized communities to enact change, 251–52, 264–65; structural Islamophobia addressed by, 251, 264–68; U.S. Constitution and White privilege, 251, 256–57; White liberals leveraging White privilege, 251–52, 258–63; and White nationalism, altering the narrative of, 262–63. *See also* holistic justice, empathy as necessary to

holistic justice, empathy as necessary to, 264–71; overview, 251, 264; definition of empathy, 264; and the (non-skin-color–based) disadvantages of White

Americans, 262; and recognition of our common humanity, 271–72; and religious interfaith diversity, cultivation of, 257, 264–72; and White liberals leveraging White privilege, 263

Holocaust, 74, 227, 268

Holocaust denial, 74, 124

Holt, Earl, 229, 230

Holy Order of Aryan Warriors. *See* Order, The

homegrown violent extremism, 21. *See also* domestic terrorism; federal statute criminalizing domestic terrorism, lack of

Hopper, Dillon Ulysses, 71

Howell, Vernon. *See* Koresh, David

Huntington, Samuel, 142, 324n8

Husayn, Imam, 93

Hutaree, 204–5

Ibn Anas, Imam Malik, 95

Ibn Hanbal, Imam Ahmad, 95

Ibn Taymiyya, Taqi ad-Din Ahmad ibn 'Abd al-Halim: overview, 94; and the Christian Crusades/Mongol-Tatar invasion, 97, 139; fatwa, 97; and jihad, formulation of, 170–71, 173; *The Religious and Moral Doctrine of Jihad (as-Siyasat ash-Shar'iyya fi Islah ar-Ra'i wa-r-Ra'iyya)*, 170–71; al-Wahhab as drawing on, 95, 97, 102; and *al-walā' wa-l-barā'* (loyalty and disavowal), 97, 106

Ibn Warraq, 325n19

Iceland, Ásatrú religion and, 270–71

identity: apocalyptic rhetoric of political violence and, 218; choice to commit violence and lack of or fragmented, 15; conflict of being a Muslim and being an American, 232; and the international rise of nationalism, 261–62; intersectional, education framework for, 257, 258, 351–52n19; lone wolf packs as community of belonging and, 108, 228–32, 240–43, 245; White identity politics, 261–63, 352n21. *See also* belonging; minoritized communities

Identity Evropa (American Identity Movement), 2, 72, 127

imago dei, 269

Immigration Act (1924), 237–38

immigration. *See* anti-immigration (immigrants of color)

"imperial judiciary," 229

incels, 80, 128

India: partition of, 92; and rise of nationalism, 261–62

Indigenous peoples: definition and use of term, 30; racism of Christianity and, 270; surveillance and criminalization of, 256; systemic racism and, 265. *See also* minoritized communities

intelligence agencies, and 'Azzam's assassination, 92

interest convergence theory (Derrick Bell), 258–59

Internet: algorithmic confounding, 221, 245, 246; as amplifying terrorist voices, 220, 221; anonymity and, 221, 225, 226, 228; Big Tech and efforts to combat terrorist content on, 225, 226, 246, 345n59, 349n98; conspiracy theory of "Radical Left" control of, 285n86; coordination of offline activities using, 226–28; cyberstalking, 128–29; Dark Web, 13–14, 221, 225, 226, 343n33; doxing and harassment, 131, 227; encrypted communication, 226; First Amendment debates around efforts to legislate terrorist content on, 226; and the ideological consolidation and division of the political far right, 23; insularity of, as reinforcing worldviews (algorithmic confounding), 221, 245, 246; Just Terror, 234, 235; and law enforcement, White nationalists and affinity for, 70; offline organization as enabled by, 221, 226–28; online disinhibition effect, 225; Open Source Jihad, 234–35; open-source messaging services, 225; and the question of whether exposure to content promoting violence compels individual actions, 221–22; and recruitment and promotion of terrorists, 221, 225–32; shorthand used on, 225; support and fundraising for terrorism on, 221; and tax protesters, 69; troll armies, 227–28; victimhood narratives and, 221. *See also* lone wolf myth, and online wolf packs; media entities and outlets; social media

intersectionality: Kimberlé Crenshaw and, 351–52n19; education framework for holistic justice and, 257, 258, 351–52n19; stereotyping of Muslim Americans as disregarding, 266

Iraq: Abu Ghraib, 154; and division of the Middle East after WWI, 143; and the Golden Age of Islam, 268; U.S.-led war in, 3, 14, 86, 92, 138, 140, 148, 213, 214

IRS (Internal Revenue Service), terrorist attack on, 68–69

ISIL. See Islamic State (Dāʿish)

ISIS. See Islamic State (Dāʿish)

Islam: Creativity and need to invalidate, 55; defined as term, 26; martyrdom and, 244–45, 348n93; stereotyped as synonymous with terrorism, 266; testimony of faith (shahāda), 102. See also caliphate; Islamophobia; Muhammad, Prophet; Muslim Americans; Muslims; Qurʾan; sunna

Islamic Caliphate (Ottoman Empire), dissolution of (1920s), 197

Islamic, defined as term, 27

Islamic State (Dāʿish): overview, 87–88; American militant Islamists and allegiance to, 83, 86, 245; apocalyptic rhetoric of political violence, 213, 214; attacks on rival militant Islamist groups, 89; attacks on Shiʿi and other religious minorities, 89; al-Baghdadi as leader of, 92–93; black flag of, 213; as caliphate, claim to, 27–28, 143, 144, 201–2; Dabiq (online magazine), 101, 150, 201, 214, 233–34, 244–45; deterritorialization of, 93, 202; "Establishment of the Islamic State" (video), 211; and Guantánamo detention center as symbol of oppression, 154, 155; How to Survive in the West: a Mujahid Guide (e-book), 343n33; "Kill the Imams of Kufr in the West," 101; lack of recognition by Muslims, 202; leaders of, denounced as apostates, 101–2; origins of, 90, 92–93, 313n35; Rumiyah (online magazine), 201–2, 214, 233–34, 235; and ash-Sham, 212; state actors in support of, 88; strategy of directly attacking apostate regimes, 89; urging Muslim Americans not to vote (2016), 101; and U.S. foreign policy as form of warfare, 148

Islamism: definition of, 25–27, 287n95; "Islam is the solution" as slogan of, 26

Islamism (militant): apocalyptic rhetoric of, 205–6, 207–8, 211–15, 216–18; black flag of, 213; defensive war equated with traditional actions of practicing Islam, 91, 172; definition of, 26, 287n95; duty for jihad equated with traditional actions of practicing Islam, 105; first incidents in the U.S., 84–85; fluidity of affiliations and memberships among, 91–92; Muslim Americans held to be

non-Muslim by, 3, 100, 101, 103–4, 141, 157, 177, 200, 231; number of Americans traveling overseas to participate in, 88; schools of jurisprudence (madhāhib), 94–96, 313n39. See also antisemitism and militant Islamism; Islamic State (Dāʿish); Islamism (militant), American terrorists expressing; Islamism (militant), foundational concepts of; Islamism (militant), literature influencing; lone wolf myth; media entities and outlets, militant Islamist; al-Qaʿida; victimhood narrative and militant Islamists

Islamism (militant), American terrorists expressing: antisemitism and, 146–47; heroic cause as recruitment lure, 88; holistic justice as antidote to, 165–68; identity and community acceptance as factor in involvement in, 108, 228–32, 240–43, 245; Islamophobia as instrumentalized by, 13–15, 155–56, 175, 250, 252–53, 265; Islamophobic rhetoric as help to, 13–15, 175; lack of religious knowledge as factor in choosing violence, 84, 86–87, 140; loss of civil liberties due to threat of, 3–4; manifestos not a tool used by, 235–36; manufacturing of cases by law enforcement agencies, 85; Muslim Americans held to be non-Muslim by, 3; new converts and vulnerability to violent worldview, 84, 86–87; as post-9/11 phenomenon, 4, 84, 250; statistics on fatalities caused by, 6–7, 85; violent attacks by, 83–84, 85–87; warfare to claim the United States as part of the Islamic State as goal of, 4, 155, 200; White nationalists converting to, 125–26; White nationalists using violence of, to validate their Islamophobia, 87–88. See also Crusader-Zionist alliance, militant Islamist conception of

Islamism (militant), foundational concepts of: overview, 93–94, 106–7; al-ʾamr bi-l-maʿrūf wa-n-nahī ʿan al-munkar (enjoining good and forbidding evil), 105–6; the Crusades and colonialism as contexts for, 106–8; farḍ ul-ʿayn (individual duty), 104–5; ḥākimiyyat Allah (nothing is outside the realm of God's sovereignty), 172, 173, 182, 198–99; jāhiliyya (immorality and ignorance), 103–4, 107, 157, 173, 174,

182–83, 198–99; and presentism, avoidance of, 94; *ṭāghūt* or *ṭawāghīt* (idolatry and man-made laws), 98–100; *takfīr* (anathematization), 96–97, 100–103, 157. *See also* Islamism (militant), foundational concepts of, *al-walā' wa-l-barā'* (loyalty and disavowal); jihad; victimhood narrative and militant Islamists

Islamism (militant), foundational concepts of, *al-walā' wa-l-barā'* (loyalty and disavowal): and absolute monotheism vs. polytheism, 97, 98; *dār ul-ḥarb*, 96; *dār ul-Islam*, 96; instrumentalization of, 106, 140–41, 205; as paralleling the trope of White genocide, 157; and separatism from the institutions and societies of non-Muslims, 97–98, 198–99, 231; and *takfīr* (excommunication of Muslims and Islamic institutions), invocation of, 96–97, 157; as term, 96; as victimhood narrative, 107–8; and war on Muslim governments, justification of, 96–97, 98, 157, 172; and war on un-Islamic governments, 96, 97, 157–58. *See also* Islamism (militant), foundational concepts of; jihad

Islamism (militant), literature influencing: *The Bitter Harvest (al-Hisad al-Murr)* (az-Zawahiri), 144; *Book of Monotheism (Kitab at-Tawhid)* (al-Wahhab), 99; *The Call for a Global Islamic Resistance (Da'wat al-Muqawama al-Islamiyya al-'Alamiyya)* (as-Suri), 224; *Clear Evidence of the Disbelief of the Saudi State (al-Kawashif al-Jaliyya fi Kufr ad-Dawla as-Sa'udiyya)* (al-Maqdisi), 98; *The Community of Abraham (Millat Ibrahim)* (al-Maqdisi), 98; "Declaration of War against the Americans Occupying the Land of the Two Holy Places" (Bin Laden), 142; *The Defense of the Muslim Lands: The First Obligation after Faith (ad-Difa 'an Aradi al-Muslimin Aham Furud al-A'yan)* ('Azzam), 91, 104–5; "Establishment of the Islamic State" (video, Islamic State), 211; *Five Tracts of the Martyr Imam Hasan al-Banna (Majmu'at Rasa'il al-Imam ash-Shahid Hasan al-Banna)* (al-Banna), 171; *How to Survive in the West: a Mujahid Guide* (Islamic State (Dā'ish) e-book), 343n33; *The Islamic Concept and Its Characteristics (al-Khasa'is at-Tasawwur al-Islami*

wa-l-Muqawwimatuh) (Qutb), 172; "Kill the Imams of Kufr in the West" (Islamic State (Dā'ish)), 101; "And Make it Known and Clear to Mankind" (speech online) (al-Aulaqi), 175; *The Meaning of Taghut (Ma'ana at-Taghut)* (al-Wahhab), 99; "A Message to the American People" (speech online) (al-Aulaqi), 175, 232; *Milestones (Ma'alim fi-t-Tariq)* (Qutb), 103; "My Life in Jihad" (al-Qa'ida), 154–55; "A Prayer to My God" (al-Khattab), 147; *The Religious and Moral Doctrine of Jihad (as-Siyasat ash-Shar'iyya fi 'Islah ar-Ra'i wa-r-Ra'iyya)* (Ibn Taymiyya), 170–71; *The Slicing Sword* (forward by al-Aulaqi), 235; "The End of Sykes-Picot" (video), 143; *The Neglected Duty (al-Farida al-Gha'iba)* (Faraj), 91, 104; *Towards Understanding Islam* (Mawdudi), 172, 173; *Under the Shade of the Qur'an (Fi Zilal al-Qur'an)* (Qutb), 105; "Why We Hate You and Why We Fight You" (Islamic State), 150; "World Islamic Front Statement Urging Jihad against Jews and Crusaders" (Bin Laden), 142–43. *See also* media entities and outlets, militant Islamist

Islamophobia: and apocalyptic rhetoric of political violence, 210, 211; Black Muslims and, 265; concentration camps threatened by White nationalists, 175; as hallmark of White nationalism, 10; increase in number of hate groups, 282n52; increase in, under Trump administration, 13, 126, 278–79n32, 282n52; and the international rise of nationalism, 261–62; Islamist violence used by White nationalists to justify, 87–88; manifestos espousing, 240–41, 244; Nazi roots of militant Islamism, claim of, 320n59; 9/11 and increase of, 265; rhetoric of, as instrumentalized by both militant Islamists and White nationalists, 13–15, 155–56, 175, 250, 252–53, 265; the shari'a claimed to be totalitarian, 325n19; stereotyping of all Muslim Americans as terrorists, 266; terrorist attacks based on, 39, 124–25, 161–63, 240–42; transnational White nationalism and, 127–28, 240–41, 261; the White ethnostate and, 124–25, 185, 253; White genocide beliefs and, 124–28, 156, 175

Islamophobia, structural: current counterterrorism efforts as engaging in, 252–54,
265–66; definition of, 251; holistic
justice as antidote to, 265–68
ul-Islam, Shaykh. See Ibn Taymiyya, Taqi
ad-Din Ahmad ibn 'Abd al-Halim
Islam vs. the West. See clash of civilizations
narrative
Israel: Arab-Israeli War (1948), 152; bias of
the U.S. toward/American Zionism, 151,
152, 153; as "enemy" in jihad, 170,
173, 174; as jāhiliyya, 157; Mossad, 92;
move of the U.S. embassy to Jerusalem,
14, 123, 140, 151, 209–10, 326n33;
pro-Zionist factions of the U.S. political
far right, 123, 209–10; and right of
return of the Palestinian diaspora, 153;
role of the U.S. in establishing the state
of, 140; settlements on confiscated
Palestinian land, 151, 152; Six-Day War
(1967), 91, 152; statehood of, 152; and
statehood of Palestine, 152. See also
antisemitism
IS. See Islamic State (Dā'ish)
Italy, 324n11

Jabhat, 89
Jabhat an-Nusra. See Hayat Tahrir
ash-Sham
Jabhat Fateh ash-Sham. See Hayat Tahrir
ash-Sham
Jackson, James Harris, 164–65, 230
Jackson, Reverend Jesse, 28
jāhiliyya (immorality and ignorance),
103–4, 107, 157, 173, 174, 182–83,
198–99
al-Jama'at al-Islamiyya (JI, Islamic
Organization), 198
Jama'at at-Tawhid wa-l-Jihad (the
Organization of Monotheism and
Struggle), 92
Japan, 324n11
Japanese Americans, internment during
WWII, 264–65
Jefferson, Thomas, 192, 334n31, 335n46
Jeffress, Pastor Robert, 11, 44
Jerusalem: move of U.S. embassy to, 14,
123, 140, 151, 209–10, 326n33;
restoration of the Jewish Temple in, as
End Times symbol, 123, 209–10
Jesus: antisemitism and beliefs about, 54,
56–57; apocalyptic rhetoric of political
violence and role of, for both White
nationalists and militant Islamists, 207,

213, 215–17; believed to advocate
violence, 166, 167, 215–16, 217, 268;
believed to be a White man (imago dei),
269; believed to require a White
ethnostate, 167; reclaiming Jesus from
White nationalism, 268–70
Jewish Federation, 147
Jewish Occupied Government, 164
Jewish people: as "enemy" in jihad, 170,
174; as "enemy" in RAHOWA, 164,
166, 167, 174; protected by Muslims
during WWII, 268. See also
antisemitism; Holocaust; Israel;
minoritized communities
jihad: beheadings and bombings, justification of, 177–78; and binaries, reduction
of Islamist scholarship to, 106–7; and
Crusader-Zionist alliance, 150, 173,
174, 175–76, 177–79, 326n33; death on
the battlefield as most high, 171;
definition and use of term, 27, 170; the
"enemy," defined, 170, 173, 174–75,
176–77; and fitna, overcoming, 176–77;
and Jesus as warrior, 217; as just and
holy war (jus ad bellum), 170–73, 174;
the Other, defined, 174; proper terms in
lieu of (qitāl or ḥarb), 27, 170–71;
RAHOWA compared to, by Ben
Klassen, 164; selectively chosen and
decontextualized Qur'anic verses and
Islamic thought to justify, 163, 170–71,
172, 175–80, 331n46; transliteration of
term, 31. See also Islamism (militant),
foundational concepts of
al-Jihad al-Islami al-Misri (Egyptian Islamic
Jihad), 90
John Birch Society, 55, 59
Johnson, Corey, 86–87
Johnson, Daryl, 6
Johnson, Greg, Counter-Currents, 233
Johnson, Lyndon B., Kerner Commission,
259–60
Jones, Alex, 122
Jordanian Muslim Brotherhood, 91
Judaism: converts from, as source of
antisemitism in militant Islamism, 146,
147. See also antisemitism
Judeo-Christian lineage. See Abrahamic
tradition
Juergensmeyer, Mark, 21
Jump Out Boys (gang), 70–71
Jung, Carl, 59
justice, American hypocrisy of, 256–57. See
also holistic justice

kafir (rejector of Islam or ingrate), 100
Kahl, Gordon, 75
Kansas Security Force, 126
Keller, Tim, 45
Kennedy, Robert F., 260
Kerner Commission, 259–60
Kerner, Otto, 259
Kessler, Jason, 1
Khan, Samir, 233
al-Khattab, Yousef (aka Joseph Leonard
    Cohen), 146–47; "A Prayer to My
    God," 147
Khorasan, black flags of, 213
al-Khulafa' ur-Rashidun (Rightly Guided
    Caliphs), 195–96, 201, 202, 203
Kingdom Identity Ministries, 211, 333n23
kingdom of God, 169
kingdom of heaven (on earth), 166, 169,
    186, 211
King, Reverend Dr. Martin Luther, Jr., 22,
    260; assassination of, 260; Letter from a
    Birmingham Jail, 259; Poor People's
    Campaign, revival of, 268, 269–70
kinism, 181–82
Kirk, Charlie, 44
Klassen, Ben: and antisemitism, 56, 57, 119,
    191–92; and apocalypse/eschatology,
    rejection of, 206, 207, 208; as atheist,
    191; background of, 55; Christianity,
    opposition to, 56–57; as coining
    RAHOWA, 164; death of, 54; and
    denial of a deity, 55, 62; and Greek and
    Roman mythology, 62; on hierarchical
    leadership vs. lone wolf strategy, 224;
    immigrants of color vilified by, 119;
    invalidation of other religions, 55–56,
    61–62, 125; on Islam, 125; "our race is
    our religion" doctrine, 56, 164, 191;
    racism of, 191–92; title given to himself,
    298n79; and violence, endorsement of,
    56, 62; and the White ethnostate, 119;
    and Whiteness, determination of, 62.
    Works: Building a Whiter and Brighter
    World, 57; Nature's Eternal Religion,
    55, 208; Racial Loyalty, 55; RAHOWA,
    55, 164; Salubrious Living, 55; The
    White Man's Bible, 55, 119, 169, 208.
    See also Creativity
Knights Templar, 240–41
Koresh, David (aka Vernon Howell),
    133–34
Ku Klux Klan (KKK): The Crusader
    (newspaper), 9–10; founding of, 73;
    growth over time of, 52, 73; hoods of,

as symbol of racism, 11; as influence on
    development of White nationalism, 59,
    223, 260–61; Wade Michael Page's
    attempt to join, 40; and religion, 63, 72,
    73; Trump endorsement by, 73, 114;
    and Unite the Right demonstration
    (2017), 2
Kurds, Islamic State (Dā'ish) attacks on,
    89

LaHaye, Tim, 209; Left Behind series, 209
Lane, David: antisemitism of, 192;
    background of, 59; and Cascadia/White
    American Bastion, 162; and Christian
    Identity, 42; as founder of Wotanism,
    40, 42, 58–59, 208–9; and the Founding
    Fathers/Constitution, 192–93;
    immigrants of color vilified by, 118; and
    the lone wolf (Wotan) strategy, 223–24;
    martyrdom narrative and, 223, 244; and
    murder of Alan Berg, 59; and The
    Order, 75, 220; Queerphobia of, 130;
    and violence, endorsement of, 62; White
    Genocide Manifesto, 118, 183–84, 237,
    239; and Whiteness, determination of,
    62; "Wotan Is Coming," 223–24; as
    writer of the Fourteen Words, 40,
    41–42, 53, 118, 239. See also Fourteen
    Words
LaPierre, Wayne, 121, 319n39
Lashkar-e-Taiba (Army of the Pure), 92,
    147
Latinx people: definition and use of term,
    30–31; evangelicals, 43; heterogeneity
    of, 265; manifestos attacking, 344n39;
    racial profiling of, 308n182; surveillance
    and criminalization of, 256; systemic
    racism and, 264–65, 355n45; terrorist
    attacks on, 7, 240, 242–43. See also
    minoritized communities
Latter-day Saints (LDS), Church of Jesus
    Christ of: antigovernment protesters
    and, 46–49, 293–94n29; Book of
    Mormon cited as inspiration by armed
    antigovernment protesters, 46, 47; as
    George W. Bush supporters, 292n18;
    The Nay Book (Nay), 48; as Mitt
    Romney supporters, 292n18; as Trump
    supporters, 292n18; and the U.S.
    Constitution, divinity of, 47–48; White
    Horse Prophecy, 47–48; White
    nationalism, denunciation of, 294n31;
    White nationalists and, 49, 294n31,
    296nn45–46

law enforcement: American militant Islamic terrorism cases manufactured by, 85; Constitutional Sheriffs, 63, 76–77, 308nn182–183; definitions of "lone wolf," 222; long association with White nationalism, 70–71; White nationalist affinity for, 70. *See also* FBI; federal statute criminalizing domestic terrorism, lack of; Ghost Skins

Lazarus, Emma, "The New Colossus," 119–20

leaderless resistance. *See* lone wolf myth

League of the South, 2, 76, 127

Lebanon, 92, 143

Lee, Robert E., 1–2, 12

Legan, Santino William, 120, 121, 148

Le Pen, Marine, 239

Lewis, Bernard, "clash of civilizations," 324n8

LGBTQ+. *See* Queer people

liberals. *See* White liberals

Liberty University, 44

Lightfoot Militia, 49

Lincoln, Bruce, 16–17

Little Rock, Arkansas. *See* Bledsoe, Carlos

Locke, John, 333n18

lone wolf myth: overview, 221, 245; definitions of "lone wolf," 222; leaderless resistance paradigm (White nationalists), 222–25; leaderless resistance paradigm/*nizām, lā tanzīm* (militant Islamists), 224–25; profiles of lone wolves as varying, 246, 340–41n11; and question of whether exposure to content promoting violence compels individual acts, 221–22; Wotan, 223–24

lone wolf myth, and online wolf packs: overview, 221, 245–46; attempts to regulate Internet content, 225, 226, 228, 246; "book clubs," 227–28; and community, belonging to, 228–32, 240–43, 245; martyrdom and, 243–45; offline actions coordinated online, 226–28; seeking narratives online to sanction real-world violence, 230–32, 245; technology involved, 225–26, 228, 232–35, 343n33; transnational White nationalism and, 240–43, 245–46; troll armies, 227. *See also* Internet; manifestos of White nationalists; media entities and outlets; social media

Los Angeles County Sheriff's Department, 70–71

lost tribes of Israel, 51–52, 57, 334n30

Lynk, Michael, 152–53

Macdonald, Andrew (alias of William Pierce), *The Turner Diaries*, 74–75, 83, 237, 239

MacDonald, Kevin, *Occidental Observer*, 233

McDowell, Benjamin T. S., 230, 345n51

McInnes, Gavin, 79

Mack, Richard, 76–77, 308n183

McMahon, Daniel, 128–29

McNallen, Stephen, 59, 270–71; *An Odinist Anthology*, 59, 300n100; "What Would Odin Say about Gun Control?," 122

McVeigh, Timothy (Oklahoma City bombing): overview, 68, 75; Elohim City/Christian Identity links, 75, 307n176; as influence, 125, 126, 162–63; martyrdom narrative about, 75, 244; Ruby Ridge/Waco events as motivating, 132, 135; and The Order, 220; *The Turner Diaries* as influence on, 75, 83, 237, 239

madāris (plural of *madrasa*), Wahhabi Islam and Saudi Arabia and, 95–96

madhāhib, 95. *See also madhhab*

madhhab. *See* Hanafi school; Hanbali school; Maliki school; Shafiʻi school

madrasa. *See madāris* (plural of *madrasa*)

MAGA ("Make America Great Again"), 11, 124, 261, 280n41

Magna Carta (England, 1215), 187

Magnum, Destinee, 161

mainstreaming of White nationalism: Frazier Glenn Miller Senate campaign and, 113–14; the Trump administration and, 120

majority-minority in the U.S., White nationalist anxiety about, 70, 117

Maktab Khadamat al-Mujahidin al-ʻArab (Arab Mujahidin Services Bureau, MAK), 90

Malcolm X. *See* X, Malcolm

Malheur National Wildlife Refuge (Oregon). *See* Bundy, Ammon

Maliki school (*madhhab*), 95

Malik, Tashfeen. *See* Farook, Syed Rizwan and Tashfeen Malik

Mamdani, Mahmood, 287n95

manifestos of White nationalists: American militant Islamists have not written manifestos, 235–36; antisemitic manifestos, 220, 242, 243, 344n39; and the

Fourteen Words, 220, 236–37; as gospel transcending religious and nonreligious affiliations, 236, 240, 243; Islamophobic manifestos, 240–41, 244; martyrdom narrative and, 236; online, as accelerating terrorist actions, 240; racist and anti-immigration manifestos, 219–20, 228–30, 237–40, 241–43, 344n39;· transnational White nationalism and, 236–37, 238–39, 240–42; and the White ethnostate, 236–37. *See also* manifesto authors; White nationalists, literature influencing

manifesto authors: Robert Bowers, 236; Breivik, Anders Behring (aka Fjotolf Hansen aka Andrew Berwick) (*2083: A European Declaration of Independence*), 240–41; Patrick Wood Crusius (*The Inconvenient Truth*), 236, 242–43, 347–48n87; John Earnest (*An Open Letter*), 236, 242; Madison Grant (*The Passing of the Great Race*), 237–38; Adolf Hitler (*Mein Kampf*), 237, 238; James Jackson, 165; David Lane (*White Genocide Manifesto*), 118, 183–84, 237, 239; "Laws for the Lone Wolf" (Metzger), 223; William Pierce (*The Turner Diaries*), 74–75, 83, 237, 239; Jean Raspail (*The Camp of the Saints*), 237, 239; Dylann Roof (*The Last Rhodesian*), 219–20, 228–30, 236, 344n39; Brandon Tarrant (*The Great Replacement*), 240, 241–42, 244

Māori people, 241

al-Maqdisi, Abu Muhammad, 14, 94, 98, 102; *Clear Evidence of the Disbelief of the Saudi State (al-Kawashif al-Jaliyya fi Kufr ad-Dawla as-Sa 'udiyya)*, 98; *The Community of Abraham (Millat Ibrahim)*, 98

Marquez, Enrique, Jr., 84

Marshall, Thurgood, 229

Martin, Trayvon, 28, 228

martyrdom narrative: Arabic term for martyr (*shahīd*), 348n93; conspiracy theories and, 244, 348n89; and dying in battle as most high, 171; killings by the U.S. government and, 232, 233, 243–44; lone wolf myth and, 243–45; manifestos of White nationalists and, 236; recruitment of terrorists and, 243–45

masājid: defined as preferred term instead of "mosques," 84; Wahhabi Islam and Saudi Arabia and, 95–96

al-Masjid an-Nabawi (Prophet's Masjid), 142

Mateen, Omar, 130, 231

Mathews, Robert Jay, 75, 162; "Declaration of War," 114–15. *See also* Order, The

Mawdudi, Abu-l-'ala, 198–99, 202; *Towards Understanding Islam*, 172, 173

Mayflower Compact (Massachusetts, 1620), 187

Mecca, 142

media entities and outlets, militant Islamist: *Amaq News Agency*, 233; *Dabiq*, 101, 150, 201, 214, 233–34, 244–45; *Fursan ar-Rafa*, 233; *Halummu*, 233; *How to Survive in the West: A Mujahid Guide*, 343n33; *Inspire*, 83, 154–55, 233, 234–35; *Invasion Brigades*, 233; *al-Minbar Jihadi Media*, 13–14; *Mutarjim*, 233; *Nashir News*, 233; *One Ummah*, 233; *The Pinnacle (Dhurwat as-Sanam)*, 233; of Revolution Muslim (defunct), 146–47; *Rumiyah*, 201–2, 214, 233–34, 235; *Voice of Hind*, 233; *Voice of Jihad (Sawt al-Jihad)*, 233. *See also* Internet; Islamism (militant), literature influencing; lone wolf myth; lone wolf myth, and online wolf packs; social media

media entities and outlets, White nationalist: *Breitbart.com*, 233, 278n31; *Counter-Currents*, 9–10, 233; *Daily Stormer*, 9–10, 227, 233, 344n39; *InfoWars*, 122; *lastrhodesian.com*, 220; *Occidental Observer*, 233; radio, 44, 49, 74, 122, 187, 225, 303n138, 333n23; *Radix Journal*, 233; *The Right Stuff*, 233; *Scribd*, 241; *Stormfront*, 73, 135, 233, 240, 244; television, 44, 56, 226; of Traditionalist Youth Network, 233. *See also* Internet; lone wolf myth; lone wolf myth, and online wolf packs; manifestos of White nationalists; social media; White nationalists, literature influencing

metagenics (inheritance of tradition and culture), 59, 300n100

methodology of text: achieving empathy through epistemic worldview analysis, 17–19; appendix with a list of terrorist actors, lack of, 22; approaches to understanding language (translation), 31–32; comparative analysis, 16–17; and defamiliarization, 17; distinguishing

methodology of text *(continued)*
violence in the name of religion from
religious violence, 15–16; interviews
with key figures, 17–19; law enforcement officials and, 17, 19; positionality
of the researcher and, 18–19; source
documents, 19; transliteration, 31,
289n108
methodology of text, definitions and
terminology: overview, 19–20; Black,
White, and Brown—capitalization and
differentiation of terms, 28–29;
Indigenous, 30; and Islamic State
(Dāʿish), name of, 27–28; Islamism,
25–27; jihad, 27; Latinx, 30–31;
militant Islamism, 26; militant White
nationalism, 23; the political far right,
22–23; Queer, 29–30; race, 25;
Salafiyya/Salafism, 27; terrorism, 20–22;
White nationalism, 23–25
Metzger, John, 226
Metzger, Tom, 223, 225–26, 228, 244;
"Laws for the Lone Wolf," 223; *Race
and Reason* (public-access TV), 56, 226
Microsoft, 226, 349n98
Middle East: division following World War
I, 143–44, 146, 152, 324n11; and the
exclusionary Immigration Act (1924),
237–38
Military Times, 71
military, U.S.: bases named after Confederate
leaders, 12; militant Islamists lambasting
Muslim Americans for supporting, 175;
Odinism legitimized as religion by, 60,
300n106; statistics on White nationalism
incidents in, 71; veteran recruitment by
right wing extremists, 6, 70. *See also*
Ghost Skins; military, U.S., terrorist
attacks on installations
military, U.S., terrorist attacks on
installations: in Chattanooga, Tennessee,
86; Fort Hood, Texas (Hasan), 137–38,
231, 231–32; Fort Stewart-Hunter Army
Airfield, Georgia (plot), 71; Little Rock
(Arkansas) military recruiting office, 85
militias and paramilitary groups, 2, 63, 69,
113, 204, 210
millenarian Christians, 123, 134, 206
millennialism or millenarianism, 206. *See also*
apocalyptic rhetoric of political violence
Miller, Frazier Glenn, Jr. (aka Frazier Glenn
Cross, Jr.), 113–14, 148; *A White Man
Speaks Out,* 113; "Declaration of War,"
114

Miller, Stephen, 239, 278–79n32,
346–47n76
Mills, Alexander Rud (aka Tasman Forth),
61
Milwaukee, Wisconsin. *See* Page, Wade
Michael
minoritized communities: "activism"
proposed as alternative term for
"terrorism," and criminalization of
political activism by, 20–21; definition
of, 251; holistic justice and amplification
of, 251; Muslim Americans allying with
other groups to enact change for holistic
justice, 251–52, 264–65; normalization
of systemic oppression of, under Trump,
13; potential of conveyor belt theory of
terrorism to be used against, 15;
surveillance of, and potential for federal
statute criminalizing domestic terrorism
to be used against, 7, 22, 246, 256,
351n16; terms for, capitalization and
use of, 28–31. *See also* anti-immigration
(immigrants of color); Black Americans;
Black Lives Matter; disabilities, people
with; Indigenous peoples; Jewish people;
Latinx people; Muslim Americans;
Other, the; people of color; Queer
people; women
misogyny and antifeminism: incels, 80, 128;
intersectionality and, 257; as militant
Islamist ideology, 196; racism as
intersecting with, 128–29; as shared by
White nationalists and militant
Islamists, 4–5; terrorist attacks based
on, 128–29, 227, 321n72; White
genocide beliefs and, 128–29, 131; of
White nationalists, 41, 227; women as
reinforcing, 5, 129. *See also* patriarchal
cisheteronormativity
Mongol/Tatar invasion (of Islamic world),
97, 139, 196
Montesquieu, 199
Moonshot CVE, 349n98
Moore, Russell, 45
Moorish sovereign citizens, 63, 68, 80
Mormons. *See* Latter-Day Saints (LDS)
mosques. *See* masājid
Mt. Rushmore, 12
mud-people, as term, 50, 52–53, 115–16
Muhammad, Abdulhakim Mujahid (aka
Carlos Bledsoe), 85
Muhammad, Prophet: al-Baghdadi's claim
to lineage of, 93, 201; the caliphate
during lifetime of, 195, 203; death of,

94–95, 195; holy sites of, 142; and title of *Inspire* online magazine, 234. *See also* al-Khulafa' ur-Rashidun (Rightly Guided Caliphs); Qur'an; Salafiyya (as-Salaf as-Salihin, "the Pious Predecessors"); sunna

Muhammad, Younes Abdullah, 146

Mujahidin. *See* Maktab Khadamat al-Mujahidin al-'Arab (Arab Mujahidin Services Bureau, MAK)

Mumbai attacks (2008) (Lashkar-e-Taiba, Army of the Pure), 147

munāfiq (hypocrite), 100, 101, 177, 231

murtadd (apostate), 100–101, 157

Muslim Americans: allying with other minoritized groups to enact change for holistic justice, 251–52, 264–65; Black Muslims, 84, 250, 265, 266–67; diversity of, 265, 266; and the early history of the U.S., 84, 250, 266–67; as "enemy" in jihad, 170, 174–75; as "enemy" in RAHOWA, 156, 164, 166, 167, 174; exhorted to carry out violent actions, 274–75; the hijab and, 266; increase of Islamophobic violence against, 13, 278–79n32; as informants to FBI, 175; as military supporters, 175; as "mud people," 115; narrative of being forced into concentration camps, 175; as non-Muslim, 3, 100, 101, 103–4, 141, 157, 177, 200, 231; population of, 266; stereotyped as terrorists, 266; urged not to vote (2016), 101. *See also* counterterrorism; holistic justice; Islamism (militant), American terrorists expressing; minoritized communities

Muslim Brotherhood (al-Ikhwan al-Muslimun), 91, 102, 171, 172

Muslim, Imam, 207

Muslim-majority nations with secular rulers: the Crusader-Zionist alliance as supporting, 141–42, 148, 150, 153, 155, 157, 200; drone strikes creating anti-American and antigovernment sentiment in, 254–55; as "enemy" in jihad, 170, 173, 174, 177; as *jāhiliyya*, 157; militant Islamic justification of war on, 96–97, 98, 102, 103, 144, 199–200

Muslims: defined as term, 26–27; as disagreeing with the methodology of violence, 140; as disagreeing with the misappropriation of religion by terrorists, 81, 163, 327n49, 331n46;

protecting Jews during the Holocaust, 268; Trump's attacks on, 12–13

Myanmar, state-sponsored genocide of the Rohingya, 3, 140, 148, 153, 154

Namkai-Meche, Taliesin Myrddin, 161–62

Napolitano, Janet, 6

Nasar, Mustafa Setmariam (aka Abu Mus'ab as-Suri), *The Call for a Global Islamic Resistance (Da'wat al-Muqawama al-Islamiyya al-'Alamiyya)*, 224

Nasser, Gamal 'Abdel, 144

National Advisory Commission on Civil Disorders, 259–60

National Alliance, 74–75

National Association of Evangelicals, 43, 269

National Defense Authorization Act (2019), 72

nationalism, as equated with patriotism, 261

Nationalist White Party, 55

National Policy Institute, 2, 9, 123, 130, 274n6, 278n31. *See also* Spencer, Richard

national security: the counterterrorism paradigm as undermining, 250, 252–55. *See also* national security, and White nationalism recognized as greater threat than militant Islamism to; U.S. Department of Homeland Security

national security, and White nationalism recognized as greater threat than militant Islamism to: overview, 6–9, 276n16; dismantling and defunding of counterterrorism programs under Obama administration, 6; dismantling and defunding of counterterrorism programs under Trump administration, 8–9; fatality statistics, 6–7, 85; Islamophobia in the name of, 265; Trump affinity for White nationalists and lack of action on, 8–9; White privilege and lack of action on, 7–8

National Socialist Movement, 2, 73, 74

Nation Institute, 6

Nation of Islam, 125

Native Americans. *See* Indigenous peoples

nativism, 261, 268

Nay, Keith Allen, 48; *The Nay Book*, 48

Nazi Germany: antisemitism and, 124; the Bible as used to justify, 190; "blood and soil," 58, 241; eugenics and, 296n47; logo of the Nazi Party, 189; militant

Nazi Germany *(continued)*
  Islamism claimed to have roots in, 146,
  320n59; neo-Nazis and, 73–74;
  Odinism and, 59–60, 74; terrorists referring to, 162. *See also* Hitler, Adolf
Nehlen, Paul, 130–31
neo-Confederates, 2, 63, 67, 76. *See also*
  Council of Conservative Citizens
neo-Nazis: antisemitism and fascist policies
  as focus of, 73–74; and atheism or
  agnosticism, 72–73, 74; logo of, 74,
  189; and religion, 63, 72–73, 74. *See
  also* National Socialist Movement
Nevada. *See* Bundy, Cliven
New Jersey. *See* Rahimi, Ahmad Khan
new right, 79. *See also* White nationalism
New World Order. *See* globalism (White
  nationalist antisemitic conspiracy theory)
New York City: first World Trade Center
  bombing (1993), 84–85. *See also*
  Jackson, James; 9/11 attacks; Rahimi,
  Ahmad Khan; Shahzad, Faisal
New Zealand: Christchurch Call to Action
  Summit (Big Tech), 239n98; first
  terrorism conviction in, 347n80. *See
  also* Tarrant, Brenton
Nichols, Terry, 68
Nietzsche, Friedrich, 59
9/11 attacks: American militant Islamism as
  arising in the wake of, 4, 84, 250; and
  Bush declaration of "crusade" of War
  on Terror, 144–45; increase of
  Islamophobia following, 265; Queer-
  phobia in reaction to, 130; Wahhabi
  Islam and, 96
Nixon, Richard M., 260
Nolen, Alton, 86
Nordic thesis, 237–38
Norse pagan religions. *See* Ásatrúers;
  Odinism; Wotanism
North, Gary, 293n28
Northwest Territorial Imperative, 162
Norway. *See* Breivik, Anders Behring
#Not1MoreDeportation, 256
NRA (National Rifle Association), 121,
  319n39

Oath Keepers, 11, 48, 49, 127
Obama administration: defunding and
  deprioritizing of White nationalist
  counterterrorism programs, 6; and drone
  strikes, 14, 232, 233, 244, 254; and
  Guantánamo prisoners, 154; and U.S.-led
  wars in Iraq and Afghanistan, 14

Obama, Barack Hussein: and myth of a
  post-racial U.S., 260; and rise in White
  nationalist groups, 73, 260; speech stating
  the U.S. is not at war with Islam, 14; on
  terrorism by tax protester, 68; terrorist
  plots against, 71; Trump's conspiracy
  theory of birtherism and, 10, 65
Ocasio-Cortez, Alexandria, 10
Odal rune, 74
Odinism: overview, 58; apocalyptic rhetoric
  of (Ragnarok), 58, 207, 208–9; and
  Aryan global community, 193;
  Christianity, rejection of, 57, 60–61;
  Creativity and invalidation of, 55,
  61–62; the eagle as symbol in, 333n29;
  and the Founding Fathers/Constitution,
  191, 192–93, 335n46; and the Great
  Seal of the U.S., 192, 335n46; growth
  of, 60; hammer of Thor (Mjölnir), 60,
  61, 271; name of, defined as term, 57;
  nonliteral interpretation of texts, 58;
  nonmilitant adherents, organizing
  against racism, 270–71; Poetic Edda
  (Elder Edda) text of, 58, 176, 179,
  208–9, 271, 333n29; Prose Edda,
  208–9; Queer people as accepted in,
  130; the Second Amendment and, 122;
  social forms of worship (e.g. *blots*), 60;
  U.S. military authorization as official
  religion, 60, 300n106; Valhalla and the
  Valkyries, 113, 169–70, 179, 209, 214,
  245; and the Vikings/Vinland, 118, 162,
  169, 193–94, 335n49; and violent
  death, preference for, 169–70, 171. *See
  also* Ásatrúers; Wotanism
Odinist Fellowship, 61
Oklahoma City bombing. *See* McVeigh,
  Timothy
Olympics (1996). *See* Rudolph, Eric
Omar, Ilhan, 10
One World Church, 211
online disinhibition effect, 225
online world. *See* Internet; lone wolf myth;
  lone wolf myth, and online wolf packs;
  media entities and outlets; social media
oppression. *See* anti-oppression; systemic
  oppression
The Order: "88" as symbol for, 220–21;
  founding of, 75; David Lane and, 40;
  Robert Jay Mathews as founder of, 114,
  220; and religion, 75; terrorist acts by
  members of, 40; *The Turner Diaries* as
  inspiring, 74–75, 237; violence
  committed by, 75

Oregon. *See* Bundy, Ammon

O'Reilly, Bill, 10

Orientalism: and "clash of civilizations" narrative, 3, 141, 274n9, 324n8; as extension of colonialism, 274n9; racialized Christendom as reifying, 9; Edward Said, 274n9

Orlando, Florida. *See* Mateen, Omar

Osred, *Odinism: Past, Present and Future*, 192

the Other: empathy and the perspective of, 264; and the international rise of nationalism, 261–62; the Internet and vilification of, 221, 230; jihad and, 174; RAHOWA and, 174

Ottoman Empire: and antisemitism as political tool, 146; the division of, after WWI, 138, 143–44, 146, 324n11; Islamic Caliphate (Ottoman Empire), dissolution of (1920s), 197; pluralism and holistic justice in, 267–68

Page, Wade Michael: as domestic terrorist, 39; as Ghost Skin, 71; as White nationalist, 39–41, 79, 148, 220, 230, 233; and White power music, 40, 162

Pakistan: antisemitic terrorist attacks from, 147; Operation Cyclone (U.S. funded program), 89; and partition of India, 92; support of al-Qa'ida by, 88; and Wahhabi Islam, 96

Palestinian Authority, 89

Palestinian Muslim Brotherhood, 91

Palestinian people: and antisemitism, 146–47; and the Arab-Israeli War (*nakba*) of 1948, 152; and the Crusader-Zionist alliance, 151–53; diaspora of, and the right to return, 153; and division of the Middle East after WWI, 143, 152; humanitarian crisis of, 152–53; Israeli settlements on confiscated land of, 151, 152; and lack of citizenship, 152, 153; and martyrdom narratives, 243; refugees, 152, 153; and the Six-Day War (*naksa*) of 1967, 152; statehood of, international failure to recognize, 151–52; and U.S. bias toward Israel/American Zionism, 151, 152, 153

pan-Arabism, 139

pan-Islamism, 90–91

pantheism, 236

paradise, as denied to Muslim Americans, 103–4

paramilitary groups and militias, 2, 63, 69, 113, 204, 210

Parrott, Matthew, 233

Parwan Detention Facility ("Bagram prison," Afghanistan), 154

Pathway to Victory, 44

patriarchal cisheteronormativity: glorification of, 227; Queer people as countering, 29–30, 128, 131; White nationalists and fear of loss of, 128–29, 136. *See also* misogyny and antifeminism

Patriot, Christian, "Tet Take Two: Eslam's 2016 European Offensive," 126–27

Patriot Front, 65

patriotism: desire for White ethnostate as, 174; nationalism as equated with, 261

Patriot movement (umbrella term), 63, 67. *See also* militias and paramilitary groups; sovereign citizens

Payne, Ryan, 293–94n29

Pelosi, Nancy, 71

Pendergraft, Andrew, 233; *The Andrew Show*, 233

people of color: "activism" proposed as alternative term for "terrorism," and criminalization of political activism by, 20–21; colorism and, 265; and the education framework for intersectional identities, 257; as "enemy" in RAHOWA, 164, 166, 167; increase of hate crimes, harassment, and intimidation since Trump's election, 13; political far right theology of (Black Hebrew Israelism), 63; Queerphobia and, 130–31; reclaiming Jesus from White nationalism, 268–70; as sovereign citizens, 63, 68; specific terms for, capitalization and use of, 28–29; as term, 355n45; Trump's attacks on, 12–13. *See also* anti-immigration (immigrants of color); minoritized communities; racism; systemic racism

Perkins, Tony, 44

Peters, Pete, 184–85, 187, 333n23

phantom cells, 222–23

Pierce, William: Cosmotheism, 54, 55, 56, 237, 298n76; on Creativity, 298–99n82; and the National Alliance, 74, 298–99n82; and RAHOWA, 56; *The Turner Diaries* (alias Andrew Macdonald), 74–75, 83, 237, 239

Pious Predecessors. *See* Salafiyya (as-Salaf as-Salahin)

Pittsburgh, Pennsylvania. *See* Bowers, Robert

Pitts, Demetrius (aka Abdur Raheem Rafeeq and Salah ad-Deen Osama Waleed), 87
Planned Parenthood, 77
pluralism: the caliphate as supporting, 141, 198–99; Islam and, 267–68; the Qur'an and, 267; religion and, 141–42, 263; White nationalist rejection of, 181, 182
police. *See* law enforcement
political correctness, 107, 131, 167, 182
political far left: as antigovernment activists, 301n124; tax protesters, 68
political far right: antisemitism as virulent throughout, 123; and Christianity upheld as encompassing Whiteness, 9; definition of, 22–23; incels, 80, 128; international rise of, 261–62; people of color and theology, 63; people of color as sovereign citizens, 63, 68; pro-Zionist factions of, 123, 209–10; and racial identities derived from White nationalist discourse, 9. *See also* American White evangelicalism; antigovernment activism; anti-immigration (immigrants of color); gun control issue; White nationalism
polygenism, 50–51, 52–54, 56–57, 115–16, 124, 145, 185, 187
Portland, Oregon: White homeland proposed for, 162. *See also* Christian, Jeremiah Joseph
Posse Comitatus, 53, 73, 75, 77
poverty: among White people, and racism, 262; intersectionality and, 257; systemic racism and, 355n45; and White nationalist victimhood narratives, 262
Poway, California. *See* Earnest, John
Praetorian Guard, 48
preppers, 63, 301n124
Pressley, Ayanna, 10
prisons, Wotanism and proselytization in, 61
Project Dox Tranny Storyline, 131
Proud Boys, 2, 79–80, 127
public-access television, *Race and Reason* (Metzger), 56, 226
Pulse shootings. *See* Mateen, Omar

al-Qa'ida: overview, 87–88; American weapons given to, 90; antisemitism and, 146–47; apocalyptic rhetoric of political violence, 213; black flag of, 213; and the caliphate, need to establish, 102; deterritorialization of Islamic State and resurgence of, 93; and DIY bomb instructions, 83; funding for, 90; and Guantánamo detention center as symbol of oppression, 154–55; *Inspire* magazine, 83, 154–55, 233, 234–35; and the lone wolf concept, 224; origins of, 89–92; rebuke of Islamic State (Dā'ish) for indiscriminate use of violence, 89; state actors in support of, 88; strategy of targeting the U.S. to force its withdrawal of support from secular Muslim-majority governments, 89, 102; and territory, need for, 200–201; and U.S. foreign policy as form of warfare, 148
QAnon, 66–67, 225, 303n136
qitāl, as term in lieu of jihad, 27, 170–71
Queer people: and definition and use of "Queer" as term, 29–30; doxing and harassment of, 131; drag queen story hour programs, 131; as "enemy" in RAHOWA, 164, 167, 174; gender fluidity, Ásatrú religion and, 271; globalism conspiracy theory and Queerphobia, 130; increase of hate crimes, harassment, and intimidation since Trump's election, 13; limited acceptance by White nationalists, 129, 130; as "mud people," 115; Queerphobia, 129–31, 257; rights of, Constitutional Sheriffs as aligned against, 77; terrorist attacks on, 130–31, 231; as threat to patriarchal cisheteronormativity, 29–30, 128, 131; transgender community and Queerphobia, 130–31; Trump's attacks on, 12–13; White ethnostate beliefs and, 185; White genocide beliefs and, 129–31. *See also* minoritized communities
Qur'an: and the Abrahamic/Judeo-Christian lineage, 267; antisemitism and, 146, 147, 325n24; apocalyptic rhetoric and, 207, 212, 216–17; Arabic as language of, 156; and the caliphate, 196, 199; desecrations of, at Gitmo, 154; enslaved Black Muslims and, 266; the Founding Fathers and, 267; on freedom of religion, 267; infallibility of, 193–94, 203; "In God we trust," 195; on Jewish people as People of the Book, 146; jihad as justified through selectively choosing and decontextualizing verses of, 163, 170–71, 172, 175–80, 331n46; orthodox Islam and belief in, 176; and pluralism, 267; on race as illusory, 267;

and reclaiming Jesus from White
nationalism, 270; and *ṭāghūt*, 99; and
takfīr, 101–2; and title of *Inspire* online
magazine, 234; translation used in text,
31–32; the U.S. Constitution and
similarities in, 267

Qutb, Sayyid: ʿAzzam and, 91; "clash of
civilizations" trope attributed to, 199;
on the Crusade as ongoing and the need
for the caliphate, 139–40, 141, 147; and
the dissolution of the Islamic Caliphate
(1920s), 197; *The Islamic Concept and
Its Characteristics (al-Khaṣaʾis
at-Tasawwur al-Islami wa-l-Muqawwimatuh)*, 172; on *jāhiliyya*, 103,
106–7; and jihad, 171, 172–73, 174,
199–200; martyrdom narrative and,
172, 244; Mawdudi as influence on,
199; *Milestones (Maʿālim fi-t-Tariq)*,
103, 172; on Muslim Americans as
apostates, 99–100; *Under the Shade of
the Qurʾan (Fi Zilal al-Qurʾan)*, 105;
az-Zawahiri and, 91

race: the capitalization of "Black" and
"White" as highlighting the artificiality
of, 29; as construct, 25, 29, 257, 263,
267; the Qurʾan on, as illusory, 267;
White nationalist use of the term as
default use in this text, 25
race realist, as term, 79
race war. *See* RAHOWA (racial holy war)
racial consciousness, 229, 258
racism: alternative terms for, as normalization of, 79; the alt-right and normalization of, 79, 80; Big Tech and complicity
in, 246; Black Muslims and, 265;
Christian movement to reclaim Jesus
from White nationalism, 268–70;
citizenship reserved for Whites, 186–87;
colorblindness, 258, 261; as "God's
will," 229; and government anti-poverty
programs, beliefs about, 117; harassment by troll army based on, 227; and
the international rise of the political far
right, 261–62; MAGA red hats as
symbol of, 11; manifestos espousing,
219–20, 228–30, 237–40, 241–43,
344n39; misogyny and antifeminism
intersecting with, 128–29; neo-Confederates and calls for secession, 76;
polygenism theory, 50–51, 52–54,
56–57, 115–16, 124, 145, 185, 187;
poverty among White people and, 262;

racial awareness of White nationalists,
229; "reverse racism" claims, 71,
262–63; terrorist attacks based on, 86,
161–63, 164–65, 219–21, 236, 242–43;
Trump's overt and covert displays of,
10–13, 41, 279–80nn40–41,
281nn43,45; the White ethnostate and,
186–87; as White nationalist narrative,
41. *See also* anti-immigration (immigrants of color); eugenics; RAHOWA
(racial holy war); systemic racism; White
nationalism
radicalism, as term, 21
radio, White nationalist, 44, 49, 74, 122,
187, 225, 303n138, 333n23
Rafeeq, Abdur Raheem. *See* Pitts, Demetrius
Rahimi, Ahmad Khan, 86
RAHOWA (racial holy war): overview,
163–64; apocalyptic rhetoric of, 209,
210–11; and the Bible, selective readings
of, 163, 166–69, 176, 179; calls for,
114–15; coded language for, 11;
Creativity religion as originators of, 54,
56; the death penalty and, 167–68;
defined as term, 163, 164; the "enemy,"
defined, 164, 166, 167–68, 174; the
Fourteen Words as battle cry of, 163,
164, 165, 173, 179, 205, 239;
interpretation of, as varying within
White nationalist groups, 165–66; and
Jesus as warrior, 217; jihad compared to,
164; neo-Confederates and, 76; the
Other and, 174; and race traitors, 239;
terrorists as justifying actions via, 39,
164–65; transnational White nationalism
and, 243; *The Turner Diaries* (William
Pierce, alias Andrew Macdonald) as
laying groundwork for, 239; violence as
pious deed necessary to defend the White
race, 164, 165–66, 166–70, 208, 220;
the White ethnostate and, 173
Ramadan, founding of Islamic State
(Dāʿish) during, 313n35
Rand, Howard, 51, 52
Rapture, 205, 209, 210. *See also* apocalyptic rhetoric of political violence
Raspail, Jean, *The Camp of the Saints*, 237,
239
Ravensblood Kindred, 72
Rawles (James Wesley, Rawles), 67, 162
Reagan, Ronald: Afghanistan policy
(Operation Cyclone), 89; and evangeli-
cals, 45; Year of the Bible (1983),
331–32n6

Reclaiming Jesus movement, 268–69, 270
Reconstructionism, Christian, 46, 123,
    185–86, 189–90, 293n28
Redbeard, Ragnar, *Might is Right,* 120–21,
    128
Red Letter Christian movement, 292–93n22
Reeves, Cory, 72
Regulators (gang), 70–71
relationships, interracial (miscegenation),
    118, 119, 185, 237, 239
religion: and the Arabic word "dīn," 16;
    decline of institutionalized religion in
    the U.S., 60; as exploited to justify/
    sanctify violence, 15–16, 26, 81;
    interfaith empathy, cultivation of, 257,
    264–72; the majority of adherents as
    appalled at misappropriation by
    terrorists, 81; pantheism, 236;
    pluralism, 141–42, 263; and the secular,
    as Western/European construct, 16;
    sparse knowledge of, as factor in
    individual choosing acts of violence, 15,
    84, 86–87, 106, 140, 174. *See also*
    American White evangelicalism; atheists
    and agnostics and the political far right;
    Christianity and Christians; evangelicals;
    Islam; Latter-day Saints (LDS), Church
    of Jesus Christ of; secularism and the
    secular; White nationalist religions
Republican Party, as plutocratic populists,
    316–17n13
"reverse racism" claims, 71, 262–63
Revolution Muslim, 146–47
Rhodesia (Zimbabwe), 220
Rida, Muhammad Rashid, 197
right wing. *See* political far right
Robertson, Pat, 123
Rockwell, George, 60
Roeder, Scott, 78
Rohingya Muslims (Myanmar), 3, 140,
    148, 153, 154
Rohr, Richard, 269
Rome (militant Islamist shorthand for the
    U.S.), 214
Rome, White nationalism harking back to
    ancient, 119, 208
Romney, Mitt, 47, 292n18
Roof, Dylann Storm, 181, 219–21, 228–30;
    as influence, 230, 240, 241, 242; *The
    Last Rhodesian* (manifesto), 219–20,
    228–30, 236, 344n39
Rousseau, Jean-Jacques, 199
Rousseau, Thomas, 65
Roy, Olivier, 26

Ruby Ridge (Idaho) standoff and shootout,
    132–33, 135, 151, 243
Rudolph, Eric, 78
Rushdoony, Rousas John, 293n28
Rushton, Edwin, 47
Russia, and division of the Middle East
    after WWI, 143
Russian Imperial Movement, 8
Ryan, Paul, 131

as-Sadat, Anwar, 144; assassination of, 91
Sagebrush Rebellion (1970s–80s), 68
Said, Edward, *Orientalism,* 274n9
as-Salaf as-Salahin. *See* Salafiyya (as-Salaf
    as-Salahin)
Salafi Islam, 98
Salafiyya (as-Salaf as-Salahin, "the Pious
    Predecessors"): definition of, 27;
    militant Islamists co-opting and
    exploiting connotations of, 27
San Bernardino, California. *See* Farook,
    Syed Rizwan and Tashfeen Malik
Sandy Hook Elementary School (Sandy
    Hook, Connecticut), 122
Saudi Arabia: and funding for al-Qaʻida,
    90; government viewed as apostate by
    militant Islamists, 144; and militant
    Islamism, support for, 88; and 9/11
    attacks, 96; and Wahhabi Islam, 95–96,
    97, 106
Schaeffer, Francis August, 77; "A Christian
    Manifesto," 77
Schiff, Adam, 351n15
Seattle, Washington. *See* Haq, Naveed
Second Amendment. *See* gun control issue
secularism and the secular: as antithetical to
    Islam's teachings for heads of state, 103;
    Christian rejection of, 46, 189–91,
    194–95, 334n39; Crusader-Zionist
    alliance (militant Islamist conception)
    and intention to replace Islam with,
    139–40, 144, 156–58; definition of, 16;
    Dominionism and rejection of, 194–95;
    militant Islamism and intention to
    replace, 156–57, 327n49; Muslim
    reformists and, 196; non–Western
    European cultures not understanding
    religion in terms of, 16. *See also*
    caliphate; Muslim-majority nations with
    secular rulers; religion; White ethnostate
separation of church and state. *See*
    secularism and the secular
Serbia, 325–26n27
Sessions, Jeff, 1, 190, 334n39

ash-Shabab (the Youth), 83
el-Shabazz, el-Hajj Malik. *See* X, Malcolm
ash-Shafi'i, Imam Muhammad Idris, 95
Shafi'i school (*madhhab*), 95
Shahzad, Faisal, 149, 150, 231
ash-Sham, 212
shari'a: overview, 93–94; anti-shari'a
   legislation, 127, 320n59; Islamophobic
   claims of totalitarianism of, 325n19;
   March against Sharia rallies, 127. *See
   also* Qur'an; sunna
Shea, Matthew, 48–49, 296n45–46; "The
   Biblical Basis of War," 49
Shi'i Muslims: and the caliphate, 196;
   Islamic State (Dā'ish) attacks on, 89;
   school of jurisprudence, 313n39;
   Wahhabi Islam and destruction of, 97
Sikhs, 39, 266, 300n106
skinhead subculture, 40, 78–79
Skousen, W. Cleon, 308n183
Smith, Jonathan Z., 17
Smith, Joseph, 47
SNAP (Supplemental Nutrition Assistance
   Program), 117
Social Darwinism, 120–21
social media: 4chan, 66, 225, 242; 8chan,
   236, 242, 347–48n87; 8chan's /pol/ and
   k/, 225; 8kun, 225; BCM (Because
   Communication Matters), 225; Dawn,
   225; Discord, 128, 225; Facebook, 83,
   220, 225, 226, 230, 244, 349n98;
   Facebook livestreaming of terrorist
   attacks, 241, 246; Gab, 123, 124, 128,
   225, 236, 242; GodTube, 211; hashtags
   (#WhiteGenocide, #SpeakFreely), 225;
   Instagram, 120, 121, 225; Pepe the
   Frog, 24, 225; Riot, 225; RocketChat,
   225; Telegram, 131, 225, 244; Twitter,
   24, 123, 129, 225, 226, 321n72;
   Twitter, Donald Trump and, 11, 24,
   79–80, 279–80nn37,40–41,
   281nn43,45, 285–86n86, 302n133,
   303n136, 309n198; Viber, 225;
   WhatsApp, 225; Yahoo Together, 225;
   YouTube, 225, 226, 233, 345n59. *See
   also* Internet; lone wolf myth; lone wolf
   myth, and online wolf packs; media
   entities and outlets; social media, Reddit
social media, Reddit: AMA ("Ask Me
   Anything"), 130; r/Braincels, 128; r/
   Europe, 225; r/MGTOW, 128; r/New
   Right, 225; r/The_Donald, 225
Soldiers of Odin, 127
Somalia, 83, 214

South Africa, apartheid, 190, 220
South Park (TV show), 146
South Poverty Law Center (SPLC), 276n16
sovereign citizens: as antigovernment
   adherents, 19, 23, 63, 68–69, 80; people
   of color as significant number of, 63, 68
Soviet Union, Afghanistan invasion by,
   89–90, 91
Spain, pluralism in medieval, 267–68
Spencer, Richard: *alt-right* coined as term
   by, 2; and antisemitism, 123, 227; as
   identitarian, 79; and the National Policy
   Institute, 2, 9, 123, 130, 274n6,
   278n31; and Nick Fuentes, 24; and
   Queer people, acceptance of, 130; *Radix
   Journal*, 233; and Dylann Roof, support
   for, 230; as Trump supporter, 9; and
   Unite the Right demonstration, 2, 273n1
Spencer, Sherry, 227
Stack, Joseph, 68–69
Standing Rock activists, 22
state laws: anti-shari'a legislation ("American Laws for American Courts"), 127;
   systemic racism enforced by, 264–65
stereotype threat, 254
structural oppression. *See* systemic
   oppression; systemic racism
Stubba, "The Menace of the Mullahs," 125
Sufism, 97
sunna: overview, 94; apocalyptic rhetoric
   and, 207–8, 212–13, 214, 217; and the
   caliphate, 196, 201; disruption of unity
   of the Muslims, 201, 337n75; and "in
   God we trust" phrase, 195; jihad as
   justified via, 178–79; questioning of, as
   rendering one an apostate, 108; and the
   U.S. Constitution, similarities with, 267
Sunni Muslims: aggrieved by division of the
   Middle East after WWI, 143–44; the
   multitude of voices on the nature of the
   caliphate, 196; persecution of, through
   systemic ethnoreligious discrimination,
   generally, 140; schools of jurisprudence
   of, 94–97. *See also* caliphate, territory
   and; Salafiyya (as-Salaf as-Salahin, "the
   Pious Predecessors")
as-Suri, Abu Mus'ab (aka Mustafa
   Setmariam Nasar), *The Call for a
   Global Islamic Resistance (Da'wat
   al-Muqawama al-Islamiyya
   al-'Alamiyya)*, 224
survivalism and survivalists, 63, 77, 162,
   210, 301n124
Survivors of the Abortion Holocaust, 77

Swift, Wesley, 51, 52–53; *God, Man, Nations, and the Races,* 53

Sykes, Mark, 143

Sykes-Picot Agreement (1916), 143–44, 146, 152, 324n11

Syria: civil war, 148, 154; and division of the Middle East after WWI, 143; government viewed as apostate by militant Islamists, 144

systemic oppression, 251, 256–57; Christianity used to justify, 46, 268–69; Whiteness and power in, 258, 263. *See also* holistic justice; minoritized communities; systemic racism

systemic racism: and acts of terrorism, prosecution of, 20; Black Lives Movement as protesting, 228; civil rights movement and, 259–60; distinct struggles of each community of color with, 264–65, 355n45; global demonstrations against, 12; health outcomes and, 355n45; holistic justice and expansion of framework of, 257; the Kerner Report on, 259–60; laws enforcing, 264–65; life expectancy and, 355n45; Barack Hussein Obama and, 260; poverty and economic discrimination and, 355n45; and terrorism as term applying to Muslims but not White nationalists, 20; Donald Trump and, 260–62; White allies and interest convergence theory, 258–60; White liberals leveraging White privilege to combat, 251–52, 258–63; White people cannot be the subjects of, by definition, 263

ṭāghūt or *ṭawāghīt* (idolatry, forces of disbelief, powers of evil), 98–100

takfīr (anathematization), 96–97, 100–103, 157

Taliban, 96

Tarrant, Brenton: and calls to account of Big Tech, 349n98; *The Great Replacement,* 240, 241–42, 244; as influence, 240, 242; martyrdom narrative and, 244; prison sentence of, 347n80; terrorist attack by, 240–42

tattoos, as White nationalist symbol, 40, 71, 79

tax protesters, 68, 303n140; terrorist incidents by, 68–69

television, White nationalist, 44, 56, 226

territory. *See* caliphate, territory and; White ethnostate

terrorism: definition of, 20–22, 283n71; systemic racism and assumption that the term applies to Muslims but not White nationalists, 20. *See also* counterterrorism; federal statute criminalizing domestic terrorism, lack of; holistic justice; Islamism (militant); lone wolf myth; White nationalism

Teutonic legend, Cosmotheism and, 298n76

Texas State Militia, 127

Theoharis, Liz, 269–70

Three Percenters, 49, 68

Tlaib, Rashida, 10

Tolimir, Zdravko, 325–26n27

Tometi, Opal, 28

Torah, orthodox Islamic view of, 176, 267

Traditionalist Worker Party, 2

Traditionalist Youth Network, 130, 233

Transjordan, and division of the Middle East after WWI, 143

transliteration in the text, 31, 289n108

transnational White nationalism: and the Fourteen Words, 236–37, 240; Ghost Skins, 304n149; Islamophobia, 127–28, 240–41, 261; manifestos and, 236–37, 238–39, 240–42; and need for a federal statute criminalizing domestic terrorism, 256; numerological symbols in, 189; racism and anti-immigration, 241–42, 261; RAHOWA and, 243; rise of the political far right, 261–62; and the White ethnostate, 236–37, 241–42; and White genocide beliefs, 261

Tree of Life Synagogue (PA). *See* Bowers, Robert

Triangle Center on Terrorism and Homeland Security, 7

troll armies, 227–28

the Troth, 271

Trump administration: anti-immigration policies of, 120, 190–91, 239, 334n4, 346–47n76; antisemitism as increasing under, 13, 153, 281n50; defunding and deprioritizing of White nationalist counterterrorism programs, 8–9; Evangelical Advisory Board, 44; Faith and Opportunity Initiative, 44; and the Fourteen Words, allusion to, 120; Islamophobic attacks on Muslims as increasing during, 278–79n32; moving the U.S. embassy in Israel to Jerusalem, 14, 123, 140, 151, 209–10, 326n33; Palestinian aid cancelled by, 153; Presidential Social Media Summit

(2019) for the political far right, 261; separation of immigrant families by, 190–91, 334n39; White House Faith Initiative, 44

Trump, Donald: advisors who are White nationalists, 239, 278nn31–32, 346–47n76; affinity for racist and exclusionary worldviews of White nationalist groups, 8–9, 24, 260–62, 268, 285n86; antigovernment activism and, 131; attacks on Black Lives Matter, 11, 279–80n40; birtherism attacks by, 10, 65; Christian consternation with rhetoric and policies of, 268; citing Raspail's *The Camp of the Saints*, 239; covert and overt racism displayed by, 10–13, 41, 279–80nn40–41, 281nn43,45; COVID-19 pandemic and, 65; decried by White nationalists as not doing enough, 124; and "Deep State," normalization of fears of, 13, 65, 302n133; economic anxiety and election of, 116; election campaign of 2016, 65, 73, 126, 260–61; election campaign of 2020, 12, 65, 281n45; election hailed by White nationalists, 9–10; endorsements by White nationalists, 73, 114; evangelicals not supporting, 45; evangelicals supporting, 43, 44–45, 292n18; globalist (antisemitic conspiracy theory) references by, 65; impeachment of, 11, 45, 281n43; Islamophobia as increasing under, 278–79n32; Islamophobic rhetoric of, seen as ammunition by both militant Islamists and White nationalists, 13–15, 145; MAGA ("Make America Great Again"), 11, 124, 261, 280n41; Mount Rushmore speech (2020), 12; and normalization of conspiracy theories, 9, 65, 66–67, 285n86, 302n133, 303n136; and normalization of White nationalism, 9, 10, 12–13, 120, 262; pardons issued by, 47, 308n182; and QAnon, 66–67, 303n136; systemic racism brought into stark relief under, 260–62; terrorist threats against, 87; and Unite the Right demonstration (2017), support for, 12, 79–80, 230; White genocide believed to be prevented by, 12–13

Tsarnaev, Dzhokhar, 149–50, 231, 235, 236, 346n68

Tsarnaev, Tamerlan, 149–50, 213, 231, 235

Turning Point USA, 44

two-seed theory (polygenism), 51, 54, 115–16, 124, 145, 185

Uighur people, 140, 153

umma (global community of Muslims), 3

Unicorn Riot, 72

United Nations: and Palestine, 151–52, 153; U.S. suspending funding for, 152

United States: Great Seal of, 188–89, 192, 333n29, 334n31, 335n46; Immigration Act (1924) as influenced by eugenics, 237–38; justice, hypocrisy of, 256–57; motto of ("In God we trust"), 195; Muslim Americans and the early history of, 84, 250, 266–67; al-Qaʿida and strategy of attacks on, 89, 102; and Whiteness as the identity marker of power, 249–50, 257; as Whore of Babylon, 99, 210. *See also* counterterrorism; Crusader-Zionist alliance, militant Islamist conception of; federal statute criminalizing domestic terrorism, lack of; government anti-poverty programs; Islamism (militant), American terrorists expressing; military, U.S.; national security; secularism and the secular; United States foreign policy, militant Islamist anger about; United States–led wars in Muslim–majority nations, militant Islamist anger about; U.S. constitution; White ethnostate; White nationalism; *headings beginning with* U.S.

United States foreign policy, militant Islamist anger about: overview, 3; and the Crusader-Zionist alliance, 140, 141–42, 148–50, 151–55, 325–26nn27,33; as motivation for American terrorists, 84, 85, 86, 138, 148–50, 254, 255

United States–led wars in Muslim-majority nations, militant Islamist anger about: overview, 3; civilian casualties and, 3, 85, 86, 148–49, 150, 153, 254–55; and the Crusader-Zionist alliance, 140, 148, 150, 153; incidents of terrorism based on, 85–87, 137–38, 148–50; and Muslim American support for, 175

Unite the Right demonstration (2017, Charlottesville, Virginia), 1–2, 65, 68, 273n1; groups participating in, 2, 65, 68, 71, 72, 79, 305–6n157; the Internet and coordination of, 226–27; killing of Heather Heyer by attendee James Alex Fields Jr., 1, 305–6n157; motivations for, 1–2; Trump's support for, 12, 79–80, 230

Unity and Security for America, 1
USA PATRIOT Act (2001), 20, 283n71
U.S. Bureau of Alcohol, Tobacco, and
    Firearms (ATF), 132, 133
U.S. Congress: deprioritizing military
    screening of White nationalists, 72; and
    Guantánamo Bay detention center, 154;
    proposed Confronting the Threat of
    Domestic Terrorism Act, 351n15;
    protesting surveillance of Black Lives
    Matter, 351n16
U.S. Constitution: Osama bin Laden on
    Muslims abiding by, 142; the Fourteen
    Amendment as insufficient to grant
    racial equality, 259; and the Qur'an,
    similarities with, 267; and reclaiming
    Jesus from White nationalism, 270;
    systemic oppression embedded within,
    251, 256–57; "We the People," 256–57,
    264. See also U.S. Constitution and the
    political far right; U.S. Constitution, as
    divine
U.S. Constitution and the political far right:
    Constitutional Sheriffs and, 76–77,
    308n183; excised of all amendments
    except the Bill of Rights, 167, 186–87;
    Fifteenth Amendment, 186; Fourteenth
    Amendment, 186, 187; neo-Confeder-
    ates and, 76; Nineteenth Amendment,
    186; Patriot movement and, 67; Ragnar
    Redbeard's attack on, 121; Thirteenth
    Amendment, 186; the White ethnostate
    and, 167, 182, 187–93, 333n29,
    334nn30–31. See also Founding Fathers
U.S. Constitution, as divine: and the Church
    of Jesus Christ of Latter-day Saints,
    47–48; and gun control issue, 121–22;
    and the White ethnostate, 184, 186–89,
    202, 331–32n6; and White nationalist
    religions, 182, 187–89, 202, 333n29,
    334nn30–31
U.S. Department of Homeland Security
    (DHS): the Fourteen Words, allusion to,
    120; Homeland Environment Threat
    Analysis Division, Extremism and
    Radicalization Branch, dismantling of,
    6; "lone offender" defined by, 222;
    Office of Community Partnerships/
    Office of Terrorism Prevention
    Partnerships defunded under Trump, 8;
    Office of Intelligence and Assessment,
    report on militant White nationalism as
    more perilous threat than militant Islam-
    ism (2009), 6; surveillance of Black
    Lives Matter movement by, 351n16;
    White nationalist tracking defunded and
    dismantled under Obama administra-
    tion, 6; White nationalist tracking
    defunded and dismantled under Trump
    administration, 8–9
U.S. Department of Veteran Affairs (VA), 60
U.S. Government Accountability Office
    (GAO), fatality statistics from domestic
    violent extremists, 6–7
U.S. Marshals Service (USMS), 132
U.S. Supreme Court: Brown v. Board of
    Education, school desegregation, 73,
    229; Cutter v. Wilkinson, nontraditional
    faiths in prisons, 61; limited rights of
    Guantánamo detention center prisoners,
    154; Muslim travel ban upheld by, 14;
    Plessy v. Ferguson, "separate but
    equal," 296n47; Roe v. Wade, abortion
    right, 77

Valhalla and the Valkyries, 113, 169–70,
    179, 209, 214, 245
Vanguard America, 2, 65, 71, 305–6n157
Vespucci, Amerigo, 193
victimhood narratives: as factor in choice to
    commit violence, 15; the Internet and
    amplification of, 221; as shared, 249
victimhood narrative and militant Islamists:
    overview, 3, 5, 155, 183; apocalyptic
    rhetoric and, 205, 212, 213–14, 217;
    and the Crusader-Zionist alliance, 143;
    as foundational to beliefs, 107–8; and
    jihad, escalation of, 105; as juxtaposed
    with narrative of imminent global
    conquest, 106
victimhood narrative and White national-
    ists: overview, 1–2, 5, 155, 183;
    apocalyptic rhetoric and, 205, 217; and
    election of Trump, 9; as foundational to
    beliefs, 107; the Fourteen Words and,
    136; holistic justice and alteration of,
    262–63; MAGA slogan and, 11; as
    self-defense of terrorism, 163; White
    genocide as, 107, 114–15; and White
    power vs. White nationalism as terms,
    25. See also White genocide
Vietnam, 140
Viking Brotherhood, 122
Vikings (gang), 70–71
Vikings: "The Shieldwall" (2017), 271;
    Wotanism/Odinism and Vinland (U.S.),
    118, 162, 169, 193–94, 335n49
Vinland. See Vikings

violence: anti-immigration, terrorist attacks based on, 7, 120–21, 240, 242–43; antisemitism, terrorist acts based on, 85, 113–14, 123–24, 147, 162, 163, 236, 242, 243; "civil war" code language as reference to, 11–12; factors leading to individual expression of, 15; Islamophobia, terrorist attacks based on, 39, 124–25, 161–63, 240–42; Jesus Christ believed to advocate, 166, 167, 215–16, 217, 268; Latinx people, terrorist attacks on, 7, 240, 242–43; mental illness used as defense of, 221; misogyny, terrorist attacks based on, 128–29, 227, 321n72; predisposition to, and seeking out narratives to justify, 75, 87; Queer people, terrorist attacks on, 130–31, 231; racism, terrorist attacks based on, 86, 161–63, 164–65, 219–21, 236, 242–43; religion exploited to justify, 15–16, 26, 81; religion, lack of knowledge/literacy as factor in individual choosing acts of, 15, 84, 86–87, 106, 140, 174; toward women, as linked with other types of violence, 4, 5. See also apocalyptic rhetoric of political violence; misogyny and antifeminism; terrorism

Voltaire, 199

Waco (Texas) siege, 132, 133–35, 151, 243

Wahhabi Islam: and the destruction of images in the Islamic world, 96; establishment of, 95–96; Hanbali school and, 95; and militant Islamist interpretations of Islam, 140; purity and, 97, 98, 102, 199–200; Muhammad Rashid Rida and endorsement of, 197; separatism and, 97–98

al-Wahhab, Muhammad ibn 'Abd, 97–98, 102; Book of Monotheism (Kitab at-Tawhid), 99; legacy of, as disproportionately revered among militant Islamists, 94, 95, 106; The Meaning of Taghut (Ma'ana at-Taghut), 99

al-walā' wa-l-barā'. See Islamism (militant), foundational concepts of, al-walā' wa-l-barā' (loyalty and disavowal)

Waleed, Salah ad-Deen Osama. See Pitts, Demetrius

Wallis, Jim, Reclaiming Jesus: A Confession of Faith in a Time of Crisis, 269

Washington, George, 187–88

Washitaw Nation, 63, 80

Watkins, Patrick, 347–48n87

Weaver, Elisheba, 133

Weaver, Pastor John, 181–82

Weaver, Rachel, 133

Weaver, Randy, 132–33, 135

Weaver, Sammy, 132, 133

Weaver, Sara, 132, 133

Weaver, Vicki, 132–33, 135

Weland, Michael, 133

welfare. See government anti-poverty programs

Whiskey Rebellion (1794), 68

White (people), capitalization and use of term, 29

White American Bastion, 162

White Americans: declining birth rates of, 115, 128; economic anxiety and, 117; White nationalists as exploiting fragility and anxiety of, 116. See also White liberals; Whiteness; White privilege

White Aryan Resistance (WAR), 56, 223, 226

White Citizens' Councils, 229

White ethnostate: overview, 2, 4, 183–84, 193; antisemitism and, 185, 186; biblical law and, 173, 182, 185–86, 189–91, 334n39; biblical prophecies and, 184–85; Christian Identity and, 62, 118–19, 182, 184–87, 198; Creativity and, 62, 119, 182, 208; and the divinity of the U.S. Constitution, 184, 186–89, 202, 331–32n6; as fending off globalism (antisemitic conspiracy theory), 185, 192; Founding Fathers believed to have intended, 165–66, 181–82, 202; the Fourteen Words and, 62, 181–82, 183, 236–37, 239; Islamophobia and, 124–25, 185, 253; Jesus believed to require, 167; and "life, liberty, and property," 186, 333n18; manifestos and, 236–37; as New Jerusalem, 184–85, 198, 202–3, 215, 217; racist religions as all emphasizing, 62; transnational White nationalism and, 236–37, 241–42; violence/militancy as foundational to, 62, 185, 202–3, 226; White nationalist evangelicalism and, 44, 185–86; Wotanism and, 62, 118, 182

White evangelicalism. See American White evangelicalism; White nationalist evangelicalism

White fragility, 258, 352n21

White genocide: overview, 107, 115–16, 135–36; antifeminism and misogyny and, 128–29, 131; antigovernment resistance and, 131–35; anti-immigration and, 117–21; antisemitism and, 119, 122–24; defined as term, 114–15; demographic changes as basis of, 115, 128, 262; the economy and, 116–17; expansion of catalogue of enemies judged to be complicit in, 115–16; and globalism (antisemitic conspiracy theory), 116, 121, 122–24, 204; gun control and, 121–22; Adolf Hitler on, 238; Islamophobia and, 124–28, 156, 175; David Lane as coining the term, 239; as paralleled by *al-walā' wa-l-barā'* (loyalty and disavowal), 157; Queer Americans and, 129–31; and "reverse racism" claims, 262–63; transnational White nationalism and, 261; Trump viewed as preventing, 12–13; as victimhood narrative, 107, 114–15; violence as justified due to threat of, 107, 115, 148, 261. *See also* RAHOWA (racial holy war)

White identitarians, 79, 81

White liberals: complicity of, 258; hypocrisy of, 259; leveraging White privilege to combat systemic racism, 251–52, 258–63

White Mountain Militia, 48

White nationalism (nonmilitant), definition of, 23

White nationalism: attempts to destigmatize and repackage, 79; binary worldview of, 136; complexity of the landscape of, 62–64, 75; definition of, 23–25; as exploiting fragility and anxiety of White Americans, 116; four main subsets of, 64; mental illness used as defense of, 221; and militancy/nonmilitancy, 23, 41; nonreligious/non-antigovernment as subset of, 78–80; normalization of, 9, 10, 12–13, 113–14, 120, 262; skinheads, 40, 78–79; statistics on numbers of terrorist acts by, 6–7, 85. *See also* antigovernment activism; antigovernment/religious organizations; antisemitism and White nationalism; conspiracy theorists and theories; counterterrorism; eugenics; federal statute criminalizing domestic terrorism, lack of; Fourteen Words; Islamophobia; media entities and outlets, White nationalist; misogyny; political far right; victimhood narrative and White nationalists; White ethnostate; White genocide; White nationalism (nonmilitant); White nationalist religions; White nationalists, literature influencing; White supremacy; xenophobia

White nationalist evangelicalism: overview, 42–43, 44; apocalyptic rhetoric of, 204–6, 207, 209–10, 211–12, 214–16, 217–18; and gun control issue, 122; immigrants of color as vilified in, 117–21; interpretation of biblical passages and, 176, 179, 186; prominent figures in, 44; and White Christian identity, 44; and the White ethnostate, 44, 185–86; and White supremacy, 44

White nationalist religions: overview, 2; immigrants of color as universally vilified by, 117–21; manifestos as transcending disparate affiliations, 236, 240, 243; White supremacy as core precept of, 81. *See also* antigovernment/religious organizations; apocalyptic rhetoric of political violence; atheists and agnostics and the political far right; Christian Identity; Creativity; Jesus; White ethnostate; White nationalist evangelicalism; Wotanism

White nationalists: converting to militant Islamism, 125–26; self-identification of, 9, 278n31. *See also* victimhood narrative and White nationalists; White nationalists, literature influencing

White nationalists, literature influencing: "The Biblical Basis of War" (Shea), 49; *Building a Whiter and Brighter World* (Klassen), 57; *The Cain-Satanic Seed Line* (Comparet), 54; *Christian Identity: Identifying God's Chosen* (film), 118; "A Christian Manifesto" (Schaeffer), 77–78; *The Creativity Handbook* (Creativity), 123; *Dearborn Independent*, 52; "Declaration of War" (Mathews), 114–15; "Declaration of War" (Miller), 114; *GOD and Lincoln on Negro-White Marriages* (Christian Identity), 119; *God, Man, Nations, and the Races* (Swift), 53; *Identification of the British Nation with Lost Israel* (Hine), 52; *Leaderless Resistance* (Beam), 222–23; *Lectures on Our Israelitish Origins* (Wilson), 51–52; *Left Behind* series (LaHaye), 209; "The Menace of the Mullahs" (Stubba), 125; *Might is Right* (Redbeard), 120–21, 128; *Nature's Eternal Religion* (Klassen), 55, 208; *The Nay Book* (Nay), 48; *Odinism: Past, Present and Future* (Osred), 192; *An Odinist Anthology* (McNallen), 59, 300n100; Poetic Edda (Elder Edda) text (Odinism), 58, 176, 179, 208–9, 271, 333n29; Prose Edda text (Odinism), 208–9; "The Protocols of the Elders of Zion," 52; *Race and Reason* (public-access TV, Metzger), 56; *Racial and National Identity* (Gale), 53, 187, 188–89; *Racial Loyalty* (newsletter, Klassen), 55; *RAHOWA* (Klassen), 55; *Salubrious Living* (Klassen), 55; "Tet Take Two: Eslam's 2016 European Offensive" (Patriot and Bracken), 126–27; "To Teach Them War" (video, Campbell), 211; *The Turner Diaries* (William Pierce, alias Andrew Macdonald), 74–75, 83, 237, 239; "What Would Odin Say about Gun Control?" (NcNallen), 122; *White Genocide Manifesto* (Lane), 118, 183–84, 237, 239; *The White Man's Bible* (Klassen), 55, 119, 169, 208; *A White Man Speaks Out* (Miller), 113; *White Revolution* (video series, Hale), 224; "Wotan Is Coming" (Lane), 223–24; *Your Heritage: An Identification of the True Israel through Biblical and Historical Sources* (Comparet), 54. *See also* manifestos of White nationalists; media entities and outlets, White nationalist

Whiteness: Christianity as encompassing, 9; determining, 62; as identity marker of power, 249–50, 263; Northern and Western Europeans as epitome of, 237; wielded as a tool to justify oppression, 257

White, Pastor Paula (aka Paula White-Cain), 44

White Patriot Party, 113

White power: tattoos symbolizing, 40; vs. White nationalism as term, 25

White power music: Jeremiah Joseph Christian and, 162; Wade Michael Page and, 40, 162; Resistance Records (National Alliance), 74; skinheads and, 79; violence glorified in, 205

White privilege: and agency, 258; definition of, 7, 258; disadvantages of Whites not

mutually exclusive with, 262; and the exclusion of White nationalism from counterterrorism programs, 8, 258; interest convergence theory and, 258–59; and lack of action against White nationalist threat to national security, 7–8; "MAGA" and nostalgic claim on, 11, 261; White fragility and protection of, 258, 352n21; White liberals leveraging, in the interest of holistic justice, 251–52, 258–63

White racialist, as term, 79

White separatism, as narrower term than White nationalism, 23, 24–25, 25

White supremacy: as core precept of White nationalist religions, 80, 229; Adolf Hitler and, 238; as narrower term than White nationalism, 23, 24; scientific proof claimed for, 50; White Northern and Western Europeans as focus of, 237. *See also* eugenics; Fourteen Words

Whore of Babylon, 99, 210

Wilson, John, 51; *Lectures on Our Israelitish Origins,* 51–52

Wolf, Chad F., 351n16

Wolin, Richard, 320n59

women: the Fourteen Words and servitude as vessels of reproduction, 42, 128; the Golden Age of Islam and equality of, 195–96; and Mawdudi's theodemocratic caliphate, 198; as reinforcing misogyny, 5, 129; in the White ethnostate, 185, 198; as White nationalists and Islamists, 4–5. *See also* misogyny and antifeminism

World Church of the Creator. *See* Creativity

World War I, division of the Middle East following, 143–44, 324n11

Wotan, 57, 192, 223–24

Wotanism: antisemitism and, 192; apocalyptic rhetoric of (Ragnarok), 58, 207, 208–9; and Aryan global community, 193; "blood and soil," 57, 58, 169, 241; calls to violence by adherents of, 114; Christianity, rejection of, 57, 60–61; the eagle as symbol and, 189, 333n29; Edda literature of, 58, 176, 179, 208–9, 271, 333n29; and the Founding Fathers/U.S. Constitution, 182, 191, 192–93; growth of, 60, 61; and gun control issue, 122; immigrants of color as vilified in, 117–18; and Islamophobia, 125; and Carl Jung, 59; and kinism, 182; David Lane as founder of, 40, 42, 58–59, 208–9; metagenics (inheritance of tradition and

Wotanism (continued)
culture), 59, 300n100; name of, defined
as term, 57–58; and Nazi Germany,
59–60; neo-Nazis as associated with, 63,
72–73, 74; and Friedrich Nietzsche, 59;
Norse mythology and, 57, 58, 59–60, 62;
and The Order, 75; and prisons,
proselytization in, 61; Queerphobia of,
130; and RAHOWA, meaning of, 165,
169–70, 179; social forms of worship
(e.g. blots), 60; terrorist acts by adherents
of, 113, 162; Thor's hammer, 61; and
Unite the Right demonstration (2017), 2;
and Vikings/Vinland, 118, 162, 169,
193–94, 335n49; and violence,
justification of, 62, 169–70; and the
White ethnostate, 62, 118, 182. See also
Odinism; Wotanism literature
Wotanism literature: White Genocide
Manifesto (Lane), 118, 183–84, 237,
239; "Wotan Is Coming" (Lane),
223–24. See also Fourteen Words
Wray, Christopher, 8

xenophobia, 22, 52, 73, 79, 113–14, 116,
120, 191, 261–62, 268, 269, 346n76
X, Malcolm (aka el-Hajj Malik el-Shabazz),
259, 260

Yazidis, Islamic State (Dā'ish) attacks on,
89
Young, Brigham, 47

az-Zarqawi, Abu Mus'ab, 89, 90, 92, 98
az-Zawahiri, 'Ayman: as Afghan Arab, 90;
and assassination of Anwar as-Sadat,
91; and assassination of 'Azzam, 92;
The Bitter Harvest (al-Hisad al-Murr),
144; on the caliphate, 200–201; on
Guantánamo prison, 154; and Islamic
State (Dā'ish), 90, 92, 102; al-Maqdisi
and, 98; on the move of the U.S.
embassy to Jerusalem, 326n33; and
al-Qa'ida, founding of, 90, 91; rebuke
of Islamic State (Dā'ish) for indiscriminate use of violence, 89; on true
Muslims (and governments) vs.
apostates, 90, 98, 144
Zimbabwe (formerly Rhodesia), 220
Zimmerman, George, 28, 228
Zionist alliance. See Crusader-Zionist
alliance, militant Islamist conception of
Zionist Occupied Government (ZOG)
(conspiracy theory), 115–16, 121,
122–23, 125, 164, 203, 210. See also
globalism (White nationalist antisemitic
conspiracy theory)